UNDERSTANDING COPYRIGHT LAW

SECOND EDITION

Marshall A. Leaffer

Professor of Law
University of Toledo

LEGAL TEXT SERIES

1995

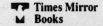
Matthew Bender

Times Mirror
Books

Library of Congress Cataloging-in-Publication Data

Leaffer, Marshall A., 1943-
    Understanding copyright law / Marshall A. Leaffer. — 2nd ed.
        p.   cm. — (Legal text series)
    "Times Mirror books."
    Includes index.
    ISBN 0-8205-2747-5
    1. Copyright—United States. I. Title. II. Series.
KF2994.L43   1995
346.7304'82—dc20   94-39940
[347.306482]   CIP

MATTHEW BENDER & CO., INC.
EDITORIAL OFFICES
11 PENN PLAZA, NEW YORK, NY 10001-2006 (212) 967-7707
2101 WEBSTER ST., OAKLAND, CA 94612-3027 (510) 446-7100

LEGAL EDUCATION PUBLICATIONS

To Nana, My Parents, Joelle, and Sarah

PREFACE

In their prefaces, most authors justify a new edition by pointing out the significant changes that have occurred since the previous edition. I am no exception. Indeed, since this book appeared in 1989, there have been important changes in the world of copyright. The trends that I noted in the First Edition have progressed in ways unpredictable five years ago. The spreading interest in copyright continues to be driven by the new digital technologies that affect the way we create and use information. Imagine, just five years ago — for better or worse — we did not have to read about the "information superhighway."

Since the First Edition, legislation has considerably altered the 1976 Act. In 1990, Congress granted "moral rights" to visual artists and conferred protection on architectural works, banned the unauthorized rental of computer software, and abrogated the states' sovereign immunity for copyright infringement. Significant new legislation appeared in 1992: copyright renewals were made automatic, the fair use defense was clarified for unpublished works, new criminal penalties were imposed, and special provisions were added to deal with home audio taping using digital media. In 1993, Congress abrogated all vestiges of the jukebox compulsory license, and abolished the Copyright Royalty Tribunal, replacing it with ad hoc arbitration panels. 1993 was a pivotal year for international relations in copyright. In that year, the United States, along with Canada and Mexico, signed the North American Free Trade Agreement (NAFTA), and the Uruguay Round of the General Agreement on Tariffs and Trade (GATT) was finally completed. Both agreements, one regional, the other multilateral, contain important provisions on copyright and intellectual property whose effects are yet to be seen. I have incorporated these legislative and international developments in this new edition.

Developments in the case law have kept up with legislative activity. Since 1989, important Supreme Court decisions have treated such diverse issues as the work-made-for-hire doctrine (*CCNV v. Reid*); the effect of the renewal term on derivative works (*Stewart v. Abend*); the standard of originality in the protection of databases (*Feist Publications, Inc. v. Rural Telephone*); parody as fair use (*Acuff-Rose v. Campbell*); and the right of a defendant as a prevailing party to recover attorneys' fees (*Fogerty v. Fantasy*). This edition also includes significant case law developments in the lower courts, such as important decisions on computer software infringement (*Computer Associates v. Altai*) and reverse engineering as fair use (*Sega v. Accolade*).

Since the First Edition, my knowledge of copyright has been greatly enriched by collaboration with three co-authors on two editions of a copyright law casebook published by Matthew Bender. (Craig Joyce, William Patry, Marshall Leaffer and Peter Jaszi, *Copyright Law* (3d ed. 1994)). My work on the casebook and the insights of my co-authors are reflected throughout this second edition of *Understanding Copyright Law*.

I extend special thanks to my assistant Debbie Levine and Jodi Booth for their help in researching and proofing the text, and to my secretary, Donna Hunt, who helped me in countless ways in completing the manuscript. I also want to thank Mary Gallagher of Matthew Bender for her editorial expertise and professional competence.

Marshall Leaffer
January 1995

PREFACE TO THE FIRST EDITION

At one time copyright law was an esoteric field, taught at a few law schools and usually by adjunct faculty. Today, courses on copyright and related areas of intellectual property are part of the regular curriculum in virtually all law schools. Why the increasing interest in copyright law? The reason lies in the ever growing importance of information in our lives. Copyright law, which concerns the right to certain kinds of intangible products called works of authorship, is *the* law for the age of information. The subject touches not only the traditional concerns of artists, writers, and musicians, but reaches the cable television and computer software industries as well. These are industries vital to the economic health of the nation. Exportation of movies, music, databases, and computer software have been a bright spot in the overall dismal balance of trade statistics during the 1980's. Adequate protection of American copyright interests abroad has become an important trade issue. The vital role played by copyright law in global affairs has been recognized in recent international trade legislation and the United States' long awaited entry into the Berne Convention, the most important of the international copyright treaties.

Understanding Copyright Law is intended as a comprehensive overview of copyright law for the student. It can be used in conjunction with the several nationally published casebooks focusing on the law of copyright. These excellent casebooks reflect two general approaches in teaching the subject. Some professors, who might be labeled "purists," teach copyright law as a self-contained subject. These persons would concentrate on the Copyright Act of 1976, its legislative history and case law, and their courses would follow the basic structure of the 1976 Act. Other teachers and scholars in the field, however, view copyright law as the centerpiece in the larger field of entertainment law. To these individuals, copyright law should be firmly situated in context, *e.g.*, movie and music industries, and a greater portion of their courses would be concerned about how copyright interacts with other bodies of related law such as unfair competition and the right of publicity. These two approaches, of course, are not mutually exclusive, nor should they be, but seem to describe the dominant tendencies in the teaching of copyright law.

Organized around the Copyright Act of 1976, this text follows the "purist" approach to the subject but tries, when appropriate, to situate the legal issue in an industry context and to relate copyright with other areas of intellectual property law. Chapter 1 provides an historical overview of copyright law and situates copyright in the larger field of intellectual property law. This chapter also evaluates the economic justification for protecting intangible property rights. Chapters 2 through 11 treat the traditional aspects of copyright law: subject matter (Chapters 2 and 3); publication and notice (Chapter 4); ownership (Chapter 5); duration, renewal and termination of transfers (Chapter 6); registration (Chapter 7); exclusive rights (Chapter 8); infringement and remedies (Chapter 9); fair use and defenses (Chapter 10); and preemption of state law (Chapter 11). The book ends with an overview of international copyright matters (Chapter 12).

Many people have encouraged and helped me in writing this book. My colleagues Bill Richman, Bruce Campbell, Henry Bourguignon, Richard Edwards, Howard Friedman, and Dan Steinbock generously read and evaluated various chapters of the text. Their comments were always incisive, challenging, and supportive. I want to express my appreciation to Pat Sinn who assisted me from the outset in researching and proofing the text. My thanks to Scott Schockling, Ken Egbert, and Rebecca Howard who provided invaluable research assistance throughout. I am especially grateful to Donna Hunt, for her patient and kind assistance in typing the text during the more than two years that this book took to complete. I also want to thank Richard Adin of Matthew Bender for his support and professional editorial judgment.

Marshall A. Leaffer
December, 1988

TABLE OF CONTENTS

Page

Preface   vii

CHAPTER 1

INTRODUCTION TO COPYRIGHT AND INTELLECTUAL PROPERTY LAW

§ 1.1   Introduction and Chapter Overview   1

PART I: HISTORICAL OVERVIEW OF COPYRIGHT

§ 1.2   The Beginnings to the Statute of Anne (1710)   3
§ 1.3   From the Constitution to the Copyright Act of 1909   5
§ 1.4   The 1909 Act   6
    [A]   General Provisions of the 1909 Act   6
    [B]   United States Exclusion From the Berne Convention   7
    [C]   Legislative Attempts to Retool the 1909 Act   7
§ 1.5   The Copyright Act of 1976   8
    [A]   Important Changes in the 1976 Act   8
    [B]   The Berne Convention Implementation Act of 1988 . . .   10
    [C]   Post-Berne Amendments   11
    [D]   The Continuing Importance of the 1909 Act and the 1976 Act As Originally Enacted   12

PART II: JUSTIFICATIONS FOR COPYRIGHT LAW

§ 1.6   In General   12
§ 1.7   The Natural Law Justification   13
§ 1.8   The Economic Rationale of Copyright Law   15
    [A]   Rationale of the Copyright Clause   15
    [B]   Why Should Property Rights be Created For Information?   15
§ 1.9   The Future of Copyright   17

PART III: COPYRIGHT, PATENT, AND TRADEMARK COMPARED

§ 1.10   In General   20

§ 1.11   Patent Law   20

    [A]   In General   20

    [B]   Procedures to Obtain a Patent   21

    [C]   Kinds of Patents   21

    [D]   Utility Patents: Requirements for Validity   22

    [E]   Patent Infringement   23

§ 1.12   Trademark Law   24

    [A]   Generally   24

    [B]   Federal Registration of Trademarks   24

    [C]   Trademark Infringement   25

§ 1.13   Chart Comparing Copyright, Patent, and Trademark   26

§ 1.14   State Intellectual Property Law   27

    [A]   Trade Secrets   27

    [B]   Unfair Competition Law   28

    [C]   Common Law Copyright   28

    [D]   The Right of Publicity   29

    [E]   Misappropriation   30

CHAPTER 2

**SUBJECT MATTER OF COPYRIGHT:
GENERAL STANDARDS**

§ 2.1   Introduction and Chapter Overview   33

PART I: FIXATION

§ 2.2   Fixation and the Distinction Between the Material Object and
    the Copyright   34

§ 2.3   Tangible Medium of Expression   35

    [A]   The Fixation Requirement   35

    [B]   The Anti-Bootleg Provisions: An Exception to the Fixation
    Requirement   36

§ 2.4   Perception by Machine or Device   38

§ 2.5   The Videogame Cases   38

§ 2.6   Works Not Fixed in a Tangible Medium of Expression: Com-
    mon Law Copyright   39

Page

PART II: ORIGINALITY

§ 2.7 Original and Creative Authorship 41
   [A] In General 41
   [B] Independent Creation 41
   [C] The Quantum of Originality: Creative Authorship . . . 42

PART III: DERIVATIVE WORKS AND COMPILATIONS

§ 2.8 Derivative Works and Compilations: An Overview 44
§ 2.9 Derivative Works 46
   [A] Originality in Derivative Works 46
   [B] Use of Derivative Works in the Public Domain 46
   [C] The Lawful Use Requirement 47
   [D] Originality in Reproductions of Works of Art 47
§ 2.10 Originality In Derivative Work Authorship: The Colorization
        Controversy 50
§ 2.11 Compilations 51
   [A] Originality in Compilations: An Overview 51
   [B] The *Feist* Case and the Demise of the Industrious Effort
        Doctrine 52
   [C] Originality in Selection and Arrangement after *Feist* . . 54
   [D] Computer Databases 55

PART IV: NON-COPYRIGHTABLE SUBJECT MATTER

§ 2.12 Ideas and Systems Under § 102(b) 56
   [A] In General 56
   [B] Idea and Expression: The Doctrine of *Baker v.
        Selden* 58
        [1] The Nature of Functional Works: Patent Policy and
             Copyright Law 58
        [2] The Merger Doctrine 60
   [C] Fictional Characters 62
   [D] Historical Research 64
§ 2.13 Other Issues on Non-Copyrightable Subject Matter 66
   [A] Copyright in Immoral, Illegal and Obscene Works . . 66
   [B] Government Works 67

Page

CHAPTER 3

WORKS OF AUTHORSHIP: CATEGORIES OF COPYRIGHTABLE SUBJECT MATTER

§ 3.1 Introduction and Chapter Overview   69

PART I: WORKS OF AUTHORSHIP: OVERVIEW

§ 3.2 The Eight Categories   69
  [A] Generally   69
  [B] Excluded Writings   70
  [C] Copyrightable Subject Matter: The 1909 and 1976 Acts
       Compared   71
  [D] Importance of How a Work is Categorized   72

PART II: LITERARY WORKS

§ 3.3 Generally   73
§ 3.4 Computer Programs (Software)   73
  [A] Historical Background: CONTU   73
  [B] Copyrightability of Programs—Initial Doubts   74
§ 3.5 Computer Technology   75
  [A] Computer Hardware: The Basics   75
  [B] Computer Software: Developmental Stages   76
  [C] Application and Operating System Programs   76
§ 3.6 Computer Programs in the Courts: *Apple Computer, Inc. v.
       Franklin Computer Corp.*   77
  [A] *Apple Computer, Inc. v. Franklin Computer Corp.*: The
       Issues Involved   77
  [B] Copyright in a Program Expressed in Object Code . .   77
  [C] Copyrightability of a Program Embedded in a ROM . .   78
  [D] Copyrightability of Operating Systems   78
§ 3.7 Computer-Generated Works   80
§ 3.8 Other Forms of Intellectual Property Protection for Computer
       Software: Trade Secret and Patent Law   81
  [A] Trade Secret Protection for Computer Software   81
  [B] Patent Law Protection for Computer Software   82
§ 3.9 Semiconductor Chips   83
  [A] The Technological Background, the Economic Stakes, and
       the Legal Dilemma   83

Page

[B] The Semiconductor Chip Act: Statutory Overview . . .   84

**PART III: PICTORIAL, GRAPHIC, AND SCULPTURAL WORKS:
THE UTILITARIAN OBJECT**

§ 3.10 Generally   85
§ 3.11 Works of Applied Art and the Design of Useful
        Objects   85
§ 3.12 Industrial Design Under the 1976 Act   87
§ 3.13 Physical Separability: *Esquire, Inc. v. Ringer*   87
§ 3.14 Conceptual Separability   89
§ 3.15 Architectural Works   91
        [A] In General   91
        [B] Architectural Works Constructed Before December 1,
             1990   91
             [1] Architectural Structures   91
             [2] Architectural Plans, Models, and Drawings   92
        [C] The Architecural Works Protection Act of 1990   93
§ 3.16 Other Forms of Protection for Works of Applied Art: Design
        Patent and Proposed Design Legislation   94
        [A] Design Patent   94
        [B] Design Legislation   96
§ 3.17 Maps   97

PART IV: OTHER CATEGORIES OF COPYRIGHTABLE SUBJECT MATTER

§ 3.18 Musical Works   98
§ 3.19 Sound Recordings   99
        [A] Distinguishing the Sound Recording From Other Works of
             Authorship and the Phonorecord   99
        [B] Originality in Sound Recordings   100
        [C] No Federal Protection for Pre-1972 Sound Record-
             ings   100
§ 3.20 Dramatic Works   101
§ 3.21 Pantomimes and Choreographic Works   101
§ 3.22 Motion Pictures and Other Audiovisual Works   103

Page

CHAPTER 4

PUBLICATION, NOTICE AND OTHER FORMALITIES

§ 4.1   Introduction and Chapter Overview   105

PART I: PUBLICATION

§ 4.2   Publication: Its Role in Copyright Law   107

[A]   In General   107

[B]   Historical Overview of the Publication Doctrine   107

[C]   Justification of the Publication Doctrine   108

§ 4.3   "Publication" Defined   109

§ 4.4   Publication Under the 1909 Act: Its Continuing Impor-
         tance   110

§ 4.5   Two Court-Made Efforts to Ameliorate the Publication Require-
         ment's Harsh Effect Under the 1909 Act   110

[A]   Generally   110

[B]   Divestive and Investive Publication   111

[C]   Limited versus General Publication   112

§ 4.6   The Importance of Publication Under the 1976 Act   114

[A]   Generally   114

[B]   Publication and Compliance with Formalities   114

[C]   Publication and International Copyright   115

[D]   Publication: Durational Consequences   115

§ 4.7   Special Publication Contexts: 1909 and 1976 Acts
         Compared   115

[A]   Performance as Publication   115

[B]   Publication by Display   116

[C]   The Distribution of Phonorecords as Publication   117

[D]   Publication of a Derivative Work   118

PART II: NOTICE

§ 4.8   Generally: Justification for Notice Requirement   119

[A]   The Background   119

[B]   Abrogation of the Notice Requirement: The Berne Con-
         vention Implementation Act of 1988   119

§ 4.9   Notice Requirements Under the 1976 Act before the Berne
         Convention Implementation Act of 1988 Amendments . . .   121

Page

§ 4.10 Form and Position of Notice Under the 1976 Act 122

[A] Form of Notice on Copies 122

[B] Form of Notice on Phonorecords for Sound Recordings 123

[C] Year Date 124

[D] Name of Copyright Owner 124

[E] Location of the Notice 124

§ 4.11 Omission of Notice 125

[A] Generally 125

[B] Omission of Notice and Forfeiture of Copyright 126

[C] Omission of Notice: The Savings Provision 127

[D] Innocent Infringement 129

§ 4.12 Error in Name and Date 130

[A] Generally 130

[B] Error in Name 130

[C] Error in Date 131

[D] Omission of Name or Date 132

§ 4.13 Special Notice Subsections 132

[A] Notice for Publications Containing Government Works 132

[B] Notice for Contribution to Collective Works 132

§ 4.14 Notice Under the 1909 Act 134

[A] Generally 134

[B] Form of Notice 134

[C] Location of Notice 135

[D] Year Date 136

[E] Omission of Notice 136

[F] U.S. Works First Published Outside the United States 137

PART III: THE MANUFACTURING CLAUSE

§ 4.15 The Demise But Continuing Importance of the Manufacturing Clause 138

§ 4.16 The Manufacturing Clause Under the 1976 Act 139

[A] Generally 139

[B] The "Preponderantly" Requirement 139

[C] Exceptions to the Manufacturing Provisions 139

[D] Effect of Non-Compliance Under the 1976 Act 139

Page

§ 4.17 The Manufacturing Clause Under the 1909 Act   140

[A] Generally   140

[B] *Ad Interim* Protection   140

[C] Forfeiture by False Affidavit and General Non-
Compliance   141

**PART IV: RESTORATION OF COPYRIGHT IN
WORKS PREVIOUSLY IN THE PUBLIC DOMAIN**

§ 4.18 Retroactivity Under Article 18 of the Berne Convention and
the Constitutional Dilemma   141

§ 4.19 Restoration of Copyright in Certain Foreign Public Domain
Works Under Section 104A: From NAFTA to the Uruguay
Round Agreements Act   142

[A] The North American Free Trade Agreement Act   142

[B] The Uruguay Round Agreements Act   143

CHAPTER 5

OWNERSHIP OF COPYRIGHT

§ 5.1 Introduction and Chapter Overview   147

PART I: INITIAL OWNERSHIP: WORKS MADE FOR HIRE AND JOINT WORKS

§ 5.2 Works Made for Hire   148

[A] Generally   148

[B] Works Made for Hire: An Overview of the Basic
Standards   148

[C] Works Made for Hire in the Courts Before *Community for
Creative Non-Violence v. Reid*: The Blurring of Distinctions Between the Two Subdivisions   150

[D] The Literal Reading of the Categories: *Community for
Creative Non-Violence v. Reid*   151

[E] *CCNV* in Perspective: Will it Help the Independent
Contractor?   153

§ 5.3 Works Made for Hire Under the 1909 Act   154

§ 5.4 Joint Works   155

[A] Generally   155

[B] Joint Works Under the 1976 Act   156

[C] Consequences of Joint Ownership   158

Page

[D] Joint Works and Derivative Works Compared 159

§ 5.5 Joint Ownership Under the 1909 Act 159

§ 5.6 Ownership of Contributions to Collective Works 161

§ 5.7 Ownership of Copyright As Distinguished from Ownership of the Material Object: The *Pushman* Doctrine 162

PART II: TRANSFERS OF COPYRIGHT INTERESTS

§ 5.8 Divisibility of Copyright 163

[A] In General 163

[B] Consequences of Divisibility: Standing to Sue 164

§ 5.9 Indivisibility of Ownership Under the 1909 Act 164

§ 5.10 Drafting and Construing Licenses: The Problem of New Media 166

§ 5.11 Transfers of Copyright: The Writing Requirement 168

[A] The 1976 Act 168

[B] The Writing Requirement Under the 1909 Act 169

§ 5.12 Recordation 170

[A] In General 170

[B] Recordation: Priority Between Conflicting Transfers (Assignments and Exclusive Licenses) 170

[C] Priority Between a Transferee and a Non-Exclusive Licensee 171

§ 5.13 Involuntary Transfers 171

CHAPTER 6

DURATION, RENEWAL AND TERMINATION OF TRANSFERS

§ 6.1 Introduction and Chapter Overview 173

PART I: DURATION

§ 6.2 In General: The 1909 and 1976 Acts Compared 174

§ 6.3 The Mechanics of Duration Under the 1976 Act 175

[A] All Terms Run to the End of the Calendar Year 175

[B] The Basic Term: Life of the Author Plus 50 Years . . . 176

[C] Anonymous and Pseudonymous Works and Works Made for Hire 176

[D] Joint Works 176

[E] Duration of Sound Recordings: The Special Status of Sound Recordings Fixed Before February 15, 1972 . . . 176

Page

[F]   Death Records   177
[G]   Duration of Copyright: Works Created But Not Published
      or Copyrighted Before January 1, 1978   177

§ 6.4   Should Duration of Copyright Be Lengthened Another 20
        Years?   178

PART II: RENEWAL

§ 6.5   Works Published or Copyrighted Before January 1, 1978: An
        Overview   179
[A]   In General   179
[B]   The Renewal Registration Requirement Under the 1976
      Act   179
[C]   Works in Their Second Term As of January 1, 1978 . .   180
[D]   Summary Chart on Duration Under the 1976 Act . . .   181
§ 6.6   Renewal: Copyrights in the First Term As of 1978   181
[A]   Generally: The Continuation of the Renewal System Under
      the 1976 Act   181
[B]   Renewal Claimants   182
§ 6.7   Exceptions to the Author's Right to the Renewal Term . .   184
[A]   Generally   184
[B]   Posthumous Works   184
[C]   Composite Works and Corporate Works   184
[D]   Employer of a Work Made for Hire   185
§ 6.8   Transfers of the Renewal Term: *Fisher v. Witmark*   186
§ 6.9   Automatic Renewal for Copyrights Originally Secured between
        January 1, 1964, and December 31, 1977   187
[A]   Generally   187
[B]   How Automatic Renewal Works   187
[C]   Continuing Incentives to Register   188
§ 6.10   The Renewal Term and Derivative Works   189
[A]   Generally   189
[B]   *Stewart v. Abend*: Demise of the New Property Theory of
      Derivative Works   190
[C]   *Stewart v. Abend* Reassessed   191

PART III: TERMINATION OF TRANSFERS

§ 6.11   Termination Generally   192

§ 6.12 Termination of the Extended Renewal Term Under § 304(c)   193

§ 6.13 Termination Formalities   196

§ 6.14 Section 304(c): Termination and Derivative Works — *Mills Music v. Snyder*   197

§ 6.15 Termination of Transfer Under § 203   198

§ 6.16 Sections 304(c) and 203 Compared   200

§ 6.17 Some Works Enjoy No Termination Right, and Other Works Have Both Termination and Renewal Rights   201

[A] Certain Grants Subject to No Termination   201

[B] Grants Subject to Both Termination and Renewal . . .   202

CHAPTER 7

COPYRIGHT REGISTRATION AND DEPOSIT

§ 7.1 Introduction and Chapter Overview   203

PART I: REGISTRATION

§ 7.2 The Copyright Office   204

§ 7.3 Why a Registration System?   204

§ 7.4 Registration of Copyright: An Overview   206

§ 7.5 Registration Procedures   207

§ 7.6 The Importance of Registration   209

[A] Prerequisite to Bringing Suit for Infringement   209

[B] Registration As *Prima Facie* Evidence of Validity . .   210

[C] Registration As a Prerequisite for Obtaining Statutory Damages and Attorney's Fees   210

[D] The Interplay of Registration and Recordation   211

§ 7.7 Refusal of Registration: § 411(a)   212

§ 7.8 Registration Under the 1909 Act: The "Prompt Deposit" and Registration Requirement   212

PART II: DEPOSIT

§ 7.9 Generally   213

§ 7.10 Mandatory Deposit for the Library of Congress   214

§ 7.11 Failure to Comply with Deposit Requirements   214

§ 7.12 Mechanics of Deposit   214

§ 7.13 Mandatory Deposit Under § 407 and the Deposit Requirement for Registration Under § 408 Compared   215

Page

Appendix to Chapter 7   217

CHAPTER 8

THE EXCLUSIVE RIGHTS AND THEIR LIMITATIONS

§ 8.1   Introduction and Chapter Overview   221

PART I: EXCLUSIVE RIGHTS, LIMITATIONS, AND COMPULSORY LICENSES

§ 8.2   Introduction to the Exclusive Rights and Their Limita-
        tions   221
§ 8.3   The Compulsory Licenses and Their Administration   223
        [A]   What is a Compulsory License?   223
        [B]   From the Copyright Royalty Tribunal to Copyright Arbi-
              tration Royalty Panels   223
        [C]   Are the Compulsory Licenses Justifiable?   225

**PART II: THE REPRODUCTION AND ADAPTATION
RIGHTS AND THEIR LIMITATIONS**

§ 8.4   The Reproduction Right: Generally   227
§ 8.5   The Right to Prepare Derivative Works: The Adaptation Right
        — Generally   227
§ 8.6   Limitations to the Reproduction and Adaptation Rights: Com-
        puter Uses — § 117   229
§ 8.7   Limitations to the Reproduction and Adaptation Rights: The
        Compulsory License for Making and Distributing Phonorecords
        (The Mechanical License) — § 115   231
        [A]   Generally   231
        [B]   How the Compulsory License Works   231
        [C]   Where the Compulsory License Does Not Apply . . .   232
        [D]   Procedures   233
§ 8.8   Limitations to the Reproduction and Adaptation Rights:
        Ephemeral Recordings — § 112(d)   233
§ 8.9   Limitations to the Reproduction and Adaptation Rights: Sound
        Recordings — § 114(b)   234
§ 8.10 Limitations to the Reproduction and Adaptation Rights: Repro-
        duction of Pictorial, Graphic, and Sculptural Works in Useful
        Articles — § 113   236
§ 8.11 Limitations to the Reproduction and Adaptation Rights: Archi-
        tectural Works   236

PART III: THE DISTRIBUTION RIGHT AND ITS LIMITATIONS

§ 8.12 The Distribution Right: Generally 237
§ 8.13 Limitations on the Distribution Right: The First Sale
Doctrine 237
    [A] Generally 237
    [B] Non-Consensual Transfers 239
§ 8.14 Modifications and Exceptions to the First Sale Doctrine 240
    [A] Record Rental 240
    [B] Software Rental 241
    [C] Imported Copies Legally Obtained Abroad: The Gray
Market 242
    [D] The Right to Dispose of Copies or Phonorecords of a Re-
stored Work 244
    [E] The Resale Royalty Right (*Droit de Suite*) 244
    [F] The Public Lending Right 246

**PART IV: THE PERFORMANCE AND DISPLAY
RIGHTS AND THEIR LIMITATIONS**

§ 8.15 The Performance Right: Generally 246
§ 8.16 What is a Public Performance? 247
    [A] Generally 247
    [B] Performances in Places Open to the Public 248
    [C] The Size and Composition of a Public Audience . . . 249
§ 8.17 Non-Profit and Other Exemptions to the Performance Right
Under § 110 250
    [A] Generally 250
    [B] Instructional Exemptions: § 110(1) (Face-to-Face);
§ 110(2) (by a Transmission) 250
    [C] Exemptions for Transmissions to the Blind and Handi-
capped: §§ 110(8) and 110(9) 251
    [D] Agricultural and Horticultural Fairs — § 110(6); Vending
Establishments — § 110(7); and Veterans and Fraternal
Organizations — § 110(10) 252
    [E] Exemption for Certain Nonprofit Performances:
§ 110(4) 252
§ 8.18 The *Aiken* Exemption—§ 110(5)—and the Multiple Performance Doctrine 254
    [A] The Multiple Performance Doctrine: The 1909 Act
Background 254

Page

[B] Secondary Transmissions and the Multiple Performance Under the 1976 Act: The *Aiken* Exemption — § 110(5)   255

[C] The *Aiken* Exemption in the Courts   257

§ 8.19 Secondary Transmissions: § 111   258

[A] In General   258

[B] Overall Structure of § 111   258

[C] General Exemptions: § 111(a)   259

[1] Clause (1): Retransmissions to Private Lodgings   259

[2] Clause (2): Instructional Transmissions   260

[3] Clause (3): The Passive Carrier Exemption   260

[4] Clause (4): The Secondary Transmitter Exemption   260

[D] The Compulsory License for Cable Systems: § 111(c)   260

[E] Reporting Requirements and Royalty Fees for Cable Systems: § 111(d)   261

[F] The Computation and Distribution of Royalty Fees . . .   262

[G] Afterthoughts: Is § 111 an Anachronism?   263

§ 8.20 The Satellite Retransmission Compulsory License   264

§ 8.21 The Jukebox License   266

[A] The Rise and Fall of the Compulsory Jukebox License   266

[B] The Jukebox Licensing Procedure: A Voluntary Negotiated License   266

§ 8.22 Performing Rights Societies   267

[A] Why They Are Needed: Capturing the Valuable But Elusive Performance Right   267

[B] How They Operate: The ASCAP Model   268

[C] Dramatic (Grand Rights) and Non-Dramatic Performing Rights (Small Rights)   269

[D] Antitrust Problems   269

§ 8.23 The Compulsory License for Public Broadcasting: § 118 . .   271

§ 8.24 Performance Rights in Sound Recordings (*Droits Voisins*)   271

§ 8.25 The Right of Public Display: § 106(5)   272

§ 8.26 Limitations on the Display Right   273

[A] Public Display of an Owned Copy: § 109(c)   273

[B] Other Exemptions to the Display Right   274

Page

PART V: BEYOND CONVENTIONAL COPYRIGHT PROTECTION: THE MORAL RIGHT FOR VISUAL ARTISTS AND THE COMPULSORY LICENSE FOR DIGITAL AUDIO TAPING DEVICES

§ 8.27 The Moral Right   275

[A] Generally   275

[B] Analogues of the Moral Right in State and Federal Law   276

[C] State Art Preservation Acts   277

§ 8.28 Copyright Protection of Moral Rights: The Visual Artists Rights Act of 1990 (VARA)   278

[A] Generally   278

[B] Summary of the Provisions of VARA   279

[C] Beyond Moral Rights for Visual Artists?   281

§ 8.29 The Audio Home Recording Act of 1992   282

[A] The Challenge of New Recording Technology   282

[B] Provisions of the Audio Home Recording Act of 1992   283

CHAPTER 9

INFRINGEMENT AND REMEDIES

§ 9.1 Introduction and Chapter Overview   285

PART I: INFRINGEMENT: SUBSTANTIVE ISSUES

§ 9.2 The Elements: Ownership, Copying, and Improper Appropriation   285

§ 9.3 Circumstantial Proof of Copying: Access and Substantial Similarity   286

§ 9.4 Access   288

§ 9.5 Substantial Similarity   289

[A] Generally   289

[B] Verbatim Similarity and Pattern Similarity Compared   290

[C] Verbatim Similarity   290

[D] Pattern Similarity   290

[E] Determining Pattern Similarity: The Learned Hand Abstractions Test   291

[F] Applying the Abstractions Test to Computer Programs: From *Whelan Associates* to *Computer Associates*

	Page
(*Altai*)	292
§ 9.6 Substantial Similarity in the Litigation Process	295
[A] Generally	295
[B] The Ordinary Observer or Audience Test	296
[C] Bifurcated Tests: *Arnstein* and *Krofft*	297
§ 9.7 Improper Appropriation: Need for a Flexible Approach	299

PART II: REMEDIES

§ 9.8 Preliminary Injunctions	300
§ 9.9 Impounding and Destruction of Infringing Articles	301
§ 9.10 Damages and Profits: Generally	301
§ 9.11 Actual Damages and Profits: The Prohibition Against Double Counting	301
§ 9.12 Recovery of Profits	302
[A] Advantages to Claiming Lost Profits	302
[B] Costs Defendant May Deduct	303
[C] Apportionment of Profits to Infringing Activity	303
§ 9.13 Statutory Damages	304
[A] Generally	304
[B] The Method of Computing Statutory Damages	304
[C] The Problem of Multiple Infringements	305
[D] Multiple Plaintiffs and Defendants	305
§ 9.14 Costs and Attorney's Fees	306
§ 9.15 Criminal Penalties	308

PART III: INFRINGEMENT: PROCEDURAL MATTERS

§ 9.16 Jurisdiction	309
[A] "Arising Under" Jurisdiction	309
[B] Pendent Jurisdiction	311
§ 9.17 Statute of Limitations	312
§ 9.18 Parties to Suit: Plaintiff's Standing	312
§ 9.19 Standing to Sue Federal and State Governments	313
[A] Federal Government	313
[B] State Government: The Eleventh Amendment Issue	313
§ 9.20 Related Defendants: Vicarious Liability and Contributory Infringement	314
[A] Generally	314

Page

[B] Actively Inducing Another to Infringe Copyright . . . 314

[C] Vicarious Liability: The Right to Supervise and a Financial
Interest 316

CHAPTER 10

FAIR USE AND OTHER DEFENSES TO COPYRIGHT INFRINGEMENT

§ 10.1 Introduction and Chapter Overview 317

PART I: FAIR USE: THE BACKGROUND

§ 10.2 In General 318

§ 10.3 Historical Origin of the Doctrine of Fair Use: *Folsom v.
Marsh* 319

§ 10.4 Section 107 of the 1976 Act: Generally 319

§ 10.5 The Preamble to § 107: Is Fair Use Productive Use? . . . 320

§ 10.6 The Four Criteria 321

PART II: THE FOUR FACTORS INDIVIDUALLY EXAMINED

§ 10.7 The Purpose and Character of the Use 323

§ 10.8 Nature of the Copyrighted Work 324

§ 10.9 The Amount and Substantiality of the Portion Used in Relation
to the Copyrighted Work as a Whole 326

§ 10.10 The Effect of the Use upon the Potential Market for, or Value
of, the Copyrighted Work 327

PART III: SPECIAL APPLICATIONS OF FAIR USE ANALYSIS: NEW TECHNOLOGIES, PARODY, AND THE FIRST AMENDMENT

§ 10.11 Fair Use and the New Reproductive Technologies: Videotaping
and Photocopying 328

[A] Copyright and the New Reproductive Technologies:
Generally 328

[B] Videotaping: The *Betamax* Case 329

[C] Photocopying: *Williams & Wilkins* 330

[D] The Failure of the Litigation Process 330

§ 10.12 Avoiding Fair Use Determinations: Industry-Wide Resolution
of the Photocopying Dilemma 332

[A] Library Photocopying Under § 108 332

[B] Multiple Copies for Classroom Use 333

Page

[C] A Private Collecting Agency: The Copyright Clearance
Center   335

§ 10.13 Reverse Engineering of Computer Software: *Sega Enterprises
Ltd. v. Accolade, Inc.*   336

§ 10.14 The Problem of Parody   338

[A] Generally   338

[B] Parody and the Four Factors: *Campbell v. Acuff-
Rose*   339

[C] How Much Can the Parody Take From the Origi-
nal?   340

[D] Parody and the Fourth Fair Use Factor: Market
Effect   341

[E] Does the Parody Have to Satirize the Copyrighted
Work?   342

§ 10.15 Fair Use and the First Amendment   343

[A] Generally: No Irreconcilable Tension   343

[B] The Merger of Idea and Expression   344

§ 10.16 Fair Use: A Synthesis   346

CHAPTER 11

COPYRIGHT LAW IN A FEDERAL SYSTEM:
PREEMPTION OF STATE LAW

§ 11.1 Introduction and Chapter Overview   349

PART I: PREEMPTION BEFORE THE 1976 ACT

§ 11.2 The Misappropriation Doctrine and Other State Attempts to
Protect Intellectual Property: The 1909 Act Background . . .   351

[A] Two Divergent Tendencies   351

[B] The Classic Statement: The *INS* Case   351

§ 11.3 Preemption Reborn: *Sears* and *Compco*   353

§ 11.4 The Aftermath of *Sears* and *Compco*   354

Part II: PREEMPTION UNDER § 301 OF THE 1976 ACT

§ 11.5 Section 301: Generally   356

§ 11.6 Rights Equivalent: The Language of the Statute and the Legislative History   358

[A] Rights Equivalent: The Peculiar Structure of § 301 . . .   358

Page

    [B]   The Legislative Odyssey of § 301   358

§ 11.7 Rights Equivalent: The Case Law Applying § 301   360

    [A]   The Extra Elements Approach   360

    [B]   The Failure of the Extra Elements Approach   363

§ 11.8 The Necessary Return to Traditional Preemption Analysis: Four Examples   364

    [A]   State Anti-Blind-Bidding Statutes   364

    [B]   State Law Conferring Broader or Narrower Rights . .   364

    [C]   Are Rights Equivalent Those Provided Under §§ 107–120?   365

    [D]   The California Resale Royalty Act   366

§ 11.9 Subject Matter: The Second Requirement for Preemption of State Law   366

    [A]   Non-Original Works, and Works in the Public Domain or Excluded by § 102(b)   367

    [B]   Subject Matter Which Congress Could Have, But Did Not Include   367

§ 11.10 Non-Preempted Works   368

§ 11.11 Other Preemption Provisions of the Copyright Act   369

    [A]   The Visual Artists Rights Act of 1990: § 301(f)   369

    [B]   The Architectural Works Protection Act of 1990: § 301(b)(4)   369

CHAPTER 12

AN OVERVIEW OF INTERNATIONAL COPYRIGHT

§ 12.1 Introduction and Chapter Overview   371

PART I: THE MAJOR INTERNATIONAL TREATIES INVOLVING COPYRIGHT

§ 12.2 Generally   372

§ 12.3 The Universal Copyright Convention (U.C.C.)   373

    [A]   Generally   373

    [B]   Basic Provisions of the U.C.C.   373

        [1]   General Obligations   374

        [2]   Basis of Protection   374

        [3]   Formalities   374

        [4]   Minimum Term of Protection   374

        [5]   Exclusive Rights   374

Page

[6] Berne Safeguard Clause   374

[C] The Paris Revision of the U.C.C.   375

§ 12.4 The Berne Convention   375

[A] Generally   375

[B] Berne Convention: Summary of its Basic Provisions . .   376

[1] Subject Matter   376

[2] Basis of Protection   376

[3] Preclusion of Formalities   377

[4] Minimum Term of Protection   377

[5] Exclusive Rights   377

§ 12.5 U.S. Entry Into Berne   378

[A] Generally   378

[B] The Berne Convention Implementation Act of 1988 . . .   379

[1] Formalities   380

[2] Architectural Works   381

[3] Jukebox Compulsory License   381

[4] Works in the Public Domain: Retroactivity   382

[5] Copyright Infringement Remedies   383

[C] Benefits to American Authors and Copyright Owners from Berne Membership   383

§ 12.6 Other Copyright-Related Conventions   383

[A] Convention for the Protection of Producers of Phonograms Against Unauthorized Duplication of Their Phonograms   383

[B] Brussels Satellite Convention   384

[C] Copyright in the Americas: Buenos Aires Convention   384

**PART II: FOREIGN AUTHORS AND CONFLICTS
OF LAW IN INTERNATIONAL COPYRIGHT**

§ 12.7 Foreign Authors   385

[A] Unpublished Works   385

[B] Published Works: The Five Bases for Protection in § 104(b)   385

§ 12.8 International Copyright and Conflicts of Law   387

[A] The Application of Foreign Copyright Law by U.S. Courts   387

[B] The Application of U.S. Law to Foreign Infringing Acts   388

Page

[C] Choice of Law Rules in International Copyright Conflicts 388

PART III: TRADE REGULATION AFFECTING INTERNATIONAL COPYRIGHT MATTERS

§ 12.9 Infringing Importation of Copies or Phonorecords 390

[A] Sections 602 and 603 of the 1976 Copyright Act . . . 390

[B] Section 337 of the Tariff Act of 1930: The U.S. International Trade Commission 391

[C] Broad Based Trade Legislation 393

PART IV: MULTILATERAL AND REGIONAL APPROACHES TO INTERNATIONAL COPYRIGHT PROTECTION

§ 12.10 Beyond the International Treaties: A GATT Solution . . . 394

[A] The Shortcomings of the International Treaties 394

[B] From the GATT to the World Trade Organization . . . 395

[C] Intellectual Property Under the WTO: The TRIPS Agreement 396

[D] WIPO Responds to GATT: The Berne Protocol 397

§ 12.11 Regional Integration and Copyright Law: The European Union and NAFTA 397

[A] The European Union (EU) 397

[B] The North American Free Trade Agreement (NAFTA) 399

Table of Cases TC-1

Table of Statutes, Regulations and Treaties TS-1

Index I-1

INTRODUCTION TO COPYRIGHT AND INTELLECTUAL PROPERTY LAW

"The general rule of law is, that the noblest of human productions — knowledge, truths ascertained, conceptions and ideas — become after voluntary communication to others, free as the air to common use." *International News Service v. Associated Press,* 248 U.S. 215, 250 (1918) (Justice Brandeis, dissenting).

"No man but a blockhead ever wrote, except for money." Samuel Johnson, as quoted in III *Boswell's Life of Johnson* 19 (Hill ed. 1934).

§ 1.1   Introduction and Chapter Overview

In a surprisingly short period of time, the United States has evolved from an industrial to an information- and services-based society. Our post-industrial era is marked by rapid technological change in which our ability to reproduce and receive information grows exponentially. It is hard to believe that motion pictures first appeared little more than seventy years ago; many of us can remember a time when cable and satellite communications belonged to a hazy future. Who can predict what new information-based technologies lie ahead? From all indications, the communications revolution is only in its infancy.

As the value of communicative expression grows, so does the legal structure that governs the rules concerning its ownership. Products of the mind are protected under three areas of "Intellectual Property" law. *Patent law* provides a limited monopoly for new and inventive products, processes and designs. *Trademark law* prohibits product imitators from passing off their goods or services as the products of others. *Copyright law* protects "original works of authorship." A separate body of state-created law provides additional protection.

The information industries are critically important to the American economy in its post-industrial stage. The numbers are staggering, as a study released in late 1992 demonstates.[1] In 1990, the copyright industries generated $331.5 billion, representing a 5.8% share of the U.S. gross domestic product — a share which, from 1977 to 1990, grew well over twice as fast as the economy as a whole. The same industries employed 5.6 million people in 1990, or 4.8% of total U.S. employment. The impact of the copyright industries on American trade is equally impressive. Taken together,

---

[1] Economists, Inc., *Copyright Industries in the U.S. Economy* (Sept. 29, 1992).

a selected sample of core copyright industries (including pre-recorded music, motion pictures, home videos, books, periodicals, newspapers, and computer software) generated foreign sales of at least $34 billion in 1990. Only aviation and agricultural exports were larger. Today, U.S.–produced software alone constitutes more than half of the world market. These figures are sure to grow in future years.

Such developments indicate clearly the growing importance of intellectual property. The transfer of information has become an ever greater component of international trade and the centerpiece of U.S. competitiveness. Unlike other areas of the economy, where intellectual property is concerned, the United States is a net exporter — indeed, the world's largest exporter by far. Whether old media (motion pictures, music) or new (computer software), this nation is preeminent in the production and distribution of copyrighted works. But there is a dark side to this success. American copyright owners have become increasingly vulnerable to piracy and expropriation abroad and to inadequate protection of their interests under foreign laws. Accordingly, the international aspects of copyright law no longer can be given secondary consideration in a serious study of the subject.[2]

In the broadest sense, copyright law creates a system of property rights for certain kinds of intangible products, generally called works of authorship. Initiated in 18th century England, the first copyright act gave authors the exclusive right to make copies of their books. Today, copyright law covers much broader ground, including not only most artistic, literary, and musical works, but computer software and databases as well.

The term *copyright* is a highly descriptive term: the right to make copies. It reflects the basic Anglo-American notion that undesirable economic results will occur if unimpeded copying is allowed of those intangible products whose production we wish to encourage. The focus of copyright law is on the benefits derived by the public from the labors of authors. By this view, reward to the copyright owner or author is a secondary concern.

Although the term "copyright" is highly descriptive in one sense, it is a misnomer in another. Today's copyright goes much farther in protecting works against copying in the strict sense of the word. Much of what we protect in copyright law today, such as performance rights, display rights and derivative work rights, are more akin to rights to *use* a work rather than to *copy* it.[3]

The analog of copyright in the civil law world is known as *droit d'auteur* (France), *derecho de autor* (Spain), *Urheberrecht* (Germany), all of which terms can be translated as *author's rights*. The difference in terminology between the common law *copyright* and the civil law *author's rights* is more than linguistic coincidence; it reveals a fundamental difference in attitude between the two legal traditions about works of authorship. The term "copyright" is an impersonal one, removed from the

---

[2] See Chapter 12, *infra*. For an overview of U.S. intellectual property law policy in a changing world order, see Marshall A. Leaffer, *Protecting American Intellectual Property Abroad: Toward a New Multilateralism,* 76 Iowa L. Rev. 273 (1991).

[3] For a development of this idea, see John M. Kernochan, *Imperatives for Enforcing Author's Rights,* 131 Revue Internationale du Droit D'Auteur [R.I.D.A.] 181 (1987).

author. It connotes a negative right, the right of the owner to prevent copying of his work. The general philosophy of copyright in the common law world is to provide material support to one who invests in producing the work, whether an individual author or corporate entity. The ultimate goal of copyright is to enhance public welfare, an essentially economic value.

By comparison, the civil law tradition views the author's work as an extension of his or her personality which springs into existence by a personal act of creation. This view reflects a more sympathetic attitude toward the author.[4] In the civil law world, an author is deemed to have a moral entitlement to control and exploit the product of his or her intellect. Under a principle of natural justice, the author, whose work is identified with his or her name throughout its existence, is given the right to publish his work as he or she sees fit, and to prevent its injury or mutilation.[5]

This introductory chapter is divided into three parts. Part I treats copyright from an historical viewpoint, beginning with developments in 16th century England to the passage of the 1976 Act, our current copyright law. Part II examines the nature of intangible property and the economic rationale for copyright law. Part III provides a broad overview of other forms of intellectual property law protection such as federal patent and trademark law and state trade secret and unfair competition law.

PART I: HISTORICAL OVERVIEW OF COPYRIGHT[6]

§ 1.2   The Beginnings to the Statute of Anne (1710)

The development of copyright law has been a continuing response to the challenge posed by new technologies that reproduce and distribute human expression. Indeed, the first copyright statute was a reaction to a new technology of the fifteenth century: the printing press.

Introduced into England in 1476 by William Caxton, the printing press, allowed large-scale reproduction of books for the first time. This new technology enriched publishers and booksellers (but not necessarily authors) and threatened the Crown, which shuddered at the thought of widespread dissemination of works advocating religious heresy and political upheaval. The Crown's solution to the problem was

---

[4] *See* Royce F. Whale & Jeremy Phillips, *Whale on Copyright* 18 (3d ed. 1983).

[5] The significance of this difference in attitude between the common law and civil law world will be discussed later in connection with 1990 amendments to U.S. copyright law providing certain "moral rights" protection for visual artists. These amendments to American copyright law suggest that the line between the two approaches — "copyright" versus "moral right" may not be as sharp as it once was. In fact, there seems to be an increasing convergence between the common law and civil law systems. Despite this convergence, however, the civil law still affords a wider scope of protection than traditional common law has been willing to allow. For example, although 1990 amendments to the Copyright Act established a moral right for visual artists, its scope is limited when compared with moral rights recognition in certain civil law countries like France. *See* §§ 8.27, 8.28 *infra*.

[6] For an excellent overview of the early development of copyright law, see L. Ray Patterson, *Copyright in Historical Perspective* (1968).

a system of regulation designed to control this "dangerous art." In 1534, a royal decree prohibited anyone from publishing without a license and without approval by official censors. The Crown conferred a publishing monopoly on the Stationer's Company, a group of London printers and booksellers, who were expected to do the Crown's bidding while handsomely lining their own pockets.[7]

After a controversial and checkered career, during which the Stationer's copyright was used as an instrument of both monopoly and press control, official licensing to publish expired in 1695, leaving the Stationer's Company unsheltered by regulation and vulnerable to competition from "upstart" publishers. Parliament listened to the Company's predictions of economic disaster and anarchy. In response to these lobbying efforts, Parliament passed the first copyright act, the Statute of Anne, in 1710.[8]

The Statute of Anne maintained Stationer's rights until 1731 in works already printed. But the Stationers' expectation of a continued monopoly over book publishing never materialized. In effect, the Statute of Anne undermined the Stationers' stranglehold on the book trade by recognizing for the first time the rights of authors to their works. The stated purpose of the Statute, as revealed in its enactment clause, was " . . . the encouragement of learned men to compose and write useful work."[9] Thus, the Statute of Anne shifted the emphasis from the Stationer's Company to authors in general and declared that its ultimate purpose was to enhance public welfare by encouraging the dissemination of knowledge.[10]

The Statute of Anne rewarded authors for their creations, but at the same time recognized the public domain by limiting these rights to a specific number of years.[11] For existing works, the Statute provided that "authors and their assigns" should have the sole right of publication for twenty-one years. New books enjoyed a different term of protection. They were given a first term of protection of 14 years for authors and their assigns, measured from the date of first publication, plus a second term of 14 years which reverted to the author if he lived to its commencement. Although the Statute appeared on its face to create a limited term of protection, the stationers claimed perpetual rights over their works and asserted that the statute was merely designed to provide them with expedited recovery against piracy. The lower courts sustained the Stationers' position for more than a half century until the famous case of *Donaldson v. Beckett.*[12] In rejecting the plaintiffs' argument for a common law right in copyright that would exist in perpetuity, the House of Lords in *Donaldson* established that the term of copyright is finite. And once that copyright term is exhausted, a work will (in today's parlance) fall into the "public domain."

---

[7] *See* Benjamin Kaplan, *An Unhurried View of Copyright* 5 (1967).

[8] 8 Anne, ch. 19 (1710).

[9] *Id.* at ch. 19 § 1.

[10] *See* Bernard A. Grossman, *Cycles in Copyright,* 22 N.Y.L. Sch. L. Rev. 653, 657 (1977).

[11] *See* Howard B. Abrams, *The Historic Foundation of American Copyright Law: Exploding the Myth of Common Law Copyright,* 29 Wayne L. Rev. 1119, 1141 (1983).

[12] 2 Bro. P.C. 129, 1 Eng. Rep. 837, 4 Burr. (4th ed) 2408, 98 Eng. Rep. 257 (H. L. 1774). In *Donaldson,* the House of Lords overruled *Millar v. Taylor,* 4 Burr. (4th ed.) 2303, 98 Eng. Rep. 201 (K.B. 1789), decided just five years before.

The Statute of Anne defined a "copy" as being "the sale, liberty of printing, and reprinting of a book." Infringement occurred when a third party printed, reprinted, or imported the book without consent. The protection granted was basically no more than a prohibition against literal copying.[13] To enforce one's rights, one had to register the title of the book with the Stationer's Company before publication.

On the whole the Statute of Anne, which became the model for copyright law in the United States, articulated a series of mixed and contradictory messages about the purposes of copyright. On the one hand, the Statute, as interpreted by the House of Lords in *Donaldson*, vindicated the the consumer interest in creating a public domain, and allowing free access to previously protected works. On the other hand, the stationers' argument for perpetual protection was favorably received by "natural rights" advocates who view authorship as a privileged category of human activity.[14] As we will see, these two approaches to copyright, one based on the natural rights of the author and the other on utilitarian principles (the economic rationale of copyright) which are the foundations of a system of copyright, are sometimes at cross purposes. These approaches will be discussed in a later section.[15]

§ 1.3   From the Constitution to the Copyright Act of 1909

Although the colonies already had their own forms of copyright laws,[16] the Framers of the Constitution recognized the need for a uniform law for copyright and patents.[17] The United States Constitution, Article I, Section 8, Clause 8, which empowers Congress to legislate copyright and patent statutes, reads as follows:

> To promote the progress of science and the useful arts, by securing for limited times, to authors and inventors, the exclusive right to their respective writings and discoveries.

The Patent and Copyright Clause was adopted in final form without debate in a secret proceeding on September 5, 1787. As a result, little is known about what the Framers had in mind in drafting this particular constitutional clause or about the scope of the various terms of the constitutional language.[18] Consequently, one is left with the language of the Clause itself, which does not even use the term "copyright."As revealed in the constitutional language, the dominant idea is to promote the dissemination of knowledge to enhance public welfare. This goal is to be

---

[13] *See generally* Part IV of L. Ray Patterson & Craig Joyce, *Monopolizing the Law: The Scope of Copyright Protection for Law Reports and Statutory Compilations,* 36 UCLA L. Rev. 719 (1989).

[14] *See generally,* Peter Jaszi, *Toward a Theory of Copyright: The Metamorphoses of "Authorship,"* 1991 Duke L.J. 455 (1991).

[15] See §§ 1.6–1.8, *infra*.

[16] Abrams, *supra* note 11, at 1173. Twelve states had adopted copyright statutes on the eve of the first federal copyright law of 1790.

[17] *See generally,* Francine Crawford, *Pre-Constitutional Copyright Statutes,* 23 Bull. Copyright Soc'y 11 (1975).

[18] *See* Ralph Oman, *The Copyright Clause: "A Charter For A Living People,"* 17 U. Balt. L. Rev. 99, 103 (1987).

accomplished through an economic incentive in the form of a monopoly right given for limited times, and the beneficiary of this monopoly right is the author.

The first Copyright Act of 1790[19] was passed pursuant to this constitutional authority, and its provisions, modeled on the Statute of Anne, set the tone for future statutes. Like the Statute of Anne, the Act of 1790 gave protection to the author or his assigns of maps, charts, and books for two 14-year terms, an original and a renewal term. Judicial constructions, including most notably *Wheaton v. Peters* in 1834,[20] followed *Donaldson v. Beckett* in insisting on the primacy of federal law, and punctilious observance of its requirements in the scheme of American copyright law. From 1790 until the 1909 Act, the copyright law underwent two general revisions[21] in addition to several important amendments which greatly elaborated many aspects of copyrightable subject matter, rights, remedies and administration.[22]

§ 1.4   The 1909 Act

[A]   General Provisions of the 1909 Act

In December 1905, President Theodore Roosevelt called for a complete revision of the copyright law to meet modern conditions. The result was the Copyright Act of 1909 which lasted for 68 years, until the enactment of the current law, the Copyright Act of 1976. Despite the four-year revision process, the 1909 Act was hardly a model of clarity, coherence or precision, but it did contain important new features. Under the 1909 Act, for instance, copyrightable subject matter was expanded to include "all the writings of an author."[23] The Act included a bifurcated durational system, a first term of 28 years and a second 28-year renewal term, conferring copyright protection for a possible 56 years.[24] Under the Act, federal copyright began at the moment of publication,[24] rather than from the time the title of the work was filed for registration, as had been previously required. Except for works not intended for reproduction (such as motion pictures and speeches), unpublished works were not covered by the Act, and a dual system of state common law

---

[19] Act of May 31, 1790, Ch. 15, 1 Stat. 124.

[20] 33 U.S. (8 Pet.) 591 (1834). The case is discussed at length in Part III of Craig Joyce, *The Rise of the Supreme Court Reporter: An Institutional Perspective on Marshall Court Ascendency,* 83 Mich. L. Rev. 1291 (1985).

[21] The general revisions took place in 1831 and 1870.

[22] Some of the more important changes occurred as follows: 1819, federal jurisdiction for copyright cases; 1831, addition of musical compositions as copyrightable subject matter and extension of the copyright term from 14 to 28 years; 1846, deposit requirements for the Library of Congress; 1856, public performance right for dramatic works; 1865, photographs as copyrightable subject matter; 1870, Library of Congress given principal responsibility for copyright and Copyright Office created; 1874, notice provisions required. For a more detailed look at the changes in the law between 1790 and 1909, *see* William F. Patry, *Copyright Law and Practice* 14–56 (1994).

[23] *See* 17 U.S.C. § 4 (1909 Act).

[24] *See* 17 U.S.C. § 24 (1909 Act).

[24] *See* 17 U.S.C. § 10 (1909 Act).

copyright for unpublished works and federal protection for published works existed. Because of its various provisions, the 1909 Act did not solve the problems which excluded the United States from joining the principal treaty governing international copyright relations, The Berne Convention for the Protection of Literary and Artistic Works.

[B] United States Exclusion from the Berne Convention

One particularly unfortunate feature of the 1909 Act was its failure to amend U.S. law to conform to the then relatively new Berne Convention for the Protection of Literary and Artistic Works. Concluded in 1886, the Berne Convention was the first, and has remained for over 100 years, the principal, international copyright convention.[25] Since its inception, the Berne Convention has been revised five times, most recently in the Paris revision in 1971. Its success as an international agreement is reflected by its large number of adherents which, by the mid-1980's, included every major country in the world except China, the Soviet Union, and the United States.

The 1909 Act retained several aspects of U.S. copyright law which constituted major stumbling blocks for United States entry into the Berne Convention. Two of the more prominent impediments were the 1909 Act's insistence on compliance with certain formalities as a prerequisite for copyright protection and the Act's shorter term of copyright.[26] The 1909 Act required notice on all published copies of a work; failure to include the required notice could inject the work into the public domain.[27] This aspect of American law was clearly in conflict with the Berne requirement that copyright protection be granted absent compliance with formalities. In addition, the 1909 Act's bifurcated durational system was not in accord with Berne's minimum durational requirement of the life of the author plus fifty years.[28] Consequently, these and other provisions of the 1909 Act prevented U.S. entry into the Berne Convention.

[C] Legislative Attempts to Retool the 1909 Act

From 1909 until the passage of the 1976 Act, changing times and technologies forced Congress to amend the 1909 Act. For example, motion pictures were added to copyrightable subject matter in 1912, and in 1952, a performance right for profit was provided for non-dramatic literary works. In 1954, the United States ratified the Universal Copyright Convention[29] which provides non-discriminatory protection to nationals of all member nations for works published within their borders. No formalities are required for unpublished works. Published works, however, must bear a prescribed notice, but a nation can require other formalities for its own nationals or for works first published within its borders, as long as these further

---

[25] For an overview, see Stephen. M. Stewart, *International Copyright and Neighboring Rights* 86–132 (1983).

[26] There were other 1909 Act provisions impeding U.S. entry into Berne. This subject is discussed in fuller detail in § 12.5, *infra*.

[27] *See* 17 U.S.C. § 10 (1909 Act).

[28] Berne Convention art. 7.

[29] Universal Copyright Convention, Sept. 6, 1962.

requirements are imposed without discrimination against nationals of foreign member states.

After some years, it became apparent that the 1909 Act was beyond repair and should be replaced by new legislation.[30] In 1955, Congress authorized a copyright revision project, followed by twenty years of reports and extensive hearings, culminating in the passage of the Copyright Act of 1976.[31]

§ 1.5   The Copyright Act of 1976

[A]   Important Changes in the 1976 Act

The 1976 Act made innovative changes in addition to clarifying certain aspects of existing law. The more important aspects of the Act include:

(1) *Preemption of common law copyright.* Section 301 of the 1976 Act preempts common law copyright, which had bedeviled the administration of the 1909 Act.[32] No longer is there the dual system of copyright, *i.e.*, federal protection for published works and state common law protection for unpublished works. Now all works fixed in a tangible medium of expression are protected under the Act from the moment of creation.

(2) *Duration.* The Act eliminated the dual 28-year terms for copyright and replaced them with a single, extended term of the life of the author plus 50 years.[33] Publication is no longer the measuring point for most works. However, an alternate term of 75 years from publication or 100 years from creation, whichever is less, is given for anonymous and pseudonymous works, and works made for hire.[34] Even here, the term is much longer than under the 1909 Act.

(3) *Formalities.* Formalities continued to be important under the 1976 Act. Notice was still required for all published works, and it was possible to forfeit copyright by failure to affix notice.[35] Registration of copyright and recordation of transfers of copyright were also a condition to bringing suits for infringement of these works until amendments which took effect in 1989 eliminated the latter requirement and modified the former.[36] These formalities have been modified by the Berne Convention Implementation Act of 1988. *See* 17 U.S.C. §§ 411, 205. A requirement, mandating the domestic manufacture of copies of copyrighted works was maintained in the Act but expired in 1986.

(4) *Subject Matter:* The 1976 Act established broad categories of subject matter which, according to the legislative history, are to be construed liberally. These are:

---

[30] For an overview of the 1909 and 1976 Acts, see Robert A. Gorman, *An Overview of the Copyright Act of 1976*, 126 U. Pa. L. Rev. 856 (1978).

[31] H.R. Rep. No. 94–1476, 94th Cong., 2d Sess. 47–50 (1976).

[32] *See* 17 U.S.C. § 301.

[33] *See* 17 U.S.C. § 302(a).

[34] *See* 17 U.S.C. § 302(c).

[35] *See* 17 U.S.C. §§ 401(a) and 405.

[36] *See* 17 U.S.C. § 411.

(1) literary works; (2) musical works; (3) dramatic works; (4) pantomimes and choreographic works; (5) pictorial, graphic, and sculptural works; (6) motion pictures and other audiovisual works; (7) sound recordings; and (8) architectural works.[37] The subject matter is broad but Congress fell short of including all the writings of an author as it could have done under its constitutional authority. Rather, the subject matter of copyright includes *original* works of authorship, set forth in the eight aforestated broad and overlapping categories. What constitutes sufficient originality for a valid copyright is a matter of judicial precedent.

(5) *The Exclusive Rights and Their Limitations.* Section 106 of the 1976 Act enumerates five exclusive rights of copyright ownership: the rights to reproduce and adapt the copyrighted work, and to distribute, perform and display it publicly. A new provision, § 106A, was added in 1990 to delineate rights in works of visual art. The sections immediately following § 106A [38] impose various limitations on the exclusive rights. Section 107, the first of those limitations, codifies the judicially developed "fair use" privilege. The 1976 Act has tried to codify the privilege of fair use, the broadest exception to the exclusive rights under § 106, by setting forth criteria to be used in determining what constitutes fair use.[39]

(6) *Compulsory Licenses and the Copyright Royalty Tribunal.* The 1976 Act has increased to five the number of compulsory licenses in copyright, allowing access to copyrighted works on payment of the statutory fees and compliance with certain formalities. Under the Act as originally passed, there were only four compulsory licenses:[40] the cable television license; the mechanical recording license; the jukebox license; and the public broadcasting license. A new license for satellite home viewing, the satellite retransmission license, was added in 1988.[41] The compulsory licenses had been administered by the Copyright Royalty Tribunal, an administrative agency established by the Act.[42] Constantly under fire, the Copyright Royalty Tribunal was abolished in 1993 and replaced by Copyright Arbitration Royalty Panels (CARPs).[43]

(7) *Ownership.* Ownership of copyright is divisible under the 1976 Act; the copyright owner can now license or assign parts of the copyright to third parties, who can bring suits for infringement of their ownership rights.[44] The Act also specifies that ownership of the material object does not entail ownership of the copyright in the work.[45]

(8) *Entry Into Berne.* Although some progress had been made toward entry into the Berne Convention, such as extending the term of copyright, other stumbling

---

[37] *See* 17 U.S.C. § 102(a). In 1990, § 102(a) was amended to include architectural works. *See* 17 U.S.C. § 102(a)(8).

[38] *See* 17 U.S.C. §§ 107–120.

[39] *See* 17 U.S.C. § 107.

[40] *See* 17 U.S.C. §§ 111, 115, 116, and 118.

[41] 17 U.S.C. § 119.

[42] *See* 17 U.S.C. §§ 801–810.

[43] The Copyright Royalty Tribunal Act of 1993, Pub. L. No. 103–198 (1993).

[44] *See* 17 U.S.C. § 201(d).

[45] *See* 17 U.S.C. § 202.

blocks impeding entry, such as formalities of notice and registration, had not been removed. It was not until the Berne Act amendments of 1988 that these impediments to U.S. adherence were overcome.

(9) *Legislative Developments from 1978 to 1988.* Major developments in copyright have occurred since passage of the 1976 Act. In 1980, a new § 117 was added to the Act, involving the protection and scope of rights in computer programs.[46] Other amendments have been added as well,[47] but perhaps the major development in copyright since 1978 is the passage of the Semiconductor Chip Protection Act of 1984.[48] Affording protection to semiconductor mask works, this Act is a legislative response to the need to protect a new technology vital to our economic well being.

[B]   The Berne Convention Implementation Act of 1988[49]

Effective March 1, 1988, the United States entered into the Berne Union, the largest and most important international copyright convention. Among the principal motivating factors for entry at this time were the United States' withdrawal from UNESCO, the United Nations agency which administers the Universal Copyright Convention (UCC), the growing importance of intellectual property in world trade, and the systematic piracy of American works in certain foreign countries. To have a say in the development of international copyright policy, and establish copyright relations with 24 more countries, it was felt that the United States should join the world copyright community as soon as possible.[50]

The Berne Convention Implementation Act of 1988 ("BCIA") amended several aspects of the 1976 Copyright Act in conflict with Berne requirements. The Implementation Act reflects a *minimalist* approach whereby Congress attempted to amend the 1976 Copyright Act only where there was a direct conflict with the provisions of the Berne Convention.[51]

The most significant changes brought about by the Berne Amendments are the modification of formalities such as notice, registration, and recordation as conditions of copyright protection. These changes were neccessitated by Berne requirements that copyright protection not be based on compliance with formalities.[52] Accordingly, the 1988 amendments have abrogated the notice requirement.[53] For works published on or after March 1, 1989, notice is permissive and a copyright owner can no longer forfeit copyright by omitting notice of publicly distributed copies of

---

[46] *See* 17 U.S.C. § 117.

[47] *See* the Record Rental Amendment of 1984, Pub. L. No. 98–450, 98 Stat. 1727 (1984), and the Satellite Home Viewer Act of 1988, Pub. L. No. 100–667, 104 Stat. 3949 (1988).

[48] Pub. L. No. 98–620, 98 Stat. 3347 (1984). For a discussion of the Act and the technology of semi-conductor mask works, see § 3.9, *infra*.

[49] Pub. L. No. 100–568, 102 Stat. 2853 (1988).

[50] H.R. Rep. No. 100–609, 100th Cong., 2d Sess. 7 (1988).

[51] *Id.* at 20.

[52] Berne Convention Art. 5(2) (Paris text).

[53] 17 U.S.C. § 401 (as amended by BCIA). For a discussion of notice, see § 4.8, *infra*.

the work.**54** The registration requirement has also been modified. For works originating from a Berne country, registration is no longer required as a prerequisite for bringing a suit for copyright infringement.**55** Finally, recordation in the Copyright Office of an interest in copyright is no longer required as a prerequisite to bringing a suit for infringement.**56**

In addition to relaxing certain formalities, the 1988 amendments include an express recognition of architectural plans in the definition of pictorial, graphic, and sculptural works,**57** a modification of the jukebox license,**58** and a doubling of the limits for statutory damages.**59**

[C] Post-Berne Amendments

In 1990, Congress made further amendments to the 1976 Act, granting new rights to visual artists**60** and protection to architectural works,**61** banning the direct or indirect commercial rental of computer software,**62** and abrogating the sovereign immunity of the states for copyright infringement.**63** Significant new legislation appeared in 1992: copyright renewals were made automatic, the fair use doctrine was clarified for unpublished works, new criminal penalties for copyright infringement were imposed, and special provisions were added to the Copyright Act to deal with home audio taping using digital media.

The year 1993 saw equally important amendments to the 1976 Act. Congress abrogated the jukebox compulsory license, replacing it in a section renumbered 116A with a voluntary negotiated license. In the same year, Congress abolished the Copyright Royalty Tribunal, replacing it with *ad hoc* arbitration panels (CARPs) which will now make royalty determinations previously made by the CRT.**64** Under the Uruguay Round Agreements Act (URAA), passed at the end of 1994 as part of the United States obligation under the General Agreement on Tariffs and Trade (GATT), Congress rewrote § 104A to restore copyright in works whose source country is a member of the World Trade Organization or the Berne Convention.**65**

---

54 17 U.S.C. § 405 (as amended by BCIA). For a discussion of omission of notice, see § 4.11, *infra.*

55 17 U.S.C. § 411 (as amended by BCIA). For a discussion of copyright registration, see §§ 7.1–7.8, *infra.*

56 17 U.S.C. § 205(d) requiring recordation to bring an infringement suit has been deleted by the BCIA. For a discussion of recordation, see § 5.12, *infra.*

57 17 U.S.C. § 101 (as amended by BCIA). For a discussion of architectural works, see § 3.15, *infra.*

58 17 U.S.C. § 116 (as amended by the BCIA). For a discussion of the jukebox license, see § 8.21, *infra.*

59 *See* 17 U.S.C. § 504(c) (as amended by BCIA). This increase in statutory damages is unrelated to the requirements of Berne adherence.

60 17 U.S.C. § 106A.

61 17 U.S.C. § 102(a)(8).

62 17 U.S.C. § 109(b).

63 17 U.S.C. § 511.

64 *See* 17 U.S.C. 801–03.

65 17 U.S.C. § 104A. See discussion in §§ 4.18-4.19 *infra.*

In addition, pursuant to the same legislation, a new Chapter 11 was added to the Copyright Act, prohibiting the unauthorized fixation of and trafficking in sound recordings and music *videos*.[66] If the recent past is any guide, we should expect Congressional activity to continue apace.

[D] The Continuing Importance of the 1909 Act and the 1976 Act As Originally Enacted

Both the 1909 Act and the provisions of the 1976 Act as originally enacted remain relevant for several reasons. Most importantly, works whose source country is the United States[67] that have gone into the public domain under the 1909 Act and the original provisions of the 1976 Act remain in the public domain. For example, if a work was published without notice under the 1909 Act, it could be injected into the public domain.[68] Such a work cannot be revived by the less harsh forfeiture provisions of the 1976 Act[69] or the total abrogation of the notice requirement under the Berne Amendments of 1988.[70] In addition, the 1976 Act has specifically incorporated provisions of the prior law, and has retained standards developed in case law decided under the 1909 Act for important issues such as the standards of orginality and copyright infringement.

A copyright scholar has a complicated task — to be conversant with the provisions of the 1909 Act, the 1976 Act as originally enacted, and subsequent amendments to the 1976 Act, and also to be able to determine which piece of legislation is applicable in a particular situation.

PART II: JUSTIFICATIONS FOR COPYRIGHT LAW

§ 1.6   In General

Whether property rights should be recognized in products of the mind is a matter of long-standing debate and challenges fundamental assumptions about why society creates a system of property rights. Few question the correctness of granting property rights in land or chattels but, when the subject turns to intangible property, the consensus breaks down. There continues to be a lively debate about the nature and scope of protection for intellectual products.[71]

---

[66] 17 U.S.C. § 1101. *See also* the companion criminal anti-bootleg provisions in 18 U.S.C. § 2319A.

[67] Section 104A, passed pursuant to U.S. obligations under the General Agreement on Tariffs and Trade (GATT), restores copyright in works whose source country is a member of the World Trade Organization or an adherent of the Berne Convention. It does not restore copyright for works in the public domain whose source country is the United States. *See* 17 U.S.C. § 104A. Copyright restoration is discussed *infra* in §§ 4.18 and 4.19.

[68] For a discussion of notice under the 1909 Act, see § 4.14, *infra*.

[69] *See* 17 U.S.C. Trans. and Suppl. Provs. § 103.

[70] *See* Berne Convention Implementation Act of 1988, Pub. L. No. 100–568 § 12 (1988).

[71] *See, e.g.*, James Boyle, *A Theory of Law and Information: Copyright, Spleens, Blackmail, and Insider Trading*, 80 Cal. L. Rev. 1413 (1992); Jessica Litman, *The Public Domain*,

Discomfort with recognizing property rights in products of the mind runs through the common law, under which property rights arose from possession. But intellectual products were quite unlike land or chattels because once disseminated publicly, ideas and other intangibles were not subject to exclusive possession. Justice Brandeis reflected this view in a famous dissent. "The general rule of law is, that the noblest of human productions — knowledge, truths ascertained, conceptions, and ideas — become, after voluntary communication to others, free as the air to common use."[72]

Despite common law resistance, however, property rights for intellectual property always have had vigorous support. In general, arguments for establishing property rights in anything (land, chattels or intangibles) are justified on two fundamental grounds: first, a person's moral right to reap the fruits of his or her own labor (an idea based on natural law philosophy); and second, a utilitarian rationale that views copyright law as an incentive system designed to produce an optimal quantity of works of authorship, and thereby enhance public welfare. The emphasis of natural rights theory, characteristic of Continental European states, focuses on the author as an individual who deserves, on moral principles, to be compensated for work done. By comparison, the utilitarian justification, historically more common in the United States and Great Britain, places consumer welfare in the forefront, treating reward to authors primarily as a means to that end. In this country, the debate beween advocates of these positions is of more than mere historical interest. It continues today.

§ 1.7 The Natural Law Justification

The natural law justification for recognizing property rights in works of authorship is based on the rights of authors to reap the fruits of their creations, to obtain rewards for their contributions to society, and to protect the integrity of their creations as extensions of their personalities. The proposition that a person is entitled to the fruits of his labor is a compelling argument in favor of property rights of any kind, tangible or intangible. The most famous proponent of this natural rights theory was John Locke, the eighteenth century English philosopher, who reasoned that persons have a natural right of property in their bodies. In owning their bodies, people also own the labor of their bodies and, by extension, the fruits of their labor.[73]

According to this natural rights approach, an individual who has created a piece of music or a work of art should have the right to control its use and be compensated

---

39 Emory L.J. 965 (1990); David Vaver, *Intellectual Property Today: Of Myths and Paradoxes*, 69 Can. Bar Rev. 98 (1990); Tom G. Palmer, *Intellectual Property: A Non-Posnerian Law and Economics Approach*, 12 Hamline L. Rev. 261 (1989); Wendy J. Gordon, *An Inquiry Into the Merits of Copyright: The Challenges of Consistency, Consent, and Encouragement Theory*, 41 Stan. L. Rev. 1343 (1989).

[72] *International News Service v. Associated Press*, 248 U.S. 215, 250 (1918).

[73] *See* John Locke, *Second Treatise of Government*, Ch. 5 (1960). For an overview of Lockean natural law theory as applied to intellectual property, see Wendy J. Gordon, *A Property Right in Self Expression: Equality and Individualism in the Natural Law of Intellectual Property*, 102 Yale L.J. 1533 (1993).

for its sale, no less than a farmer reaps the benefits of his crop. In addition, because the author has enriched society through his creation, the author has a fundamental right to obtain a reward commensurate with the value of her contribution. Thus, copyright law, which confers an exclusive property right in an author's work, vindicates the natural right of individuals to control their works and be justly compensated for their contributions to society.[74]

The natural law justification for copyright law is not without its critics. First, natural law theory maintains that the author should have control over his work, but indicates little about how much control the author should have, how long that control should last, and who should benefit from the copyrighted work. The reality of positive law thus conflicts with the natural rights ideal. The United States has adopted a positive law approach, under which rights are granted solely as a matter of statute. The content of such rights is to be determined as the legislature sees fit, in accordance with the constitutional goal of promoting the progress of science.

Second, some have questioned whether copyright law satisfies the ideal of just compensation for the author's contribution to society. Empirically, copyright law has not particularly rewarded works of enduring social value, but more often the contrary. Again, the reality of positive law departs from the abstractions of natural rights theory. As a theoretical matter, the goal of fair compensation is at best a vague concept. No one can show what is the "fair" price for any commodity, service, or work of authorship. Normally, for most endeavors, we prefer to allow the market to set its price, and believe the consumer is benefited when competition pushes that price toward the marginal cost of production. But even if it were possible to determine "just" compensation, society generally seems unconcerned about ensuring compensation in a sum equal to what any given individual — whether schoolteacher, farmer, auto worker, or nurse — contributes. Indeed, virtually all salaried workers and entrepreneurs are rewarded in lesser measure than the value they contribute — the difference being profit.

Despite such difficulties, the natural law justification for copyright enjoys considerable support both in the United States and throughout the world.[75] It has motivated the successive revisions of the Berne Convention for the Protection of Literary and Artistic Property, which has continued to attract additional adherents including the United States. To many, however, natural law theory provides no more than a starting point and limited justification for copyright law. As an alternative to natural law propositions, one must turn to a utilitarian justification for the protection of intangible property rights. Based on economic principles, the utilitarian approach vindicates copyright law as an incentive system for authors to create works of authorship and thereby enhance the public welfare. As the next section shows, this view of copyright is deeply engrained in American law.

---

[74] For an overview of natural rights theory, see Alfred C. Yen, *Restoring the Natural Law: Copyright as Labor and Possession*, 51 Ohio St. L. J. 517 (1990).

[75] *See also* the 1948 Universal Declaration of Human Rights, Article 27(2), which gives the rights of authors a dignity coequal with that afforded to the most basic entitlements of humankind. The Article reads: "Everyone has the right to the protections of the moral and material interests resulting from any scientific, literary, or artistic creation of which he is the author."

§ 1.8   The Economic Rationale of Copyright Law

[A]   Rationale of the Copyright Clause

Without specifying the form of protection, Art. 1, § 8, cl. 8 of the Constitution empowers Congress to legislate copyright and patent statutes, conferring a limited monopoly on writings and inventions. By implication, the Constitution recognizes that copyright law plays an important role in our market economy. Rather than encouraging production of works by government subsidy, or awards or prizes, the author is given, through the limited monopoly of copyright law, a private property right over his creation whose worth will ultimately be determined by the market. The underlying policy of this constitutional provision is to promote the public welfare through private market incentives. The U.S. Supreme Court, in *Mazer v. Stein*, stated the rationale underlying the Copyright Clause as follows:

> The economic philosophy behind the clause empowering Congress to grant patents and copyrights is the conviction that encouragement of individual effort by personal gain is the best way to advance the public welfare through the talents of authors and inventors in science and the useful arts.[76]

[B]   Why Should Property Rights be Created for Information?

The law confers property rights on most things of value which we normally think of as being tangible things, occupying physical space, such as land or movable objects. The law, however, also recognizes property rights in information, an intangible product. This is hardly surprising. Information can be of great value as well as costly to produce, and without a legal regime protecting certain informational products, we would not produce the optimal amount of information for the public welfare. For this reason, copyright law recognizes property rights in certain kinds of expressive information called "works of authorship."

Protecting informational products presents special difficulties for the law because of their inherent intangible nature. Products of information, a piece of music, a computer program, or a radio signal, have characteristics which differentiate them from tangible products, such as a chair, an apple, or a television set. Once information is created, it can never be used up, and it can be used at little cost. A song can be sung endlessly, a computer program reproduced over and over, without ever using it up or depriving anyone else of its use. Information does not present the allocation problems that physical property does. If someone steals my automobile, I am deprived of it. My automobile is finite and exhaustible; whereas my song is infinite and inexhaustible.

This characteristic of intellectual property leads to an economic dilemma. Creating property rights in information imposes costs on the public. Why confer a life-plus-50-years monopoly for a work of art, a computer program, or a piece of music, if each of these products can be used infinitely and simultaneously without depriving anyone else of their use? Free market economics would prohibit creation of monopolies without an economic justification. As a monopolist, the owner of the

[76] 347 U.S. 201, 219 (1954).

copyright can charge a higher than competitive price for his or her product, causing people to buy less of it and to seek less useful substitutes for it. In economic terms, consumer welfare is distorted by this property right (copyright) which results in a less than maximum diffusion of information.[77]

The above analysis is not entirely accurate because it applies only to information already created.[78] Without a proper return on investment, a producer, for example, will not invest the millions of dollars it takes to create a movie, if it can be copied by a free rider who has none of the development costs. The creator who cannot recoup his investment will not create. Thus, if the author cannot exclude others from his work, the result will be either non-production or non-disclosure. Viewed in this way, copyright law represents an economic trade-off between optimal creation of works of authorship and their optimal use.[79]

In the absence of copyright protection, self-help through market headstart is the traditional means by which an author or inventor can obtain a return on investment. By being the first to print and sell a book, could the creator earn enough profit to justify his investment and induce his or her continued creation? If so, headstart is a sufficient incentive for continued production; as a result, granting a copyright monopoly is unnecessary and harms the consumer.[80] A headstart advantage may

---

[77] According to economists, informational products have *public goods* characteristics — non-rivalrous consumption and non-appropriability. For example, a television signal carrying a copyrighted movie can be consumed non-rivalrously (one person's use of the signal does not deprive another consumer's use of the same signal). In addition, the signal is non-appropriable because it is difficult for its producer to appropriate its value through its sale. Consumers will tend to become "free riders" of the signal, which can be easily captured and used at little or no cost. Because the producer cannot appropriate its true value through its sale, a suboptimal amount of information will be produced. The solution to the public goods problem (to encourage optimal production) is either direct government subsidy or giving limited monopoly rights to authors through copyright law. *See* A. Alchian & W. Allen, *Exchange and Production: Competition, Coordination and Control* 99–101 (3d ed. 1983). For an excellent discussion of property rights in information and the public goods problem, *see* Robert Cooter & Thomas Ulen, *Law and Economics* 135–68 (1988).

[78] *See* Frank H. Easterbrook, *The Supreme Court and the Economic System*, 98 Harv. L. Rev. 4 (1984). Judge Easterbrook takes the position that intellectual property cases often reflect a trade-off between optimal creation of information and its optimal use. As a result, he advocates an *ex ante* approach as opposed to an *ex post* approach in deciding intellectual property cases. The *ex ante* approach is forward looking and is concerned with making rules which encourage the optimal creation and use of information. By comparison, the *ex post* approach is one that is solely concerned with settling a dispute between the parties.

[79] *Id.* at 25. Another way of putting it: a system of copyright that promotes economic efficiency will be one in which its principal doctrines "maximize the benefits from creating additional works, minus both the losses from limiting access and the costs of administering copyright protection." *See* William M. Landes & Richard A. Posner, *An Economic Analysis of Copyright Law*, 28 J. of Legal Stud. 325, 326 (1989).

[80] This argument is elaborately made in a famous article, Stephen Breyer, *The Uneasy Case for Copyright: A Study in Copyright of Books, Photocopies and Computer Programs*, 84 Harv. L. Rev. 281 (1970); *compare* Barry W. Tyerman, *The Economic Rationale for Copyright Protection for Published Books: A Reply to Professor Breyer*, 18 UCLA L. Rev. 1100 (1971),

adequately reward some inventors and authors, particularly when the costs of reproduction are significantly less than the costs of creation. But a headstart advantage is only as good as the length of time it takes another to copy your product. A company spending millions in developing a computer operating system program or motion picture could hardly compete with an imitator, which has no development costs, and is able to copy the program quickly and cheaply and enter the market immediately thereafter. Consequently, market headstart may be inadequate to encourage the optimal creation of works of authorship and inventions.

In place of an unregulated market, the government regulates reproduction through copyright law by conferring a limited monopoly on works of authorship. On the one hand, copyright law provides the incentive to create information and a shelter to develop and protect it. On the other hand, the copyright monopoly is a limited one. It is limited in time and scope by such doctrines as idea/expression, originality, and fair use. Viewed in this way, copyright law represents an economic trade-off between encouraging the optimal creation of works of authorship through monopoly incentives, and providing for their optimal access, use, and distribution through limiting doctrines. As Justice Stewart, in *Twentieth Century Music Corporation v. Aiken*,[81] said:

> The immediate effect of our copyright law is to secure a fair return for an author's creative labor. But the ultimate aim is, by this incentive, to stimulate artistic creativity for the public good. "The sole interest of the United States and the primary object in conferring the monopoly," the Supreme Court has said, "lie in the general benefits derived by the public from the labors of authors."

§ 1.9   The Future of Copyright

Does the current system of copyright work as intended? Just as the printing press gave rise to the need for copyright law, new technologies have created the further need for legislative response. After a 20-year revision process, the Copyright Act of 1976 was passed with the hope that the law could meet the challenges of new technologies. But what seemed to be a far-sighted, intelligently drafted statute is already obsolete in some ways. The reason is the time lag between technological and legal change. Technological change always seems to outstrip the law's ability for adaptation. This is no better exemplified than in the law of copyright, a victim of the reprographic revolution.

Reproductive technologies are getting better and cheaper all the time. With today's reprographic technologies anyone can be a publisher; photocopying machines run faster and more efficiently, and threaten the existence of marginal, high

---

with Stephen Breyer, *Copyright: A Rejoinder*, 20 UCLA L. Rev. 75 (1972). For a discussion of the strengths and weaknesses of the economic theory of copyright, *see* Wendy J. Gordon, *An Inquiry into the Merits of Copyright: The Challenges of Consistency, Consent, and Encouragement Theory*, 41 Stan. L. Rev. 1343 (1989).

[81] 422 U.S. 151, 156 (1975).

cost publications. Digital audio tape produces the best sound and the worst nightmares for the music industry, already besieged by the ubiquitous cassette recorder. The digital audio sampler, widely used in rap and hip-hop music, copies prerecorded sounds, stores them in the sampler's database digitally, and by the use of computer software, reproduces them on another recording in the same or altered forms. Art to some, high tech theft to others, sampling has developed into a common and cheap way to create musical compositions.[82] All these new technologies allow access to copyrighted works and enable their diffusion in ways recently thought impossible.

The creation of copyrighted works, however, is just as difficult as ever. We can copy, store and retrieve a novel like *War and Peace* quickly and effortlessly, but the art of creation has no fast forward button. Today's author would take no less time, and incur no lesser expense, to produce *War and Peace* than Tolstoy did decades ago. Perhaps he would not bother to exert himself today without being able to adequately recover his investment. Because of this imbalance, we will no doubt create new mechanisms, legislative and private, for protecting and rewarding works of authors. Without effective protection for authors, the supply of works of authorship may diminish such that we will be left with sophisticated copying techniques but with nothing worth copying.

Perceived threats posed by the new technology should not overshadow the fact that a copyright is a monopoly and a long one at that.[83] There is perhaps a tendency today to overreact, looking to copyright law as a panacea in protecting all technologies and all intangible values.[84] Should designs for useful articles receive life-plus-50-years protection? Should copyright protection be extended to genetically engendered bacteria,[85] literary titles, or microcode? Some new and old technologies seem inappropriate for copyright protection. For some intangible values, *sui generis* protection of shorter duration may be preferable. Other countries already do this for industrial design and computer programs, believing that a full copyright term is unnecessarily long when one takes into account the relatively short commercial life of such products.

While changes in copying technologies may dramatically affect incentives to produce works of authorship, other current changes in technology call into question the very notion of authorship and of copyright law itself.[86] Traditionally, a reference

---

[82] Only one case has considered the legality of sampling. *See Grand Upright Music, Ltd. v. Warner Bros. Records.*, 780 F. Supp. 182 (S.D.N.Y. 1991) (infringement found in defendant's unlicensed use of a three word sample and its unaccompanied music). For an overview of the subject, see David Goldberg & Robert J. Bernstein, *Reflections on Sampling*, New York Law Journal, Jan. 15, 1993, p. 3.

[83] The basic term of copyright lasts the life of the author plus 50 years.

[84] *See* John M. Kernochan, *Imperatives for Enforcing Author's Rights,* 131 R.I.D.A. 181 (1987).

[85] For a proposal to grant copyright protection for genetically engendered bacteria, see Irving Kayton, *Copyright in Living Genetically Engineered Works*, 50 Geo. Wash. L. Rev. 191 (1982).

[86] *See* Pamela Samuelson, *Digital Media and the Changing Face of Intellectual Property Law*, 16 Rutgers Computer & Tech. L.J. 323 (1990).

to the "author" of a work, calls to mind a person, such as a novelist, composer, or artist. This "individualistic" notion of authorship (also called the "romantic" model of authorship) is ingrained in popular thinking and inscribed in the law of copyright.[87] But is this individualistic model of creation, on which so much of copyright law is based, appropriate to the world of digital electronic technologies where sounds, images, and words are duplicated, rearranged, and disseminated over vast, reticulated electronic networks?[88] Unlike our individualistic model of creation, this is a world of shared texts — electronic bulletin boards, news groups, and electronic documents — where the identities of individual contributors are either unknown or obscure, and whose contribution is fused into a multifaceted group effort. Who is the author, and who is the publisher of these valuable informational products that result from these group efforts? Application of traditional copyright principles requires answers to such basic questions, but none are forthcoming. Unquestionably, these collaborations will present a multitude of legal and ethical issues about the ownership of the material produced. But can traditional copyright principles be adapted to the electronic network without stifling a dynamic, rapidly evolving cultural "commons"? Some have forcefully argued that, although copyright will have a role to play in allocating ownership rights in the electronic network environment, traditional copyright principles based on individualistic notions of authorship are inappropriate for the proper development of this new technology.[89]

[87] The history, meaning, and ideology of authorship are examined comprehensively in Peter Jaszi, *Toward a Theory of Copyright: The Metamorphoses of "Authorship"*, 1991 Duke L.J. 455. (1991); *see also* Jessica Litman, *Copyright as Myth*, 53 U. Pitt. L. Rev. 235 (1991); Robert H. Rotstein, *Beyond Metaphor: Copyright Infringement and the Fiction of the Work*, 68 Chi.-Kent L. Rev. 725 (1992–1993); Martha Woodmansee, *The Author, the Arts, and the Market: Rereading the History of Aesthetics* (1993).

[88] The best known of these networks is the so-called "Information Superhighway." Legislation creating the "Information Superhighway" would establish a new, federally-funded, high speed network within the Internet (the Research and Education Network, or NREN).

The "Information Highway" will be used for electronic assembly, such as virtual town halls and village greens, and will include not only shared text, but multimedia transmissions of images, voice and video as well. In addition, the network will be a publications medium, distributing electronic newspapers, video clips, and other material. The challenge of adapting copyright to the digital age is explained and examined in Pamela Samuelson & Robert J. Glushko, *Intellectual Property Rights for Digital Library and Hypertext Publishing Systems*, 6 Harv. J. Law & Tech. 237 (1993). Proposals to amend the Copyright Act to accommodate copyright to the digital age and cyberspace are presented in *Intellectual Property and the National Information Infrastructure: A Preliminary Draft of a Report of the Working Group on Intellectual Property Rights* (1994).

[89] Peter Jaszi, *On The Author Effect: Contemporary Copyright and Collective Creativity*, 10 Cardozo Arts & Ent. L.J. 293, 320 (1992).

PART III: COPYRIGHT, PATENT, AND TRADEMARK COMPARED

§ 1.10   In General

Anyone who seeks a thorough understanding of copyright law should be well acquainted with the other major bodies of intellectual property protection, particularly patent and trademark law. Although based on different statutes, goals, and theories, these three forms of intellectual property law protection (copyright, patent and trademark) are interrelated and often overlap in the same subject matter. The purpose of the next section is to paint these relationships in broad brush, starting first with the federal intellectual property law and then proceeding to an analogous body of law arising out of state causes of action.

All forms of intellectual property share similarities. First, as to its nature, all intellectual property involves property rights to information: copyright (expressive information); patent (technological information); and trademark (symbolic information). Second, as to its administration by the federal government, a large body of intellectual property law is governed by federal statutes, and specific federal agencies are involved in administering patents, trademarks, and copyrights. Third, as to its international dimension, intellectual property is found in its most developed form in Western industrialized countries and is the subject of international conventions. Fourth, as to its esoteric subject matter, although intellectual property becomes more and more important from a practical, economic standpoint in our information age, this body of law is woefully misunderstood and shunned by the non-specialist.

§ 1.11   Patent Law

[A]   In General

The patent grant encourages investment in research and development to produce valuable technological information. It creates a limited monopoly over this information in return for its public disclosure. Once issued, the patent becomes a public record, accessible to those wishing to use the information to improve or invent around the invention and to those wishing to use the patent once its term expires.

Patents are the only branch of intellectual property dependent on governmental grant. A copyright does not begin by an act of government, but by the act of an author in creating a work. Similarly, trademark rights do not begin with registration, but by the use of the mark on a product or service. This basic difference between patents and other forms of intellectual property is often misunderstood by the non-specialist. The misunderstanding arises from the fact that federal agencies, the Copyright Office and Trademark Office, issue registrations in their respective fields. Copyright and trademark registrations can confer valuable rights, but registration does not create the copyright or the ownership of a trademark.

[B] Procedures to Obtain a Patent

A patent is granted by a governmental agency, the Patent Office, and lasts exactly 20 years from the date of application.[90] The decision to grant the patent is made after the patent examiner evaluates the application to determine whether it meets the standards of patentability.

The application is usually drafted by a patent attorney, one admitted to practice before the Patent Office. The patent attorney's special technical expertise is needed to properly draft the patent application and nurture its prosecution through the administrative procedures. The patent application consists of three parts:[91] the claims, the drawings, and the specification. The numbered claims, found at the end of the patent document, determine the scope of the patent and are critical in deciding if the patent has been infringed. The specification and drawings show the preferred embodiment of the invention and disclose the best means of making and using it.

The administrative process leading to issuance of a patent can take years, and thousands of dollars in legal fees. Thus, a patent should be sought only after careful consideration as to the chances of success for its issuance and its eventual validity if challenged in a court of law.

[C] Kinds of Patents

A patent confers a legal right to exclude others for a limited time from making, using, or selling the patented invention throughout the United States. There are three kinds of patents: a utility patent having a 20-year term measured from the date of application, a plant patent having the same term, and a design patent having a 14-year term as measured from the date of the grant. The utility patent is the one most often referred to when patents are discussed, and is the most important from an economic standpoint.

Utility patents are given for new, useful, and non-obvious products and processes.[92] Plant patents are given for inventing and discovering, and then asexually reproducing new and distinct plant varieties.[93] Design patents are granted for new, original, and ornamental designs for an article of manufacture.[94]

---

[90] *See* 35 U.S.C. § 154. Legislation related to obligations under the GATT changed the term to 20 years from the date of application. Previously, patents had lasted 17 years from the moment of issuance. The Uruguay Round Agreements Act (URAA), effective December 8, 1994, changed the basic term of patent. Current transitional provisions provide that 'the term of a patent that is in force on or that results from an obligation before the date that is six months after the date of the enactment of the Uruguay Round Agreements Act shall be the greater of the 20-year term . . . or 17 years from the grant. *See* 35 U.S.C. § 154(c)(1) (as amended by the URAA.)

[91] *See* 35 U.S.C. §§ 111–115.

[92] *See* 35 U.S.C. § 101.

[93] *See* 35 U.S.C. § 161.

[94] *See* 35 U.S.C. § 171. For a discussion of design patents see § 3.16, *infra.*

[D] Utility Patents: Requirements for Validity

The patent statute sets forth the requirements for patentability in § 101.[95] A patent is conferred on one who " . . . invents or discovers any new and useful process, machine, manufacture or composition of matter, or any new improvement thereof." To obtain a patent one must show (1) patentable subject matter, (2) novelty, (3) usefulness, and (4) non-obviousness.

Patentable subject matter covers the full range of technological information as physically implemented in a product or process. Products are things: machines, chemical compounds, or objects. A process is a method of achieving a result. In addition to the more familiar patents covering mechanical, electrical and chemical products or processes, patents have been granted for inventions in biotechnology (*e.g.,* man-made microbes)[96] and processes using computer software.[97]

Only *novel* products or processes are patentable. One cannot patent a preexisting natural substance. Nor can one patent a product or process which is already patented in another country or described in a printed publication.[98] Lack of novelty will preclude patentability if the invention is known, used, or sold in the United States by third parties before the patent applicant's claimed date of invention.[99] Moreover, an invention is not considered novel if an application for it is not filed in the Patent Office within a year from the time the invention is used, sold, or described in a printed publication by either third parties or by the inventor.[100] In this way, the patent statute encourages early disclosure of the invention through application in the Patent Office.

The novelty requirement reveals a fundamental difference between copyright and patent. To be copyrightable, a work must be original, the author's own work, not copied from another work. Theoretically, there could be two copyright owners of the same work created at different points in time. The originality requirement also explains why, to prove copyright infringement, the plaintiff must prove that the defendant actually copied the work, and that it was not a product of the defendant's original effort.

On the other hand, novelty in patent is an absolute concept. Once an invention exists, it is forever barred from patentability by future inventors, even if the second inventor does not copy from the first but independently arrives at the same result. The novelty requirement also explains the nature of patent infringement, which occurs if the defendant makes, uses, or sells the patented invention.[101] Originality or independent invention is no defense in an action for patent infringement as it is in copyright infringement.

---

[95] *See* 35 U.S.C. § 101.
[96] *See Diamond v. Chakrabarty*, 447 U.S. 303 (1980).
[97] *See Diamond v. Diehr*, 450 U.S. 175 (1981).
[98] *See* 35 U.S.C. § 102(b).
[99] *See* 35 U.S.C. § 102(a).
[100] *See* 35 U.S.C. § 102(b).
[101] *See* 35 U.S.C. § 271(a).

Even if the subject matter is new, patentability is precluded if the invention would be obvious to one with ordinary skill in the art. In other words, the invention sought to be patented must be nonobvious.[102] Applying the nonobviousness standard is one of the most troublesome tasks in patent law. Determination of obviousness is ultimately a question of law based on several factual conclusions. The leading case of *Graham v. John Deere Co.*[103] sets forth the process of inquiry to determine nonobviousness. First, the scope and content of the prior "art" must be determined. Next, the differences between the prior art and the claim must be ascertained. Finally, the level of ordinary skill of the practitioner in the pertinent art must be resolved. Secondary considerations such as commercial success and the failure of others to make the discovery are also taken into account. It is easy to see why obviousness determinations in courtroom settings are often lengthy proceedings involving battles of technical experts testifying why a certain invention is obvious or not.

Nothing in copyright or trademark approximates the obviousness standard. The same can be said for the utility requirement in patent law, requiring that the invention be useful.[104] The requirment of "utility" means that the invention must work as described in the patent application. Utility also means that the invention must confer some benefit upon mankind.[105]

[E] Patent Infringement

The patentee can enforce the patent against those making, using, and selling the patented invention.[106] It is the most exclusive right in intellectual property law, and original creation and innocent infringement cannot be asserted as defenses to patent infringement. The Patent Act allows for injunctive relief and up to three times actual damages for certain infringements.[107] Patent infringement suits brought in federal district court can be appealed to the Court of Appeals for the Federal Circuit, a special appeals court created in 1981 in large part to handle the technicalities of patent litigation and to add a rational uniformity to patent law. Although the patentee enjoys a legislative presumption of validity of the patent, some courts have become notorious for appearing eager to strike down patents as being invalid. Thus, in litigation, the patentee runs the risk of having the patent invalidated after incurring the expense of obtaining the patent and defending it in the patent litigation. The effect can be economically devastating to a patentee who made these substantial expenditures in expectation that the patent would be validated.

---

[102] *See* 35 U.S.C. § 103.
[103] 383 U.S. 1 (1966).
[104] *See* 35 U.S.C. § 101.
[105] *See Brenner v. Mason*, 383 U.S. 519 (1966).
[106] *See* 35 U.S.C. § 271.
[107] *See* 35 U.S.C. §§ 281–294.

§ 1.12   Trademark Law

[A]   Generally

Trademark law confers rights in symbolic information. A trademark is a brand name which can be a word, a symbol, or a device so long as it is used by a business to distinguish its goods from those of others.[108] Trademarks — brand names and other symbols of identity — such as Coca-Cola, the Pillsbury Dough Boy, and the golden arches of McDonald's — surround us. These trade symbols are valuable to businesses and consumers. To their owners, a trade symbol is a marketing device, a focus of brand loyalty. To consumers, trade symbols allow the saving of time in deciding which product to buy and where to buy it. On the negative side, critics of trademark law believe that trade symbols create irrational brand loyalty, permitting the owner of a well-known mark to set his price for the product above the competitive price. As such, an overly strong trademark law creates entry barriers to new competition from lower-priced products and more efficient competitors. Whatever the merits of these arguments, trademark law, as well as the other branches of intellectual property law, is strongest and most developed in the Western countries.

Trademarks, unlike patents and copyrights, can theoretically last forever so long as they are used to distinguish goods or services. Trademarks can be abandoned by non-use or can fall into the public domain — become the generic name of a product — if they no longer distinguish the goods or services. But ownership of a trademark is not subject to a specific duration and can theoretically endure in perpetuity.

Unlike copyright and patent law, trademark law is not the exclusive domain of federal law. Whereas a federal statute is the only source of copyright and patent law, trademark rights arise out of the state common law.[109] Consequently, Congress' power to legislate is limited to interstate transactions. Trademark, and the related body of unfair competition law, exists in all states but, only when a mark is used in interstate commerce, can the owner look to federal law and the right to register a trademark in the Trademark Office.[110]

[B]   Federal Registration of Trademarks

The federal trademark statute, the Lanham Act,[111] is important from a practical standpoint. The Act sets forth a registration system, administered by the U.S. Trademark Office, which confers substantial advantages on the registrant. Among these benefits are that: (1) the certificate of registration is *prima facie* evidence of

---

[108] *See* 15 U.S.C. § 1127; *see generally* Restatement (Third) of Unfair Competition § 9 (Tent. Draft No. 2, Mar. 23, 1990).

[109] *See Trademark Cases,* 100 U.S. 82 (1879).

[110] Effective November, 1989, an applicant for federal trademark registration can base his or her application on an *intent* to use the mark in commerce as well as on its actual use. However, not until the applicant has proved actual use will registration issue. *See* 15 U.S.C. § 1051(b)(1)(A) (as amended by the Trademark Law Revision Act of 1988).

[111] *See* 15 U.S.C. §§ 1051–1127.

the validity of the registration;[112] (2) registration is constructive notice to others of the claim of ownership;[113] (3) registration confers federal jurisdiction without regard to diversity of citizenship or amount in controversy;[114] (4) registration can become incontestable after five years of continuous use of the mark and will constitute the exclusive right to use of the mark;[115] (5) registration provides the right to treble damages, attorney's fees, and other remedies in an action for infringement;[116] and (6) registration provides the right to request customs officials to bar importation of goods bearing infringing trademarks.[117] Taken as a whole, these advantages are a powerful inducement to register.

Federal trademark registration is obtained by filing an application in the Trademark Office. Once filed, an application is reviewed by a trademark examiner who verifies, among other things, that: (1) the mark is not deceptive; (2) the mark is not confusingly similar to another mark; and (3) the mark is not merely descriptive of the goods or misdescriptive of them, geographically descriptive or misdescriptive, or primarily merely a surname.[118]

The trademark examination process is neither as lengthy nor as costly as an examination of a patent. The trademark application is relatively simple to complete as compared with the patent application. Further, in contrast to patent, prosecution before the Trademark Office does not require the aid of a special attorney admitted to practice before the agency. The trademark registration process, however, can be much more intricate and costly than filing for copyright registration.

[C]   Trademark Infringement

A trademark is infringed when a third party without authorization uses a confusingly similar mark on similar goods or services.[119] The ultimate test is whether the concurrent use of the two marks would cause consumers to be mistaken or confused about the source of origin or sponsorship of the goods or services. Thus, the marks neither have to be identical, nor used on identical products to be confusingly similar.

---

[112] See 15 U.S.C. § 1057(b).
[113] See 15 U.S.C. § 1072.
[114] See 15 U.S.C. § 1111.
[115] See 15 U.S.C. § 1065.
[116] See 15 U.S.C. §§ 1116–1120.
[117] See 15 U.S.C. § 1124.
[118] See 15 U.S.C. § 1052(a), (d)–(e).
[119] See 15 U.S.C. § 1052(d).

§ 1.13 Chart Comparing Copyright, Patent, and Trademark

A COMPARISON OF COPYRIGHT, PATENT, AND TRADEMARK

	COPYRIGHT	PATENT	TRADEMARK
SUBJECT MATTER	Literary, musical, artistic works	Utility Patents: Functional features of products and processes Design Patents: Ornamental designs for manufactured goods	Words, names, symbols or devices
STANDARDS FOR VALIDITY	Originality	Utility Patents: Novelty, obviousness, utility Design Patents: Novelty and nonobviousness of the design	Use of the mark to distinguish one's goods or services
WHEN DOES PROTECTION BEGIN?	On creation, i.e. fixation in a tangible medium of expression	Utility Patents: application date in U.S. Patent and Trademark Office Design Patents: Date of grant by U.S. Patent and Trademark Office	On use of the mark
DURATION OF PROTECTION	Life of the author plus 50 years, or 75 years from publication or 100 years from creation whichever is less	Utility Patents: 20 years from application date* Design Patents: 14 years from date of grant.	So long as properly used as a trademark
STANDARDS FOR INFRINGEMENT	Copying and substantial similarity	Utility Patents: Making, using, or selling the patented invention. Design Patents: Similarity of designs to ordinary observer	Likelihood of confusion

*The Uruguay Round Agreements Act changed the basic term of patent from 17 years from the date of grant to 20 years from the date of application. Subsisting patents on December 8, 1994, or applications filed within six months after that date will endure the greater of 17 years from the date of grant, or 20 years from the application date.

§ 1.14   State Intellectual Property Law

A diverse system of state intellectual property law plays a significant role in protecting intangible property. These areas of state law are variously known as: trade secret; unfair competition; common law copyright; right to publicity; and misappropriation. Two of the more important areas of traditional state protection are trade secret and unfair competition, which are analogous to patent and trademark law, respectively. Of less practical importance is common law copyright, which is almost entirely preempted by federal law. In addition to these traditional forms of state law protection, the right to publicity represents a relatively new body of law having similarities to both copyright and trademark law. Finally, an older form of state law, misappropriation law, still is available in appropriate cases. State protection of intangible property interests supplements federal protection, and fills in gaps unattended by federal law.

[A]   Trade Secrets

The *First Restatement of Torts*[120] defines a trade secret as consisting of:

> . . . any formula, pattern, device or compilation of information which is used in one's business, which gives him an opportunity to obtain an advantage over competitors who do not know or use it. [A trade secret] may be a formula for a chemical compound; a process of manufacturing, treating or preserving materials; a pattern for a machine or other device; or a list of customers.

Trade secret law protects much the same technological information as does patent law, but trade secret subject matter is even broader, extending to customer lists, marketing plans, and other information not included within patentable subject matter.[121] In addition, a trade secret does not have to meet the rigorous standards of inventiveness required by patent law. For these reasons, some businesses decide not to seek patent protection if the risk of being rejected for lack of patentable subject matter or inventiveness is substantial and/or does not justify the time and expense of the patent application process.

A valid trade secret exists only if it is substantially "secret" within the trade secret's owner's industry. Absolute secrecy is not required, but if the trade secret is widely used within the industry, it is less likely that it can be protected as a property right. Other factors which courts consider in determining whether secrecy exists are: the extent to which the subject matter is known by the employees in the trade secret owner's business, and the extent of measures taken to guard the secrecy of the subject matter.[122]

Trade secrets have the attributes of property, and can be licensed, taxed, and inherited. But if an attribute of property is the right to exclude others from using it, the trade secret is a weak form of property protection. A trade secret can only

---

[120] *Restatement of Torts* § 757, comment b (1939).

[121] *Id.*

[122] *See Roger M. Milgrim on Trade Secrets* § 2.01 (1988).

be enforced against improper appropriation, such as theft by an industrial spy,[123] or a breach of a confidential relationship not to divulge the trade secret. This is why it is often said that trade secret protects a relationship rather than a property interest.

Trade secrets are a particularly appropriate form of protection for processes. By its nature, a process, such as the formula for making Coca-Cola, can be practiced secretly by a few people and is often difficult to determine by reverse engineering. Compared with the 17-year patent monopoly, a trade secret may exist forever, so long as substantial secrecy exists. Thus, instead of seeking a patent for a process which will have to be publicly disclosed in the patent grant and whose patent protection will last only 17 years, many businesses prefer the trade secret status of their information in a gamble for a much longer term of protection.

[B] Unfair Competition Law

The term "unfair competition" is defined in two ways. It is sometimes used to mean a general area of law covering various commercial torts. This would include actions for trade secret misappropriation, interference with contractual relations, predatory pricing, trademark infringement, product disparagement, and any other activity contrary to our notions of fair competitive practices.

Unfair competition law is also used in a narrower preferred sense, referring to an action brought when one company passes off its goods or services as someone else's. An action for unfair competition may involve trademark infringement, use of confusingly similar corporate names, use of similar titles of literary works, products, or containers, and trade dress similarities. False representations and false advertising would fall under this definition of unfair competition as well.[124]

[C] Common Law Copyright

Under the 1909 Act, federal copyright protection began when an author published his work. Unpublished works were given protection, if at all, under state common law copyright. In contrast, the 1976 Act now protects works from the moment of creation — that is, when they are fixed in a tangible medium of expression.[125] In so doing, the 1976 Act specifically preempts state common law copyright.[126] Federal preemption will occur for a work *fixed in a tangible medium of expression,* if the state law covers the subject matter of copyright and confers the same kinds of exclusive rights found in the federal Copyright Act.

Although federal preemption casts a long shadow, state common law copyright might play a role when a work is not fixed in a tangible medium of expression. Examples would include an oral interview or jazz improvisation. The States would

---

[123] *See, e.g., E.I. du Pont de Nemours & Co. v. Christopher,* 431 F.2d 1012 (5th Cir. 1970) (aerial photography of a plant undergoing construction was an improper means of appropriating a trade secret).

[124] *See generally* Restatement (Third) of Unfair Competition §§ 2–6 (Tent. Draft No. 1, April, 12, 1988).

[125] *See* 17 U.S.C. § 102(a).

[126] *See* 17 U.S.C. § 301(a).

not be precluded from protecting these non-fixed works under their own copyright laws. The underlying authority lies in the United States Constitution which allows Congress to pass laws protecting "writings of authors."[127] Writings are generally recognized as works embodied in some kind of material form, the opposite of a purely oral or other non-fixed work.[128] Falling outside the constitutional authority of Congress, protection of oral or other non-fixed works could validly be regulated by state law. In practice, however, few courts have even considered copyright protection for oral works, but they have recognized its possibility.[129]

[D] The Right of Publicity

In 1953, a court[130] recognized for the first time an intangible property right called the "right of publicity." A body of law had already developed around the right of privacy, prohibiting appropriation for commercial benefit of a person's name or likeness. If a private person's name or likeness is used to advertise a commercial product,[131] for example, the law would allow issuance of an injunction, and would award appropriate damages for this invasion of private life and the right to be let alone as a private citizen. However, when the persona of an athlete, a movie star, or other celebrity is exploited in this way, one cannot argue as persuasively that a privacy interest is invaded. Celebrities, by implication, have waived aspects of their privacy. The harm that occurs in these circumstances is a commercial one, because the celebrity has been deprived of a property right in the fruit of his labors — *i.e.,* the ability to exploit commercially his name or picture. The right to privacy relates to dignitary harm, whereas the right to publicity involves commercial harm. The two rights rest on distinct legal theories.

Some states have statutes protecting the right of publicity;[132] in others the right is protected under the common law.[133] Whatever its form, the right of publicity is a more absolute right than either trademark or unfair competition rights and is based on a theory of unjust enrichment. An action for the right of publicity does not have to show confusion of source or sponsorship or falsity, only theft of goodwill in a third party's use of a name or likeness.

The right of publicity has continued to expand beyond its traditional domain of names and likenesses. Recent case law has used the publicity doctrine to protect attributes concerning other aspects of the identity and image of a celebrity. These have included prohibitions against a Bette Midler sound-alike in a commercial,[134]

---

[127] U.S. Const. art. I, § 8, cl. 8.

[128] *See Goldstein v. California,* 412 U.S. 546, 567–68 (1973).

[129] *See, e.g., Estate of Hemingway v. Random House, Inc.,* 23 N.Y.2d 341, 244 N.E.2d 250, 296 N.Y.S.2d 771 (1968). For a discussion of this case, see § 2.6, *infra.*

[130] *Haelan Laboratories, Inc. v. Topps Chewing Gum, Inc.,* 202 F.2d 866 (2d Cir.), *cert. denied,* 346 U.S. 816 (1953).

[131] *See Pavesich v. New England Life Ins. Co.,* 122 Ga. 190, 50 S.E. 68 (1905).

[132] *See* Cal. Civ. Code § 3344.

[133] *See Hirsch v. S.C. Johnson & Son, Inc.,* 90 Wis. 2d 379, 280 N.W.2d 129 (1979).

[134] *Midler v. Ford Motor Co.,* 849 F.2d 460 (9th Cir. 1988).

the use of the phrase "Here's Johnny" by a seller of portable toilets,[135] and an advertisement showing a robot resembling Vanna White in a game show.[136]

In addition to the ever expanding scope of the publicity right, the duration of the right is another controversial area. Whether the right of publicity survives the death of a celebrity is an open question. Some courts[137] and state statutes[138] have recognized its descendibility, while others have declared that it ends on death,[139] like the right to privacy. Some recent statutes recognize its descendibility but, like copyright law, limit its duration to life-plus-50-years to prevent distant generations from claiming the right. The policy favoring the right of publicity, much less its descendibility, is dubious at best. Supporters of the right and its descendibility maintain that it encourages artistic creativity, as does federal copyright law. Those opposing the right argue that, even if it encourages commercial exploitation of celebrity persona, other branches of intellectual property, such as trademark and unfair competition, rest on sounder assumptions which support many of the same interests as the right of publicity.[140]

[E] Misappropriation

The misappropriation doctrine is the broadest, if not the vaguest, theory protecting intangibles under state law. The doctrine traces its name to the United States Supreme Court decision in *International News Service v. Associated Press.*[141] In this case, the INS, a news gathering organization, systematically gathered from the AP's publicly distributed newspapers and bulletin boards "hot" news stories which it was able to send to its subscribers on the West Coast, sometimes actually beating AP newspapers to publication. The activity engaged in by INS, the appropriation of news, did not fit into the traditional areas of intellectual property. Gathering the news from public sources involved no breach of trust on which to base an action for theft of trade secrets; there was no passing-off to justify an action for unfair

---

[135] *Carson v. Here's Johnny Portable Toilets, Inc.*, 698 F.2d 831 (6th Cir. 1983).

[136] *Vanna White v. Samsung Electronics America, Inc.*, 971 F.2d 1395 (9th Cir. 1992), *pet. for reh'g and reh'g en banc den.*, 989 F.2d 1512 (9th Cir. 1993) (worthy of particular attention is Judge Alex Kozinski's dissenting opinion questioning the overprotection of celebrity image under an ever expanding cause of action for right of publicity. "Overprotecting intellectual property is as harmful as underprotecting it. Creativity is impossible without a rich public domain").

[137] *See, e.g., Martin Luther King, Jr. Center for Social Change, Inc. v. American Heritage Products, Inc.*, 694 F.2d 674 (11th Cir. 1983).

[138] *See, e.g.,* Cal. Civ. Code § 990.

[139] *See, e.g., Memphis Development Found. v. Factors, Etc.*, 616 F.2d 956 (6th Cir. 1980) (declining to recognize a *post mortem* right of publicity in Elvis Presley's persona).

[140] *Cf.* David Lange, *Recognizing the Public Domain*, 44 Law & Contemp. Probs. 147 (1981). *But see* Peter L. Felcher & Edward L. Rubin, *The Descendibility of the Right of Publicity: Is There Commercial Life After Death?*, 89 Yale L.J. 1125 (1980).

[141] 248 U.S. 215 (1918) For an overview of the doctrine, see Leo Raskind, *The Misappropriation Doctrine as a Competitive Norm of Intellectual Property Law*, 75 Minn. L. Rev. 875 (1991). For further discussion of this case in the context of federal preemption, see § 11.2[B], *infra.*

competition; nor did the INS engage in copyright infringement. Despite this lack of traditional intellectual property protection, the Supreme Court held that the INS activities constituted a new variety of unfair competition called "misappropriation." It enjoined the INS from using AP news reports until the commercial value of the news (its "hotness") had dissipated. The Court recognized not a general property right in the news, but a quasi-property right in "hot," breaking news which protected the originator from its competitor. In his dissent, Justice Brandeis stated that the majority was conferring monopoly rights in an idea that should be in the public domain and that protection of intangibles should be left to traditional forms of intellectual property protection.

The misappropriation doctrine is essentially an equitable doctrine existing on the fringes of intellectual property law. Applied equitably, causes of action for misappropriation have been successful where the traditional forms of intellectual property protection do not apply, but where a need for protection exists. The strong cases have typically arisen when (1) A, by substantial investment has created an intangible of value not protected by patent, trademark, copyright law, or breach of confidence, which is (2) appropriated by B, a free rider, at little cost, (3) thereby injuring A and jeopardizing A's continued production of the intangible.[142] Under this theory, the Metropolitan Opera was able to enjoin the unauthorized recording of its broadcasts,[143] and before sound recordings were given protection by a federal law in 1971, tape piracy was attacked under the misappropriation doctrine.[144] In both situations, plaintiffs could not base their claim on traditional bodies of intellectual property law, but were successful under the equitable reaches of the misappropriation doctrine.

Some courts have expressed a hostility toward the misappropriation doctrine, claiming that it conflicts with the policy underlying federal patent and copyright law and is therefore preempted under the Supremacy Clause of the Constitution. In 1929, Judge Learned Hand refused to apply the doctrine to dress design piracy on this ground,[145] and in the 1964 *Sears, Roebuck and Co. v. Stiffel Co.*[146] and *Compco Corp. v. Day-Brite Lighting, Inc.*[147] cases, the Supreme Court struck down Illinois unfair competition law as clashing with the policies of federal patent law. In addition to case law hostile to the doctrine, § 301 of the 1976 Copyright Act expressly preempts state laws which cover the same ground as federal copyright.[148] Despite these contrary trends, the misappropriation doctrine appears to be still alive for application in the occasional, appropriate case.[149]

---

[142] *See* J. Thomas McCarthy, *Trademarks and Unfair Competition* § 10.23 (2d ed. 1984).

[143] *Metropolitan Opera Association v. Wagner-Nichols Recorder Corp.*, 199 Misc. 787, 101 N.Y.S.2d 483 (Sup. Ct. 1950), *aff'd*, 279 A.D. 632, 107 N.Y.S. 795 (1951).

[144] *See Goldstein v. California*, 412 U.S. 546 (1973).

[145] *Cheney Bros. v. Doris Silk Corp.*, 35 F.2d 279 (2d Cir. 1929).

[146] 376 U.S. 225 (1964).

[147] 376 U.S. 234 (1964).

[148] For a full discussion of the misappropriation doctrine and the preemptive effect of 17 U.S.C. § 301(a), see Chapter 11, *infra*.

[149] For example, misappropriation was the theory used to enjoin the Chicago Board of Trade when it proposed the sale of stock market index contracts based on the Dow Jones

Average. The intangible value was the valuable information embodied in the Dow Jones Average. *See Board of Trade v. Dow Jones & Co.*, 98 Ill. 2d 109, 439 N.E.2d 526 (1982); *Standard & Poor's Corp. v. Commodities Exchange, Inc.*, 683 F.2d 704 (2d Cir. 1982). Whether the doctrine will survive the 90's is an open question.

CHAPTER 2

SUBJECT MATTER OF COPYRIGHT: GENERAL STANDARDS

§ 2.1 Introduction and Chapter Overview

The threshold requirement for copyrightability is set forth in § 102(a) of the Copyright Act:

> Copyright protection subsists, in accordance with this title, in original works of authorship fixed in any tangible medium of expression, now known or later developed, from which they can be perceived, reproduced, or otherwise communicated, either directly or with the aid of a machine or device.[1]

This section establishes two fundamental requirements for copyright protection: originality and fixation. By comparison, § 102(b) denies protection to any "idea, procedure, process, system, method of operation, concept, principle, or discovery. . . ."[2] This chapter examines the meaning of these statutory provisions to understand what Congress can do pursuant to its constitutional empowerment "To Promote the Progress of Science . . . , by securing for limited Times to Authors . . . the exclusive Right to their . . . Writings. . . ."[3]

This chapter, which is divided into four parts, examines the basic standards for copyrightability. Parts I and II examine the meaning of fixation and originality. Part III involves the copyrightability of derivative works and compilations. The focus in this part is on what constitutes originality for works which are substantially based on other copyrighted works or on public domain materials. Part IV is concerned with the non-copyrightable subject matter set forth in § 102(b). It includes other related topics as well, such as the copyrightability of "immoral" works and governmental works.

---

[1] 17 U.S.C. § 102(a).

[2] 17 U.S.C. § 102(b).

[3] As to whether the writings of authors constitute "Science" or "useful Arts," even the Supreme Court has seemed uncertain. In *Bleistein v. Donaldson Lithographing Co.*, 188 U.S. 239 (1903), the Court assumed the latter. But more recently, in *Graham v. John Deere Co.*, 383 U.S. 1 (1966), the Court proceeded on the view that, in eighteenth century usage, "Science" referred to the products of authors and "useful Arts" to the works of inventors. In light of the order in which the Framers placed both "Authors and Inventors" and "Writings and Discoveries," the better view probably is that "Science and useful Arts" have the meanings attributed to them in *Graham*. Hence, the usage in the text above.

PART I: Fixation

§ 2.2 Fixation and the Distinction Between the Material Object and the Copyright

Under the Copyright Clause of the U.S. Constitution, Congress may make laws to protect the "Writings" of authors. This "writings" requirement has been construed by the Supreme Court to mean any "physical rendering" of the fruits of the author's creativity.[4] Under the terminology of the present statute, a work is incapable of protection under federal law unless it is "fixed" in a "tangible medium of expression."

As the statutory language indicates, copyright subsists in "works of authorship." An "author" in the constitutional sense means *the person to whom anything owes its origin.* The creator of a work is its author.[5] Thus, a copyright comes into existence when an author takes the affirmative step of placing his or her work on a material object such as a piece of paper, a magnetic tape, or a block of marble. Unlike a patent, which is conferred by act of the government, a copyright is created by the act of an author in fixing the work in a tangible medium of expression.[6] After creating the work in this manner, the author may register[7] his or her claim to copyright in the Copyright Office, but the act of registration does not *create* the copyright.

An important preliminary distinction must be made between the copyright and the material object.[8] Copyright is an interest in an intangible property right called a work of authorship, which to qualify for statutory protection must be fixed in a material object. A copyright springs into existence when both a work of authorship and a material object merge through the act of fixation. The Copyright Act enumerates seven broad categories of works of authorship,[9] each of which may be embodied in a variety of material objects. Suppose, for example, that A writes a novel. For copyright purposes, A's novel would fall under the category of a literary work,[10] one composed of words or symbols. A's novel could be embodied on paper,

---

[4] *Goldstein v. California*, 412 U.S. 546 (1973).

[5] *See Bleistein v. Donaldson Lithographing Co.*, 188 U.S. 239 (1903); *Burrow-Giles Lithographic Co. v. Sarony*, 111 U.S. 53, 58 (1884). It can be assumed that the term "author" means human author. For a discussion of computer authored works, see § 3.7, *infra.*

[6] 17 U.S.C. § 102(a).

[7] 17 U.S.C. § 408.

[8] 17 U.S.C. § 202. The Copyright Act establishes that

> Ownership of the material object or any of the exclusive rights under a copyright is distinct from ownership of any material object in which the work is embodied. Transfer of ownership of any material object . . . does not in itself convey rights in the copyrighted work embodied in the object.

[9] These are: (1) literary works, (2) musical works (including words), (3) dramatic works, (4) pantomimes and choreographic works, (5) pictorial works, (6) motion pictures and other audiovisual works, and (7) sound recordings. *See* 17 U.S.C. § 102. Included as well are compilations and derivative works. *See* 17 U.S.C. § 103.

[10] Literary works are works . . . expressed in words, numbers, or other verbal or numerical symbols or indicia, regardless of the nature of the material objects, such as books,

printed on microfiche, or recorded on magnetic tape. There is but a single work of authorship, the literary work,[11] no matter how numerous or diverse the material objects on which the work is placed.[12]

Although fixation of a work may take place on an infinite variety of material objects, the Copyright Act defines all material objects in terms of two broad categories, copies and phonorecords. Phonorecords are objects in which sounds are fixed, whereas copies are a residual category consisting of all material objects not phonorecords.[13] Thus, copies and phonorecords comprise all the material objects in which works are capable of being fixed.

§ 2.3　Tangible Medium of Expression

[A]　The Fixation Requirement

The fixation requirement directly relates to the Copyright Clause of the Constitution which limits the grant of copyright to writings of authors.[14] Only works which qualify as writings may claim federal copyright protection. The Supreme Court has construed the "writings" requirement to mean any physical rendering of the fruits of intellectual activity.[15] Thus, the physical rendering should take some material form capable of identification and having a more or less permanent endurance.

For the purpose of the Copyright Act, a work is fixed in a tangible form when it is placed in a relatively stable and permanent embodiment. In effect, it must be recorded or written in some manner. Thus, mere performance of a work does not qualify under this provision. No matter how innovative, ingenious, or beautiful a performance by an improvisational theater group or jazz musician, the basic standard of fixation would not be met, and statutory copyright protection could not be obtained without a recordation in some form. Similarly, other creations such as a live broadcast over radio or television, an ice sculpture, or sand castle would be too evanescent or transient to meet the requirement of tangibility.

---

periodicals, manuscripts, phonorecords, film, tapes, disks, or cards, in which they are embodied.

17 U.S.C. § 101 (literary works). The term "literary works" also includes computer databases. *See* H.R. Rep. No. 94–1476, 94th Cong., 2d Sess. 54 (1976).

[11] See 17 U.S.C. § 101 for the definition of a literary work.

[12] H.R. Rep. No. 94–1476, 94th Cong., 2d Sess. 53 (1976).

[13] Professor Nimmer argues that

an unnecessary complexity in a necessarily complex statute could have been avoided by defining copies to include all material objects in which works of authorship are fixed regardless of whether or not the work consists of sound.

1 *Nimmer on Copyright* § 2.03[C] (1993).

[14] U.S. Const. Art. I, § 8, cl. 8:

To promote the Progress of Science and useful Arts, by securing for limited Times to Authors and Inventors the exclusive Right to their respective Writings and Discoveries.

[15] *Goldstein v. California*, 412 U.S. 546 (1973).

On the other hand, the recordation or writing need not have to last a long time. For example, in *MAI Systems Corp. v. Peak Computer Inc.*,[16] the court held that the loading of the plaintiff's copyrighted software into RAM memory consitutes a fixation and qualifies as a copy under the Copyright Act. Permanence and stability requirements were met even though the text will vanish forever when the computer is turned off at the end of the work session, unless, of course, it first is stored in some other way — for example, on a disk.

To obtain copyright, the author herself or someone under her authorization [17] must reduce the work to a relatively stable form. Only then may an author control the performance of her work by third parties. Suppose, for example, that A, a performance artist, recites a spontaneous poetic monologue which is recorded by B, a member of the audience. The recordation would not constitute a "fixation" for the purpose of copyright because it was not authorized by the author, with the result that A would not be able to control B's exploitation of the piece. What A should do to avoid this problem is to record the poetic work on magnetic tape *before* the performance. The work would then be fixed and third parties would infringe the copyright if they reproduced the work or performed it without permission.

Obviously, the author should "fix" her work beforehand. This is not always possible, however, for works which are created spontaneously. But would a simultaneous fixation of the work as it is being performed qualify for copyright? For live broadcasts, the Copyright Act provides protection when the work is being simultaneously recorded. Customarily, a simultaneous recording is carried out for most broadcasts. There is, however, a gap in the law for non-broadcasted works, that is, for works which are not being simultaneously transmitted [18] beyond the place where they are being performed. Even though they may be simultaneously recorded, they are not covered by this provision, which requires transmission. Non-broadcasted works would thus be in jeopardy of appropriation by someone in the audience making an unauthorized recording. One solution to this problem is to have the performance telephoned to another location, thereby meeting the transmission requirement.[19]

[B] The Anti-Bootleg Provisions: An Exception to the Fixation Requirement

Until the passage of the anti-bootleg provisions under the Uruguay Round Agreements Act,[20] the fixation requirement constituted a major obstacle to an effective remedy for the unauthorized fixation of live performances. Effective December 8, 1994, the unauthorized fixation of sound recordings and music videos of live *musical* performances is rendered illegal.

---

[16] 991 F.2d 511 (9th Cir. 1993).

[17] H.R. Rep. No. 94–1476, 94th Cong., 2d Sess. 53 (1976).

[18] To transmit is to communicate a performance "by any device or process whereby images or sounds are received beyond the place from which they are sent." 17 U.S.C. § 101.

[19] 1 *Nimmer on Copyright* § 1.08[B] (1993).

[20] Pub. L. No. 103–465, 108 Stat. 4809 (1994).

The practice of bootlegging live musical performances of U.S. artists has presented a legal quandary for performers of music. As discussed above, federal copyright with its fixation requirement has deprived performing artists of an effective cause of action against the unauthorized fixation of live performances. The problem was addressed in the past through various state anti-bootlegging and unfair competition laws, and by common law copyright. Performers have sought relief against acts taking place in individual states, with varying success, but recourse against international trade in bootleg sound recordings has been largely elusive. Effective copyright enforcement against international bootlegging depends on the U.S Customs Service stopping entry of the recording at the border. The Customs Service does not, as a rule, enforce rights under state law. Once bootleg recordings make their way into the stream of commerce, from a practical standpoint, their further sale and distribution become impossible to curtail. Consequently, lack of effective border enforcement, pursuant to a uniform federal law, has led to a vibrant international trade in bootleg recordings.

The Uruguay Round Agreements Act, designed to implement U.S. obligations under the new World Trade Organization (previously known as the General Agreement on Tariffs and Trade or GATT), has provided civil and criminal remedies to combat the bootleg trade. A new Chapter 11 of the Copyright Act grants performers a civil cause of action for the unauthorized making, fixation, and trafficking [21] in sound recordings and music videos. Section 1101 of the Act makes it illegal to fix the sounds or sounds and images of a live musical performance in a copy or phonorecord, or to reproduce copies or phonorecords of such a performance from an unauthorized fixation. [22] It is also illegal to transmit to the public or distribute any copy or phonorecord embodying the unauthorized recording. Persons who engage in such activities are subject to all the remedies for infringement under copyright. [23] Supplementing the civil cause of action are criminal provisions that subject the unauthorized fixation of and trafficking in sound recordings, music videos, or live musical performances to criminal penalties. [24]

The anti-bootleg provisions in the new Chapter 11 of the Copyright Act represent a departure from a basic tenet of U.S copyright law. For the first time, a remedy is given to works that are not fixed by the author in a tangible medium of expression. Although the anti-bootleg provisions are limited to musical works, one may ask whether these provisions will be extended eventually to prohibit the unauthorized fixation of live performances covering the entire range of copyrightable subject matter — i.e., literary and dramatic works.

---

[21] " . . . [T]he term 'traffic in' means transport, transfer, or otherwise dispose of, to another, as consideration for anything of value, or make or obtain control of with intent to transport, transfer or dispose of." Id.

[22] 17 U.S.C. § 1101(a)(1).

[23] For infringement remedies, see 17 U.S.C. §§ 502–505.

[24] 18 U.S.C. § 2319A.

§ 2.4 Perception by Machine or Device

The fixation requirement will be satisfied if the work as fixed can be perceived either directly or with the aid of a machine or device.[25] The fixation can take place in any manner, form, or medium. It makes no difference if the work is written in words, numbers, notes, sounds, pictures, or other symbols, so long as they can be perceived either directly or by any machine or device existing now or developed at a later time. The broad language of the Copyright Act is intended to overturn a famous and much criticized case under the 1909 Act, *White-Smith Music Publishing Co. v. Apollo Co.*,[26] which held that a piano roll was not a copy of the musical composition embodied on it and therefore did not qualify for copyright because there must be a printed record in intelligible notation, readable to the eye. The *White-Smith* doctrine was applied to both phonorecords and magnetic tape, neither of which embody intelligible, eye-readable written notation. Today, under the Copyright Act, the *White-Smith* doctrine is completely overruled, allowing copyrightability for sound recordings, computer programs, motion pictures, and other works embodied on objects which cannot be read without a machine or device.[27]

§ 2.5 The Videogame Cases

The most recent analysis of the fixation requirement has involved actions for infringement of copyrighted video games.[28] For this kind of entertainment, visual images and sounds are produced by computer programs stored in various memory devices. When the game is not being played, the images are repetitive but during play, they are subject to variation by human intervention.[29] The defendants in several cases have claimed that they were free to copy the plaintiff's games because they were not fixed in a tangible medium of expression but were rather ephemeral projections on a cathode ray tube. In addition, the variations of image patterns due to the different skills of those playing the games prevented a sufficiently consistent pattern to constitute a fixation of the work. The case law has universally renounced this reasoning.

---

[25] 17 U.S.C. § 102(a).

[26] 209 U.S. 1 (1908).

[27] The House Report makes this clear:

This broad language is intended to avoid the artificial and largely unjustifiable distinctions, derived from cases such as *White-Smith Music Publishing Co. v. Apollo Co.*, 209 U.S. 1 (1908).

H.R. Rep. No. 94–1476, 94th Cong., 2d Sess. 52 (1976).

[28] *Tandy Corp. v. Personal Micro Computers, Inc.*, 524 F. Supp. 171 (N.D. Cal. 1981); *Stern Electronics, Inc. v. Kaufman*, 523 F. Supp. 635 (E.D.N.Y. 1981), *aff'd*, 669 F.2d 852 (2d Cir. 1982); *Atari, Inc. v. Amusement World, Inc.*, 547 F. Supp. 222 (D. Md. 1981); *Atari, Inc. v. North Am. Philips Consumer Electronics Corp.*, 672 F. Supp. 607 (7th Cir. 1982); *Williams Electronic, Inc. v. Artic Int'l, Inc.*, 685 F.2d 870 (3d Cir. 1982).

[29] "Video games . . . can roughly be described as computers programmed to create on a television screen cartoons in which some of the action is controlled by the player." *Stern Elec., Inc. v. Kaufman*, 669 F.2d 852, 853 (2d Cir. 1982).

In *Stern Electronics, Inc. v. Kaufman*,[30] the question whether the statutory fixation requirement was met arose since the audiovisual images were transient and could not be fixed. The court held that the audiovisual game was "permanently embodied in a material object, the memory devices, from which it could be perceived with the aid of the other components of the game."[31] These memory devices, called ROMs (read only memory), are tiny computer chips containing thousands of pieces of data which store the instructions of the computer program. A microprocessor executes the program, causing the game to operate. The fixation requirement is met when the computer program is embodied in the ROM device. There is nothing startling about the holding in *Stern* once it is understood that the ROM is the material object, and the copyrighted work is the computer program embodied in it.

Another issue litigated in the videogame cases is whether the player's participation prevents the fixing of the audiovisual patterns. In *Williams Electronics Inc. v. Artic International, Inc.*,[32] the court rejected this claim, concluding that there is always a repetitive sequence of a substantial portion of the sights and sounds of the game. Many aspects of the display remain constant from game to game regardless of how the player operates the controls. Thus, the fixation requirement does not require that the work be written down or recorded somewhere exactly as it is perceived by the eye. Rather, all that is necessary is that the work is capable of being perceived with the aid of a machine or device.[33]

§ 2.6   Works Not Fixed in a Tangible Medium of Expression: Common Law Copyright

So far the discussion has focused on works fixed in a tangible medium of expression and qualifying for federal copyright protection.[34] How, if at all, can one protect the creative effort of those works which are not fixed and so do not qualify for protection under federal copyright law? Due to their inherently vague nature, oral works present difficult problems of proof of their existence and ownership. Apart from these difficult practical problems, there is little case law directly

---

[30] 669 F.2d 852 (2d Cir. 1982).

[31] 669 F.2d 852, 856 (2d Cir. 1982).

[32] 685 F.2d 870 (3d Cir. 1982).

[33] *See Midway Mfg. Co. v. Artic Int'l, Inc.*, 547 F. Supp. 999 (N.D. Ill. 1982), *aff'd*, 704 F.2d 1009 (7th Cir. 1983).

[34] Until the 1976 Copyright Act, the American law of copyright was based on the dichotomy between federal and state law. Unpublished works were the domain of state common law copyright. Once a work was published, federal protection began and the state law or common law copyright was divested. Under the 1976 Act, federal protection begins when a work is fixed. 17 U.S.C. § 102(a). Thus, if common law copyright is still available at all, it would apply to works not fixed in a tangible medium, consisting of oral works and performances. Unlike the 1976 Act, many "authors' rights" laws around the world do not differentiate between fixed and unfixed works as a basis for copyright protection. Neither the Berne Convention for the Protection of Literary and Artistic Works, to which the United States acceded effective March 1, 1989, nor the Universal Copyright Convention, to which the U.S. has been a party since 1955, limits member states to protecting fixed works.

establishing state protection under a common law copyright theory.[35] Only one state court has suggested that protection could be effected by this means. In *Hemingway v. Random House, Inc.*,[36] the Nobel Prize winning author's friend, A. E. Hochner, kept a meticulous record of Hemingway's reflections on a range of matters and published a book, *Papa Hemingway*, based largely on these oral musings. Although the New York Court of Appeals did not find common law copyright infringement on the part of Hochner's publisher, Random House, the court suggested that there may be situations in which an interlocutor utters statements protectable under state law. But it must be clear from the circumstances that the speaker intended to create a property interest in his oral work. The speaker should, at least, mark off the utterance from common speech to demonstrate that he meant to adopt it as a unique statement and to control its publication. The court was apparently concerned about the problem of determining under these circumstances what constituted the work in question and whether an infringement or misuse of the work by third parties had taken place.

In *Falwell v. Penthouse International, Ltd.*,[37] the court once again suggested that common law copyright for oral statements is an available form of protection in the appropriate case, but refused to allow Jerry Falwell's claim on this basis. Falwell had given an interview to a reporter from *Penthouse Magazine* which was published without his consent in the magazine. In rejecting Falwell's claim of common law copyright infringement, the court found that nowhere had the Reverend identified the subject matter of his claim by design or implication. In addition, the court expressed a fear of nuisance suits brought by celebrities claiming protection for their oral statements. The court did leave open the possibility, however, of common law copyright protection of oral expression under narrow circumstances, but failed to define the appropriate circumstances in which this protection would occur.

The reluctance of the courts to entertain suits under a common law copyright theory reveals the policy behind the fixation requirement. Unlike real and personal property, a copyright is an intangible property right whose boundaries do not have natural physical limits. The fixation requirement renders those boundaries somewhat more concrete. At least, when a work is embodied in a tangible medium of expression, one can point to something, enabling a court to determine whether infringement has taken place. It also simplifies market transactions because buyers and sellers are better able to specify what rights are being acquired. Thus, the fixation requirement serves a useful economic goal by facilitating the organization of a market for copyrighted works, and at the same time, keeping ownership rights within reasonable limits.[38] The lack of boundaries appears to influence the courts, as in *Hemingway* and *Falwell*, who generally deny the claims of common law copyright. The fixation requirement is perhaps the clearest example of a boundary setting

---

[35] One state, California, by statute protects works of authorship not fixed in a tangible medium of expression. *See* Cal. Civ. Code § 980(a) (West 1982).

[36] 23 N.Y.2d 341, 244 N.E.2d 250, 296 N.Y.S.2d 771 (1968).

[37] 521 F. Supp. 1204 (W.D. Va. 1981).

[38] See Wendy S. Gordon, *An Inquiry into the Merits of Copyright: The Challenges of Consistency, Consent, and Encouragement Theory*, 41 Stan. L. Rev. 1343, 1378-84 (1989), for a stimulating elaboration of this idea.

device that demarcates and delimits the grant of copyright. But there are others, and one can find a number of "boundary-making" doctrines throughout the 1976 Act, including the intricate texture of the ennumerated rights and their limitations, the idea/expression dichotomy, and the requirement of originality.

PART II: ORIGINALITY

§ 2.7 Original and Creative Authorship

[A] In General

Although the essence of copyright is originality, this key term is purposely left undefined by the Copyright Act. According to the House Report, the reason for this lack of explicit definition is the legislative intention to incorporate the standard for originality as established by courts under the 1909 Act.[39] As developed by the case law, there are two aspects to originality: independent creation and a modest quantum of creativity. With *Feist Publications, Inc. v. Rural Telephone Service Company, Inc.* 499 U.S. 340 (1990), the Supreme Court declared that originality (independent creation plus a modicum of creativity), the *"sine qua non* of copyright" is a constitutional requirement for copyright protection.[40] The influence of *Feist* will have a significant impact on the law of copyright in two important ways. First, although the *Feist* case itself concerned the copyrightability of compilations of fact, the case will affect all varieties of works of authorship when the issue of originality arises, particularly for categories of works often manifesting low degrees of authorship, such as maps, and computer software programs. Second, in constitution-alizing the originality requirement, *Feist* clearly constrains Congress' power to legislate under the copyright and patent clause of the Constitution in protecting works that do not meet the constititutional requirement of originality, that is, independent creation and the requisite quantum of creativity.[41]

[B] Independent Creation

An original work is one that is independently created, owing its origin to an author. Simply put, it is a work not copied from another. Courts have inferred the requirement of originality from the constitutional language which limits copyright to writings of authors.[42] It follows that one can not be an author unless he originated

---

[39] H.R. Rep. No. 94–1476, 94th Cong., 2d Sess. 51 (1976).

[40] Justice O'Connor's opinion referred no fewer than thirteen times to the constitutional basis of the originality requirement.

[41] For a discussion of constitutional issues involving attempts by Congress under the Commerce Clause or the states to circumvent *Feist*, see Paul J. Heald, *The Vices of Originality*, 1991 Sup. Ct. Rev. 143, 168–177 (arguing that neither Congress under the Commerce Clause nor the States have the authority to circumvent *Feist* by special legislation to protect unoriginal works).

[42] According to H.R. Rep. No. 94–1476, 94th Cong., 2d Sess. 51 (1976), this standard of originality does not include requirements of novelty and there is no intention to enlarge the standard of copyright protection to require them.

something. This standard for originality should be compared with the much more rigorous patent standard of novelty. To qualify for a patent, an invention must be novel, not known or practiced previously.[43] As a corollary, a patentee may establish infringement by showing that the alleged infringing product or process is substantially similar to the patented invention.[44] In patent law, infringement will be found even if the third party had independently created the invention.

By contrast, in copyright law all that is required for protection is independent creation,[45] not striking uniqueness, ingenuity, or novelty.[46] Paradoxically, nothing prevents a valid claim of copyright on two or more substantially similar works so long as they were independently created. An action for copyright reflects this principle by requiring the copyright owner to prove both substantial similarity and copying. Unlike a case for patent infringement, proving substantial similarity alone will not be enough to prove copyright infringement; one must prove by direct or circumstantial evidence that the infringer actually copied another's work. In a famous passage, Judge Learned Hand phrased the issue as follows:

> If by some magic a man who had never known it were to compose anew Keats's *Ode on a Grecian Urn*, he would be an "author" and, if he copyrighted it, others might not copy that poem, though they might of course copy Keats's [public domain poem].[47]

[C]   The Quantum of Originality: Creative Authorship

Even if a work is an independent creation it must demonstrate a minimal amount of creative authorship. The standard is a *de minimis* one; almost any distinguishable variation of a prior work will constitute a sufficient quantity of originality. Thus, courts have found originality in such banal creations as the label on a box of cake[48] and plastic flowers.[49] Copyright, however, has been denied to fragmentary words or phrases,[50] slogans,[51] slight variations of musical compositions,[52] and

---

[43] 35 U.S.C. §§ 101, 102.

[44] 35 U.S.C. § 271.

[45] 17 U.S.C. § 101.

[46] *Alfred Bell & Co. v. Catalda Fine Arts, Inc.*, 191 F.2d 99 (2d Cir. 1951).

[47] *Sheldon v. Metro-Goldwyn Pictures Corp.*, 81 F.2d 49, 54 (2d Cir. 1936).

[48] *See, e.g., Kitchens of Sara Lee, Inc. v. Nifty Foods Corp.*, 266 F.2d 541, 545 (2d Cir. 1959) ("[t]he pictures of the cakes used by plaintiff on its labels although possibly not achieving the quality of a Leonardo 'Still Life' nevertheless have sufficient commercial artistry to entitle them to protection against obvious copying . . ."). *But cf. Bailie v. Fisher*, 258 F.2d 425 (D.C. Cir. 1958) (holding that a standing cardboard star does not fall within the historical and ordinary conception of a work of art).

[49] *See, e.g., Prestige Floral S.A. v. California Artificial Flower Co.*, 201 F. Supp. 287 (S.D.N.Y. 1962). *But cf. Gardenia Flowers, Inc. v. Joseph Markovits, Inc.*, 280 F. Supp. 776 (S.D.N.Y. 1968) (holding that plaintiff's artificial corsages lacked the creativity and originality necessary for a work of art under the 1909 Act).

[50] For example, the Copyright Office reflected this view in one of its regulations under the 1909 Act. Words and short phrases, such as names, titles and slogans, familiar symbols or designs are not copyrightable. 37 C.F.R. § 202.1(a) (1959). *See Alberto-Culver Co. v. Andrea Dumon, Inc.*, 466 F.2d 705 (7th Cir. 1972) (holding that the phrase "most personal

paraphrases of standard business forms as not meeting the *de minimis* standard.[53]

In determining whether a work meets the quantum of originality, the work must be evaluated as a whole, not dissected as to its individual components. In *Atari Games Corp. v. Oman*,[54] the court held that the Copyright Office improperly denied registration to a videogame screen. The Office erred because it focused on the independent components of the screens made up of simple geometric shapes. The Office should have evaluated the work as a whole because even simple geometric shapes, when selected and combined in a distinctive manner, may meet the modest standard for creative authorship.[55]

Why require a quantum of originality? One justification is the idea of a *quid pro quo* for the copyright monopoly. We should reward with a copyright only an author who has contributed to our fund of culture. Judge Kaplan has phrased this idea as follows:

> we can . . . conclude that to make the copyright turnstile revolve, the author should have to deposit more than a penny in the box, and some like measure ought to apply to infringement.[56]

Although the requirement of creative authorship entails a certain *de minimis* amount of originality, it embodies no conception of artistic merit or beauty. A celebrated case decided early in the century, *Bleistein v. Donaldson Lithographing Co.*,[57] involving the copyrightability of a circus poster, explicitly established that, in deciding questions of copyrightability, courts should not inject their own views on what constitutes artistic merit. Justice Holmes expressed this idea as follows:

---

sort of deodorant" is not copyrightable). *See also* 37 C.F.R. § 202.1 (1982), in which, under "Materials not subject to copyright," "words and short phrases such as names, titles and slogans" are included. *But see* 1 *Nimmer on Copyright* § 2.01[B] (1993), for arguments that even a short phrase, if sufficiently creative, might be entitled to copyright protection.

[51] Slogans can be protected in certain circumstances under the law of unfair competition. *See generally* J. Thomas McCarthy, *Trademarks and the Law of Unfair Competition* (1973). *See also* Samuel W. Tannenbaum, *Uses of Titles for Copyrighted and Public Domain Works*, 6 Bull. Copyright Soc'y 64 (1959).

[52] *See, e.g., Shapiro, Bernstein & Co. v. Miracle Record Co., Inc.*, 91 F. Supp. 473 (N.D. Ill. 1950), and *McIntyre v. Double-A Music Corp.*, 179 F. Supp. 160 (S.D. Cal. 1959). *But cf. Wihtol v. Wells*, 231 F.2d 550 (7th Cir. 1956) (holding that a composition based on a folk song was copyrightable). *See also* Joel L. Friedman, *Copyright and the Musical Arrangement: An Analysis of the Law and Problems Pertaining to This Specialized Form of Derivative Work*, 7 Pepperdine L. Rev. 125 (1979).

[53] *See, e.g., Donald v. Zack Meyer's T.V. Sales and Service*, 426 F.2d 1027, 1031 (5th Cir. 1970), *cert. denied*, 400 U.S. 992 (1971) (holding that the plaintiff's legal form was not entitled to protection, the court stated, "[w]e reward creativity and originality with a copyright but we do not accord copyright protection to a mere copycat").

[54] 888 F.2d 878 (D.C. Cir. 1989); *Atari Games Corp. v. Oman*, 979 F.2d 242 (D.C. Cir. 1992).

[55] *See Atari*, 979 F.2d at 244 (the work would be copyrightable "if the requisite level of creativity is met by either the individual screens or the relationship of each screen to the others and/or the accompanying sound effects").

[56] Benjamin Kaplan, *An Unhurried View of Copyright* 46 (1967).

[57] 188 U.S. 239 (1903).

It would be a dangerous undertaking for persons trained only to the law to constitute themselves final judges of the worth of pictorial illustrations, outside of the narrowest and most obvious limits. At one extreme some works of genius would be sure to miss appreciation. Their very novelty would make them repulsive until the public had learned the new language in which their author spoke. . . . At the other end, copyright would be denied to pictures which appealed to a public less educated than the judge.[58]

Since *Bleistein*, both courts and the Copyright Office have avoided aesthetic decisions in deciding questions of originality.

The *Bleistein* case involved the corollary question of whether copyright could be claimed for a work intended for advertising purposes. Under an earlier view, copyright protection was denied to advertisements on the ground that they lacked artistic merit. Most courts have followed Justice Holmes' statement that "[a] picture is none the less a picture and none the less a subject of copyright that it is used for an advertisement."[59] To name a few dimensions of copyrightability in an advertisement, today, textual aspects of an advertisement may be protected as a literary work and the pictorial elements as an artistic or graphic work.[60] In sum, so long as the work contains the required original elements, courts will not look to the intended purpose of the work or the audience to whom it is directed.

PART III: DERIVATIVE WORKS AND COMPILATIONS

§ 2.8 Derivative Works and Compilations: An Overview

Derivative works and compilations are specifically recognized by § 103[61] of the 1976 Act as copyrightable subject matter. They join the seven protected categories of works of authorship set forth in § 102.[62]

Section 101 defines a derivative work as:

. . . a work based upon one or more preexisting works, such as a translation, musical arrangement, dramatization, fictionalization, motion picture version, sound recording, art reproduction, abridgement, condensation, or any other form in which a work may be recast, transformed, or adapted. A work consisting of editorial revisions, annotations, elaborations, or other modifications which, as a whole, represent an original work of authorship, is a "derivative work."[63]

All works to a certain degree borrow from others, but in the case of a derivative work, a substantial copying has taken place. In other words, a derivative work would be an infringement of the work on which it is based. To avoid infringement, the

[58] *Id.* at 251–52.
[59] *Id.* at 251.
[60] *Ansehl v. Puritan Pharmaceutical Co.*, 61 F.2d 131 (8th Cir. 1932).
[61] 17 U.S.C. § 103.
[62] 17 U.S.C. § 102.
[63] 17 U.S.C. § 101.

derivative work author of a translation, musical arrangement, or art reproduction must either base his work on one in the public domain or obtain permission from the author of the preexisting copyrighted work.[64] Any recasting, reforming, abridgement, or editorial revision can be copyrighted as a derivative work so long as the standard of originality is met.

Compilations are similar to derivative works because they too are substantially based on preexisting materials and data. A compilation is defined in the Act as:

> . . . a work formed by the collection and assembling of preexisting materials or of data that are selected, coordinated, or arranged in such a way that the resulting work as a whole constitutes an original work of authorship. The term "compilation" includes collective works.[65]

The compilation differs from the derivative work in one significant way. Unlike the derivative work author, the creator of a compilation does not recast, reform, or change the underlying materials but rather compiles (or assembles) them in his own manner. Thus, a compilation can include the selection, coordination, and arrangement of facts, data, or materials that are in the public domain. Examples of factual assemblage of this type are telephone books, case reporters, and catalogs of various kinds. The term "compilation" encompasses "collective works," defined as including works such as periodicals, anthologies, or encyclopedias, in which separate works are assembled into a collective whole. Instead of an assembly of facts or data, a collective work is made up an assembly of independent works such as an anthology of poems, or articles in a monthly magazine.

To be copyrightable, the derivative work, compilation, or collective work must satisfy the standard of originality, and the work must display a variation on the preexisting work that is more than merely trivial, that is sufficient to render the work distinguishable from the prior work in a meaningful way.[66]

---

[64] If a work borrows only the ideas of a preexisting work and not the *expression* of those ideas, it is not a derivative work because there has been no infringement of the preexisting work. *See Reyher v. Children's Television Workshop*, 533 F.2d 87 (2d Cir. 1976); Paul Goldstein, *Derivative Rights and Derivative Words in Copyright*, 30 J. Copyright Soc'y 209 (1983).

[65] 17 U.S.C. § 101 (compilation).

[66] For cases finding sufficient originality, see *Hesse v. Brunner*, 172 F. Supp. 284 (S.D.N.Y. 1959) (original photograph of a public domain building); *Roth Greeting Cards v. United Card Co.*, 429 F.2d 1106 (9th Cir. 1970) (greeting card considered as a whole, including text, arrangement of text, art work, and association between art and text, constitutes sufficient originality). Cases finding insufficient originality include: *Shapiro, Bernstein & Co. v. Jerry Vogel Music Co.*, 73 F. Supp. 165 (S.D.N.Y. 1947) (a change in rhythm and a slight variation in the bass of the accompaniment of a song); *Eggers v. Sun Sales Corp.*, 263 F. 373 (2d Cir. 1920) (new and original pagination for a public domain work); *Carter v. Hawaii Transportation Co.*, 201 F. Supp. 301 (D. Hawaii 1961) (selection of cities to be included in public domain map).

§ 2.9 Derivative Works

[A] Originality in Derivative Works

Original authorship in a derivative work consists of modifying the pre-existing work into a new work. For example, if a person translates Flaubert's *Madame Bovary*, his copyright extends to the original aspects of the translation, such as finding the proper word equivalents, and patterning the syntax to read properly in English. The derivative work copyright extends only to those original elements added by the derivative work author, not to the underlying work. Copyright in the resulting derivative work is unrelated to any exclusive right in the pre-existing material. It is independent of, and does not affect or enlarge the scope, duration, ownership, or subsistence of, any copyright protection in the pre-existing material. In the Flaubert example, anyone could go to the public domain source and make his own independently copyrighted work.

The above example involved a derivative work based on a public domain work, but a derivative work can be based on a copyrighted work as well. Take, for example, a motion picture version of a copyrighted dramatic work such as *Death of a Salesman*. In this instance, the derivative work copyright would cover the original elements added to the underlying copyrighted work, for example, the original dialogue, the camera angles, and the montage. If the play went into the public domain, anyone could freely reproduce it, perform it or make a motion picture based on it so long as they did not copy the original elements of the copyrighted derivative work.

[B] Use of Derivative Works in the Public Domain

Difficult conceptual problems arise when the derivative work goes into the public domain while the underlying work remains copyrighted. The problems are most complex when the original elements of the derivative work are inextricably intertwined with the pre-existing work, such as when a screenplay is based on a novel, or an English translation of a novel originally written in a foreign langauge.

In Grove Press, Inc. v. Greenleaf Publishing Co.,[67] an English translation of Jean Genet's *Journal du Voleur* entered the public domain for failure to comply with the *ad interim* provisions of the manufacturing clause.[68] The underlying French version, however, was protected by a valid copyright. Suit was brought by the copyright owner to enjoin reproduction and distribution of the public domain English translation. The court held that in copying the translation, the defendant had infringed the copyrighted aspects of the preexisting French language work. In theory, a third party could use the original aspects added by the translation to the underlying work. But these public domain aspects, the new matter of the translation, were so intertwined and fused with the underlying work that they could not be used without

---

[67] 247 F. Supp. 518 (E.D.N.Y. 1965).

[68] For a discussion of the *ad interim* provisions of the manufacturing clause under the 1909 Act, see § 4.17[B], *infra*.

infringing the underlying work. Paradoxically, the effect of the court's ruling was to keep the public domain translation out of the public domain.[69]

Grove supports protection of the copyright owner, but undermines an equally important policy in copyright law, that of enriching the public domain. Perhaps the better result would have been to allow copying of the public domain translation. This would have deprived the copyright owner of royalties for that translation, but solely as to that one version in that medium only. The copyright owner could still license other translations of his work, while the public could have access to what should properly belong in the public domain.

[C] The Lawful Use Requirement

A derivative work copyright can only be obtained when the author legally used the material on which the derivative work was based. Section 103(a)[70] of the Copyright Act states that no copyright can be claimed for any part of a derivative or collective work that has used the pre-existing material unlawfully. This prevents an unlawful user of the underlying work from profiting from unlawful use, and protects aspects of the work that were unlawfully derived from preexisting material. The effect of this section is to deny copyright to derivative works which unlawfully use pre-existing material throughout the entire work. If one can separate the unlawful aspects from the other parts of a work which were created lawfully, those latter aspects could qualify for copyright. Thus, an unauthorized translation of a novel could not be copyrighted at all. But the owner of the copyright for an anthology of poetry, as the collective work author, could sue anyone who infringed the whole anthology, even if the infringer showed that one or more poems in the collection were unlawfully used.

[D] Originality in Reproductions of Works of Art

Courts have had particular difficulty in applying the standard of originality for reproductions or works of art.[71] An artistic reproduction is a derivative work, one which is substantially based on an underlying or preexisting work, and, like any other

---

[69] The *Grove* reasoning was also applied in *Russell v. Price*, 612 F.2d 1123 (9th Cir. 1979), *cert. denied*, 446 U.S. 1952 (1980), where a derivative work film based on the Shaw play *Pygmalion* and prepared during the first term of the play's copyright, had entered the public domain because of failure to renew the copyright. Defendant, who wanted to exploit the film, argued that because the copyright for the film had expired, the film was in the public domain free for all to use. The court disagreed. Only the original elements of the film entered the public domain, but the material used in the film from the underlying play was left unaffected. Because the film could not be used without using the play, the defendant would be liable for infringement. *See also Stewart v. Abend*, 495 U.S. 207 (1990) (author's grant of short story gave the defendant no right to exploit the picture *Rear Window*, based on the story, during the story's renewal term, since the author had died before the renewal term vested). *Stewart* is discussed at § 6.10 [B], *infra*.

[70] 17 U.S.C. § 103(a).

[71] Art reproductions are specifically included in the definition of pictorial, graphic, and sculptural works. *See* 17 U.S.C. § 101.

kind of work of authorship, it must meet the standard of originality. But the nature and extent of this originality have been the subjects of long-standing controversy.

In general, an artistic reproduction which merely makes an exact copy of a prior work would lack sufficient originality. If the copy, however, entails the independent creative judgment of the artist in its production, those aspects will render the work original. In *Alfred Bell & Co. v. Catalda Fine Arts, Inc.*,[72] the copyrightability of mezzotint engravings based on public domain paintings were questioned as lacking originality. The court held that the engravings were sufficiently original as to be entitled to copyright, because the author contributed something more than a merely trivial variation on the preexisting work, something that was more recognizably his own. As applied to the mezzotints, that something more entailed the creative efforts of engravers and artists in selecting the colors and in their using the engraving process, which introduced variations on the original painting. Under the court's view, a modest grade of originality is all that is required for copyrightability. This is, in effect, little more than a prohibition against actual copying.

Recent cases, particularly in the Second and Seventh Circuits, appear to run counter to *Catalda*'s *de minimis* standard for originality as applied to identical reproductions of works of art. Some courts have declined to award a derivative work copyright protection to the labor involved in transferring a work from one medium into another. To provide copyright protection under these circumstances would, in effect, confer copyright on the medium itself. In *L. Batlin & Son, Inc. v. Snyder*,[73] the Second Circuit Court of Appeals refused to grant copyright protection to the plaintiff's virtually exact copy in plastic of a cast iron, public domain, Uncle Sam bank. The court held that the standard for originality was not met because the variations were merely trivial and that the physical skill and special training to convert the cast iron bank were insufficient to support copyright.

Batlin was affirmed, if not extended, in *Durham Industries v. Tomy Corp.*,[74] a more recent Second Circuit case involving the copyrightability of three dimensional reproductions of the famous Walt Disney characters, Mickey Mouse, Donald Duck, and Pluto. The court held that the toys did not display sufficient originality because copying from one medium to another requires nothing more than physical as compared with artistic skill.

Cases dealing with copyright for artistic reproduction conflict and are hard to reconcile even in the same circuit. *Batlin* and *Tomy* should be compared with *Alva Studios, Inc. v. Winninger*,[75] which involved the copyrightability of a small-scale reproduction of Rodin's famous public domain sculpture, the *Hand of God*. Here the court held that the work was copyrightable, requiring great skill and originality to reproduce a scale reproduction with such exactitude. *Alva* differs from *Batlin* and *Tomy* in the complexity and exactitude required in the resulting reduction of the

[72] 191 F.2d 99 (2d Cir. 1951).
[73] 536 F.2d 486 (2d Cir. 1976).
[74] 630 F.2d 905 (2d Cir. 1980).
[75] 177 F. Supp. 265 (S.D.N.Y. 1959).

Rodin sculpture, and perhaps the cases can be reconciled by the proposition that a scale reproduction *without more* should not support copyright.[76]

These Second Circuit cases have imposed what seems to be a more rigorous standard of originality for artistic reproductions than for other works of authorship. A standard requiring artistic as opposed to physical skill may inevitably lead to judicial considerations of artistic merit. This would conflict with the traditional copyright principles that judges should stay away from such matters. In addition, these decisions create a paradox where greater protection would be conferred on sloppy, inaccurate copies as opposed to highly accurate, skillful ones. At the very least, *Batlin* and *Tomy* require a greater showing of creative authorship for artistic reproductions, a substantial variation on the public domain rather than the *de minimis* or trivial variation standard enunciated in *Catalda.*

Why require a greater degree of originality for reproductions of works of art? In *Gracen v. Bradford Exchange*,[77] the Seventh Circuit Court of Appeals refused copyright to an artist's rendering of a photograph of Judy Garland's Dorothy for lack of substantial variation. According to Judge Posner, the originality standard, particularly for derivative works such as artistic reproductions, should be higher than for preexisting works, to prevent potential overlapping claims and harassment by claimants of derivative work copyrights. His reasoning went like this: Without requiring a quantum of originality, it may be very difficult to determine whether a third party has copied from a public domain source or copied from the copyrighted work. We should require a sufficiently gross difference between the underlying and the derivative work to avoid entangling subsequent artists depicting the underlying work with copyright problems. Thus, too liberal construction of the originality standard may paradoxically inhibit rather than promote the creation of works based on those in the public domain.[78]

The *Gracen* court, by requiring a substantial variation for derivative works such as artistic reproductions, has imposed a *de facto* novelty standard for certain works of authorship. Its justification for the higher standard was based on the practicality of judicial administration in deciding claims of infringement. Even if the court did not overstate the evidentiary problem in deciding whether the second derivative

---

[76] Although there appears to be some discrepancy in how far the courts will go in conferring copyright on art reproductions, the historical tendency has been expansive. *Cf. Eden Toys v. Florelee Undergarment Co.*, 697 F.2d 27 (2d Cir. 1982), holding that a gift wrap design based on sketches of Paddington Bear was copyrightable because the "cleaner look" of the gift wrap design satisfied the minimal requirements for originality under the Copyright Act.

[77] 698 F.2d 300 (7th Cir. 1983).

[78] As the court pointed out, the concept of originality serves an important legal function, to prevent overlapping claims. Suppose Artist A produces a reproduction of the *Mona Lisa*, a painting in the public domain, which differs slightly from the original. B also makes a reproduction of the *Mona Lisa*. A, who has copyrighted his derivative work, sues B for infringement. B's defense is that he was copying the original, not A's reproduction. "[I]f the difference between A's reproduction and the original is slight, the difference between A's and B's reproductions will also be slight, so that if B had access to A's reproductions, the trier of fact will be hard-pressed to decide whether B was copying A or copying the *Mona Lisa* itself." *Id.* at 304.

work author copied the public domain work or the copyrighted derivative work, one of the costs of a low standard for originality may be the encouragement of a certain number of infringement suits brought by overzealous owners of derivative works. Alternatively, the standard set forth in *Gracen* may impede production of highly competent artistic renderings which cannot be protected by copyright.

§ 2.10 Originality In Derivative Work Authorship: The Colorization Controversy

Thanks to a process called "colorization," copyright owners have been able to inject new value into commercially dormant black and white films. Film purists and artists are outraged at what they believe is the mutilation of an artistic creation. Colorization is a technological advance which has challenged the fundamental basis of copyright law. Apart from the ethics of adding color to a film originally created in black and white by its originator,[79] some have questioned whether a colorized film meets the standard of authorship sufficient to constitute a valid derivative work.

The process of colorization involves the use of a computer which scans a black and white film transferred on videotape for its spectrum of grey tones.[80] From these grey tones, an individual versed in this technique must choose an appropriate color corresponding to the object, the decor and the epoch portrayed in the film. The colorization process is time-consuming and costly.

The copyright issue is whether colorizers have added the requisite amount of human authorship to a preexisting work to meet the standard of copyrightability for a derivative work. Colorizers argue that they use a computer as a painter uses a brush or a novelist uses a typewriter and that the arrangement and combination of colors constitutes the requisite amount of creative authorship for a copyrightable derivative work. They would view their work as analogous to a musical arrangement or a translation which modifies a preexisting work in adding original authorship.[81] The contrary view holds that colorizers are mere computer technicians whose choices are governed by a predetermined process made possible by a new form of computer

---

[79] Colorization has engendered scathing attacks from those who see it as a destruction of America's cultural heritage and the mutilation of a work of art. *See* Alberta I. Cook, *Colorization; Actors and Directors: Color Them Mad as Hell*, Nat'l Law J., July 27, 1987 at 10, 11. Legislation has been introduced to amend the Copyright Act to make it unlawful to publicly perform a materially altered film without certain disclosures. *See* Film Integrity Act of 1987, H.R. 2400, 100th Cong., 1st Sess. (1987). For a discussion of the moral right of an author to prevent mutilation or alteration of his work, see §§ 8.27, 8.28 *infra*.

[80] For an overview of the subject and a detailed explanation of the colorization process, see James Thomas Duggan & Neil V. Pennella, *The Case for Copyrights in "Colorized" Versions of Public Domain Feature Films*, 34 J. Copyright Soc'y 333 (1987).

[81] Proponents emphasize that the requisite amount of authorship is governed by a *de minimis* standard. *See, e.g., Pantone, Inc. v. A. I. Friedman, Inc.*, 294 F. Supp. 545 (S.D.N.Y. 1968) (color chart in a "how-to" book on mixing colors); *Sargent v. American Greetings Corp.*, 588 F. Supp. 912 (N.D. Ohio 1984) (painting colorized by adding color to line drawings).

technology.[82] Whatever human authorship is added by the colorizer, it is too trivial to meet the standard of originality.[83]

Colorization has not been tested in the courts but the Copyright Office has decided that colorized films are entitled to copyright registration as derivative works if the colorized work manifests a sufficient modification of the preexisting work that is more than a trivial variation.[84]

§ 2.11 Compilations

[A] Originality in Compilations: An Overview

As discussed previously, compilations are works of authorship created by collecting, selecting, and assembling pre-exisiting materials or data. The compiled materials may consist of individually copyrighted works, as in an anthology of contemporary short stories, or may only include public domain materials, such as facts or data. Consider a compilation composed of factual matter such as a telephone book, a catalog of prices, or a list of potential customers, each element of which is in the public domain. Often, unearthing facts and putting them into a compilation requires skill and hard work. Copyright law, however, does not protect facts *per se*, nor the talent that went into discovering them. Rather, copyright protects original works of authorship. One cannot author a fact because facts simply exist, even if they sometimes have to be discovered at great effort and expense. This principle is embodied in § 102(b) of the 1976 Act which denies copyright to any "discovery, regardless of the form in which it is described. . . ."[85]

Copyright in a compilation consists of the original elements an author has added to the assembled pre-existing materials or data. They vary widely in original authorship. Some compilations contain facts plus extensive authorial analysis and judgment in the selection and organization of the pre-existing data; other compilations contain nothing more than an arrangement of facts, such as certain indexes. For all varieties of compilations, however, copyright in the compilation extends not to the pre-existing materials or data themselves, but to the author's judgment in selecting and arranging the disparate materials or data and organizing them into a unified work. Other indicia of authorship would include analysis, description, and

---

[82] Copyright does not extend to a process. *See* 17 U.S.C. § 102(b). For a discussion of § 102(b), see § 2.12, *infra*.

[83] *See, e.g., McIntyre v. Double-A Music Corp.*, 166 F. Supp. 681 (S.D. Cal. 1958), and cases cited at 683 (transposition of music to another key or arrangement using common chords not copyrightable).

[84] 37 C.F.R. § 202 (1987). The Copyright Office has developed a set of criteria to determine whether the colorized film meets the requisite standard for a derivative work. In effect, the regulation requires that numerous color selections must be made by human beings from an extensive color inventory whose range and extent of colors added must represent more than a trivial variation. The colorization must modify the overall appearance of the motion picture. In addition, neither the removal of color from a motion picture, nor mere variations of color will justify registration.

[85] 17 U.S.C. § 102(b).

instruction accompanying the individual elements making up the compilation. Like any other work of authorship, the compilation must contain more than a trivial variation on what is in the public domain, but a compilation need not be novel or unique. It must be independently created and display a *de minimis* amount of creative, intellectual, or aesthetic labor. This fundamental principle about the requisite standard for copyright protection was raised to the level of a constitutional requirement in *Feist Publications, Inc. v. Rural Telephone Service Co.*[86]

[B]   The *Feist* Case and the Demise of the Industrious Effort Doctrine

Compilations, particularly those which assemble public domain materials, reflect basic tensions in copyright policy. Modern copyright law has had difficulty with works that are low in personal authorship even though the works themselves may be high in commercial value.[87] Consider the following situation. Suppose B, without doing independent research, appropriates the factual information contained in a compilation produced at great expense by A, such as a telephone book or other catalog. Suppose also that B has not taken the original elements added to the public domain, such as A's subjective arrangement or organization of the compilation. Can A be protected under copyright law from B's total appropriation of A's hard work in gathering the facts? Under traditional copyright law principles, facts *per se* are not protectible. Nevertheless, some courts have stretched copyright law to protect a compilation from similar "free riders" like B who have appropriated the fruits of another's labor. To limit protection to the expressive elements in this instance would seem to confer inadequate protection on a compilation containing little expression.[88] The sentiment favoring protection is understandable and may be justified on a natural law theory that people are entitled to the fruits of their labor. Moreover, uninhibited free riding may well undermine the incentive to create such informational works. But, however motivated by equitable considerations, if carried to its logical conclusion, this expansive "sweat of the brow" approach to copyright would risk turning copyright into a general misappropriation law.

Although the "sweat of the brow" doctrine has enjoyed a persistent success through the years, it was specifically rejected by the United States Supreme Court

---

[86] 499 U.S. 340 (1991).

[87] For an elaboration of this idea, see Jane C. Ginsburg, *Creation and Commercial Value: Copyright Protection of Works of Information*, 90 Colum. L. Rev 1865 (1990).

[88] The expansive view is represented by *Leon v. Pacific Telephone & Telegraph Co.*, 91 F.2d 484 (9th Cir. 1937). In *Leon*, the plaintiff compiled a telephone directory with the names and telephone numbers arranged in alphabetical order. The defendant took the same names and numbers and rearranged them by the numerical order of the numbers, creating a reverse telephone book. *See also Rand McNally & Co. v. Fleet Management Sys., Inc.,* 600 F. Supp. 933, 941 (N.D. Ill. 1984); *National Business Lists, Inc. v. Dun & Bradstreet, Inc.*, 552 F. Supp. 89 (N.D. Ill. 1982). Other cases involving similar fact situations present a rationale closer to the traditional purpose of copyright law; *see Schroeder v. William Morrow and Co.*, 566 F.2d 3 (7th Cir. 1977) (infringement found in a catalog of names and addresses where defendant copied the selection, order and arrangement of the names), and *Southern Bell Tel. & Tel. Co. v. Associated Tel. Directory Publishers*, 756 F.2d 801, 811 (11th Cir. 1985).

in 1991 in *Feist Publications, Inc. v. Rural Telephone Service Co.* [89] Here, the Court specifically discarded industrious effort as a standard for copyrightability separate from the effort's embodiment in the creative arrangement, selection, and coordination of the subject matter in the work.

In *Feist*, plaintiff Rural Telephone provided telephone service to several communities in northwest Kansas and published white pages containing an alphabetical listing of subscriber's names, towns, and telephone numbers. Defendant Feist also published telephone books and tried to license Rural's list of names but was refused. Feist used Rural's listings without permission, copying about 1,300 names and numbers from Rural's white pages, including four fictitious listings that Rural had inserted to detect copying.

The Supreme Court found that Rural's copyright in its telephone directory did not protect the names and numbers copied by Feist. In her opinion, Justice O'Connor based her decision on the bedrock constitutional principle that a protectible work must be original with the author. "Original" in the copyright sense means that the work was independently created and possesses at least some minimal degree of creativity. Factual works may possess the requisite creativity, *e.g.,* where the author chooses which facts to include, in what order, and their arrangement for effective use. But the protection extends only to those parts of the work original to the author and not to the facts themselves. In sum, protection of a factual work extends only to its *original* selection or arrangement. The *Feist* Court ruled that Rural's alphabetical arrangement of its telephone listings could not have been more obvious or banal, lacking the minimal modicum of creativity necessary to constitute original authorship. Thus, even though Feist took a substantial amount of factual information from Rural's directory, it did not take anything that amounted to original authorship. Accordingly, Feist's copying did not constitute copyright infringement.

Feist is unequivocal on one point: an alphabetical listing of telephone subscribers and their numbers cannot be protected as a compilation under copyright unless the selection, coordination, or arrangement of the facts is original. This in itself is a dramatic holding and from a copyright standpoint, will have a substantial impact on the numerous publishers of telephone books.

---

[89] The commentary on *Feist* and the question of originality in copyright law is voluminous. *See* Howard B. Abrams, *Originality and Creativity in Copyright Law*, 55 Law & Contemp. Probs. 3 (1992), Jane C. Ginsburg, *"No Sweat?," Copyright and Other Protection of Works of Information After* Feist v. Rural Telephone, 92 Colum. L. Rev. 338 (1992), Robert A. Gorman, *The* Feist *Case: Reflections on a Pathbreaking Copyright Decision*, 18 Rutgers Computer & Tech. L. J. 731 (1992); Marci A. Hamilton, *Justice O'Connor's Opinion in* Feist Publications Inc. v. Rural Telephone Service Co., *An Uncommon Though Characteristic Approach*, 38 J. Copyright Soc'y 83 (1990); Paul J. Heald, The Vices of Originality, *Sup. Ct. Rev. 143 (1991); Shira Perlmutter, The Scope of Copyright in Telephone Directories: Keeping Listing Information in the Public Domain*, 38 J. Copyright Soc'y 1 (1990); *Symposium, Copyright Protection for Computer Databases, CD-ROMS and Factual Compilations* (pts. l, ll) 17 U. Dayton L. Rev. 323, 331 (1992); Russ VerSteeg, *Rethinking Originality*, 34 Wm. & Mary L. Rev. 801 (1993).

[C] Originality in Selection and Arrangement after *Feist*

Feist does not, however, answer what kind of selection or arrangement is original and protectible authorship. For this we must wait for the case law to fill in the gaps. A series of Yellow Pages cases demonstrates the difficulties in determining originality in compilations. For the most part, Yellow Pages directories require more organization and arrangement than the white pages held uncopyrightable in *Feist*. Plaintiffs have, nevertheless, had difficulty in enforcing their rights. In *Key Publications, Inc. v. Chinatown Today Publishing Enterprises, Inc.*,[90] the Second Circuit upheld the copyright in a listing of businesses located in New York's Chinatown of interest to the Chinese community. However, it found no infringement, even though defendant had copied 1500 of the 9000 entries found in plaintiff's directory, because defendant had used a different selection and arrangement of the material. The copied listings made up of 75% of defendant's directory, and represented 17% of plaintiff's. Thus, it makes no difference what percentage or how many facts are taken from the plaintiff's work so long as the compiler does not appropriate the copyrightable selection and arrangement of the prior work. In *Bellsouth Advtg. & Pub. Corp. v. Donnelley Information Pub., Inc.*,[91] another Yellow Pages case, defendant copied into a computer both the directory's listings and the classification headings. The Court did not find sufficient originality in the structure of the compilation headings to be protectible. Although more intricate than Feist's alphabetical ordering of the White Pages, one could characterize plaintiff's Yellow Page classifications as obvious, typical, or commonplace. As the court stated: "[Bellsouth] can claim no copyright in the idea of dividing churches by denomination or attorneys by area of specialty."[92]

A compilation may display sufficient originality for copyright purposes if the work as a whole constitutes either original selection or original arrangement. Thus, a work may be arranged in a commonplace way (*e.g.*, an alphabetical arrangement of a telephone book), but may nevertheless be copyrightable if the data are selected in an original way. An example of creative selection occured in *Eckes v. Card Prices Update*,[93] in which a selection of 5,000 premium baseball cards from approximately 18,000 cards was held copyrightable. Here, the selection of data required creative rather than merely mechanical decisions of inclusion.[94] Alternatively, a compilation may be copyrightable if the arrangement is original.[95] Unfortunately for enterprising compilers seeking copyright protection, the most useful ordering systems for compilations would not meet the *Feist* criteria for originality. By contrast, highly original

[90] 945 F.2d 509 (2d Cir. 1991).
[91] 999 F.2d 1436 (11th Cir. 1993).
[92] *Id.* at 1444.
[93] 736 F.2d 859 (2d Cir. 1984).
[94] *Compare Financial Information v. Moody's Investors Service*, 751 F.2d 501 (2d Cir. 1984), discussed below, where the court held that a compilation of bond redemptions culled from bond tombstones in newspapers was not copyrightable. No selection was involved in the compilation, and the actual gathering of information was purely mechanical.
[95] *See, e.g., Kregos v. Associated Press*, 937 F.2d 700 (2d Cir. 1991) (baseball pitching performance chart, which set forth nine categories of past performance statistics for the day's starting pitchers to aid in predicting outcome of game, held copyrightable).

systems of arrangement often are of limited value. For example, an alphabetical list of lawyers might be highly useful and valuable but uncopyrightable from the standpoint of arrangement. On the other hand, a list of local lawyers arranged according to the size of their libraries or the square footage in their waiting rooms may contain sufficient originality in arrangement for copyright protection. But who needs such a compilation? Accordingly, one might expect the issue of originality in compilations to arise with greater frequency over the selection rather than the arrangement of the facts or data.

[D]   Computer Databases[96]

Quickly updated, easy-to-use, automated databases disseminate information which was previously obtained by laboriously thumbing through such sources as card catalogs, dictionaries, or legal encyclopedias. Automated databases are copyrightable as compilations and[97] as such, they present the same doctrinal problems of scope and protection as the traditional database. Rather than being fixed on pages of a book, automated data is fixed in electromagnetic media that require the intervention of a computer in order to communicate the content. Automated databases are different from hard copy dictionaries or encyclopedias because they are so easy to retrieve and copy, and from a practical standpoint, are difficult to protect. Essentially, the legal issues concerning the protection of computer databases are similar to those related to protection of any other compilation which, after *Feist*, must embody some creative authorship.

The difficult conceptual problems for compilations in copyright most often arise when a compilation manifests a low degree of authorship, *i.e.*, where the author has added little more than an arrangement of facts. Such compilations often occur in connection with an automated database.

A good example of the difficult issues of originality for this kind of database occurred in a pre-*Feist* case, *West Publishing Co. v. Mead Data Central Inc.*,[98] The *Mead Data* case concerned the copyrightability of West's arrangement of legal decisions (the star pagination system) in its National Reporter System. Lexis had planned to add star pagination to the text of opinions stored in its legal database to enable viewers to use Lexis without having to consult West reporters for page citations. West contended that Lexis's wholesale appropriation of pagination from West's reporters infringed West's copyright in its compilation of cases. The court rejected Mead's argument that West was trying to protect the numbers on its pages. It found instead that Mead infringed the copyright in West's case arrangement, an important part of which was the internal page citations. The court distinguished taking the numbering system and isolated factual data from the wholesale taking of the plaintiff's arrangement of the data. In sum, a numbering system and its factual data are not copyrightable, but the overall arrangement of the actual data is.

---

[96] For a discussion of the issue, see Note, *Jack B. Hicks, Copyright and Computer Databases: Is Traditional Compilation Law Adequate?*, 65 Tex. L. Rev. 993 (1987); and CONTU *Final Report* at 41.

[97] 17 U.S.C. § 101 (compilation).

[98] 799 F.2d 1219 (8th Cir. 1986).

Is *West* still viable after *Feist* with its requirement of original selection or arrangement of factual matter? Specifically, what is original about a numeric arrangement — consecutive numbering — of the pages in a given legal opinion or set of opinions? Unquestionably, West could prevent Mead from publishing a competing volume of the Supreme Court Reporter using West's system of pagination. But *West* goes much further than this, finding an infringement because Mead's database showed where a specific group of words are found on a certain page in the West reporters. This holding is questionable in the post-*Feist* world. The two decisions can only be reconciled on the difficult premise that West's consecutive arrangement of pages in its reporter system manifests a greater degree of originality than Feist's uncopyrightable alphabetical arrangement of a telephone book.

Another database compilation with low authorship content was involved in *Financial Information, Inc. v. Moody's Investors Service, Inc.*[99] As compared with *West,* this case shows that (even before *Feist*) the courts would not protect individual facts despite a "free-riding" defendant. Financial Information, Inc. (FII) mailed to subscribers the *Daily Bond Card,* consisting of index cards containing information about municipal bonds. The cards were a pure compilation of financial facts, and the information collected on them required little, if any, editorial skill. Moody's copied the information from these cards, which it incorporated into *Moody's News Reports.* The District Court took an expansive view on the daily fact cards, stating "[t]o accord copyright protection to the annual compilation but deny it to each daily component would negate the value of the protection accorded the yearly compilation."[100] In other words, why should the serial thief go free, while the thief who waited to copy the final compilation is punished as an infringer? The Court of Appeals was troubled by this paradox, but rejected the District Court's decision in favor of the plaintiff and remanded the case to decide whether the data on the FII cards involved a modicum of selection, coordination, or arrangement by FII.

The decision in *FII* supports the basic principle for protection of compilations in copyright law as articulated in *Feist.* Facts *per se* are not protected under copyright law no matter how sympathetic one might be toward the author who expended the effort to compile them. A compilation should be entitled to copyright protection only if the author has added original authorship to public domain facts in the selection, coordination, and arrangement of the data.

PART IV: NON-COPYRIGHTABLE SUBJECT MATTER

§ 2.12 Ideas and Systems Under § 102(b)

[A] In General

One of the most pervasive and oft-cited principles in copyright law is that copyright protects the expression of an idea but not the idea itself. Section 102(b) of the Copyright Act codifies this principle by denying copyright protection to any

---

[99] 751 F.2d 501 (2d Cir. 1984).
[100] *Id.* at 506.

idea, procedure, process, system, method of operation, concept, principle, or discovery, regardless of the form in which it is described, explained, illustrated, or embodied in such work.[101]

Once an author reveals his work to the public, he injects the idea into the public domain and must be content to maintain control only over the *form* in which the idea is expressed. Copyright extends only to the specific, concrete, expressive vehicle through which the writer's ideas appear, leaving the substance of the ideas outside the scope of the author's monopoly. This fundamental principle of copyright law cuts across the entire range of copyrightable subject matter. It is consistent with the purpose of copyright law, which is to encourage the creation of an optimal variety of artistic expression. To create new works, future authors must have access to a well-endowed public domain, the place where fundamental building materials — concepts, discoveries, and technological solutions — reside and are freely available for those wishing to embellish them with their own original expression.[102]

As a result, copyright law does not preclude others from using ideas or information revealed in an author's work. Accordingly, a discoverer of a scientific principle or historical fact, or someone who unearths an unknown play by Shakespeare cannot claim copyright despite the effort and ingenuity expended. Ideas, discoveries, principles and facts are freely accessible to the public, and to confer property status on them would hinder rather than promote "the progress of science and the useful arts," undermining the constitutionally declared purpose of copyright. Any lower standard would intolerably burden future creative activity and the dissemination of knowledge, and might even conflict with the First Amendment. It has been said that copyright does not significantly interfere with the First Amendment because it protects only the form of expression contained in the copyrighted work and allows the author's ideas to circulate freely.[103]

Once an abstract idea is disclosed to the public, it becomes a part of our common reservoir of knowledge, and it will not matter whether the originator has spent vast sums of money developing it, advertising it, or making it popular. It may, however, be possible to protect the private disclosure of an original idea, plan, or scheme to others under circumstances which suggest a confidential relationship or an implication of contract. But an action for the misappropriation of an idea must be sought under a state law cause of action such as breach of trust or contract, not under federal copyright law.[104]

---

[101] 17 U.S.C. § 102(b).

[102] For an excellent overview of the idea-expression dichotomy in copyright, see Leslie A. Kurtz, *Speaking to the Ghost: Idea and Expression in Copyright*, 47 U. Miami L. Rev. 1221 (1993).

[103] *See* 1 *Nimmer on Copyright* § 1.10 (1993).

[104] *See, e.g., Desny v. Wilder*, 46 Cal. 2d 715, 299 P.2d 257 (1956) (writer alleged express promise by movie producer to pay for story). The California Supreme Court stated:

> The person who can and does convey a valuable idea to a producer who commercially solicits the service or who voluntarily accepts it knowing that it is tendered for a price should likewise be entitled to recover.

Id. at 734, 299 P.2d at 267. *See also Davies v. Krasna*, 245 Cal. App. 2d 535, 54 Cal. Rptr. 37 (1966); *Donahue v. Ziv Television Programs, Inc.*, 245 Cal. App. 2d 593, 54 Cal. Rptr.

As in the case of originality, the idea-expression distinction is left undefined in the Copyright Act. Its application is to be determined by standards developed in case law under the 1909 Act. The idea-expression issue often arises in a suit for copyright infringement. To prove infringement, the copyright owner must prove substantial similarity between his work and the defendant's. The plaintiff must show that the alleged infringer took more than an abstract idea from his work, copying the *expression* of that idea.[105]

The idea-expression dichotomy, which cuts across all copyrightable subject matter, is easy to state but is more difficult and elusive to apply in practice. Separating an idea from its expression is an *ad hoc* process, and how broadly a court defines what constitutes the idea as compared to the expression depends on the nature of the subject matter at issue. In every situation, the court must strike a balance between two conflicting interests. If the idea is defined too broadly, it will create a bottleneck impeding production of future works. On the other hand, if the idea is defined too narrowly, future authors will not have sufficient economic incentive to create new works. Because the idea-expression dichotomy is best examined in a specific context, the discussion now turns to three applications of the idea-expression principle: the doctrine of *Baker v. Selden*; the protection of literary characters; and the protection of historical fact and research.

[B]   Idea and Expression: The Doctrine of *Baker v. Selden*

[1]   The Nature of Functional Works: Patent Policy and Copyright Law

Functional works, such as computer programs, architectural plans, and legal forms, appeal less to the individual intelligence and aesthetic sensibility than carry out a specific task or achieve a certain result. These works are found in all varieties of copyrightable subject matter. For example, although computer programs are literary works and architectural blueprints are pictorial works, both are also functional works because they share a common task-oriented dimension. They differ from a poem or painting because their aesthetic aspect is only incidental to their primary purpose: to accomplish a given task. Because functional works often closely integrate idea and expression, they tend to conflict with copyright law's protection of original expression. This basic principle is embodied in § 102(b), which precludes copyright protection not only for ideas, but also for systems, processes, and methods of operation. As Professor Goldstein points out, interests of utility will frequently compel expression in functional works "to hew closely to the underlying — and unprotectible — idea, procedure, process, system or method of operation that it expresses."[106]

130 (1966); and *Minniear v. Tors*, 266 Cal. App. 2d 495, 72 Cal. Rptr. 287 (1968). For an extensive discussion of protection under state law, see 3 *Nimmer on Copyright* § 16.03 (1993).

[105] *See Nichols v. Universal Pictures Corp.*, 45 F.2d 119 (2d Cir. 1930); Edward Samuels, *The Idea-Expression Dichotomy in Copyright Law*, 56 Tenn. L. Rev. 321 (1989); Amy B. Cohen, *Copyright Law and the Myth of Objectivity: The Idea-Expression Dichotomy and the Inevitability of Artistic Value Judgments*, 66 Ind. L. J. 175 (1990).

[106] Paul Goldstein, 1 *Copyright*, 195 (1989).

When encountering a functional work, the courts will limit protection to avoid conferring a *de facto* monopoly over the unprotectible, utilitarian aspects of the work. Distinguishing between idea and expression is a difficult but necessary task because of the policies that differentiate copyright from patent law. Copyright law encourages production of a broad range of artistic, literary, and musical works. Its standard of validity, based on originality, is relatively easy to meet and a rigorous formal examination process is not required. Once obtained, a copyright confers a relatively thin but lengthy term of property rights (life of the author plus fifty years). Despite the lengthy term, the exclusionary force of the copyright grant is relatively weak because the consumer generally can turn to satisfactory substitutes for any given novel, film, or work of art, a multitude of which compete for the consumer's dollar. If satisfactory substitutes are available, the seller will enjoy no market power for the work. Thus, even though the copyright grant is long, it confers a legal rather than an economic monopoly.

By contrast, the patent laws encourage protection of works in the realm of technology. The patent grant, however, is conferred only on those inventions that represent a substantial advance over the prior art.[107] Unlike a copyright, a patentable invention must demonstrate considerably more than originality and must meet the rigorous tests of novelty and nonobviousness.[108] Failure to meet these standards would result in conferring monopoly protection on an insubstantial advance over the public domain. The patent grant provides a more powerful set of exclusive rights although of relatively short (seventeen years) duration.[109]

In contrast to copyright, the patent grant may confer a powerful economic monopoly in the absence of satisfactory substitutes that compete in the market for the patented product or process. Thus, the courts are justifiably concerned given the risk of providing copyright protection of such long duration over subject matter failing to meet the more rigorous standards of patent law. The conflict between copyright and patent policy often arises when a work of utility contains expressive elements. In this situation, the courts must develop a principled approach by which the expressive elements of a work are rendered discrete from the work's underlying ideas and utilitarian aspects.

These principles concerning the protectibility of functional works were established in the leading case of *Baker v. Selden* ,[110] In *Baker,* copyright protection was sought for a work entitled *Selden's Condensed Ledger of Bookkeeping Simplified*, which explained a new system of bookkeeping. Included in the work were a set of blank forms consisting of ruled lines and headings specially designed for use with the system. Those forms permitted the entire operations of a day or a week to be reported on a single page or on two pages facing each other. The defendant published a book with forms achieving the same result but with different arrangements of the columns and headings. The Supreme Court could have decided the case simply by finding that there was an absence of similarity in the expression of the idea promoted

---

[107] See Section 1.11, *supra*, for a discussion of patents.

[108] 35 U.S.C. § 102, 103.

[109] 35 U.S.C. § 154.

[110] 101 U.S. 99 (1879).

by Selden's book. The Supreme Court, however, reversed a judgment for the plaintiff, reasoning that the system could not be used absent the methods and diagrams in the book.[111] Thus, according to the Court, the ledger was actually a utilitarian object rather than an expressive work. Unless copyright were denied in this instance, a monopoly could in effect be granted over the underlying idea of the system. The Court stated that monopolies over systems or processes should be difficult to obtain, and the claimant should have to meet the rigorous examination for novelty and invention used by the Patent Office. Moreover, a grant of the patent monopoly lasts only 17 years while that of copyright, at that time, lasted 56 years. In other words, we should not allow a creator of inherently patentable subject matter, *i.e.*, a system or process, to use copyright law to circumvent the patent system.

[2] The Merger Doctrine

The Court's views on distinguishing patent from copyright law have become universally accepted. But the *Baker* Court enunciated another rationale in denying copyrightability. It is known as the doctrine of *Baker v. Selden*, which may be summarized as follows: Where the use of an idea requires the copying of the work itself, such copying will not constitute infringement. On the other hand, if the copying does not involve the use of the art but instead its explanation, then such copying will constitute an infringement. No one is exactly sure of what the Court really meant by its use-explanation dichotomy. For that matter, the case is oracle-like, permeated with obscure language, and we can only speculate about what the Court actually had in mind.

One interpretation goes by the name of the "merger doctrine." According to this view, the doctrine of *Baker v. Selden* implies that there are some instances where the use of a system or process necessitates the identical copying of the author's expression of the system or process. In other words, if the underlying idea (or system, process, or method of operation) can effectively be expressed in only one way, the idea and expression are said to have "merged." When this occurs, the work cannot receive protection under copyright law. To allow copyright protection in such an instance would undermine the distinction between copyright and patent law.

Does the doctrine of *Baker v. Selden*, the "merger doctrine" as it is often called, have an empirical basis? As a factual matter, is there any system or method which can be performed by the use of only one particular form of written expression? Some commentators have challenged this basic assumption of the merger doctrine.[112] Nevertheless, the doctrine has found support in Copyright Office regulations[113] denying copyright to works designed for recording information which works do not in themselves convey information. Support has also been found in the case law where verbatim copying of a contract form was allowed because it was for use rather

---

[111] *Id.* at 103.

[112] 1 *Nimmer on Copyright* § 2.18[D] (1993).

[113] 37 C.F.R. §§ 202.1(b), (c) (1987). *See also Taylor Instrument Co. v. Fawley-Brost Co.*, 139 F.2d 98 (7th Cir. 1943) (chart for recording temperatures held not copyrightable); and *Aldrich v. Remington Rand, Inc.*, 52 F. Supp. 732 (N.D. Tex. 1942) (forms for keeping tax records held not copyrightable).

than explanation.[114] And in *Morrissey v. Procter & Gamble Co.*,[115] the court allowed verbatim copying of contest instructions, even though more than one form of expression was possible, because there existed only a limited number of possible forms of expression. Similarly, in *Kern River Gas Transmission Co. v. Coastal Corp.*,[116] the plaintiff's depiction of its proposed natural gas pipeline route on government survey maps was not copyrightable. The maps may have been original, but, according to the court, they expressed the idea of the location of the pipeline in the only effective way. Thus, when idea and expression are inseparable they merge, precluding copyright protection.[117]

Not all courts have followed the doctrine of *Baker v. Selden*.[118] In *Harcourt, Brace & World, Inc. v. Graphic Controls Corp.*,[119] copyright was allowed for answer sheet forms which not only provided spaces for the correct answers, but also provided minimal information. Other courts have stated that the question of liability should turn on whether the defendant has copied the copyrightable elements of the work — for which it originally received protection — no matter what kind of use is to be made of the copied material.

Regardless of the policy goals, the merger doctrine has provided little direction or predictability in deciding actual cases, and courts often have difficulty discerning when idea and expression are inextricably fused. Whether idea and expression have merged will depend on how broadly or narrowly "idea" is defined. Defining the idea of a work is by no means easy, but it is not a mystical process. The result of this determination is critical in deciding whether a work is copyrightable and whether a third party has improperly appropriated protected expression. Ultimately, how broadly the "idea" is defined will depend on competitive considerations.

A number of hard-fought computer screen display cases illustrate the complex nature of the definitional process. Computer-generated screen displays,[120] such as Apple's graphical user interface (GUI), provide a good example. These displays

---

[114] *Crume v. Pacific Mutual Life Ins. Co.*, 140 F.2d 182 (7th Cir.), *cert. denied*, 332 U.S. 755 (1944).

[115] 379 F.2d 675, 678 (1st Cir. 1967).

[116] 899 F.2d 1458 (5th Cir. 1990).

[117] One should compare *Kern* with *Mason v. Montgomery Data, Inc.*, 967 F.2d 135 (2d Cir. 1992) (no merger in real estate ownership maps based on public domain sources because presentation of factual subject matter (placement, size, dimensions of survey tracts, etc.) could be expressed in many different ways); *see also Herbert Rosenthal Jewelry Corp. v. Kalpakian*, 446 F.2d 738 (9th Cir. 1971) (plaintiff's jewel-encrusted pin, shaped like a bee, was not copyrightable because the jeweled bee-shaped pin was an idea that defendant could freely copy).

[118] The Supreme Court stated in *Mazer v. Stein*, 347 U.S. 201, 218 (1954):

> We find nothing in the copyright statute to support the argument that the intended use or use in industry of an article eligible for copyright bars or invalidates its registration. We do not read such a limitation into the copyright law.

[119] 329 F. Supp. 517 (S.D.N.Y. 1971). *See also Continental Casualty Co. v. Beardsley*, 253 F.2d 702 (2d Cir. 1958) (blanket bond forms held copyrightable).

[120] The graphical user interface is one aspect of the user interface that governs how people interact with the computer. *See Que's Computer User's Dictionary* 634 (4th ed. 1993).

contain attractive aesthetic features while facilitating efficient use and can become, over time, an industry standard. A computer programmer's design choices (not just for screen displays but for all aspects of the user interface) are often determined by many considerations, both aesthetic and utilitarian, such as mechanical specifications, compatibility requirements, and industry demands.[121] Generally, the courts will allow protection for the artistic features of an interface while denying protection to clearly functional features, such as centered headings, and underscored program names.[122] Courts have also denied protection to user interfaces and other features that have become industry standards, even though those features were completely arbitrary at the time they were adopted.[123] Thus, what consitutes an idea, process, or system for a user interface (or any other work for that matter) is not self-defining. Inevitably, complicated competitive considerations, which may regulate an entire industry, loom large in determining the scope of protection for computer interfaces and programs. The ultimate determination may be stated as follows: if a third party were deprived of copying a particular feature, how serious would be the resulting social costs of the monopoly on consumer welfare?

In sum, separating idea from expression is often a complex task but an unavoidable one. Here, a court, in close cases, must engage in a delicate balancing process, based on competitive concerns, to determine whether society should have access to a certain technological solution. In applying the idea-expression doctrine, a court should focus on these competitive considerations more explicitly, rather than framing the debate under the merger doctrine.

[C] Fictional Characters

The protection of fictional literary characters such as Sam Spade, James Bond, and Superman, presents a recurring question in copyright law and an interesting variation on the idea-expression dichotomy. First, some primary distinctions should be made. This discussion focuses on literary characters, those described in *words*, whether in a novel or a play, and not on cartoon, or other pictorial characters that are copyrightable as part of a drawing, painting, or other visual work.[124] Second, names of characters may be protected under unfair competition law[125] and possibly

---

[121] *Computer Assocs. Int'l, Inc., v. Altai, Inc.*, 982 F.2d 936, 709–10 (2d Cir. 1992).

[122] *See Manufacturers Technologies, Inc. v. Cams, Inc.*, 706 F. Supp. 984 (D. Conn. 1989) (protection denied to elements that represent a narrow range of possibilities); *Lotus Dev. v. Paperback Software Int'l*, 740 F. Supp. 37 (D. Mass. 1990) (protection conferred on spreadsheet program's command structure).

[123] *Apple Computer, Inc. v. Microsoft Corp.*, 799 F. Supp. 1006 (N.D. Cal. 1992).

[124] For protection of graphic characters, see *Walt Disney Prod. v. Air Pirates*, 345 F. Supp. 108 (N.D. Cal. 1972) (holding Walt Disney characters, particularly Mickey Mouse, were protectible).

[125] *DC Comics, Inc. v. Filmation Assocs.*, 486 F. Supp. 1273 (S.D.N.Y. 1980). *See generally* E. Fulton Brylawski, *Protection of Characters — Sam Spade Revisited*, 22 Bull. Copyright L. Soc'y 77 (1974); for a particularly comprehensive review of the issue, see Leslie A. Kurtz, *The Independent Legal Lives of Fictional Characters*, 1986 Wis. L. Rev. 429. *See also* Michael T. Helfand, *When Mickey Mouse is as Strong as Superman: The Convergence of Intellectual Property Laws to Protect Fictional Literary and Pictorial Characters*, 44 Stan. L. Rev. 623 (1992); Francis M. Nevins, *Copyright + Character = Catastrophe*, 39 J. Copyright Soc'y 303 (1992).

trademark law, but not under copyright law. This leaves open the important question: what protection, if any, may be claimed for the delineation of a literary character, apart from the character's name and visual appearance?

Perhaps the most famous comment on the copyrightability of literary characters is that of Judge Learned Hand in *Nichols v. Universal Pictures Corp.,*[126]

> If *Twelfth Night* were copyrighted, it is quite possible that a second comer might so closely imitate Sir Toby Belch or Malvolio as to infringe, but it would not be enough to cast as one of the characters a riotous knight who keeps wassail to the discomfort of the household, or a vain and foppish steward who becomes amorous towards his mistress. These would be no more than Shakespeare's ideas in the play, as little capable of monopoly as Einstein's *Doctrine of Relativity*, or Darwin's theory of the *Origin of Species*. It follows that the less developed the characters, the less they can be copyrighted; that is the penalty an author must bear for marking them too indistinctly.[127]

Judge Hand suggests that there are two aspects of character protection: the infringed character must be sufficiently delineated and the infringing character must closely imitate the infringed character. Under this test, the line must be drawn between mere ideas sketching the general nature of the character and more fully developed characterization. In this sense, the protectability of the literary dimension of a character is no different from the protectibility of other elements in literary works, such as the details of plot and setting.

Courts have differed on the principle involved in the protection of literary characters. In *Warner Bros. Pictures, Inc. v. Columbia Broadcasting System,*[128] the court suggested another test, stating that copyright might cover a fictional character if the character constitutes the story being told, rather than merely a chessman or vehicle in the telling of the story. This somewhat more restrictive view of copyright for literary characters arose out of a contractual dispute covering the rights to Dashiell Hammet's fictional detective Sam Spade. In this case, the Ninth Circuit Court of Appeals held that the contract assigning the motion picture, radio, and television rights to the book, *The Maltese Falcon*, did not cover a copyright in the character of Sam Spade because characters *per se* are not copyrightable. This holding goes far beyond Judge Hand's statement and would deny copyright protection, even against direct copying of a unique and developed character, unless the character really constitutes the story being told.

---

[126] 45 F.2d 119 (2d Cir. 1930). In *Nichols*, the author of the play, *Abie's Irish Rose*, sued the producer of the movie, *The Cohens and the Kellys*. Both were comedies dealing with religious intermarriage. Judge Learned Hand held for the defendant on the grounds that the theme of the play fell in the realm of unprotected "ideas." *Warner Bros, Inc. v. American Broadcasting Co., Inc.*, 654 F.2d 204 (2d Cir. 1981) (holding that the television comedy, *The Greatest American Hero*, did not infringe the copyright in cartoon strips and movies of *Superman* because the idea of a character with superhuman powers who battles the forces of evil is not copyrightable, although the expression of such an idea could be). For an excellent discussion of the protection of dramatic characters, see *Authors League Symposium on Copyright*, 29 J. Copyright Soc'y 611 (1982).

[127] 45 F.2d 119, 121.

[128] 216 F.2d 945 (9th Cir. 1954) (also known as the *Sam Spade* case).

This Sam Spade standard would rarely be met, virtually excluding protection of literary characters. It has not been widely approved by either the bench or commentators.[129] The *Sam Spade* case may be distinguished as a contracts rather than a copyright case, with the statements on character rights mere *dicta*. Perhaps the better view is Judge Hand's, which presents the proper question concerning rights in fictional characters: has the infringer taken the expressive details of an adequately delineated character rather than the general abstract idea of a character?[130]

[D] Historical Research

Copyright protection has been denied to historical fact, whether part of an historical novel, biography, or news story. The discovery of a fact is simply not an original work of authorship.[131] The discoverer does not create facts; he finds and records them, making him an author neither in a constitutional nor in a statutory sense. As a corollary, copyright protection does not extend to the interpretation of historical fact. Suppose, for example, A proposed a new theory about the true identity of Shakespeare, or why the Watergate break-in took place. Here again, protection is denied for much the same reasons. For one, an interpretation of fact is simply a fact derived from other facts. For another, an interpretation is very much like an abstract idea, and when published, it becomes part of the public domain.

Copyright for any non-fiction narrative, whether history, biography, or news story, covers the literal form of the author's expression. Thus, anyone may relate a writer's theory of Shakespeare's identity or of the Watergate break-in, but may not copy or closely paraphrase the another's expression of the theory. Moreover, even literal copying may be allowed if the form of the expression is not original with the author, such as a purported actual conversation between the Watergate participants, even if unearthed from the public domain sources at great expense to and labor by the author.

Historical works, news stories, and biographies present much the same questions of copyrightability as encountered in compilations and collective works. As in all works using public domain materials, disparate or individual facts are freely appropriable by third parties, whereas their selection, patterning, and arrangement are protected under copyright.[132]

---

[129] *See* 1 *Nimmer on Copyright* § 2.12 (1993).

[130] For an application of Hand's principle of delineation to a group of characters in the *Rocky I, II,* and *III* films, see *Anderson v. Stallone*, 11 U.S.P.Q.2d 1161 (C.D. Cal. 1989) (defendant's script using the *Rocky* characters was infringing because the *Rocky* characters were so highly developed and central to the three movies that they constituted the story being told).

[131] *Rubin v. Boston Magazine Co.*, 645 F.2d 80 (1st Cir. 1981).

[132] Although historical facts in themselves, even newly discovered ones, may not be entitled to copyright, it may be argued that their selection and arrangement in a particular work provide sufficient originality to warrant protection. This problem displays the inherent tension in copyright law between the underlying and competing policies of protecting the interests of an author who may have spent great time and effort on his product, and the benefit to the public in the wide dissemination of facts. *See generally* Robert C. Denicola, *Copyright in*

After *Feist v. Rural Telephone Service Co.*[133] and the demise of the "sweat of the brow" as a basis of copyright protection, the trend in the case law should weigh against protecting the industrious effort involved in unearthing historical fact. Pre-*Feist* cases manifested a tension between protection of the efforts of the researcher and the need to allow dissemination of historical knowledge. Some cases have come very close to allowing protection for the general body of historical research resulting from the labor of the researcher. For example, in *Toksvig v. Bruce Publishing Co.*,[134] the plaintiff had written a biography of Hans Christian Anderson, exhaustively researching Anderson's life from original Danish sources. The defendant based his biography on the plaintiff's work and other English language books. Although the court could have found infringement because of the defendant's literal copying, it suggested that the defendant was free to obtain the same material by going to the public domain sources, but could not make a substantial and unfair use of the plaintiff's work. Other cases following this view have analogized the *Toksvig* principle to the protection of compilations, like city directories, where infringement has been found based on the defendant's copying of the entire directory.[135]

Despite some pronouncements in the case law that historical research in itself can be the basis of copyright, the recent trend in the case law, even before *Feist*, was to refuse copyright protection based on the industrious effort of the researcher. For example, in *Miller v. Universal Studios, Inc.*,[136] the plaintiff had spent some 2500 hours in the preparation of a book involving a notorious Georgia kidnapping in which the victim was imprisoned in an underground coffin. The kidnapping victim and the reporter collaborated on the book. Universal Studios, after unsuccessful attempts to secure movie rights, nevertheless made a movie based entirely on the book. The District Court declared itself in favor of the copyrightability of research. Its justification was based on a rationale similar to the telephone directory compilation cases: to reward the effort and ingenuity involved in giving expression to facts and to the effort required to unearth the facts.

Collections of Facts: A Theory for the Protection of Nonfiction Literary Works, 81 Colum. L. Rev. 516 (1981); Robert A. Gorman, *Copyright Protection for the Collection and Representation of Facts*, 76 Harv. L. Rev. 1569 (1963); and Robert A. Gorman, *Fact or Fancy? The Implications for Copyright*, 29 J. Copyright Soc'y 560 (1982). The question of the copyrightability of research often arises when a second work, *e.g.* , a television movie, is based upon facts uncovered in an earlier work. *See, e.g., Rosemont Enterprises, Inc. v. Random House, Inc.*, 366 F.2d 303 (2d Cir. 1966), *cert. denied*, 385 U.S. 1009 (1967) (the life story of Howard Hughes); *Miller v. Universal City Studios, Inc.*, 650 F.2d 1365 (5th Cir. 1981) (kidnapped victim who was buried alive); and *Hoehling v. Universal City Studios, Inc.*, 618 F.2d 972 (2d Cir. 1980) (the destruction of the Hindenberg). This decision is extensively criticized in Jane C. Ginsburg, *Sabotaging and Reconstructing History: A Comment on the Scope of Copyright Protection in Works of History After* Hoehling v. Universal Studios, 29 J. Copyright Soc'y 647 (1982). *Nash v. CBS*, 899 F.2d 1537 (7th Cir. 1990) (novel version of the shooting of the gangster John Dillinger).

[133] 499 U.S. 340 (1991).
[134] 181 F.2d 664 (7th Cir. 1950).
[135] *Miller v. Universal City Studios, Inc.*, 460 F. Supp. 984 (S.D. Fla. 1978).
[136] 650 F.2d 1365 (5th Cir. 1981).

The Court of Appeals reversed the District Court decision because it was unable to identify any appropriation of original expression. The court distinguished the telephone directory cases as constituting a category in themselves rather than extending their questionable logic to another setting.[137] According to the Fifth Circuit, copyright should be based only on the resulting writing and the original elements of authorship expressed in the work. The court could find "no rational basis for distinguishing between facts and the research involved in obtaining facts."[138] To hold that research is copyrightable is the same as holding that the facts discovered by research are entitled to copyright protection. *Id.* Whether the material in question is considered to be historical fact depends largely on how the author characterizes the work. If the historian holds out the events as factual matter, they enter into the public domain, despite their strangeness or the improbability of their occurrence. For example, in *Nash v. CBS,*[139] the plaintiff had a novel theory about the killing of the famous gangster, John Dillinger. In his work, *Dillinger Dead or Alive*, the author purported to show, among other things, that Dillinger was not killed in an assassination ambush when leaving a Chicago restaurant. Rather, the gangster, on learning of the trap, sent another person — a Dillinger lookalike — who was shot instead. This bizarre story, which received no legitimacy from reputable historians, became the subject of a CBS television show and subsequently, the basis of a suit for copyright infringement. The Court of Appeals for the Seventh Circuit held that CBS had copied historical fact but not its expression. Judge Easterbrook stated:

> Nash does not portray The Dillinger Dossier . . . as (a) work of fiction . . . which makes all the difference. The inventor of Sherlock Holmes controls that character's fate while copyright lasts; the first person to conclude that Dillinger survived does not get dibs on history. If Dillinger survived, that fact is available to all. Nash's rights lie in his expression: in his words, in his arrangement of facts (his deployment of narration interspersed with interviews, for example), but not in the naked "truth."[140]

If Nash had characterized his work as historical fiction, CBS may well have been found to have infringed the work.

§ 2.13 Other Issues on Non-Copyrightable Subject Matter

[A] Copyright in Immoral, Illegal, and Obscene Works

Copyright infringers have sometimes asserted as an affirmative defense that the plaintiff's work was obscene, immoral or fraudulent. This form of the unclean hands defense, despite some older authority,[141] has been rejected in more recent times.[142]

---

[137] *Id.* at 1371.

[138] *Id.* at 1372.

[139] 899 F.2d 1537 (7th Cir. 1990).

[140] *Id.* at 1541.

[141] *See* William F. Patry, *Copyright Law and Practice* 127 (1994).

[142] *See, e.g., Belcher v. Tarbox*, 486 F.2d 1087 (9th Cir. 1973) (racing forms are copyrightable); and *Jartech Inc. v. Clancy*, 666 F.2d 403 (9th Cir. 1982) (obscenity is not a defense to claim of copyright infringement).

In *Mitchell Brothers Film Group v. Cinema Adult Theater*,[143] the court rejected an unclean hands defense by defendants who obtained and exhibited the pornographic motion picture *Behind the Green Door*. The court found no implied exception in the Copyright Act for obscene works, and also found that the Copyright Clause of the Constitution is best served when read without restrictions on content imposed by governmental officials. The court feared that an obscenity determination, based on community standards, would fragment the law of copyright. As a result of these differing standards, copyright protection would vary from locality to locality and generation to generation. In place of a uniform copyright law which is national in scope, one community might allow piracy, while another would enforce the copyright in the same work. The goal of a uniform copyright law would be undermined by incorporating the obscenity standard.[144]

The question remains whether the Copyright Office could reject registration based on obscenity or fraudulent content. The Copyright Office would have to imply this authority but has declined to do so, despite a Department of Justice opinion concluding that the Copyright Office has the discretion to reject registration on morality grounds.[145]

Unlike the Copyright Act, which is silent on matters of morality, the Federal Trademark Act expressly forbids registration for a trademark of immoral, deceptive, or scandalous matter.[146] The federal government, however, may be ill-suited for such determinations of morality. The Trademark Office, for example, has made decisions totally arbitrary in appearance, denying registration to Booby Trap[147] as a mark for brassieres, while allowing Weekend Sex[148] for a magazine. Fortunately, the Copyright Office has formally decided not to make such decisions.[149]

[B]　Government Works

Section 105 of the Copyright Act provides:

> Copyright protection under this title is not available for any work of the United States Government, but the United States Government is not precluded from receiving and holding copyrights transferred to it by assignment, bequest, or otherwise.

By this section, the United States Government cannot claim copyright in works prepared by employees of the government in the course of their official duties. Thus, all reports, manuals, videotapes, musical or artistic works produced by a government employee pursuant to his official duties are in the public domain. According to the House Report, a government worker's official work product is similar to work made

---

[143] 604 F.2d 852 (5th Cir. 1979), *cert. denied*, 445 U.S. 917 (1980).

[144] Although *Mitchell Bros.* was based on the 1909 Act, its reasoning has been adopted by the 1976 Act case *Jartech Inc. v. Clancy*, 666 F.2d 403 (9th Cir. 1982), *cert. denied*, 459 U.S. 826 (1982).

[145] *Op. Att'y Gen.* 73, 171 U.S.P.Q. (BNA) 329 (1958).

[146] 15 U.S.C. § 1052(a).

[147] *In re Runsdorf*, 171 U.S.P.Q. (BNA) 443 (TMTAB 1971).

[148] *In re Madsen*, 180 U.S.P.Q. (BNA) 334 (TMTAB 1973).

[149] *Compendium II of Copyright Office Practices* § 108.10.

for hire.[150] Accordingly, a government employee could claim copyright only in a work written at his or her own volition outside formal duties. Whether a work is deemed created pursuant to, or independent of, official duties will turn on a series of factual considerations varying from case to case.[151]

Section 105 does not preclude the U.S. government from owning copyright in a work when the copyright is obtained by a transfer. For example, the government can obtain copyright ownership by assignment, bequest, or otherwise. The question is how to treat a governmentally commissioned work — a work created at governmental insistence by an independent contractor pursuant to a contract in which the independent contractor agrees to assign the work to the government. According to the House Report, where the government commissions a work in this manner, as an alternative to having one of its employees do the same work, it should be unable to claim copyright through contract with the independent contractor.[152] Otherwise, the government would be able by subterfuge to circumvent the statute disallowing copyright in works of the government. On the other hand, if the commissioned work is not related to the specific duties of an employee of an agency, the Government can obtain the copyright by a contract for its assignment.[153]

The above rules apply to the federal government only; state and local governments have no § 105 constraints on their ownership in copyrighted works created by public officials as part of their official duties. There are, however, certain categories applicable to all governmental works, state or federal, which are inherently in the public domain. This category of inherently non-copyrightable works includes statutes, ordinances, regulations, and judicial opinions. Accordingly, in *Georgia v. The Harrison Company*,[154] the State of Georgia could not claim copyright in its new code. The court held that the code was a public domain work, owned by the people of Georgia, who as citizens, must have free access to the laws governing them.[155]

---

[150] H.R. Rep. No. 94–1476, 94th Cong., 2d Sess. 58 (1976).

[151] *See, e.g., Scherr v. Universal Match Co.*, 297 F. Supp. 107 (S.D.N.Y. 1967), *aff'd on other grounds*, 417 F.2d 497 (2d Cir. 1969), *cert. denied*, 397 U.S. 936 (1970). For a discussion of the work made for hire doctrine, see § 5.2, *infra*.

[152] H.R. Rep. No. 94–1476, 94th Cong., 2d Sess. 59 (1976).

[153] *See Schnapper v. Foley*, 667 F.2d 102 (D.C. Cir. 1981). *Contra*: Professor Nimmer argues that such a contract should be void since the statute does not refer to commissioned works, because Congress wished that independent contractors be allowed to retain copyright in their works. Interpreted in this way, any contract for assignment of a work created by an independent contractor would subvert the statute. 1 *Nimmer on Copyright* § 5.06[B][3] (1993).

[154] 548 F. Supp. 110 (N.D. Ga. 1982), *vacated by agreement between the parties*, 559 F. Supp. 37 (N.D. Ga. 1983).

[155] *See also Building Officials & Code Admin. v. Code Technology, Inc.*, 628 F.2d 730 (1st Cir. 1980) (code written by private body and afterwards adopted into law is in public domain).

CHAPTER **3**

WORKS OF AUTHORSHIP: CATEGORIES OF COPYRIGHTABLE SUBJECT MATTER

§ 3.1 Introduction and Chapter Overview

The types of works which may qualify for copyright protection are enumerated in eight broad, overlapping categories of copyrightable subject matter called "works of authorship." While focusing on the types of works which may qualify for copyright protection, this chapter elaborates, as well, on the general standards of copyrightability such as originality, fixation, and idea-expression treated in Chapter 2.

This chapter is divided into four parts. Part I examines the meaning of the term "works of authorship" and the importance of how a work is categorized. Parts II and III have a unifying theme: the difficulty copyright law has had in assimilating works of utility, *i.e.*, those works which combine the useful and the expressive, such as computer programs and works of applied art. Part II treats literary works, focusing on the protection of computer programs. Part III concerns graphic, pictorial, and sculptural works. Most of the discussion emphasizes the scope of copyright protection for works of applied art. Part IV introduces the other categories of copyrightable subject matter, namely: musical works, sound recordings, dramatic works, choreographic works, pantomimes, and motion pictures.

PART I: WORKS OF AUTHORSHIP: OVERVIEW

§ 3.2 The Eight Categories

[A] Generally

Section 102(a)[1] of the 1976 Act sets forth eight illustrative categories of works of authorship:

    (1) literary works;

    (2) musical works, including any accompanying words;

    (3) dramatic works, including any accompanying music;

    (4) pantomimes and choreographic works;

---

[1] 17 U.S.C. § 102(a). See note 12, *infra*.

    (5) pictorial, graphic, and sculptural works;

    (6) motion pictures and other audiovisual works;

    (7) sound recordings; and

    (8) architectural works.

Congress purposely chose the term "works of authorship" in § 102(a) of the 1976 Act rather than the more inclusive term "all the writings of an author" as is found in the 1909 Act.[2] By choosing the more restrictive term, Congress indicated its intention not to exhaust the full scope of its constitutional authority to protect all writings.[3] One reason for Congress's choice of terminology was to avoid an ambiguity inherent in the 1909 Act which conferred copyright on "all the writings of an author." This seemingly all-inclusive language, however, had been construed by the courts as conferring copyrightability on less than all writings.[4] Thus, Congress has made explicit in the 1976 Act what the courts had imposed on the 1909 Act by their restrictive interpretation of the term "writings."

The term "works of authorship" is purposely left undefined in the 1976 Act. According to the House Report,[5] this omission was intended to provide for coverage which would be both extensive and flexible enough to accommodate new technologies and new ways which authors find to express themselves, but still less extensive than the full scope of constitutional authority to protect all writings. In short, copyright protection will be extended not only to works clearly falling into the eight specified categories but to analogous works as well.

[B] Excluded Writings

The question remains, which writings of authors are excluded from protection under the less-than-comprehensive term "works of authorship"? The legislative history is not explicit on this point. In general, deciding whether a writing will be considered a work of authorship is a two-step process. First, one must determine whether the legislative history has expressly excluded it. Examples of express exclusion are industrial design[6] and typeface design,[7] which Congress has explicitly indicated are not to be considered works of authorship. Second, even absent express exclusion, one must determine whether the writing has been *historically* excluded.

---

    [2] 17 U.S.C. § 4 (1909 Act).

    [3] "Writings" may be defined as "any physical rendering of the fruits of creative intellectual and aesthetic labor." *See Goldstein v. California*, 412 U.S. 546, 561 (1973).

    [4] *See id.* at 567; *Capitol Records, Inc. v. Mercury Records Corp.*, 221 F.2d 657, 660 (2d Cir. 1955).

    [5] H.R. Rep. No. 94–1476, 94th Cong., 2d Sess. 51 (1976).

    [6] For a discussion of industrial design, see § 3.12, *infra*.

    [7] "Typeface" is defined as a set of letters, numbers or other symbolic characters whose forms are related to repeating design elements consistently applied in a notational system and are intended to be embodied in articles whose intrinsic utilitarian function is for use in composing text or other cognizable combinations of characters. The House Report indicates an intent to exclude typeface designs from protection despite their status as writings. H.R. Rep. 94–1476, 94th Cong., 2d Sess. 55 (1976). *See Eltra v. Ringer*, 579 F.2d 294 (4th Cir. 1978) (typefaces are not copyrightable as works of art).

This determination requries a return to the case law under the 1909 Act. An example of writings which have been historically excluded and which have not been expressly included by the Copyright Act or the legislative history are literary characters[8] and titles.

One could easily make a persuasive case for the protection of titles under copyright law. As writings, they fall within the scope of feasible copyright subject matter. Consisting of words and symbols, titles meet the definitional requirement of a literary work under § 102(a). The title of a work can be commercially valuable. Catchy and clever titles such as *Everything You Always Wanted to Know About Sex But Were Afraid to Ask* can have great market impact.

Although not specifically excluded from copyright protection by the 1976 Act or its Committee Reports, titles are regarded as uncopyrightable subject matter despite a declared legislative intent for flexibility in § 102(a).[9] Thus, even if titles are writings, and look like literary works, they are excluded. The reason lies in their *de minimis* nature, as reflected in the Copyright Office circular which lumps together titles, short words and phrases, and trademarks as uncopyrightable.[10] Title protection must be sought elsewhere, primarily under state or federal unfair competition law on a theory of "passing off."[11]

[C] Copyrightable Subject Matter: The 1909 and 1976 Acts Compared

The categories listed in § 102(a) of the 1976 Act are meant to be illustrative, rather than limitative.[12] By this approach, Congress wanted to avoid the definitional rigidities of the 1909 Act and give as much flexibility to the courts as possible to adapt the law to new technologies and media. This rigidity was reflected in § 5 of the 1909 Act, which set forth fourteen categories of works of authorship ostensibly to provide administrative categories for registration in the Copyright Office.[13] Although these categories were meant only for administrative convenience, courts tended not to find a work copyrightable unless it fit into one of the categories.[14] The list lacked logic and coherency. It was no more than a grab bag of specific categories, some of which were based on the material object embodying a work — such as books and periodicals — and others on broad subject matter categories — such as sound recordings and motion pictures. More importantly, however, it was

---

[8] Literary characters *per se* are not copyrightable. For a discussion of literary characters, see § 2.12[C], *supra*.

[9] *Arthur Retlaw & Assocs., Inc. v. Travenol Laboratories, Inc.*, 582 F. Supp. 1010, 1014 (N.D. Ill. 1984).

[10] *See* Copyright Office *Circular No. 34*. Copyright Office *Compendium II*, § 202.021 states that " . . . words and short phrases such as names, titles, and slogans are not copyrightable."

[11] *See, e.g., Davis v. United Artists, Inc.*, 547 F. Supp. 722 (S.D.N.Y. 1982).

[12] As stated in the House Report:

> the seven categories do not necessarily exhaust the scope of "original works of authorship" that the bill is intended to protect.

H.R. Rep. No. 94–1476, 94th Cong., 2d Sess. 53 (1976).

[13] 17 U.S.C. § 5 (a–n) (1909 Act).

[14] *See Capitol Records, Inc. v. Mercury Records Corp.*, 221 F.2d 657 (2d Cir. 1955).

often difficult to determine whether a work fit into one or another of the classes. This determination could have important substantive consequences as to the form and location of notice, the manufacturing clause requirements, protection in unpublished form, and whether the work enjoyed the right of public performance for profit.

In comparison, the 1976 Act has conceptually streamlined the classification of copyrightable subject matter. The current Act is consistent in separating the work of authorship from the material object — the copy or phonorecord — in which it is embodied. For example, a literary work may be embodied in a book or recorded on tape, a musical work may be fixed on tape or written as sheet music, and a choreographic work may be written in specialized notation or filmed on tape. Regardless of the medium in which it is embodied, the work of authorship remains a literary or musical work under § 102(a).

The categories set forth in § 102(a) of the 1976 Act are not only broad but also overlapping. For example, a "literary work," defined in the Act as consisting of words and syllables, overlaps the dramatic work category; lyrics for a song can fit into either the literary work or musical work category; pantomimes and choreographic works can, in certain instances, double as dramatic works.

This overlapping aspect of copyrightable subject matter is reflected in the Register of Copyright's classification system for registration purposes [15] which has collapsed the eight statutory categories into four broader ones: Class TX (non-dramatic literary works); Class PA (performing arts); Class VA (visual arts); Class SR (sound recordings). When reviewing the copyright application, the Register may determine whether the claim fits into one of the categories.

[D]   Importance of How a Work is Categorized

How a work is categorized can have important legal consequences, particularly as to the scope of the copyright owner's exclusive rights. The exclusive rights are extensively covered in Chapter 8 of this treatise, but to provide a few examples: an owner of a copyright in a sound recording does not enjoy a performance right;[16] only non-dramatic musical works are subject to compulsory license for reproduction and distribution under § 115;[17] and a library's reproduction right under § 108(h) is much wider for literary and dramatic works than for other categories.[18] Thus, the classification of a work is more than just a formality.

Who decides whether a work fits into one category or another? Ultimately, a court would make this decision. The Copyright Office, however, has an influential role in determining into which category a work falls. Section 408(c)(1) of the Act[19] authorizes the Copyright Office to promulgate regulations specifying administrative classes for registration purposes. Despite that section's proviso that "[t]his administrative classification of works has no significance with respect to the subject matter

---

[15] Copyright Office Regulations § 202.3 (Registration of Copyright).

[16] 17 U.S.C. § 114.

[17] 17 U.S.C. § 115.

[18] 17 U.S.C. § 108(h).

[19] 17 U.S.C. § 408(c)(1).

of copyright or the exclusive rights provided by this title," the Office's administrative classification can, as a practical matter, have a significant influence on a court's determination on classification.[20]

PART II: LITERARY WORKS

§ 3.3   Generally

Literary works are defined by the 1976 Act as

> works, other than audiovisual works, expressed in words, numbers, or other verbal or numerical symbols or indicia, regardless of the nature of the material objects, such as books, periodicals, manuscripts, phonorecords, film, tapes, disks, or cards, in which they are embodied.[21]

This category encompasses all works written in words or symbols of any kind, regardless of the material objects in which they are embodied. The word "literary," in this context, implies no idea of literary merit. A literary work can be a computer program, a catalog, a data base, or a poem written on a piece of paper or recorded on cassette. Copyright in computer programs is one form of literary work which has caused much controversy in recent years.

Computer programs are now a fundamental part of copyright law, and issues concerning them are discussed at various points in this text.[22] The following two sections introduce the computer question in an historical overview, and present the basic terminology of computer technology. These two sections are followed by an examination of the leading case of *Apple Computer, Inc. v. Franklin Computer Corp.*[23]

§ 3.4   Computer Programs (Software)

[A]   Historical Background: CONTU

Formal recognition of computer programs as copyrightable subject matter did not come about until 1980 with an amendment to the Copyright Act.[24] Under the original version of § 117, the 1976 Act kept the legal status quo of computer programs as it existed on December 31, 1977.[25] But it was widely accepted that

---

[20] *See Esquire, Inc. v. Ringer*, 591 F.2d 796, 802 (D.C. Cir. 1978).

[21] 17 U.S.C. § 101 (literary works).

[22] For a discussion of the video game cases, see § 2.5, *supra*. For a discussion of limitations on the exclusive rights to a computer program, see § 3.6, *infra*.

[23] 714 F.2d 1240 (3d Cir. 1983), *cert. dismissed*, 464 U.S. 1033 (1984).

[24] Act of December 12, 1980, Pub. L. No. 96–517, § 10(b), 94 Stat. 3028.

[25] As early as 1964, the Copyright Office registered the first computer program in the book category under the Office's Rule of Doubt (policy favoring the applicant when uncertainties about copyrightability arise), and continued this practice as long as the programs were deposited in humanly readable form.

computer programs were copyrightable as literary works. According to the House Report, the definition of literary works included

> computer data bases, and computer programs, to the extent that they incorporate authorship in the programmer's expression of original ideas, as distinguished from the ideas themselves.[26]

Although copyrightability of computer programs was clearly favored by the legislative history of the 1976 Act, doubts remained after its passage because computer programs did not fit neatly into the more traditional forms of literary works. Because of this uncertainty, the complexity of the issues, and the economic stakes, Congress appointed the National Commission of New Technological Uses of Copyrighted Works (CONTU) to study the computer program issue. Their final report in 1979 made specific recommendations to amend the Copyright Act which were adopted in their entirety.[27] The revisions included a new definition of "computer program" in § 101, and § 117's Limitations on Exclusive Rights: Computer Programs.

Computer programs are now defined in § 101 as

> a set of statements or instructions to be used directly or indirectly in a computer in order to bring about a certain result.[28]

In addition, the Act now contains a revised § 117 setting forth the scope of exclusive rights in computer programs.[29] Thus, the Copyright Act, its legislative history and, with little exception, the case law, have fully recognized computer programs as a mainstream form of copyrightable subject matter.[30]

[B] Copyrightability of Programs — Initial Doubts

Computer programs have a different look and feel as compared to more traditional forms of copyrightable subject matter. Reservations on this basis concerning the wholesale inclusion of computer programs in copyright law were expressed in the dissenting and concurring comments of Commissioners Hershey and Nimmer to the CONTU *Final Report*. Hershey argued against protection because computer programs, unlike other forms of copyrightable subject matter, such as sound recordings or motion pictures, do not communicate with people, but are essentially mechanical, labor-saving devices, which transmit electronic impulses to operate machines called computers.[31] Professor Nimmer, in his concurring opinion, wrote

---

[26] H.R. Rep. No. 94–1476, 94th Cong., 2d Sess. 54 (1976).

[27] Pub. L. No. 96–517, § 10, 94 Stat. 3015, 3028. One should note the minor deviation from the CONTU language in § 117. Nat'l Commission on New Technological Uses of Copyrighted Works, *Final Report* 12 (1979).

[28] 17 U.S.C. § 101 (computer programs).

[29] 17 U.S.C. § 117. For a discussion of § 117, see § 8.6, *infra*.

[30] For an overview of copyright law on computers since passage of the computer program amendments, see Arthur R. Miller, *Copyright Protection for Computer Programs, Databases, and Computer-Generated Works: Is There Anything New Since CONTU?*, 106 Harv. L. Rev. 977 (1993).

[31] *See* CONTU *Final Report, Dissent of Commissioner Hershey* at 27–28.

that full protection of computer programs under copyright law would strain the meaning of "writings" and "authors" under the Constitution, broadening copyright law to where it becomes a general misappropriation law, and covering subject matter more appropriate for patent protection. Nimmer's solution for this overbreadth was to grant copyright protection only to programs producing a copyrightable output. Thus, a program producing a video game whose output is an audio-visual work, or one producing a database whose output is a compilation, would be copyrightable.[32] But a program that controlled the air conditioning in a building, a non-copyrightable output, would not be eligible for copyright protection. Neither Hershey's nor Nimmer's approach was adopted, and all programs are now copyrightable, regardless of their nature or output.

To grasp the legal issues surrounding the scope of protection for computer programs requires a basic understanding of the technology involved.

§ 3.5   Computer Technology

[A]   Computer Hardware: The Basics[33]

Phenomenal progress in computer technology has dramatically altered the way in which we use, store, record, and transmit information. The first room-sized computers of the late 1940's could do no more than today's personal desktop models, which are becoming smaller, faster, and cheaper all the time.

This technological process is reflected in the key elements of computer hardware which have gone through four generally acknowledged generations: vacuum tubes, transistors, printed circuits, and integrated circuits. With each change in the fundamental building blocks, the new technology has reduced the computer's energy requirements and price. For example, first generation vacuum tubes, unreliable and energy inefficient, were replaced in the late 1940's by the second generation transistor. Smaller and more efficient, the transistor marked the beginning of the semiconductor industry's use of silicon material. Next followed the printed circuits, replaced by today's fourth generation integrated circuits, which place all essential components and connectors in silicon material. The revolution is continuing, and one can expect newer, smaller, faster, more efficient configurations.

The integrated circuitry of a digital computer (the hardware), housed in the central processing unit (CPU) of the computer, can do nothing without being instructed. The computer program, or software, as it is called in the industry, instructs the computer how to carry out its logical functions to produce the intended result or perform a task, such as producing patterns for a video game or the columns in a spreadsheet, or performing the "spell check" in a word processing program. The design of the program is based on an algorithm, a procedure for solving a given type of mathematical problem. The algorithm is sometimes called the "logic" of the program.

---

[32] *Id.* at 26–27 (concurring opinion of Professor Nimmer).

[33] For an overview of the subject, see Steven Mandell, *Computers and Data Processing Today With Basic* 28–44 (1983); CONTU *Final Report* at 9–12.

[B]   Computer Software: Developmental Stages[34]

A program goes through various developmental stages before it is ready to instruct the CPU. The first task of the program designer is to express the logical structure of the program, which was traditionally done through an elaborate set of charts. Flow charting has given way to other more expedient methods, but a basic recitation in English to define the program logic is a necessary first step. The program is then implemented by coding it first into human-readable language, using English symbols, such as BASIC, FORTRAN or PASCAL, called high-level languages. The program is then rewritten into an intermediate level language called Basic Assembly Language, which in turn is translated into machine language for execution by the computer. Both high-level language and Basic Assembly are written in "source code," and are intelligible to humans. The CPU, however, can only follow directions in machine language, called "object code," a binary code written in zeros and ones. Object code is unintelligible to a human reader. Because object code cannot be read by the human eye, many software proprietors, in order to impede copying, distribute their programs only in that form, never in source code.

Computer programs are fixed in a variety of devices, *e.g.,* on paper, floppy disks, or semiconductor chips. One such device is the ROM (Read Only Memory),[35] a semiconductor chip containing the computer programs permanently embedded into it in object code. ROMs are manufactured separately and then placed into the circuitry of the computer. As the name indicates, information stored on the ROM can only be read, not erased.

[C]   Application and Operating System Programs

Computer programs can be classified functionally as either application or operating system programs. Application programs perform precise tasks or solve specific problems, such as word processing, checkbook balancing, or game playing. Operating system programs generally manage the internal functions of the computer, or facilitate operations of applications programs, performing tasks common to any applications program. An operating system program, for example, might start the computer and activate its circuits, preparing it to accept instructions.

The discussion now turns to an application of these technological concerns in a leading case which examined the key aspects of copyright in computer software.[36]

---

[34] For a discussion of the process, see Raymond T. Nimmer, *Law of Computer Technology* §§ 1–12 to 1–20 (1985). See also the useful glossary of terms at xxix–xxii.

[35] Other kinds of memory chips, such as the widely used RAM (Random Access Memory) are more versatile than the ROM, because the computer can erase them and write into them new data or instructions.

[36] For commentary on the subject, see I.T. Hardy, *Six Copyright Theories for the Protection of Computer Object Programs*, 26 Ariz. L. Rev. 845 (1984); Peter S. Menell, *Tailoring Legal Protection for Computer Software*, 39 Stan. L. Rev. 1329 (1987); Pamela Samuelson, *CONTU Revisited: The Case Against Copyright Protection for Computer Programs in Machine Readable Form*, 1984 Duke L.J. 663; Note, *Copyright Protection of Computer Program Object Code*, 96 Harv. L. Rev. 1723 (1983).

§ 3.6 Computer Programs in the Courts: *Apple Computer, Inc. v. Franklin Computer Corp.* [37]

[A] *Apple Computer, Inc. v. Franklin Computer Corp.*: The Issues Involved

Computer programs have received expansive protection in the courts, as exemplified in the leading case of *Apple Computer, Inc. v. Franklin Computer Corp.* [38] In *Apple*, defendant Franklin copied Apple's operating system program to manufacture an Apple compatible computer. With minor variation, Franklin copied the system identically from the ROMs in which it was embedded. Having the identical operating system permitted the defendant's Franklin ACE Computer to use the vast number of application programs written for the Apple II computer. On these facts the court was confronted with three basic issues about the scope of protection for computer programs: (1) whether copyright can exist in a computer program expressed in object code; (2) whether copyright can exist in a computer program embedded in a ROM; and (3) whether copyright can exist in an operating system program. The first two questions had already been considered in other litigation ultimately favorable to the plaintiffs;[39] the third issue involving the copyrightability of operating systems constituted the novel aspect of the case. The court answered all three issues affirmatively, both reaffirming and expanding the scope of protection for computer programs.

[B] Copyright in a Program Expressed in Object Code

The court had little trouble in concluding that a work written in object code unintelligible to humans would qualify as a literary work.[40] Section 102(a) states that copyright protection extends to works fixed in any tangible means of expression "from which they can be perceived . . . with the aid of a machine or device," and does not require that they be intelligible to humans.[41] As to whether object code is a literary work, the court stated that the definition of "literary works" as those expressed in " . . . numbers, or other . . . numerical symbols or indicia . . . ,"[42] clearly encompasses the zeros and ones of a binary language object code.

---

[37] 714 F.2d 1240 (3d Cir. 1983).

[38] 714 F.2d 1240 (3d Cir. 1983), *cert. dismissed.* 464 U.S. 1033 (1984).

[39] *See Williams Elec., Inc. v. Artic Int'l, Inc.*, 685 F.2d 870 (3d Cir. 1982); *Stern Elec., Inc. v. Kaufman*, 669 F.2d 852, 855-56 (2d Cir. 1982).

[40] The first case holding that computer software embedded in a ROM was copyrightable was *Tandy Corp. v. Personal Micro Computers, Inc.*, 524 F. Supp. 171 (N.D. Cal. 1981). The copyrightability of the object code embedded in a ROM was much in doubt under 1909 Act case law. *Data Cash Systems, Inc. v. JS & A Group, Inc.*, 480 F. Supp. 1063 (N.D. Ill. 1979), *aff'd on other grounds*, 628 F.2d 1038 (7th Cir. 1980) (non-protectible because not intelligible to human readers). The court's holding was based on the early decision of *White-Smith Music Publishing Co. v. Apollo Co.*, 209 U.S. 1 (1908), which held that a piano roll was not a copy of the musical composition because it was not in a form humans could perceive. *White* has been specifically discarded by the 1976 Act, leading to the protection of non-human readable fixations. See § 2.4, *supra*.

[41] 17 U.S.C. § 102(a).

[42] 17 U.S.C. § 101 (literary works).

[C]   Copyrightability of a Program Embedded in a ROM

The defendant also argued that the embodiment of a program on a ROM precluded its protection because ROMs are utilitarian objects or machine parts. This argument had previously been rejected in the video game cases,[43] and the court had no difficulty repeating that the statutory requirement of fixation was satisfied because the ROM computer chip constituted the material object in which the copyrighted work, *i.e.*, the program, was embedded.[44]

[D]   Copyrightability of Operating Systems

The key issue in *Franklin* involved the copyrightability of the operating system programs, which Franklin claimed were *per se* uncopyrightable under *Baker v. Selden*[45] and its extension in *Morrissey v. Procter & Gamble Co.*[46] The defendant argued that there were a limited number of ways to write an operating system program which would run most Apple Computer software. This argument states the doctrine of "merger" in which a work is uncopyrightable if its idea and expression merge, or are so closely related that one cannot be used without the other. Here, the Third Circuit found that the trial court had made insufficient findings as to whether idea and expression had merged, and remanded the case on this issue.[47] The court, however, unequivocally upheld the copyrightability of computer programs, whether application or operating systems:

> Both types of programs instruct the computer to do something. Therefore, it should make no difference for purposes of Section 102(b) whether these instructions tell the computer to help prepare an income tax return (the task of an application program) or to translate a high level language program from source code into its binary language object code form (the task of the operating system . . .).[48]

Franklin has established the copyrightability of operating system programs and the illegality of copying the programmer's expression manifested in the program.[49] The pertinent question in forthcoming cases will be the scope of that protection and what constitutes infringement of a program. In that regard, the court did not define the difference between idea and expression as applied to computer programs. This distinction is not easy to show in the case of computer programs because they are

---

[43] *See Williams Elec., Inc. v. Artic Int'l, Inc.*, 685 F.2d 870, 876 (3d Cir. 1982).

[44] 714 F.2d 1240, 1249 (3d Cir. 1983).

[45] 101 U.S. 99 (1879). For a discussion of *Baker*, see § 2.12[B], *supra*.

[46] 379 F.2d 675 (1st Cir. 1967).

[47] 714 F.2d 1240, 1253 (3d Cir. 1983).

[48] *Id.* at 1251.

[49] The basic holdings in *Franklin* have been strengthened in *Apple Computer, Inc. v. Formula Int'l, Inc.*, 562 F. Supp. 775 (C.D. Cal. 1983), *aff'd*, 725 F.2d 521 (9th Cir. 1984) (object code in ROM is copyrightable); *NEC Corp. v. Intel Corp.*, 645 F. Supp. 590 (N.D. Cal. 1986) (microcode and microprograms are copyrightable computer programs within the meaning of the Copyright Act. Microprograms were defined by the court as "a set of statements used, directly or indirectly to bring about the result of interpreting the INTEL 8086 instruction set." *Id.* at 593).

essentially different from most other copyrighted works. The idea-expression doctrine as applied to a painting, a novel, or a piece of music has a long tradition developed over the years through case law. To separate idea from expression is sometimes a difficult task, but one which is possible because of their inherent nature. These familiar forms communicate with people, and their design is dictated by aesthetics. On the other hand, computer programs are inherently functional, and are designed to perform specialized tasks. In a novel, for example, the idea could be viewed as the general theme, whereas the copyrightable expression lies in the details, scenes, events, and characterizations.[50]

In the computer program context, one can equate idea with the accomplishment of a given task or function. Thus, if there are other ways to achieve the same result, there are alternative means of expression, and the doctrine of merger does not apply. Copyright should not be used to monopolize a result: the very essence of § 102(b). But stating this proposition does not answer the hard question: how broadly or narrowly do you define the result in the operating system context? Franklin wished to define the result broadly as 100% Apple compatibility in order to use the vast library of application programs written for the Apple system. Assuming Apple compatibility is the uncopyrightable result, and total compatibility could only be achieved by identical copying, the doctrine of merger would apply, rendering the operating system virtually uncopyrightable. The *Franklin* court, however, fell short of establishing 100% compatibility as the uncopyrightable "idea." In addition, it did not indicate either what degree of compatibility or how this compatibility could be achieved.

Franklin may wish to achieve total compatibility . . . but that is a commercial and competitive objective which does not enter into the somewhat metaphysical issue of whether particular ideas and expressions have merged.[51]

Now that computer programs are copyrightable regardless of their form or expressive content, the next set of issues, as suggested above, will be to determine the scope of their protection. This issue arises when the defendant (unlike in *Franklin*) has not engaged in verbatim copying of the program but has copied the sequence and organization of the program. The difficult question in this context is to determine when a programmer's protectable expression has been taken.[52]

Another currently debated scope-of-protection issue is whether a defendant can copy a plaintiff's program to develop a non-infringing, competing or compatible program. This process of reverse engineering, called "disassembly and decompilation," has been successfully defended as a fair use and has presented intricate problems of copyright and competitive policy.[53]

---

[50] *Reyher v. Children's Television Workshop*, 533 F.2d 87 (2d Cir. 1976).

[51] *Apple Computer, Inc. v. Franklin Computer Corp.*, 714 F.2d 1240, 1253 (3d Cir. 1983).

[52] *See, e.g., Whelan Assoc., Inc. v. Jaslow Dental Laboratory, Inc.*, 797 F.2d 1222 (3d Cir. 1986) and *Computer Assoc. Int'l v. Altai, Inc.*, 982 F.2d 693 (2d Cir. 1992). For a discussion of these cases, see § 9.5[F], *infra*.

[53] *See Sega Enter. v. Accolade, Inc.*, 977 F.2d 1510 (9th Cir. 1992); See § 10.13, *infra*, for a discussion of the issue.

§ 3.7 Computer-Generated Works[54]

Authors have always used machines such as quill pens, typewriters, and cameras while creating their works. Computers, the latest development in this line, are machines which organize information and do nothing unless instructed by a program. Some programs, word processing programs for example, are inert tools for creation and a computer so programmed works much like a camera or typewriter, where virtually all choices are made by a human author. Other programs, however, contribute to creative authorship, such as those that compose music or graphic images with only the slightest human input.

Can computers be authors? Neither the Constitution nor the Copyright Act indicates that authors have to be human. It is universally assumed, however, that the copyright monopoly was intended for human authors and that granting copyright to a machine would be an absurdity. The reason relates to the purpose of copyright (and all intellectual property law, for that matter), which is to provide incentives to create. Machines do not need these monopoly incentives; they just need electricity.

If a machine cannot be an author for copyright purposes, who is the author of a computer-generated work? The choice is between the user of the program and the programmer. CONTU found that the author was the one who employed the computer.[55] This is an overstatement because an author must demonstrate originality and a quantum of creativity which justifies the copyright. One who simply turns on a computer and inserts a program that composes music would be hard put to claim originality in the result. There must be some evidence of choice, selection, or intellectual labor constituting originality. The range of user originality is quite easy to find in the output generated through use of a word processing program, but at the other end of the continuum, for computer-generated works involving significant or no user discretion, copyright should be denied. As in any other legal determination, there will be different line-drawing processes within these extremes to determine whether the user of the program has supplied sufficient original authorship to the computer-generated work.

The programmer is the other person who may have a claim to authorship in a computer-generated work. The right to the copyright in the program is clear, but does the same principle apply to what the program produces? Despite the significant intellectual effort put into creating the program, there are fundamental reasons why the programmer should not be allowed to claim the output. First, the programmer did not himself fix the work. He created the possibility of a work, but did not embody it in the tangible medium of expression. The user is the one who did that, and copyright law confers authorship on the person who fixes the work. Second, for computer-generated works the output is randomly determined and unpredictable. Copyright should only be conferred upon an author who conceives as well as fixes

---

[54] For an overview, see Pamela Samuelson, *Allocating Ownership Rights in Computer-Generated Works*, 47 U. Pitt. L. Rev. 1185 (1986).

[55] *See* CONTU *Final Report* at 43–46. *See also* Raymond T. Nimmer, *The Law of Computer Technology* §§ 1–35 to 1–37 (1981).

a work. From the above, the raw output of a computer-generated work should be treated as fact, without ownership rights in anybody. In short, copyright protection should be conferred on the user of the program, not the programmer, but only when the user has added original authorship to the raw output.

§ 3.8   Other Forms of Intellectual Property Protection for Computer Software: Trade Secret and Patent Law

[A]   Trade Secret Protection[56] for Computer Software

Copyright law is only one means of intellectual property law protection for computer software. Trade secret law and patent law also have important roles to play. Traditionally, trade secret protection has been the body of law that owners of computer programs have used to protect their creations.

A trade secret has been defined as

> any formula, pattern, device or compilation of information which is used in one's business, and which gives him an opportunity to obtain an advantage over competitors who do not know or use it.[57]

Providing a broader range of subject matter protection than copyright law, trade secret law has been the law of choice through the years for the computer software industry.[58]

Trade secret protection is in some important ways more limited than copyright and patent law protection. Trade secrets are protected only as long as the subject matter has not become generally known in the industry.[59] Moreover, trade secrets are only protected against misappropriation by breach of a confidential relationship, not against discovery by innocent means such as reverse engineering.[60] These general standards place computer programs in a precarious position once the program is distributed to the public, where its design could be easily discovered by third parties. Thus, trade secret protection is of most value during a program's developmental stage where it can be protected against improper disclosure by breach of confidence. Nevertheless, even for publicly distributed programs, the computer software industry has tried a variety of ingenious techniques designed to retain the trade secret status of the program either by licensing it to customers under an obligation of confidence or nondisclosure, or by distributing the program only in machine readable object code. Despite these techniques, any publicly distributed program is vulnerable to discovery by reverse engineering, and once it becomes generally known within the industry, the trade secret protection is lost.

[56] For a discussion of trade secret law, see § 1.14[A], *supra*.
[57] *Restatement of Torts* § 757, Comment b (1939).
[58] *See* Duncan M. Davidson, *Protecting Computer Software: A Comprehensive Analysis*, 1983 Ariz. St. L.J. 611; and Glen T. MacGrady, *Protection of Computer Software — An Upgrade and Practical Synthesis*, 20 Hous. L. Rev. 1033 (1983).
[59] *See* Roger M. Milgrim, *Trade Secrets*, § 2–74 (1988) (absolute secrecy is not required).
[60] *See, e.g., Telex Corp. v. I.B.M. Corp.*, 510 F.2d 894 (10th Cir. 1975).

[B] Patent Law Protection for Computer Software

Patent law,[61] which confers a 20-year monopoly on products and processes, is another possible source of intellectual property protection for computer software.[62] The advantage of patent protection is that, unlike copyright law whose threshold of protection is originality, patent protects its owner against all users and sellers of the patented invention, even an independent discoverer.[63] The disadvantage of patent protection is its cost — the time and money it takes to obtain a patent. The Patent Office scrutinizes the application thoroughly to determine whether it meets the rigorous standards of patentability, namely: novelty[64] and non-obviousness.[65] The examination process may take years if there are complications, and the filing costs and legal fees can amount to thousands of dollars, even for an application ultimately denied protection. Because of the time and expense involved, patent law protection is not the appropriate route for most computer software. The decision to seek patent protection depends on the anticipated long market life and significant commercial value of the program. For example, a novel operating system program may be more appropriate for patent protection than an applications program for a video game which has a relatively short market appeal.

The patentability of inventions using computer software was uncertain until *Diamond v. Diehr*,[66] where the Supreme Court, in a five-to-four decision, established that an invention is no less patentable because it makes use of computer software. *Diehr* involved the patentability of a process for curing raw synthetic rubber. The process used computer software to compute time, temperature, and pressure accurately, so that rubber would retain its shape after molding was completed. The process employed a well-known mathematical formula for which no claim was made. The Court held that

> . . . a claim drawn to subject matter otherwise statutory does not become nonstatutory simply because it uses a mathematical formula, computer program, or digital computer.[67]

In sum, software embodied in an otherwise patentable process or apparatus can qualify for patent protection so long as protection is not sought for a mathematical formula or method of calculation.[68] The case law after *Diehr* has expanded protection for computer programs[69] to allow increasingly broad claim coverage.[70]

---

[61] For a discussion of patent law, see § 1.11, *supra*.

[62] *See* 35 U.S.C. § 101.

[63] *See* 35 U.S.C. § 271.

[64] 35 U.S.C. § 102.

[65] 35 U.S.C. § 103.

[66] 450 U.S. 175 (1981).

[67] *Id.* at 187.

[68] *See In re Walter*, 618 F.2d 758 (C.C.P.A. 1980).

[69] *See, e.g., In re Pardo*, 684 F.2d 912 (C.C.P.A. 1982).

[70] *See, e.g., Arrhythmia Research Technology, Inc. v. Corazonix Corp.*, 958 F.2d 1053 (Fed. Cir. 1992). It has also engendered much controversy. For differing views about the patentability of computer software, see, e.g., Pamela Samuelson, Benson *Revisited: The Case Against Patent Protection for Algorithms and Other Computer Program-Related Inventions*,

Following the trend in the case law, the U.S. Patent and Trademark Office issues yearly a greater number of software patents.[71] Considering the greater number and breadth of software patents issuing today, and the ever-increasing number of companies computerizing their manufacturing processes, patenting computer software has become an increasingly attractive method of protecting computer software.[72]

§ 3.9 Semiconductor Chips

[A] The Technological Background, the Economic Stakes, and the Legal Dilemma[73]

Semiconductor chips, tiny integrated circuits embodied in silicon base material, have become exceedingly important to the electronics industry, the nation's economy, and our daily lives. They seem to run almost everything from television sets and cardiac pacemakers to robots and printing presses.

To compact thousands of switching devices on this fingernail-size wafer is a complex and expensive task, often involving thousands of engineering hours and millions of dollars. The process generally begins by producing a series of drawings representing the electronic circuitry. From these drawings, a series of stencils, called masks, are produced. Each mask corresponds to one layer of the final chip, and is layered into the final chip by a chemical process. Creation of these masks is a costly and critical element of microchip production; copying them is the goal of the microchip pirate.

Although masks are expensive and time-consuming to produce, they are relatively cheap and can be copied quickly. The microchip pirate simply removes a chip's casing and photographs its individual layers. Having no research and development costs, the pirate is often able to undersell the original producer. This gross discrepancy between the cost of creation and the cost of reproduction has led microchip producers to seek the law's protection to ensure that they will receive an adequate return on their investment.

Traditional forms of intellectual property protection, however, have been unavailable for semiconductor chips, for several reasons. First, trade secret protection is impractical. Relatively easy to reverse engineer, chips lose trade secret protection quickly following an unrestricted sale. Second, patent protection is largely unavailable. Despite their high production costs, chips have difficulty meeting the rigorous

---

39 Emory L.J. 1025 (1990) (opposing patent protection and advocating *sui generis* protection); Samuel Oddi, *An Uneasier Case for Copyright Than for Patent Protection of Computer Programs*, 72 Neb. L. Rev. 351 (1993) (somewhat easier case can be made for patent protection of computer programs than under copyright or a *sui generis* system).

[71] Office of Technology Assessment, *Finding a Balance: Computer Software, Intellectual Property and the Challenge of Technological Change* 55 (1992).

[72] *See* Roger L. Cook, *The Software Industry Anticipates a Flood of Patent Litigation*, National Law Journal, January 24, 1994, at S2.

[73] *See generally* H.R. Rep. No. 98–781, 98th Cong., 2d Sess. (1984).

patent standard of inventiveness. Third, copyright law has not provided a source of protection. The Copyright Office reflects the current thinking. To the Copyright Office, chips are uncopyrightable utilitarian objects. The Copyright Office has registered the schematic drawings of the electrical interconnections of the chip, but protection extends only to the drawings, not to the chip itself. The reason for this anomaly lies in § 113(b) of the Copyright Act,[74] which states that copyright in a pictorial, graphic, or sculptural work portraying a useful article does not extend to the manufacture of the article itself. Similarly, architectural drawings of a building or technical drawings for a motorcycle are protectible under copyright law, but the building or motorcycle they portray is not.[75]

[B] The Semiconductor Chip Act: Statutory Overview

Lack of significant protection for this important industry under traditional intellectual property law led to *sui generis* protection in the Semiconductor Chip Protection Act of 1984.[76] A hybrid of patent and copyright law (but closer to copyright in nature), the Act provides protection upon registration or first commercial use,[77] whichever occurs first, and then lasts ten years from that date.[78]

Mask works must meet a copyright-like standard of originality. Protection is available for original mask works independently created, but is not available for commonplace staple designs, or their trivial variations.[79] As in copyright law, protection does not extend to an idea, concept, principle, or discovery used in the mask work design. Procedures, processes, and methods of operation described or embodied in a mask work are not eligible for protection; for this, one must seek patent protection. To avoid forfeiture, registration in the Copyright Office must be sought within two years of commercial exploitation anywhere in the world.[80] The Copyright Office will issue registration if the formal elements of the application are present and the subject matter is apparent, but it will conduct no search for conflicting prior registrations. The effective date of registration is the date on which a complete and allowable registration is filed in the Copyright Office.[81]

Notice on mask works is permissive, but strongly recommended because it constitutes *prima facie* notice that the mask work is protected.[82] Notice consists of the symbol "M" in a circle, plus the name or recognized abbreviation of the mask owner.[83] A mask owner must affix notice in a way that gives reasonable notice of his claim.

---

[74] 17 U.S.C. § 113(b). For a discussion of § 113(b), see § 8.10, *infra*.

[75] For a discussion of architectural works, see § 3.15, *infra*.

[76] Act of November 8, 1984, Pub. L. No. 98–620, 98 Stat. 3347; 17 U.S.C. §§ 900 *et seq.*

[77] 17 U.S.C. § 904.

[78] 17 U.S.C. § 905.

[79] 17 U.S.C. §§ 902(b)(1) and (2).

[80] 17 U.S.C. § 908(a).

[81] 17 U.S.C. § 908(e).

[82] 17 U.S.C. § 909(a).

[83] 17 U.S.C. § 909(b).

The federal district courts are given exclusive jurisdiction over claims for infringement of a mask work. Registration or application for registration of the work is a prerequisite to bringing suit.[84] Remedies include injunction, damages, and profits. As in copyright law, the owner of the work may elect an award of statutory damages to a maximum of $250,000 for infringement of any one mask work, in lieu of damages and profits.[85] The Act establishes a three-year statute of limitations.[86]

PART III: PICTORIAL, GRAPHIC, AND SCULPTURAL WORKS: THE UTILITARIAN OBJECT

§ 3.10 Generally

Section 102(a)(5) of the 1976 Act provides protection to pictorial, graphic, and sculptural works, a category which

> include[s] two-dimensional and three-dimensional works of fine, graphic, and applied art, photographs, prints and art reproductions, maps, globes, charts, technical drawings, diagrams and models.[87]

The term "graphic, pictorial, and sculptural works" encompasses works of fine art as well as applied art and implies no criteria of aesthetic value or taste.[88] The aspect of this category which has engendered the most controversy is the role of copyright in protecting artistic creations embodying utilitarian objects. The following sections concentrate on this issue by examining the question of industrial design and architectural works.

§ 3.11 Works of Applied Art and the Design of Useful Objects[89]

The designer's art fuses the functional with the aesthetic, producing objects of everyday life — telephones, lighting fixtures, automobiles, tableware — which are both beautiful and useful. Excellence comes at a price, and designers must recoup

---

[84] 17 U.S.C. §§ 910(a) and (b).

[85] 17 U.S.C. § 911.

[86] 17 U.S.C. § 911(d).

[87] 17 U.S.C. § 101 (pictorial, graphic, and sculptural works).

[88] H.R. Rep. No. 94–1476, 94th Cong., 2d Sess. 55 (1976).

[89] For comprehensive reviews of the subject, see Ralph S. Brown, *Design Protection: An Overview*, 34 UCLA L. Rev. 1341 (1987); Robert C. Denicola, *Applied Art and Industrial Design: A Suggested Approach to Copyright in Useful Articles*, 67 Minn. L. Rev. 707 (1983); Michael J. Lynch, *Copyright in Utilitarian Objects: Beneath Metaphysics*, 16 U. Dayton L. Rev. 647 (1991); Shira Perlmutter, *Conceptual Separability and Copyright in Designs of Useful Articles*, 37 J. Copyright Soc'y 339 (1990); J. H. Reichman, *Design Protection and the Legislative Agenda*, 55 Law & Contemp. Probs. 281 (1992); J.H. Reichman, *Design Protection After the Copyright Act of 1976: A Comparative View of the Emerging Interim Models*, 31 J. Copyright Soc'y 267 (1984); J.H. Reichman, *Design Protection in Domestic and Foreign Copyright Law: From the Berne Revision of 1948 to the Copyright Act of 1976*, 1983 Duke L.J. 1143.

their investment to stay in business. They wish to protect their designs from free-riding imitators who are able to sell their imitations at a lower price than the originator's.

These objects of utility have presented a difficult issue for the law of copyright. The reason for this difficulty lies in their fusion of the utilitarian and the aesthetic. The goal of the law has been to grant protection to the aesthetic features of an object without unduly extending the monopoly to its functional or mechanical features. It is often impossible, however, to separate in a rational way the aesthetic aspect of the article from its utilitarian dimension.

Until the leading case of *Mazer v. Stein*,[90] it was unclear whether copyright protection was available for works of art embodied in industrial objects or whether protection was limited to the design patent laws.[91] The Copyright Office took the position that copyright protection was limited to works of artistic craftsmanship insofar as their form, but not as to their mechanical or utilitarian aspects, as in jewelry, enamels, glassware, and tapestries.[92]

Mazer involved the copyrightability of male and female statuettes of Balinese dancers used for bases of table lamps. Petitioners, who had copied these lamp stands, argued against the validity of a copyright for a work of art made as part of a mass-produced good. The Supreme Court disagreed, however, upholding the Copyright Office's regulation allowing copyright for works embodied in useful objects as to their form, but not as to their mechanical or utilitarian features. In addition, the Court also held that protection by design patent did not bar copyright protection.[93] The Court justified the overlapping forms of intellectual property protection because the copyright monopoly is of a different nature than patent. It is less exclusive than the patent monopoly and protects originality rather than novelty or invention.

After *Mazer v. Stein*, the use to which a work of art was put became irrelevant, but the question remained whether the whole range of industrial design in useful articles could qualify for copyright. From Balinese dancers used as a lamp base, courts extended protection to an antique telephone shape used as a pencil sharpener,[94] and a coin bank in the shape of a dog.[95] In addition to these mass-produced objects, graphic designs for textiles were also included within copyrightable subject matter.[96]

If a statuette of a Balinese dancer was copyrightable, why not an automobile, a toaster, or a modernistic lighting fixture. The difference between these useful objects and the *Mazer* statuettes is that their artistic aspects are of an abstract nature often fused with the functional attributes of the object. To deny copyright to these objects, however, would run contrary to the basic tenet of American copyright law, that

---

[90] 347 U.S. 201 (1954).

[91] *See* Brown, n. 84, *supra*, at 1344.

[92] 37 C.F.R. § 202.8(a) (1949).

[93] 347 U.S. at 215 (1954).

[94] *Ted Arnold Ltd. v. Silvercraft Co.*, 259 F. Supp. 733 (S.D.N.Y. 1966).

[95] *Royalty Designs, Inc. v. Thrifticheck Serv. Corp.*, 204 F. Supp. 702 (S.D.N.Y. 1962).

[96] *See, e.g., Peter Pan Fabrics, Inc. v. Martin Weiner Corp.*, 274 F.2d 487, 489 (2d Cir. 1960).

individual perception of the beautiful is too varied a power to permit a narrow or rigid conception of art.[97] Despite this tradition, which prevented judges and bureaucrats from discriminating against art forms, the Copyright Office wished not to incorporate the entire range of mass-produced objects into copyright law. By regulation, the Copyright Office adopted the separability standard[98] which continues to be the focus of debate under the 1976 Act.

§ 3.12   Industrial Design Under the 1976 Act

Section 101 provides that:

> the design of a useful article . . . shall be considered a pictorial, graphic, or sculptural work only if, and only to the extent that, such design incorporates pictorial, graphic, or sculptural features that can be identified separately from, and are capable of existing independently of, the utilitarian aspects of the article.[99]

As explained in the House Report, this section is designed to draw a line between copyrightable works of applied art and uncopyrightable industrial design.[100] The pertinent section of the House Report reads as follows:

> Unless the shape of an automobile, airplane, lady's dress, food processor, television set, or any other industrial product contains some element that, *physically or conceptually*, can be identified as separable from the utilitarian aspects of the article, the design would not be copyrighted under the bill.

(Emphasis added.)[101] In effect, the House Report would deny protection to the overall design of the useful article even if aesthetic considerations govern some aspects of the article.

§ 3.13   Physical Separability: *Esquire, Inc. v. Ringer*

In *Esquire, Inc. v. Ringer*,[102] the Court of Appeals for the District of Columbia held that the overall shape of certain outdoor lighting fixtures was ineligible for copyright as a work of art. The Register of Copyright had denied copyright to the fixtures, based on Office regulations which precluded registration of a design of a utilitarian object when

---

[97] *Bleistein v. Donaldson Lithographing Co.*, 188 U.S. 239, 243 (1903).

[98] 37 C.F.R. § 202.10(c) (1959):

> If the sole intrinsic function of an article is its utility, the fact that the article is unique and attractively shaped will not qualify it as a work of art. However, if the shape of a utilitarian article incorporates features, such as artistic sculpture, carving, or pictorial representation, which can be identified separately and are capable of existing independently as a work of art, such features will be eligible for registration.

[99] 17 U.S.C. § 101 (pictorial, graphic, and sculptural works).

[100] H.R. Rep. No. 94–1476, 94th Cong., 2d Sess. 55 (1976).

[101] *Id.*

[102] 591 F.2d 796 (D.C. Cir. 1978).

the fixtures . . . did not contain elements, either alone or in combination, which are capable of independent existence as a copyrightable pictorial, graphic, or sculptural work apart from the utilitarian aspect.[103]

Unlike the statuettes in *Mazer*, which could exist independently as a sculptural work when removed from the lamp mechanism, the modernistic abstract form of the lighting fixture was inextricably fused with its utilitarian function.

The *Esquire* court upheld the Register's interpretation of its regulations and the denial of copyright. Although a pre-1976 Act case, the court looked to the recently passed 1976 Act's provisions and its legislative history. Section 101 was considered to be a codification of 1909 Act practices and was deemed to reflect congressional understanding of the design problem.

In applying § 101 of the recently passed Copyright Act of 1976 and reviewing the House Report's analysis, the *Esquire* court denied copyright, finding no aspect of the lighting fixture physically separable from its overall configuration. In so doing, the court refused to apply the other aspect of the conceptual separability test suggested by the House Report. Instead, the court preferred to read the legislative history as a whole, which indicated an intent "to draw as clear a line as possible between copyrightable works of applied art and uncopyrighted works of industrial design."[104] The court focused on the phrase in the House Report which stated that

the overall design or configuration of the utilitarian object, even if it is determined by aesthetic as well as functional considerations, is not eligible for copyright.[105]

In short, the *Esquire* court took a narrow view of the separability issue: first, holding that the overall design of an industrial object is never eligible for copyright and, second, that only those aspects removable from the object and that maintain an independent existence as a graphic, pictorial, or sculptural work qualify for copyright protection. Several courts have employed the *Esquire* approach, denying copyright protection to toy airplanes[106] and automobile hubcaps.[107]

Physical separability, as adopted by *Esquire*, has been largely rejected by both courts and commentators as being contrary to the intent of Congress. Professor Nimmer has pointed out that, from the simplest instance of a statuette on the hood of a car, there are very few objects that could pass the physical separability test. Moreover, even the *Mazer* statuettes could exist independently if their utilitarian lamp bases were removed.[108] Another shortcoming in the *Esquire* approach lies in its holding that the overall configuration of a useful object cannot be protected. This approach leads to irrational results. Carried to its logical conclusion, a physical separability approach would protect the *Mazer* statuettes because they were only a

---

[103] *Id.* at 798.

[104] *Id.* at 803, *quoting* H.R. Rep. No. 94–1476, 94th Cong., 2d Sess. 55 (1976).

[105] *Id.* at 804.

[106] *See Gay Toys, Inc. v. Buddy L. Corp.*, 522 F. Supp. 622 (E.D. Mich. 1981).

[107] *See Norris Indus., Inc. v. International Tel. & Tel. Corp.*, 212 U.S.P.Q. (BNA) 754 (N.D. Fla. 1981), *aff'd*, 696 F.2d 918 (11th Cir. 1983).

[108] 1 *Nimmer on Copyright* § 2.08[B] (1993).

part of the object's entire configuration, while it would deny protection to a statuette used as a receptacle for collecting coins. Finally, under the same reasoning, a fabric design could not be protected under copyright because the design, dyed into a textile, cannot be physically separated and exist independently of the material. For these reasons, other courts, particularly the Second Circuit, have looked to the House Report's statement that separability could be determined *physically or conceptually.*[109]

§ 3.14 Conceptual Separability

In *Kieselstein-Cord v. Accessories By Pearl, Inc.,*[110] the Second Circuit Court of Appeals applied the conceptual-separability test to the highly ornamental surfaces of two belt buckles. To the court, the ornamental surfaces of these belt buckles were conceptually separable from their composite design because they were unrelated to the utilitarian function of the buckles. As evidence of this aesthetic appeal, some persons were wearing the buckles as jewelry other than at the waist, which indicated that "the primary ornamental aspect of the . . . buckles is conceptually separable from their subsidiary utilitarian function."[111] The court suggested that conceptual separability exists where an article would be marketed as an aesthetic object even if it had no useful function.[112]

More recently, the majority in *Carol Barnhart Inc. v. Economy Cover Corp.*[113] appeared to return implicitly to a standard of physical separability. In *Barnhart,* the copyrightability of four human torso mannequins used for clothing display was at issue. The court found that the claimed artistic features, the life-size breast form and the width of the shoulders, were inextricably related to their utilitarian function, *i.e.,* the display of clothes. The case was distinguished from *Kieselstein* where, by comparison, the ornamental aspect of the belt buckle was unrelated to its utilitarian function.[114]

Judge Newman, in dissent, was troubled by the outcome of the case and by its absence of a unifying test for conceptual separability. He proposed the following test: for design features to be conceptually separate from the utilitarian aspects of the useful article that embodies the design, the article must stimulate in the mind of the beholder a concept that is entirely separable from the utilitarian functions.[115]

---

[109] H.R. Rep. No. 94–1476, 94th Cong., 2d Sess. 55 (1976). For the pertinent quote from the House Report, see § 3.12, *supra.*

[110] 632 F.2d 989 (2d Cir. 1980).

[111] *Id.* at 993.

[112] Some case law has followed this likelihood-of-marketability approach to conceptual separability. *See, e.g., Poe v. Missing Persons,* 745 F.2d 1238 (9th Cir. 1984). Nimmer has criticized this approach as discriminating against non-representational art, being too difficult to prove, and being too restrictive in result. 1 *Nimmer on Copyright* § 2.08[B] (1993).

[113] 773 F.2d 411 (2d Cir. 1985).

[114] *Id.* at 419.

[115] *Id.* at 422.

To the dissent, these *Barnhart* forms created in the observer's mind's eye were not just a useful object but a work of art as well.[116]

The design of a bicycle rack was at issue in *Brandir Int'l, Inc. v. Cascade Pacific Lumber Co.*[117] In denying copyrightability to the racks, the majority adopted a test proposed by Professor Denicola[118] to determine the fine line between protectable works of applied art and unprotectible industrial design: if the design elements reflect the merger of aesthetic and functional considerations, the artistic aspects are not conceptually separable. Alternatively, if the design elements reflect the designer's artistic judgment independent of functional considerations, there is conceptual separability. As applied to the bicycle rack, the court found that the form of the rack was significantly influenced by functional concerns so that the conceptual elements were not conceptually separate from the utilitarian.[119]

Judge Winter, in dissent, would not have focused on the process used by the designer, but rather on how the rack was perceived. Thus the test should be whether the design of a useful object, however intertwined with its functional aspects, is perceived as an aesthetic concept not related to the article's function.[120]

The problem of industrial design will continue to plague the courts. Although a consensus has formed around some form of conceptual separability, the courts have yet to formulate a test that will separate the utilitarian from the artistic, does not discriminate between various art forms, and is formulated clearly enough so that the trier of fact can come to a reasoned judgment. This is perhaps an impossible task given the inherently illogical nature of the subject. One point of view (the majority in *Brandir*) would judge the separability as revealed in the design process and whether the designer was motivated by aesthetic choices. This test has the virtue of separating the aesthetic from the utilitarian, but at the same time, it will often necessitate a lengthy procedure with expert testimony. The alternate view (the dissent in *Brandir*) would judge separability from the standpoint of the ordinary observer — whether the design engenders an aesthetic reaction in the eye of the beholder. The advantage of this approach, advocated by Judges Newman and Winter, is that it presents the question of separability in a more administratively convenient form for the trier of fact.

[116] *Id.* at 426.

[117] 834 F.2d 1142 (2d Cir. 1987).

[118] *Id.* at 1145. Professor Denicola is the author of an important article on the design issue which proposes the text adopted by the Court. *See* Robert C. Denicola, *Applied Art and Industrial Design: A Suggested Approach to Copyright in Useful Articles*, 67 Minn. L. Rev. 707, 741 (1973).

[119] *Id.* at 1146.

[120] *Id.* at 1151.

§ 3.15   Architectural Works[121]

[A]   In General

As works of applied art, architectural works present many of the same problems encountered in the discussion on industrial objects. There are two aspects to the copyrightability of architectural works: the plans and models which represent the structure, and the architectural structure itself. Both received protection under copyright law, but that protection was limited. Architectural works were viewed as useful objects, subject to the same constraints discussed previously. This changed with the passage of The Architectural Works Protection Act of 1990.[122] This legislation, designed to comply with Berne Convention obligations, conferred full protection on architectural structures and officially recognized that architectual works are the eighth category of copyrightable subject matter under § 102(a)(8).[123] The new Act, however, does not apply to architectural structures constructed before the effective date of the Act, December 1, 1990. Thus, it is necessary to understand the pre-1990 law governing architectural plans and structures for the overwhelmingly greater number of buildings constructed before that date.

[B]   Architectical Works Constructed Before December 1, 1990

[1]   Architectural Structures

The scope of protection in a three-dimensional architectural structure is the same as the protection afforded to all pictorial, graphic, or sculptural works embodied in useful objects. After all, architectural structures are simply useful objects that fuse the aesthetic and the functional in a three-dimentional object. Thus, as is the case for the design of useful objects, copyright protection extended only to those elements in a building which were physically or conceptually separable from its overall design. For example, a gargoyle on a building would receive copyright protection but not the overall appearance of the building or the arrangement of the spaces and shapes within and outside the building.

This rule was not above criticism. The separability test as applied to architectural structures might discriminate against the truly artistic output of the architect's craft. Thus, the overall configuration of a "modernist" Mies Van der Rohe building would be excluded from protection whereas the crudest add-on surface ornamentation would be copyrightable. In other words, a modernist building would run into the same separability problems as the unadorned lighting fixture in *Esquire v. Ringer*.[124] In sum, for a standing structure, infringement does not occur unless the copier

---

[121] For a comprehensive overview, see Jane C. Ginsburg, *Copyright in the 101st Congress: Commentary on the Visual Artists' Rights Act and the Architectural Works Copyright Protection Act of 1990*, 14 Colum.–VLA J.L. & Arts 477 (1990); David E. Shipley, *Copyright Protection for Architectural Works*, 37 S.C. L. Rev. 393 (1986); Rafael Winick, *Copyright Protection for Architecture After the Architectural Works Copyright Protection Act of 1990*, 41 Duke L. J. 1598 (1992).

[122] Pub. L. No. 101–650, 104 Stat. 5089, 5133 (1990).

[123] 17 U.S.C. 102(a)(8).

[124] 591 F.2d 796 (D.C. Cir. 1978).

has reproduced the building's "separable" pictoral, graphic, or sculptural features that are capable of existing independently of its utilitarian aspects.[125]

[2] Architectural Plans, Models, and Drawings

Under § 101's definition of pictorial, graphic, and sculptural works, diagrams, models, and technical drawings and architectural plans were included as copyrightable subject matter.[126] Unlike buildings, architectural plans, models or drawings are not useful articles and are not subject to a "separability" limitation because their purpose is to "merely portray the appearance of the article or to convey information."[127]

Although not subject to the separability limitation, architectural plans did not receive first class citizenship under the original 1976 Act.[128] Architectural plans and models could be infringed by their reproduction as such, but the unauthorized construction of a building by using the plans was not an infringement of the plans. Thus, under the copyright law before the 1990 amendments, a structure was not a copy of a plan or model. If a lawful copy of an architectural plan were obtained, it could be used to construct the building that it portrayed so long as no copies of the plans were made. In short, copyright in architectural plans or models did not convey a right to control their use.[129] This rupture between the plan and the building it portrays is an exception to the normal rule that a substantially similar three-dimensional sculptural work can infringe a two dimensional graphic or pictorial work.[130]

Imperial Homes Corp. v. Lamont[131] provides an example of this gap in protection for architectural plans and drawings. In *Imperial Homes*, defendants, the Lamonts, had visited one of Imperial's residences where they made detailed observations and measurements of its architecture. In addition, the Lamonts had obtained copies of the copyrighted advertising brochures containing floor plans. The court concluded that infringement could be found if they had copied in whole or in part the floor plans from the brochures in making their own architectural plans, even if these same

---

[125] 17 U.S.C. § 101 (pictorial, graphic, and sculptural works).

[126] *See* 17 U.S.C. § 101; *see also* H.R. Rep. No. 94–1476, 94th Cong., 2d Sess. 53 (1976). As for the case law, *see, e.g., Aitken, Hazen, Hoffman, Miller P.C. v. Empire Constr. Co.,* 542 F. Supp. 252 (D. Neb. 1982). The 1988 amendments to the 1976 Copyright Act were not intended to change the scope of copyright in either architectural plans or the structures they represent. *See* H.R. Rep. No. 100–609, 100th Cong., 2d Sess. 49 (1988).

[127] 17 U.S.C. § 101 (useful article).

[128] *See* 17 U.S.C. § 113(b) (specifying that the body of law existing at the passage of the 1976 Act governs the scope of protection for architectural plans).

[129] The reason for this anomalous rule relates to the doctrine of *Baker v. Selden* that would allow copying for the purpose of use but not for the purpose of explanation. For a discussion of the doctrine of *Baker v. Selden,* see § 2.12[B], *supra.*

[130] *See, e.g., Ideal Toy Corp. v. Kenner Products Division,* 443 F. Supp. 291 (S.D.N.Y. 1977).

[131] 458 F.2d 895 (5th Cir. 1972).

plans would give the copyright owner no claim over the features they detail.[132] As we will see, these limitations on copyright for architecture have been removed by the 1990 amendments.

[C] The Architectural Works Protection Act of 1990

Under the 1990 amendments to the Copyright Act, architectural works are explicitly recognized as the eighth form of copyrightable subject matter under Section 102(a).[133] Architectural works are defined as "the design of a building, architectural plans, or drawings." The work includes "the overall form as well as the arrangement and composition of spaces and elements in the design, but does not include individual standard features."[134] The term "building" is intended to cover habitable structures (and those used by people, *e.g.*, churches, gazebos, etc.) and would exclude three-dimensional non-habitable structures such as highways, bridges, and pedestrian walkways.

The Act confers full protection on works of architecture. Buildings constructed on or after December 1, 1990 will no longer be subject to the separability limitation. And any features, including external and interior architecture, which reflect the architect's creativity will be covered by the amendments. Of course, there will be subject matter limitations under Section 102(b), prohibiting copyright protection for functional features of the building, including individual standard features, such as common windows, doors, and other staple building components.

Determining the scope of protection for an architectural work will involve a two-step process. First, one must examine the work to determine if there are original design elements, including the overall shape and interior architecture. Second, if such design elements are present, one must then determine whether the elements are functionally required. If these elements are not functionally required, the work will be protected without applying physical or conceptual separability tests.[135] Otherwise, architectural works will be subject to the standard of originality as for all works of authorship, as developed by the case law. Determinations of originality are generally made *ad hoc* by the courts. It will take some time before they create a body of law providing significant guidance on what constitutes originality for architectural works.

The 1990 amendments have also changed the relationship between the copyright in the architectural work and the copyright in the plans and drawings. As discussed above, under the original 1976 law, a defendant who had access to the plans or drawings could construct a building and escape liability if the plans and drawings were not copied. Now, infringement may lie even though access to the three-dimensional work is obtained from its two-dimensional or three-dimensional depiction.

---

[132] *See also Demetriades v. Kaufmann,* 680 F. Supp. 658 (S.D.N.Y. 1988) (unauthorized copying of architectural plans an infringement, but injunction against further construction of structure denied).

[133] 17 U.S.C. § 102(a)(8).

[134] 17 U.S.C. § 101 (architectural works).

[135] *See* H.R. Rep. No. 101–735, 101st Cong., 2d Sess. 20–21 (1990).

The Act covers only those architectural works created on or after the date of enactment, December 1, 1990, and will include architectural works that are unconstructed and embodied in unpublished plans and drawings. As an incentive to construct these works, the legislation terminates protection on December 31, 2002, if the architectural work has not been constructed by that date. If the work is constructed by that date, its term of protection will not expire before December 31, 2027.[136]

Owners of architectural works are granted the same exclusive rights as other copyright owners with two exceptions. First, under section 120(a),[137] the owner cannot prevent the making, distributing, and displaying of pictures, photographs, or other pictorial representations of an architectural work visible from a public place. This would allow an author to publish a book on architecture using photographs of copyrighted architectural works without infringing the copyrights in the works. Second, under Section 120(b),[138] the owner of a building embodying a protected architectural work may make alterations to the building and even destroy it, notwithstanding the exclusive rights of the copyright owner to prepare derivative works under section 106(2).[139]

§ 3.16 Other Forms of Protection for Works of Applied Art: Design Patent and Proposed Design Legislation[140]

[A] Design Patent

In addition to copyright law, industrial designers can protect their creations under design patent law.[141] Section 171 of the Patent Act[142] confers a design patent for a 14-year term to whomever invents a new, original, and ornamental design for an article of manufacture. As for subject matter, design patents may be issued for the appearance of articles of manufacture for their shape, surface ornamentation, or both. Design patents have been issued for the appearance of a stadium grandstand,[143] the design of jets of water in a fountain,[144] and the shank of a drill bit.[145] A patentable

---

[136] Pub. L. No. 101–650, Stat. 5089 (1990). *See* 17 U.S.C. § 303. Duration under § 303 is discussed at § 6.3[G] *infra*.
[137] 17 U.S.C. § 120(a) (added by Pub. L. No. 101–650, Stat. 5089, 5133 (1990)).
[138] 17 U.S.C. § 120(b) (added by Pub. L. No. 101–650, Stat. 5089, 5133 (1990)).
[139] 17 U.S.C. § 106(2).
[140] This section focuses on two statutory forms of design protection. The form of useful objects, including aspects of architecture, can also be protected under trademark and unfair competition law. Generally, protection extends to nonfunctional aspects of the work. In addition, secondary meaning must be shown in these nonfunctional aspects. For an overview, see Ralph S. Brown, *Design Protection: An Overview*, 34 UCLA L. Rev. 1341, 1357–95 (1987). For an excellent case reviewing the entire area and providing an integrated theory, see Judge Posner's opinion in *W. T. Rogers Co., Inc. v. Keene*, 778 F.2d 334 (7th Cir. 1985).
[141] *See generally,* Donald S. Chisum, *Patents* § 1.04 (1980).
[142] 35 U.S.C. § 171.
[143] *In re Hadden*, 20 F.2d 275 (D.C. Cir. 1927).
[144] *In re Hruby*, 373 F.2d 997 (C.C.P.A. 1967).
[145] *In re Zahn*, 617 F.2d 261 (C.C.P.A. 1980).

design must be ornamental, appealing to the aesthetic sense as a thing of beauty. Unlike copyright, the courts are directly involved in questions of aesthetics in determining the validity of design patents.[146]

Despite their seeming appropriateness, design patents have not afforded a practical means for the protection of industrial design. The reasons are the time and expense required to obtain a design patent, the difficulty that many designs have in meeting the standards of patentability, and their marked tendency of being declared invalid when challenged in federal court.

By comparison with copyright, whose key standard is originality, the standards for obtaining a design patent, novelty and non-obviousness, are much more rigorous and difficult to meet. As for novelty, the design must differ from prior art, and not merely modify it. Moreover, even if novel, the design must meet the standard of non-obviousness. Here the question presented is whether the design would be nonobvious to ordinary skilled designers in the field.[147] One can think of very few designs which arguably could not be challenged on one or both of these grounds. As a result, design patents are often declared invalid when challenged in federal court.[148]

The costs of obtaining a design patent, including filing fees, issuance fees, and attorney's fees, are substantial, particularly when compared with copyright. The complicated application process requires hiring a patent attorney, one specifically admitted to practice before the Patent Office. The examination procedure takes time because the Patent Office conducts a search to determine novelty and non-obviousness.[149] A design patent can be more valuable to its owner than a copyright. Unlike a copyright, the design can be enforced against all persons creating a design substantially similar in appearance, even those persons who have not copied the design.

Copyright and design patent have overlapping subject matter. Thus, the question arises whether a design patent can be obtained for a copyrighted work, or whether a copyright can concurrently protect a design patent. In the leading case on the issue, *In re Yardley*,[150] the Court of Customs and Patent Appeals allowed a design patent to be issued on a watch design, even though the applicant had previously registered a claim for copyright.

---

[146] *See, e.g., Blisscraft of Hollywood v. United Plastics Co.*, 294 F.2d 694 (2d Cir. 1961).

[147] *In re Nalbandian*, 661 F.2d 1214 (C.C.P.A. 1981).

[148] For an overview and survey of design patent litigation, see Thomas B. Lindgren, *The Sanctity of the Design Patent: Illusion or Reality? Twenty Years of Design Patent Litigation Since* Compco v. Day-Brite Lighting, Inc., *and* Sears Roebuck & Co. v. Stiffel Co., 10 Okla. City U. L. Rev. 195 (1985). Despite the hurdles in obtaining a design patent, between 4000 and 5000 design patents are issued each year on about double the number of applications. *Id.* at 205.

[149] Recent statistics show that the process takes on average two years and six months for issuance of a design patent. *See* 1986 *PTO Annual Report* at 21.

[150] 493 F.2d 1389 (C.C.P.A. 1974).

The effect of a design patent on the validity of a copyright was unclear before the 1976 Act.[151] The rationale was that the public act of filing for a patent dedicated the work to the public. The 1976 Act would appear to undermine this public domain rationale because a copyright subsists from the moment of creation — and not just from the moment of publication.[152] Thus, both copyright and design patent protection could exist concurrently in the same object.

[B] Design Legislation

Because of the limited protection provided by design patent and copyright law, *sui generis* design protection legislation has been introduced in Congress virtually every year for the past thirty years.[153] Most proposals for industrial design legislation provide protection for original ornamental designs of a useful article, including both two-dimensional and three-dimensional aspects of shape and surface. Protection would be denied to the utilitarian features of a design as well as to staple commonplace designs.

Industrial design legislation is closer in spirit to copyright law than patent law. All recent proposals have used the less strict standard of originality, as opposed to the more rigorous novelty standard of patent law. Infringement of the design would be based on copyright principles, and evidence of copying would have to be shown to sustain the action.

Unlike copyright law, design legislation requires registration of the design. After the design is made public, its registration would have to take place within six months of its publication in order to avoid forfeiture. A governmental agency would examine registration applications for *prima facie* subject matter, but would conduct no search for previously registered, confusingly similar designs. Protection would last for 10 years, beginning from the date when the design was made public by exhibition, sale, or offer to sell. Most design legislation provides for flexible notice requirements, (*i.e.*, a "d" in a circle). Failure to affix notice would not forfeit protection but would significantly limit remedies against infringers.

Proposed design legislation has taken varying approaches to whether design patent, design protection, and copyright could exist concurrently in the same object. In other words, should these forms of intellectual property be mutually exclusive or cumulative? For example, some versions of design legislation would require a choice between design protection, copyright, and design patent.[154] Thus, copyright

---

[151] *Compare Korzybski v. Underwood & Underwood, Inc.*, 36 F.2d 727 (2d Cir. 1929) (design patent bars copyright) *with Zachary v. Western Publishing Co.*, 75 Cal. App. 3d 911 (1977) (publication by government does not dedicate copyright to public domain).

[152] For a discussion of publication under copyright law, see §§ 4.2–4.7, *infra*.

[153] *See, e.g.*, S. Rep. No. 100–791, 100th Cong., 1st Sess. (1987). Industrial design is protected internationally in many countries as part of the Union of Paris for the Protection of Industrial Property. To enjoy protection under the Convention, an author or owner of a design must comply with national law, which varies from country to country. *See* Stephen P. Ladas, *Patents, Trademarks, and Related Rights* § 490 (1975).

[154] *E.g.*, Title II of S. Rep. No. 94–22, 94th Cong. 2d Sess. (1976). *See* H.R. Rep. No. 94–1476, 94th Cong., 2d Sess. 49–50 (1976).

would terminate on registration of the design. Alternatively, issuance of a design patent would terminate protection under the design legislation. Other versions would allow concurrent copyright protection, but the design protection would cease on issuance of a design patent.[155]

§ 3.17 Maps[156]

Maps have been recognized as copyrightable works since the first American copyright statute was enacted in 1790. Under the 1976 Act, maps are not explicitly included as copyrightable subject matter but qualify as pictorial, graphic, and sculptural works.[157] Although their copyrightability has never been in doubt, the element of originality required in maps involved controversy because some case law under the 1909 Act imposed a higher standard of originality for maps than for other varieties of copyrightable subject matter.

Maps are generally a rearrangement of factual matter, and the map maker must go either to public domain sources for this information or to the terrain itself.[158] Whether the creator of a map must directly observe the terrain to claim copyright in his creation has long been a controversial issue. In *Amsterdam v. Triangle Publications, Inc.*,[159] the court held that, to meet the standard of originality, the publisher of a map must engage in some direct observation, that is, some original work of surveying or calculation or investigating the terrain. By this approach, a mere rearrangement of public domain sources would not meet the standard. *Amsterdam* imposes a special kind of "sweat of the brow" requirement on the author, and, as such, this direct observation standard imposed a stricter standard of originality on maps than on other copyrightable works. With the demise of the "sweat of the brow" doctrine under *Feist Publications v. Rural Telephone Service Co.*,[160] the validity of the case law requiring direct observation is all the more doubtful.

Even before *Feist*, the recent case law had rejected the direct observation rule, treating the standard of originality for maps the same as for any other compilation or factual work. In *United States v. Hamilton*,[161] for instance, the court rejected the defendant's argument that the copied map was not subject to copyright since it was simply a synthesis of information already in the public domain. The court viewed maps as any other copyrightable work, requiring only that the work display

[155] *See, e.g.,* S. Rep. No. 100–791, 100th Cong. 2d Sess. §§ 1027–28 (1988).

[156] For an overview of the subject placed in the context of copyrightability of factual works, see Robert A. Gorman, *Fact or Fancy? The Implications for Copyright*, 29 J. Copyright Soc'y 560 (1982); David B. Wolf, *Is There Any Copyright Protection for Maps After* Feist, 39 J. Copyright Soc'y 224 (1992).

[157] H.R. Rep. No. 94–1476, 94th Cong., 2d Sess. 54 (1976).

[158] Maps present the same issues as other factual compilations. For a discussion of compilations, see § 2.11, *supra*.

[159] 93 F. Supp. 79 (E.D. Pa. 1950), *aff'd on opinion below,* 189 F.2d 104 (3d Cir. 1951).

[160] 499 U.S. 340 (1991).

[161] 583 F.2d 448 (9th Cir. 1978).

something original, and held that arrangements and combinations of facts are copyrightable so long as they are not merely trivial variations of information within the public domain. The elements of authorship of selection, design, and synthesis were enough to meet the standard. *Hamilton* puts the cartographer in the same position as any other author creating a pictorial, graphic, or sculptural work.[162] There seems to be little justification in discouraging creative arrangement in the cartographic arts by holding the cartographer to a higher standard of originality. Of course, some originality must be shown, and merely copying the outline of the United States or selecting the principal cities of North America from memory will not constitute sufficient originality for the issuance of copyright registration.[163]

PART IV: OTHER CATEGORIES OF COPYRIGHTABLE SUBJECT MATTER

§ 3.18 Musical Works

Although the 1976 Act does not define "musical works" because of a commonly understood definition for this category,[164] it does clarify one important point of controversy under the 1909 Act. Section 102(a)(2) specifies that the category of musical works encompasses both the words of a song and its instrumental component. A "musical work" can be embodied in various material objects such as musical notation on written paper or directly recorded on a phonorecord.[165]

Musical works, like other works of authorship, must display a quantum of originality and creativity, manifested in melody, harmony, or rhythm, individually or in some combination.[166] Much music is based on public domain sources, and issues regarding the standard of originality arise with relative frequency for arrangements of these public domain sources. The same issue arises when an action is brought by a copyright owner of a popular song. Popular songs resemble one another — there are only a finite number of possibilities for this genre. But originality, not novelty, is required, and the author need add very little to the public

---

[162] Questions of originality and merger of idea and expression arise in map cases: *compare Mason v. Montgomery Data, Inc.*, 967 F.2d 135 (5th Cir. 1992) (plaintiff's real estate ownership maps using information from public domain sources were capable of a variety of expression and were sufficiently original in their selection and arrangement of facts, as well as in their pictorial and graphic elements, to meet the *Feist* standard of originality) *with Kern River Gas Transmission Co. v. Costal Corp.*, 899 F.2d 1458 (5th Cir. 1990) (plaintiff's representation of a proposed national gas pipeline route on government survey maps was not copyrightable even though it may have been original, because it was the only effective way the idea of the location of the pipeline could be expressed).

[163] *Carter v. Hawaii Transp. Co.*, 201 F. Supp. 301 (D. Haw. 1961).

[164] H.R. Rep. No. 94–1476, 94th Cong., 2d Sess. 53 (1976).

[165] For deposit purposes, however, the Copyright Office will accept, in place of the written work, a recorded version of the musical work if it exists only in this form. *See* 37 C.F.R. § 202.20 and Copyright Office, *Circular 50.*

[166] Rhythm, however, is the least likely aspect of music in which originality may be manifested. *See Northern Music Corp. v. King Record Distributing Co.*, 105 F. Supp. 393 (S.D.N.Y. 1952); 1 *Nimmer on Copyright* § 2.05[D] (1993).

domain to meet the standard of originality. Similarly, musical arrangements, a form of derivative work, are copyrightable, so long as the arranger adds the requisite amount of original authorship.[167]

§ 3.19   Sound Recordings[168]

[A]   Distinguishing the Sound Recording From Other Works of Authorship and the Phonorecord

"Sound recordings" as defined in Section 101 [169] are

> works that result from the fixation of a series of musical, spoken, or other sounds, but do not include the sounds accompanying a motion picture or other audio visual work, regardless of the nature of the material objects, such as disks, tapes, or other phonorecords, in which they are embodied.

This statutory definition sets forth the basic features of a sound recording which distinguish this form of copyrightable subject matter from other works. Essentially, a sound recording is a captured performance. The performance captured in the sound recording may be a musical, literary, or dramatic work. These works of authorship should be distinguished from the copyright in the sound recording. This area of ambiguity exists because both the musical or literary work are embodied in the same material object, the phonorecord. The distinction is of more than academic interest because the owner of a sound recording copyright enjoys different exclusive rights than the copyright owner of the musical or literary work captured in the sound recording. Most importantly, the copyright owner of a sound recording may not control its performance, while the copyright owner of a literary, musical, or dramatic work enjoys a full performance right.[170]

The sound recording must also be distinguished from the material object in which it is embodied. Sound recordings are embodied in phonorecords which, under the Copyright Act, include anything capturing sound, such as tapes, disks, or computer chips.[171] To illustrate these distinctions, if CBS issues a compact disc recording of Copeland's *Third Symphony* performed by the New York Philharmonic, the musical copyright would be of the *Third Symphony*, and the sound recording would be the aural version of the work fixed in the material object, the compact disc. The sound recording copyright confers no ownership right to either the material object or to the underlying musical work.

---

[167] *See Plymouth Music Co. v. Magnus Organ Corp.*, 456 F. Supp. 676 (S.D.N.Y. 1978).
[168] For an overview, see Diamond, *Sound Recordings, and Phonorecords: History and Current Law*, 1979 Ill. L.F. 337 (1979).
[169] 17 U.S.C. § 101 (sound recordings).
[170] 17 U.S.C. § 114. For a discussion of the less than full exclusive rights in sound recordings, see § 8.9, *infra*.
[171] 17 U.S.C. § 101 (phonorecords).

[B] Originality in Sound Recordings

As with any copyrightable subject matter, sound recordings must meet the standard of originality. The source of originality in sound recordings may emanate from the performers whose performance is being captured, or from the record producer who sets up the recording and processes, compiles, and edits the sounds. Performer originality consists of all the choices a performer makes in interpreting a tune, a story, or a literary work, such as tone, inflections of voice, or musical timing. Almost any conscious performance by a human being would add the degree of originality necessary for copyrightability in a sound recording.

Originality can also emanate from the producer who sets up the recording, even if no performer is involved in the rendition. One can think of such examples as a recording of sea sounds, bird calls, or motor traffic. Here the acts of capturing the performance, processing the sounds, and then compiling and editing them would supply the requisite originality. Of course, the author of the sound recording must add something of his own; a purely mechanical recording involving no authorial choice would fail for lack of originality.[172]

Sound recordings are by nature derivative works that often combine original contributions by several original authors. Determining who among these several authors owns the sound recording can present difficult legal and factual issues. The ownership of a sound recording is essentially a matter to be determined by the participants who create the recording. Absent a contractual provision to the contrary, and assuming originality by both a record producer and a performer, the sound recording would be owned jointly by performer and record producer.[173] To avoid creating a joint ownership, contract negotiations should be employed to resolve questions about who owns copyright to the sound recording.

[C] No Federal Protection for Pre-1972 Sound Recordings

Sound recordings were formally recognized by federal law for the first time in the Sound Recording Act of 1971. The need for nationally uniform protection under copyright law was critically important to the recording industry at that time because pirates were inflicting substantial losses on the industry by unauthorized recordings. Bearing only a fraction of the production costs, they could often undersell the original producers who would, as a result, be unable to recoup their investments. Thus, the need for federal protection was apparent, despite a patchwork of state laws conferring common law protection for sound recordings before 1972.

Sound recordings were finally recognized in a systematic way by the Copyright Act of 1976, but the Act only applies to sound recordings fixed after 1972. Sound recordings fixed before 1972 are not subject to statutory protection under federal copyright law. These pre-1972 sound recordings are not, however, as a group thrown into the public domain but are subject to continuing protection by state law. Section 301(c) of the 1976 Act confers continuing protection on sound recordings first fixed before 1972, providing that "any rights and remedies under common law and statutes

---

[172] *See* H.R. Rep. No. 94–1476, 94th Cong., 2d Sess. 57 (1976).

[173] For a discussion of the implications of joint ownership, see § 5.4, *infra*.

of any state shall not be annulled or limited . . . until February 15, 2047."[174] Thus, the plaintiff in any action for infringement of a sound recording fixed before 1972 must look to state copyright law, if any, for his remedies.

§ 3.20   Dramatic Works

Dramatic works are a separate category of copyrightable subject matter purposefully left undefined in the 1976 Act because of a generally accepted definition. For administrative reasons, the Copyright Office has defined a "dramatic work" as

> one that portrays a story by means of dialogue or acting and [that] is intended to be performed. It gives directions for performance or actually represents all or a substantial portion of the action as actually occurring, rather than merely being narrated or described.[175]

Whether a work is categorized as a dramatic work, rather than a non-dramatic literary or musical work, can be of legal and practical importance. Under the 1976 Act, for example, exceptions for performance and display of works for non-profit or governmental entities apply only in certain instances to non-dramatic literary and non-dramatic musical works.[176] The compulsory license to make sound recordings under § 115 is limited to non-dramatic musical works,[177] and the manufacturing clause pertains to works consisting preponderantly of non-dramatic literary works in English.[178] In addition, performing rights societies, such as ASCAP and BMI, and licensing organizations, such as Harry Fox, limit their activities to non-dramatic musical works.[179]

§ 3.21   Pantomimes and Choreographic Works[180]

The 1976 Copyright Act has for the first time added pantomimes[181] and choreographic works to the categories of copyrightable subject matter in Section

---

[174] 17 U.S.C. § 301(c).

[175] *Compendium II of Copyright Office Practices* § 431.

[176] 17 U.S.C. § 110(2).

[177] 17 U.S.C. § 115.

[178] 17 U.S.C. § 601.

[179] For a discussion of these organizations and the licensing of non-dramatic musical works, see § 8.22, *infra*.

[180] For a useful overview of the subject, see Martha M. Traylor, *Choreography, Pantomime and the Copyright Revision Act of 1976*, 16 New Eng. L. Rev. 227 (1981).

[181] Pantomimes as well as choreography were recognized for the first time in the 1976 Act. "Pantomimes" may be defined as

> the art of imitating or acting out situations, characters, or some other events with gestures and body movement. Mime is included in this category. Pantomimes need not tell a story or be presented before an audience to be protected by copyright.

Compendium II of Copyright Office Practices § 460.01. Pantomimes are distinct from choreographic works as copyrightable subject matter. Many of the same concepts, however, are involved in the protection of these two art forms. The discussion in this section is limited to choreography, which has drawn the most commentary and case law.

106. Along with musical and dramatic works, choreographic works and pantomimes are not defined in the Act. The House Report indicates that this absence of definition was purposeful because these categories have settled, generally accepted meanings.[182]

The only specific mention of choreographic works in the House Report states that the category does not include social dance steps and simple routines.[183] This statement appears to reiterate nothing more than the basic *de minimis* standard of originality as it would apply to a choreographic work.

The Copyright Office has defined choreography in its compendium of practices as

> the composition and arrangement of dance movements and patterns, usually intended to be accompanied by music. Dance is defined as static and kinetic successions of bodily movement in certain rhythmic and special relationships. Choreographic works need not tell a story in order to be protected by copyright.[184]

This definition gives choreography a broader scope of protection as compared to the 1909 Act which protected choreography only as a dramatic work, that is, if it told a story. This narrow view of choreography under the 1909 Act left abstract forms of dance in a state of uncertain protection.[185] Because choreography now constitutes copyrightable subject matter in its own right, it would appear that a dramatic content requirement is no longer required.[186]

To meet the originality standard, the choreographer need only add something recognizably her own. This standard could be met even though the choreographer was heavily influenced by a style of dance such as that of Balanchine or Martha Graham. Artistic style *per se* is not copyrightable. Expression in choreography involves the concrete details worked out by the choreographer, within the school or technique of dance movement, such as the sequencing and organization of the dance. For much the same reason that style is uncopyrightable, so too the invention of a new dance step is not copyrightable.

Choreography is usually fixed either in notation or in film. Two systems specific to dance, Laba notation and Benesh notation, are generally used. These systems of symbolic choreographic language are known by few choreographers. Film, despite certain limitations, is the most widely used method of fixing a choreographic work.

---

[182] H.R. Rep. No. 94–1476, 94th Cong., 2d Sess. 53 (1976).

[183] *Id.* at 54.

[184] *Compendium II of Copyright Office Practices* § 450.01.

[185] *See* 1 *Nimmer on Copyright* § 2.07[B] (1993).

[186] *See Horgan v. MacMillan, Inc.*, 789 F.2d 157 (2d Cir. 1986). Some choreographic works, as well as pantomimes, qualified for protection under the 1909 Act and were registered by the Copyright Office as either a "dramatic work" or as a "book." These works will receive continued protection under the 1976 Act. A more difficult issue involves the status of choreographic works or pantomimes not published under the 1909 Act. No cases have treated this issue, but it would appear that these works would now be protected under the 1976 Act. *See* 1 *Nimmer on Copyright* § 2.07[D] (1993).

§ 3.22 Motion Pictures and Other Audiovisual Works

Motion pictures and audiovisual works are accorded separate status as copyrightable subject matter under the 1976 Act. The broader category of audiovisual work is defined as

> works that consist of a series of related images which are intrinsically intended to be shown by the use of machines or devices such as projectors, viewers, or electronic equipment, together with accompanying sounds, if any, regardless of the nature of the material objects, such as films or tapes, in which the works are embodied.[187]

A work can qualify as an audiovisual work, even though it consists of individually copyrightable works, so long as it communicates related images. These images do not have to occur in sequential order. In *Stern Electronics, Inc. v. Kaufman*,[188] the Second Circuit Court of Appeals upheld copyright in the audiovisual display of a video game even though the display was predetermined by a computer program embodied in a microchip memory device, and the repetitive series of images were affected by the intervention of a player. In addition, the court held that the images did not have to be sequential to be copyrightable:

> [t]he repetitive sequence of a substantial portion of the sights and sounds of the game qualifies for copyright protection as an audiovisual work.[189]

As is the case for all works of authorship, originality in an audiovisual work is determined by evaluating the work as a whole. In *Atari Games Corp. v. Oman*,[190] the District of Columbia Court of Appeals held that, even if the individual graphic elements of a videogame screen were not copyrightable, the audiovisual work as a whole would be copyrightable if the requisite level of creativity were satisfied by the individual screens or the relationship of each screen to the others and/or the accompanying sound effects. In this way, an audiovisual work resembles a compilation of facts where the individual components may not be copyrightable, but their selection and arrangement may supply the minimal degree of creativity needed for the purposes of copyright.

Motion pictures are a subcategory of audiovisual works and are defined as

---

[187] 17 U.S.C. § 101 (audiovisual works).

[188] 669 F.2d 852 (2d Cir. 1982).

[189] *Id.* at 856. The notion of an audiovisual work was further broadened in *WGN Continental Broadcasting Co. v. United Video, Inc.*, 693 F.2d 622 (7th Cir. 1982), where the court held that copyright in a television news program included the teletext in the vertical blanking interval. The defendant, a satellite carrier, picked up WGN's news program but did not retransmit the teletext, instead substituting another service on the vertical blanking interval. The court held that the defendant was an infringer even though the teletext could not be viewed simultaneously with the television program. In effect, the plaintiff's news program was a two-channel program consistent with the expansive definition of an audiovisual work, a series of related images which do not have to be seen in sequence.

[190] 979 F.2d 242 (D.C. Cir. 1992).

. . . works consisting of a series of related images which, when shown in succession, impart an impression of motion, together with accompanying sounds, if any.[191]

This definition clarifies a long-standing ambiguity in copyright about the status of motion picture sound tracks.[192] Now motion picture sound tracks are an integral part of the copyright in a motion picture.[193]

From the above definition, the essence of a motion picture is a series of related images which can be shown in successive order and give the impression of motion. As for any work, the motion picture must be fixed in a tangible medium of expression. Thus, mere live performances, such as telecasts of live sports events, are not covered unless simultaneously fixed in at least one copy.[194] Absent such a fixation, protection must be sought under the common law.[195]

---

[191] 17 U.S.C. § 101 (motion pictures).

[192] H.R. Rep. No. 94–1476, 94th Cong., 2d Sess. 56 (1976).

[193] The importance of categorization lies in the exclusive rights which vary according to the category. Thus, if the sound track were considered a sound recording instead of part of the motion picture copyright, it would not enjoy a performance right. For a discussion of the lack of a performance right in a sound recording, see § 8.24, *infra*.

[194] H.R. Rep. No. 94–1476, 94th Cong., 2d Sess. 52 (1976).

[195] For a discussion of unfixed works protectable under common law copyright, see § 2.6, *supra*.

CHAPTER 4

PUBLICATION, NOTICE AND OTHER FORMALITIES

§ 4.1 Introduction and Chapter Overview

An author's dissemination of his or her work to the public — *i.e.,* publication — is a significant event from a copyright standpoint. Under the 1909 Act, a work of authorship enjoyed perpetual protection until it was published. At that moment, the work became subject to federal protection which limited the duration of the copyright to two 28-year terms — a first term and a renewal term — for a total of 56 years. The 1909 Act also required the copyright owner to affix proper notice to each publicly distributed copy of the work. Non-compliance with the notice requirement could inject the work into the public domain. It was a trap for the unwary, and many an author inadvertently forfeited copyright in his work in this manner.

By having federal copyright begin when a work is created, the 1976 Act reduces, but does not eliminate, the role that publication plays in the overall scheme of copyright protection. For works publicly distributed on or after January 1, 1978, and before March 1, 1989, the 1976 Act retains the notice requirement. Failure to affix proper notice on a publicly distributed work between these two dates could inject the work into the public domain unless the copyright owner took certain affirmative steps within five years of the publication to "cure" the improper notice. Until the 1988 amendments to the Copyright Act, the United States was alone in the world in requiring compliance with notice formalities as a prerequisite for copyright protection. Insistence on this formality was a major impediment to United States entry into the Berne Copyright Convention, which requires, as a condition of membership, the protection of copyright without requiring compliance with formalities.[1]

With the passage of the Berne Convention Implementation Act of 1988 ("BCIA"), affixation of notice is no longer required on published copies or phonorecords of a work publicly distributed on or after March 1, 1989, the effective date of U.S. entry into the Berne Convention. Instead, affixation of notice is permissive, and omission of notice on however many publicly distributed copies will not inject a work into the public domain. By adopting permissive notice, the BCIA amendments removed a major stumbling block to United States' entry into the Berne Union, the major international copyright convention.

---

[1] *See* Berne Convention art. 5(2) (Paris text).

The Berne amendments operate prospectively. In so doing, they leave undisturbed copyrights that had been injected into the public domain for failure to comply with formalities such as proper notice, renewal registration, and manufacturing requirements. The desire to forge international trade agreements, and achieve reciprocal treatment of U.S. works in foreign countries, forced a rethinking of the status of these public domain copyrights.

The first break with traditional practice came about with the Act implementing the North American Free Trade Agreement (NAFTA) in 1993 that restored copyrights in certain Mexican and Canadian films that had fallen into the public domain. One year later, the Uruguay Round Agreements Act, in more dramatic fashion, restored copyright in a much larger group of foreign public domain copyrights. Under the Act, copyright is automatically restored for works originating with a World Trade Organization (WTO) or Berne country, that had been ejected into the public domain for failure to comply with copyright formalities. These restored works will be given the remainder of the copyright term that they would have enjoyed if they had not entered the public domain.

Despite the abrogation of the notice requirement, the 1909 Act and the original provisions of the 1976 Act are still relevant to determining the status of a work. First, the 1976 Act as originally passed is not retroactive and does not revive a work of U.S. origin falling into the public domain under the 1909 Act. Second, the 1988 amendments to the 1976 Act are not retroactive and any work of U.S. origin falling into the public domain for failure to comply with the notice provisions of the 1976 Act in effect before March 1, 1989, will remain permanently in the public domain. Third, for a work publicly distributed on or after January 1, 1978, and before March 1, 1989, omission of notice can be overcome, and copyright in a work saved, if the copyright owner took certain steps to cure the omitted notice.[2]

The copyright practitioner has a complicated task in determining when a work was published to evaluate its current validity. First, he must keep in mind three time frames: for works published before January 1, 1978, the harsh notice provisions of the 1909 Act will apply; for works published on January 1, 1978 and before March 1, 1989, the less strict notice provisions of the 1976 Act as originally enacted will apply; and for works published on or after March 1, 1989, the permissive notice provisions of the BCIA amendments will apply. Second, to determine whether a copyright has been restored under the Uruguay Round Agreements Act, a practitioner must ascertain whether the work originates from a WTO or Berne member country.

This chapter is divided into four parts. Part I examines publication doctrine under the 1909 and 1976 Acts. Much of Part I examines the important role publication plays in copyright law. This Part also demonstrates how the courts carved exceptions out of the publication doctrine to avoid forfeiture of copyright. Part II considers the notice requirement, focusing on what constitutes adequate notice and the consequences of publishing a work without affixing proper notice under the 1909 Act and

---

[2] The copyright owner must register a work within five years and make a reasonable effort to add notice to copies distributed to the public in the United States after discovery of notice. *See* 17 U.S.C. § 405(a). For a discussion of this provision, see § 4.11, *infra.*

the 1976 Act as originally enacted, as well as the effect of the BCIA amendments which have abrogated the notice requirement. Part III treats the now abrogated curiosity of American law known as the "manufacturing clause," which had required certain books written by American authors to be manufactured in the United States. Although no longer a part of the law, the manufacturing clause may still have a limited effect on previously distributed works not complying with its provisions. Part IV discusses restoration of copyrights from the public domain under the Uruguay Round Agreements Act.

PART I: PUBLICATION

§ 4.2   Publication: Its Role in Copyright Law

[A]   In General

Under the Copyright Act of 1976, copyright protection begins on creation, that is, when an author has fixed a work in a tangible medium of expression.[3] At that moment, copyright protection begins as a matter of federal law and endures, generally, for the life of the author plus 50 years.[4] State common law copyright may still apply to works not fixed in a tangible medium, such as oral works, but the 1976 Act effectively federalizes copyright.[5] This is a fundamental change from the 1909 Act, which recognized a dual system of copyright in which the dividing line was publication. Under the 1909 Act, unpublished works were protected by state common law copyright, and so long as a work remained unpublished, common law copyright could theoretically endure forever. Once a work was published, state common law protection ended (divested) and federal protection began (invested).[6] To encourage authors to disclose their works to the public, the 1909 Act gave the advantages of federal protection but with limited duration. As measured from the moment of publication, federal copyright protection lasted for a maximum of 56 years: 28 years for the initial term plus a 28-year renewal term.[7]

[B]   Historical Overview of the Publication Doctrine

Divestiture of common law rights on publication of a work is a doctrine that originated in England with *Millar v. Taylor*,[8] a case decided several decades after passage of the Statute of Anne,[9] the first English copyright statute. In *Millar,* the court of the King's Bench concluded that common law rights were perpetual, lost neither by publication nor by the expiration of copyright. According to the court,

---

[3] *See* 17 U.S.C. § 102(a).

[4] *See* 17 U.S.C. § 302(a).

[5] *See* 17 U.S.C. § 301.

[6] For an excellent overview of the subject of publication, see Fulton E. Brylawski, *Publication: Its Role in Copyright Matters, Both Past and Present*, 31 J. Copyright L. Soc'y 507 (1984).

[7] *See* 17 U.S.C. § 24 (1909 Act).

[8] 98 Eng. Rep. 201 (K.B. 1769).

[9] 8 Anne ch. 19 (1710).

the Statute of Anne provided extra remedies during the term of copyright but did not abrogate common law rights.

Five years later, the House of Lords, in *Donaldson v. Becket,*[10] considered what effect the Statute of Anne had on common law rights. The House of Lords narrowly overruled *Millar v. Taylor*, holding that common law rights were divested on publication by operation of the Statute. Whether the House of Lords misconstrued the law is still a matter of historical controversy.[11]

The effect of publication on common law rights was first considered in the United States in *Wheaton v. Peters*[12] in which the Supreme Court agreed with the House of Lords' view in *Donaldson*. Reviewing the history of the publication doctrine, the Court held that the copyright owner could not claim common law copyright protection in his published works. Thus, until the passage of the 1976 Act, the principle that publication divests common law rights was universally accepted.

[C]   Justification of the Publication Doctrine

Why should the act of publication divest common law copyright? One can look to the Patent and Copyright Clause in the Constitution authorizing Congress to protect writings of authors only for "limited times."[13] The "limited times" provision attempts to promote the public interest by creating an environment for the optimum production and dissemination of works of authorship. On the one hand, we encourage production of works of authorship by providing a limited monopoly to the copyright owner. On the other hand, we encourage dissemination by allowing the public free access to these works upon expiration of the copyright term, when a work enters the public domain. Common law copyright for unpublished works, which could last in perpetuity, recognized the author's right to privacy in his work. This privacy interest prevailed over the public's access right until the author decided to exploit his work economically by publishing it. So, a bargain was struck: the author could enjoy the economic fruits of his labor and could have access to the remedies conferred by federal copyright protection. In exchange, she would have to accept the limitations imposed on her monopoly by the eventual dedication of her work to the public domain.

Because it constituted the dividing line between common law and federal copyright, the concept of publication was perhaps the most important single concept under the 1909 Act. It was also criticized as the 1909 Act's major defect. As developed in case law, publication became a highly technical concept, often difficult to apply in a practical context. Although the 1976 Act removed the central role of publication in copyright law, the concept of publication remains of utmost

---

[10] 4 Burr. 2408 (H.L. 1774).

[11] For an extensive examination of the English common law copyright and its American legacy, particularly regarding the interpretation of *Donaldson v. Becket* as construed by *Wheaton v. Peters,* see Howard B. Abrams, *The Historic Foundation of American Copyright Law: Exploding the Myth of Common Law Copyright*, 29 Wayne L. Rev. 1119 (1983).

[12] 33 U.S. (8 Pet.) 591 (1834).

[13] U.S. Const. Art. I, § 8, cl. 8.

importance for works published both before and after January 1, 1978, the effective date of the 1976 Act.

§ 4.3 "Publication" Defined

What constitutes "publication"?[14] This most important concept was purposely left undefined by the drafters of the 1909 Act, leaving publication doctrine to develop, sometimes inconsistently, through the case law. The 1976 Act, however, has attempted to codify and clarify this decisional law, defining publication as

> . . . the distribution of copies or phonorecords of a work to the public by sale or other transfer of ownership, or by rental, lease or lending. The offering to distribute copies or phonorecords to a group of persons for purposes of further distribution, public performance, or public display, constitutes publication. A public performance or display of a work does not of itself constitute publication.[15]

By this definition, publication occurs when the copyright owner voluntarily sells, leases, loans, or gives away the original or a tangible copy of the work to the general public. However, publication is not limited to situations where tangible copies are conveyed to the public. Even if no sale or other disposition of the work has taken place, publication will occur if the work is offered to the public in any manner authorized by the copyright owner. Publication has been found, for instance, when the copyright owner has distributed work to retail dealers for sale to the general public.[16] Alternatively, publication does not occur by a public performance or display[17] of a work, so long as the public performance or display occurs without a sale, offer to sell, or other disposition of tangible copies of the work. In short, publication generally occurs, but is not limited to situations where the public has obtained a possessory right in the work.

Two other curiosities of publication doctrine should be noted. One is that the copyright owner's subjective intent to publish is irrelevant. Thus, publication can take place even if the copyright owner does not realize that, as a matter of law, he is committing or consenting to acts which would publish the work. The second is that even *de minimis* distribution constitutes publication so long as the general public has obtained or is offered a possessory right in the work.[18] Publication may occur

---

[14] For a general discussion of publication concepts under the 1909 Act, the Universal Copyright Convention, and the Berne Convention, see 1 *Nimmer on Copyright* § 4.04 n. 5 (1993).

[15] 17 U.S.C. § 101.

[16] *See Data Cash Sys., Inc. v. JS & A Group, Inc.*, 628 F.2d 1038 (7th Cir. 1980).

[17] The statutory definition of "publication" excludes publication by display. This differs from the case law under the 1909 Act which indicated that an unrestricted display could be considered a publication. *See, e.g., Letter Edged in Black Press, Inc. v. Public Bldg. Comm.*, 320 F. Supp. 1303 (N.D. Ill. 1970). For a discussion of publication by display under the 1909 Act, see § 4.7[B], *infra*.

[18] When a work is offered to a limited class of the public, the courts have found no publication at all under the limited publication doctrine. *See* § 4.5[C], *infra*.

upon distribution of just one copy of the work.[19] Thus, to publish a work does not mean that the public's need is satisfied by sufficient public distribution of the work.

§ 4.4   Publication Under the 1909 Act: Its Continuing Importance

For works published before January 1, 1978, the provisions of the 1909 Act apply. Once a work enters the public domain (unless restored under the Uruguay Round Agreements Act),[20] it remains there irrevocably, unaffected either by the provisions of the 1976 Act, as originally passed, or the BCIA amendments which have abrogated the notice requirement. To decide whether a work has entered the public domain before January 1, 1978, one must look to the 1909 Act provisions governing publication and notice. Under the 1909 Act, every time a work was published, the copyright owner was required to affix proper copyright notice to each copy of the work.[21] Failure to do so could inject the work into the public domain. Thus, if in 1989, A brought an action for copyright infringement of a work published in 1970 without proper notice, B, the alleged infringer, could assert as a defense that the work was published without proper notice and was therefore in the public domain. Indeed, many authors and copyright owners have forfeited the copyright to their work through the harsh terms of the 1909 Act. Unless restored under the Uruguay Round Agreements Act,[22] these works remain in the public domain and are not retrievable by the 1976 Act.[23] Because of the enormous amount of works published before January 1, 1978, today's copyright practitioner must be well aware of publication doctrine as it existed under the 1909 Act.

§ 4.5   Two Court-Made Efforts to Ameliorate the Publication Requirement's Harsh Effect Under the 1909 Act

[A]   Generally

By failing to comply with the formalities required under the 1909 Act, copyright owners often unwittingly injected their works into the public domain. This would typically occur when the author distributed his work to members of the public

---

[19] *See Burke v. National Broadcasting Co., Inc.*, 598 F.2d 688 (1st Cir. 1979), *cert. denied*, 444 U.S. 869 (1979); *Stern v. Remick & Co.*, 175 F. 282 (S.D.N.Y. 1910).

[20] Under the Uruguay Round Agreements Act, copyright is restored for works originating from Berne or World Trade Organization countries that were injected into the public domain for failure to comply with U.S. copyright formalities. *See* 17 U.S.C. § 104A. These restoration provisions are discussed at §§ 4.18–4.19 *infra*.

[21] 17 U.S.C. § 10 (1909 Act):

> Any person entitled thereto by this title may secure copyright for his work by publication thereof with notice of copyright required by this title.

[22] Restoration of copyrights in certain foreign works that were injected into the public domain for noncompliance with U.S. formalities is discussed at §§ 4.18–4.19 *infra*.

[23] 17 U.S.C. Trans. & Supp. Provs. § 103. See §§ 4.18–4.19 *infra*, for a discussion of these copyright restoration provisions.

without affixing the requisite notice. The act of publication was said to have "divested" the author's common law rights, and because the author did not properly secure federal rights available through meeting the requisite formalities, federal copyright was not "invested." Divestment of common law rights without investment of federal rights resulted in the work's "dedication" to the public domain.

It is often said that "the law abhors a forfeiture"; the same is true for the law of copyright. Courts gradually developed doctrines to mitigate the harsh effects of the 1909 Act's mechanistic rules regarding publication without notice.

[B]   Divestive and Investive Publication

To avoid forfeiture of copyright, some courts required a larger public distribution of a work for a publication to divest common law protection than to invest federal copyright. The leading statement of this doctrine was made in *American Visuals Corp. v. Holland*,[24] where Judge Frank concluded:

> [T]he courts apply different tests of publication depending on whether plaintiff is claiming protection because he did not publish and hence has a common law claim of infringement — in which case the distribution must be quite large to constitute "publication" — or whether he is claiming under the copyright statute — in which case the requirements for publication are quite narrow. In each case the courts appear so to treat the concept of publication as to prevent piracy.[25]

In short, it takes a greater degree of publication to divest common law copyright than to invest federal statutory copyright.[26]

The investive/divestive distinction can be considered *dictum*, never adopted as the law in a specific case. It is a difficult doctrine to apply in a systematic, non-arbitrary way because it leaves two basic questions unanswered: first, how extensive must a public distribution be for a divestive publication to take place? Second, how small must the distribution be for an investive publication? It comes as no surprise that these questions have never been properly answered in the case law. Accordingly, it is virtually impossible for an author to determine with any certainty whether common law rights have been divested and/or federal rights invested. The doctrine imposes another level of complexity on the already elusive determination of when publication has occurred.

Despite its dubious status as a rule of law, the *investive/divestive doctrine* may still be relevant in practice under the 1976 Act, and it may have important consequences in a given case, if adopted. First, if a work were published without proper notice and the publication were found to be divestive, federal protection would not invest and the work would fall into the public domain. As a second possibility, if the publication were considered divestive, but copyright was secured by proper affixation of notice, federal protection would have begun. In this instance,

---

[24] 239 F.2d 740 (2d Cir. 1956).

[25] *Id.* at 744.

[26] *See American Vitagraph, Inc. v. Levy*, 659 F.2d 1023 (9th Cir. 1981); *Hirshon v. United Artists Corp.*, 243 F.2d 640 (D.C. Cir. 1957).

the copyright would endure for an initial term of 28 years plus a renewal term of another 47 years.[27] If, as a third possibility, a court found the publication was neither investive nor divestive, the work would be considered unpublished. The consequence is that for works unpublished on January 1, 1978, copyright duration would be determined under the 1976 Act, whose main term is life of the author plus 50 years.[28] Because of the important consequences involving duration and validity of copyright, copyright owners will try to invoke the investive/divestive distinction for years to come.

[C] Limited versus General Publication

Another court-made doctrine, ostensibly developed under the 1909 Act to avoid forfeiture of copyright, is the distinction between limited and general publication.[29] A limited publication is a non-divestive publication which communicates the contents of a work to a narrowly selected group for a limited purpose, without transferring the rights of diffusion, reproduction, distribution, or sale.[30] For example, a limited publication would occur where copies of manuscripts are distributed to trade members for criticism or review[31] or where copies of architectural plans are distributed to contractors for bidding purposes.[32] The essential point is this: a limited publication is one in which circulation of the work is restricted *both* as to the persons who receive it and the purpose for its distribution. Otherwise it is considered a general (divestive) publication. Because it focuses on the copyright owner's purpose in publishing the work, the limited publication doctrine contradicts the general rule that a person's subjective intent is irrelevant in deciding whether a publication has taken place.

Despite noticeable exceptions, for the most part, the courts have pushed the limited publication doctrine to its farthest reaches to avoid a forfeiture of copyright. In *King v. Mister Maestro, Inc.*,[33] the court found a limited publication where advance copies of Martin Luther King's *I Have a Dream* speech were given to the press. The speech was later broadcast to millions of people. The advance copies of the text which were given to the press contained no copyright notice and were distributed with no apparent limitation. The court found this to be a limited publication because the tangible copies of the speech were given to a limited group, the press, and not to the general public. In addition, the copies were distributed to serve a limited purpose only, which was to assist the press in covering the event.

The *King* case is questionable in its reasoning. Although the press, a limited group, was initially given the speech, it was simply a conduit for the eventual dissemination of the speech to the general public. If the essential feature of a general publication

---

[27] *See* 17 U.S.C. § 304.

[28] *See* 17 U.S.C. § 302(a).

[29] *See generally* 1 *Nimmer on Copyright* § 4.13 (1993).

[30] *See White v. Kimmell*, 193 F.2d 744, 746 (9th Cir.), *cert. denied*, 343 U.S. 957 (1952).

[31] *See, e.g., Hemingway v. Random House, Inc.* , 23 N.Y.2d 341, 296 N.Y.S.2d 771, 244 N.E.2d 250 (1968).

[32] *See Nucor Corp. v. Tennessee Forging Steel Serv., Inc.* , 476 F.2d 386 (8th Cir. 1973).

[33] 224 F. Supp. 101 (S.D.N.Y. 1963).

is the public's possessory right in tangible copies of the work, it is hard to imagine a more general publication than the one that took place in this case. Despite its questionable reasoning, placing in doubt its status as "good" law, *King* does show the lengths to which some courts have gone to avoid forfeiture of copyright, a trend that appears ever more apparent.

King, despite its strained reasoning, represents a clear tendency to stretch the definition of "limited publication to avoid forfeiture of copyright."[34] The trend continued, for example, in *Academy of Motion Pictures Arts and Sciences v. Creative House Promotions, Inc.,*[35] the Academy had distributed 158 copies of its famed Oscar statuette to award winners between 1929 and 1941, without notice of copyright and without any express restriction on the recipient's right to sell or dispose of their Oscars. In 1941, the Academy registered their claim to copyright, and from that time, all Oscars have borne notice of copyright. In 1976, the defendant commissioned a trophy sculptor to create a sculpture strikingly similar to the Oscar, which it sold to various corporate buyers. In an infringement suit, the District Court ruled that the Oscar had entered the public domain before 1941, because the Academy's divestive and general publication, without notice, triggered the loss of copyright. Although distributed to a limited group of persons (a highly select group of award winners), the Academy's distribution was not sufficiently limited as to purpose. The Academy asserted that its publication was limited and non-divestive because the Oscars were distributed to a select group of persons for a limited purpose. The Court of Appeals agreed with the Academy's limited publication theory, reversing the District Court.

Although no express restrictions on the use or distribution of the Oscar existed before 1941, the Ninth Circuit held that such were restrictions were implied. First, neither the Academy nor any living Oscar recipient had ever offered to transfer an Oscar to the general public. Second, each Oscar was personalized with the name of the original winner. Third, the Academy never gave the recipients the permission to sell, distribute, or make other copies of their Oscars.

The publication in *King* and the Oscar case should be compared with the general publication found in *Public Affairs Associates, Inc. v. Rickover,*[36] involving copyright in speeches given by Admiral Rickover on various occasions. In this pre-1976 Act case, the Admiral made his speeches available to the press, sent them to individuals both on request and unsolicited, and gave printed copies to sponsors for further distribution. The general nature of the publication lay in the unrestricted ability of the public to obtain tangible copies of the speeches. Failure to affix notice on the speeches coupled with their general publication injected the speeches into the public domain.

---

[34] *See, e.g., Burke v. National Broadcasting Co., Inc.,* 598 F.2d 688 (1st Cir.), *cert. denied,* 444 U.S. 869 (1979) (limited non-divestive publication found where author authorized one copy of film to be made to be shown on German non-commercial television and for lecture purposes, even though there was no explicit prohibition on further distribution of the film).

[35] 944 F.2d 1446 (9th Cir. 1991).

[36] 284 F.2d 262 (D.C. Cir. 1960), *vacated on other grounds,* 369 U.S. 111 (1962). *See also* 1 *Nimmer on Copyright* § 4.04 (1993).

Although it may appear that the case stands for a rule that the subjective intent is determinative on whether a general publication has occurred, the court rejected this rationale for its decision. *Id.* at 103. Unlike *King* and the Oscar case, the unrestricted distribution of the Admiral's speeches to the public rendered a claim of limited publication too difficult to sustain with any plausibility.

§ 4.6 The Importance of Publication Under the 1976 Act

[A] Generally

For works published on or after January 1, 1978, publication remains a pivotal point in many aspects of the law of copyright. First, the act of publication necessitates compliance with formalities, including notice and deposit. The one exception is that, for works publicly distributed before March 1, 1989, affixation of notice is permissive. Second, the act of publication has important consequences in international copyright relations. Third, the act of publication can determine the duration of copyright. In addition to these contexts, the act of publication is significant in a number of other situations.[37]

[B] Publication and Compliance with Formalities

The act of publication is important in determining whether one must or should comply with certain formalities. Most importantly, for works published after January 1, 1978, and before March 1, 1989, notice showing the date of publication was required on all publicly distributed copies of the work.[38] Failure to affix proper notice on published copies of a work could lead to a forfeiture of copyright.[39] With the passage of the BCIA amendments, notice is no longer required, although it is still highly recommended, for a work published on or after March 1, 1989.

Other than this modification brought about by the BCIA amendments, the other important consequences of publication remain unchanged. The basic deposit requirements are the same. For all works published in the United States, one must fulfill the deposit requirements of the Library of Congress within three months after publication.[40] Noncompliance can lead to criminal fines.[41] After having published a work, one must register a claim for copyright or lose certain advantages in an infringement suit.[42] For example, registration in the Copyright Office within five

---

[37] *See* 17 U.S.C. § 203(a)(3) (termination of transfers covering publication rights); 17 U.S.C. § 108(b) (right of libraries to reproduce certain works depends on whether the work is published); 17 U.S.C. §§ 118(b) and (d) (non-commercial compulsory broadcast performance license applies only for published works).

[38] *See* 17 U.S.C. §§ 401(a), 402(a).

[39] 17 U.S.C. § 405. For a discussion of forfeiture of copyright by omitting notice, see § 4.11, *infra.*

[40] *See* 17 U.S.C. § 407(a). For a discussion of deposit requirements for the Library of Congress, see § 7.8, *infra.*

[41] *See* 17 U.S.C. § 407(d).

[42] *See generally* 17 U.S.C. §§ 408–412. For a discussion of remedies, see §§ 9.8–9.15, *infra.*

years of publication confers *prima facie* evidence of validity of the copyright.[43] Moreover, one can obtain statutory damages and attorney's fees for published works only if registration preceded the infringement or if the work was registered three months after publication.[44]

[C] Publication and International Copyright

The act of publication has great significance in international copyright relations. For both the Universal Copyright Convention and the Berne Convention, works first published in a member state or by a national of a member state must be given the same protection in every other member state as works first published in the member's own territory.[45]

[D] Publication: Durational Consequences

The date of publication determines the duration of copyright for certain categories of works. Under the 1976 Act, the term for anonymous and pseudonymous works, and works made for hire is measured from the year of first publication.[46] The normal copyright term is the life of the author plus 50 years,[47] and, unless Copyright Office records reveal otherwise, the author may be presumed dead for at least 50 years, 75 years after publication.[48] For these and other reasons,[49] publication plays an important role for works published on or after January 1, 1978.[50]

§ 4.7 Special Publication Contexts: 1909 and 1976 Acts Compared

[A] Performance as Publication

A performance is not a publication. No matter how large the audience or to whom it is directed, an oral dissemination of a musical or literary work does not constitute a publication.[51] The Martin Luther King case [52] graphically illustrates this basic tenet of copyright law. Although Martin Luther King delivered his *I Have a Dream*

---

[43] 17 U.S.C. § 410(c).

[44] 17 U.S.C. § 412.

[45] For a discussion of international copyright matters, see §§ 12.1–12.11, *infra*.

[46] 17 U.S.C. § 302(c). For a discussion of duration, see §§ 6.1–6.4, *infra*.

[47] 17 U.S.C. §§ 302(a) and (d).

[48] 17 U.S.C. §§ 302(c), (d) and (e).

[49] The rights of foreign authors under United States copyright law are dependent upon whether the work is published. 17 U.S.C. § 104. Archival reproduction rights for libraries are permitted for unpublished works. 17 U.S.C. § 108. *See also* 17 U.S.C. §§ 118 and 504(c)(2)(ii) (availability of public broadcasting license).

[50] Another durational consequence of publication is found in 17 U.S.C. § 303, which extends the period of protection of a work unpublished as of January 1, 1978, if the work is published before 2003.

[51] *See Ferris v. Frohman*, 223 U.S. 424 (1912) (public performance of a written drama not a publication).

[52] *King v. Mister Maestro, Inc.*, 224 F. Supp. 101 (S.D.N.Y. 1963).

speech to millions of people through the media, the court held that he did not publish the work by performing it.

That a performance is not a publication seems contradictory to the rationale of the *publication doctrine*. Publication enables an author to exploit his work economically. In return, the author must eventually dedicate his work to the public domain. From this standpoint, a performance should be a publication. Authors profit enormously from the performance of their works, even though no tangible copies of the work are distributed to the public. Nevertheless, the basic rule that a performance is not a publication is ingrained in 1909 Act case law and is now codified in the 1976 Act.[53] In addition, the 1976 Act explicitly provides that a public display is not a publication.[54]

[B] Publication by Display

By expressly providing that a public display is not a publication, the 1976 Act has clarified a matter of some uncertainty under the 1909 Act. What little case law exists on this topic indicates that a public display of a work of art in a gallery, museum, or other public place, even without an accompanying offer to sell, constitutes a publication if the public viewing the work were not restricted from copying it. In *Letter Edged in Black Press, Inc. v. Public Building Comm. of Chicago*,[55] an unrestricted public display forfeited copyright in a Picasso sculpture. The plaintiff, Chicago's Public Building Commission, erected a monumental Picasso sculpture, built from a maquette which it publicly displayed without proper copyright notice. The court found that the maquette was an original tangible work of authorship and that the monumental sculpture was merely a large copy of it. When the maquette was displayed, there were no restrictions on its being photographed or copied in any way. This "unrestricted" display was found to be a general publication, not a limited one. As a result, the work was injected into the public domain.[56] Thus, the unrestricted display dedicated the work to the public domain.

Alternatively, a display would not constitute a publication if the public were admitted to view the work with an express or implied understanding that copying was not allowed. In the leading case of *American Tobacco Co. v. Werckmeister*,[57] gallery guards strictly enforced a no copying policy for a painting on public display. In these circumstances, failure to affix copyright notice did not inject the work into the public domain, and only a limited publication took place.

---

[53] *See* 17 U.S.C. § 101.

[54] *Id.*

[55] 320 F. Supp. 1303 (N.D. Ill. 1970).

[56] The unrestricted display was only one of the ways in which the work was injected into the public domain. The Commission sent out pictures of the maquette without copyright notice for use in a publicity drive which appeared in national magazines. Souvenir booklets, containing drawings and photographs of the maquette, were distributed without copyright notice. The Art Institute of Chicago sold postcards of the maquette, again without notice of copyright.

[57] 207 U.S. 284 (1907).

[C]   The Distribution of Phonorecords as Publication

Under the 1976 Act, a publication of a sound recording publishes both the sound recording and the recorded musical work embodied on the phonorecord. This rule applies to works distributed on or after January 1, 1978. Until the Sound Recording Act of 1971, the 1909 Act took the opposite approach, that publication of a sound recording did not publish the musical work. For example, suppose A in 1970 recorded and distributed records of his copyrighted song to the public in phonorecord form. This distribution would neither publish the sound recording nor the musical work no matter how wide the distribution or how many records were sold. Even if the phonorecord were distributed without notice, no forfeiture of copyright on the sound recording or musical work would occur because no publication had occurred.

What is the explanation for this deviation from the law and policy of the publication doctrine? An historical quirk may explain these inconsistencies. In *White-Smith Music Publishing Co. v. Apollo Co.*,[58] the Supreme Court held that a recordation of a musical composition by mechanical means in a piano roll (later extended by analogy to phonorecords) was not a copy of the musical composition. Thus, because a phonorecord was not a copy of the work embodied on it, its sale did not publish the musical work. The record industry relied on the *White-Smith* doctrine, and it became an industry practice to make and distribute recordings without registering the musical work or publishing the work in any other way. The *White-Smith* doctrine was overturned with the 1976 Act, and now all material objects, whether copy or phonorecord, are treated alike for the purpose of the law. In short, sale of a phonorecord will now publish both the musical work and the sound recording.

The Sound Recording Act of 1971,[59] the first federal act to protect sound recordings, amended the 1909 Act to include phonorecords in the definition of "copies" to protect the copyright owners of musical works and sound recordings. But sound recordings were not treated the same as musical works under the amendment. As for the sound recording, the publication of a phonorecord divested common law rights, and the copyright owner was required to comply with the 1909 Act's notice requirements to avoid forfeiture of copyright. On the other hand, the musical composition, *i.e.*, the words and the music, was unaffected by failure to affix notice on the phonorecord.[60] Thus, under the 1971 amendment, a publication of the sound recording on a phonorecord without notice would inject the sound recording into the public domain while the musical work embodied on the same phonorecord would be unaffected.

The 1976 Act has eliminated the *White-Smith* doctrine, and now the public distribution of a phonorecord publishes both the sound recording and the musical work embodied on it. The 1909 Act rules, however, remain important to determine the public domain status of works published before the effective date of the 1976 Act.

---

[58] 209 U.S. 1 (1908).

[59] Sound Recording Amendment, Pub. L. No. 92–140, 85 Stat. 391 (1971).

[60] *See Rosette v. Rainbo Record Mfg. Corp.*, 354 F. Supp. 1183 (S.D.N.Y. 1973).

[D] Publication of a Derivative Work

Another unsettled issue under the 1909 Act was whether publication of a derivative work[61] constituted publication of the preexisting work on which it was based. For example, if A writes a screenplay and authorizes B to make a movie of it, does publication of the movie publish the underlying work? One could argue that a derivative work is a copy of the preexisting work. The reason is that a derivative work, by definition, is one which substantially reproduces the underlying work.[62] As always, the issue is important because the 1909 Act required notice on all copies of a published work, and failure to affix notice injected the work into the public domain.

Derivative works can be created in the same medium, such as a second edition of a textbook or an enlargement of a photograph, or in a different medium, such as a three-dimensional rendition of a cartoon character or a movie based on a play. Case law under the 1909 Act held that when the two works were in the same medium, publication of the derivative work published the preexisting work.[63] The derivative work was regarded as a copy of the preexisting work, and failure to affix notice on the derivative work injected the preexisting work into the public domain.

When the derivative work was reproduced in a different medium, such as a screenplay into a film, or a photograph of a three-dimensional work, some courts, under the 1909 Act, expressed the contrary view that the publication of the derivative work did not publish the underlying work.[64] These cases are hard to reconcile with the basic justification for the publication doctrine because the owner of the underlying work is obtaining an economic benefit from the exploitation of his work. Perhaps this anomaly can be explained as another attempt to avoid the forfeiture of copyright under the notice provisions of the 1909 Act.

Under the 1976 Act, publication of the derivative work would appear to publish the preexisting work. This principle is not specifically stated in the 1976 Act but is implied in § 401(b)(2),[65] which provides that

> in the case of compilations or derivative works . . . the year contained in the year date of first publication of the compilation or derivative work is sufficient.

---

[61] *See* 17 U.S.C. § 101 (derivative work). For a discussion of derivative works, see §§ 2.8–2.9, *supra*.

[62] Professor Nimmer takes this position. *See* 1 *Nimmer on Copyright* § 4.12[A] (1993).

[63] *See First Am. Artificial Flowers, Inc. v. Joseph Markovits, Inc.*, 42 F. Supp. 178 (S.D.N.Y. 1972).

[64] *See Key West Hand Print Fabrics, Inc. v. Serbin, Inc.*, 244 F. Supp. 287 (S.D. Fla. 1965) (publication of photograph of plaintiff's fabric design in magazine did not inject the fabric design into the public domain despite lack of notice); *O'Neill v. General Film Co.*, 171 A.D. 854, 157 N.Y.S. 1028 (1916) (publication of film based on play will divest common law rights in film only).

[65] 17 U.S.C. § 401(b)(2).

PART II: NOTICE

§ 4.8   Generally: Justification for Notice Requirement

[A]   The Background

In general, notice of copyright consists of affixing the name of the copyright owner, the date of first publication of the work and a symbol (© , copr. or copyright) in a reasonably noticeable location on the work. Before the effective date of the Berne Convention Implementation Act of 1988 ("BCIA"), March 1, 1989, the 1976 Act, as did the preceding Acts, required notice of copyright for all publicly distributed copies of a work of authorship.[66] The notice requirement was unique to American law, the United States being the only major country where noncompliance with the affixation of notice on a work could lead to a forfeiture of copyright.[67] Our insistence on this formality (among other reasons) impeded U.S. entry into the Berne Convention, the preeminent international copyright convention, for over 100 years.[68] With the entry of the United States into the Berne Convention, notice of copyright is no longer required for works publicly distributed on or after March 1, 1989.

Why did we insist on notice in our law? According to the House Report accompanying the 1976 Act, notice serves several purposes. It places into the public domain works in which no one has an interest in maintaining copyright. It also informs the public of a claim for copyright. In addition, it identifies the copyright owner and shows the date of publication.[69]

It is doubtful that the value of these functions of notice outweighed its unfairness to authors or our inability to enter into the Berne Convention. In addition to these basic objections, the notice on a work can often be misleading. Notice presumably informs a user of the copyright owner's identity. But this is not always the case. A copyrighted work may be transferred while copies of the work may continue to circulate for years containing the name of the previous copyright owner.

[B]   Abrogation of the Notice Requirement: The Berne Convention Implementation Act of 1988

As of March 1, 1989, notice is no longer required on a publicly distributed work, and omission of notice can no longer result in forfeiture of copyright. Notice is permissive, a choice left to the copyright owner's discretion. But even for works distributed on or after March 1, 1989, notice of a claim for copyright is recommended and may be particularly useful in litigation where a defendant asserts a defense of innocent infringement. Under § 401(d), as amended by the BCIA, if

---

[66] 17 U.S.C. § 401(a). H.R. Rep. No. 94–1476, 94th Cong., 2d Sess. 143 (1976).

[67] 2 *Nimmer on Copyright* § 7.02 (1993).

[68] The Berne Convention prohibits imposition of formalities as a prerequisite to protecting works by the nationals of other signatory states or works first or simultaneously published in such states. Berne Convention art. 5(2) (Paris text, 1971). For a discussion of the Berne Convention, see § 12.4, *infra*.

[69] H.R. Rep. No. 94–1476, 94th Cong., 2d Sess. 143 (1976).

reasonable notice is given as specified in the 1976 Act, then no weight shall be given to a defendant's interposition of a defense based on innocent infringement to mitigate actual or statutory damages.[70] In effect, although notice is permissive for works published after March 1, 1989, it is still encouraged by the 1976 Act because it cuts off the defense of innocent infringement. As a result, the copyright owner must continue to be concerned about the technical rules of proper notice, no longer to avoid forfeiture, but to enjoy the full extent of remedies allowed in a suit for copyright infringement. These rules of proper notice are discussed in § 4.10, *infra*.

Despite the abrogation of the notice requirement for publicly distributed works after March 1, 1989, the notice provisions of both the 1976 Act and the 1909 Act are very much alive. The reason is that works that have entered the public domain under a previous statute are not revived by the subsequent legal regime, unless restored under the Uruguay Round Agreements Act.[71] Thus, a work falling into the public domain because of failure to affix notice under the 1909 Act is not revived by the less harsh provisions of the 1976 Act. Similarly, a work entering the public domain for omission of notice under the provisions of the 1976 Act is not revived by the permissive notice provisions of the BCIA amendments.[72] In short, the copyright practitioner must be conversant with the 1909 Act, the 1976 Act as originally enacted, the BCIA amendments, and be able to apply the appropriate statute.

The three statutory frameworks can be viewed as follows:

---

[70] *See* 17 U.S.C. § 401(d) ("If a notice of copyright . . . appears on the published copy or copies . . . , then no weight shall be given to . . . a defense based on "innocent infringement. . . .").

[71] *See* 17 U.S.C. 104A, which automatically restores copyright to works originating in Berne or WTO countries which lost copyright protection for failure to comply with U.S. formalities. For a discussion of the restoration provisions, see §§ 4.18–4.19 *infra*.

[72] In only one narrow instance has Congress resurrected works from the public for failure to publish with notice. 17 U.S.C. § 104A, passed pursuant to requirements for entering the North American Free Trade Agreement, resurrects copyright in Mexican and Canadian motion pictures that had entered the public domain for failure to comply with the notice provisions of the 1976 Act as originally passed).

Before 1/1/78	On or after 1/1/78 and before 3/1/89	On or after 3/1/89
1909 Act	1976 Act as originally enacted	Berne Act Amendments of 1988
Notice required.	Required notice with savings provisions (*see* 17 U.S.C. § 405(a)).	Notice permissive.

§ 4.9 Notice Requirements Under the 1976 Act Before the Berne Convention Implementation Act of 1988 Amendments

For works publicly distributed on or after January 1, 1978, and before March 1, 1989, the 1976 Act, while easing the harsh forfeiture provisions of the 1909 Act,[73] nevertheless forced the copyright owner to comply with notice formalities. Section 401(a) provided:

> Whenever a work protected under this title is published in the United States or elsewhere by authority of the copyright owner, a notice of copyright as provided by this section shall be placed on all publicly distributed copies from which the work can be visually perceived, either directly or with the aid of a machine or device.[74]

Certain important general points arise from this statutory language. First, notice was not a permissive act but was a requirement for copyright protection[75] any time a work was published.[76] Second, the notice requirement was limited to published

---

[73] The 1976 Act intended to avoid the "arbitrary and unjust forfeitures" resulting under the 1909 Act from "unintentional or relatively unimportant omissions or errors in the copyright notice." H.R. Rep. No. 94–1476, 94th Cong., 2d Sess. 143 (1976).

[74] 17 U.S.C. § 401(a). The BCIA has changed the language "shall be placed on" to "may be placed on." *See* 17 U.S.C. § 401(a).

[75] Strict adherence to statutory formalities became the American viewpoint as early as 1824 in *Ewer v. Coxe*, 8 F. Cas. 917 (C.C.E.D. Pa. 1824). The most famous case holding that formalities be strictly observed was decided by the Supreme Court in 1834, *Wheaton v. Peters*, 33 U.S. (8 Pet.) 591 (1834). The *Wheaton* doctrine is extensively explored in Craig Joyce, *The Rise of the Supreme Court Reporter: An Institutional Perspective on Marshall Court Ascendancy*, 83 Mich. L. Rev. 1291 (1985).

[76] 17 U.S.C. § 101. Section 101 defines "publication" as

works in all copies visually perceived with the naked eye or with the aid of a machine or device.[77] Third, notice had to be affixed to copies of a work whether published in the United States or abroad; it was not solely limited to United States publications.[78] Fourth, notice was required on all tangible copies published by or under the authority of the copyright owner;[79] the rules of notice did not apply to unauthorized publication of the work.[80] From these general considerations, the discussion now turns to the technical aspects of complying with the notice requirements.

Even though improper notice can no longer forfeit copyright for works publicly distributed on or after March 1, 1989, the rules of proper notice remain important because affixation of proper notice on copies or phonorecords deprives a defendant of the defense of innocent infringement in the mitigation of actual or statutory damages for causes of action arising after the effective date of the BCIA. Thus, a copyright practitioner should be concerned about the rules of proper notice regardless of when the work was published.[81]

§ 4.10   Form and Position of Notice Under the 1976 Act

[A]   Form of Notice on Copies

As specified by § 401(b), notice of copyright consists of three elements: (1) the symbol "©," or the abbreviation "Copr.," or the word "Copyright"; (2) the name of the owner of the copyright; and (3) the date of first publication. For example, a typical notice may look like this: © John Doe 1986. The three elements constituting notice may be placed in any order.

To inform copyright owners of the correct form of notice, the 1976 Act authorizes the Register of Copyrights to prescribe by regulation the proper form and position of notice for various kinds of works.[82] In questionable cases, the Register's regulations should be consulted, but, as the 1976 Act specifically provides, these regulations are not to be considered exhaustive.[83]

. . . the distribution of copies or phonorecords of a work to the public by sale or other transfer of ownership, or by rental, lease, or lending. The offering to distribute copies or phonorecords to a group of persons for purposes of further distribution, public performance, or public display, constitutes publication. A public performance or display of a work does not of itself constitute publication.

[77] 17 U.S.C. § 401(a).

[78] H.R. Rep. No. 94-1476, 94th Cong., 2d Sess. 144 (1976). The phrase, "or elsewhere," which does not appear in the present law, makes the notice requirements applicable to copies or phonorecords distributed to the public anywhere in the world, regardless of where and when the work was first published.

[79] 17 U.S.C. § 401(a).

[80] 17 U.S.C. § 405(c); *see Fantastic Fakes, Inc. v. Pickwick Int'l, Inc.*, 661 F.2d 479 (5th Cir. 1981).

[81] *See* 17 U.S.C. §§ 401(d) and 402(d).

[82] 17 U.S.C. § 401(c). *See* H.R. Rep. No. 94-1476, 94th Cong., 2d Sess. 144 (1976).

[83] 17 U.S.C. § 401(c).

Requirements for proper notice can become ridiculously formalistic. For example, to constitute proper notice, must the "c" be surrounded by a circle (©), or will some other form of enclosure suffice, such as "c" in parentheses ((c))? The Copyright Office's final regulations reject anything but © , "Copr." or "Copyright" as specified in the 1976 Act. One court, however, has disagreed, holding that "c" surrounded by a hexagon constitutes adequate notice.[84]

What should the rule be regarding the copyright symbol? Flexibility should govern rather than technical rules about circles or parentheses, and decisions should be based on a reasonableness standard.[85] Moreover, the burden should be on the party asserting improper notice to show that the notice as given was inadequate to inform a reasonable person about a claim to copyright.[86]

[B] Form of Notice on Phonorecords for Sound Recordings

Further complicating an already technical subject, the 1976 Act sets forth a special form and position of notice for phonorecords of sound recordings.[87] For phonorecords the Act requires the symbol ℗, the year of first publication, and the name of the owner of the copyright.[88] The notice has to be placed on the surface of the phonorecord or phonorecord label or container " . . . to give reasonable notice of the claim of copyright."[89]

The form of notice required for phonorecords embodying a sound recording differs from that imposed for "copies."[90] For copies (all material objects other than phonorecords), the Act specifies three variations for the copyright symbol: ©, "Copr." or "Copyright."[91] On the other hand, for a phonorecord embodying a sound recording, only one form is specified: the symbol ℗.[92]

What justifies the special form for phonorecords of sound recordings, the symbol ℗, rather than the universal © for all tangible embodiments   copyrighted works? The House Report provides two principal reasons: the first is to distinguish claims

---

[84] 17 U.S.C. § 401(b)(1). Use of the symbol "c" without a circle around it was said to be defective in *Goldsmith v. Max*, 1978–1981 Copyright Dec. ¶ 25,248 (S.D.N.Y. 1981). In *Videotronics, Inc. v. Bend Elec.* , 586 F. Supp. 478 (D. Nev. 1984), the court suggested that the letter "c" within a parenthesis instead of a circle might constitute a defective notice, but held that a hexagonal figure which completely surrounded the "c" was an adequate substitute for a circle as used on a video screen which was incapable of producing a perfect circle.

[85] 17 U.S.C. § 401(c). H.R. Rep. No. 94–1476, 94th Cong., 2d Sess. 144 (1976):

. . . notice "shall be affixed to the copies in such manner and location as to give reasonable notice of the claim of copyright."

Subsection (c) follows " . . . the flexible approach. . . ."

[86] *Quinto v. Legal Times of Washington, Inc.*, 506 F. Supp. 554 (D.D.C. 1981); 17 U.S.C. § 406(a).

[87] 17 U.S.C. §§ 402(b) and (c).

[88] 17 U.S.C. § 402(b).

[89] 17 U.S.C. § 402(c).

[90] 17 U.S.C. §§ 401 and 402.

[91] 17 U.S.C. § 401(b)(1).

[92] 17 U.S.C. § 402(b)(1).

in the sound recording from the musical work, artistic work, or literary work embodied on it or contained on the phonorecord, album cover, or liner notes. Second, the symbol ℗ has been adopted as the international symbol by the phonogram convention.[93] These justifications hardly justify the added complexity needed to comply with copyright formalities under the 1976 Act.

[C] Year Date

Proper notice must include the year date of first publication of the work[94] on all categories of copyrightable works with one exception. The

> date may be omitted where a pictorial, graphic, or sculptural work with accompanying text matter, if any, is reproduced in or on greeting cards, postcards, stationary, jewelry, dolls, toys or any useful articles.[95]

Apart from this narrow exception, the date of first publication (not creation) must be placed on all copies or phonorecords to constitute proper notice.

[D] Name of Copyright Owner

To constitute proper notice, copies of a work have to include the name of the copyright owner.[96] The full name need not be affixed; an abbreviation by which the name can be recognized or an alternative designation of the owner is sufficient.[97] For a sound recording, when the producer of the sound recording is named on the phonorecord labels or containers and no other name appears with the symbol ℗ and year date, the producer's name shall be considered a part of the notice.[98]

[E] Location of the Notice

In contrast with the 1909 Act, the 1976 Act does not specify where on a particular work copyright notice must be affixed to constitute proper notice. The 1976 Act provides that notice shall be affixed in such a manner and location as to give reasonable notice of the claim of copyright.[99] The Register of Copyrights, pursuant to legislative authority, has issued regulations indicating where notice should be placed on various kinds of works to comply with reasonable notice requirements.[100]

---

[93] H.R. Rep. No. 94–1476, 94th Cong., 2d Sess. 145 (1976).

[94] 17 U.S.C. §§ 401(b)(2) and 402(b)(2).

[95] 17 U.S.C. § 401(b)(2).

[96] 17 U.S.C. §§ 401(b)(3) and 402(b)(3).

[97] *Id.*

[98] 17 U.S.C. § 402(b)(3).

[99] As stated in the House Report:

> A notice placed or affixed in accordance with the regulations would clearly meet the requirements but, since the Register's specifications are not to "be considered exhaustive," a notice placed or affixed in some other way might also comply with the law if it were found to "give reasonable notice" of the copyright claim.

H.R. Rep. No. 94–1476, 94th Cong., 2d Sess. 144 (1976); *see* 37 C.F.R. § 201.20 (1987).

[100] The Copyright Office's regulations pertaining to methods of affixation and position of notice are found at 37 C.F.R. § 201.20 (1987). For explanatory comment, see 46 Fed. Reg. 58,307–14 (1981).

§ 4.11   Omission of Notice

[A]   Generally

The notice provisions of the 1909 Act threatened the copyright owner with a possible loss of copyright for non-compliance.[101] Under the 1976 Act, for works published on or after January 1, 1978, and before March 1, 1989, non-compliance with notice formalities can forfeit copyright, but forfeiture is more difficult.[102] One can inject a work into the public domain under § 405 of the 1976 Act as originally enacted if notice was omitted from a substantial number of copies and if registration of the work is not made within five years of publication.[103] In addition to registration, a reasonable effort is required, upon discovering the omissions, to add notice to copies or phonorecords publicly distributed in the United States.[104] These provisions reveal that omission need not be fatal to the copyright so long as two further formalities were complied with, that is, registration of the work and an attempt to affix notice after discovery of the omission.

The BCIA amendments abrogated the notice requirement, but their effect was not retroactive. Thus, copyright owners, to save their work from falling into the public domain, were still required to use these cure provisions for omitted notice on works publicly distributed before March 1, 1989. Accordingly, a copyright owner had to avail himself of these savings provisions for all public distribution of the work even after the effective date of the BCIA. For example, suppose that a public distribution of a work with omitted notice took place on February 28, 1989, the last day before the effective date of the BCIA amendments. To save the work from forfeiture, the copyright owner had five years, until March 1, 1994, to cure omitted notice by registering the work and making a reasonable effort to add notice to works distributed after discovery of the omission.

As stated above, the BCIA amendments were prospective in effect and did not revive a work falling into the public domain for failure to apply notice after publication of the work. This conforms to the basic policy of the 1976 Act, which did not revive works in the public domain before 1978.[105] In 1993, pursuant to its responsibilities in joining the North American Free Trade Agreement (NAFTA), Congress enacted implementing legislation that would resurrect certain copyrights from the public domain. A new § 104A of the Copyright Act would restore copyrights in Mexican and Canadian motion pictures that had fallen into the United States public domain for failure to comply with the 1976 Act notice requirement.

---

[101] *See* 37 C.F.R. § 202 (1987); *Original Appalachian Artworks, Inc. v. Toy Loft, Inc.*, 684 F.2d 821, 826 (11th Cir. 1982) (copyright would have been forfeited had dolls been published in 1977). *See also* 17 U.S.C. § 10 (1909 Act).

[102] H.R. Rep. No. 94–1476, 94th Cong., 2d Sess. 147 (1976):

> Section 405(a) takes a middle-ground approach in an effort to encourage use of a copyright notice without causing unfair and unjustifiable forfeitures on technical grounds.

[103] 17 U.S.C. § 405(a).

[104] 17 U.S.C. § 405(a)(2).

[105] *See* 17 U.S.C. Transitional and Supplementary Provisions § 103.

The legislation would allow the continued use for one year of copies owned before the effective date of the amendment.[106]

The relatively modest restoration provisions of NAFTA were greatly extended the following year by the Uruguay Round Agreements Act.[107] On January 1, 1996, copyright will be automatically restored in certain works of foreign origin that entered the public domain for failure to comply with U.S. copyright formalities such as notice and renewal registration. This legislation, however, does not revive works of *U.S.* origin from the public domain. Thus, despite, the BCIA's abrogation of formalities, and the Uruguay Round's restoration provisions, a large number of works — those of U.S. origin — are unaffected by these dramatic changes in United States copyright law. Their public domain status will still be determined by compliance with notice and other formalities under prior U.S. law.

[B] Omission of Notice and Forfeiture of Copyright

For a work publicly distributed on or after January 1, 1978, and before March 1, 1989, omission of notice sufficient to forfeit copyright could only take place if the act of omission was authorized by the copyright owner.[108] Copyright is not affected if notice is somehow removed from published copies or phonorecords of the work without the authorization of the copyright owner.[109] Moreover, even if the copyright owner authorized a third party to distribute his work, these notice provisions do not apply if notice was omitted pursuant to an express written agreement between the parties that the distributor comply with the notice provisions of the 1976 Copyright Act.[110]

Even if omission of notice has taken place by authority of the copyright owner, forfeiture cannot occur (and the cure provisions need not be used) unless notice had been omitted from "more than a relatively small number of copies or phonorecords."[111] The meaning of what constitutes "more than a relatively small number"

---

[106] *See* Pub. L. No. 103–182, 107 Stat. 2115 (1993).

[107] *See* Pub. L. No. 103–465, 108 Stat. 4809 (1994); the Act's provisions are codified at 17 U.S.C. § 104A. For a discussion of restoration, see §§ 4.18–4.19 *infra*.

[108] *See Beacon Looms, Inc. v. S. Lichtenberg & Co., Inc.*, 552 F. Supp. 1305 (S.D.N.Y. 1982). *But cf.* 17 U.S.C. §§ 405(a), (b).

[109] 17 U.S.C. § 405(c). S. Rep. No. 94–473, 94th Cong., 1st Sess. 131 (1975):

> Subsection (c) of section 405 involves the situation that arises when someone in the chain of distribution removes, destroys, or obliterates the notice. The courts dealing with this problem under the present law, especially in connection with copyright notices on the selvage of textile fabrics, have generally upheld the validity of a notice that was securely attached to the copies when they left the control of the copyright owner, even though removal of the notice at some later stage was likely. This conclusion is incorporated in subsection (c).

See, e.g., Peter Pan Fabrics, Inc. v. Martin Weiner Corp., 274 F.2d 487 (2d Cir. 1960) (at least in the case of a deliberate copyist, the absence of notice is a defense that the copyist must prove, and the burden is on him to show that notice could have been embodied in the design without impairing its market value).

[110] 17 U.S.C. § 405(a)(3).

[111] 17 U.S.C. § 405(a)(1).

of copies has led to some debate. By "small number," does the Act refer to a percentage of the total distribution or to some absolute number equivalent to a small amount? The House Report is silent on this issue except to say that the provision is intended to be less restrictive than the analogous provision in § 21 of the 1909 Act.[112]

Although the case law is not totally consistent, the percentage formula has generally been adopted. Thus, the omission of notice from nine percent of garments made from fabric designs was excused,[113] while the omission of notice from 22 to 37 percent of 1,335 publicly distributed sculptural reproductions was deemed to constitute more than a relatively small number.[114] Most other courts have taken this percentage approach as well.[115]

[C] Omission of Notice: The Savings Provision

The 1976 Act includes a savings provision where notice has been omitted on more than a relatively small number of copies or phonorecords publicly distributed on or after January 1, 1978 and before March 1, 1989.[116] Under § 405(a)(2) of the 1976 Act, the copyright owner must take the following two steps:

(1) register the work before or within five years after the publication is made, and

(2) make a reasonable effort to add notice to all copies or phonorecords publicly distributed in the United States after discovery of the omission.

This important savings provision contains several ambiguities that the case law is just beginning to resolve.

The registration requirement in § 405(a)(2) is relatively straightforward. Registration can take place before or after the public distribution without notice, so long as it is accomplished within five years.[117] The effective date of registration is the day on which an application, deposit, and fee are received in the Copyright Office.[118] However, registration occurring after the five-year period will not save the copyright if notice has been omitted from more than a relatively small number of copies of the work.[119]

---

[112] H.R. Rep. No. 94–1476, 94th Cong., 2d Sess. 147 (1976).

[113] *Flora Kung, Inc. v. Items of Cal., Inc.*, 29 Pat. Trademark & Copyright J. (BNA) No. 721, at 515 (S.D.N.Y. Nov. 16, 1984).

[114] *King v. Burnett*, 1981–1983 Copy. Dec. ¶ 25,489 at 17,913 (D.D.C. 1982).

[115] *See e.g., Ford Motor Co. v. Summit Motor Prods., Inc.*, 930 F.2d 277 (3d Cir. 1991), *cert. denied*, 112 S. Ct. 373, 116 L. Ed. 2d 325 (1991) (four million copies without notice out of 100 million constituted a relatively small number).

[116] 17 U.S.C. § 405(a)(2).

[117] *See Original Appalachian Artworks, Inc. v. Toy Loft, Inc.*, 684 F.2d 821 (11th Cir. 1982) (registration effectuated within five years of the date of first publication).

[118] 17 U.S.C. § 410(d):

Where the three necessary elements [of application, deposit, and fee] are received at different times, the date of receipt of the last of them is controlling. . . .

H.R. Rep. No. 94–1476, 94th Cong., 2d Sess. 157 (1976).

[119] *Id.* at 147.

The second aspect of § 405(a)(2), requires a reasonable effort to add notice to all copies or phonorecords that are publicly distributed in the United States after the omission has been discovered.[120] This section presents two particularly controversial issues. First, what constitutes a reasonable effort after discovery? Second, can deliberate omissions of notice be cured under § 405(a)(3)?

The second question has spawned litigation despite a clear indication in the legislative history that deliberate omissions can be cured. According to the House Report, a work published without any copyright notice will be subject to statutory protection for at least five years whether the omission was partial or total, unintentional or deliberate.[121]

The Second Circuit, in *Hasbro Bradley, Inc. v. Sparkle Toys, Inc.*,[122] adopted the House Report's view that the cure provisions of § 405(a)(2) extend to deliberate as well as inadvertent omissions of notice. In this case, the plaintiff, a toy manufacturer, brought an action to enjoin an admitted copyist from distributing its *Transformer* brand robot toys in the United States. The defendant claimed that copyright was forfeited by the Japanese company, the assignor to Hasbro and the originator of the toys, in deliberately omitting notice from 213,000 of the toys sold in Asia. The defendant relied on *Beacon Looms, Inc. v. S. Lichtenberg & Co., Inc.*,[123] which held that a deliberate omission of notice cannot be cured because, under the words of the statute, such an omission cannot be "discovered."[124] The defendant reasoned that this would preclude a cure for a deliberate omission of notice. The court rejected this premise, stating that the assignor's deliberate omission of notice was indeed discovered by the assignee who was then attempting to cure the omission. The Second Circuit also relied on the drafters' desire to avoid murky questions of proof relating to subjective intent.

In addition to registration, § 405(a)(2) requires that the copyright owner make a reasonable effort to add notice to all copies or phonorecords that are publicly distributed before March 1, 1989 in the United States after the omission has been discovered.[125] By this provision, the copyright owner does not have to make a reasonable effort to add notice to copies already possessed by members of the public.[126] On the other hand, the copyright owner has a clear duty to affix notice

120 17 U.S.C. § 405(a)(2). *See Original Appalachian Artworks, Inc. v. Toy Loft, Inc.*, 684 F.2d 821 (11th Cir. 1982) (registration without "reasonable effort" will not excuse notice omission).
121 H.R. Rep. No. 94–1476, 94th Cong., 2d Sess. 147 (1976).
122 780 F.2d 189 (2d Cir. 1985).
123 552 F. Supp. 1305 (S.D.N.Y. 1982).
124 17 U.S.C. § 405(a)(2).
125 *See generally* 2 *Nimmer on Copyright* § 7.13[B] (1993).
126 *See, e.g., Midway Mfg. Co. v. Artic Int'l, Inc.*, 704 F.2d 1009, 1013 (7th Cir.), *cert. denied*, 464 U.S. 823 (1983) (plaintiff did not lose copyright in video games, even if published without notice in Japan, when copyright was registered within five years and all copies distributed in United States contained notice); *Hagendorf v. Brown*, 707 F.2d 1018, 1019 (9th Cir. 1983) (publication without notice did not forfeit protection if registration occurred within five years of publication and no copies were distributed in United States after omission was discovered or, if distribution occurred, the author made a reasonable effort to add notice to copies distributed).

to copies still in his possession awaiting distribution.[127] Does the duty of reasonable effort to affix notice extend to copies distributed before discovery, no longer in the copyright owner's possession, but which have not yet reached the public? In other words, does the copyright owner have to make a reasonable effort to add notice to copies held by wholesalers or retailers?[128] Some sort of reasonable effort to add notice must be made by the copyright owner. From the language of the statute, copies held by retailers and wholesalers are still to be distributed to the public.

It is unclear what constitutes a reasonable effort in attempting to affix notice for those copies.[129] The reasonable effort requirement is a question of fact to be worked out under the circumstances of each case. But as one court states:

> Implicit in the concept . . . is the expectation that an expenditure of time and money over and above that required in the normal course of business will be made.[130]

In short, until the courts have filled in more details, a prudent copyright owner should promptly supply retailers with a sufficient means to affix notice to the pertinent copies.

[D]　Innocent Infringement

As previously indicated, the most severe consequence of omission of notice for works publicly distributed on or after January 1, 1978 and before March 1, 1989, is that it may lead to an eventual forfeiture of copyright.[131] Omitted notice can lead to another adverse consequence which also applies to works distributed after March 1, 1989. Section 405(b) limits remedies against innocent infringers misled by lack of notice.[132]

Section 405(b) applies only to innocent infringers who can prove they were misled by omission of notice from an authorized copy of the work. Once the infringer meets this burden, this section shields him against liability for actual damages and statutory

---

[127] *See Videotronics, Inc. v. Bend Elec.*, 586 F. Supp. 478 (D. Nev. 1984) (fact that notice was omitted from only 28 copies was irrelevant in view of "all copies" requirement).

[128] *See Shapiro & Son Bedspread Corp. v. Royal Mills Associates*, 568 F. Supp. 972 (S.D.N.Y. 1983), *rev'd on other grounds*, 764 F.2d 69 (2d Cir. 1985) (plaintiff's motion for preliminary injunction denied because it had not made reasonable efforts to replace defective notice with proper notice); *Beacon Looms, Inc. v. S. Lichtenberg & Co.*, 552 F. Supp. 1305, 1313 (S.D.N.Y. 1982).

[129] *Beacon Looms, Inc. v. S. Lichtenberg & Co.*, 552 F. Supp. 1305 (S.D.N.Y. 1982) (held that where some 900,000 units not bearing a copyright notice had been sold to retail dealers, the sending of only 50,000 labels bearing a notice to such dealers, without ascertaining the number of units still held in the dealers' inventories, failed to comply with the "reasonable effort" requirement).

[130] *Videotronics, Inc. v. Bend Elec.*, 586 F. Supp. 478, 483 (D. Nev. 1984).

[131] Where copyright notice is required and its omission is not excused under 17 U.S.C. § 405(a), the legal consequence is forfeiture of the copyright and release of the work into the public domain. *Shapiro & Son Bedspread Corp. v. Royal Mills Assoc.*, 568 F. Supp. 972 (S.D.N.Y. 1983), *rev'd on other grounds*, 764 F.2d 69 (2d Cir. 1985).

[132] *See* 17 U.S.C. § 405(b).

damages and, although not specified, probably attorney's fees as well.[133] This limitation lasts until the infringer is put on notice of the claim to copyright, as actual knowledge bars innocent infringement.[134] On the other hand, the court has the discretion to allow recovery for profits made by the infringing acts and to enjoin further infringements or, in the appropriate case, to allow the infringing acts to continue upon payment of a reasonable license fee.

Despite the concern for those who may have innocently relied on omission of notice from an authorized copy of the work, it seems contradictory that there can be any innocent infringement when copyright protection, on or after January 1, 1978, begins automatically on creation.[135] Further, as indicated by the House Report, persons who plan to undertake major enterprises based on copies of works lacking notice should check the records of the Copyright Office before starting a project.[136] In accordance with this view, one court has held that one cannot be an innocent infringer misled by lack of notice if a search of the Copyright Office records would have revealed the registration.[137]

§ 4.12 Error in Name and Date

[A] Generally

Under the 1909 Act, errors in name and date could inject copyright into the public domain.[138] By comparison, the 1976 Act specifies that an error in name will not affect the validity or ownership of copyright. However, certain errors in date for works publicly distributed on or after January 1, 1978 and before March 1, 1989 are considered omissions of notice subjecting the copyright owner to possible forfeiture. For errors in both name and date, innocent infringers can avoid liability if misled by these errors.[139] For works publicly distributed on or after March 1, 1989, errors in name or date will not affect validity or duration of copyright, but the copyright owner will not benefit from the evidentiary weight of proper notice provided in §§ 401(d) and 402(d), which deprive a defendant of an innocent infringement defense in mitigation of actual or statutory damages.

[B] Error in Name

When the name of the copyright owner is incorrect in the copyright notice, copyright validity or ownership is not affected.[140] However, § 406 provides a

---

[133] 17 U.S.C. § 405(b). 3 *Nimmer on Copyright* § 14.10[D] (1993); S. Rep. No. 473, 94th Cong., 1st Sess. 131 (1975) (courts have broad discretion to grant or limit damages, depending upon the specific situation).

[134] *See Aitken, Hazen, Hoffman, Miller, P.C. v. Empire Constr. Co.*, 542 F. Supp. 252 (D. Neb. 1982).

[135] 17 U.S.C. § 102(a).

[136] H.R. Rep. No. 94–1476, 94th Cong., 2d Sess. 148 (1976).

[137] *Quinto v. Legal Times of Washington, Inc.*, 506 F. Supp. 554 (D.D.C. 1981).

[138] 17 U.S.C. § 10 (1909 Act). *See* 17 C.F.R. § 202.2 (1987).

[139] 17 U.S.C. §§ 405(b) and 406(a).

[140] 17 U.S.C. § 406(a) (the BCIA). *See Fantastic Fakes, Inc. v. Pickwick Int'l, Inc.*, 661 F.2d 479 (5th Cir. 1981).

complete defense to a person

> . . . who innocently begins an undertaking that infringes the copyright . . .
> if such person proves that he or she was misled by the notice and began the
> undertaking in good faith under a purported transfer . . . from the person
> named therein. . . .[141]

What constitutes "an undertaking begun in good faith" was examined in *Quinto
v. Legal Times of Washington, Inc.*[142] In *Quinto,* the defendant reprinted an article
that had been published in the Harvard Law Review. The article did not bear
copyright notice, although there was a blanket notice in the masthead of the
publication. The defendant published the article verbatim after receiving general
permission to do so from the editor of the student journal, but without inquiring
further into the copyright status of the article and without trying to contact the author.
The court concluded that the good faith defense was not available and

> . . . that good faith in the context of this case entails not only honesty in fact
> but reasonableness as well.[143]

Accordingly, the defendant had a duty to inquire as to who owned the copyright.[144]

Even if a person shows he or she was misled by the notice and began the undertaking in good faith under a transfer from the person named in the notice, the defense
of good faith does not apply if before the undertaking was begun:

> (1) registration for the work had been made in the name of the owner of
> copyright; or

> (2) a document executed by the person named in the notice and showing the
> ownership of the copyright had been recorded.[145]

[C] Error in Date

Antedated and post-dated notices are governed by § 406(b).[146] For works
publicly distributed on or after January 1, 1978, and before March 1, 1989, bearing
an antedated notice (stating a date of publication earlier than the actual publication
date), duration of copyright is measured from that date. On the other hand, if the
year date in the notice was more than one year later than the year date of publication,
such notice is deemed to be an omission of notice and is treated under the provisions
of § 405. For example, if A publishes his work on Feburary 28, 1989, but affixes
at that time a notice date of 1991, the post-dated notice is treated as no notice at
all, being more than one year later than the actual publication date for the work.
Here the copyright owner must avail himself of the cure provisions of § 405
(registration within five years and reasonable attempt to add notice) or face forfeiture
of copyright. For works published on or after March 1, 1989, neither antedated nor

---

[141] 17 U.S.C. § 406(a).
[142] 506 F. Supp. 554 (D.D.C. 1981).
[143] *Id.* at 562.
[144] *Id.* at 563.
[145] 17 U.S.C. §§ 406(a)(1) and (2).
[146] 17 U.S.C. § 406(b).

post-dated notice has any effect on duration or validity of copyright, but the provisions of §§ 401(d) and 402(d), concerning the evidentiary weight of proper notice, will not benefit the copyright owner.

[D] Omission of Name or Date

For works publicly distributed on or after January 1, 1978, and before March 1, 1989, complete omission of the name or date from copyright notice is treated as an omission of notice under § 405.[147] The 1976 Act contains no provision that the elements of notice must be directly contiguous or accompany one another.[148] On the other hand, if the elements of notice are too widely separated for their relationship to be reasonably apparent, this situation will be treated as an omission of notice.[149]

§ 4.13   Special Notice Subsections

[A] Notice for Publications Containing Government Works

Works produced by the United States Government are precluded from copyright protection and are in the public domain.[150] Often government documents are published commercially along with new matter added by the publisher, such as introductions, illustrations, and editing. Although copyrightable subject matter is added by the publisher, the great bulk of the work may consist of a public domain governmental work. Section 403 attempts to avoid the misleading nature of a notice of copyright in publications containing government works by requiring that when copies or phonorecords consist preponderantly of one or more works of the United States Government, the copyright notice must identify that part of the work in which copyright is claimed.[151] For works published on or after January 1, 1978 and before March 1, 1989, failure to do so is treated as an omission of notice under § 405.[152] Section 403 has now been amended by the BCIA. For works published on or after March 1, 1989, an absence of an identifying statement will deprive the copyright owner of the evidentiary weight of proper notice under §§ 401(d) and 402(d), but will not invalidate copyright in the work.[153]

[B] Notice for Contribution to Collective Works

Under the 1909 Act, it was unclear what constituted proper notice for a contribution to a collective work. Section 404 of the 1976 Act attempted to solve

---

[147] 17 U.S.C. § 406(c).

[148] H.R. Rep. No. 94–1476, 94th Cong., 2d Sess. 150 (1976). •

[149] *Id.*

[150] 17 U.S.C. § 105.

[151] 17 U.S.C. § 403.

[152] H.R. Rep. No. 94–1476, 94th Cong., 2d Sess. 146 (1976).

[153] *See* 17 U.S.C. § 403.

this traditionally troublesome problem.[154] The basic approach of this section is summarized in the House Report[155] as follows:

(1) to permit but not require a separate contribution to bear its own notice;

(2) to make a single notice covering the entire collective work as a whole sufficient to satisfy the notice requirement for each contribution it contains; and

(3) to protect the interests of the innocent infringer of copyright in a contribution that does not bear its own notice, who has dealt in good faith with the person named in the notice covering the collective work as a whole.

Section 404 provides that for works publicly distributed before March 1, 1989, the copyright owner of an individual contribution need not affix notice to his individual work to protect the copyright from forfeiture, so long as notice is affixed by the owner of the collective work.[156] However, for works publicly distributed on or after January 1, 1978, and before March 1, 1989, the 1976 Act allows a defense of good faith infringement by a person misled by an improper name in the notice.[157]

For works publicly distributed on or after March 1, 1989, there is no longer any obligation to affix notice to protect the validity of copyright in a separate contribution to a collective work. However, so long as a single notice appears in the name of the collective work owner, the owner of a contribution can benefit from the new §§ 401(d) and 402(d), which disallow the defense of innocent infringement in mitigation of actual or statutory damages.[158]

A special problem occurs where an advertisement is placed in a collective work by persons other than the owners of copyright in the collective work.[159] For example, suppose that an advertisement is placed in a magazine consisting of several articles written by outside authors. The general copyright notice in the collective work does not protect the advertisement as it did the authors of the individual contributions to the collective work. For works publicly distributed on or after January 1, 1978, and before March 1, 1989, the copyright in the advertisement is not protected by notice in the collective work, and if notice was not affixed to the advertisement, the work faces forfeiture of copyright by this omission of notice.[160] For works publicly distributed on or after March 1, 1989, copyright in the advertisement cannot be invalidated by this omission of notice, but the provisions of §§ 401(d) and 402(d), which disallow the defense of innocent infringement in mitigation of actual or statutory damages, will not benefit the copyright owner.

---

[154] 17 U.S.C. § 404.

[155] H.R. Rep. No. 94–1476, 94th Cong., 2d Sess. 146 (1976).

[156] *See Quinto v. Legal Times of Washington, Inc.*, 506 F. Supp. 554 (D.D.C. 1981).

[157] *See* 17 U.S.C. § 406(a).

[158] *See* 17 U.S.C. §§ 401(d) and 402(d). These sections allow no evidentiary weight to be given to a defense of innocent infringement when proper notice has been affixed to the work.

[159] *See* 17 U.S.C. § 404(a).

[160] H.R. Rep. No. 94–1476, 94th Cong., 2d Sess. 146 (1976).

§ 4.14 Notice Under the 1909 Act

[A] Generally

The highly technical notice provisions of the 1909 Act, with all their pitfalls, often led to the inadvertent forfeiture of copyright.[161] These notice provisions are still important today. The reason is that neither the 1976 Act as originally enacted nor the BCIA amendments will revive a work that went into the public domain before January 1, 1978. With passage of the Uruguay Round Agreements Act, copyrighted works originating from Berne or WTO countries that were injected into the public domain for failure to comply with U.S. copyright formalities are automatically restored to copyright. Works of U.S. origin, however, will stay in the public domain.[162] Thus, determination of the status of a work published before January 1, 1978, requires looking to the provisions of the 1909 Act.[163]

The important notice provision under the 1909 Act is § 10, specifying that

> [a]ny person entitled thereto by this title may secure copyright for his work by publication thereof with the notice of copyright required by this title; and such notice shall be affixed to each copy thereof published or offered for sale in the United States by authority of the copyright proprietor. . . .[164]

Section 10, by its use of the words "may secure copyright," appears to treat affixation of notice as discretionary for the protection of copyright. To the contrary, however, proper notice was required under the 1909 Act, and an omitted or defective notice on published copies of the work could inject it into the public domain.[165] Moreover, the savings provisions found in § 405(a)[166] of the 1976 Act are not available in the 1909 Act.[167]

[B] Form of Notice

Sections 19 through 21 of the 1909 Act[168] set forth the requirements for proper notice, consisting of the three common elements: the copyright symbol, the proprietor's name, and the year date of first publication. Despite this broad similarity, the requirements for proper notice under the 1909 Act differ from those under the 1976 Act.

As for the copyright symbol: "©," "Copr.," or "Copyright" was sufficient.[169] The

---

[161] Id.

[162] See 17 U.S.C. § 104A. The restoration provisions are discussed at §§ 4.18–4.19 infra.

[163] 17 U.S.C. § 301(a).

[164] 17 U.S.C. § 10 (1909 Act).

[165] 17 U.S.C. § 10 (1909 Act). See, e.g., Original Appalachian Artworks, Inc. v. Toy Loft, Inc., 684 F.2d 821, 826 (11th Cir. 1982) (copyright would have been forfeited had work been published in 1977); Bessett v. Germain, 18 F. Supp. 249 (D. Mass. 1937); United Thrift Plan, Inc. v. National Thrift Plan, Inc., 34 F.2d 300 (E.D.N.Y. 1929).

[166] 17 U.S.C. § 405(a).

[167] H.R. Rep. No. 94–1476, 94th Cong., 2d Sess. 146 (1976).

[168] 17 U.S.C. §§ 19–21 (1909 Act).

[169] 17 U.S.C. § 19 (1909 Act).

1909 Act did not recognize wide variations from these three recognized forms.[170] However, to promote a minimum of disfigurement for works of art,[171] the 1909 Act allowed a short form of notice for pictorial, graphic, and sculptural works. Here, an initial monogram or trade symbol accompanied by "©" constitutes proper notice.[172] However, if the symbol was not identified with the copyright owner, his name had to appear on some accessible portion of the work such as a margin, back or permanent base, or pedestal.[173] Although the 1976 Act does not provide a similar short form of notice, works published before January 1, 1978 may continue to affix the same short form of notice on copies published afterwards.[174]

[C] Location of Notice

The 1909 Act prescribed specific locations for notice on books, periodicals, and musical works.[175] If the copyright owner did not comply with these specific location provisions, the work could be injected into the public domain for lack of proper notice.[176] A reasonable notice standard applied for other kinds of works such as motion pictures and pictorial, graphic, or sculptural works.[177]

Often highly technical questions arose about the location of notice on repetitive designs such as gift wrapping or dress fabric. One early case required notice of copyright on each design.[178] Later case law loosened this formalistic approach. For example, in *H. M. Kolbe Co., Inc. v. Armgus Textile Co.*,[179] the court held that notice placed every sixteen inches on the selvage of the plaintiff's checkerboard rose design constituted proper notice. Similarly, in *Peter Pan Fabrics, Inc. v. Martin Weiner Corp.*,[180] a flexible approach was taken to notice of copyright placed on the selvage of a fabric design which would either be cut off from the fabric or rendered undetectable on a dress. Here, Learned Hand adopted a "commercial impairment test" in which, at least in the case of a deliberate copyist, the defendant has the burden to show that notice could have been embodied in the design without impairing its market value.

---

[170] *Fleischer Studios, Inc. v. Ralph A. Freundlich, Inc.*, 73 F.2d 276 (2d Cir. 1934); *American Code Co. v. Bensinger*, 282 F. 829 (2d Cir. 1922).

[171] *Hearings on S. 6330 and H.R. 19–853 Before the Committees on Patents*, 59th Cong., 1st Sess. 97–100 (1906).

[172] *See* 17 U.S.C. § 19 (1909 Act); *Puddu v. Buonamici Statuary, Inc.*, 450 F.2d 401 (2d Cir. 1971); *Dan Kasoff, Inc. v. Palmer Jewelry Mfg. Co.*, 171 F. Supp. 603 (S.D.N.Y. 1959); *Hollywood Jewelry Mfg. Co. v. Dushkin*, 136 F. Supp. 738 (S.D.N.Y. 1955).

[173] 17 U.S.C. § 19 (1909 Act).

[174] 17 U.S.C. Trans. & Supp. Prov. § 108.

[175] 17 U.S.C. § 20 (1909 Act).

[176] *See, e.g., United Thrift Plan v. National Thrift Plan*, 34 F.2d 300 (E.D.N.Y. 1929) (a notice in proper form but on the last page of a ten-page booklet was held equivalent to no notice at all).

[177] *See Coventry Ware, Inc. v. Reliance Picture Frame Co.*, 288 F.2d 193 (2d Cir. 1961); *Scarves by Vera, Inc. v. United Merchants and Mfrs., Inc.*, 173 F. Supp. 625 (S.D.N.Y. 1959); *Trifari, Krussman & Fishel, Inc. v. Charel Co., Inc.*, 134 F. Supp. 551 (S.D.N.Y. 1955).

[178] *DeJonge & Co. v. Breaker de Kassler Co.*, 235 U.S. 33 (1914).

[179] 315 F.2d 70 (2d Cir. 1963).

[180] 274 F.2d 487 (2d Cir. 1960).

[D]   Year Date

The requirements for affixing the year date are less specific under the 1909 Act than under the 1976 Act. The year date of first publication was required only for printed literary, musical, dramatic works[181] and sound recordings.[182] For other works, such as motion pictures and pictorial works, the copyright symbol and copyright owner's name sufficed.[183]

[E]   Omission of Notice

Section 21 of the 1909 Act provided:

> Where the copyright proprietor has sought to comply with the provisions of this title with respect to notice, the omission by accident or mistake of the prescribed notice from a particular copy or copies shall not invalidate the copyright or prevent recovery for infringement against any person who, after actual notice of the copyright, begins an undertaking to infringe it. . . .[184]

This provision appears to be similar to that of the original notice provisions of the 1976 Act,[185] but there are significant differences. Section 21 applied only to accidents or mistakes due to some sort of mechanical failure[186] in affixing notice, and not to inadvertence[187] or mistake of law.[188] In addition, the copyright owner must have omitted notice on a particular copy or copies; an omission of notice from all of the copies would not be excused by § 21.[189] How "few" are a "few"? The

---

[181] 17 U.S.C. § 19 (1909 Act); *see Wildman v. New York Times Co.*, 42 F. Supp. 412 (S.D.N.Y. 1941).

[182] 17 U.S.C. § 19 (1909 Act).

[183] *Advertisers Exch., Inc. v. Anderson*, 144 F.2d 907 (8th Cir. 1944); *Abli, Inc. v. Standard Brands Paint Co.*, 323 F. Supp. 1400 (C.D. Cal. 1970); *Florence Art Co. v. Quartite Creative Corp.*, 158 U.S.P.Q. 382 (N.D. Ill. 1968); *Leigh v. Gerber,* 86 F. Supp. 320 (S.D.N.Y. 1949).

[184] 17 U.S.C. § 21 (1909 Act).

[185] 17 U.S.C. § 405(a)(1).

[186] *Leon B. Rosenblatt Textiles, Ltd. v. M. Lowenstein & Sons, Inc.*, 321 F. Supp. 186 (S.D.N.Y. 1970); *Florence Art Co., Inc. v. Quartite Creative Corp.*, 158 U.S.P.Q. 382 (N.D. Ill. 1968) (copyright upheld where mechanical difficulties led to partial obliteration of notice on some copies—§ 21 not expressly invoked); *Strauss v. Penn Printing & Publishing Co.*, 220 F. 977 (E.D. Pa. 1915).

[187] *Seiff v. Continental Auto Supply, Inc.*, 39 F. Supp. 683 (D. Minn. 1941); *Basevi v. Edward O'Toole Co.*, 26 F. Supp. 41 (S.D.N.Y. 1939). *But cf. Rexnord, Inc. v. Modern Handling Sys., Inc.*, 379 F. Supp. 1190, 1197 (D. Del. 1974) (omission of notice " . . . must occur despite [the claimant's] efforts to the contrary; it must be, in short, inadvertent").

[188] *Puddu v. Buonamici Statuary, Inc.*, 450 F.2d 401 (2d Cir. 1971); *Rexnord, Inc. v. Modern Handling Sys., Inc.*, 379 F. Supp. 1190 (D. Del. 1974); *Gardenia Flowers, Inc. v. Joseph Markovits, Inc.*, 280 F. Supp. 776 (S.D.N.Y. 1968); *Wildman v. New York Times Co.*, 42 F. Supp. 412 (S.D.N.Y. 1941).

[189] *Data Cash Systems, Inc. v. JS & A Group, Inc.*, 628 F.2d 1038 (7th Cir. 1980); *Puddu v. Buonamici Statuary, Inc.*, 450 F.2d 401 (2d Cir. 1971); *Krafft v. Cohen*, 117 F.2d 579 (3d Cir. 1941); *J. A. Richards, Inc. v. New York Post, Inc.*, 23 F. Supp. 619 (S.D.N.Y. 1938).

case law suggests a percentage test. The court in *American Greetings Corp. v. Kleinfarb Corp.*[190] indicated that § 21 applied where the copyright owner omitted notice from 500,000 of 22 million copies, or two percent of the total number of copies.

[F]   U.S. Works First Published Outside the United States

The notice requirement is not just limited to works published in the United States. The 1976 Act, as originally enacted, required that notice be placed on works published here or abroad.[191] The House Report justifies this requirement because of the great flow of works across national boundaries.[192] To protect economic and proprietary interests in this intellectual material, the notice requirement applied equally to works published abroad.[193]

Whether the copyright owner had to abide by the formalities of the 1909 Act for works published abroad has never been resolved.[194] This, of course, is a relevant consideration as stated before. First, one may have to determine whether a work has entered the public domain before 1978 for failure to comply with the notice requirement.[195] Second, for works published after 1978, the copyright owner has the option to choose the 1909 or 1976 Act's notice requirements.[196]

The leading case interpreting the 1909 Act's requirement for works published abroad is *Heim v. Universal Pictures Co.*[197] In *Heim,* the court took the position that publication abroad without notice did not place a work into the public domain. Justice Frank argued that because § 9 of the 1909 Act merely required that "notice be affixed to each copy published or offered for sale in the United States,"[198] its provisions apply only to U.S. publications.[199] The contrary view argues that § 10's first clause,

---

[190] 400 F. Supp. 228, 231 (S.D.N.Y. 1975).

[191] 17 U.S.C. § 401(a). The use of the phrase "or elsewhere" indicates that the requirements of notice are applicable to foreign editions of works copyrighted in the United States. H.R. Rep. No. 94–1476, 94th Cong., 2d Sess. 144 (1976).

[192] H.R. Rep. No. 94–1476, 94th Cong., 2d Sess. 144 (1976).

[193] *See Hasbro Bradley, Inc. v. Sparkle Toys, Inc.,* 780 F.2d 189 (2d Cir. 1985) (U.S. law requires notice even on copies of the work distributed outside the United States).

[194] Common law copyright protection in the United States was lost upon publication of the work, even if publication occurred abroad. *Hill & Range Songs, Inc. v. London Records, Inc.,* 142 N.Y.S.2d 311 (Sup. Ct. 1955). *See McKay v. Barbour,* 199 Misc. 893, 107 N.Y.S.2d 113 (Sup. Ct. 1950). Publications occurring within the United States must bear the required notice under the 1909 Act to command statutory copyright protection.

[195] *Data Cash Systems, Inc. v. JS & A Group, Inc.,* 628 F.2d 1038 (7th Cir. 1980); *Conner v. Mark I, Inc.,* 509 F. Supp. 1179 (N.D. Ill. 1981); *Excel Promotions Corp. v. Babylon Beacon, Inc.,* 207 U.S.P.Q. 616 (E.D.N.Y. 1979).

[196] 17 U.S.C. Trans. & Supp. Prov. § 108.

[197] 154 F.2d 480 (2d Cir. 1946).

[198] *Id.* at 486.

[199] 17 U.S.C. § 10 (1909 Act); *G. & C. Merriam Co. v. United Dictionary Co.,* 146 F. 354 (7th Cir. 1906), *aff'd,* 208 U.S. 260 (1908).

[a]ny person entitled thereto by this title may secure copyright for his work by publication thereof with the notice of copyright required by this title . . .,[200]

would require notice as set forth in §§ 19 and 20,[201] and that the second clause of the section applies only to preservation of copyright for works on which copyright has already been secured.[202]

PART III: THE MANUFACTURING CLAUSE

§ 4.15 The Demise But Continuing Importance of the Manufacturing Clause

The manufacturing clause, a prominent feature of both the 1909 and 1976 Copyright Acts, prohibited importation into the United States of English language literary works by American authors unless the works were manufactured, printed, and bound in the United States or Canada.[203]

The manufacturing clause was in effect protectionist legislation, benefiting American printers at the expense of American authors. A unique and much criticized feature of American law since 1891,[204] the manufacturing clause has been a trap for unwary authors, a barrier to United States' participation in the Berne Union, and a violation of the General Agreement on Tariffs and Trade.[205] Fortunately, by its own terms, § 601 of the 1976 Act expired on July 1, 1986.[206]

Even though the manufacturing clause is currently dead, it cannot be totally ignored. It is of continuing, though limited importance, because of its effect on non-complying works under both the 1976 Act and the 1909 Act. The following sections outline the 1976 and 1909 Acts' versions of the manufacturing clause, examining first what it entailed and then turning to the effect of non-compliance with its provisions.

---

[200] 17 U.S.C. § 10 (1909 Act).

[201] 17 U.S.C. §§ 19, 20 (1909 Act).

[202] 2 *Nimmer on Copyright* § 7.12[D][2][a] (1993).

[203] Under the 1976 Act, the work could be manufactured in Canada as well as the United States. *See* 17 U.S.C. § 601(a). Under the 1909 Act, only the United States could be the place of manufacture. *See* 17 U.S.C. § 16 (1909 Act).

[204] 26 Stat. 1106 (1891).

[205] General Agreement on Tariffs and Trade (GATT), 55 U.N.T.S. 194, T.I.A.S. No. 1700.

[206] Section 601 was originally to be repealed as of July 1, 1982, though the House Report suggests the even earlier date of January 1, 1981. *See* H.R. Rep. No. 94–1476, 94th Cong., 2d Sess. 166 (1976). Section 602 was amended by Pub. L. No. 97–215, 96 Stat. 178 (1982), to extend the date of repeal to July 1, 1986. President Reagan vetoed the Act of July 13, 1982, but the veto was overridden by the House and the Senate, and § 601 expired on July 1, 1986.

§ 4.16 The Manufacturing Clause Under the 1976 Act

[A] Generally

The subject matter of the manufacturing clause extends to " . . . copies of a work consisting preponderantly of nondramatic literary material that is in the English language. . . ."[207] Other varieties of copyrightable subject matter such as pictorial, graphic, and sculptural works were exempted from the provisions of the manufacturing clause. Importation of copies falling into these narrow confines is prohibited if these works were not manufactured[208] in the United States or Canada.

[B] The "Preponderantly" Requirement

Works were subject to the manufacturing requirement only if "preponderantly" of nondramatic literary material in English; the non-dramatic literary material must have exceeded the exempted material in "importance." Thus, a book consisting of graphics, photographs or illustrations with a short preface, brief captions, and an index in English would not meet the "preponderantly" standard.[209] But even if the English language portions of the book were extensive enough to meet the "preponderantly" test, only those aspects would be required to be manufactured in the United States. The manufacture of the pictorial portion of the book outside the United States or Canada would not be a violation of the manufacturing clause.

[C] Exceptions to the Manufacturing Provisions

The manufacturing clause was subject to several exceptions.[210] It applied only to American authors and domiciliaries on the date of importation or distribution of a work into the United States. Copies imported for personal use, use by federal or state government, educational, scholarly or religious purposes, and works in Braille were exempt. In addition, two thousand copies of a non-complying work could be imported pursuant to certain formalities. Finally, individual authors who arranged for manufacture of the first publication abroad were exempt.

[D] Effect of Non-Compliance Under the 1976 Act

Failure to comply with the manufacturing clause did not result in forfeiture of copyright. The sanctions imposed were less drastic but nonetheless serious. The

---

[207] 17 U.S.C. § 601(a).

[208] What constitutes "manufacture" is a highly technical question. Some of these complexities are reflected in *The Compendium of Copyright Office Practices,* Chs. 1210, 1211 (1984), which tries to define the meaning of the term in light of 17 U.S.C. § 601(c).

[209] *See generally* H.R. Rep. No. 94–1476, 94th Cong., 2d Sess. 166–67 (1976). However, in *Stonehill Communications, Inc. v. Martuge,* 512 F. Supp. 349 (S.D.N.Y. 1981), the court found the "importance" test suggested by the House Report too vague for practical application. The court adopted instead an objective or mechanical test such that " . . . a book 'consists of preponderantly nondram[a]tic literary material . . . in the English language' when more than half of its surface area, exclusive of margins, consists of English-language text." *Id.* at 352.

[210] *See* 17 U.S.C. § 601(b).

non-complying copies could be seized, forfeited, and destroyed by the Department of the Treasury and U.S. Postal Service.[211] In addition, violation constituted a complete defense in any civil or criminal action for infringement of the copyright owner's exclusive rights to reproduce and distribute his work.[212] To raise this defense the infringer had to prove: (1) that the copyright owner imported non-complying copies of the work, (2) that the infringing copies were manufactured in the U.S. or Canada, and (3) "that the infringement was commenced before the effective date of registration for an authorized edition of the work. . . ."[213] The defense extended not only to the non-dramatic literary aspects of the work, but also to aspects such as photographs or foreign language materials, if the same copyright owner owned both types of materials. Although the manufacturing clause has expired, its violation can arguably be used as a defense against a non-complying work publicly distributed between January 1, 1978 and July 1, 1986, the expiration date of the manufacturing clause. Thus, the possibility of a defense based on plaintiff's noncompliance remains until the copyright owner registers an American edition in compliance with the law.

§ 4.17   The Manufacturing Clause Under the 1909 Act

[A]   Generally

The manufacturing clause under the 1909 Act was more restrictive than under the 1976 Copyright Act. Section 16 of the 1909 Act established the major requirements.[214] Under its terms, any printed book or periodical in the English language, as well as foreign language books of American authors, had to be manufactured in the United States. Canadian manufacture was prohibited under the 1909 Act as well. The manufacturing clause requirements encompassed not just the texts of books, but the illustrations as well.

[B]   *Ad Interim* Protection

Under the 1909 Act manufacturing clause, *ad interim* copyright protection could be obtained for English language books and periodicals manufactured abroad.[215] To secure *ad interim* protection, the claimant had to deposit and register the *ad interim* claim in the U.S. Copyright Office within six months of first publication abroad. Fifteen hundred copies of the work could then be imported into the United States within six months of foreign publication. *Ad interim* protection endured for five years, measured from the date of publication abroad. If, within the five year period, an edition of the work was published in compliance with the manufacturing clause, the work could claim a 28-year copyright term, measured from the date of its first publication. According to some case law, failure to register within the

---

[211] *See* 17 U.S.C. § 603(a).

[212] *See* 17 U.S.C. § 601(d).

[213] *See* 17 U.S.C. § 601(d)(3).

[214] 17 U.S.C. § 16 (1909 Act).

[215] *See generally* 2 *Nimmer on Copyright* § 7.23[F] (1988).

six-month period and failure to publish the complying edition within the five-year period resulted in the loss of copyright protection.[216]

[C] Forfeiture by False Affidavit and General Non-Compliance

Under § 17 of the 1909 Act,[217] anyone depositing a work with the Copyright Office also had to submit an affidavit swearing that manufacturing clause requirements had been met. Section 18 provided that knowingly making a false affidavit forfeited copyright.[218] It was unclear, however, whether failure to comply with manufacturing clause requirements without making a knowingly false affidavit resulted in forfeiture of copyright.

Whether the work was injected into the public domain is a matter of controversy. The answer to this question is important because works going into the public domain are not revived by the 1976 Act or by the subsequent Berne Convention Implementation Act amendments. Although the case law is not clear on this issue, the better view is that non-compliance did not inject a work into the public domain.[219] Section 18 specifically provided for forfeiture when a knowingly false affidavit is submitted, whereas forfeiture is not mentioned as the result of general non-compliance with manufacturing requirements. This implies that forfeiture did not occur except where expressly stated.

PART IV: RESTORATION OF COPYRIGHT IN WORKS PREVIOUSLY IN THE PUBLIC DOMAIN

§ 4.18   Retroactivity Under Article 18 of the Berne Convention and the Constitutional Dilemma

When the United States adhered to the Berne Convention, it took a minimalist position about the necessity of changing United States law to comply with the requirements of Berne. In so doing, it sidestepped Article 18 of Berne. Known as the "retroactivity" provision, Article 18 requires new member nations on accession to protect all works from other member countries whose copyrights have not yet

---

[216] See H.R. Rep. No. 94–1476, 94th Cong., 2d Sess. 164 (1976). The issue is whether failure to comply with manufacturing clause provisions and *ad interim* requirements places the work in the public domain or invalidates an author's copyright enforcement rights. *See Hoffenberg v. Kaminstein*, 396 F.2d 684 (D.C. Cir.), *cert. denied*, 393 U.S. 913 (1968) (failure to comply justified Copyright Office's refusal to register a work); *Bentley v. Tibbals*, 223 F. 247 (2d Cir. 1915).

[217] 17 U.S.C. § 17 (1909 Act).

[218] 17 U.S.C. § 18 (1909 Act).

[219] See, e.g., *Hoffenberg v. Kaminstein*, 396 F.2d 684 (D.C. Cir. 1968); *but see Meccano, Ltd. v. Wagner*, 234 F. 912 (S.D. Ohio 1916). Professor Nimmer argues that copyright in a work would not be forfeited if non-compliance was not accompanied by a knowingly false affidavit in connection with a claim for registration. In this situation, copyright would have been suspended during the period of the 1909 Act, but would have been revived under the 1976 Act. Thus, non-compliance with the *ad interim* provisions under the 1909 Act is a moot issue today. *See* 2 *Nimmer on Copyright* § 7.23[E] (1988).

expired in their countries of origin.[220] This would include restoration of copyright protection for foreign works that had fallen into the public domain in the United States for failure to comply with formalities, such as notice and renewal. Aside from Berne requirements, it was thought that restoration of copyright for foreign works would facilitate efforts to secure effective protection of U.S. works in foreign markets. At least, restoration of copyright would improve the position of the U.S. in future negotiations to extend the rights of U.S. authors in Berne member countries. Despite these cogent arguments supporting restoration of copyright in the public domain, Congress determined that no special legislation was necessary to implement Article 18 of the Berne Convention. The issue was thought to merit further study, particularly the question whether Congress had the constitutional authority to revive public domain copyrights.

The constitutional issue presents itself on two fronts: the limited times language of the Patent and Copyright Clause,[221] and the Due Process Clause of the Fifth Amendment.[222] Restoring a dead copyright would not appear to violate the limited times provision, which prohibits *perpetual* copyrights. Thus, so long as the copyright will eventually expire, the limited times provision, would not appear to require that copyright protection be confined to a single and uninterrupted term. The second constitutional concern, the "Takings" Clause of the Fifth Amendment, offers the more challenging question. One could legitimately ask: Would a resurrection of copyright impair the Due Process rights of those who have used a work in reliance on its public domain status? To avoid the reliance issue and its Due Process implications, Congress took these concerns into account. In both the NAFTA and Uruguay Round restoration provisions, Congress exculpated past uses of a restored work. In addition, it provided a one-year grace period for certain other uses to allow those who had relied on the public domain status to adjust to the new realities.

§ 4.19 Restoration of Copyright in Certain Foreign Public Domain Works Under Section 104A: From NAFTA to the Uruguay Round Agreements Act

[A] The North American Free Trade Agreement Act

The North American Free Trade Agreement (NAFTA) Act[223] implemented the first provisions to restore copyright protection for foreign works. The NAFTA amendments restored copyright in certain Mexican and Canadian motion pictures, and works that were included in them, that had fallen into the public domain for failure to comply with the notice formality. To reclaim copyright from the public

---

[220] Berne Convention art. 18 (Paris Text). The pertinent subsections 1 and 4 read: (1) This Convention shall apply to all works which, at the moment of its coming into force, have not yet fallen into the public domain in the country of origin through expiry of the term of protection. . . . (4) The preceding provisions shall also apply in the case of new accessions to the Union. . . .

[221] U.S. Const. Art. I, § 8 cl. 8.

[222] U.S. Const. Amend. V.

[223] Pub. L. No. 103–182, 107 Stat. 2057 (1993).

domain, copyright owners of eligible works had to file a statement of intent with the Copyright Office between January 1 and December 31, 1994.[224] A restored copyright will endure for the remainder of the copyright term that the work would have enjoyed if it had had proper notice affixed.

However interesting they are from a theoretical standpoint, the restoration provisions of NAFTA are narrow in scope. For one, they apply only to Mexican and Canadian motion pictures, not to audio-visual works generally. Moreover, for works published on or after January 1, 1978 and before March 1, 1989, the NAFTA amendments apply only to works that entered the public domain for failure to affix proper notice. Thus, works in the public domain before 1978, or those that entered the public domain for failure to comply with other formalities, e.g., renewal registration, are not revived.

[B] The Uruguay Round Agreements Act

One year after the NAFTA amendments, the Uruguay Round Agreements Act[225] restored copyrights for certain foreign works in the public domain in a much more dramatic fashion. This legislation, which implements the negotiations completed under the Uruguay Round of the General Agreement on Tariffs and Trade (GATT),[226] rewrites § 104A of the Copyright Act. Under the Act,[227] copyright

---

[224] 17 U.S.C. § 104A(b).

[225] Pub. L. No. 103–465, 108 Stat. 4809 (1994).

[226] United States obligations under the new World Trade Organization are based on the Uruguay Round negotiations pursuant to the General Agreement on Tariffs and Trade (GATT). One result of the negotiations was the Agreement on Trade Related Aspects of Intellectual Property (TRIPS), which is the basis for the amendments to the Copyright Act retroactively restoring copyright. Article 9 of TRIPS stipulates that "members shall comply with Articles 1–21 and the Appendix of the Berne Convention." See the Dunkel Draft from the GATT Secretariat, Annex III 57, 59 (William S. Hein, 1992). Thus, compliance with the retroactivity provisions of the Berne Convention Article 18 is required. See § 4.11 supra for a discussion of retroactivity under Berne. GATT, now renamed the World Trade Organization, is discussed at § 12.10 infra.

[227] The restoration provisions of the Uruguay Round Agreements Act are not clear about the date on which copyright is restored for works previously in the public domain — whether that date is January 1, 1995, January 1, 1996, or perhaps some date in between. The date of restoration is of critical importance to copyright owners, to public domain users, and to the Copyright Office in the exercise of its administrative obligations. The language of the Act supports the January 1, 1995 date: section 514(h)(2)(A) states the "the date of restoration . . . is the date on which the Agreement on Trade Related Aspects of Intellectual Property enters into force with respect to the United States." That date was January 1, 1995. Another view maintains that the date of restoration is January 1, 1996. This position is based on legislative intent, fairness to public domain users, and administrative convenience. For example, the Copyright Office must publish not later than 90 days before the date of United States entry into the WTO, regulations governing filings for notices of intent to enforce restored copyright. Clearly, the Copyright Office cannot comply with the three-month publication obligation if the Act's restoration provisions go into effect on January 1, 1995. In addition, Article 65 of the TRIPS Agreement allows developed countries one year to implement the Agreement. These are cogent arguments for a January 1, 1996 restoration date. Nonetheless, the legislative

is restored in certain foreign works that have lost U.S copyright protection because of noncompliance with formalities or because the work did not originate in a country with which the United States had copyright relations. To ensure that the legislation does not result in such restorations being "takings" of property under the Fifth Amendment, the legislation includes provisions to protect the interests of parties who had relied on the loss of copyright protection for such works. These users of public domain works are called "reliance parties."[228]

Restorable works must meet several requirements. First, they must enjoy copyright protection in their source country to be eligible for restoration.[229] Thus, a work that lies in the public domain in the source country,[230] for whatever reason, will not be restored in the United States. Second, at the time the work was created, at least one author or rightholder must have been a national or domiciliary of an eligible country and, if the work was published, it must have been first published in an eligible country and not published in the United States during the 30-day period following publication in such eligible country.[231] An eligible country is one other than the United States, that is a World Trade Organization (WTO) member, adheres to the Berne Convention, or is subject to a Presidential proclamation.[232] Thus, the Uruguay Round restoration provisions do not affect public domain status of works of U.S. authors who forfeited copyright for failure to comply with formalities. Similarly, even works of foreign authors, who first published their works in the United States, will also remain in the public domain. Third, restorable works must have fallen into the public domain under U.S. law for any of the following reasons: failure to comply with any of the formalities such as copyright notice, registration, renewal, or the manufacturing requirement; the lack of copyright relations between the U.S. and the source country; or that the work in question was a sound recording published before February 15, 1972.[233] If these three requirements are met, copyright will be restored for the remainder of the term of copyright as if the work had not gone into the public domain.

Ownership rights of restored works will vest initially in the author as determined by the law of the source country. Subsequent transfers will determine ownership status. The term of protection for restored works is the same term the work would have enjoyed if it had not lost copyright protection.[234] For example, a 1942 French film that entered the public domain in 1970 for failure to renew, would enjoy the remainder of its original, 75–year term, enduring until December 31, 2017. Similarly, a Chinese work from 1980, before China joined the Berne Convention, will have a term of protection measured by its author's life plus 50 years. In other

---

intent is not clear, the TRIPS Agreement is not self-executing, and the statutory language indicates the earlier date. This suggests that an amendment to the Act, clarifying the restoration date, is sorely needed.

[228] 17 U.S.C. § 104A(h)(4).

[229] See 17 U.S.C. § 104A(h)(6)(B) for a definition of "source country."

[230] *See* 17 U.S.C. § 104A(h)(8).

[231] 17 U.S.C. § 104A(h)(6)(D).

[232] 17 U.S.C. § 104A(h)(3).

[233] 17 U.S.C. § 104A(h)(6)(C).

[234] 17 U.S.C. § 104A(a)(1)(B).

words, copyright protection for restored works will resume for the remainder of the original term as if it had run without interruption.

A work protected by a restored copyright will be treated like any other copyrighted work. Thus, full liability for infringement will attach.[235] To avoid unfairness and possible constitutional problems, provision has been made for persons who have relied on the absence of copyright protection. The rights of these "reliance parties" — persons who have made extensive use of such works and have invested substantially in their exploitation — are given special consideration under § 104A.[236]

Reliance parties are prospectively liable for unauthorized use of a restored work, but only on receipt of notice of restoration.[237] Effective notice may be given to reliance parties in either of two ways. The copyright owner of a restored work may, within 24 months after the date of restoration of copyright, file a notice with the Copyright Office. The Copyright Office will periodically publish these filed notices, which will constitute constructive notice of restoration. Alternatively, the copyright owner can serve a reliance party with actual notice indicating an intent to enforce the restored copyright. In either instance, a reliance party may continue the performance, distribution, or display of the work for twelve months from the earliest notice.[238] Copies of the work made before the date of restoration of copyright may be sold or otherwise disposed of without the authorization of the restored work's copyright owner, only during the twelve-month period commencing on the date of receipt of actual notice or of publication in the Federal Register of the notice of intent, whichever occurs first.[239]

Reliance parties are subject to the remedies provided for infringement of copyright. But what about the continuing exploitation of derivative works, such as a movie based on a public domain novel? Here, if the derivative work was created before the enactment of the Uruguay Round Agreements Act (December 8, 1994), a reliance party may continue to exploit that work for the duration of the restored copyright if the reliance party pays to the owner of the restored copyright reasonable compensation for its use. This provision is designed to encourage private negotiations between the parties. In the absence of private negotiations, the District Courts are directed to determine such compensation by considering the market effect of this use on the restored work, and the relative contributions of expression of the author of the restored work and of the reliance party to the derivative work.[240] Thus, little if any compensation may be forthcoming for such insubstantial uses as an instructional book containing a single paragraph from a restored work, or a motion picture vaguely based on a restored novel.

---

[235] 17 U.S.C. 104A(d).
[236] 17 U.S.C. § 104A(h).
[237] 17 U.S.C. § 104A(e)(1).
[238] 17 U.S.C. § 104A(c).
[239] 17 U.S.C. § 109(a).
[240] 17 U.S.C. § 104A(d)(3)(B).

CHAPTER 5

OWNERSHIP OF COPYRIGHT

§ 5.1 Introduction and Chapter Overview

Chapter Two of the 1976 Copyright Act concerns ownership and transfer of copyright. It begins with the proposition that copyright vests initially in the author or authors of a work.[1] This key term, "author," is left undefined by the Act, but it is generally accepted that an author is the person who originates a work. The author is most frequently the creator of a work, but this is not always the case. For example, an employer is considered the author of a work made for hire.

Initial ownership of copyright is easy to determine when a person creates a work on his own motivation. Many works of authorship, however, are created pursuant to employment (works made for hire), and others are created by the collaborative efforts of several authors who may contribute their authorship at different times (joint works). Under the 1909 Act, these two situations presented difficult conceptual problems in determining the nature and scope of copyright ownership. The 1976 Act has done much to clarify some of the more unsatisfactory doctrines under the 1909 Act. Even with this added clarity, important questions about copyright ownership are left open. For this reason, the case law developed under the 1909 Act is sometimes used to fill-in those gaps left unattended by the 1976 Act. Moreover, rules that were developed under the 1909 Act and its case law are of utmost importance in determining the ownership status of works created before January 1, 1978, the effective date of the 1976 Act.[2]

This chapter, which is divided into two parts, concerns ownership of copyright. Part I examines how copyright ownership vests, focusing on two important situations: works made for hire and joint works. Part II concerns the special nature of contracts transferring some or all of the bundle of rights which comprise copyright ownership. This part examines the doctrine of divisibility, how copyright assignments and licenses are drafted and construed, and the importance of recording documents in the Copyright Office.

---

[1] 17 U.S.C. § 201(a).

[2] For an overview of the extent to which the 1976 Act is retroactive, see Susan K. Beckett, *The Copyright Act of 1976: When Is It Effective?*, 24 Bull. Copyright Off. Soc'y 391 (1977).

PART I: Initial Ownership: Works Made for Hire and Joint Works

§ 5.2 Works Made for Hire

[A] Generally

In copyright law, works created as part of one's job, called "works made for hire," are treated differently than works created by individual authors on their own motivation. For a work made for hire, initial ownership vests in the employer, who is considered the author of the work.[3] From a practical, economic standpoint, this category is significant. Works created in the course of employment constitute a large percentage of all copyrighted works.

Important legal consequences spring from categorizing a work as one made for hire. First, the employer-author has the entire right to the work; the employee-creator has no ownership rights whatsoever. Second, a work made for hire is not subject to the termination provisions of the 1976 Act.[4] Third, the normal duration for a copyrighted work is the life of the author plus 50 years. Works made for hire, however, have copyright protection for 75 years from publication, or 100 years from creation, whichever is less.[5] Fourth, because the employer is the author of a work made for hire, the nationality and status of the employer can have important consequences. For example, if the employer is the United States government, copyright cannot be claimed at all.[6] In addition, if the employer is a foreign national, the manufacturing clause[7] will not apply, and questions of copyrightability may be determined in certain circumstances by the foreign employer/author's nationality or domicile.[8]

[B] Works Made for Hire: An Overview of the Basic Standards

Section 101[9] defines a work made for hire as:

(1) a work prepared by an employee within the scope of his or her employment; or (2) a work specially ordered or commissioned for use as a

---

[3] 17 U.S.C. § 201(b):

In the case of a work made for hire, the employer or other person for whom the work was prepared is considered the author for purposes of this title, and, unless the parties have expressly agreed otherwise in a written instrument signed by them, owns all of the rights comprised in the copyright.

[4] Under the 1976 Act, an author can terminate a transfer of a copyright interest between the 35th and 40th years under § 203 and for the 19-year extension of the renewal under § 304. These termination of transfer provisions do not apply to works made for hire. For a discussion of termination of transfer, see §§ 6.11–6.17, *infra*.

[5] *See* 17 U.S.C. § 302(c). For works copyrighted before 1978, the employer-author of a work made for hire has the right to claim the second 28-year renewal term. For a discussion of copyright renewal, see §§ 6.5–6.10, *infra*.

[6] *See* 17 U.S.C. § 105.

[7] For a discussion of the now-defunct manufacturing clause which required works published in English to be manufactured in the United States, see §§ 4.15–4.17 *supra*.

[8] *See* 17 U.S.C. § 104. For a discussion of foreign authors, see §§ 12.7–12.8, *infra*.

[9] 17 U.S.C. § 101 (work made for hire).

contribution to a collective work, as a part of a motion picture or other audiovisual work, as a translation, as a supplementary work, as a compilation, as an instructional text, as a test, as answer material for a test, or as an atlas, if the parties expressly agree in a written instrument signed by them that the work shall be considered a work made for hire.

There are two ways in which a work made for hire can be created. Under subdivision (1), a work made for hire may arise from works created within the scope of employment. This subsection must be read in connection with § 201(b),[10] which provides:

. . . the employer or other person for whom the work was prepared is considered the author for purposes of this title, and, unless the parties have expressly agreed otherwise in a written instrument signed by them, owns all of the rights comprised in the copyright.

In other words, when a work is created by an employee, it is presumed to be made for hire unless the parties agree otherwise in a written instrument. Thus, a graphic artist who works full time as an employee for an advertising agency will not own the copyright on his drawings made for a client of the firm unless he and his firm enter into a written contract designating the employee as author.[11]

Subdivision (2) concerns specially commissioned works, those which are created by independent contractors[12] — persons who are not salaried workers of the commissioning party. First, for specially commissioned works, subdivision (2) limits the creation of a work made for hire to nine enumerated categories.

These nine categories are: (1) a contribution to a collective work;[13] (2) a part of a motion picture or other audiovisual work; (3) a translation; (4) a supplementary

---

[10] 17 U.S.C. § 201(b).

[11] Are an academic's writings created in a university setting works made for hire whose ownership vests in the employer-university? This question has been discussed extensively in the literature. *See* Rochelle Cooper Dreyfuss, *The Creative Employee and the Copyright Act of 1976*, 54 U. Chi. L. Rev. 590 (1987); Leonard D. DuBoff, *An Academic's Copyright: Publish and Perish*, 32 J. Copyright Soc'y 17 (1984); Laura G. Lape, *Ownership of Copyrightable Works of University Professors: The Interplay Between the Copyright Act and University Copyright Policies*, 37 Vill. L. Rev. 223 (1992); Todd F. Simon, *Faculty Writings: Are They "Works Made for Hire" Under the 1976 Copyright Act?*, 9 J.C. & U. L. 485 (1982–83); Russ VerSteeg, *Copyright and the Educational Process: The Right of Teacher Inception*, 75 Iowa L. Rev. 381 (1990); *but see Weinstein v. University of Illinois*, 811 F.2d 1091 (7th Cir. 1987) (rejecting university's claim to copyright ownership for a work prepared by academic in the course of employment and with university funds).

[12] An independent contractor may be defined as

[o]ne who renders service in the course of independent employment or occupation, and who follows employer's desires only as to results of work, and not as to means whereby it is to be accomplished.

Black's Law Dictionary 693 (5th ed. 1979).

[13] 17 U.S.C. § 101 defines a "collective work" as

a work, such as a periodical issue, anthology, or encyclopedia, in which a number of contributions, constituting separate and independent works in themselves, are assembled into a collective whole.

work;[14] (5) a compilation; (6) an instructional text; (7) a test; (8) answer material for a test; or (9) an atlas. Second, falling into one of these categories is not enough; to qualify as a work made for hire, the parties must "expressly agree in a written instrument signed by them that the work shall be considered a work made for hire."[15] In other words, even if a contribution to a collective work is specially commissioned from an independent contractor, a work made for hire is not created unless the parties have explicitly stated their intention to do so in a signed writing. In addition, this writing differs from other written contracts in that it must be signed by *both* parties,[16] and that it must consist of explicit wording that the work be considered a "work made for hire." Thus, if A commissions B to make a sculpture for his home, a work made for hire cannot be created even if the parties so agree in a written contract, because B's creation does not fit into one of the nine categories.[17] In sum, subdivision (2) makes it more difficult to create a work made for hire for a work commissioned from an independent contractor than one created in the scope of employment.

The treatment of commissioned works as works made for hire was quite different under 1909 Act case law. This body of law established a presumption that the commissioning party was the author of a work made for hire, unless the parties intended the contrary. The 1976 Act has clearly reversed that presumption. The reason for this change, according to the legislative history, was to remedy an inequitable situation where the copyright on a work created by an independent contractor would presumptively fall into the hands of a commissioning party.[18]

[C] Works Made for Hire in the Courts Before *Community for Creative Non-Violence v. Reid*: The Blurring of Distinctions Between the Two Subdivisions

What had appeared to be a relatively clear statutory framework, in which Congress intended to limit works made for hire to two bright-line categories, did not prove to be so once the courts got into the act. The problem arose in interpreting the meaning of "employee" and "scope of employment" in subdivision (1) and "specially ordered or commissioned works" in subdivision (2), key terms undefined

---

[14] [A] supplementary work is a work prepared for publication as a secondary adjunct to a work by another author for the purpose of introducing, concluding, illustrating, explaining, revising, commenting upon, or assisting in the use of the other work, such as forewords, afterwords, pictorial illustrations, maps, charts, tables, editorial notes, musical arrangements, answer material for tests, bibliographies, appendixes, and indexes.

See 17 U.S.C. § 101 (work made for hire).

[15] 17 U.S.C. § 101 (work made for hire).

[16] *Schiller & Schmidt, Inc. v. Nordisco Corp.*, 969 F.2d 410, 412 (7th Cir. 1992).

[17] Despite congressional intent to limit strictly the creation of works made for hire for commissioned works, a broad interpretation of supplementary and collective works would encompass a large percentage of work done by free-lance artists and writers. *See* Note, *Free Lance Artists, Works for Hire, and the Copyright Act of 1976*, 15 U.C. Davis L. Rev. 703, 708 (1982).

[18] H.R. Rep. No. 94-1476, 94th Cong., 2d Sess. 121 (1976).

in the Act and undiscussed in the committee reports. Some courts refused to accept this radical break with past practice. They blurred the distinction between the two subdivisions in the definition of a work made for hire. The issue which has divided the case law is whether the clause "employee within the scope of his or her employment" in subdivision (1) can encompass an independent contractor in some circumstances. One line of cases interpreted the term "employee" expansively, extending its meaning to employment relationships involving independent contractors.[19] In contrast, another line of cases narrowly interpreted "employee," limiting it, for example, to the master-servant relationship in agency law.[20]

[D]   The Literal Reading of the Categories: *Community for Creative Non-Violence v. Reid*

The meaning of "employee" was resolved in *Community for Creative Non-Violence v. Reid*,[21] where the Supreme Court literally read the statute. In so doing, it limited the definition of employee in subdivision (1) to the master-servant relationship. In *CCNV*, a charitable organization dedicated to eliminating homelessness claimed copyright ownership of a statue called "Third World America." CCNV had commissioned the sculptor, Reid, to create a sculpture dramatizing the plight of the homeless for a Christmas pageant in Washington, D.C. CCNV supplied the plans and sketches, ultimately executed by Reid. On that basis, CCNV claimed ownership of the copyright in the sculpture as an employer for hire.

The Supreme Court, in finding that the work could not be a work made for hire, reviewed the four bases for a work made for hire that had emerged in the case law: (1) a work made for hire comes into existence when the hiring party retains the right to control the work;[22] (2) a work made for hire comes into existence when the hiring

---

[19] *See, e.g., Aldon Accessories, Ltd. v. Spiegel, Inc.*, 738 F.2d 548 (2d Cir.), *cert. denied*, 469 U.S. 982 (1984) (an independent contractor can be considered an employee under subdivision (1) of the work made for hire definition if the hiring author directed and supervised the independent contractor). Courts in subsequent cases had difficulty applying *Aldon*'s supervision standard and produced inconsistent results. One point of controversy was whether the right to direct and supervise meant that the right had to be actually and actively exercised. Or was the right to supervise the independent contractor enough in itself to create a work made for hire? The cases were in conflict on this point. In *Peregrine v. Lauren Corp.*, 601 F. Supp. 828 (D. Colo. 1985), the court found a work made for hire where the commissioning party had the right to supervise the way in which a free-lance photographer did the work, though the court did not define the actual degree to which the employer exercised this right. Alternatively, in *Sygma Photo News, Inc. v. Globe International, Inc.*, 616 F. Supp. 1153 (S.D.N.Y. 1985), official photographs of the British royal family taken at their insistence, and with their right to supervise and approve the photographs, were not a work made for hire. Here, the court found that the royal family insufficiently exercised its right to supervise. Also adopting *Aldon* is *Evans Newton, Inc. v. Chicago Systems Software*, 793 F.2d 889, 894 (7th Cir.), *cert. denied*, 479 U.S. 949 (1986).

[20] *See Restatement (Second) of Agency* § 220 (1958). *See, e.g., Easter Seal Society for Crippled Children and Adults of Louisiana, Inc. v. Playboy Enterprises*, 815 F.2d 323, 335–36 (5th Cir. 1987).

[21] 490 U.S. 730 (1989).

[22] *Peregrine v. Lauren Corp.*, 601 F. Supp. 828 (D. Colo. 1985).

party actually retains control in the creation of the work;[23] (3) the term "employee" applies only to those persons so defined under agency law; and[24] (4) the term "employee" only refers to formal salaried employees.[25] The Court rejected the right to control or actual control tests. Instead, it selected the third alternative, holding that the words "employee" and "employment" describe the conventional master-servant relationship as understood by the common law of agency. In addition to complying with the legislative history, the court pointed out that this interpretation seems more consistent with the logic of the work-made-for-hire provisions. Why have a subdivision (2) which limits the creation of a work made for hire to nine situations for a commissioned work if subdivision (1) can be read so broadly as to cover commissioned works as well?[26] The rationale is that the ambiguous words "employee," "employer," and "independent contractor" would be rendered more precise by tying their meanings to agency law. As a result, a more precise definition for these key terms will provide buyers and sellers with greater predictability in their dealings.

Thus, to determine if someone is an employee under the law of agency, the following factual matters must be considered:

> right to control the manner and means by which the product is accomplished . . . the skill required; the source of the instrumentalities and tools; the location of the work; the duration of the relationship between the parties; whether the hiring party has the right to assign additional projects to the hired party's discretion over when and how long to work; the method of payment; the hired party's role in hiring and paying assistants; whether the work is part of the regular business of the hiring party; whether the hiring party is in business; the provision of employee benefits; and the tax treatment of the hired party.[27] Here, Reid had all the attributes of an independent contractor. He supplied his own tools, worked for a limited time on a specific project, hired his own assistants at his own discretion, and was paid a flat sum for his work. In addition, Reid neither received employee benefits nor contributed to the unemployment insurance of the worker's compensation club. Thus, Reid was not an employee for hire and, as an independent contractor, retained copyright in the work. However, the evidence indicated that the work might be a joint work if the commissioning party contributed sufficient authorship.

The *CCNV* approach will hardly eliminate problems in deciding who is an employee under the statute.[28] Multifactor tests, such as that of the *Restatement*

---

[23] *See, e.g., Aldon Accessories Ltd. v. Spiegel, Inc.*, 738 F.2d 548 (2d Cir.), *cert. denied*, 469 U.S. 982 (1984).

[24] *See, e.g., Easter Seal Society for Crippled Children and Adults of Louisiana, Inc. v. Playboy Enterprises*, 815 F.2d 323, 335–36 (5th Cir. 1987).

[25] *See, e.g., Dumas v. Gommerman*, 865 F.2d 1093 (9th Cir. 1989).

[26] H.R. Rep. No. 94–1476, 94th Cong., 2d Sess. 121 (1976). See the excellent discussion of the legislative history in William F. Patry, *Copyright Law and Practice* 373–82 (1994) and Jessica D. Litman, *Copyright, Compromise, and Legislative History*, 72 Cornell L. Rev. 857, 900–01 (1987).

[27] *CCNV*, 490 U.S. at 745.

[28] For a comprehensive overview of the issues involved in applying the common law agency test, see Robert Kreiss, *Scope of Employment and Being an Employee Under the Work-Made-*

(Second) of Agency, are often difficult to apply.[29] The *Restatement* factors are intensely factual, and none of them are independently determinative. As expected, most courts since *CCNV* have weighed the factors variously, according to the relation between the parties.[30] Some factors, however, will be more important and will undoubtedly be considered in every case. These more salient factors may include the hiring party's right to control the manner and means of creation, the skill required, the provision of employee benefits, the tax treatment of the hired party, and whether the hiring party has the right to assign additional projects to the hired party.[31]

[E] *CCNV* In Perspective: Will It Help the Independent Contractor?

CCNV seems to be a substantial victory for free-lance (independent contractor) authors. Now, the work made for hire category can only be created in certain narrow contexts (the nine categories) and only if the parties sign a written contract. The statute, however, does not delineate which parties are required to sign the written contract, or when in the parties' relationship they must agree. In answer to this question, the Seventh Circuit held that the writing must be signed by both the hiring and the hired party and that the writing must be executed before the work has been created.[32] Even if the agreement has to occur before creation of the work, must it be contemporaneous? For example, suppose a photographer and a magazine enter into a written agreement creating a work made for hire relationship concerning all future pictures the photographer takes for the magazine. If such a blanket agreement would not literally violate the statute, would it violate the spirit of the work made for hire provisions? Even though blanket contracts may be efficient in reducing transaction costs between the parties, they might well transgress the pro-author bias of the work-made-for-hire provisions.

After *CCNV*, contractual arrangements creating a work made for hire are more difficult. The question is how will rational hiring parties react to these contractual constraints. In other words, has *CCNV* really changed things from a practical standpoint? One result may be that more employers will try to circumvent the

---

for-Hire Provision of the Copyright Law: Applying the Common-Law Agency Tests, 40 U. Kan. L. Rev. 119 (1991).

[29] The unsettled state of the work-made-for-hire doctrine has prompted calls for an amendment to the 1976 Copyright Act clarifying the meaning of the phrase, "a work prepared by an employee within the scope of his or her employment." One attempt would limit scope of employment situations where the employee receives all employment benefits due under applicable state and federal law and the employer withholds taxes from such payments to the employee, remitting such taxes to the Internal Revenue Service. Under this provision, free-lance authors would not be considered employees for hire. *See* S. 1253 101st Cong., 1st Sess. (1989).

[30] *See, e.g., Marco v. Accent Publishing Co.*, 969 F.2d 1547 (3d Cir. 1992) (holding that a photographer was an independent contractor, while ignoring some factors and noting that some were "indeterminate" and should not be considered).

[31] *Aymes v. Bonelli*, 980 F.2d 857 (2d Cir. 1992) (some factors will often have little or no significance while others will be significant in almost every situation).

[32] *Shiller & Schmidt, Inc. v. Nordisco Corp.*, 969 F.2d 410, 412 (7th Cir. 1992).

uncertainties of the work-made-for-hire doctrine, with its fact-intensive definition of "employee." Employers will adopt a rule of thumb: when in doubt, insist on an assignment of copyright from the prospective employee. Although an assignment of copyright provides a somewhat shorter duration of copyright ownership than a work made for hire, it may satisfy the needs of most employers. The major drawback to an assignment of copyright when compared with a work made for hire is that an assignment (or any transfer of copyright) can be terminated between the thirty-fifth and fortieth years of the grant if the author or her heirs decide to do so.[33] Realistically, not many employers will be concerned about termination of their ownership rights after thirty-five years. Most works, including advertising jingles, commercial artwork, or computer software, have a much shorter economic life than that. From this point of view, are free-lance authors really better off after *CCNV* now that employers, who usually have greater bargaining power, will mechanically insist on an assignment of copyright from their independent contractors?

§ 5.3 Works Made For Hire Under the 1909 Act

Section 26 of the 1909 Act recognized the work-made-for-hire doctrine in providing that "the word 'author' shall include an employer in the case of works made for hire."[34] The 1909 Act did not define the key terms in this phrase, and the courts were forced to create their own standards for construing the statute. The case law clearly favored employers over creators in determining whether a work made for hire was created.

Under the 1909 Act, whether a work was created in the scope of employment or commissioned from an independent contractor, courts applied a presumption that ownership of the copyright vested in the employer as a work made for hire.[35] The presumption could be overcome by an agreement to the contrary.[36] Absent an agreement, the employee could rebut the presumption by showing a contrary intent of the parties.[37] For this purpose, the court would look to such evidentiary factors as industry custom, pattern of dealing, at whose expense and insistence the work was created, and the supervision and control of the work.[38] Of these factors, the most important was the supervision and control exercised by the employer.[39]

The concern with 1909 Act case law is of more than historical interest because the 1976 Act is not applied retroactively in determining copyright ownership. Such

[33] *See* 17 U.S.C. § 203(a). An assignment of copyright will not confer absolute ownership rights on the assignee because the author can still terminate the transfer between the thirty-fifth and fortieth years of the grant. But despite this, some commissioning parties prefer the security of an assignment of copyright to the unpredictable nature of the work-made-for-hire doctrine as construed in the courts. For a discussion of termination of transfer, see §§ 6.11–6.17, *infra*.

[34] 17 U.S.C. § 26 (1909 Act).

[35] *May v. Morganelli-Heumann & Assoc.*, 618 F.2d 1363 (9th Cir. 1980).

[36] *See Roth v. Pritikin*, 710 F.2d 934 (2d Cir.), *cert. denied*, 464 U.S. 961 (1983).

[37] *See Meltzer v. Zoller*, 520 F. Supp. 847, 851 (D.N.J. 1981).

[38] *Brattleboro Publishing Co v. Winmill Publishing Corp.*, 369 F.2d 565 (2d Cir. 1966).

[39] *See Murray v. Gelderman*, 566 F.2d 1307, 1310 (5th Cir. 1978).

retroactivity would raise serious constitutional problems. The leading case regarding the non-retroactivity of the 1976 Act is *Roth v. Pritikin*,[40] where the plaintiff, a free-lance author, delivered recipes for a successful diet book under an oral contract in October 1977, and received payment for her work. The book became a best seller. Roth argued that the 1976 Act should be applied retroactively and that, because the 1976 Act required a written contract to create a work made for hire, the pre-1978 oral contract was ineffective. The court held that transactions taking place before 1978 should be governed by the 1909 Act, which would give ownership to the commissioning parties, at whose insistence and expense the work was created, and to those who retained the right to supervise and control Roth's free-lance work.[41]

The rationale for looking to the 1909 Act was based on constitutional principles. Divesting the commissioning parties of their ownership status under the new 1976 Act definition of "work made for hire" would raise serious constitutional Due Process issues under the Fifth and Fourteenth Amendments, and would possibly violate the Fifth Amendment prohibition on the federal government's right to take public property for public use without just compensation.[42]

§ 5.4   Joint Works

[A]   Generally

Works of authorship are often created by two or more persons and are treated as joint works. Section 101 of the 1976 Copyright Act defines a "joint work" as

> a work prepared by two or more authors with the intention that their contributions be merged into inseparable or interdependent parts of a unitary whole.[43]

The key terms in the definition, "inseparable" and "interdependent," are not defined. The House Report gives as examples of "inseparable" a novel or a painting, while examples of *interdependent* include a motion picture, opera, or words and music.[44] Whether a work entails interdependent or inseparable elements is irrelevant in determining whether a joint work has been created. What counts is that the authors intended their respective labors to be integrated into one work. The contributions of the individual authors do not have to be equal in quantity and quality. Thus, a joint work can be created even if the collaborative efforts of the authors are unequal,

---

[40] 710 F.2d 934 (2d Cir.), *cert. denied*, 464 U.S. 961 (1983).

[41] *Id.* at 937.

[42] *Id.* at 939; *see also* 1 *Nimmer on Copyright* § 1.11 (1993) (applying the 1976 Act to ownership would constitute a violation of the Due Process Clause of the Fifth and Fourteenth Amendments, and a violation of the Fifth Amendment limitation on the federal government's right to take private property for public use without just compensation).

[43] 17 U.S.C. § 101 (joint works).

[44] H.R. Rep. No. 94–1476, 94th Cong., 2d Sess. 120 (1976). It appears that the House Report, in referring to "inseparable," means a work which has been recast, reformed, or adapted as opposed to an interdependent work, *i.e.*, one which is made of assembled parts, such as various collective works. *See* 1 *Nimmer on Copyright* § 6.04 (1993). In any event, whether a work is transformed or assembled, the intent is the critical aspect for creating a joint work.

but the Act does not indicate whether all the authors must make a copyrightable contribution to the collaborative effort. Despite this uncertainty, courts have unanimously denied joint authorship claims where an individual contribution is not itself copyrightable. Thus, a joint author must not only intend that his contribution be part of a joint work but must contribute more than *de minimis* authorship to the resulting work.[45] In other words, a hiring party who contributes general ideas, factual matter, or describes to another what the commissioned work should do or look like does not become a joint author of the work. As one court stated, "To be an author, one must supply more than mere direction or ideas: one must translate[] an idea into a fixed, tangible expression entitled to copyright protection. The supplier of an idea is no more an 'author' of a [computer program] than is the supplier of the disk on which the program is stored."[46]

Why this insistence upon copyrightable contributions from all joint authors? First, it seems more consistent with the spirit of copyright law to oblige all joint authors to make copyrightable contributions. Second, this rule may prevent spurious claims by those who might otherwise try to share the fruits of the efforts of a sole author of a copyrightable work. Third, and most important, it may encourage those with non-copyrightable contributions to protect their rights through contract, because if they neglect to do so, the copyright will remain with the one or more persons who created the copyrightable material. Thus, the rule should tend to force the parties to specify their rights in a written contract, such as an assignment of the copyright or to establish a work make for hire in the appropriate situation.[47]

This definition of joint works describes only one way in which a joint work is created — by a process of joint authorship. A joint work, however, can also result in several other ways:[48] when a copyright owner transfers the copyright to more than one person, or when the copyright passes by will or intestacy to two or more persons, or when the work is subject to state community property laws. In addition, a joint work is created when renewal rights or rights terminated under the termination of transfers provision vest in a class made up of two or more persons.[49] Thus, a joint work may be more broadly defined as one in which copyright is owned in undivided shares by two or more persons, whether created by joint authorship or some other way.

[B] Joint Works Under the 1976 Act

Joint works are created when the authors intend, at the time of the writing, that their contributions become part of a joint work.[50] Although intent is the essential element of a joint work, it does not matter when the *fulfillment* of that intent takes place. Returning to the songwriting example, a joint work could be created if A's

[45] *See Donna v. Dodd, Mead & Co., Inc.,* 374 F. Supp. 429 (S.D.N.Y. 1974); *Erickson v. Trinity Theatre,* 13 F.3d 1061 (7th Cir. 1994).

[46] *See, e.g., S.O.S., Inc. v. Payday, Inc.,* 886 F.2d 1081 (9th Cir. 1989).

[47] *Childress v. Taylor,* 945 F.2d 500 (2d Cir. 1991).

[48] *See 1 Nimmer on Copyright* § 6.01 (1993).

[49] See §§ 6.11–6.17, *infra,* for a discussion of renewal rights and termination of transfers.

[50] H.R. Rep. No. 94–1476, 94th Cong., 2d Sess. 120 (1976).

words were created in 1946 and B's music was created in 1978, with their integration into the final song taking place in 1988. Each composer's intent to create a joint work at the time of creation is the essential requirement. It is irrelevant that the composers were unknown to each other or had no idea which words or music would eventually be used. Nor do the authors have to have collaborated together at the same time and place so long as each author intended at the time of the creation that his or her contribution would be combined in some way with another's work.

Alternatively, a joint work is not created if an author did not intend at the time of creation that his work be merged into an inseparable or interdependent work. By this principle, a joint work would not be created when, for example, A, the writer of the words, intended them to be nothing more than a poem, but later decided that they should be integrated with music into a song. Nor would a joint work be created if a poet, a playwright, or a novelist were to show that he merely hoped that someday his work would be integrated into a song, an opera, or a motion picture without an explicit intention for this to occur.

Does the joint authorship of an underlying work confer any joint ownership rights in a new work created by one of the joint authors that is substantially based on the underlying work? Suppose that A and B create a joint work, for example, an article in a scientific journal. At a later time after a falling out between the two parties, A uses a substantial portion of the original article but adds substantial original authorship to the new article. Is B a joint author of the second article?[51] Here, joint ownership would not attach to the second work unless there was evidence that the authors intended their joint product to be forever indivisible. Without such evidence, a derivative work would be created and B would not be a joint author of the resulting derivative work. A contrary rule, as one court stated: "would convert all derivative works based upon jointly authored works into joint works, regardless of whether there had been any joint labor on the subsequent version. If such were the law, it would eviscerate the independent copyright protection that attaches to a derivative work that is wholly independent of the protection afforded the preexisting work."[52]

In sum, what counts is primary intent to create a joint work. The appropriate question to ask in the songwriting example is whether each author created his work primarily for the purpose that it be integrated at some future time into a joint work. In many cases, deciding such nuances of intent is a difficult task, particularly if a court has to decide the primary intent of a deceased author who never explicitly indicated his intent during his lifetime. This task becomes all the more difficult in situations involving more than two authors, as in a movie or theater collaboration.[53] Nevertheless, much rides on this elusive concept of intent in determining whether a work is, on the one hand a joint work, or, on the other, a derivative or collective work.

---

[51] *See, e.g., Weissman v. Freeman*, 868 F.2d 1313 (2d Cir. 1989), *cert. denied*, 493 U.S. 883 (2d Cir. 1989) (holding, under similar facts, that the second work was not a joint work).

[52] *Weissman*, 868 F.2d at 1317.

[53] For an excellent overview of these problems, see Susan Keller, *Collaboration in Theater: Problems and Copyright Solutions*, 33 UCLA L. Rev. 891 (1986).

Childress v. Taylor[54] illustrates the requirements of sufficient authorship and intent and their interplay in the creation of a joint work. In *Childress*, the defendant Taylor contacted Childress to write a play based on the life of the legendary comedienne "Moms" Mabley. Although Taylor, a professional actress, wrote none of the script, she provided Childress with her research on "Moms" Mabley's life, and suggested that certain scenes be included in the play. The relationship between the parties deteriorated before the rights between them were specified by contract. Taylor then had another author modify the script and shortly thereafter, using this new version, she performed the work publicly. In response to Childress's suit for copyright infringement, Taylor contended she was a joint author and shared with Childress the rights to the play. The Second Circuit rejected Taylor's claim of joint authorship because her efforts lacked the two basic elements needed to create a joint work. First, Taylor, who supplied only certain ideas and research, did not contribute the requisite degree of authorship. Second, even if Taylor's contribution was independently copyrightable, a joint work was not created due to a lack of intent. Nothing indicated that the putative joint authors ever regarded themselves as joint authors. Critical to the absence of intent was a lack of understanding on the question of billing and credit. Here, there was no evidence that Childress ever considered, or would even have agreed, that Childress and Taylor would be "billed" and "credited" as joint authors of the play. *Childress* shows how a court will set up a presumption against a finding of a joint work when a putative co-author has contributed only a relatively small amount to the work. In this situation, the court will require convincing evidence of intent to create a joint work.

[C] Consequences of Joint Ownership

Whether a joint work is created by joint authorship or in some other way, the authors are co-owners of copyright in the work. As co-owners, the authors are deemed to be tenants-in-common,[55] a term borrowed from real property law, which means that each of the co-owners has an undivided ownership in the entire work.[56] As a result, each co-owner can use or license the whole work as he wishes, and the only obligation is a duty to account for profits to the other joint owner. What a joint owner cannot do is transfer all interest in the work — that is, assign the work or grant an exclusive license in it without the written consent of the other co-owners.[57]

---

[54] 945 F.2d 500 (2d Cir. 1991).

[55] Absent an agreement to the contrary between joint owners, their relationship is one of tenancy-in-common, not a joint tenancy. The basic difference between the two is that on the death of a co-tenant, the ownership right passes to his heirs, whereas in a joint tenancy, the right passes to the surviving joint tenant. *See* 1 *Nimmer on Copyright* § 6.09 (1993); *Picture Music, Inc. v. Bourne, Inc.*, 314 F. Supp. 640 (S.D.N.Y. 1970), *aff'd*, 457 F.2d 1213 (2d Cir. 1972).

[56] Absent an agreement otherwise, joint authors share an equal percentage of ownership in the joint work. The joint authors share equally despite the degree of individual authorship contributed. *See, e.g., Sweet Music, Inc. v. Melrose Music Corp.*, 189 F. Supp. 655 (S.D. Cal. 1960).

[57] 17 U.S.C. § 204(a).

The paradigm of joint authorship is a collaboration between songwriters[58] A, who composes the music, and B, who composes the words. Assuming that A and B intend at the time of the writing of their respective works to create a joint work, either can use the work or grant a *nonexclusive* license (but not an exclusive license or assignment) to others. No consent is needed in granting these rights, but the joint authors must share the profits from any exploitation of the work.[59]

[D] Joint Works and Derivative Works Compared

Rights of ownership in a derivative or collective work vary substantially from joint ownership. For a derivative or collective work, the contributing author owns his own contribution only. There is no undivided interest in the whole work as in the case of joint ownership. The practical effect of this difference can be quite significant.

Take, for example, the authors of the words and the music to the song discussed above. Assume that neither A nor B had the intention at the time of creation that their works be integrated into a joint work. The ensuing song would be considered a derivative work. As owner of the derivative work, each author owns nothing more than his original contribution — one the words, the other the music. Absent a specific contractual agreement, each author would have to obtain permission for every use of the song from the owner of the underlying work.

Other consequences result from joint ownership, as compared with ownership of a derivative or collective work. The entire joint work passes to the heirs or devisees of each joint author, and the term of protection is life-plus-50-years as measured from the life of the last living joint author.[60] By comparison, the owner of a derivative or collective work can convey no more than his individual contribution to his heirs or devisees, and the term of protection is measured from the life of each individual author. In the songwriting example, this would result in the heirs of A owning the words and the heirs of B owning the music.

§ 5.5 Joint Ownership Under the 1909 Act

Section 24 of the 1909 Act[61] indirectly acknowledged the principle of joint ownership by allowing a renewal of copyright to be owned jointly by more than

---

[58] Joint works have arisen out of a variety of situations. *See, e.g., Donna v. Dodd, Mead & Co., Inc.*, 374 F. Supp. 429 (S.D.N.Y. 1974) (photographer and writer of a text); *Meltzer v. Zoller*, 520 F. Supp. 847 (D.N.J. 1981) (architect and home owner); *Community for Creative Non-Violence v. Reid*, 846 F.2d 1485 (D.C. Cir. 1988), *aff'd*, 490 U.S. 730 (1989) (suggesting that a sculpture may have been a joint work of the sculptor and commissioning party because both parties contributed to it. The court remanded the case to determine whether the two parties' contributions were intended to be inseparable parts of a whole and whether each contribution was substantial enough to meet the test of originality and authorship), *aff'd*, 490 US. 730 (1989).

[59] *See Oddo v. Ries*, 743 F.2d 630 (9th Cir. 1984).

[60] For a discussion of duration of copyright, see §§ 6.2–6.4, *infra.*

[61] 17 U.S.C. § 24 (1909 Act).

one person. The Act, however, did not specify how joint ownership could be created. The principles of joint authorship developed through case law culminating in the *12th Street Rag* doctrine, which the 1976 Act was designed to overrule.[62]

Until the *12th Street Rag* decision[63] in 1955, the case law under the 1909 Act essentially reflected the codification of joint authorship principles in the 1976 Act. The key element in creating a joint work was the common design or intent of the authors to merge their contributions into an indivisible whole at the time of creation. This intent could be found even if the authors wrote their works at different times, did not work together or did not even know one another.[64]

A major departure in the case law occurred in the *12th Street Rag* decision.[65] This controversial decision removed the requirement that the intent to create a joint work be shown at the time of creation. In *12th Street Rag*, a composer created an instrumental piano solo, never intending that it eventually be accompanied by words. The composer assigned his rights to a publisher who commissioned lyrics for the piano solo. Was the song a joint work? The court held that it was, even though the author did not intend to create a joint work.

The *12th Street Rag* holding greatly increased the potential number of joint works, and departed from prior case law in two ways. First, the intent to create a joint work no longer had to be shown at the time of creation; it could be shown at anytime thereafter. Second, this intent could be supplied by the copyright owner, in this case the assignee, who might or might not necessarily be the author.

The *12th Street Rag* doctrine has been vigorously criticized.[66] The major objection is that it throws an element of uncertainty into determining ownership rights for derivative or collective works created under licenses given by a copyright owner before 1978.[67] The doctrine also has a tendency to extend the copyright term for works that may have fallen into the public domain.[68] For these and other reasons, the doctrine has been overruled by the 1976 Act.

The question remains, must a court today apply the *12th Street Rag* doctrine in construing ownership rights for transactions taking place before 1978? The 1909

[62] *See Shapiro, Bernstein & Co., Inc. v. Jerry Vogel Music Co., Inc.*, 221 F.2d 569 (2d Cir.), *modified on rehearing*, 223 F.2d 252 (2d Cir. 1955) (*12th Street Rag* case).

[63] *Id.*

[64] *See Shapiro, Bernstein & Co., Inc. v. Jerry Vogel Music Co., Inc.*, 161 F.2d 406 (2d Cir. 1946), *cert. denied*, 331 U.S. 820 (1947) (*Melancholy Baby* case).

[65] *Shapiro, Bernstein & Co. v. Jerry Vogel Music Co.*, 221 F.2d 569 (2d Cir.), *modified on rehearing*, 223 F.2d 252 (2d Cir. 1955) (*12th Street Rag* case).

[66] *See, e.g.,* 1 *Nimmer on Copyright* § 6.06[B] (1993).

[67] For the difference in ownership between derivative and collective works, *see* § 2.8, *supra*. For example, in a situation where A writes the music and B the words for a song, neither A nor B has any rights to the other's work absent agreement, whereas if a joint work is created each can grant nonexclusive licenses to the whole work without the other's consent.

[68] For example, consider the songwriting example where A writes the words and B the music. Assume that the song is a derivative work. If the copyright term in the song ends, anyone could use A's words. But if the work is considered a joint work, the copyright term under § 302(b) of the 1976 Act endures for the life of the last surviving author plus 50 years.

Act case law is still important because nothing indicates that the 1976 Act is to be applied retroactively, and to do so in some instances would raise serious constitutional problems.[69] Unlike the relatively well-settled 1909 Act case law on works made for hire, the *12th Street Rag* case is more an aberration than a decision supported by the mainstream case law. Thus, a court could reasonably ignore the doctrine as being inconsistent with better-reasoned authority, virtually identical to the 1976 Act conception of joint authorship.

§ 5.6   Ownership of Contributions to Collective Works

A "collective work" is defined in § 101 as

> . . . a work, such as a periodical issue, anthology, or encyclopedia, in which a number of contributions, constituting separate and independent works in themselves, are assembled into a collective whole.[70]

A collective work is, in effect, a species of compilation,[71] but unlike other types of compilations it consists of separate and independent copyrighted works. The distinction is also made between a joint work, where the separate elements merge into a unified whole, and a collective work where they remain separate and distinct.[72]

Under the 1909 Act, there was much confusion about the relation between copyright in the collective work and copyright in the individual work. Section 201(c) of the 1976 Act is intended to clarify the confusion.[73] It provides:

> Copyright in each separate contribution to a collective work is distinct from copyright in the collective work as a whole, and vests initially in the author of the contribution. In the absence of an express transfer of the copyright or of any rights under it, the owner of copyright in the collective work is presumed to have acquired only the privilege of reproducing and distributing the contribution as part of that particular collective work, any revision of that collective work, and any later collective work in the same series.

Under § 201(c), one should distinguish copyright in the contribution to the collective work from copyright in the collective work. Collective work authorship is similar to authorship in a compilation, and extends to the elements of compilation

---

[69] *See Roth v. Pritikin*, 710 F.2d 934 (2d Cir.), *cert. denied*, 464 U.S. 961 (1983). Retroactive application of the 1976 Act law regarding works made for hire may well violate the due process clause under the Fifth and Fourteenth Amendments and possibly the Fifth Amendment's limitation on the federal government's taking of private property for public use.

[70] 17 U.S.C. § 101 (collective work).

[71] *Id.* (compilation):

> A "compilation" is a work formed by the collection and assembling of preexisting materials or of data that are selected, coordinated, or arranged in such a way that the resulting work as a whole constitutes an original work of authorship. The term "compilation" includes collective works.

[72] H.R. Rep. No. 94–1476, 94th Cong., 2d Sess. 122 (1976).

[73] 17 U.S.C. § 201(c).

and editing that went into creating the collective work as a whole, including contributions written by employees of the collective work's author. For example, collective work authorship in an anthology of poetry would extend to the selection and arrangement of the poems, and other editing, such as an introduction to the poems, but not to the poems themselves.

Under this section, the individual contributors to the collective work retain the copyrights in their works, absent a written agreement stating the contrary.[74] In addition, the section sets up a presumption that the copyright owner in the collective work has the right to reproduce and distribute the contribution as part of that particular collective work, a revision of the collective work, or as part of any later collective work in the same series. Take, for example, an issue of a magazine which is comprised of several individually copyrighted articles. Absent a written agreement to the contrary, the magazine could not republish individually one of those copyrighted articles. The publisher of the magazine, however, does have the right to republish that entire issue, or a revision of it, without consent of the copyright owner of the article. In addition, the collective work author has no implied right to revise the individual contribution without the author's consent.

These rules involving collective works were designed to clarify a somewhat uncertain situation existing under the 1909 Act, as well as to improve the legal position of authors to contributions.[75] The legal presumptions set forth in § 201(c) require the copyright owner of the collective work — the encyclopedia, anthology or symposia — to obtain written contracts for the right to reprint the contribution or for the transfer of its copyright.

§ 5.7 Ownership of Copyright as Distinguished from Ownership of the Material Object: The *Pushman* Doctrine

Section 202 of the 1976 Act codifies a fundamental principle in copyright law: the distinction between ownership of the material object and ownership of the copyright. As discussed earlier, an outright sale of a material object, such as a book, canvas, or master tape recording of a musical work, does not transfer copyright.[76] One possible exception to this rule is the *Pushman* doctrine [77] under which an author or artist who has sold an unpublished work of art or a manuscript is presumed to have transferred his *common law* [78] copyright, unless the copyright has been specifically reserved. In *Pushman*, an artist sold an unpublished painting, one which had not yet been divested of its common law copyright. As to who owned the

---

[74] *See, e.g., Quinto v. Legal Times of Washington, Inc.*, 506 F. Supp. 554 (D.D.C. 1981).

[75] H.R. Rep. No. 94–1476, 94th Cong., 2d Sess. 122 (1976).

[76] For a discussion of this concept, see § 2.2, *supra*.

[77] *Pushman v. New York Graphic Society, Inc.*, 287 N.Y. 302, 39 N.E.2d 249 (1942).

[78] Recall that under the 1909 Act, before a work was published it was protected by state common law copyright. Publication was the dividing line between state and federal protection. The *Pushman doctrine* applies only to the sale of an object embodying an unpublished work and, therefore, protected by common law copyright. For a discussion of publication see §§ 4.2–4.7, *supra*.

copyright in the painting, the court held that the sale of the material object, *i.e.*, the canvas, was presumed to have conveyed the common law copyright as well.

The legislative history[79] of § 202 indicates that this section was drafted in part to overturn the *Pushman* doctrine. Its demise began even before the 1976 Act when California[80] and New York[81] enacted statutes reversing the presumption that an unconditional sale of an unpublished work of art transferred copyright along with the material object. Despite these attempts to overrule it, the *Pushman doctrine* is not entirely dead. The reason is that the 1976 Act does not operate retroactively for transactions involving pre-January 1978 transfers of copyright. Thus, the *Pushman* doctrine is really still alive, and one should scrutinize all pre-1978 transfers of a material object embodying a work then protected under common law copyright to determine the ownership rule in the pertinent state jurisdiction.[82]

PART II: TRANSFERS OF COPYRIGHT INTERESTS

§ 5.8 Divisibility of Copyright

[A] In General

Copyright in a work may be regarded as a bundle of rights that may be transferred in its entirety or individually. The 1976 Act in § 201(d)(2)[83] explicitly recognizes the principle of the divisibility of copyright in providing:

> Any of the exclusive rights comprised in a copyright, including any subdivision of any of the rights specified by Section 106, may be transferred . . . and owned separately. The owner of any particular exclusive right is entitled, to the extent of that right, to all of the protection and remedies accorded to the copyright owner by this title.

Divisibility of ownership applies to transfer of copyright ownership, defined in § 101 as:

> an assignment, mortgage, exclusive license, or any other conveyance, alienation, or hypothecation of a copyright or of any of the exclusive rights comprised in a copyright, whether or not it is limited in time or place of effect, but not including a nonexclusive license.[84]

---

[79] H.R. Rep. No. 94–1476, 94th Cong., 2d Sess. 124 (1976).

[80] Cal. Civ. Code § 982(c) (West Supp. 1976).

[81] N.Y. Gen. Bus. Law §§ 223–24 (McKinney 1968).

[82] Even in New York and California, states which have abrogated the *Pushman* doctrine by statute, the doctrine may well be applicable to transactions taking place before the effective date of those statutes. Moreover, the statutes in New York and California apply to the sale of works of fine art. There remains the question of whether the *Pushman* doctrine is still viable in those states for works other than fine art even after the effective date of the abrogating statutes.

[83] 17 U.S.C. § 201(d)(2).

[84] 17 U.S.C. § 101 (transfer of copyright ownership).

To be effective, transfers of copyright must be written and signed by the copyright owner.[85]

Section 201(d) recognizes the concept of divisibility of copyright, which allows the copyright owner to transfer less than the full ownership interest in the copyright. Section 201(d) explicitly provides that each of the exclusive rights set forth in § 106 — those of reproduction, adaptation, publication, performance, and display — may be infinitely subdivided and each of these subdivided rights may be owned and enforced separately.[86] For example, A, a novelist, could grant an exclusive license in his writing to B to write a screenplay from the novel, another to C to write a play based on a chapter of the novel, and a third to D to perform the work in the state of Ohio during the month of July 1993. All of the above conveyances are transfers of copyright, and each transferee enjoys all the rights of a copyright owner.[87]

[B] Consequences of Divisibility: Standing to Sue

All transferees of copyright are given standing to sue without having to join the copyright proprietor. This right is particularly important to the exclusive licensee who can bring suit on his own behalf to protect his ownership interest in the copyright. By contrast, under the 1909 Act the exclusive licensee was not considered an owner of copyright and was forced to join the copyright owner.[88] This requirement could be quite burdensome on the exclusive licensee whose rights were infringed, and could result in the exclusive licensee's exclusion from the courts because of inability to join a copyright owner as an indispensable party.[89] Now, given standing to sue, the exclusive licensee can effectively protect his ownership interest.

§ 5.9   Indivisibility of Ownership Under the 1909 Act

Under the 1909 Act, a copyright was perceived as an indivisible entity incapable of being broken up into smaller rights. This doctrine of indivisibility, as it was known, was justified mainly as protecting infringers against harassment from successive law suits. Only an assignee of the entire copyright could bring suit, whereas licensees could not; this effectively cut down on the number of persons who sue.

---

[85] 17 U.S.C. § 204.

[86] H.R. Rep. No. 94–1476, 94th Cong., 2d Sess. 123 (1976).

[87] *See, e.g., Hubbard Broadcasting, Inc. v. Southern Satellite Systems, Inc.*, 777 F.2d 393 (8th Cir. 1985) (exclusive license to local television broadcaster confers standing to sue); *Library Publications, Inc. v. Medical Economics Co.*, 714 F.2d 123 (3d Cir. 1983) (exclusive license to newsstand dealer confers standing to sue).

[88] The 1909 Act considered copyright to be an indivisible entity, and the copyright owner could not transfer ownership of the copyright in part. *See* § 5.9, *infra*.

[89] *See, e.g., Ilyin v. Avon Publications, Inc.*, 144 F. Supp. 368, 374–75 (S.D.N.Y. 1956) (exclusive licensee unable to join foreign copyright owners as indispensable parties).

Under the 1909 Act, the distinction between a license and an assignment[90] led to important consequences other than the inability to bring suit in one's own name. The most serious consequence of indivisibility involved the right to claim copyright. Under the 1909 Act, copyright could be secured only if notice appeared in the name of the copyright owner.[91] If no notice or improper notice such as notice in a name other than the copyright owner was given, the work could be injected into the public domain.

These requirements caused problems in many copyright industries, but their effect was particularly evident in magazine publishing.[92] For example, assume that A, author of an unpublished and uncopyrighted article, granted to B magazine in 1970 the right to publish the article in B magazine. If B magazine carried a copyright notice only in the magazine's name, A's copyright was jeopardized. The reason is that B magazine was a licensee of A, not a copyright owner of A's article, and correct notice had to bear the name of the copyright owner. Thus, the general notice in the name of B magazine was incorrect, and the article was published without notice. The result was a possible injection of A's article into the public domain.[93]

These problems forced authors to use various means, artificial and inconvenient, to protect their works. By one method, the author would assign all rights to the publisher, who would agree to transfer the rights back to the owner after publication. Not many authors were aware of the notice requirement and its consequences, much less the complicated practices built up to avoid the problems created by the doctrine of indivisibility. In short, to circumvent problems created by indivisibility, authors tried to create ingenious methods which sometimes, but not always, worked.[94]

Because of its unfairness to authors, indivisibility was one of the most criticized doctrines in copyright law.[95] It was dealt a severe blow in *Goodis v. United Artists Television, Inc.*,[96] which held that where a magazine purchases the right of first publication of an article, copyright notice in the magazine's name is sufficient to secure copyright for the author. Since *Goodis*, most courts have refused to forfeit copyright in a work containing the name of the licensee rather than the copyright owner.[97]

---

[90] In general, a grant is an assignment if the grantee is given full rights; a grant is a license if the grantor retains some of those rights. *See* Harry G. Henn, *"Magazine Rights" — A Division of Indivisible Copyright*, 40 Cornell L.Q. 411, 430–31 (1955).

[91] 17 U.S.C. §§ 10, 19 (1909 Act).

[92] *See* Henn, n. 80, *supra.*

[93] *Letter Edged in Black Press, Inc. v. Public Bldg. Comm'n of Chicago*, 320 F. Supp. 1303 (N.D. Ill. 1970).

[94] To avoid forfeiture, some courts would interpret the agreement as an assignment, instead of a license, in which the magazine acquired legal title to the contribution and the author retained beneficial title. *See* 3 *Nimmer on Copyright* § 10.01[C] (1993).

[95] *See* Kaminstein, *Divisibility of Copyright*, Copyright Office *Study No. 11*, 86th Cong., 2d Sess. (Comm. Print 1960).

[96] 425 F.2d 397 (2d Cir. 1970).

[97] *See, e.g., Fantastic Fakes, Inc. v. Pickwick International, Inc.*, 661 F.2d 479 (5th Cir. 1981). *But see Letter Edged in Black Press, Inc. v. Public Bldg. Comm'n of Chicago*, 320 F. Supp. 1303 (N.D. Ill. 1970) (*Goodis* distinguished as applying to magazine publishing only).

The result in *Goodis* foreshadowed the total abrogation of indivisibility in the 1976 Act. It also explains § 404 of the 1976 Act, which specifically provides that:

> a single notice applicable to the collective work as a whole is sufficient to satisfy [notice requirements] . . . with respect to the separate contributions it contains . . . regardless of the ownership of copyright in the contributions and whether or not they have been previously published.[98]

These notice provisions have freed the contributor to a collective work from having to worry about the loss of copyright through improper notice. In addition, the author no longer has to worry about setting up artificial means, such as the transfer arrangements described above, to avoid the problems of copyright indivisibility.

§ 5.10   Drafting and Construing Licenses: The Problem of New Media

For the most part, transfers and non-exclusive licenses of copyright present no greater problem in legal drafting and interpretation than in any other specialized area of the law. No set form exists for drafting an assignment or license, but most agreements include provisions, among others, for (1) royalties, (2) duration of the agreement, (3) its geographical scope, (4) manner in which the work may be exploited, (5) termination circumstances, (6) name to be carried on the notice of copyright, and (7) responsibilities for maintaining an infringement suit. Once in court, these provisions are no more or less difficult to construe than any other kind of legal writing.

One issue of contract construction, however, has proved to be particularly challenging: the determination of the scope of media to which the transfer pertains. This problem results from the rapid and revolutionary change in communications media. Sometimes the parties fail to take into account a new medium. Other times they are either unaware of the medium or it was not in existence at the time the grant was executed.

To decide scope-of-media issues, courts generally search for the intent of the parties by analyzing the language of the agreement, along with permissible extraneous evidence. The intent may be clear from a specifically worded contract, or implied by other circumstances including the general custom and expectation of the author in the particular industry.[99] When the parties knew or should have known about a new medium, the courts adopt an interpretation most consistent with all the terms of the license. For example, in *Manners v. Morosco*[100] an exclusive licensing agreement which included the right "to produce, perform and represent" a play did not include the motion picture rights. This interpretation was consistent with the terms of the license mainly because the parties were aware of the new medium but failed to mention it in the agreement.[101] Here, the court applied a general principle

---

[98] 17 U.S.C. § 404(a).
[99] *See, e.g., Goodis v. United Artists Television, Inc.*, 425 F.2d 397 (2d Cir. 1970).
[100] 252 U.S. 317 (1920).
[101] *See also Klein v. Beach*, 232 F. 240 (S.D.N.Y. 1916).

of contract construction, *i.e.*, the contract must be viewed as a whole, one part interpreted in connection with its other parts.[102]

A more difficult problem of interpretation is presented when a court has to decide whether new or undeveloped media fall within the grant. Here the traditional quest for the intent of the parties will not work when the issue involves media of which they could not have been aware. This is not a new problem; technology changes more rapidly than our ability to describe it, even in the best-drafted contracts. For example, in *L.C. Page & Co. v. Fox Film Corp.*,[103] the court construed a grant of motion picture rights in 1923, before "talkies," to include the right to produce the film with sound.

When faced with this problem, courts have followed two approaches. A strict approach, which generally favors the licensor, would limit media use to the literal terms of the agreement. The second approach would apply a "reasonableness" standard in which media use would include all uses reasonably falling within the media described in the license. This approach generally favors the grantee and promotes a wider distribution of copyrighted works in new media.

Cohen v. Paramount Pictures Corp.[104] provides an example of the stricter approach to construing contractual language, one that would take a more literal reading of the contractual terms. In *Cohen*, the issue was whether a license conferring the right to exhibit a film "by means of television" included the right to distribute videocassettes of the films. When executed in 1969, the videocassette was not envisaged. The court sided with Cohen, the plaintiff-licensor, who wished to prevent distribution of the videocassettes. The court scrutinized the contractual terms of the Cohen-Paramount license and found that it lacked broad enough language to encompass distribution by videocassette. The court distinguished the other cases allowing distribution by the new media. In these cases, the language of the contract expressly conferred the right to exhibit films by methods yet to be invented. By contrast, the Cohen-Paramount license lacked such broad terms, while expressly reserving to the copyright owner all rights not expressly granted.

In its meticulous examination of the contractual language, the court claimed to be guided by the purpose of copyright law, which is to protect authors and encourage them to create. Thus, it would frustrate the purpose of the Act to construe the license as granting a right in a medium unknown at the time the parties entered into the agreement. The implication is that, in construing agreements, close questions concerning the rights granted should be resolved in favor of the grantor, to provide authors adequate incentives to create. This is hard to understand. The author of a new work may be motivated by the expectation of a certain return on her investment of time and effort, and this motivation will be based on known uses, not unforeseen ones. Thus, from an incentive standpoint it makes little difference in whose favor the agreement is construed.

By comparison with *Cohen*, the court in *Bartsch v. Metro-Goldwyn-Mayer, Inc.*[105] would place the burden on the licensor to show that the terms of the license

---

[102] *Restatement (Second) of Contracts* § 202(2) (1981).

[103] 83 F.2d 196 (2d Cir. 1936).

[104] 845 F.2d 851 (9th Cir. 1988).

[105] 391 F.2d 150 (2d Cir. 1968).

do not extend to the new medium. *Bartsch* concerned a 1930 assignment of a musical play, in which the assignee was given the right

> . . . to project, transmit and otherwise reproduce the said work or any adaptation or version thereof, visually or audibly by the art of cinematography or any process analogous thereto. . . .[106]

The assignee argued that this clause gave the right to broadcast the work by live telecast. The court did not agree because transmission of a work by cinematography is not analogous to its transmission by live telecast.[107] The *Bartsch* court did, however, discuss the principles of construction to be applied when dealing with media unknown to the parties and when the language of the contract is ambiguous. By general proposition, if the words are broad enough to cover the new use, it is fairer that the burden of framing and negotiating the exception should fall on the grantor.[108] In addition, the broader definition supports diffusion of copyrighted works, allowing the person in the best position to distribute the work in the new media to do so. Alternatively, the narrower definition might impede distribution of works in the new media by creating a deadlock between grantor and grantee. Thus, the expansive approach benefits the public by encouraging greater distribution of copyrighted works.[109]

§ 5.11 Transfers of Copyright: The Writing Requirement

[A] The 1976 Act

Under § 204(a) of the Copyright Act, when copyright ownership is transferred other than by operation of law, it is not *valid*

> . . . unless an instrument of conveyance, or a note or memorandum of transfer, is in writing and signed by the owner of the rights conveyed. . . .[110]

The writing requirement in § 101 applies to transfers of copyright which include

> an assignment, mortgage, exclusive license, or any other conveyance, . . . of any of the exclusive rights . . . but not including a nonexclusive license.[111]

---

[106] *Id.* at 151.

[107] The court did, however, allow the defendant's use of the work in live telecasts based on another provision in an assignment from Bartsch which transferred the motion picture rights throughout the world. *Id.* at 153. Thus, the analysis used by the court in how it would construe transfers of copyright involving a scope of media problem is essentially *dictum*. It has been influential, however, and represents the current view. *See* 3 *Nimmer on Copyright* § 10.10[B] (1993).

[108] *Bartsch v. Metro-Goldwyn-Mayer, Inc.*, 391 F.2d 150, 155 (2d Cir. 1968).

[109] *Bartsch* was cited in *Platinum Record Co., Inc. v. Lucasfilm, Ltd.*, 566 F. Supp. 226 (D.N.J. 1983) (license, which gave grantee rights to exhibit and distribute film containing copyrighted songs throughout the world by any means or methods now or hereafter known, covered the right to distribute videocassettes and discs of the film. Such distribution was allowed even though plaintiff might have anticipated future developments in exhibiting motion pictures).

[110] 17 U.S.C. § 204(a).

[111] 17 U.S.C. § 101 (transfer of copyright ownership).

The writing requirement ensures that the copyright owner will not inadvertently give away his or her copyright. In addition, a writing serves as a guidepost to resolve disputes by rendering the ownership rights clear and defininte. To serve these functions, the writing must be executed contemporaneously with the agreement.[112]

To determine whether a writing is necessary, one must distinguish between transfers on the one hand, that require a writing, and nonexclusive licenses that do not. Nonexclusive licenses, that may be transferred orally, are those in which the grantor retains the right to license the same right to others.

The writing requirement is a flexible one. There is no prescribed form for the writing transferring copyright except that it be signed by the copyright owner.[113] Although the "writing" may take many forms, it can be viewed as a simple, straightforward, and absolute requirement for a valid transfer (assignment or exclusive license) of copyright. Accordingly, courts have not relaxed the writing requirement to allow for industry practices, *e.g.*, in the movie industry, where written contracts are not the way business is done.[114]

By contrast with transfers of copyright, nonexclusive licenses may be granted orally. They may also be implied from conduct or the relationship between the parties. For example, courts have implied a license arising out a partnership relation.[115] In other instances, a nonexclusive license is construed where a copy of the work is delivered to a hiring party who has commissioned the work.[116]

[B] The Writing Requirement Under the 1909 Act

Under § 28 of the 1909 Act, total transfers of copyright, such as assignment, were required to be in writing.[117] Unlike the 1976 Act, however, there was no similar requirement for licenses, exclusive or nonexclusive. Thus, under the 1909 Act, an oral contract could convey an exclusive license to copyright, and an assignment of state common law copyright could be either oral or implied by conduct. These rules are still important today to determine the status of grants executed before 1978, because it is doubtful that the current Act could be applied retroactively in such an instance without raising serious constitutional problems.[118]

---

[112] *Kongsberg Int'l, Inc. v. Rice,* 16 F.3d 355 (9th Cir. 1994) (copyright owner's letter written three and one half years after alleged oral agreement is not substantially contemporaneous with oral agreement); *but see Eden Toys, Inc. v. Florelee Undergarment Co.,* 967 F.2d 27, 36 (2d Cir. 1982) (memorandum of transfer made within year of oral agreement and during term of exclusive license validated agreement *ab initio*).

[113] Although not a requirement, it is recommended that the instrument be notarized. Under 17 U.S.C. § 204(b), proper notarization constitutes *prima facie* evidence of execution of the transfer.

[114] *See, e.g., Effects Assocs. Inc. v. Cohen,* 908 F.2d 555 (9th Cir. 1990).

[115] *See, e.g., Oddo v. Ries,* 743 F.2d 630 (9th Cir. 1984) (manuscript prepared pursuant to partnership duties impliedly gave other members of the partnership right to use manuscript).

[116] *Effects Associates, Inc. v. Cohen,* 908 F.2d 555 (9th Cir. 1990) (nonexclusive license implied where author created a work at defendant's request and delivered it intending that defendant copy and distribute it).

[117] 17 U.S.C. § 28 (1909 Act).

[118] For a discussion of these constitutional problems, see § 5.3, *supra*.

§ 5.12 Recordation

[A] In General

Section 205 of the Copyright Act of 1976[119] allows recordation in the Copyright Office of all documents of copyright ownership whether assignments, exclusive licenses, or nonexclusive licenses. To fully enjoy the benefits of the 1976 Act, an owner of a copyright interest should accompany the recordation with a registration of the underlying work.

An owner of a copyright interest is rewarded by prompt recordation. For causes of action arising before March 1, 1989, recordation of a copyright interest is a prerequisite to bringing a suit for copyright infringement.[120] For example, an owner of an exclusive license to perform a copyrighted work cannot defend his rights in a court of law without recording his exclusive license in the Copyright Office.[121]

For causes of action arising on or after March 1, 1989, recordation as a prerequisite to bringing a copyright infringement suit is no longer required.[122]

Although recordation is no longer required to bring an infringement suit, it is highly recommended for other reasons. First, recordation specifically identifying the work will give notice to the world of the terms set forth in the document.[123] Thus, even if a person did not have actual notice of the document, he is presumed to have had that information when a transfer is recorded. This important constructive notice aspect of recordation applies only if the underlying work is registered.[124] Second, recordation establishes priority of ownership between conflicting transfers of copyright as well as conflicts between a transfer and a nonexclusive license.[125]

[B] Recordation: Priority Between Conflicting Transfers (Assignments and Exclusive Licenses)

Section 205(d)[126] of the 1976 Act establishes priorities of ownership between conflicting transfers of copyright, including any combination of conflicting assignments and exclusive licenses. Consider the following hypothetical situation: suppose

---

[119] 17 U.S.C. § 205.

[120] 17 U.S.C. § 205(d). This section has been deleted by the BCIA.

[121] See, e.g., Burns v. Rockwood Dist. Co., 481 F. Supp. 841 (N.D. Ill. 1979) (recordation is a jurisdictional prerequisite to bringing an infringement action); see also Swarovski, Ltd. v. Silver Deer Ltd., 537 F. Supp. 1201 (D. Colo. 1982) (proper recordation for the purpose of bringing an infringement suit imposes no obligation to record each instrument of transfer in a chain of title. Plaintiff need only record the immediate transfer to him to comply with § 205(d)).

[122] Recordation as a prequisite to bringing an infringement suit was deemed to be a formality incompatible with membership in the Berne Convention and was abrogated by the Berne Convention Implementation Act of 1988. For a discussion of the Berne Convention, see §§ 12.4–12.5, infra.

[123] 17 U.S.C. § 205(c).

[124] 17 U.S.C. § 205(c)(2).

[125] 17 U.S.C. §§ 205(d) and (e) (before the 1988 amendments, these sections were 205(e) and (f), respectively).

[126] 17 U.S.C. § 205(d).

that A, a writer, assigns to B the copyright of his novel in December 1989, and then conveys the same rights to C in January 1990. The question is who owns the copyright? Under the terms of this section, the first transferee, B, will prevail if he records within one month after execution of the agreement (two months if the agreement was executed outside the country). When the one-month grace period terminates, it then becomes a race between the two transferees of record, and if the first transferee, B, is the last to record, he loses his ownership to the copyright in the novel.

These priority provisions apply only if the work was registered in addition to being recorded.[127] If the work has not been registered, these provisions will not apply, and the court will decide priority based on proof submitted by the parties.

Two exceptions attach to these priority rules. First, one cannot enjoy a priority if he has received a transfer in bad faith, *e.g.,* with actual knowledge about the prior transfer. The second exception involves a transfer given without valuable consideration, such as by gift or bequest. In these two situations, the later transferee will not prevail over the first even if the first transferee fails to record his transfer. In summary, later transferees, even if they record first, cannot prevail over a prior transferee if they receive an ownership right in bad faith or without valuable consideration.

[C] Priority Between a Transferee and a Non-Exclusive Licensee

Section 205(e)[128] concerns priority between a transferee and a nonexclusive licensee. Under this section, a nonexclusive licensee will prevail over a transferee (assignee or exclusive licensee), but only in certain circumstances. First, the nonexclusive license must be evidenced in a written instrument signed by the copyright owner, and the license must be taken before execution of the transfer. Second, even if the nonexclusive license were taken after the transfer, it would prevail if evidenced in a writing and taken in good faith before recordation of the transfer without notice of it. For example, suppose a playwright assigned his copyright in his play to B, and one month later gave a nonexclusive license to C to perform the play. Here, the nonexclusive license would continue to be effective if B failed to record the work in the Copyright Office, and if C took his nonexclusive license in good faith.

§ 5.13 Involuntary Transfers

Section 201(e)[129] of the Copyright Act provides:

> . . . When an individual author's ownership of a copyright, or any of the exclusive rights under a copyright, has not previously been transferred

---

[127] Section 205(d) incorporates § 205(c)'s requirements for constructive notice: that the recorded document so identifies the work, that its ownership status be revealed by a reasonable search, and that the work be registered.

[128] 17 U.S.C. § 205(e).

[129] 17 U.S.C. § 201(e).

voluntarily by that individual author, no action by any governmental body or other official or organization purporting to seize, expropriate, transfer, or exercise rights of ownership with respect to the copyright, or any of the exclusive rights under a copyright shall be given effect, . . . except as provided under Title 11.

The purpose of this provision is to impede possible attempts by foreign governments, *i.e.*, China, to seize copyright from a dissident writer and prohibit the distribution of the work in the United States.[130] Other *involuntary* transfers are exempt from § 201(e). These include bankruptcy proceedings and mortgage foreclosures to which the author in such instances has voluntarily consented.[131]

---

[130] H.R. Rep. No. 94–1476, 94th Cong., 2d Sess. 123 (1976).

[131] *Id.* at 124. In addition, § 201(e) does not apply to involuntary bankruptcy provisions under Title 11 of the Federal Bankruptcy Act.

DURATION, RENEWAL AND TERMINATION OF TRANSFERS

§ 6.1 Introduction and Chapter Overview

How long should a copyright last?[1] In a speech on copyright before the House of Commons in 1841, Lord Macaulay reflected on the length of the copyright term:[2]

> It is good that authors should be remunerated; and the least exceptionable way of remunerating them is by a monopoly. Yet monopoly is an evil. For the sake of the good we must submit to the evil; but the evil ought not to last a day longer than is necessary for the purpose of securing the good.

In much the same spirit, Article I, § 8 of the U.S. Constitution[3] allows Congress to pass laws protecting writings of authors for "limited times" only. Although copyright is "limited" in duration, it does last a long time: the basic term of copyright is measured by the life of the author plus fifty years. Is such a long duration of copyright consistent with the constitutional language, "to promote the progress of science and the useful arts"? Macaulay, who called copyright "a tax on readers to give bounty to writers,"[4] certainly would not have thought so. On an intuitive level, one might conclude that such a long term is not warranted to encourage the optimum production of advertising jingles, computer programs, and commercial art, all of which fall within the broad range of copyrightable subject matter.

The fact is that it is impossible to determine the minimum duration sufficient to encourage the optimum amount of investment for the enormous range and variety of works of authorship. But even if the length of protection exceeds the ideal from a consumer welfare standpoint, we need not fear the copyright monopoly with the same intensity as, for example, the patent monopoly.[5] Despite the length of the copyright term, and the burdens it imposes, the copyright monopoly is tempered by various limiting doctrines such as the requirement of originality, the idea-expression

---

[1] For an overview of the subject, see Saul Cohen, *Duration*, 24 UCLA L. Rev. 1180 (1977).

[2] I Thomas Babington Macaulay, *Macaulay's Speeches and Poems* 285 (A.C. Armstrong & Son 1874). Lord Macaulay gave his speech pursuant to a legislative proposal to extend the copyright term to the life of the author plus sixty years.

[3] U.S. Const., Art. 1, § 8, cl. 8.

[4] *See* Macaulay, n. 2, *supra*.

[5] The patent monopoly is much more exclusive than that of copyright. It provides a 17-year monopoly encompassing the right to make, use, and sell the patented invention. For a discussion, see § 1.11, *supra*.

dichotomy, and the privilege of fair use.[6] In sum, the copyright monopoly is long but relatively weak.

This chapter, which is divided into three parts, is concerned broadly with the duration of copyright. Part I treats duration under the 1976 Act, whose basic term is life of the author plus fifty years. The 1976 Act has retained the bifurcated two-term system of copyright for works published before January 1, 1978. For works published before January 1, 1964, the author was required to file for renewal in the Copyright Office during the twenty-eighth year of the first copyright term. For works published between January 1, 1964 and December 31, 1977, renewal is automatic, and a copyright owner is no longer required to file a renewal registration in the Copyright Office. Part II discusses renewal and the continuing importance of 1909 Act case law in construing questions relating to the second copyright term. Part III then considers termination of transfers whereby an author or his designated successor(s) may terminate transfers and nonexclusive licenses in two situations. Section 304(c) of the 1976 Act[7] allows termination of the extended nineteen-year renewal term in certain circumstances, while § 203 of the 1976 Act[8] permits the termination of transfers and nonexclusive licenses for works enjoying a duration of life-plus-fifty-years.

PART I: DURATION

§ 6.2 In General: The 1909 and 1976 Acts Compared

As stated above, for most works created after January 1, 1978, the copyright term is measured by the life of the author plus 50 years. By comparison, the 1909 Act used a radically different system of duration, measured by the date of publication[9] (or the date of registration in unpublished form),[10] and continued for 28 years, followed by a renewal term of 28 years, for a total of 56 years.[11] This change in the duration of copyright is the centerpiece of the 1976 Act. Was there a need for it?

The House Report[12] offers a series of justifications for the longer term, summarized as follows:

(1) The longer term is needed to ensure an author and his dependents a fair remuneration for his works, particularly since life expectancy is longer than it was when the 1909 Act was passed.

(2) A shorter term would discriminate against works whose value is not recognized until many years later, particularly in our era where new communications media have greatly increased the commercial life of works.

---

[6] For a discussion of originality and idea-expression, see § 2.12, *supra*. For a discussion of fair use, see Chapter 10, *infra*.

[7] *See* 17 U.S.C. § 304(c).

[8] *See* 17 U.S.C. § 203.

[9] *See* 17 U.S.C. § 10 (1909 Act).

[10] *See* 17 U.S.C. § 12 (1909 Act).

[11] *See* 17 U.S.C. § 24 (1909 Act).

[12] H.R. Rep. No. 94–1476, 94th Cong., 2d Sess. 134–35 (1976).

(3) The public will not be hurt by a longer term but rather will benefit from its effect on encouraging increased production and dissemination of works.

(4) Based on a certain moment (death), the life-plus-50 system is a more precise measure as compared with the 1909 Act's use of "publication" to determine duration of copyright.

(5) The life-plus-50 system replaces the 1909 Act's burdensome, expensive renewal system with all its pitfalls.

(6) Although authors lose perpetual protection under common law copyright, they are fairly compensated for this loss by a term of life-plus-50-years.

(7) Without a life-plus-50 system, entry into the Berne Convention, the major international copyright convention, would be impossible.[13]

These justifications address three major concerns: fairness to authors, administrative convenience, and entry into Berne. The fairness, arguments are speculative and sometimes dubious. Although some authors will benefit from the longer term, it is uncertain whether the public will benefit accordingly. There are costs to any monopoly. The longer the monopoly, the greater the costs to the public, which will have less access to the copyrighted work and will have to pay higher prices for it. This point is not mentioned by the House Report. In general, the optimum term for copyright is a question of endless debate, and fairness to authors is only one aspect of the durational puzzle. The second group of arguments, based on administrative efficiency, are accurate for the most part. Abolishing the two-term copyright and replacing it with a single life-plus-50-years term simplifies administration even though, as a practical matter, the date of an author's death may sometimes be difficult to determine. The last justification concerning entry into Berne, arguably provides the most persuasive reason for the current term of copyright. Without a life-plus-50 term, the United States could not have hoped to join the Berne Convention and, thus, the world copyright community.[14]

§ 6.3   The Mechanics of Duration Under the 1976 Act

[A]   All Terms Run to the End of the Calendar Year

Under § 305 of the 1976 Act,[15] all copyright terms run to the end of the calendar year in which they would otherwise expire. This provision applies to all important time-limit formalities, such as renewals and terminations of transfers. Expiration of the term at the end of the calendar year provides an administrative convenience to both the Copyright Office and the copyright owner. For example, suppose that A copyrighted his work on April 10, 1972. Instead of the renewal deadline falling on

---

[13] *See* Berne Convention art. 7(1). Entry into the Berne Convention requires a life-plus-50-year term as a minimum term of copyright protection.

[14] For a discussion of the Berne Convention and the United States' entry, effective March 1, 1989, see §§ 12.4-12.5, *infra*.

[15] *See* 17 U.S.C. § 305.

April 10, 2000, as it would have under the 1909 Act, the deadline extends to December 31, 2000.

[B] The Basic Term: Life of the Author Plus 50 Years

Copyright in works created after January 1, 1978 subsists for the life of the author plus 50 years.[16] The basic term is relatively easy to apply. Assume that A creates works in 1980, 1985, and 1990, and dies in 2000. All of these works will enter into the public domain on the same date, after December 31, 2050, because all of A's copyrights will be measured by his life plus 50 years. That all of A's works enter the public domain at the same time simplifies copyright administration.

[C] Anonymous and Pseudonymous Works and Works Made for Hire

Anonymous works, pseudonymous works, and works made for hire constitute a major exception to the basic term of copyright. Under § 302(c),[17] the term for these works is 75 years from the first publication, or 100 years from creation, whichever is shorter. Thus, if A creates a work in 1978 in the course of employment, *i.e.*, a work made for hire, and publishes it in 1980, the work will go into the public domain after 2055. As compared with the basic copyright term, the term for anonymous, pseudonymous, and works made for hire is much less precise from an administrative standpoint. This alternative term of copyright is measured by creation or publication, events which are sometimes difficult to determine with any precision.

[D] Joint Works

The life-plus-50-years term also applies to joint works, but with an important difference. Under § 302(b),[18] copyright is measured from the last surviving author's death plus 50 years. For example, suppose A and B create a joint work in 1980. A dies in 1990 and B dies in 2000. The copyright will enter the public domain after 2050, 50 years after B's death (the last surviving author). Because of this provision, joint works have a chance of lasting much longer than works of individual authors, particularly if one of the joint authors is young.

[E] Duration of Sound Recordings: The Special Status of Sound Recordings Fixed Before February 15, 1972

Sound recordings were not recognized as copyrightable subject matter by federal copyright law until February 15, 1972.[19] Before that date, a sound recording author had to look to state law for protection of his creation against infringement. The 1976 Act has not changed the pre-1972 status of sound recordings. Section 301(c) provides that

---

[16] *See* 17 U.S.C. § 302(a).

[17] 17 U.S.C. § 302(c).

[18] *See* 17 U.S.C. § 302(b).

[19] Act of Oct. 15, 1971, Pub. L. No. 92–140, 85 Stat. 391.

any rights or remedies [for pre-1972 sound recordings] under the common law or statutes of any State shall not be annulled or limited by this title until February 15, 2047.[20]

Section 301(c) leaves sound recordings created before 1972 in a netherworld of uncertain state law protection.

Other than their peculiar status before 1972, sound recordings are treated the same as any other work. Thus, sound recordings created between February 15, 1972 and December 31, 1977 will have a 28-year first term and a 47-year renewal term. For sound recordings created after 1977, however, the basic life-plus-50-years term will apply.[21]

[F] Death Records

The year date of an author's death is the critical measure in computing the length of copyright. Because of its importance, § 302(d)[22] requires that the Register of Copyrights keep a public record containing information about the death of authors of copyrighted works. This section allows anyone having an interest in a copyright to file a statement in the Copyright Office that an author is living or dead. Section 302(e)[23] also creates a presumption of death, taking effect 75 years after publication or 100 years after creation, whichever is less. Any person who obtains a certified report from the Copyright Office that there is no indication that the author of the work is living, or had died less than 50 years before, is entitled to a presumption that the author has been dead for at least 50 years. Good faith reliance on this presumption is a complete defense to copyright infringement.[24]

[G] Duration of Copyright: Works Created But Not Published or Copyrighted Before January 1, 1978

Section 303[25] provides that all works created, but not copyrighted or published before 1978, will be treated under the basic term of copyright set forth in § 302,[26] and their copyrights will not expire before December 31, 2002. But if these works are published before this expiration date, copyright protection will last until December 31, 2027.

These works typically include letters, diaries, and other manuscripts never sold, exhibited, or reproduced for public distribution. Suppose, for example, that A owns a copyright on a letter sent to B in 1911, which has never been published. A dies in 1927. The copyright on the letter lasts until December 31, 2002. But if the copyright owner publishes the letter before this date, he will receive another 25 years

[20] See 17 U.S.C. § 301(c).
[21] However, when an anonymous, pseudonymous, or work made for hire is created, the 75/100 year term applies. See 17 U.S.C. § 302(c).
[22] See 17 U.S.C. § 302(d).
[23] See 17 U.S.C. § 302(e).
[24] Id.
[25] See 17 U.S.C. § 303.
[26] That is, life of the author plus 50 years. See 17 U.S.C. § 302.

of protection — until December 31, 2027. A sizable number of these works are likely to be in existence. Failure to publish them before 2003 will forfeit copyright protection, and the copyright owner will be deprived of an extra 25 years of protection. In short, December 31, 2002 will be a significant date for the public domain. This provision demonstrates once again the continuing importance of publication under the 1976 Act.

§ 6.4   Should Duration of Copyright Be Lengthened Another 20 Years?

Now that the United States has had a number of years of experience with the life-plus-50 term, momentum has been gaining to extend the basic copyright term for another 20 years (life plus 70) and to lengthen the second term of copyright from 47 to 67 years. Favoring the extension of the term are authors and their heirs who would benefit from greater duration. By contrast, others would argue that the copyright is long enough already, perhaps too long, for the true commercial life of most works. Moreover, a longer duration would undermine the function of the public domain. By extending the term of copyright, the public would not have access to these works of authorship, and future authors would be deprived of basic material with which to produce new works.

The most cogent argument for an extension of the copyright term is the United States' role as a net exporter of copyrighted materials. At this time, United States works, published over 75 years ago, are progressively entering the public domain every year.[27] At the same, they are also entering the public domain in foreign countries, even in those countries that have a longer term of protection than the United States, *e.g.*, life plus 70 years. How is this explained? Under section 7(8) of the Berne Convention, a member country must provide a term of protection for copyright governed by the legislation of the country where protection is claimed. This section, however, establishes an exception to the basic nondiscrimination principle known as "the rule of the shorter term." Unless the legislature of that country otherwise provides, the term shall not exceed the term fixed in the work's country of origin.[28] The "rule of the shorter term" has significant ramifications for works whose origin is the United States. For instance, the European Community, a major consumer of United States works, has adopted a uniform life-plus-70 term, but applies the Berne Convention's "rule of the shorter term."

How this affects United States works is best illustrated by an example. Suppose an author who publishes a work in 1925 dies in 1975. The work will enter the public domain in the United States in the year 2000.[29] Under the "rule of the shorter term," the work will also enter the public domain in that same year in France. On the other hand, if the United States provided another twenty years of protection (ninety-five years of protection), the work would not enter the public domain of both the United

---

27 See § 6.5[C], *infra*, for duration of copyright for works published before 1978.
28 Berne Convention art. 7(8) (Paris text). For a discussion of Berne, see §§ 12.4-12.5 *infra*.
29 There is a 75-year duration for works published before 1977. *See* § 6.5[C], *infra*.

States and France until 2020. Thus, the result of an extended duration would be to enrich United States authors and nurture a favorable balance of trade.

PART II: Renewal

§ 6.5　Works Published or Copyrighted Before January 1, 1978: An Overview

[A]　In General

For works published before 1978, the 1976 Act continues the bifurcated durational structure of the 1909 Act. The 1909 Act set up statutory copyright protection for two consecutive terms, a first term of twenty-eight years, measured from the date of publication, and a second or renewal term of twenty-eight years, for a total of fifty-six years.[30] The renewal term reverted to the author automatically, if he properly filed for renewal registration during the 28th year. Failure to comply with renewal formalities meant forfeiture of copyright to the public domain. As a result, many works entered the public domain through an author's ignorance of the formalities. Paradoxically, renewal formalities, designed to protect an author and his family, often operated to deprive an author of his work. With the passage of the Uruguay Round Agreements, copyright will be restored in works for the remainder of the term of copyright if the work entered the public domain for failure to comply with formalities such as renewal. But these provisions apply only to works whose origin is a Berne or WTO country. Copyright will not be restored for failure to renew in works whose origin is the United States.

[B]　The Renewal Registration Requirement Under the 1976 Act

The 1976 Act has progressively modified the nature and effect of the renewal system in three significant ways. First, as originally enacted, the 1976 Act retained the bifurcated durational system for works copyrighted before 1978, with one major difference:[31] the second term of copyright has been lengthened from 28 to 47 years. The second change occurred in 1992, with legislation establishing automatic renewal of all works.[32] Before these amendments, renewal registration had to be filed in the Copyright Office during the 28th year of the first term of copyright for all works still in their first terms on January 1, 1978. Failure to comply with this formality injected the work into the public domain. The Automatic Renewal Amendment abrogates the registration requirement. Now, for works first published between 1964 and 1977 (inclusive), an author will enjoy a full 75-year copyright term, without having to file for renewal during the 28th year. The Automatic Renewal Amendment, however, does not revive a first term copyright, published before 1964, that went into the public domain for failure to file a renewal registration.

---

[30] 17 U.S.C. § 24 (1909 Act).

[31] *See* 17 U.S.C. § 304(a).

[32] Pub. L. No. 102–307, 106 Stat. 264 (1992).

The third major change occurred with the Uruguay Round Agreements Act passed at the end of 1994. Under its provisions, copyright in certain foreign works that entered the public domain for failure to comply with formalities such as renewal registration will be restored.[33] The term of protection for restored works is the same term the work would have enjoyed if it had not lost U.S. copyright protection. For example, a 1940 Italian movie which had lost protection for failure to renew in 1967 will endure until December 31, 2015. The restoration provisions do not revive *all* works that fell into the public domain for failure to renew. They only apply to certain foreign works whose source country is a member of the WTO, or an adherent of Berne. By contrast, the Uruguay Round amendments do not revive copyright in a work whose country of origin is the United States.[34] Thus, the renewal requirement remains an important consideration in determining whether a work of U.S. origin — a large number of works — is in the public domain.

[C] **Works in Their Second Term as of January 1, 1978**

The second kind of subsisting copyright is found in works in their second or renewal terms between December 31, 1976 and December 31, 1977. These copyrights receive an extra nineteen years added to the second term, extending copyright to a total term of seventy-five years. Extension of the term is automatic, and the copyright owner need do nothing to receive the extra nineteen years. For example, suppose that a work was copyrighted in 1930 and renewal was properly claimed in 1958. The second term of copyright now lasts forty-seven years, expiring after December 31, 2005.

A special status is given to older copyrights that were extended in duration by a series of congressional enactments in 1962.[35] Congress believed that passage of a new Copyright Act was imminent and thought it was unfair to allow these works to fall into the public domain. To avoid this result, Congress from 1962 until the passage of the 1976 Act extended the term of these copyrights every year. As for other copyrights subsisting as of January 1, 1978, these specially extended copyrights automatically receive a seventy-five year term.[36] For example, a work that

---

[33] The date on which a public domain copyright is restored is not clearly indicated in the Act. One view suggests that copyright is restored when the United States enters into the new World Trade Organization — *i.e.*, on January 1, 1995. The other view maintains that legislative intent, fairness to public domain users, and the administrative obligations of the Copyright Office indicate a January 1, 1996 date of restoration. See Section 4.19[B] note 227 *supra* for a more complete discussion.

[34] A work eligible for restoration under 17 U.S.C. § 104A(h)(6)(D) must have entered the public domain for failure to comply with U.S. copyright formalities. In addition, it must have at least one author or rightholder who at the time the work was created, was a national or domiciliary of a WTO or Berne country and it must not have been published in the United States during the 30-day period following publication in such eligible country. Restoration of copyright is discussed in §§ 4.18–4.19 *supra*.

[35] *See Copyright Office Circular R 15t.*

[36] Congress passed a private law in 1971 (Priv. L. No. 92–60, 85 Stat. 857 (1971)) which provided extended protection for the works of Mary Baker Eddy, founder of the Christian Science Church. The clause was declared unconstitutional as violating the Establishment Clause of the First Amendment. *United Christian Scientists v. Christian Science Bd.*, 616 F. Supp. 476 (D.D.C. 1985), *aff'd*, 829 F.2d 1152 (D.D.C. 1987).

was copyrighted on April 10, 1915, and renewed by April 10, 1943, would have expired in 1971, but was kept alive by yearly congressional enactments. It will now receive a seventy-five year term which will last through December 31, 1990. In sum, to determine whether a work is in the public domain, one should subtract seventy-five years from the present date, and if copyright was secured before that date, the work is in the public domain.[37]

[D]   Summary Chart on Duration Under the 1976 Act

The following chart summarizes the basic duration for works created before and after January 1, 1978:

Before 1/1/78	On or After 1/1/78
Published or Copyrighted	*Created, i.e., Fixed*
75 years (2 terms: 28 + 47 = 75)[38]	Life-plus-50-years or 75 years from publication or 100 years from creation, whichever is less, if an anonymous or pseudonymous work, or a work made for hire
Unpublished	
Life-plus-50-years but all unpublished works on 1/1/78 will last until 2002, and if published, through 2027.	

§ 6.6   Renewal: Copyrights in the First Term as of 1978

[A]   Generally: The Continuation of the Renewal System Under the 1976 Act

Section 24 of the 1909 Act, now incorporated into § 304(a) of the 1976 Act, establishes a bifurcated copyright term. The first term lasts twenty-eight years, followed by a forty-seven year second or renewal term which automatically reverts to the author and his family. The original rationale of the renewal term was a paternalistic one: to protect authors and their families against unremunerative transfers which may have been given under economic duress or without knowledge of a work's potential value. Thus, authors have been given a special status in copyright law, as persons who should be helped out of bad deals they may have struck.

Renewal procedures are straightforward. To claim renewal, one must file for renewal in the Copyright Office during the 28th year of the first copyright term.[39]

---

[37] For example, suppose today's date is April 4, 1989. By subtracting 75 years, one can determine that works published before January 1, 1914 would have fallen into the public domain, but works published after that date could still be protected by copyright if the proper renewal were filed.

[38] Renewal registration is no longer required for works published between 1964 and 1977.

[39] 17 U.S.C. § 24 (1909 Act).

A renewal application can be filed by anyone on behalf of someone else, but it has to be filed in the name of one entitled to the renewal term.[40] Timely filing is required to obtain the term and failure to do so will dedicate the work to the public domain. As a result, through inadvertence or ignorance, many authors have forfeited and will continue to forfeit their works to the public domain by failing to comply with renewal formalities.[41]

The renewal system has proved to be neither fair to authors nor easy to administer. But despite its obvious drawbacks, § 304(a)[42] of the 1976 Act has incorporated the renewal system, faults included, as it existed under the prior law.[43] Congress has done so perhaps less for paternalistic reasons than to avoid the unfairness of changing rules on which authors and copyright owners have relied.[44] As a result, today's practitioner must understand the renewal system under the 1909 Act.

Understanding the renewal system under the 1909 Act, and the case law interpreting it, is important for determining the validity of works which would currently be in their second renewal term. First, for works whose origin is the United States,[45] the 1976 Act does not revive copyrights entering the public domain before 1978, and failure to renew was frequently the way works entered the public domain under the 1909 Act. Thus, the 1909 Act concerning renewal becomes important for evaluating whether a work has gone into the public domain. Second, one must look to the 1909 Act and its case law to determine the ownership status of a copyrighted work, because the 1976 Act will not be applied retroactively for such matters.[46]

[B] Renewal Claimants

Section 24 of the 1909 Act and § 304(a)[47] of the 1976 Act provide that the renewal term vests in the author of the work.[48] As for joint works,[49] the renewal

---

[40] See 2 Nimmer on Copyright § 9.05[D] (1993).

[41] See Barbara A. Ringer, Renewal of Copyright, Copyright Office Study No. 31 (Arthur Fisher mem. ed. 1963).

[42] 17 U.S.C. § 304(a).

[43] By incorporating the language of § 24 of the 1909 Act, the present Copyright Act has adopted some of the most obscure language in a notoriously obscure piece of legislation.

[44] H.R. Rep. No. 94–1476, 94th Cong., 2d Sess. 139 (1976).

[45] The Uruguay Round Agreements Act has restored copyright in certain foreign works that were injected into the public domain for failure to comply with U.S. copyright formalities such as notice and renewal. Works of U.S. origin, however, that were ejected into the public domain for failure to renew, remain there. See §§ 4.18–4.19 supra, for a discussion of copyright restoration.

[46] See Roth v. Pritikin, 710 F.2d 934 (2d Cir.), cert. denied, 464 U.S. 961 (1983) (the 1976 Act definition of work made for hire will not be applied retroactively to transactions occurring under the 1909 Act).

[47] 17 U.S.C. § 24 (1909 Act) has been completely incorporated into 17 U.S.C. § 304(a) of the 1976 Act; see H.R. Rep. No. 94–1476, 94th Cong., 2d Sess. 139 (1976).

[48] This would include vesting of the renewal term in the employer of a work made for hire. For a discussion of works made for hire, see § 5.2, supra.

[49] A joint work is a work prepared by two or more authors with the intention that their contributions be merged into inseparable or interdependent parts of a unitary whole. See 17 U.S.C. § 101 (joint works). For a discussion of joint works, see § 5.4, supra.

right vests in the joint authors, and renewal by one joint author or statutory successor is deemed a renewal for all the other joint authors.[50]

If an author is not living at the vesting of the renewal term, §§ 24 and 304(a) designate other classes of persons who can claim copyright. Both sections provide that if the author is not living, the widow, widower, *or* children will own the renewal term. Despite the use of the disjunctive, the Supreme Court in *DeSylva v. Ballentine*[51] construed this language to mean that renewal rights vested in the widow or widower *and* children of an author, who would take as a class.

This works as follows: suppose an author dies before the vesting of the renewal term in his work, leaving a widow and one child. Here, widow and child would each take a 50% share as joint owners of the copyright. But what if the author left a widow with more than one child? In the previous example, if the author left two children instead of one, would each survivor take a 33-1/3% share, or would the widow take 50%, with each child taking a 25% share? The case law under the 1909 Act indicates the equal share solution.[52] Once it is decided who owns what shares in the copyright, all the owners are considered tenants-in-common.

If neither the author's widow nor any children are alive, the rights vest in the author's executor, to be distributed to the legatees under his will.[53] Absent a will, renewal rights vest in the author's next of kin, determined by the laws of intestacy in the state where author is domiciled at death.[54]

The definitions of "widow" and "children" are no longer a matter of state law, as they were under the 1909 Act.[55] Section 101 of the 1976 Act now provides a statutory definition for these terms.[56] The term "children" now includes the author's illegitimate[57] and adopted children, and the term "widow(er)" includes the author's surviving spouse under the law of the author's domicile at death, whether or not the spouse has later remarried.[58]

---

[50] *See* 2 *Nimmer on Copyright* § 9.05[E] (1993).

[51] 351 U.S. 570 (1956).

[52] *See Bartok v. Boosey & Hawkes, Inc.*, 523 F.2d 941 (2d Cir. 1975). Whether the courts will adopt the 1909 Act's equal share solution is an open question. A court might be persuaded to look to the termination of transfer provisions under the 1976 Act, which provide that the widow would take a one-half interest and the children would apportion the other half *per stirpes*. For a discussion of these provisions, see § 6.12, *infra*.

[53] *See* 17 U.S.C. § 304(a).

[54] *See DeSylva v. Ballentine*, 351 U.S. 570, 580–81 (1956).

[55] *Id.*

[56] *See* 17 U.S.C. § 101 (children).

[57] *See Stone v. Williams*, 970 F.2d 1043 (2d Cir. 1992) ("children" are to be determined by state law).

[58] *See* 17 U.S.C. § 101 (widow).

§ 6.7 Exceptions to the Author's Right to the Renewal Term

[A] Generally

Section 304(a) of the 1976 Act sets forth four exceptions to the rule that the author and his family are the proper claimants for the renewal term. The copyright owner, rather than the author or his family, can claim the renewal term for: (1) posthumous works, (2) periodical, cyclopedic, or other composite works, (3) works copyrighted by a corporate body, and (4) works copyrighted by an employer as a work made for hire. The language in § 304(a) is identical to that of the 1909 Act.[59] Accordingly, one must look to the case law developed under the 1909 Act to construe these terms.

[B] Posthumous Works

To most people, the term "posthumous work" would mean any work published after the author's death. This dictionary definition of "posthumous" has not been adopted in § 304(a) of the 1976 Act. According to the House Report,[60] a posthumous work is to be defined more narrowly, as in *Bartok v. Boosey & Hawkes, Inc.*[61] This case concerned Bartok's *Concerto for Orchestra*, created toward the end of his life and assigned to his publisher before his death. Both the publisher and Bartok's son claimed the renewal rights to the work on expiration of the initial term of copyright in 1974.

The court held that this was not a posthumous work under § 24 of the 1909 Act. Although the work was published after Bartok's death, the court held that a posthumous work was a work for which no copyright assignment or other contract for exploitation of the work has occurred during the author's lifetime and which is unpublished before the author's death. Although the work was unpublished, Bartok had assigned rights to it before his death. Therefore, it was not a posthumous work as the court construed this term. Accordingly, the renewal term could be claimed by Bartok's son rather than the proprietor of the initial term.

Although this usage of "posthumous" deviates from the dictionary meaning of the term, the definition of "posthumous work" is consistent with the congressional purpose of the renewal term. It favors the author's family versus transferees, and protects the author's family from unremunerative transfers given by the author.

[C] Composite Works and Corporate Works

The proprietor owns the renewal term for composite and corporate works. A composite work is one in which several authors have contributed individual work. It is much like a collective work,[62] except that it does not encompass anthologies of a single author. The composite work author can claim renewal for the entire work, but each individual author has a claim to the renewal rights in his individual contribution.[63]

---

[59] 17 U.S.C. § 24 (1909 Act).
[60] H.R. Rep. No. 94–1476, 94th Cong., 2d Sess. 139 (1976).
[61] 523 F.2d 941 (2d Cir. 1975).
[62] *See* 17 U.S.C. § 101 (collective work).
[63] *Compendium II of Copyright Office Practices* § 1310 (1984).

For a work copyrighted by a corporate body (other than as an assignee or licensee of the individual author), renewal vests not in the author but in the corporate body. What this arcane category encompasses is not entirely clear, and it would appear to overlap the category of works made for hire. It has been applied in very few cases without satisfactory elucidation of its basis as an independent ground for a claim to the renewal term.[64] The Copyright Office discourages renewal registration on this basis except in certain narrow circumstances, but has not clarified what those cases are or how they differ from the work-made-for-hire category.[65]

[D] Employer of a Work Made for Hire

The fourth situation in which renewal may be claimed by the proprietor occurs in the case of an employer of a work made for hire. Although the 1976 Act has significantly modified the definition of a "work made for hire," this significant change in the law will not be applied retroactively.[66] Thus, for works published before 1978 in their first renewal term, one must apply the work-made-for-hire doctrine developed under the 1909 Act.

Epoch Producing Corp. v. Killiam Shows, Inc.[67] demonstrates some of the difficulties involved in this retroactive application to determine who, if anyone, owns the renewal term in a copyrighted work. Plaintiff Epoch, in a suit for infringement, asserted ownership as an employer for hire of D. W. Griffith's *Birth of a Nation*, and argued that it had the right to claim the renewal term in the work. Epoch had renewed the work in 1942 and brought its suit for infringement against Killiam in 1969. The defendant argued that Epoch had no right to claim the renewal term because it did not qualify as an employer for hire. Thus, according to the defendant, the work had entered the public domain because it had not been renewed by the proper party.

The court agreed that, under the circumstances, no work for hire was created and that, unlike an original registration of copyright, a renewal registration carried no presumption of validity.[68] In addition, the author, D. W. Griffith, nowhere explicitly stated his intent to convey the renewal right.[69] Thus, the work had entered the public domain after the first twenty-eight-year term of copyright. This case is instructive because it reveals the problems of both proof and legal standards that may arise when today's courts apply the 1909 Act to transactions of the distant past.

[64] See *Schmid Bros., Inc. v. W. Goebel Porzellanfabrik, K.G.*, 589 F. Supp. 497, 505 (E.D.N.Y. 1984).

[65] *Compendium II* at § 1317.06(c) (1984) (an example given in the *Compendium* is: works to which stockholders of a corporation have contributed indistinguishable parts).

[66] See *Roth v. Pritikin*, 710 F.2d 934, 939 (2d Cir.), *cert. denied*, 464 U.S. 961 (1983) (retroactive application of the 1976 Act's definition of "work made for hire" to pre-1978 transactions would raise a due process violation and be a taking of property without just compensation).

[67] 522 F.2d 737 (2d Cir. 1975), *cert. denied*, 424 U.S. 955 (1976).

[68] *Id.* at 745.

[69] *Id.* at 747.

§ 6.8 Transfers of the Renewal Term: *Fisher v. Witmark*

The stated congressional purpose of the two-term copyright protection was to protect authors against unremunerative transfers. This paternalistic goal, however, was undermined by 1909 Act case law. In *Fred Fisher Music Co. v. M. Witmark & Sons,*[70] the Supreme Court held that an assignment by an author of the renewal term, before that right had vested, was binding on the author. It soon became industry practice to require an assignment of the author's renewal rights in the initial contract. In order to sell their works, authors were pressured into conveying their renewal rights in the second copyright term.

There was one limitation on an author's power to assign the renewal term before its expiration. The author had to survive until the renewal term vested.[71] In *Miller Music Corp. v. Charles N. Daniels, Inc.,*[72] the Supreme Court held that, when an assigning author died before the renewal vested, the right to the second term would vest in the statutory successors under § 24 of the 1909 Act. To circumvent this risk, assignees of renewal rights sought to bind all the potential statutory successors, such as the author's spouse, by written contract. Again, contrary to the paternalistic objective of the renewal term, courts upheld these agreements so long as they were supported by adequate consideration and were written in express language granting rights in the renewal term.[73] In sum, *Fred Fisher* and its progeny undermined the basic policy of the renewal grant, which was to protect the unequal bargaining position of many authors.

Although no renewal application need be filed after December 31, 2005,[74] the problems arising in *Fred Fisher*, as well as in *Epoch* and *DeSylva*, will arise well into the twenty-first century so long as ownership of renewal rights must be determined.

---

[70] 318 U.S. 643 (1943).

[71] It was not clear exactly when the renewal vested. The issue was never decided under the 1909 Act, and the 1976 Act did not fill the gap. There are three possibilities for the vesting date: any time during the 28th year; when renewal is registered, *see, e.g., Frederick Music Co. v. Sickler*, 108 F. Supp. 587 (S.D.N.Y. 1989); and at the beginning of the renewal term, *see, e.g., Masascalco v. Fantasy, Inc.*, 953 F.2d 469 (9th Cir. 1991). *See generally* 2 *Nimmer on Copyright* § 9.05[C] (1993). The Copyright Renewal Act of 1992 (Pub. L. No. 102–302, 106 Stat. 264 (1992)) has resolved the issue of the vesting date for copyrights originally secured between January 1, 1964 and December 31, 1977. Under the automatic renewal provisions, renwal vests on either of two dates: when the registration is filed, or if no registration is filed, at the beginning of the renewal term. 17 U.S.C. 304(a)(2)(A)(i) and (2)(B)(i). Automatic renewal is discussed at § 6.9, *infra*.

[72] 362 U.S. 373 (1963).

[73] *See* 2 *Nimmer on Copyright* § 9.06[C] (1993).

[74] Works published in 1977 will be the last group of works for which a renewal application will be required. For these works, a renewal application will have to be filed in 2005 to claim the renewal term of 47 years.

§ 6.9   Automatic Renewal for Copyrights Originally Secured Between January 1, 1964 and December 31, 1977

[A]   Generally

After enactment of the 1976 Act, the momentum has increased to eliminate all copyright formalities. This movement gathered steam with the United States' entry into the Berne Convention. One of the fundamental provisions of Berne is that the enjoyment and exercise of rights shall not be subject to any formality,[75] and to many, the renewal requirement in United States law appeared inconsistent with Berne obligations. At the same time, very little practical justification could be found for retaining renewal formalities.

Originally, the renewal provisions were designed to allow authors to reclaim copyright and to provide certainty about copyright ownership. The renewal requirements, rather than achieving these laudatory goals, caused the opposite effect: they proved to be unfair to authors and bred legal uncertainty. First, as to fairness, renewal requirements dispossessed authors of their works. They erected a trap for many authors who failed to file for timely renewal in a procedurally correct way, thereby injecting their works into the public domain.

Second, rather than clarifying ownership, renewal provisions provoked uncertainty about copyright ownership. Much of this uncertainty can be traced to the confusion over when the renewal term "vested" under applicable statutory principles.

The problem here is obvious. Suppose that an author granted an assignment of renewal rights and that renewal was timely claimed, *i.e.*, during the twenty-eighth year, and suppose further that the author died before the renewal term began. Who owned the rights to the renewal term: the author's statutory beneficiaries or the grantee of the renewal term? Under the case law, the answer depended upon *when* the renewal term had vested. Some courts held that the renewal vested on the date of the renewal registration, which could occur at any time during the twenty-eighth year. Other courts held that the author had to survive until the beginning of the renewal term.[76]

Congress enacted the Copyright Renewal Act of 1992[77] to remedy the various difficulties of the preceding renewal system.

[B]   How Automatic Renewal Works

For works whose copyright was secured between 1964 and 1977, renewal is conferred automatically when the first term ends.[78] These works will enjoy the

---

[75] Berne Convention Paris Text (Art. 5(2)).

[76] *Compare Frederick Music Co. v. Sickler*, 708 F. Supp. 587 (S.D.N.Y. 1989) (renewal vests when the first qualified claim is filed) *with Marascalco v. Fantasy, Inc.*, 953 F.2d 469 (9th Cir. 1991) (section 304(a) requires an author to survive until the start of the renewal term in order for the renewal copyright interest to vest in his assignees).

[77] 102 Pub. L. No. 102–307, 106 Stat. 264 (1992).

[78] From a practical standpoint, this means that the first works automatically renewed were those whose renewal term began on January 1, 1993.

forty-seven year renewal term without having to file a renewal registration. An author may still file for renewal, and will want to do so because of certain advantages that flow from a renewal registration, but compliance with renewal formalities is permissive and will not affect the validity of the work. On the other hand, pre-1964 works are not affected by the automatic renewal amendment. It does not alter the public domain status for pre-1964 works that have failed to comply with the renewal requirements.

The vesting problem discussed above is resolved by automatic renewal in favor of early vesting.[79] Under the Renewal Act, the renewal term will vest when the copyright owner applies for renewal (during the twenty-eighth year after publication), even if he or she dies before the renewal term begins. For example, suppose an author of a musical work secured copyright in 1966. The renewal term will begin automatically on January 1, 1995. The renewal term will vest in the author if he or she applies for renewal in 1994. If the renewal term does not vest in the author for lack of a renewal application or because he or she dies before January 1, 1995, the new term will vest in the author's widow(er) or children alive when any of them obtained a 28th year registration. If no registration was obtained, renewal will vest in those persons alive on December 31, 1994. If none of the statutory beneficiaries is alive, the renewal term will vest in the author's executor.

[C] Continuing Incentives to Register

Despite an automatic renewal term, the Act provides three powerful incentives to file timely for renewal. Thanks to automatic renewal, the owner of the renewal term will no longer lose copyright for failure to comply with renewal formalities. But the owner may not be able to enjoy the economic benefits of copyright ownership without a timely claim for renewal.

The first major incentive in the 1992 Renewal Act concerns derivative works prepared under an authorization granted during the original term of copyright. If a timely renewal is filed, first-term grants of renewal rights may be nullified. Thus, the principles of *Stewart v. Abend* [80] still apply but only if a renewal registration is obtained during the twenty-eighth year of publication. If no registration is filed, a derivative work made pursuant to the grant can still be exploited, but no new derivative work can be made after the new term begins. For example, suppose an author of a play secures copyright in the play and grants motion picture and renewal rights to a film company. If the renewal right vests in the author, he is bound by the grant, and the film company will own the renewal rights. On the other hand, if the author dies before renewal vests, the author's statutory beneficiaries can prevent the motion picture from being exploited, but only if renewal registration is timely claimed. Without a timely renewal registration, an authorized film, translation, or other derivative work prepared under the grant can continue to be exploited under the terms of grant.

The second benefit of timely registration concerns the evidentiary weight accorded the registration. If registration is made during the last year of the first term,

---

[79] 17 U.S.C. 304(a)(2)(B) (as amended by 102 Pub. L. No. 307, 106 Stat. 264 (1992)).
[80] 495 U.S. 207 (1990) (discussed at § 6.10, *infra*).

the certificate of renewal registration shall constitute *prima facie* evidence as to the validity of the facts stated in the certificate. The evidentiary weight to be given to the certificates for registrations made after the end of that one-year period will be within the discretion of the court.

A third incentive to register concerns the remedies available to those who have registered their renewals. Remedies for copyright infringement are narrowed for authors who fail to file a timely renewal registration. Failure to file for renewal disallows statutory and actual damages, attorney's fees, and seizure and forfeiture (*see* sections 504, 505, and 509 of the Act) for all infringements that commence before registration. Registration at any time during the second term make the above remedies available for acts taking place after registration.

§ 6.10   The Renewal Term and Derivative Works[81]

[A]   Generally

When an author has licensed another, during the first copyright term, to create a derivative work, to what extent can the owner of the copyright in the derivative work continue to exploit the work in the second copyright term? The issue arises as follows: suppose R has licensed E, during the first copyright term, to create a motion picture of R's novel. E's motion picture is a derivative work based on the underlying work, *i.e.*, the novel. Can E's motion picture, a derivative work, continue to be exploited without R's consent during the renewal term?

This situation involves a conflict between the rationale of the renewal term and the theory of derivative rights. On the one hand, the renewal term creates an entirely new right, one that reverts automatically to the author and his family, unencumbered by assignments and licenses granted during the initial term. This suggests that a license to prepare a derivative work would terminate at the end of the initial term, as would the right to exploit the derivative work prepared under that license.

On the other hand, a derivative work may be individually copyrighted, and the derivative work author will own the copyright in the original elements added to the underlying work. Some derivative works surpass the underlying works in their creative and commercial value. Thus, to impede exploitation of the derivative work after the first term has expired may be both unfair to derivative work authors and costly to the public, who may be deprived of access to the work.

Until the Supreme Court case of *Stewart v. Abend*,[82] the case law was very much in conflict on the issue of the right to continued exploitation of a derivative work after expiration of the first copyright term. One line of cases implied that the derivative work cannot be exploited without the consent of the copyright owner of

---

[81] For a detailed overview, see Peter Jaszi, *When Works Collide: Derivative Motion Pictures, Underlying Rights, and the Public Interest*, 28 UCLA L. Rev. 715 (1981); Carol A. Ellingson, *The Copyright Exception for Derivative Works and the Scope of Utilization*, 56 Ind. L. J. 1 (1980).

[82] 495 U.S. 207 (1990).

the underlying work.[83] The opposite approach would permit continued exploitation of a derivative work in the second copyright term absent authorization of the owner of the renewal term.[84]

This latter approach views the derivative work as an independent work — a "new property" — in its own right and in its entirety, unattached to the underlying work.[85] Because it runs counter to the principle that derivative work authors own only the original elements added to the underlying work, this "new property rights" theory of derivative works received harsh criticism by commentators,[86] and even subsequent Second Circuit cases challenged its authority.[87] But it was not until 1990, with *Stewart v. Abend*, that the Supreme Court reconciled this conflict about the effect of expiration of the first term of copyright on the continuing right to exploit a derivative work made pursuant to a first-term grant.

[B] *Stewart v. Abend:* Demise of the New Property Theory of Derivative Works

In *Stewart v. Abend*,[88] the Supreme Court explicitly rejected the new property rights theory of derivative works, holding that the assignment of renewal rights by

---

[83] *Ricordi & Co. v. Paramount Pictures, Inc.*, 189 F.2d 469 (2d Cir.), *cert. denied*, 342 U.S. 849 (1951). *See also Fitch v. Shubert*, 20 F. Supp. 314 (S.D.N.Y. 1937) and *Grove Press, Inc. v. Greenleaf Pub. Co.*, 247 F. Supp. 518 (E.D.N.Y. 1965). *See* § 2.9[B], *supra*.

[84] The leading case is *Rohauer v. Killiam Shows*, 551 F.2d 484 (2d Cir.), *cert. denied*, 431 U.S. 949 (1977). In *Rohauer*, a movie, *Son of the Sheik*, based on a preexisting novel, could continue to be exploited even though the author died before vesting of the renewal term and successors to the renewal term assigned their rights to a third party. Defendant's right to continued exploitation of the derivative work was limited to the version created under the grant and gave no right to make second generation derivative works. In so holding, the court was heavily influenced by the policy behind the not-yet-effective termination of transfer provisions of the 1976 Act, which allow the author to recover interests transferred for the last 19 years of the renewal term (17 U.S.C. § 304(c)), and allow termination of all transfers at the end of their 35th year (17 U.S.C. (§ 203)). Under these provisions, a grant may be terminated, but is allowed continued exploitation of a derivative work prepared under the grants. See discussion of termination of transfers in § 6.11.

[85] Professor Nimmer called this the "new property rights" theory of the derivative work. *See* 1 *Nimmer on Copyright* § 3.07[A] (1993).

[86] *See* Malcolm L. Mimms, Jr., *Reversion and Derivative Works Under the Copyright Acts of 1909 and 1976*, 25 N.Y.L. Sch. L. Rev. 595 (1980); 1 *Nimmer on Copyright* § 3.07[A] (1993); Ralph S. Brown, *The Widening Gyre: Are Derivative Works Getting Out of Hand?*, 3 Cardozo Arts & Ent. L.J. 2 (1984).

[87] *Russell v. Price*, 612 F.2d 1123 (9th Cir. 1979), *cert. denied*, 446 U.S. 952 (1980) (Although a derivative work film based on the Shaw play, *Pygmalion*, prepared during the first term of the play's copyright, had entered the public domain for failure to renew, defendant could not exploit the public domain because to do so would infringe the underlying work (the play) which was not in the public domain. Only the original elements of the film entered the public domain, but the material used in the film from the underlying play was left unaffected. Thus, because the film could not be used without using the play, defendant would be liable for infringement). *See also Filmvideo Releasing Corp. v. Hastings*, 668 F.2d 91 (2d Cir. 1981) (entry into public domain of derivative work motion picture for failure to renew had no effect on valid copyright in underlying stories).

[88] 495 U.S. 207 (1990).

an author does not defeat the right of the author's statutory successor(s) to those rights if the author dies before the renewal right vests. In other words, when the grant of rights in the preexisting work lapses, the right to use parts of it in the derivative work ceases, and its continued use will infringe the preexisting work.

Stewart involved the film rights to a short story, "It Had to Be Murder," first published in 1942. The author, Cornell Woolrich, assigned the film rights to the short story to a production company and agreed to renew the copyright and assign the rights to the second term. Actor Jimmy Stewart and director Alfred Hitchcock acquired these rights and released the film version, *Rear Window*, in 1954. Woolrich died in 1968 before he could renew his copyright. In 1969, the executor of Woolrich's estate renewed the copyright and assigned the renewal term to Abend, who was acquiring the renewal copyrights to a number of stories based on films. On the re-release of the film in various media, Abend sued for copyright infringement, claiming that the right to use the film version terminated when Woolrich died before renewing copyright.

The Supreme Court agreed with the plaintiff, holding that the derivative work film could not be exploited without the permission of the owner of the underlying work. Justice O'Connor, writing for the majority, based her decision on a general principle: one may exploit only such copyrighted material as one owns or is authorized to use. Under this basic principle, a derivative work author cannot escape his obligations to the owner of the renewal copyright merely because he created a new version under an assignment or license that ended with the first copyright term. By implication, it would not change matters even if the derivative work author had contributed as much or more than the author of the underlying work. The Court also rejected the defendant's assertion that the termination of transfer provisions of the 1976 Act, allowing continued exploitation of a derivative work created before termination, manifested congressional intent to alter the delicate balance between the rights of authors of preexisting and derivative works.

[C]   *Stewart v. Abend* Reassessed

Simply stated, *Stewart* denies continued exploitation during the renewal term of a derivative work prepared during the initial term, unless rights during the renewal term were properly obtained. It gives primacy to authors of preexisting works at the expense of derivative work authors. Of course, the derivative work author owns the original elements added to the underlying work and can continue to use them as he wishes, unless this use would infringe the underlying work. This traditional principle, however, presents intractable problems for the continued exploitation of certain works, such as an opera based on a play, a film based on a novel, or a translation. In these kinds of derivative works, the new elements are so inextricably fused with the underlying work that one cannot be used without the other. In such instances, the practical effect will be to deny the derivative work author the right to his own original authorship.

Given the extensive number of movies, plays, television programs, sound recordings, etc., that are based on preexisting works in which copyright was secured before 1978, *Stewart* will change the way licenses for these derivative works are negotiated. For example, suppose a short story published in 1977 is made into a tele-movie in 1999, under a grant conveying the renewal term, and the author dies before the renewal terms vests. If the statutory beneficiaries comply with renewal formalities, all rights to the continued exploitation of the film terminate. For the most part, continued use of the derivative work will have to be renegotiated, and the new terms will be subject to the bargaining process. But this renegotiation process may often involve heavy transaction costs, thereby diminishing the value of both the preexisting and derivative works. Moreover, some derivative work owners may be faced with a tough decision: either pay the price of a new license or assignment (including the costs of negotiation) or stop using the derivative work. An inability to meet the new contract price may prevent the dissemination of some valuable derivative works, ultimately depriving the consumer of access to these works. Even so, one might conclude that at least the practical effect is beneficial to a worthy group of persons: the heirs of authors of preexisting works. One might view *Stewart* as a ruling that transfers wealth from derivative work authors to heirs of authors of preexisting works. But it is uncertain that the heirs of authors will really benefit from the "windfall" they apparently gain from *Stewart*. Instead, the heirs of authors may obtain less than anticipated if future derivative work authors, to avert the risks and uncertainties of renegotiation, avoid using pre-1978 works on which to base their derivative works. Thus, the unintended effect of *Stewart* may well be to reduce the value of pre-1978 works, harming the very heirs of the authors it appears to champion.

PART III: TERMINATION OF TRANSFERS

§ 6.11 Termination Generally[89]

The termination of transfer provisions of the 1976 Act serve much the same purpose as the renewal term of the 1909 Act. Their purpose is paternalistic, protecting authors from unremunerative transfers which may be given because of an author's "unequal bargaining position . . . , resulting in part from the impossibility of determining a work's value until it has been exploited."[90] These termination provisions allow an author and her family a second chance to reap the benefits from the author's works, but avoid the objectionable features of the two-term copyright.

Termination provisions cover two different situations. Section 304(c)[91] applies to works in their second renewal term as of January 1, 1978, and allows the author and his family to terminate transfers made before 1978 in order to recover the

---

[89] For an overview, see Frank R. Curtis, *Caveat Emptor in Copyright: A Practical Guide to the Termination of Transfer Provisions of the New Copyright Act*, 25 Bull. Copyright Soc'y 19 (1977); Harold See, *Copyright Ownership of Joint Works and Terminations of Transfers*, 30 U. Kan. L. Rev. 517 (1982); Marc R. Stein, *Termination of Transfers and Licenses Under the New Copyright Act: Thorny Problems for the Copyright Bar*, 24 UCLA L. Rev. 1141 (1977).

[90] H.R. Rep. No. 94–1476, 94th Cong., 2d Sess. 124 (1976).

[91] *See* 17 U.S.C. § 304(c).

nineteen years of the extended renewal term.[92] The other termination of transfer provision, § 203,[93] applies to transfers made after 1977. These two provisions give the author and her family the right to terminate, which must be effected according to the procedures established by statute and regulation. In other words, termination is not automatic, and if the author or her family neglect to take the necessary steps within the statutory time period, the transfer will continue in accordance with the original contract.[94]

In either case, the right to terminate cannot be assigned away in advance.[95] Thus, the termination provisions avoid the problem created by 1909 Act case law, whereby renewal rights may be assigned before their vesting.[96] This case law is still relevant to construing assignments of the renewal copyright, but does not apply to the extra nineteen years of the extended renewal term or to an author's termination right for post-1977 transfers. Despite the invalidity of agreements to surrender the termination right, one may speculate about various techniques to reach the same goal. One method might include a periodic termination of contract and renegotiation of a new contract which would extend the termination period. Whether a court would validate such an agreement is an open question, but such a ploy would appear to be contrary to the protective purpose of the termination provision.[97]

§ 6.12   Termination of the Extended Renewal Term Under § 304(c)

The grants covered by § 304(c) should not be confused with an author or family making advance assignments of the renewal term. These transfers of the renewal term are still binding. The provisions in § 304(c) concern only recovery of the nineteen years of the extended renewal term for grants executed before 1978. The legislative history justifies the recovery, stating that the 1976 Act created a new property right in extending the renewal term nineteen years, and that right should be enjoyed by the authors and their families rather than as a windfall for transferees.[98]

The intricate mechanics of § 304(c) termination can be broken down into six questions:

(1) *What grants are covered?*

---

[92] For example, suppose that the second 28-year term would have expired in 1990. Section 304(c) extends the renewal term for another 19 years, until 2009.

[93] *See* 17 U.S.C. § 203.

[94] *See* 17 U.S.C. §§ 203(b)(6) and 304(c)(6)(F).

[95] *See* 17 U.S.C. §§ 203(a)(5) and 304(c)(5). *See also* H.R. Rep. No. 94–1476, 94th Cong., 2d Sess. 125 (1976).

[96] *See Fred Fisher Music Co. v. M. Witmark & Sons*, 318 U.S. 643 (1943).

[97] For other contractual ploys to circumvent the provision rendering invalid agreements to restrict the right to terminate, see Paul Goldstein, *Termination of Transfers and Licenses Under the New Copyright Act: Thorny Problems for the Copyright Bar*, 24 UCLA L. Rev. 1107, 1152 (1977).

[98] H.R. Rep. No. 94–1476, 94th Cong., 2d Sess. 140 (1976).

(a) Grants executed before January 1, 1978, by the author or his successors who could claim the renewal term of any transfer covering renewal rights, including exclusive and nonexclusive licenses.[99]

(b) Exceptions are works made for hire and dispositions by will.

(2) *Who can terminate?*[100]

(a) The author or a majority of authors of a joint work.

(b) If the author is dead:

(i) If the author dies without children, leaving only a widow or widower, then the widow or widower owns the entire termination.

(ii) If the author leaves surviving children, without a widow or widower, then the children take the entire interest.

(iii) If both a widow(er) and children are surviving, the widow(er) takes a 50% share and the children take the other 50%. The rights of the children and grandchildren are exercised *per stirpes*. This means that the children take the share that their parents would have taken. Suppose, for example, the author's widow and two of his three children are living and a third is deceased:[101]

---

[99] *See* 17 U.S.C. § 304(c).

[100] *See* 17 U.S.C. §§ 304(c)(1) and (2).

[101] H.R. Rep. No. 94–1476, 94th Cong., 2d Sess. 125 (1976).

In this example, the widow will take 50% and the children will take 50%. The share of each child will be 16–2/3%, but if child 3 is dead, leaving three children, each of the three grandchildren will get 5–5/9%. Because a majority interest is needed to terminate a right, the widow must be joined by one of the children to terminate. If neither child 1 nor child 2 joins, then the widow must obtain a *majority* consent of the third child's children to terminate the right. The result is consistent with the principle that the interest of a deceased child can be exercised only by majority action of his or her surviving children.[102] One grandchild will not be enough, even though it would look as if the ownership would constitute 55–5/9%.

(c) When a grant is given by one other than the author, all surviving grantors are required to terminate.

(3) *When may termination take place?*[103]

(a) During the five-year period beginning at the end of fifty-six years from the date copyright was originally secured, or beginning on January 1, 1978, whichever is later.[104]

(4) *How may termination be effected?*[105]

(a) By serving written notice on the grantee, or his successor in title. If the grant was executed by a person or persons other than the author, all of those who executed the grant and survive must sign the notice.

---

[102] *Id.*

[103] *See* 17 U.S.C. § 304(c)(3).

[104] For example, suppose the author copyrighted the work in 1920 and conveyed the renewal term to B. The author or the statutory beneficiaries would have the right to claim the extended term beginning in 1978 during the five-year period until 1983. Remember that the copyright would have expired in 1976 but was kept alive by special legislation. *See* discussion § 6.4[C], *supra.* Thus, 1978 is later than 56 years from the date copyright was secured, and the grant could be terminated at any time between 1978 and 1983. Note that the work will fall into the public domain in 1995.

[105] *See* 17 U.S.C. § 304(c)(4).

(b) Notice must comply with Copyright Office regulations.[106]

(c) A copy of notice must be recorded in the Copyright Office before the effective date of termination.

(5) *What is the effect of termination?*[107]

(a) All rights revert to those having the right to terminate.

(b) The exception is that derivative works prepared before termination may continue to be exploited under the terms of the grant.

(c) No new derivative works may be prepared after the termination date.

(d) Termination rights vest on the date notice is served.

(6) *Who can make further grants?*[108]

(a) Owners are tenants-in-common who can authorize further grants if signed by the same number and proportion as are required to terminate. The right granted is effective for all owners, even non-signers.

§ 6.13 Termination Formalities

The 1976 Act sets forth the general formalities for termination of transfer, and the Copyright Office has issued the form, content, and manner of service for proper notice of termination.[109] There remain, however, several open questions which will have to be answered by case law. For example, the 1976 Act states that "termination shall be effected by serving an advance notice in writing upon the grantee or grantee's successor in title."[110] The meaning of "successor in title" is nowhere indicated in the Act.

This and other issues concerning § 304(c) terminations were examined in *Burroughs v. Metro-Goldwyn-Mayer, Inc.*,[111] which involved an attempt to terminate a 1931 nonexclusive license to film rights with use of certain *Tarzan* characters. The nonexclusive license in question was given by a family-owned corporation, ERB, Inc., to MGM's predecessor in title. The author's heirs served notice of termination on the family-owned corporation, but not on MGM, in 1977, before the effective date of the 1976 Act. The plaintiffs contended that the *Tarzan* grant was effectively terminated and that a 1981 remake of *Tarzan* by MGM infringed their rights. The District Court held that the character, Tarzan, was sufficiently delineated to be a copyrightable interest and as such could be terminated.[112] The termination was ineffective, however, because it was premature (the Act was not yet in effect in 1977) and because it was served on the family-owned

[106] *See* 37 C.F.R. § 201.10.
[107] *See* 17 U.S.C. § 304(c)(6).
[108] 17 U.S.C. §§ 304(c)(6)(C) and (D).
[109] *See* 37 C.F.R. § 201.10.
[110] *See* 17 U.S.C. § 304(c)(4).
[111] 519 F. Supp. 388 (S.D.N.Y. 1981), *aff'd*, 683 F.2d 610 (2d Cir. 1982).
[112] *Id.* at 519 F. Supp. 388.

corporation (the original grantee) and not on the "current successor in title," MGM, as it should have been.

On appeal, the Second Circuit affirmed the decision, but on different grounds, stating that the Copyright Office regulations require that notice of termination be accompanied by a short statement as to the grants covered. The plaintiffs, however, failed to list five titles of works in their notice of termination. The court concluded that this omission rendered the termination ineffective because the grant gave the right to use the Tarzan character for each of these titles. Thus, the grant remained intact because, to be effective, a notice of termination must clearly identify the grant to which the notice applies.[113]

Burroughs still leaves open the question of whether a notice of termination, to be effective, must be served on the grantee, the grantee's successor in title, or both. The Act provides that the notice must be served on the grantee *or* the grantee's successor in title.[114] Does use of the disjunctive in the statutory language mean that the terminating party has the choice? Judge Newman, in a concurring opinion,[115] suggested that notice was ineffective because it was not served on MGM. To allow the notice to be served on the family-owned corporation would be like allowing the heirs to serve notice on themselves. In the circumstances of this case, the heirs should have at least served notice on a realistic grantee, which was MGM.

Clearly, an obligation to serve all nonexclusive licensees of an original grantee would place an enormous burden on the author, particularly if the author's grantee has conveyed a large number of nonexclusive licenses. On the other hand, to allow notice on the original grantee would undermine a basic policy of the notice provisions, which is to provide adequate notice for the person whose interest is being terminated. One intermediate solution, supporting both the interest of the author and his grantee, would require the author to serve notice on the original grantee and his exclusive licensees, but not on nonexclusive licensees. Such a requirement would impose the minimum amount of hardship for all concerned.[116]

§ 6.14   Section 304(c): Termination and Derivative Works — *Mills Music v. Snyder*

A derivative work prepared under a grant can continue to be used under its terms even after termination of the grant.[117] Continued exploitation is limited to the specific derivative work and does not extend to preparation of other derivative works based on the copyright covered by the terminated grant.

In *Mills Music, Inc. v. Snyder*[118] the issue was whether an author's termination of a music publisher's interest in a copyright also terminated the publisher's

---

[113] See 37 C.F.R. § 201.10(b)(ii).

[114] 17 U.S.C. §§ 203(a)(4) and 304(c)(4).

[115] *Burroughs v. Metro-Goldwyn-Mayer, Inc.*, 683 F.2d 610, 635 (2d Cir. 1982) (Newman, J., concurring).

[116] See 3 *Nimmer on Copyright* § 11.06[B] (1993).

[117] See 17 U.S.C. § 304(c)(6)(A).

[118] 469 U.S. 153 (1985).

contractual right to share in the royalties from those whom he had sublicensed to make derivative works. Ted Snyder, author of the song *Who's Sorry Now*, had assigned the renewal term to Mills Music. As owner of the renewal term to the song, Mills Music had sublicensed the song to more than 400 record companies, each of which had prepared separate derivative works and paid royalties. The author's family served on Mills Music notice of termination covering the nineteen-year extended renewal term and demanded that royalties revert to them. The Supreme Court, reversing a decision in favor of Snyder, held that the use of the term "grant" three times in § 304(c)(6)(A) revealed a legislative intent to cover not only the original grant but the sublicense made under that grant as well.[119] The Court acknowledged that the principal purpose of § 304 was to benefit authors, but recognized that this was not its sole rationale. Its other purpose was to enable continued public accessibility to derivative works after termination. The Court concluded that upholding the status quo did justice to both policies.[120]

Justice White, in a dissenting opinion, sharply criticized the majority's reading of the statutory language and legislative history of § 304(c). He concluded that a middleman assignee's right to receive continued royalties had nothing to do with continued public access to a work, but would undermine the other policy of the 1976 Act, which is to benefit authors.[121] Moreover, a rule benefiting authors in this instance would not disturb any system of economic incentives which the 1976 Copyright Act was intended to provide, because neither author nor middleman assignee acted in reliance on § 304(c) when they entered into their contractual relations. In other words, from a policy standpoint, if someone should obtain an extra nineteen-year windfall, it should be the author who was the intended beneficiary of the renewal term.[122] Displeasure with *Mills* has led to legislative efforts to overturn the opinion.[123]

§ 6.15   Termination of Transfer Under § 203[124]

Terminations of transfers under § 203 provisions apply to grants made after 1977. Because the first terminations under § 203 will take place beginning in 2013 for grants given in 1978, they are not of such immediate importance as terminations covering the last nineteen years of the renewal term under § 304(c). The practical effect of § 203 termination provisions, however, will be felt where parties to transfers of copyright take these provisions into account in drafting their agreements. As was the case with § 304(c) terminations, a termination of transfer under § 203 requires

---

[119] *Id.* at 170–72.

[120] *Id.* at 177.

[121] 469 U.S. at 186 (White, J., dissenting). For other criticism of the majority opinion's rationale, see Howard B. Abrams, *Who's Sorry Now? Termination Rights and the Derivative Works Exception*, 62 U. Det. L. Rev. 181 (1985); William F. Patry, *Copyright Law and Practice* 489–96 (1994).

[122] H.R. Rep. No. 94–1476, 94th Cong., 2d Sess. 140 (1976).

[123] *See, e.g.*, H.R. 3163, 99th Cong., 2d Sess. (1985).

[124] *See* 17 U.S.C. § 203.

the author or his successors to affirmatively follow procedures set forth in the Act. If the termination right is not exercised, the grant will last the entire term unless otherwise stated in the contract. In addition, the right to terminate cannot be contracted away, including an agreement to make a will or to make a future grant.[125]

Section 203 is similar, but not identical, to the termination provisions of § 304(c).[126] The same questions, however, should be considered in analyzing § 203 terminations as were considered for § 304(c) terminations:

(1) *What grants are covered?*[127]

(a) Grants by the author of any copyright interest, including exclusive and nonexclusive licenses.

(b) Grants made on or after January 1, 1978, for works created before or after 1978.

(c) Grants not covered are of works made for hire and dispositions by will.

(2) *Who can terminate?*[128]

(a) The author or, for joint works, a majority of authors who executed the grant.

(b) If the author is deceased, a majority of owners of his termination interest.[129]

(3) *When may termination take place?*[130]

(a) During the five years beginning at the end of thirty-five years from the date of the grant, or, if the grant covers the right of publication, thirty-five years from the date of publication, or forty years from the date of the grant, whichever is earlier.

(4) *How may termination be effected?*[131]

(a) By serving a written notice no less than two nor more than ten years before termination is to occur.

(b) Notice must comply with Copyright Office regulations.[132]

(c) A copy of notice must be recorded in the Copyright Office before the effective date of termination.

(5) *What is the effect of termination?*[133]

(a) All rights revert to those having the right to terminate.

---

[125] 17 U.S.C. § 304(c)(5).
[126] For a discussion of the differences, see § 6.16, *infra.*
[127] 17 U.S.C. § 203(a).
[128] 17 U.S.C. §§ 203(a)(1) and (2).
[129] See discussion in § 6.12, *supra.*
[130] 17 U.S.C. § 203(a)(3).
[131] 17 U.S.C. § 203(a)(4).
[132] 37 C.F.R. § 201.10.
[133] 17 U.S.C. § 203(b)(3).

(b) The exception is for derivative works prepared before termination, which may continue to be exploited under the terms of the grant.[134]

(c) No new derivative works may be prepared after the date of termination.

(6) *Who can make further grants?*[135]

(a) Further grants are valid if signed by the same number and proportion of owners as are required for termination. All owners are bound, even non-signers.[136]

§ 6.16   Sections 304(c) and 203 Compared

Although the two termination provisions are essentially the same in both their goals and procedures, they do contain significant differences. The following discussion summarizes these differences.

(1) *Grants covered.*

(a) The grants covered by § 304(c) are different from those covered in § 203. Section 304(c) applies only to grants executed before January 1, 1978, while § 203 applies only to grants executed after that date.

(b) Section 304(c) applies to grants given by the author or renewal beneficiary under the second provision of § 304(a). Section 203 applies only to grants given by the author.

(c) Section 304 applies to grants covering the renewal term for copyrighted works. Section 203 applies to any interest in copyright.

(2) *Who may terminate?*

Persons who may qualify to terminate the extended renewal term under § 304(c)(1)(2) are slightly different than those who can terminate under § 203(a)(1)(2) for post-1977 grants.

(3) *When may termination take place?*

For § 304(c), termination takes place during a five-year period beginning at the end of fifty-six years from the date copyright was originally secured. For § 203, termination takes place during the five years beginning at the end of thirty-five years from the grant, *i.e.*, between the 35th and 40th years of the grant, or, if the grant covers the right of publication, thirty-five years from the date of publication or forty years from the grant, whichever is less.

(4) *How may termination be effected?*

The same for both sections.

(5) *What is the effect of termination?*

---

[134] 17 U.S.C. § 203(b)(1). See discussion of § 304(c) and *Mills Music, Inc. v. Snyder*, 469 U.S. 153 (1985), in § 6.14, *supra.*

[135] 17 U.S.C. § 203(b).

[136] 17 U.S.C. § 203(b)(3).

The same for both sections.

(6) *Who is entitled to make further grants?*

Owners of a reverted right are tenants-in-common under § 304(c)(6) and can deal separately with the right except, when the right is shared, further grants require majority action as to that shared. Under § 203(b), no tenancy-in-common exists, and, for further grants, the same number and proportion as required for termination are required.

§ 6.17   Some Works Enjoy No Termination Right, and Other Works Have Both Termination and Renewal Rights

The following two subsections present several situations revealing how some works will have neither termination nor renewal rights, while other works will enjoy rights of both termination and renewal. These situations provide a good review of termination and renewal principles and their possible interplay. They also indicate that the drafters of the termination provisions may not have taken into account certain anomalies arising out of gaps in the termination and renewal provisions, which could have been avoided by careful drafting.

[A]   Certain Grants Subject to No Termination

Some works will not enjoy termination rights at all. Section 304(c) applies only to grants covering *subsisting copyrights* made before January 1, 1978, whereas § 203 applies only to grants made after that date. In addition, § 203 termination will apply only to grants made by the *author*. Thus, grants of common law rights are excluded from termination, that is, a grant made before 1977 for an unpublished work. For example, suppose that in 1977 a publisher buys the rights for a forthcoming novel and the work is not completed until 1980. The grant cannot be terminated because § 304(c) applies to subsisting copyrights only, whereas § 203 applies to post-1977 grants. In addition, the copyright term will simply be the basic life-plus-fifty-years term. No renewal term will revert to the author because renewal applies only to works copyrighted before 1978.

A second example involves a novel completed and published in 1977. Suppose the author dies in 1980 and the author's widow assigns the copyright in 1981 to a third party. No termination can be effected because § 203 applies only to an *author's* grant. Furthermore, although copyright did subsist in the work at the time of the grant, § 304(c) cannot be invoked because that section applies to grants made before 1978. The widow will, however, enjoy a renewal right after 2005 at the end of the first twenty-eight-year term.

If, however, in the above example, the work was created in 1977 but not published, and the widow assigns the copyright in 1980, the widow would have neither a termination right nor a right to the renewal term. Again, the reason is that the § 203 termination applies to grants made by the author, whereas § 304(c) applies to subsisting copyrights. There will be no renewal rights because renewal applies only to works in their first or second term of copyright. In this example, however, the work was not yet copyrighted as of January 1, 1978.

[B]   Grants Subject to Both Termination and Renewal

The interplay between §§ 304(a) and 203 will permit some works to enjoy both a renewal term and a right of termination. For example, assume that A copyrights a work in 1962 and, in 1978, assigns to B his renewal interest, which will vest in 1990. If A does not live until the vesting of renewal, the term will simply revert to his widow and family. But if A lives until the vesting of the renewal (1989), B will enjoy the rights to the forty-seven-year renewal term — until 2037. But here the author or his family can terminate the transfer pursuant to § 203, beginning in 2013 (thirty-five years after the 1978 grant), thus cutting short B's renewal term by twenty-four years.

CHAPTER 7

COPYRIGHT REGISTRATION AND DEPOSIT

§ 7.1 Introduction and Chapter Overview

Copyright registration (and the important role it plays) is a unique feature of American law. The act of registration does not create a copyright; copyright begins when an author fixes his work in a tangible medium of expression. Registration, however, can be critically important to the copyright owner because it can preserve copyright,[1] and for works which originated in the United States, it is a prerequisite for bringing an infringement suit. In order to register a claim for copyright, the applicant is required to deposit a specified number of copies of the work with the Register. The deposit serves two purposes: it identifies the work and satisfies the mandatory deposit requirement for the Library of Congress. Both registration and deposit, covered in §§ 401 through 412[2] of the Act, are administered by the Copyright Office.

This chapter, which is divided into two parts, presents a brief overview of copyright registration and the deposit requirements for the Library of Congress. Part I examines the mechanics and the importance of registering a claim of copyright in the Copyright Office. Part II reviews the mandatory deposit requirements designed to enrich the collection of the Library of Congress and the interplay of the deposit requirement with registration of a claim for copyright. In both parts of this chapter, the central role played by the Copyright Office is emphasized.

---

[1] *See* 17 U.S.C. § 405(a)(2). For works publicly distributed before March 1, 1989, copyright can be invalidated by omitting notice from more than a relatively small number of copies or phonorecords publicly distributed unless

> registration for the work has been made before or is made within five years after the publication without notice, and a reasonable effort is made to add notice to all copies or phonorecords that are distributed to the public in the United States after the omission has been discovered. . . .

For works publicly distributed after March 1, 1989, notice is permissive and omission of notice can no longer forfeit copyright. *See* 17 U.S.C. § 401(a). For a discussion of this provision, see § 4.11, *supra*.

[2] 17 U.S.C. §§ 401–412.

PART I: REGISTRATION

§ 7.2   The Copyright Office

Ever since it was created in 1897 to administer copyright registrations and deposits, the Copyright Office has remained a separate department of the Library of Congress.[3] In addition to its principal administrative function, the registration of copyright, the Copyright Office promotes the overall policies of the Library of Congress. Its chief officer, the Register of Copyrights, is appointed by the Librarian of Congress and is the Assistant Librarian of Congress for Copyright Services.[4]

From modest beginnings, today the Copyright Office, located in Washington, D.C., has over 500 employees and processes over 500,000 registrations every year. Its public information office responds to hundreds of thousands of letters and telephone calls about general copyright matters.. The Office plays a large role in advising Congress on national and international copyright policy.

In conjunction with its registration activities, the Copyright Office keeps elaborate records.[5] The Copyright Card Catalog and post-1977 automated files provide an index to United States copyright registrations from 1870 to the present.[6] These records are open for public inspection. In addition, the Office keeps an Assignment and Related Documents Index pertaining to the recordation of assignments, licenses, and other ownership interests in a copyright. For persons not wishing to do their own research, the Certifications and Document section of the Copyright Office, for a fee, will search the records and issue a report concerning the copyright status or ownership of a work.[7] Reproduction of deposit copies,[8] obtained for a fee pursuant to regulations established by the Copyright Office,[9] are available in three situations: when requested by the claimant, when requested by an attorney for litigation purposes, or when ordered by a court for litigation.[10]

§ 7.3   Why a Registration System?

Copyright registration is a unique aspect of American law. No other country has anything quite like our elaborate system, carefully administered by a governmental

---

[3] *Compendium II of Copyright Office Practices* § 104.

[4] *See* 17 U.S.C. § 701(a).

[5] *See* 17 U.S.C. § 705.

[6] *See Copyright Office Circular* R23.

[7] *See Copyright Office Circular* R22.

[8] One must deposit the required number of copies or, in some instances, identifying material to register a claim for copyright. For a discussion of the deposit requirement, see §§ 7.9–7.13, *infra*.

[9] *See* 17 U.S.C. § 706; 37 C.F.R. §§ 201.1–201.2 (1987); *see also Copyright Office Circulars* R6 and R96.

[10] *See* 37 C.F.R. § 201.2(d) (1987).

agency. Is there a need for a system of copyright registration?[11] If copyright protection begins on creation, what purpose is served by registration?

Registration has been justified in that it provides benefits to both users and owners.[12] It protects owners against the unauthorized use of their works by establishing priority of authorship, and it confers *prima facie* evidence of the validity of the copyright and the facts stated in the certificate.[13] Generally, a registration system produces a more efficient, readier market for copyrighted works. It facilitates transfers, assignments, and licenses of copyrighted works because prospective transferees have more confidence in the validity of a registered copyright. In this way, the Copyright Office registry aids prospective purchasers in determining the status of a work, and provides them information about what may be available on the market.[14]

Despite these benefits, the system has been criticized as not working according to its ideal. Fundamentally, a registration system is only as good as the information reflected in the records. Unfortunately, a search of Copyright Office records may often be unrewarding or even misleading. The absence of any mention of a work in the records does not mean it is unprotected. The reason is that copyright registration is essentially voluntary and many copyright owners choose not to register. The only exception to voluntary registration is for works copyrighted before 1978 (published with notice). For pre–1978 copyrights, the copyright owner must file a renewal registration to claim the second term.[15] Renewal registration, however, is only required for published works. For works unpublished before 1978, protection was perpetual without the need to register one's claim in the Copyright Office. Moreover, works created after 1978 are no longer subject to a renewal term, and for these works copyright registration is purely voluntary. In short, searches of the Copyright Office records are rarely conclusive.

Copyright Office records can be unreliable because the information contained in them may be inaccurate or incomplete or both.[16] To understand why, one must look at how the Office gathers, accepts and catalogs this information which ultimately

---

[11] In British copyright law, the registration system was abrogated by The Act of 1911. In 1908, Britain had provisionally entered the Berne Convention, which required that the works of an author of a member state must be protected without formality. It was believed that the registration system was such a formality. *See* Benjamin Kaplan, *Registration of Copyright,* Copyright Office *Study No. 17* (1958). *See also* Berne Convention art. 5(2) (Paris text) ("[t]he enjoyment and the exercise of these rights shall not be subject to any formality. . . .").

[12] For a comprehensive overview of the advantages and disadvantages of a registration system, see Kaplan, *supra,* note 11.

[13] *See* 17 U.S.C. § 410(c).

[14] *See* Arthur J. Levine & Jeffrey L. Squires, *Notice, Deposit and Registration: The Importance of Being Formal,* 24 UCLA L. Rev. 1232, 1254 (1977).

[15] *See* 17 U.S.C. § 304(a).

[16] To promote accuracy and and completeness in Copyright Office records, the 1976 Copyright Act authorizes the Register to establish procedures by which claimants may correct or supplement information in a registration. *See* 17 U.S.C. § 408(d); 37 C.F.R. § 201.5 (1987). No such statutory procedures existed under the 1909 Act.

finds its way into its records. Except for obvious discrepancies, the Copyright Office accepts all information provided by the applicant for registration as true, and does not make factual findings on matters external to the Copyright Office.[17] Consistent with this general policy, the Office will record[18] virtually any instrument involving an interest in the copyright without evaluating its legal sufficiency.[19] Added to these problems of reliability, the work may not yet have been catalogued, or the work may have been registered under a different title as part of larger work. Whether these inadequacies of the system undermine its justification is debatable, but one must keep them in mind whenever using Copyright Office records.

§ 7.4   Registration of Copyright: An Overview

Copyright protection begins not with registration, but when an author creates a work by fixing it in a tangible medium of expression.[20] Registration is a legal formality, and an important one, but in only two instances can it be viewed as a condition of copyright itself. First, works copyrighted (published with notice) before January 1, 1964, must have been registered and renewed during the 28th year to maintain copyright protection.[21] Second, under §§ 405 and 406 of the 1976 Act,[22] copyright registration is a required step in preserving a copyright when copyright notice has been omitted from more than a relatively small number of publicly distributed copies of the work.[23] This aspect of registration is no longer required for works publicly distributed on or after March 1, 1989, the effective date of the BCIA amendments.[24] After that date, notice is permissive and copyright can no longer be forfeited by omitting notice.

Other than in these two instances, registration is permissive, voluntary, and can be effected at any time during the term of copyright.[25] Although permissive, registration confers important advantages on the registrant and early registration is rewarded. Generally, the advantages of registration are: (1) it establishes a public record of the claim of copyright; (2) it secures the right to file an infringement suit for works whose country of origin is the United States;[26] (3) it establishes *prima*

---

[17] *Compendium II of Copyright Office Practices* § 108.05.

[18] For a discussion of recordation of ownership interests in copyright and its significance in establishing priorities among conflicting transfers, see § 5.12, *supra*.

[19] *Compendium II of Copyright Office Practices* § 1603.01.

[20] *See* 17 U.S.C. § 102(a).

[21] *See* 17 U.S.C. § 304(a). For works published on or after January 1, 1964 and before January 1, 1978, (for works whose twenty-eighth year begins January 1, 1993), renewal is automatic and copyright cannot be lost for failure to register and renew. See § 6.9 for a discussion of automatic renewal).

[22] *See* 17 U.S.C. §§ 405, 406.

[23] *See* 17 U.S.C. § 405(a).

[24] *See* 17 U.S.C. § 401(a).

[25] *See* 17 U.S.C. § 408(a).

[26] *See* 17 U.S.C. § 411. Before March 1, 1989, all persons were required to register a claim for copyright before they could bring a suit for copyright infringement. After March 1, 1989, registration as a prerequisite for bringing an infringement suit will no longer be required of works whose country of origin is a Berne Convention country. *See* 17 U.S.C. § 101 (Berne Convention Works) and § 104(b).

facie validity of the copyright;[27] (4) it makes available a broader range of remedies in an infringement suit, allowing recovery of statutory damages and attorney's fees;[28] and (5) only if registration is made, will recordation of a document in the Copyright Office give constructive notice of the facts stated in the recorded document.[29] These substantial advantages provide a strong inducement to register, particularly because registration is relatively inexpensive and involves no examination for basic validity of the copyright, in contrast to the procedure for obtaining a patent.

§ 7.5   Registration Procedures

Any copyright owner, including an owner of an exclusive license to a work, may register a claim for copyright. The claimant must send three elements in the same envelope to the Register of Copyrights.[30] These are (1) a properly completed application form; (2) a non-refundable fee[31] for each application; and (3) a deposit copy of the work to be registered. Copyright registration is effective on the date of receipt in the Copyright Office of all the required elements in acceptable form, no matter how long it takes for the actual registration to issue from the Copyright Office.[32] For persons needing a rapid issuance of a certificate, the Copyright Office has instituted a procedure called "special handling" to expedite the registration process.[33]

The application forms are printed by the Copyright Office, and only these official forms can be used; photocopies are not allowed. For example, form TX[34] is designated for published and unpublished non-dramatic literary works (books, computer programs, etc.), and form SR is designated for published and unpublished sound recordings.[35] The forms are basically self-explanatory, and relatively easy to complete.

---

[27] *See* 17 U.S.C. § 410(c).

[28] *See* 17 U.S.C. § 412.

[29] *See* 17 U.S.C. § 205(c).

[30] *See* 17 U.S.C. §§ 408, 409.

[31] Currently $20.00 up from $10.00 under the 1976 Act as orginally promulgated. Beginning in 1995, the Register of Copyrights, at five-year intervals, has been authorized to increase fees, including the fee for registration, to reflect changes in the Consumer Price Index. For fee schedules for such services as recordation, searches, and special handling, see Copyright Fees, *Copyright Office Circular 4.*

[32] *See* 17 U.S.C. § 410(d).

[33] Special handling will be granted only in cases involving pending or prospective litigation, customs matters, or contract or publishing deadlines that necessitate the expedited process. The current fee for special handling is $200. *See* Copyright Office, *Policy Decision Fixing Fees for the Special Handling of Import Statements and Documents*, ML–341 (November 1985).

[34] *See* Appendix to Chapter 7, *infra*, for a sample TX form for registration of a literary work.

[35] The other forms are VA, for pictorial, graphic, and sculptural works; PA, for the performing arts; SE, for serials; and GR/CP, an adjunct application for copyright registration covering a group of contributions to a periodical. *See Copyright Office Circular* Rlc.

The second and third elements of registration, the deposit copies and the application fee, must accompany the application form.[36] The deposit copies must comply with the statutory requirements and regulations established by the Copyright Office.[37] The Register of Copyrights has exempted certain categories of works from the deposit requirement, allowing identifying material to be sent instead.[38]

Under § 410(a),[39] the Register of Copyright shall register, after examination, a claim to copyright if

> the material deposited constitutes copyrightable subject matter and that the other legal and formal requirements . . . have been met.[40]

Alternatively, the Register of Copyright is given the authority to refuse registration when the claim is invalid and most courts defer to the Register's decision in refusing the claim.[41] The examination is carried out by the Examining Division of the Copyright Office which limits its inquiry to the material deposited and the application for registration.[42] The examiner scrutinizes the application for obvious discrepancies, but does not try to verify the facts set forth in it.[43] The examination conducted by the Copyright Office has little in common with the Patent Office's search of the prior art or the Trademark Office's search of registered marks confusingly similar to the applicant's. Unlike the Patent and Trademark Office, the Copyright Office does not institute interference proceedings to determine who has the priority between two conflicting applications.[44]

---

[36] *See* 17 U.S.C. § 409.

[37] *See* 37 C.F.R. § 202.20 (1987).

[38] *See, e.g.,* 37 C.F.R. § 202.21 (1987), which allows in certain cases identifying material instead of an actual copy of the work. For a discussion of the deposit requirement, see §§ 7.9–7.13, *infra.*

[39] *See* 17 U.S.C. § 410(a).

[40] *Id.* The Copyright Office has adopted a long-standing principle that all copyrightable elements embodied in the work are covered by a single registration. *See* 37 C.F.R. § 202.3(b)(2)(3). For example, the Office will accept registration on a single form to cover all copyrightable expressions in a computer program including screen displays. However, if a screen display is claimed in the registration of a computer program, deposit must include a reproduction of the screen display. *See* 37 C.F.R. § 202.20(c)(2)(vii)(C) (1989); 53 Fed. Reg. 21817, June 10, 1988. Most courts have followed the Copyright Office approach. They have held that the program code and the screen display are integrally related and form one work, even though the nature of authorship on screens may be different from computer program code authorship. In sum, copyright in a computer program extends to screen displays as well, and infringement of one will infringe the other. *See Whelan Associates, Inc. v. Jaslow Dental Laboratory, Inc.,* 797 F.2d 1222 (3d Cir. 1986), *cert. denied,* 479 U.S. 1031 (1987). *But see Digital Communications Associates, Inc. v. Softklone Distributing Corp.,* 659 F. Supp. 449 (N.D Ga. 1987).

[41] *See, e.g., Norris Indus., Inc. v. International Tel. & Tel. Corp.,* 696 F.2d 918 (11th Cir.), *cert. denied,* 464 U.S. 818 (1983).

[42] *Compendium II of Copyright Office Practices* § 108.

[43] *Id.* at § 108.05.

[44] The Copyright Office has adopted a principle of interpretation, known as the "Rule of Doubt," which is consistent with the passive role it takes in the examination process. Under the Rule of Doubt, the Office

§ 7.6   The Importance of Registration

[A]   Prerequisite to Bringing Suit for Infringement

The 1976 Act, as originally enacted, required registration of a claim for copyright as a prerequisite for bringing a suit for infringement. Effective March 1, 1989,[45] registration as a prerequisite for bringing an infringement suit is required only for works whose country of origin is the United States. In general, a work which is first published in the United States is considered a work whose country of origin is the United States. For these works, the registration requirement is jurisdictional, and a federal court cannot hear the case unless the requirement is met.[46] The only exception to the registration requirement for works of U.S. origin applies to an action brought for a violation of the rights of attribution and integrity for works of visual arts under section 106A of the Copyright Act.[47] Apart from this exception, the requirement is absolute. Moreover, parties cannot agree to waive the requirement for registration.[48] These rules apply regardless of the remedy sought, whether money damages, injunction, or impoundment.[49] Once registration has taken place, suit can be brought for all infringing acts occurring before or after registration.[50]

Alternatively, for a work whose country of origin is a Berne Convention country, registration is not required to bring an infringement suit. In general, a Berne Convention work is one which is first published in a Berne member country.[51] The important consideration for determining what is a Berne Convention work is the situs of the publication, not the nationality of the author. For example, a Chinese national who first publishes his work in Canada (a Berne country) would not have to register his work to bring a suit for infringement. However, if he had published his work

---

will register the claim even though there is a reasonable doubt about the ultimate action which might be taken under the same circumstances by an appropriate "court" with respect to whether the material deposited for registration constitutes copyrightable subject matter or the other legal and formal requirements of the statute have been met. *Id.* at § 108.07.

[45] *See* 17 U.S.C. § 411(a).

[46] *See Proulx v. Hennepin Technical Centers*, 1981–1983 Copy. Dec. ¶ 25,389 (D. Minn. 1981).

[47] 17 U.S.C. § 411(a).

[48] *See* 2 *Nimmer on Copyright* § 7.16[B] (1993).

[49] H.R. Rep. No. 94–1476, 94th Cong., 2d Sess. 157 (1976).

[50] *See International Trade Management, Inc. v. United States*, 553 F. Supp. 402 (Cl. Ct. 1982).

[51] A Berne Convention work is defined as:

. . . in the case of an unpublished work, one or more of the authors is a national of a nation adhering to the Berne Convention, or in the case of a published work, one or more of the authors is a national of a nation adhering to the Berne Convention on the date of first publication.

The work must either be first published in a Berne country or published simultaneously in a non-Berne and a Berne country. *See* 17 U.S.C. § 101. For a discussion of the Berne Convention, see §§ 12.4–12.5, *infra*.

first in China (a non-Berne country), registration would be required for bringing an infringement suit.[52]

Even for Berne works, registration, though not required, is strongly encouraged by the 1976 Act. First, for all works regardless of their country of origin, registration within five years of its publication confers *prima facie* validity of originality and ownership. Second, and even more important, under § 412 of the Act, registration is a prerequisite to statutory damages and attorney's fees.[53] Third, recordation of a document in the Copyright Office gives all persons constructive notice of the facts stated in the recorded document but only if the work is registered.[54] In short, prompt registration for all works, whether originating from Berne countries or not, can be critically important in effectively enforcing one's rights in a suit for infringement.

[B] Registration As *Prima Facie* Evidence of Validity

Under § 410(c),[55] a certificate of registration constitutes *prima facie* evidence of the validity of the copyright and the facts stated in the certificate. A copyright registration reorders the burden of proof, creating a rebuttable presumption of validity of the copyright claimed in the registration.[56] The *prima facie* validity effect applies only if the registration takes place within five years of publication of the work.[57] This can be especially valuable to a plaintiff seeking a preliminary injunction because the registration confers *prima facie* validity of the work's originality and ownership.[58] If registration is accomplished after five years, the court has the discretion to decide what evidentiary weight the registration will receive.[59]

[C] Registration As a Prerequisite for Obtaining Statutory Damages and Attorney's Fees

Early registration is also rewarded by § 412,[60] which allows recovery of statutory damages, costs and attorney's fees if registration has taken place before the infringing acts occurred. Even if the infringing acts take place before registration, statutory damages and attorney's fees can be recovered in two situations: (1) for

---

[52] *See* 17 U.S.C. § 411(a). The prerequisite of registration for U.S. authors under § 411(a) appears ripe for repeal because it discriminates against U.S. authors and cannot be forcefully justified as a means to enrich the Library's resources. *See, e.g.,* The Copyright Reform Bill of 1993, H.R. 897, 103d Cong., 1st Sess. (1993).

[53] *See* 17 U.S.C. § 412. Section 412 appears ripe for repeal despite arguments that its repeal (as well as the repeal of the registration requirement in § 411) would adversely affect the Library of Congress' acquisition of deposits. *See, e.g.,* The Copyright Reform Bill of 1993, H.R. 897, 103d Cong., 1st Sess. (1993).

[54] *See* 17 U.S.C. § 205(c). For a discussion of recordation see § 5.12, *supra.*

[55] *See* 17 U.S.C. § 410(c). This section applies to all works whether originating from the United States or a Berne Convention country.

[56] H.R. Rep. No. 94–1476, 94th Cong., 2d Sess. 156 (1976).

[57] *See* 17 U.S.C. § 410(c).

[58] *See* William F. Patry, *Copyright Law and Practice* 455 (1994).

[59] *See* 17 U.S.C. § 410(c).

[60] *See* 17 U.S.C. § 412.

infringement of an unpublished work;[61] and (2) for infringement of copyright which began after first publication of the work, if registration was made within three months of its first publication.[62] From a practical standpoint, § 412 provides a powerful inducement for early registration because in some instances, statutory damages[63] may be the only viable remedy for the copyright owner. Registration is still required to obtain statutory damages for works originating from Berne Convention countries, even though registration is no longer a prerequisite for bringing an infringement suit for these works on or after March 1, 1989.[64]

[D]   The Interplay of Registration and Recordation

For causes of action arising on or after March 1, 1989, the BCIA amendments have totally abrogated the recordation of a transfer of copyright ownership as a requirement to bring a suit for infringement.[65] Recordation, however, is still required under § 205(c)[66] to give constructive notice of the facts stated in the recorded document. This constructive notice provision applies only if *registration* is made for the work. The constructive notice effect of recordation is particularly important if there arises a conflict between two transfers of an interest in copyright. Priority will be given to the transfer executed first, but only if it is recorded within one month of its execution in the United States (two months in a foreign country), and recordation is made in the manner required to give constructive notice. Otherwise the later transfer will prevail if it is first properly recorded and the transfer

---

[61] *See* 17 U.S.C. § 412(1).

[62] *See* 17 U.S.C. § 412(2). A third exception is found in § 411(b), which involves an infringement of a work consisting of sounds, images, or both, the first fixation of which is made simultaneously with its transmission and registration of which is accomplished within three months after its first transmission.

[63] Statutory damages can be chosen as an alternative to actual damages and profits. They can be the only viable measure of damages when the plaintiff cannot, for practical reasons, prove actual damages and profits. By 1988 amendments to the Copyright Act, effective March 1, 1989, the range of recovery is between $500 (increased from $250) and $20,000 (increased from $10,000) and is determined at the discretion of the court. *See* 17 U.S.C. § 504(c).

[64] Recent legislation has proposed the elimination of §§ 411(a) (requiring registration as a prerequisite for bringing suit) and 412 (prerequisite to obtaining statutory damages and attorney's fees). Advocates of this legislation maintain that the registration requirement is an anachronism that discriminates against U.S. authors. Moreover, the incentives to register provided by §§ 411(a) and 412 do not in fact serve any other practical purpose such as enriching the collections of the Library of Congress. In addition, the § 412 requirement discriminates against small copyright owners who either do not know of the benefits of prompt registration or do not have the time or money to register within the short grace period provided. *See, e.g.* The Copyright Reform Bill of 1993, H.R. 897, 103d Cong. 1st Sess. (1993).

[65] Before passage of the Berne amendments, 17 U.S.C. § 205(d) required recordation of a transfer of an interest in copyright in order to bring an infringement suit. This section has been abrogated for causes of action arising after March 1, 1989, but will be required for causes of action arising before that date. For a discussion of recordation see § 5.12, *supra*.

[66] *See* 17 U.S.C. § 205(c).

was taken in good faith.[67] These constructive notice provisions strongly encourage prompt registration and recordation.

§ 7.7   Refusal of Registration: § 411(a)

What happens when the claimant is refused registration but wishes to bring suit for infringement? Section 411(a)[68] takes into account the situation in which the applicant has delivered the application, deposit and fee in proper form but registration has been refused. In this instance, § 411(a) permits the applicant to bring suit for infringement if notice and a copy of the complaint is served on the Register of Copyrights.[69] The Register has the discretion to become a party to the suit on the issue of registrability. Even if the Register does not make an appearance within 60 days of service, the court is not precluded from determining questions of registerability.[70]

Section 411(a) applies only when the applicant has complied with all the formal requirements of registration; that is, when the application, deposit and fee are delivered in proper form. For example, in *Proulx v. Hennepin Technical Centers*,[71] the applicant refused to deposit a complete copy of his 137-hour set of videotaped lectures, as required by Copyright Office regulations, depositing identifying material instead. Plaintiff also failed to respond to the Register's request for clarification as to certain inconsistencies in his application and deposit. The court held that registration had not been refused by the Copyright Office within the meaning of § 411(a):

> The term "refused" as used in Section 411(a) contemplates a final decision by the Copyright Office on the merits of the registrability of the plaintiff's submission.[72]

In this case, the plaintiff failed to exhaust his administrative remedies since he did not respond properly to the Register's requests, or obtain a final refusal to register before proceeding with his claim in federal court.

§ 7.8   Registration Under the 1909 Act: The "Prompt" Deposit and Registration Requirement

Under the 1909 Act, federal statutory copyright began not on registration but when the work was published with proper notice.[73] Section 13 of the 1909 Act[74] provided

---

[67] *See* 17 U.S.C. § 205(d).

[68] *See* 17 U.S.C. § 411(a).

[69] This is an intentional change from 1909 Act law which required the applicant to bring an action against the Register of Copyrights to compel issuance of a certificate before an infringement suit could be brought. *Id.*

[70] *Id.*

[71] 1981–1983 Copy. Dec. ¶ 25,389.

[72] *Id.* at 17,249.

[73] There was one minor exception under § 13 of the 1909 Act for certain works "not produced for sale," *i.e.*, unpublished works. *See* 2 *Nimmer on Copyright* § 7.16[A][2][c][i] (1993).

that once a work was copyrighted by publication with notice, "there shall be promptly deposited" the required copies and the claim for registration. The question has arisen whether failure to comply with this apparent requirement for prompt deposit would inject a work into the public domain. The meaning of the term *promptly* under the 1909 Act is still important to determining whether a failure to promptly deposit ejected a work into the public domain. If so, the work cannot be retrieved from the public domain because all works going into the public domain before 1978 remain there, unaffected by the 1976 Act.[75]

The case law under the 1909 Act has undermined the meaning of the "promptly" requirement. The process began with *Washingtonian Publishing Co. v. Pearson.*[76] In *Washingtonian*, plaintiff had published with proper notice an issue of *The Washingtonian* magazine. Fourteen months later, copies were deposited in the Copyright Office, and a certificate of registration was secured. Defendant argued that although prompt deposit is not a prerequisite to copyright, no action could be brought for an infringement occurring before the tardy deposit. The Supreme Court disagreed, holding that an infringement action can be brought for acts committed before and after registration.

The *Washingtonian* reasoning was pushed one step further in *Shapiro, Bernstein & Co., Inc. v. Jerry Vogel Music Co., Inc.,*[77] excusing a 27-year delay in deposit and registration. *Shapiro* effectively removed any meaning from the word "prompt," except when deposit is specifically requested from the Register of Copyright.[78] Only then may copyright be forfeited in a work. But for the purpose of bringing an infringement suit under the 1909 Act, deposit and registration could be made any time during the first term of copyright.

PART II: DEPOSIT

§ 7.9   Generally

The deposit of copies of copyrighted works serves two purposes. The first is to provide copies of the work for the collections of the Library of Congress. The second is to identify the work in conjunction with copyright registration. These two deposit requirements are intertwined because a single deposit of copies for registration will satisfy both purposes.[79]

---

[74] *See* 17 U.S.C. § 13 (1909 Act).

[75] *See* 17 U.S.C. § 103 (Trans. & Supp. Prov., 1976 Act).

[76] 306 U.S. 30 (1939).

[77] 161 F.2d 406 (2d Cir. 1946), *cert. denied*, 331 U.S. 820 (1947).

[78] *See* 17 U.S.C. § 14 (1909 Act) (noncompliance within three months of Register's demand for deposit of copies results in forfeiture of copyright).

[79] Since 1870, a single deposit has been accepted for both Library of Congress and registration purposes. *See* Dunne, *Deposit of Copyrighted Works*, Copyright Office *Study No. 20* (1960).

§ 7.10   Mandatory Deposit for the Library of Congress

With some exceptions, the deposit for the Library of Congress is mandatory and applies to all types of works.[80] These mandatory deposit requirements, designed to build up the collection of our national library, the Library of Congress, have been a feature of American law since 1790. The Register of Copyrights has been given the authority to establish regulations specifying the mechanics of the deposit requirement.[81]

Section 407 outlines the basic procedure. Within three months after a work is published with notice of copyright in the United States, the owner of copyright, or the owner of the exclusive right of publication, must deposit two copies or phonorecords of the work in the Copyright Office.[82] Works excluded from the deposit requirement are unpublished works,[83] published works not having notice, works published in foreign countries and certain categories exempted by the Register of Copyright.[84] Generally, though, once a work is published in the United States, even if it was first published abroad, deposit is mandatory.[85]

§ 7.11   Failure to Comply With Deposit Requirements

Failure to comply with deposit requirements will not forfeit copyright. Rather, mandatory deposit requirements are enforced by a graduated series of fines. For failure to deposit within three months of publication, the Register of Copyright may impose an initial fine of no more than $250 plus the cost of acquiring the requested copies and an additional fine of $2500 for willful refusal to comply with a demand for deposit.[86] By comparison, the 1909 Act treated deposit and registration as a unit and failure to comply with prompt deposit after a demand by the Register of Copyrights would not only subject the claimant to a fine, but would void copyright as well.[87] The deposit provisions of the 1909 Act should be kept in mind, despite the changes made by the 1976 Act, because the current Act will not revive a work going into the public domain before January 1, 1978.

§ 7.12   Mechanics of Deposit

Section 407 of the 1976 Act requires that deposit of a work consist of

---

[80] See 17 U.S.C. § 407.

[81] See 17 U.S.C. § 407(c).

[82] See 17 U.S.C. § 407(a)(1) and (2).

[83] Once registration is sought for an unpublished work, the claimant must comply with deposit requirements. See 17 U.S.C. § 408.

[84] See 37 C.F.R. §§ 202.19–202.21 (1987).

[85] The deposit requirement has withstood constitutional challenges on First and Fifth Amendment grounds. See Ladd v. Law and Technology Press, 762 F.2d 809 (9th Cir. 1985).

[86] See 17 U.S.C. § 407(d)(3).

[87] See 17 U.S.C. § 13 (1909 Act).

(1) two complete copies of the best edition; or (2) if the work is a sound recording, two complete phonorecords of the best edition, together with any printed or other visually perceptible material published with such phonorecords.[88]

The key term is "best edition," which means that the Library of Congress is entitled to receive the copies of phonorecords best suiting its needs.[89] In concrete terms, the best edition is the one of the highest quality relative to other published editions of the work.[90]

Many deposits are not suitable for the Library of Congress' collections and the Register of Copyright has exempted certain categories of works from the deposit requirement.[91] For example, three–dimensional sculptural works, most advertising material and individual contributions to collective works are exempt. One should consult the regulations for the entire list of exemptions.[92]

Even if the work is not specifically exempted, a person may apply for special relief from deposit requirements.[93] Special relief is most often given when an undue burden or cost would be imposed on the copyright owner if the deposit requirement for a non-exempt work were required. The grant of special relief is discretionary with the Copyright Office, which balances the needs of the Library of Congress with the hardship to the copyright owner.

§ 7.13　Mandatory Deposit Under § 407 and the Deposit Requirement for Registration Under § 408 Compared

Even though closely related and largely overlapping, deposit requirements for the Library of Congress, § 407, should be distinguished from deposit requirements for registration purposes, § 408. Deposit for the Library of Congress is mandatory, whether one registers or not. An applicant for registration need only supply one deposit copy to meet the requirements for registration and the mandatory deposit for the Library of Congress. An applicant for registration can satisfy both requirements in a single deposit. The reverse is not true. If registration is made after deposit for the Library of Congress, another deposit copy is required. For practical reasons, most parties choose to register and deposit at the same time, accompanying the deposit with the application and the fee.[94]

Because they serve somewhat different purposes, mandatory deposit with the Library of Congress and deposit for registration with the Copyright Office are not entirely identical. Because deposit for registration serves an identifying function, one copy is generally required for registration of works not subject to the mandatory

---

[88] *See* 17 U.S.C. §§ 407(a)(1) and (2).
[89] *See* 17 U.S.C. § 101 (definition of "best edition").
[90] 37 C.F.R. § 202.19(b)(iii) (1987).
[91] *See* 17 U.S.C. § 407(c).
[92] *See* 37 C.F.R. §§ 202.20–202.21 (1987).
[93] *Id.* at § 202.20.
[94] *See* 37 C.F.R. § 202.19(f) (1987).

deposit with the Library of Congress. First, one copy of an individual contribution to a collective work must be deposited for registration, but is not mandatory for the Library of Congress. Second, registration requires deposit of one complete copy or phonorecord of any unpublished work, whereas unpublished works are completely exempt from deposit with the Library of Congress.[95] Third, only works published outside the United States are exempt from the mandatory deposit, but not deposit for registration purposes.[96] With these exceptions, the mandatory deposit provisions of the Library of Congress are virtually identical to the deposit requirements for registration purposes.[97]

---

[95] *See* 17 U.S.C. § 408(b)(1).

[96] *See* 17 U.S.C. § 408(b)(3).

[97] Deposit requirements for both the Library of Congress and the Copyright Office may be modified in special cases. The Register of Copyrights has the authority to issue regulations covering the deposit requirements for registration in order to meet the practical needs of the parties, the Library of Congress, and the Copyright Office. Thus, under the regulations, one deposit copy is required instead of two, and identifying material can be deposited, instead of the actual work, where such works are cumbersome or very valuable. *See* 37 C.F.R. § 202.19 (1987).

Appendix to Chapter 7

FORM TX
For a Literary Work
UNITED STATES COPYRIGHT OFFICE

REGISTRATION NUMBER

_____

TX _____ TXU _____
EFFECTIVE DATE OF REGISTRATION

_____

Month   Day   Year

DO NOT WRITE ABOVE THIS LINE. IF YOU NEED MORE SPACE, USE A SEPARATE CONTINUATION SHEET.

1

TITLE OF THIS WORK ▼

PREVIOUS OR ALTERNATIVE TITLES ▼

PUBLICATION AS A CONTRIBUTION If this work was published as a contribution to a periodical, serial, or collection, give information about the collective work in which the contribution appeared.   Title of Collective Work ▼

If published in a periodical or serial give: Volume ▼   Number ▼   Issue Date ▼   On Pages ▼

2 **a**

NAME OF AUTHOR ▼

DATES OF BIRTH AND DEATH
Year Born ▼   Year Died ▼

Was this contribution to the work a "work made for hire"?
☐ Yes
☐ No

AUTHOR'S NATIONALITY OR DOMICILE
Name of Country
OR { Citizen of ▶
     Domiciled in▶

WAS THIS AUTHOR'S CONTRIBUTION TO THE WORK
Anonymous?   ☐ Yes ☐ No
Pseudonymous? ☐ Yes ☐ No

If the answer to either of these questions is "Yes," see detailed instructions.

NATURE OF AUTHORSHIP Briefly describe nature of material created by this author in which copyright is claimed. ▼

NOTE

Under the law, the "author" of a "work made for hire" is generally the employer, not the employee (see instructions). For any part of this work that was "made for hire" check "Yes" in the space provided, give the employer (or other person for whom the work was prepared) as "Author" of that part, and leave the space for dates of birth and death blank.

b

NAME OF AUTHOR ▼

DATES OF BIRTH AND DEATH
Year Born ▼   Year Died ▼

Was this contribution to the work a "work made for hire"?
☐ Yes
☐ No

AUTHOR'S NATIONALITY OR DOMICILE
Name of Country
OR { Citizen of ▶
     Domiciled in▶

WAS THIS AUTHOR'S CONTRIBUTION TO THE WORK
Anonymous?   ☐ Yes ☐ No
Pseudonymous? ☐ Yes ☐ No

If the answer to either of these questions is "Yes," see detailed instructions.

NATURE OF AUTHORSHIP Briefly describe nature of material created by this author in which copyright is claimed. ▼

c

NAME OF AUTHOR ▼

DATES OF BIRTH AND DEATH
Year Born ▼   Year Died ▼

Was this contribution to the work a "work made for hire"?
☐ Yes
☐ No

AUTHOR'S NATIONALITY OR DOMICILE
Name of Country
OR { Citizen of ▶
     Domiciled in▶

WAS THIS AUTHOR'S CONTRIBUTION TO THE WORK
Anonymous?   ☐ Yes ☐ No
Pseudonymous? ☐ Yes ☐ No

If the answer to either of these questions is "Yes," see detailed instructions.

NATURE OF AUTHORSHIP Briefly describe nature of material created by this author in which copyright is claimed. ▼

3 **a**

YEAR IN WHICH CREATION OF THIS WORK WAS COMPLETED This information must be given
◄ Year in all cases.

b DATE AND NATION OF FIRST PUBLICATION OF THIS PARTICULAR WORK
Complete this information ONLY if this work has been published.   Month ▶   Day ▶   Year ▶   ◄ Nation

4

See instructions before completing this space.

COPYRIGHT CLAIMANT(S) Name and address must be given even if the claimant is the same as the author given in space 2. ▼

TRANSFER If the claimant(s) named here in space 4 is (are) different from the author(s) named in space 2, give a brief statement of how the claimant(s) obtained ownership of the copyright. ▼

APPLICATION RECEIVED

ONE DEPOSIT RECEIVED

TWO DEPOSITS RECEIVED

REMITTANCE NUMBER AND DATE

DO NOT WRITE HERE
OFFICE USE ONLY

MORE ON BACK ▶ • Complete all applicable spaces (numbers 5-11) on the reverse side of this page.
                • See detailed instructions.   • Sign the form at line 10.

DO NOT WRITE HERE
Page 1 of _____ pages

EXAMINED BY	FORM TX
CHECKED BY	
☐ CORRESPONDENCE Yes	FOR- COPYRIGHT OFFICE USE ONLY

DO NOT WRITE ABOVE THIS LINE. IF YOU NEED MORE SPACE, USE A SEPARATE CONTINUATION SHEET.

PREVIOUS REGISTRATION Has registration for this work, or for an earlier version of this work, already been made in the Copyright Office?

☐ Yes ☐ No If your answer is "Yes," why is another registration being sought? (Check appropriate box) ▼

a. ☐ This is the first published edition of a work previously registered in unpublished form.

b. ☐ This is the first application submitted by this author as copyright claimant.

c. ☐ This is a changed version of the work, as shown by space 6 on this application.

If your answer is "Yes," give: **Previous Registration Number** ▼   **Year of Registration** ▼

5

DERIVATIVE WORK OR COMPILATION Complete both space 6a and 6b for a derivative work; complete only 6b for a compilation.

a. **Preexisting Material** Identify any preexisting work or works that this work is based on or incorporates. ▼

b. **Material Added to This Work** Give a brief, general statement of the material that has been added to this work and in which copyright is claimed. ▼

6

See instructions
before completing
this space.

—space deleted—

7

REPRODUCTION FOR USE OF BLIND OR PHYSICALLY HANDICAPPED INDIVIDUALS A signature on this form at space 10 and a check in one of the boxes here in space 8 constitutes a non-exclusive grant of permission to the Library of Congress to reproduce and distribute solely for the blind and physically handicapped and under the conditions and limitations prescribed by the regulations of the Copyright Office: (1) copies of the work identified in space 1 of this application in Braille (or similar tactile symbols); or (2) phonorecords embodying a fixation of a reading of that work; or (3) both.

a ☐ Copies and Phonorecords   b ☐ Copies Only   c ☐ Phonorecords Only

8

See instructions.

DEPOSIT ACCOUNT If the registration fee is to be charged to a Deposit Account established in the Copyright Office, give name and number of Account.

Name ▼   **Account Number** ▼

9

CORRESPONDENCE Give name and address to which correspondence about this application should be sent.   Name/Address/Apt/City/State/ZIP ▼

Area Code and Telephone Number ▶

Be sure to
give your
daytime phone
◀ number

CERTIFICATION* I, the undersigned, hereby certify that I am the

Check only one ▶

☐ author
☐ other copyright claimant
☐ owner of exclusive right(s)
☐ authorized agent of ....

of the work identified in this application and that the statements made by me in this application are correct to the best of my knowledge.

Name of author or other copyright claimant, or owner of exclusive right(s) ▲

10

Typed or printed name and date ▼ If this application gives a date of publication in space 3, do not sign and submit it before that date.

date ▶

☞   Handwritten signature (X) ▼

MAIL CERTIFI-CATE TO

Name ▼

Number/Street/Apartment Number ▼

City/State/ZIP ▼

Certificate
will be
mailed in
window
envelope

YOU MUST:
• Complete all necessary spaces
• Sign your application in space 10

SEND ALL 3 ELEMENTS IN THE SAME PACKAGE
1. Application form
2. Nonrefundable $20 filing fee in check or money order payable to *Register of Copyrights*
3. Deposit material

MAIL TO:
Register of Copyrights
Library of Congress
Washington, D.C. 20559

11

The Copyright Office has the authority to adjust fees at 5-year intervals, based on changes in the Consumer Price Index. The next adjustment is due in 1996. Please contact the Copyright Office after July 1995 to determine the actual fee schedule.

February 1993—100.000

✩U.S. GOVERNMENT PRINTING OFFICE: 1993-342-581/60,504

CHAPTER 8

THE EXCLUSIVE RIGHTS AND THEIR LIMITATIONS

§ 8.1 Introduction and Chapter Overview

The five exclusive rights of reproduction, adaptation, distribution, performance, and display create the boundaries of copyright ownership, and their violation constitutes copyright infringement. Each exclusive right is subject to a series of limitations set forth in §§ 107–120 of the Copyright Act. Describing these limitations is a complex, detailed task, and the length of this chapter reflects the nature of the subject.

This chapter is organized around the pertinent exclusive rights and the various limitations on them. Part I presents an overview of the subject focusing on the structure of the exclusive rights and their limitations. It introduces the concept of the compulsory license, whereby access to a copyrighted work can be obtained without negotiation with the copyright owner so long as the user meets the statutory terms and royalties. Compulsory licenses constitute a developing but controversial trend in copyright law, and their justification and administration are examined in the first part of this chapter. Part II concerns the reproduction and adaptation rights and the various limitations on them. Part III continues with the distribution right, devoting most of the discussion to the major limitation on the distribution right called the "first sale doctrine." Part IV is structured around the performance and display rights whose limitations, such as the compulsory license for cable television, are perhaps the most complicated in the Copyright Act. Part V examines the moral right, given explicit recognition for the first time in the Visual Artists Rights Act of 1990. It also treats the regulation of digital audio recording devices in the Audio Home Recording Act of 1992.

PART I: EXCLUSIVE RIGHTS, LIMITATIONS, AND COMPULSORY LICENSES

§ 8.2 Introduction to the Exclusive Rights and Their Limitations

A copyright consists of a bundle of exclusive rights which empower the copyright owner to exclude others from certain uses of his work. The exclusive rights of reproduction, adaptation, distribution, performance, and display enumerated in § 106[1] define the boundaries of copyright ownership, and their violation constitutes

---

[1] 17 U.S.C. § 106.

copyright infringement.[2] In short, they are the essence of copyright ownership. Exclusive rights can be subdivided infinitely and each can be owned and enforced separately.[3] For example, the copyright owner of a novel may grant exclusive licenses for the reproduction, distribution, and performance rights to different parties, each of whom can sue for infringement in his own right.[4]

The exclusive rights are cumulative and, to a certain extent, overlap. The same act may simultaneously infringe both the reproduction and adaptation rights, for example, by making an unauthorized translation of a copyrighted work. Here, the infringer has reproduced the work and has also adapted it in the translation. Other than this reproduction/adaptation rights overlap, it takes separate acts to infringe the other exclusive rights. If the infringer in the above example sold copies of the translation and authorized readings of it, the distribution and performance rights of the copyright owner would also be infringed.

The exclusive rights of the copyright owner are subject to important limitations set forth in §§ 107 through 120.[5] Although the most complex set of limitations are set forth in these sections, limitations begin to appear in § 106.[6] First, not all copyrightable subject matter as defined under § 102[7] enjoys the same degree of copyright protection. Neither graphic, pictorial, sculptural works nor sound recordings enjoy the same full range of exclusive rights as do literary, musical, and dramatic works. For example, the copyright owner of a sound recording cannot control the right of performance and display of the work. In addition, graphic, pictorial, or sculptural works do not enjoy a performance right. Second, § 106 limits the exclusive rights of performance and display to *public* performance and display. Accordingly, the copyright owner has no control over private performances or displays of his work.[8]

Limitations on the exclusive rights are specified in §§ 107 through 120. The longest and most complicated sections in the 1976 Act, they vary in concreteness and detail. For example, the fair use provision of § 107 is a broad limitation covering all varieties and uses of copyrighted works, whereas § 111, the cable television provision, constructs a relatively concrete and intricate system of regulation for a specific industry. Sections 111, 115, 118 and 119, which contain a system of five compulsory licenses, were once regulated by an administrative body called the Copyright Royalty Tribunal (CRT). In 1993, Congress abolished the CRT, reassigning its functions to Copyright Arbitration Royalty Panels (CARPs) convened by the Librarian of Congress on recommendation of the Register of Copyrights. The membership and the proceeding of the arbitration panels are set forth in § 802 of

---

[2] *See* 17 U.S.C. § 501(a) ("Anyone who violates any of the exclusive rights . . . is an infringer of the copyright.")

[3] *See* 17 U.S.C. § 201(d)(2). For a discussion of ownership matters, see §§ 5.8–5.9, *supra*.

[4] For discussion of transfers of copyright ownership, see § 5.8[B], *supra*.

[5] 17 U.S.C. §§ 107–120.

[6] 17 U.S.C. § 106.

[7] 17 U.S.C. § 102.

[8] For a discussion of the meaning of *public* performance and display, see § 8.16, *infra*.

the Act.[9] The following section introduces five compulsory licenses and their administration.

§ 8.3   The Compulsory Licenses and Their Administration

[A]   What is a Compulsory License?

To use a copyrighted work, normally one must obtain a license from the copyright owner, whose terms are determined through negotiation. If A, for example, wishes to reproduce B's copyrighted painting in a poster, he must obtain authorization from B, and the terms of the ensuing agreement will depend on market conditions. In five instances, however, the Copyright Act supersedes the normal market mechanism for distributing copyrighted works, and allows the prospective user the right to obtain a compulsory license under which he can use the work without the copyright owner's permission. So long as the licensee complies with the statutory procedure and pays the established royalties, the compulsory license applies.

The five compulsory licenses, including the now repealed (in 1993) jukebox license, will be discussed in more detail at various points in this chapter. By way of introduction, they are:

(1) The Cable License of § 111,[10] which establishes a compulsory license for secondary transmissions by cable television systems;

(2) The Mechanical License of § 115,[11] which establishes a compulsory license for production and distribution of phonorecords of non-dramatic musical works;

(3) The Public Broadcasting License of § 118,[12] which establishes a compulsory license for the use of certain copyrighted works by non-commercial broadcasting entities.

(4) The Satellite Retransmission License of § 119[13] which establishes a compulsory license for satellite retransmissions to the public for private viewing.

(5) The Digital Audio Tape Device License[14] which establishes immunity from liability for copyright infringement for manufacturers and importers of digital recording devices, but imposes a levy on these devices, the proceeds from which are to be distributed to copyright owners.

[B]   From the Copyright Royalty Tribunal[15] to Copyright Arbitration Royalty Panels

The now defunct Copyright Royalty Tribunal[16] was a major and controversial

---

[9] 17 U.S.C. § 802.

[10] 17 U.S.C. § 111.

[11] 17 U.S.C. § 115.

[12] 17 U.S.C. § 118.

[13] 17 U.S.C. § 119.

[14] The Audio Home Recording Act of 1992 Pub. L. No. 102–563, 106 Stat. 4237 (1992) added a new Chapter 10 to Title 17 of the U.S. Code, §§ 1001–1010.

[15] For an overview and background, see Fulton E. Brylawski, *The Copyright Royalty Tribunal*, 24 UCLA L. Rev. 1265 (1977).

[16] *See* 17 U.S.C. §§ 801–810.

creation of the 1976 Act. It was an independent agency functioning within the legislative branch of the government, and was set up to administer copyright's five compulsory licenses.[17] Members of the agency were nominated by the President for staggered seven-year terms.[18] The Copyright Royalty Tribunal served two functions.[19] The first was to set the statutory royalty rates for the compulsory licenses.[20] The second was to settle disputes concerning the distribution of monies collected for cable television and jukebox performances.[21] Although the statute provided relatively clear direction for the Tribunal's rate-making activities, it gave little indication how the Tribunal should distribute royalties. As a result of this vagueness, the Tribunal's activities had become embroiled in a constant stream of litigation and criticism.[22] Legislative hearings pointed out in detail the inadequacies[23] of the system, and sunset bills[24] were constantly proposed to phase out aspects of the compulsory licenses. From an international copyright perspective, the jukebox license, even after its amendment by the BCIA, had come under particularly

---

[17] The Tribunal had the authority to create its own rules of procedure if consistent with the Administrative Procedure Act. *See* 17 U.S.C. § 803(a).

[18] 17 U.S.C. § 802. There was no requirement that the members appointed have any copyright experience.

[19] *See* Barbara A. Ringer, *The Unfinished Business of Copyright Revision*, 24 UCLA L. Rev. 951, 974 (1977).

[20] The Tribunal had the authority to raise rates periodically. It had been criticized as being too pro-copyright owner in its rate-making activities rather than balancing the rights of creators and users. Generally, the Tribunal tried to approximate the actual market value of the works. By its actions, jukebox royalties were raised from $8.00 to $64.00 and the mechanical royalty rate was raised from 2.75 cents to 6.60 cents.

[21] The Copyright Royalty Tribunal did not distribute royalties for the mechanical license or for non-commercial broadcasting. For these licenses, the parties involved arrange the distribution for themselves. For a discussion of these compulsory licenses, see § 8.7, *infra.*

[22] Review of Tribunal decisions was before the United States Courts of Appeals. *See* 17 U.S.C. § 810. The following cases are representative of this litigation: *National Association of Broadcasters v. Copyright Royalty Tribunal*, 809 F.2d 172 (2d Cir. 1986) (cable television); *Christian Broadcasting Network, Inc. v. Copyright Royalty Tribunal*, 720 F.2d 1295 (D.C. Cir. 1983) (cable television); *Amusement & Music Operators Ass'n v. Copyright Royalty Tribunal*, 676 F.2d 1144 (7th Cir.), *cert. denied*, 459 U.S. 907 (1982) (jukebox); *Recording Industry Association of America v. Copyright Royalty Tribunal*, 662 F.2d 1 (D.C. Cir. 1981) (mechanical license).

[23] The first systematic review of the Tribunal by the General Accounting Office revealed serious deficiencies in the system. Among other things, the Tribunal had not been given clear criteria by which to act. the royalty funds could not be distributed efficiently because of legal challenge, and the commissioners themselves had little copyright experience. *See Hearings Before the Subcomm. on Courts of the House Comm. on the Judiciary, Civil Liberties, and the Administration of Justice*, 96th Cong., 2d Sess. (1981). *See also Oversight Hearing on the Copyright Royalty Tribunal and Copyright Office Before the Subcomm. on Courts, Civil Liberties, and the Administration of Justice of the House Comm. on the Judiciary*, 99th Cong., 1st Sess. (1985).

[24] *See, e.g.*, H.R. Rep. No. 2752, 99th Cong., 1st Sess. (1985).

vigorous attack as impeding American efforts to join the Berne Union, the preeminent international copyright convention.[25]

In 1993, Congress abolished the Copyright Royalty Tribunal, replacing it with Copyright Arbitration Royalty Panels to be convened, as the need arises, by the Librarian of Congress with the recommendation of the Register of Copyrights.[26]

[C]   Are the Compulsory Licenses Justifiable?

If the compulsory licenses are a major departure from the ordinary way of obtaining the right to use a copyrighted work, how did they come about and are they justifiable?[27]

The compulsory licenses are essentially products of political compromise where certain user interest groups have carved out for themselves an exception to the way in which a license is normally negotiated.[28] The cable television compulsory license provides an excellent example of this political compromise. As embodied in § 111, it reflects the intense negotiations between powerful interest groups, copyright owners and the cable television industry, resulting in a complicated system of regulation.[29]

What justifications are there for these compulsory licenses which have been attacked as undermining the fundamental rights of authors?[30] Supporters of compulsory licensing justify this preemption of an author's control over the use and distribution of a work on economic grounds. The argument is that the compulsory license serves both owners and users by reducing the transaction costs involved in licensing works through the private market system. Thus, the cable systems and copyright owners are spared the costs of hiring lawyers who would individually negotiate a license on their behalf. Without the compulsory license mechanism, these transaction costs could be so high that negotiations would not take place at all, impoverishing owners, users, and the public. Instead, the cable systems, mechanical licensees, and the public broadcasting system know exactly what they must pay and what procedures they must follow to use a copyrighted work. In sum, transaction costs and uncertainties of the marketplace are avoided, and dissemination of copyrighted works is facilitated.

---

[25] The other compulsory licenses appear compatible with Berne. *See* Ralph Oman, *The Compulsory License Redux: Will It Survive in a Changing Marketplace?*, 5 Cardozo Arts & Ent. L.J. 37, 49 (1986). For a discussion of U.S. entry into the Berne Union, see § 12.5, *infra*.

[26] The Copyright Royalty Tribunal Reform Act of 1993, Pub. L. No. 103–198, 107 Stat. 2304 (1993); H.R. Rep. No. 286, 103d Cong. 1st Sess. 2954 (1993).

[27] For an overview of the compulsory licenses, see Paul Goldstein, *Preempted State Doctrines, Involuntary Transfers and Compulsory Licenses: Testing the Limits of Copyright*, 24 UCLA L. Rev. 1107, 1127–39 (1977).

[28] For the nature of the political compromise leading to the compulsory licenses, see Barbara A. Ringer, *Copyright and the Future of Authorship*, 101 Lib. L.J. 229 (1976).

[29] For a background, overview and critique of the cable television compulsory license, recommending its elimination and return to normal market mechanisms, see David Ladd, Dorothy M. Schrader, David Leibowitz & Harriet L. Oler, *Copyright, Cable, the Compulsory License: A Second Chance*, 3 Comm. & Law 3 (1981).

[30] *See* Ringer, *Copyright in the 1980's*, 23 Bull. Copyright Soc'y 299 (1976).

Despite this ideal, compulsory licensing and its administration by the Copyright Royalty Tribunal had come under intense criticism during its entire 15-year life. Almost from the outset, the Tribunal came under siege. Its decisions on the distribution of royalties never operated smoothly and provoked protracted litigation. To the critics (invariably author groups), whatever advantages were derived from the compulsory licenses were outweighed by the costly and wasteful system of regulation, which is not only unfair to authors but economically unsound. As for the argument that compulsory licenses reduce transaction costs, critics of compulsory licenses maintain that there are private clearinghouse mechanisms, such as ASCAP and BMI, which could accomplish the same result at a fraction of the administrative cost and without government intervention.[31] Rather than abolishing the compulsory licenses, Congress responded to the shortcomings of the regulatory system. This ever increasing dissatisfaction with the CRT led to its abolition in 1993.

With the Copyright Royalty Tribunal Act of 1993, Congress has abolished an entrenched administrative agency and radically changed the regulatory landscape of the compulsory licenses. In place of the CRT, the Act has created a more flexible alternative, Copyright Arbitration Royalty Panels (CARPs). These expert panels will be convened from time to time by the Librarian of Congress, on advice of the Register of Copyrights, to reconsider particular rates or resolve disputes over the distribution of royalties. The goal of this new system is to reduce the cost of administering the compulsory licenses and shift these costs to the parties involved.[32] If it works as planned, the CARPs should provide a more limber mechanism for resolving disputes, while assuring that the decision-making process is conducted by qualified experts.

The Copyright Royalty Tribunal Act of 1993 indicates that compulsory licensing is here to stay despite its vigorous denunciation in certain quarters.[33] Whether administered by a CRT or CARPs, the compulsory licenses reflect political reality and have become an integral aspect of the way the system functions. Economic relationships and certain copyright industries are organized around the compulsory licenses. Rather than their demise, we may probably see more compulsory licenses created as a result of political expediency.[34] In addition to compulsory licenses, other forms of comprehensive regulatory schemes, such as that embodied in the Audio Home Recording Act, may become more common in subsequent years.[35]

[31] See generally Paul Goldstein, The Private Consumption of Public Goods: A Comment on Williams and Wilkins Co. v. United States, 21 Bull. Copyright Soc'y 204, 210–11 (1974). For a discussion of these Performing Rights Societies, see § 8.22, infra.

[32] See H. R. Rep. No. 286, 103d Cong., 1st Sess. 2956 (1993).

[33] For a transnational view and criticism of compulsory licenses in copyright, see Andre Francon, The Future of Copyright, 132 RIDA 2 (1987).

[34] Compulsory license solutions have been proposed for off-the-air videotaping and audio taping, see, e.g., S. 31, 98th Cong., 1st Sess. (1983) (video); S. 1739, 99th Cong., lst Sess. (1985) (audio); and for performance rights in sound recording, see H.R. 1805, 97th Cong., 2d Sess. (1981).

[35] See the Audio Home Recording Act of 1992, 102 P.L. 563; 106 Stat. 4237 (1992), discussed at § 8.29, infra.

PART II: THE REPRODUCTION AND ADAPTATION
RIGHTS AND THEIR LIMITATIONS

§ 8.4 The Reproduction Right: Generally

The exclusive right to reproduce a copyrighted work in copies or phonorecords[36] may be regarded as the most fundamental right granted by the copyright law. To reproduce a work is to fix it in a tangible and relatively permanent form in a material object, as specified in § 101.[37] One should distinguish reproduction from the broader concept of copying. Reproduction takes place when a work is copied in a material object, as when an artist puts paint on canvas or a singer records a work on a phonorecord. Copying, a broader concept, can take place without a fixation, such as by a performance or display. One unauthorized fixation can infringe the reproduction right even though the copy made is not sold or otherwise distributed to others.

§ 8.5 The Right to Prepare Derivative Works:[38] The Adaptation Right — Generally

The adaptation right is infringed when a third party makes an unauthorized derivative work[39] in which a pre-existing work is recast, reformed, or adapted, such as a translation, musical arrangement, or dramatization. The exclusive right to prepare derivative works enables the copyright owner to exploit markets other than the one in which the work was first published. Today, these derivative markets can often be more valuable than the market of first publication. Motion picture rights to a successful novel, or merchandising rights for characters in a motion picture, are examples of these highly lucrative derivative markets.[40] Through the adaptation right, American law has expanded the concept of "copying" to cover much broader ground than suggested by the ordinary meaning of that word. In one sense, to recast or transform — to adapt the work — is to "copy" it. A derivative work author, however, often involves much more than mere copying. By transforming another's work, the derivative work author may add his own substantial authorship to the underlying work. As a result, some derivative works greatly outstrip the value of the underlying work, but without recognition of the adaptation right, the copyright owner would have recourse only against verbatim forms of copying in the same medium.

Derivative right cases can run the gamut from those in which the infringing work completely incorporates the underlying work to those in which the underlying work is imperceptible, the question being always whether the second work is based upon

---

[36] 17 U.S.C. § 106(1).

[37] 17 U.S.C. § 101.

[38] 17 U.S.C. § 106(2).

[39] For a discussion of derivative works, see §§ 2.8–2.11, *supra*.

[40] For an excellent overview of the subject, see Paul Goldstein, *Derivative Rights and Derivative Works in Copyright*, 30 J. Copyright Soc'y 209 (1983).

the first. At the other end of the spectrum, the underlying work is easily recognized as in a translation or an abridgment of a novel.[41] In the middle are more difficult cases involving, for example, the stage dramatization of a novel.[42] Finally, at the other end of the spectrum, the underlying work may not appear at all in the derivative work. For example, in one case, infringement was found in the publication of a manual providing answers to questions presented in a well-known physics book.[43] Of course, the critical question is the point along this continuum at which courts should draw the line in protecting the work under § 106(2). But cases like the above seem to stretch the derivative work concept too far, transforming copyright law into a general law of misappropriation. Even though one might agree that infringement extends beyond verbatim copying, there are limits. To violate the adaptation right, the infringing work must, at least, transform, recast, or adapt a portion of the copyrighted work in some form.[44]

Some courts seem to disregard this principle. For example, in *Mirage Editions, Inc. v. Albuquerque A.R.T. Co.*,[45] the defendant cut out photographs of works of art from a commemorative book and transferred them to individual ceramic tiles. The court incorrectly found this to be an infringement of the derivative right, chiefly because defendant's work supplanted the demand for the the underlying work. From these facts, it is difficult to understand how the derivative right was infringed. Here, the defendant merely took copies that he lawfully owned and remounted them. He did so without recasting, transforming, or adapting the copyrighted work in any significant way.[46] This case illustrates a tendency of some courts to push the derivative right beyond reasonable limits to achieve an "equitable" result.

The adaptation right overlaps the reproduction and performance rights, and with few exceptions, infringement of the adaptation right infringes either the reproduction right, performance right, or both. Thus, if a person writes a play based on a novel without permission from the copyright owner, and if the play substantially embodies the copyrighted work, the copyright owner could bring an action for infringement of both the adaptation and reproduction rights. If the play were then performed, the performance right in the novel would also be infringed.

Although the adaptation right overlaps the reproduction right, it is not merely superfluous, but can constitute a valuable and separate exclusive right for the

---

[41] *See, e.g., Grove Press, Inc. v. Greenleaf Publishing Co.*, 247 F. Supp. 518 (E.D.N.Y. 1965) (translation).

[42] *See, e.g., Metro-Goldwyn-Mayer, Inc. v. Showcase Atlanta Cooperative Productions, Inc.*, 479 F. Supp. 351 (N.D. Ga. 1979).

[43] *See, e.g., Addison-Wesley Publishing Co. v. Brown*, 223 F. Supp. 219 (E.D.N.Y. 1963).

[44] But to violate the derivative right, the work need *not* be reproduced in concrete form. A performance can violate this right. For an example of a case applying this principle, *see Lewis Galoob Toys, Inc. v. Nintendo of Am. Inc.*, 964 F.2d 965 (9th Cir. 1992) (defendant's devices that allowed users of a plaintiff's videogame to alter its display did not infringe the adaptation right, because the altered displays did not incorporate a portion of the copyrighted work in some concrete or permanent form.

[45] 856 F.2d 1341 (9th Cir. 1988).

[46] For a case with virtually identical facts finding no infringement of the adaptation right, see *C. M. Paula Co. v. Logan*, 355 F. Supp. 189 (N.D. Tex. 1973).

copyright owner. In one significant instance, it is possible to infringe the adaptation right without infringing simultaneously the reproduction or performance rights.[47] This could occur when the copyright owner has licensed another to reproduce or perform the work, but has not specifically licensed the right to make a derivative work. For example, suppose A has licensed B to reproduce (make copies of) and perform his copyrighted play, and B, as a matter of convenience, abridges the play (sells copies of it in the abridged form) and performs it in its new version. If the contract were silent on the right to abridge, i.e. , adapt, a court might find an infringement of the adaptation right even though the licensee has infringed neither the performance nor the reproduction rights.[48] Thus, a prospective user of a copyrighted work should negotiate, in the appropriate situation, a license to adapt, as well as the rights to reproduce and perform, the work.[49]

§ 8.6 Limitations to the Reproduction and Adaptation Rights: Computer Uses — § 117[50]

A 1980 amendment to the 1976 Act, § 117,[51] was drafted by a specially appointed presidential commission, CONTU,[52] to meet the needs of the users and producers of computer software. The original version of § 117 served as a holding measure until CONTU had an opportunity to examine the issue. Once CONTU issued its final report, Congress quickly adopted CONTU's proposed amendment virtually in its entirety.

[47] See generally 2 Nimmer on Copyright § 8.09[A] (1993).
[48] The leading case is Gilliam v. American Broadcasting Co., Inc., 538 F.2d 14 (2d Cir. 1976), where ABC obtained a license to broadcast Monty Python programs in their entirety except for minor editing to insert commercials. ABC substantially abridged the programs, cutting twenty-four of ninety minutes from them. The court held that the unauthorized editing of the underlying work constituted an infringement of the copyright.
[49] There are common sense limits and courts have recognized that licensees are entitled to some degree of latitude in arranging the licensed work for presentation to the public, consistent with the licensee's style or standards. See Stratchborneo v. Arc Music Corp., 357 F. Supp. 1393 (S.D.N.Y. 1973), and Gilliam v. American Broadcasting Co., Inc., 538 F.2d 14 (2d Cir. 1976).
[50] For an excellent overview of the subject, see Robert A. Kreiss, Section 117 of the Copyright Act, 1991 B.Y.U. L. Rev. 1497. See also Raymond. T. Nimmer, The Law of Computer Technology (2d ed. 1992), covering all aspects of computer law.
[51] 17 U.S.C. § 117. See Pub. L. No. 96–517, 94 Stat. 3015, 3028 (1980).
[52] National Commission on New Technological Uses of Copyrighted Works (CONTU). The Commission was established to study the issue of computer uses of copyrighted works. Its recommendations for an amended § 117, as part of its Final Report of the Commission on New Technological Uses of Copyrighted Works (1979) (hereinafter CONTU Final Report), were adopted in their entirety. The one major change in the final version of § 117 from CONTU's version is Congress's substitution of the word "owner" for "rightful possessor." CONTU's version would have conferred on licensees the same rights as an owner. The legislative history does not reveal the purpose of the change. See Midway Mfg. Co. v. Artic Int'l, Inc., 704 F.2d 1009 (7th Cir.), cert. denied, 464 U.S. 823 (1983).

Section 117 creates a limited exception to the reproduction and adaptation rights by allowing the *owner* (not a licensee) of a copy of a computer program to copy it or adapt it if (1) the new copy or adaptation is created as an essential[53] step toward using the program in a computer or (2) the copy or adaptation is for archival purposes and "that all archival copies are destroyed in the event that continued possession of the computer program should cease to be rightful."[54] In addition, the last unnumbered paragraph in the section allows transfer of the exact copy made, but only along with the original copy. An adaptation of the program can only be transferred with the authorization of the copyright owner.

Section 117 supports the needs of users but is designed as well to protect the rights of creators. The above provisions apply only to a rightful owner of a copy of a program for use in his own computer.[55] Thus, the program owner's right to make archival copies ceases once the original copy is resold, and the previous owner must destroy an archival copy unless it is an exact copy of the program, which may then be transferred to the new owner instead of destroying it. The reason for this rule is to prevent the owner of a copy from both profiting from a sale of the copy and at the same time keeping an archival copy for continued use.

Section 117 exceptions to the reproduction and adaptation rights are dictated by the special needs of the software medium. The first, the adaptation of a program, is often necessary because program languages are not standardized.[56] The second, the right to make archival copies of a program, recognizes the fragility of the medium supported by the long-standing practice of computer users of making back-up copies as a precaution against mechanical or electronic failure. The privilege to make these back-up copies applies only when the program faces a legitimate threat of mechanical failure, and does not apply where no substantial risk is present, such as for a copy printed on paper.[57]

While providing access to the copyrighted work, § 117 protects the rights of the copyright owner by strictly limiting reproduction and adaptation to the peculiarities

---

[53] 17 U.S.C. § 117(1). The case law has not explicitly interpreted what is an *essential* step. One commentator has suggested that it be interpreted broadly to include any adjustments which optimize the personal use of the program. *See* Raymond T. Nimmer, *The Law of Computer Technology* at 1–66 (1985). *But see Apple Computer, Inc. v. Formula International, Inc.*, 594 F. Supp. 617 (C.D. Cal. 1984) (defendant owner of diskette program not permitted to put a program on a silicon chip. The use was for convenience, and was not an essential use, *i.e.*, indispensable and necessary).

[54] 17 U.S.C. § 117(2).

[55] *See* 2 *Nimmer on Copyright* § 8.08 at 8–105 (1993), and *Apple Computer, Inc. v. Formula International, Inc.*, 594 F. Supp. 617 (C.D. Cal. 1984).

[56] CONTU *Final Report, supra*, note 41, at 13–14.

[57] *Micro-Sparc Inc. v. Amtype Corp.*, 592 F. Supp. 33 (D. Mass. 1984); *see also Atari, Inc. v. JS & A Group, Inc.*, 747 F.2d 1422 (Fed. Cir. 1984) (the right to prepare an archival copy does not apply to programs distributed in a read only memory (ROM) because these chips were not susceptible to risks of *mechanical or electrical* failure. *But see Vault Corp. v. Quaid Software Ltd.*, 847 F.2d 255, 267 (5th Cir. 1988) (An owner of a program is entitled to make an archival copy of that program to guard against *all* types of risks, including physical and human mishap as well as mechanical and electrical failure).

of the medium. In effect, one might view § 117 as setting forth explicitly what would certainly have constituted a fair use [58] of a copyrighted computer program absent the § 117 exception. Thus, the possibility exists that fair use under 107 may be applied to computer uses that transcend the limited exception to the reproduction right set forth in § 117.[59]

§ 8.7 Limitations to the Reproduction and Adaptation Rights: The Compulsory License for Making and Distributing Phonorecords (The Mechanical License) — § 115[60]

[A] Generally

Section 115, known as the "mechanical license," places substantial limits on the reproduction, adaptation, and distribution rights of musical copyright owners.[61] It sets up a compulsory licensing system for the making and distribution of phonorecords of non-dramatic musical works. The mechanical license, which first appeared in the 1909 Act,[62] was adopted out of a fear of monopoly control of recorded music by powerful turn-of-the-century music companies.[63] Although times have changed in the music industry, the compulsory license is a mainstay of the 1976 Copyright Act.

[B] How the Compulsory License Works

Once a phonorecord of a non-dramatic musical work is distributed to the public, any other person can make a sound recording of the work for sale to the public. Section 115 gives the musical copyright owner the right to make the first distribution to the public. Thereafter, the compulsory license provisions are triggered and the musical work is fair game for anyone else wishing to make independent recordings of the work to sell to the public. To illustrate, suppose A composes a song and licenses B to gather musicians and singers for a recording. Once B's recording is distributed to the public in cassette or record, C can make his own recording of the song under the terms of the compulsory license. To obtain the compulsory license, C must follow the procedures set forth in the 1976 Act,[64] and pay the statutory royalty to the copyright owner on each record distributed under the license.[65]

---

[58] For a discussion of fair use, see Chapter 10, *infra*.

[59] *See, e.g., Sega Enters., Ltd. v. Accolade, Inc.*, 977 F.2d 1510, 1520 (9th Cir. 1992) (Section 117 does not protect a user who disassembles object code, converts it from source code, and makes printouts and photocopies of the version in source code). *See* § 10.13, *infra*, for a discussion of *Sega*.

[60] For an overview of the mechanical license, see Fredrick F. Greenman, Jr. & Alvin Deutsch, *The Copyright Royalty Tribunal and the Statutory Mechanical Royalty: History and Prospect*, 1 Cardozo Arts & Ent. L.J. 1 (1982).

[61] 17 U.S.C. § 115.

[62] 17 U.S.C. § 1(e) (1909 Act).

[63] H.R. Rep. No. 2222, 60th Cong., 2d Sess. 6 (1909).

[64] 17 U.S.C. § 115(b)(1).

[65] The royalty rate has been adjusted periodically by the Copyright Royalty Tribunal. It started out as 2.75 cents per record or .5 cent per minute of playing time, whichever is greater.

[C]   Where the Compulsory License Does Not Apply

The compulsory license applies only to non-dramatic[66] musical works; it cannot be obtained for a recording of an opera, motion picture sound track, a ballet score, or a medley of tunes from a Broadway show. To use a *dramatic* musical work, one must first negotiate with the copyright owner. Second, a person can obtain the compulsory license only if her primary purpose is to distribute the work to the public for private use.[67] This excludes recordings intended primarily for jukeboxes and background music. Third, the compulsory license can be obtained only if the original sound recording was lawfully made; that is, a first distribution was made or authorized by the copyright owner.

The compulsory license allows a person to make his own recording by assembling his own musicians for an independent recording. This provision precludes someone from reproducing the sound recording of another and using the compulsory license as his defense.[68] When making the recording, the compulsory licensee may arrange the work to conform it to his style of performance.[69] The privilege, however, is a limited one; it does not extend to changes in the basic melody or fundamental character of the work, and if the privilege is exceeded, the licensee has infringed the copyright owner's adaptation right.[70] Thus, a substantially modified

---

Since 1986, the royalty has been the larger of 5 cents or .95 cent per minute of playing time or fraction thereof. *See* 37 C.F.R. § 307 (1981). For every phonorecord made and distributed on or after January 1, 1988, the royalty payable for each work embodied in the phonorecord become either 5.25 cents or 1 cent per minute of playing time or fraction thereof, whichever amount is larger. *See* 37 C.F.R. § 307.3; *Recording Industry Ass'n v. Copyright Royalty Tribunal*, 662 F.2d 1, 17 (D.C. Cir. 1981) (" . . . (n)othing in the statute preclud(es) the Tribunal from adopting a reasonable mechanism for automatic rate changes in interim years").

Section 115(c)(3) adds to the obligation to pay royalties on records sold to the public the further requirement to pay a proportionate royalty for every rental of a record made with the authority of the copyright owner. This section was added pursuant to the Record Rental Amendment of 1984, now codified in 17 U.S.C. § 109(b). To date, there has been no activity under this provision, the record companies preferring an outright prohibition of rentals rather than obtaining royalties under the licensing system. For a discussion of the Record Rental Amendment, see § 8.14[A], *infra*. For the problems of determining Record Rental Royalties and their interplay with 17 U.S.C. § 115(c)(3), see 2 *Nimmer on Copyright* § 8.04[H] (1993).

[66] For a discussion of the distinction between non-dramatic and dramatic rights, see § 8.22[C], *infra*.

[67] 17 U.S.C. § 115(a)(1).

[68] *Id.*

. . . A person is not entitled to a compulsory license of copyrighted musical works for the purpose of making an unauthorized duplication of a musical sound recording originally developed and produced by another.

H.R. Rep. No. 94–1476, 94th Cong., 2d Sess. 108 (1976) (*citing Duchess Music Corp. v. Stern*, 458 F.2d 1305 (9th Cir.), *cert. denied*, 409 U.S. 847 (1972)).

[69] Even though the authorized recording contains words and music, the courts have allowed a purely instrumental work under the compulsory license. *See Edward B. Marks Music Corp. v. Foullon*, 171 F.2d 905 (2d Cir. 1949).

[70] 17 U.S.C. § 115(a)(2).

arrangement will be protected as a derivative work only with the copyright owner's consent. This narrow privilege places the licensee in a delicate position, because how much change is too much remains an open question. The general rule is that the changes must be minimal, designed only to conform the musical work to the range and style of the licensee's performers.[71] In short, a licensee must be faithful to the work as presented by the copyright owner and cannot distort it in any way.

[D] Procedures

Obtaining the compulsory license requires compliance with the procedures set forth in the statute plus the regulations promulgated by the Register of Copyrights. The process begins with a notice of intention to obtain the compulsory license.[72] The notice must be served on the copyright owner, or in the Copyright Office, if the copyright owner's address is unknown. The notice must be filed before distribution of the phonorecords or within thirty days of making the new recording. A compulsory license will not be issued if there is failure to comply with notice, and non-compliance constitutes infringement.[73]

The compulsory licensee must pay a monthly statutory royalty, known in the trade as "mechanical royalties." In practice, the royalty rate works as a ceiling price for a privately negotiated agreement. The 1976 Act does not prevent the parties from negotiating the terms of the license privately. Indeed, most parties find a privately negotiated agreement more convenient. They usually work through an agent, such as the Harry Fox Agency,[74] which specializes in licensing mechanical rights.

§ 8.8   Limitations to the Reproduction and Adaptation Rights: Ephemeral Recordings — § 112(d)[75]

Ephemeral recordings are copies or phonorecords of a work made for transmission[76] by a broadcasting organization legally entitled to transmit the work. The right to make ephemeral recordings is a narrow limitation on the exclusive reproduction right created to accommodate the needs of the broadcasting industry. A broadcaster may have a right to perform or display a work, but may not have the right to make

---

[71] See *Stratchborneo v. Arc Music Corp.*, 357 F. Supp. 1393 (S.D.N.Y. 1973), and 2 *Nimmer on Copyright* § 8.04[F] (1993).

[72] 17 U.S.C. § 115(b)(1).

[73] 17 U.S.C. § 115(b)(2).

[74] The Harry Fox Agency is a clearinghouse which is active in licensing synchronization rights as well. The Agency represents virtually every major music publisher in negotiations for mechanical and synchronization rights. *See generally* Ralph Oman, *Source Licensing: The Latest Skirmish in an Old Battle*, 11 Colum.-VLA J. L. & Arts 251 (1987).

[75] 17 U.S.C. § 112.

[76] Section 101 defines "transmit" as follows:

> To "transmit" a performance or display is to communicate it by any device or process whereby images or sounds are received beyond the place from which they are sent

as in a television, radio or cable transmission.

copies of it. Under this section, a broadcaster who has obtained a license to perform the work (or fits under an exception to do so) may make an ephemeral recording of the work. Section 112 may be briefly summarized as follows:

(1) *Licensed Broadcasters*: Under § 112(a),[77] a licensed broadcaster may make one copy of a work, provided that the copy is retained and used solely by the organization that made it, for the organization's own transmissions within its local service area. No further copies or phonorecords can be made of it. In addition, unless the copy is preserved exclusively for archival purposes, it must be destroyed within six months.

(2) *Government and Non-Profit*: § 112(b)[78] provides a wider privilege for governmental bodies and non-profit organizations entitled to transmit a performance or display of a work under § 110(2),[79] or to make sound recordings under § 114(a).[80] These entities may make up to thirty copies or phonorecords of the transmission embodying the performance or display, provided that no further copies are made. All copies must be destroyed within seven years of the first transmission. However, one copy may be kept for archival purposes.

(3) *Governmental and Non-profit Religious Broadcasts*: § 112(c)[81] covers religious broadcasts. It allows a governmental or non-profit organization to make one copy of a transmitted non-dramatic musical religious work if there is no charge for the copy, and the broadcaster is under a license or transfer of the copyright. All copies, except one for archival purposes, must be destroyed within one year of the first transmission.

(4) *Handicapped Audiences*: § 112(d)[82] grants the right to governmental or non-profit organizations to make ephemeral recordings for transmissions to handicapped audiences as authorized under § 110(8).[83]

(5) Section 112(e)[84] states that ephemeral recordings are not copyrightable as derivative works, unless the copyright owner gives her consent.

§ 8.9 Limitations to Reproduction and Adaptation Rights: Sound Recordings[85] — § 114(b)

This section limits the exclusive rights of reproduction, adaptation, and

---

[77] 17 U.S.C. § 112(a).

[78] 17 U.S.C. § 112(b).

[79] *See* 17 U.S.C. § 110(2) which exempts transmitted performances and displays in certain instructional settings. *See* § 8.17[B], *infra*.

[80] 17 U.S.C. § 114(a).

[81] 17 U.S.C. § 112(c).

[82] 17 U.S.C. § 112(d).

[83] 17 U.S.C. § 110(8).

[84] 17 U.S.C. § 112(e).

[85] "Sound recordings" are works that result from the fixation of a series of musical, spoken, or other sounds, but not including the sounds accompanying a motion picture or

performance in sound recordings, illustrating that sound recordings receive much less protection under copyright as compared with other copyrightable subject matter, in particular musical works.[86] Under § 114(b),[87] infringement of copyright in a sound recording occurs by either (1) reproducing it by mechanical means, or (2) rearranging, remixing, or altering it in some way by mechanical[88] means. Alternatively, one does not infringe the copyright in a sound recording by making an independent fixation, despite the extent to which the new recording imitates the preexisting sound recording. To illustrate, suppose a sound recording were made of the New York Philharmonic's rendition of Beethoven's *Fifth Symphony*. Under the limitation set forth in 114(b), another orchestra could legally imitate the New York Philharmonic's performance down to the last detail so long as the orchestra hired its own musicians and made an independent recording of the subsequent live performance.

The limitation of § 114(b) relates to the copyright in the sound recording. One should not confuse the rights in a sound recording with the rights in the musical work embodied on the same phonorecord.[89] This confusion arises from a failure to distinguish two forms of copyrightable subject matter, the musical work and the sound recording, both of which are embodied on the same material object, the phonorecord. For example, suppose record company A is the owner of the copyright of a sound recording of Irving Berlin's *White Christmas*. Under § 114(b), record company B can imitate, without permission, the style and sound of A's recording down to its smallest detail without infringing A's reproduction right or adaptation right in the sound recording. Even though the copyright in the *sound recording* cannot be infringed in this manner, B could still infringe the copyright, specifically the reproduction and adaptation rights, in the musical composition *White Christmas* by making the unauthorized recording.[90] The point is that one should always distinguish between the copyright in the sound recording and that in the musical work.

---

other audiovisual work, regardless of the nature of the material objects, such as discs, tapes, or other phonorecords, in which they are embodied.

17 U.S.C. § 101.

[86] Sound recordings enjoy a much more limited scope of protection than, for example, musical works. A sound recording does not enjoy a performance right as does a musical work. *See* 17 U.S.C. §§ 106(4) and 114(a). For a discussion of the lack of protection given to performance rights in sound recordings, see § 8.24, *infra*.

[87] 17 U.S.C. § 114(b).

[88] Infringement by "mechanical means" takes place where the actual sounds in a sound recording are reproduced by repressing, transcribing, recapturing off the air or reproducing them by other technology. *See* H.R. Rep. No 94–1476, 94th Cong., 2d Sess. 106 (1976).

[89] 17 U.S.C. § 114(c).

[90] The same conceptual difficulty in distinguishing between copyright in a sound recording and copyright in a musical work will arise again for performance rights, which musical works enjoy, but which sound recordings do not.

§ 8.10   Limitations to the Reproduction and Adaptation Rights: Reproduction of Pictorial, Graphic, and Sculptural Works in Useful Articles — § 113

Section 113(a)[91] reconfirms the general rule under 1909 Act case law[92] that copyright in a pictorial, graphic, or sculptural work is not affected when the work is used as the design for a useful object. In other words, a work may be protected under copyright law regardless of whether it is embodied in a useful or purely aesthetic object. Thus, a statuette on the hood of a car, a gargoyle on a building, and a lamp base resembling a Balinese dancer are all copyrightable works of art. That they are embodied in a useful object — car, building, or lamp — has no bearing on their copyrightability.

Section 113(b),[93] however, limits the reproduction right of useful objects. It provides that

> . . . the owner of copyright in a work that portrays a useful article as such, [is not afforded] any greater or lesser rights with respect to the making, distribution, or display of the useful article so portrayed . . .

than under the law as it developed under the 1909 Act. This codifies and reconfirms the basic rule that a drawing or model of a lighting fixture, a building, or an automobile is copyrightable as such, but the copyright does not give the artist the exclusive right to make the lighting fixture, building or automobile. In sum, a copyright in a pictorial, graphic, or sculptural work portraying a useful object does not extend to the manufacture of the useful object.[94]

Section 113(c)[95] further limits the reproduction right of a work embodied in a useful object. Under this subsection, the copyright owner cannot prevent the making, distribution, or display of pictures or photographs of such articles in connection with advertisements, commentaries, or news reports relating to the useful object.

§ 8.11   Limitations to the Reproduction and Adaptation Rights: Architectural Works

Section 120(a) of the Copyright Act provides that once an architectural work has been constructed and is publicly visible, "no right exists to prevent the making, distributing, or public display of pictures, paintings, photographs, or other pictorial representations of the work." Thus, photographers will not only be able to take pictures of publicly visible buildings but will be able to commercialize their photos as well in posters, postcards, and slides.

---

[91] 17 U.S.C. § 113(a).

[92] *Mazer v. Stein*, 347 U.S. 201 (1954). For a discussion of the copyrightability of the design of useful objects, see §§ 3.10–3.14, *supra*.

[93] 17 U.S.C. § 113(b).

[94] H.R. Rep. No. 94–1476, 94th Cong., 2d Sess. 105 (1976).

[95] 17 U.S.C. § 113(c).

Section 120(b) operates as a limitation to the adaptation right. Under this section "the owners of a building embodying an architectual work may without the consent of the author or copyright owner of the architectural work, make or authorize the making of alterations to such building, and destroy or authorize the destruction of such building. If the building embodies a work of visual art as defined in § 101, the owner of the building may be subject to liability under section 113(d)(2) for failure to procure the required permission from the artist.[96]

PART III: THE DISTRIBUTION RIGHT AND ITS LIMITATIONS

§ 8.12 The Distribution Right: Generally

Section 106(3)[97] creates the exclusive right

> to distribute copies or phonorecords of the copyrighted work to the public by sale or other transfer of ownership, or by rental, lease, or lending.

The distribution right gives the copyright owner the right to control the first public distribution of the work.[98] It differs from the other rights in § 106 which involve copying in one way or another. Rather than the right to copy, the distribution right involves the right to transfer physical copies or phonorecords of the work.

The distribution right is frequently infringed simultaneously with the reproduction right, but can also be infringed alone. Infringement of the distribution right alone commonly occurs in the music industry when unlawfully made audio or video tapes are acquired by a retailer and sold to the public. Although the retail seller may not have copied the work in any way and may not have known that the works were made unlawfully, he nevertheless infringes the distribution right by their sale. The seller's innocent intent is not a valid defense to an action for copyright infringement, which allows the copyright owner to proceed against any member in the chain of distribution.[99]

§ 8.13 Limitations on the Distribution Right: The First Sale Doctrine

[A] Generally

Section 109(a)[100] creates a basic exception to the distribution right known as the "first sale doctrine," which limits the copyright owner's control over copies of the work to their first sale or transfer. Section 109(a) provides:

> Notwithstanding the provisions of section 106(3) [citation omitted], the owner
> of a particular copy or phonorecord lawfully made under this title [citation

---

[96] See section 8.28 *infra* for a discussion of the Visual Artists Rights Act of 1990.
[97] 17 U.S.C. § 106(3).
[98] The first public distribution may be by sale, rental, lease or lending. *See* H.R. Rep. No. 94–1476, 94th Cong., 2d Sess. 62 (1976).
[99] *Costello Publications Co. v. Rotelle*, 670 F.2d 1035, 1044 (D.C. Cir. 1981).
[100] 17 U.S.C. § 109(a).

omitted], or any person authorized by such owner, is entitled, without the authority of the copyright owner, to sell or otherwise dispose of the possession of that copy or phonorecord.

Under this provision, once the work is lawfully sold or even transferred gratuitously,[101] the copyright owner's interest in the material object, the copy or phonorecord, is exhausted; the owner of that copy can then dispose of it as he sees fit. The first sale doctrine entitles the owner of a copy to dispose of it physically. Thus, one who buys a copy of a book is entitled to resell it, rent it out, give it away, rebind it, or destroy it. This same owner, however, would infringe copyright by reproducing it or performing it publicly without the consent of the copyright owner.[102] Alternatively, the first sale doctrine is not triggered when the copyright owner has rented, leased, or loaned the copy without actually transferring ownership of it.[103] The first sale doctrine can be modified by the parties,[104] but any agreement would be enforced under the law of contract rather than copyright law.[105]

The rationale of the first sale doctrine is to prevent the copyright owner from restraining the free alienability of goods. Without a first sale doctrine, a possessor of a copy or phonorecord of a copyrighted work would have to negotiate with the copyright owner every time he wished to dispose of his copy or phonorecord. This principle sometimes clashes with the copyright owner's reproduction and adaptation rights, forcing the court to make delicate distinctions. In *C.M. Paula Co. v. Logan*,[106] defendant bought plaintiff's greeting cards, transferred the designs on the cards to ceramic plaques, and sold the plaques commercially. The court held that neither the reproduction nor adaptation right was infringed and that the sale of the plaques was immunized by the first sale doctrine.[107] The defendant was not reproducing the work but simply disposing of it physically:

[e]ach ceramic plaque sold by defendant with a Paula print affixed thereto requires the purchase and use of an individual piece of artwork marketed by the plaintiff.[108]

As for infringement of the adaptation right, the court found no adaptation, rearrangement, or compilation sufficient to violate the right. Using similar reasoning, other courts have found no infringement of the distribution right where individuals have lawfully purchased copies of paper-bound books and rebound them in hard covers,

---

[101] *Walt Disney Productions v. Basmajian*, 600 F. Supp. 439 (S.D.N.Y. 1984).

[102] 17 U.S.C. § 202. *See* H.R. Rep. No. 94–1476, 94th Cong., 2d Sess. 79 (1976).

[103] *See United States v. Atherton*, 561 F.2d 747 (9th Cir. 1977), for problems in determining where a transfer of title has taken place involving motion picture prints.

[104] *United States v. Wise*, 550 F.2d 1180 (9th Cir.), *cert. denied*, 434 U.S. 929 (1977).

[105] H.R. Rep. No. 94–1476, 94th Cong., 2d Sess. 79 (1976). For an excellent article discussing the techniques used to modify the first sale doctrine by restrictive notices, see Mark A. Fischer, *Reserving All Rights Beyond Copyright: Non-Statutory Restrictive Notices*, 34 J. Copyright Soc'y 249 (1987).

[106] 355 F. Supp. 189 (N.D. Tex. 1973).

[107] The first sale doctrine was incorporated into the 1909 Act in 17 U.S.C. § 27 (1909 Act).

[108] *C.M. Paula Co. v. Logan*, 355 F. Supp. 189, 191 (N.D. Tex. 1973).

even when combined with other works.[109] The case law reveals that courts in close cases will often side with the defendant when the rights of the copyright owner encroach on the right of an owner to dispose of physical copies of the work.[110]

The above freedom of disposition of physical copies of the work applies only where the book is lawfully made.[111] Any resale or other disposition of a pirated copy would constitute an infringing act, even if the defendant had no knowledge of the piracy. Accordingly, a retail record store which has unknowingly sold pirated copies of a popular album is an infringer of copyright. Lack of knowledge that one is infringing is not a defense to an action for an infringement of the distribution right.

[B] Non-Consensual Transfers

Normally § 109(a) comes into play when the copyright owner consents to the sale of a copy or phonorecord of the work. The question has arisen whether the first sale doctrine applies to a non-consensual transfer of ownership, for instance, where a creditor acquires a work through a court compelled assignment or judicial sale. In *Platt & Munk Co. v. Republic Graphics, Inc.,*[112] plaintiff contracted with defendant to manufacture toys over which plaintiff retained copyright. Plaintiff refused to accept the delivery, claiming improper manufacture and breach of contract. Defendant, in turn, threatened summary sale under New York Personal Property and Lien Law.[113] In response to an action for infringement, defendant asserted that because he had title to the work under New York law, he could dispose of the copies under the first sale doctrine. The court held that defendant could sell the copies because of the contractual default, but not until a court properly determined the claim on the merits based on plaintiff's refusal to accept the goods.

---

[109] *See Fawcett Publications, Inc. v. Eliot Pub. Co.*, 46 F. Supp. 717 (S.D.N.Y. 1942); *but see National Geographic Soc'y v. Classified Geographic*, 27 F. Supp. 655 (D. Mass. 1939) (defendant infringed the adaptation right by taking individual articles from *National Geographic Magazine* and reassembling and rebinding them with his own index).

[110] *But see Mirage Editions, Inc. v. Albuquerque A.R.T. Co.*, 856 F.2d 1341 (9th Cir. 1988) (adaptation right infringed where defendant transferred artworks from a commemorative book to individual ceramic tiles, because, by borrowing and mounting the preexisting copyrighted art images, defendant prepared derivative works whose sales supplanted purchasers' demand for the underlying works).

[111] According to the House Report, the burden of proving whether a particular copy was lawfully made or acquired should rest on the defendant. *See* H.R. Rep. No. 1476, 94th Cong., 2d Sess. 80–81 (1976). This indicates a legislative intention to overturn the rule developed by 1909 Act case law that copyright owners in civil cases, and the government in criminal cases, had the burden of proving absence of a first sale. *See United States v. Atherton*, 561 F.2d 747, 749 (9th Cir. 1977) (sale of motion picture prints). Due process considerations may prevent imposing the burden of proof on a criminal defendant. *See, e.g., United States v. Moore*, 604 F.2d 1228 (9th Cir. 1979).

[112] 315 F.2d 847 (2d Cir. 1963).

[113] Uniform Sales Act § 60; *see also* Uniform Commercial Code §§ 2–703 and 2–706.

§ 8.14 Modifications and Exceptions to the First Sale Doctrine

[A] Record Rental[114]

The Record Rental Amendment of 1984[115] prohibits an owner of a phonorecord which embodies a sound recording or musical work from renting it to the public for direct or indirect commercial advantage. This exception to the first sale doctrine was directed against the increasing number of record stores renting records, cassettes and compact discs to their customers. The purpose of these rentals was to facilitate home copying, thereby displacing sales that could have been made by the copyright owner.[116] Thus, instead of buying a compact disc for $15.99, the client would rent the disc and purchase a blank tape for a fraction of the price. This practice was perceived as a major threat to the record-producing industry, and § 109(b) was added as an amendment to the 1976 Copyright Act in 1984.[117]

Section 109(b) constitutes a limited exception to the first sale doctrine. It applies to rentals of phonorecords[118] of a sound recording containing a musical work only,[119] and not to a resale or other transfer of a phonorecord. In addition, it is limited to rentals by commercial establishments, whereas non-profit rentals by libraries and educational institutions are specifically excluded from its provisions.

Copyright owners have long wished to benefit from lucrative secondary markets from which they were barred by the first sale doctrine. Authors, who earn their living by selling tangible copies of their works, such as textbook writers, would naturally like a percentage of sales in the organized used book market. They feel disfavored by copyright law, which appears more generous to authors who rely on the performance right for renumeration, such as composers of music. A musical copyright owner does benefit from the reproduction right, but even more from the performance right, which is not limited by the first sale doctrine. To the musical

---

[114] 17 U.S.C. § 109(b). For an overview of the subject, see David H. Horowitz, *The Record Rental Amendment of 1984: A Case Study in the Effort to Adapt Copyright Law to New Technology*, 12 Law & Arts 31 (1987).

[115] Pub. L. No. 98–450, 98 Stat. 1727 (1984).

[116] H.R. Rep. No. 98–987, 98th Cong., 2d Sess. 2 (1984).

[117] Non-retroactivity and sunset provisions were attached to § 109(b), codified in Pub. L. No. 98–450, 98 Stat. 1727 § 4. The effective date of the Act is October 4, 1984. *Id.* at § 4(a). Records bought before that date still enjoyed the first sale exemption under § 109(a). *Id.* at § 4(b). The Act also contained a five-year sunset provision. *Id.* at § 4(c). Rentals of records made after October 3, 1989, were to be once again exempt under § 109(a). The purpose of the sunset provision was to give Congress a chance to evaluate the Record Rental Amendment. *See* H.R. Rep. No. 98–987, 98th Cong., 2d Sess. 6 (1984). On November 5, 1988, President Reagan signed into law (Pub. L. No. 100–617) a bill (S. 2201) extending the Record Rental Amendment of 1984 for an additional eight years. In 1993, as a part of the North American Free Trade amendments, the sunset provisions were completely repealed. *See* Pub. L. No. 103–182, Title III, § 332, 107 Stat. 2114 (1993).

[118] *See* 17 U.S.C. § 101 for the definition of "phonorecords."

[119] It would appear that the amendment applies only to musical works, which would exclude rentals of literary works on tape as rented by the various book on tape companies. *See* 2 *Nimmer on Copyright* § 8.12[c] (1993).

copyright owner, every performance of his work represents a possible source of revenue.[120]

[B] Software Rental

Until the Record Rental Amendment was enacted, most efforts to carve out exceptions to the first sale doctrine were unsuccessful. The record producers achieved their goal because they were able to point out a real threat to their survival made plausible by the ease with which records can be copied. As predicted, it was only a matter of time before other industry groups [121] would persuade Congress to protect them as well by creating a similar exception to the first sale doctrine.[122] So far only the software industry has successfully made their case for an exception to § 109(a). The arguments for a software rental exception were similar to those made by the record industry. Here the focus was on businesses specializing in the rental of such popular programs as Wordperfect and Lotus 1-2-3. Software owners claimed that an organized rental industry would facilitate unauthorized private copying, threatening the economic heath of the industry.[123]

The Copyright Software Rental Amendments Act of 1990[124] amended section 109(b) to prohibit the rental of computer software for direct or indirect commercial advantage.[125] The Software Rental Amendments are limited to the *rental* of a program. Otherwise, the owner of a copy of a program is as free to transfer that copy as any other owner of a copy of a work, such as a book, painting or phonorecord. Unauthorized software rental constitutes copyright infringement. As with the Record Rental Amendment, no criminal liability lies. The restrictions on software rental are not absolute. First, the amendments do not apply to the lending of a copy by a nonprofit library for non-profit purposes, provided the library has affixed an appropriate copyright warning.[126] Second, the new provisions exempt from their scope "a computer program embodied in or used in conduction with a limited purpose computer that is designed for playing video games and may be designed for other purposes."[127] This odd provision overturns the decision in *Red Baron-Franklin Park, Inc. v. Taito Corp.*[128] In *Red Baron*, the court held that the first sale doctrine did not allow the operator of a video arcade, who had acquired video game circuit boards overseas, to perform the game publicly without the copyright owner's

---

[120] For a discussion of the performance right as it relates to the musical copyright owner, see § 8.22, *infra*.

[121] *See* Ralph Oman, *1976 Copyright Revision Revisited*, 34 J. Copyright L. Soc'y 29 (1987) (the movie industry would like their own exception to the first sale doctrine).

[122] *See, e.g.*, H.R. Rep. No. 1029, 98th Cong., 2d Sess. (1984), repealing the first sale doctrine for videocassettes embodying copyrighted works. *See also* discussion of the State Resale Royalty Act, § 8.14[E], *infra*, and the Public Lending Right, § 8.14[F], *infra*.

[123] *See* remarks of Senator Hatch, Cong. Rec. S17,577 (Oct. 27, 1990).

[124] Pub. L. No. 101–650, 104 Stat. 5089 (1990). The law contains a sunset clause, remaining in effect until October 1, 1997). Its duration may be extended by further legislation.

[125] 17 U.S.C. § 109(b)(1)(A).

[126] 17 U.S.C. 109(b)(2)(A).

[127] 17 U.S.C. § 109(b)(1)(B)(ii) and § 109(e).

[128] 883 F.2d 275 (4th Cir. 1989), *cert. denied*, 493 U.S. 1058 (1990).

consent. Section 109(e) permits the owner of a copy of a lawfully made video game to perform or display that game publicly on coin-operated equipment. This exemption is apparently designed to favor American video arcade owners at the expense of "foreign" (*i.e.*, Japanese) copyright owners of video game software.[129]

[C] Imported Copies Legally Obtained Abroad: The Gray Market

Gray market dealers typically buy goods in foreign countries at a significant discount from U.S. prices. They import these goods into the United States and sell them to discount retailers who are then able to undersell authorized U.S. dealers. The gray market exists because of various economic factors, particularly rapid fluctuations in foreign currencies. These fluctuations result in price differentials which may exceed tariff, freight, and related importation costs.

The distribution of genuine products outside a manufacturer's authorized channels is big business. Gray market importation has been estimated to be at various times between 5 to 7 billion dollars.[130] Gray market goods are disruptive to the authorized distribution network. Gray marketeers typically incur lower overhead costs than competing authorized dealers because they take a free ride on the advertising provided by the domestic suppliers, and rarely service the warranties accompanying the goods. The result is that gray market goods are able to undersell those of authorized distributors. On the other hand, consumer advocates point out that the public should be able to purchase cheaper genuine goods, and that these goods often do not have a warranty or service dimension at all.

Authorized dealers have attacked the importation of gray market goods under the trademark law and, with increasing success, under copyright law.[131] Section 602 of the Copyright Act covers unlawful importation in two situations. Section 602(b) deals with piratical copies — those made abroad without the copyright owner's consent. From a legal standpoint, one can always prevent piratical copies from entering the United States. The issue is one of enforcement.

By contrast Subsection (a) has generated difficult legal issues. Section 602(a) covers situations where the copyright owner has authorized the production of the goods. On its face, 602(a) would appear to clash with the first sale doctrine.[132] The

---

[129] Section 109(e) contains a sunset clause, remaining in effect until October 1, 1995.

[130] *See* Note, *The Use of Copyright Law to Block the Importation of Gray-Market Goods: The Black and White of It All*, 23 Loy. L.A. L. Rev. 645, 646 (1990).

[131] A major drawback to the use of trademark law against the gray market has been U.S. Customs Office refusal to prohibit importation of gray market goods so long as the trademark and goods are legitimate and subject to the common control of the trademark owner. *See K Mart Corp. v. Cartier, Inc.*, 486 U.S. 281 (1988). By contrast, courts have not imposed these limitations in their application of copyright law. *See Parfums Givenchy, Inc. v. Drug Emporium, Inc.*, 38 F.3d 477, 500 (9th Cir. 1994) (rationale for the parent-subsidiary exception to the import protection of the Lanham (Trademark) Act is inapplicable to copyright law).

[132] 17 U.S.C. § 602(a):

   Importation into the United States, without the authority of the owner of copyright . . . of copies or phonorecords of a work that have been acquired outside the United issue is whether § 109(a) supersedes § 602(a)'s prohibition against importation without consent of copies or phonorecords lawfully made and sold abroad. In *Columbia Broadcasting System v. Scorpio Music Distributors, Inc.*,[133] plaintiff CBS, as musical copyright owner, authorized the manufacture and sale of certain phonorecords in the Philippines. Through an intermediate buyer in the Philippines, defendant imported about 6,000 of the phonorecords into the United States. When CBS sued for infringement of the distribution right under § 602, defendant asserted that the sale of the records exhausted the distribution under the first sale doctrine. The court rejected the defense since it would render virtually meaningless § 602's prohibition against importation, without the copyright owner's consent, of copies made and sold abroad.[134] In so ruling, the court limited the scope of the first sale doctrine to situations in which copies have been legally manufactured and sold within the United States. Other cases[135] have reconfirmed *Scorpio*, enabling the copyright owner to exercise control over copies of the work which enter the American market in competition with copies lawfully manufactured and distributed within the United States.

The effectiveness of § 602(a) to curtail lawfully obtained goods abroad was thrown into doubt by *Sebastian Int'l, Inc. v. Consumer Contacts Ltd.*[136] In this case, a U.S. manufacturer of hair care products with copyrighted labels brought an infringement action against a foreign purchaser of the products who had reshipped them to the United States for resale. The district court held that the exclusive importation right under section 602 superseded the first sale doctrine. The Third Circuit reversed, holding that the manufacturer, having sold its goods with copyright labels to foreign distributors, was barred by the first sale doctrine from establishing infringement through an unauthorized importation. The court distinguished *Scorpio*, where copies were produced abroad and the sales occurred overseas. However, it held that the place of manufacture is not the key factor in determining whether § 602(a) controls. More important is policy underlying the first sale doctrine, based on a long standing common law aversion to limiting the alienability of property. In addition, the copyright proprietor had received whatever reward it was entitled to with payment of the purchase price.

The major problem with *Sebastian* is that it renders § 602(a) meaningless. This was the position taken in *BMG Music v. Perez*[137] which found that 602(a) was not

---

States is an infringement of the exclusive right to distribute copies or phonorecords under Section 106, actionable under Section 501.

(Citations omitted.)

[133] 569 F. Supp. 47 (E.D. Pa. 1983), *aff'd mem.*, 738 F.2d 424 (3d Cir. 1984).

[134] "Third-party purchasers who import phonorecords could thereby circumvent the statute . . . by simply buying the recordings indirectly." *Id.* at 49.

[135] *See, e.g., Hearst Corp. v. Stark*, 639 F. Supp. 970 (N.D. Cal. 1986) (rejecting First Amendment defense for the importation of out-of-print books); *Nintendo of America, Inc. v. Elcon Industries, Inc.*, 564 F. Supp. 937 (E.D. Mich. 1982). In addition, copyright owners' exclusive licensing agreements with authors did not violate antitrust laws). *But see Cosmair, Inc. v. Dynamite Enterprises, Inc.*, 226 U.S.P.Q. 344 (S.D. Fla. 1985), questioning the *Scorpio* decision's reasoning.

[136] 847 F.2d 1093 (3d Cir. 1988).

[137] 952 F.2d 318 (9th Cir. 1991), *cert. denied*, 112 S. Ct. 2997 (1992).

superseded by the first sale doctrine. Plaintiff BMG Music licensed the manufacture and sale of its recordings in foreign countries. It brought an infringement action against a defendant who had bought those recordings abroad and sold them in the United States. In finding a violation of § 602(a), the Ninth Circuit held that the words "lawfully made under this title" in § 109(a) afforded first-sale protection only to copies legally made and sold in the United States. Thus, § 109(a) did not apply to importation of recordings manufactured and sold abroad. It distinguished *Sebastian* as a case in which the copyrighted material was initially manufactured in the United States and exported abroad where it was bought by a third party and imported back. The distinction that the court makes, based on the place of manufacture, might be unconvincing but it does keep § 602(a) from being completely subsumed by the first sale doctrine, a position more consistent with the Congressional intent behind this section of the Act.[138]

[D] The Right to Dispose of Copies or Phonorecords of a Restored Work

Pursuant to the Uruguay Round Agreements Act of 1994,[139] copyright is automatically restored in certain foreign works that fell into the public domain for failure to comply with U.S. copyright formalities.[140] These restored copyrights will endure for the remainder of the term of copyright as if they had not fallen into the public domain. Restored copyrights will enjoy the same rights as any other. Once copyright is restored in these works, it is illegal for third parties to make further copies of the work.

But what about copies that were made before restoration — before restoration? Section 109(a) would allow owners of such copies to sell or otherwise dispose of them without authorization of the owner of the restored copyright. This right to dispose of copies, however, is limited to a twelve-month period beginning on "(1) the date of publication in the Federal Register of the notice of intent filed with the Copyright Office under section 104A(d)(2)(A), or (2) the date of receipt of actual notice served under section 104A(d)(2)(B)."[141]

[E] The Resale Royalty Right (*Droit de Suite*)[142]

The resale royalty right (*droit de suite*) is a European concept, not as yet recognized in United States copyright law. The "resale royalty right" is the right of an artist to recover a percentage of the resale value from a work of art, and as such, runs counter to the basic policy of the first sale doctrine in U.S. law. Whether

---

138 *BMG Music* was reaffirmed in *Parfums Givenchy, Inc. v. Drug Emporium, Inc.*, 38 F.3d 477 (9th Cir. 1994).

139 Pub. L. No. 103–465, 108 Stat. 4809 (1994).

140 Whether the date of restoration is January 1, 1995 or January 1, 1996 is not clearly indicated in the statute. The issue is discussed at § 4.19[B] note 227 *supra*.

141 17 U.S.C. § 104A(d)(2)(A) and (B). Restoration of copyright in certain foreign works is discussed at §§ 4.18–4.19 *supra*.

142 *See generally* John Henry Merryman, *Law, Ethics and the Visual Arts* 213–28 (2d ed. 1987); Shira Perlmutter, *Resale Royalties for Artists: An Analysis of the Register of Copyrights Report*, 16 Colum.–VLA J.L. & Arts 395 (1992).

to adopt a resale royalty on a national basis remains a subject of continuing debate.[143] Those favoring *droit de suite* maintain that a resale royalty is needed for fine artists who, unlike other authors, create one-of-a-kind works, and do not have the opportunity to exploit the work in multiples. One can think of examples where an artist sells a unique work for a pittance and the work is soon sold for many times more. To advocates of the resale royalty right, fairness to artists calls for an equitable sharing of the resale price.[144]

Critics of the resale royalty argue that it is both unfair to buyers and harms artists. The reason is that investment in art is a highly risky endeavor. More often than not contemporary art works sell at a loss rather than a profit. Even recognized artists can have periods where they produce works which decrease in value. But the resale royalty is a one-way street, and the artist whose work declines in value is not expected to compensate disappointed buyers. Moreover, art works increase in value for many reasons, some of which have little to do with the artist. The resale royalty, however, fails to take into account the value added by other persons and institutions in the art world such as critics, museums, collectors, dealers, and auction houses. Finally, its critics maintain that the resale royalty will hurt the very group it purports to help. In essence, the resale royalty, operates as a five percent sales tax, and like any tax, reduces the demand for the product. Thus, many artists may receive no actual benefit because a buyer will negotiate a lower price on the initial sale, anticipating the reduced value of the art object he or she is buying.[145]

Despite the controversial nature of the resale royalty, the State of California, the only common law jurisdiction to have done so, has adopted a version.[146] Effective January 1, 1977, the California Act covers fine art only, defined as "an original painting, sculpture, drawing or an original work of art in glass." Whenever a work of fine art is either sold by a California resident or sold in California, the seller must pay the artist a five percent royalty on a sale of $1,000 or more. The Act does not apply to sales of less than $1,000, those made twenty years after the artist's death, or to certain resales by an art dealer to a purchaser within ten years of the initial sale.

The California Act has also been criticized as benefiting too few artists and hurting the California art market.[147] Moreover, because the Resale Royalty Act applies only to sales transacted in California or by California residents, buyers simply avoid the California art market. As a result, unless a uniform national act is passed, the California art market may well suffer.

---

[143] *See* U.S Copyright Office, *Droit de Suite: The Artists Resale Royalty* (1992) [Report] summarized at 16 Colum.-VLA J.L. & Arts 381 (1992).

[144] *See generally* Monroe E. Price, *Government Policy and Economic Security for Artists: The Case of the* Droit de Suite, 77 Yale L.J. 1333 (1968).

[145] For a summary of the arguments, pro and con, see Marshall Leaffer, *Of Moral Rights and Resale Royalties: The Kennedy Bill*, 7 Cardozo L. & Ent. J. 234 (1991); John Henry Merryman, *The Wrath of Robert Rauschenberg*, 40 J. Copyright Soc'y 241 (1993).

[146] The California Resale Royalties Act, Cal. Civ. Code § 986 (1977, as amended 1983).

[147] For a general critique, see Weil, *Resale Royalties: Nobody Benefits*, Art News (March 1978).

Another reason calling for a uniform national act is that conflicts would arise if another state passed a Resale Royalty Act. For example, if New York passed a similar statute and a California resident sold a painting in New York, would two resale royalties be imposed on the seller? Because of this type of conflict, some have proposed national uniform legislation as a solution.[148] Finally, whether the California Act is preempted by the federal Copyright Act remains an open question, despite a pre-1976 Act case, *Morseburg v. Balyon*,[149] which found no preemptive effect under the 1909 Act.[150]

[F] The Public Lending Right[151]

The public lending right entitles an author of a book to royalties any time a book is borrowed from a public library. The rationale is that the authors should be able to benefit from organized borrowing of their books from libraries, much as a musical copyright owner can capture the performance right in a work. Like the resale royalty right and the Record Rental Amendment, it is an exemption to the § 109(a) first sale doctrine, in which a copyright owner's right over physical copies of the work is exhausted on their sale. Contrary to this fundamental notion in American law, the public lending right has never been close to adoption in the United States.[152]

The public lending right is found in a number of countries and the concept appears to be slowly gathering support in the United States.[153] The United Kingdom's Public Lending Right Act of 1979 illustrates how the public lending right works. The Act applies to books only, not phonorecords or video cassettes, and only to British citizens or nationals of the European community whose homes are in the United Kingdom. For an author to benefit, her book must be at least 32 pages, and it must be registered with the Register of Public Lending Right. Thereafter, the author is entitled to a modest statutory royalty based on samples conducted to determine how often the book has been checked out. The right is transferable and endures for the term of copyright.

PART IV: The Performance and Display Rights and Their Limitations

§ 8.15 The Performance Right: Generally

Section 106(4) of the Copyright Act provides that the owner of the copyright in

---

[148] *See* Leonard D. DuBoff, *Art Law* 243 (1984).

[149] 621 F.2d 972 (9th Cir.), *cert. denied*, 449 U.S. 983 (1980).

[150] For a discussion of preemption and how it relates to the Resale Royalty Act, see § 11.8[D], *infra*.

[151] *See generally* William R. Cornish, *Intellectual Property: Patents, Copyright, Trademarks and Allied Rights* 449–552 (1981); Seemann, *A Look at the Public Lending Right*, 30 Copyright L. Symp. (ASCAP) 71 (1983).

[152] 17 U.S.C. § 109(a). For a discussion of the first sale doctrine, see § 8.13, *supra*.

[153] West Germany, Netherlands, the Scandinavian countries and Australia have versions of a public lending right. *See* Cornish, n. 144, at 449.

> literary, musical, dramatic, and choreographic works, pantomimes, . . . and other . . . audiovisual works

has the exclusive right "to perform the copyrighted work publicly." Not all the categories of copyrightable subject matter under § 102 enjoy a performance right. Pictorial, graphic, and sculptural works are excluded, as are sound recordings. As defined in § 101,

> to "perform" a work means to recite, render, play, dance, or act it, either directly or by means of any device or process. . . .

So defined, a performance includes not only the initial rendition but any further act by which that rendition is transmitted to the public.[154] Thus, one performs by reciting a poem, singing a song, playing a cassette on a VCR, or simply turning on a radio. Likewise, a broadcaster performs whenever he transmits a live performance or one captured on a phonorecord. Modern technologies have provided endless opportunities to perform copyrighted works. Because of an infinite number of situations where performances take place, the right to perform can be the most valuable exclusive right for the copyright owner.

There are substantial limitations, however, on the performance right. First, the copyright owner can only control *public* performances of his work. Second, the 1976 Act specifically limits the performance right in §§ 107–120 through an elaborate set of exemptions and compulsory licenses.

§ 8.16   What is a Public Performance?

[A]   Generally

The exclusive right to perform is limited to public performances. Clearly, the 1976 Copyright Act was not designed to keep people from singing in their bathtubs or playing their favorite records during dinner in their homes. These are essentially private performances which cannot be controlled by copyright owners. What distinguishes a public from a private performance is set forth in two clauses of § 101.

Under the first clause, "publicly" means:

> (1) to perform . . . it at a place open to the public or at any place where a substantial number of persons outside of a normal circle of a family and its social acquaintances is gathered; or

> (2) to transmit or otherwise communicate a performance . . . of the work to a place specified by clause (1) or to the public, by means of any device or process, whether the members of the public capable of receiving the performance . . . receive it in the same place or in separate places and at the same time or at different times.[155]

---

[154] H.R. Rep. No. 94–1476, 94th Cong., 2d Sess. 63 (1976).
[155] 17 U.S.C. § 101.

A public performance is one which takes place in a public setting or before a public group. Thus, one can rent a movie and show it in one's house to neighbors and friends without infringing the performance right. Showing the film is "performing" it, but the performance is a private not a public one. Alternately, if the movie were shown in a semi-public place such as a club, factory, or summer camp, rather than at home, a public, and therefore infringing performance would occur.[156]

Under the second clause, a public performance takes place when a work is transmitted. As defined in the Act, a work is transmitted when it is communicated by a "process whereby images or sounds are received beyond the place from which they are sent."[157] This clause allows the copyright owner to control transmission of the work, such as by radio or television, even though the recipients are not gathered in a single place or do not receive it at the same time. The same principles apply for transmissions to limited segments of the public, such as occupants of hotel rooms or subscribers to a cable television service.[158]

[B] Performances in Places Open to the Public

The various aspects of what constitutes a "public" performance are nicely illustrated in *Columbia Pictures Industries, Inc. v. Redd Horne, Inc.*[159] In *Redd Horne*, defendant operators of videocassette stores provided television sets in private screening rooms where up to four people could rent and watch a movie of their choice. While the viewers were in the room, the movie was transmitted from a central location in the store. The videocassettes were clearly being "performed," but was the performance "public"? In finding there was a public performance, the court read the definition of "public" in the statute disjunctively, holding that if a place is public, the size and composition of the audience is irrelevant. Alternatively, if a place is not public, the size and composition of the audience will be determinative.[160] Here, the performance was public because the place where the showing took place was open to the public, even though the actual viewing audience was restricted

---

[156] H.R. Rep. No. 94–1476, 94th Cong., 2d Sess. 64 (1976).

[157] 17 U.S.C. § 101. This subsection of the definition has become an issue in the reception of satellite transmissions by individual receive-only earth stations (satellite dishes). Broadcasters have become alarmed at the increasing use of these dishes which constantly decrease in price. The law has not provided much relief against their private use. Although transmission by satellite dish to the the public would constitute a public performance, reception for private use in one's own home would be a private performance and move from copyright owner control. *See* James C. Robinson, *Private Reception of Satellite Transmissions by Earth Stations*, 48 Alb. L. Rev. 426 (1984). Absent relief under copyright law, satellite broadcasters have looked to other bodies of law. Section 705(a) (formerly § 605) of the Federal Communications Act, 47 U.S.C. § 705(a), does not apply to signals communicated to the general public, but scrambled signals such as subscription services are protected under this provision. *See, e.g., Movie Systems, Inc. v. Heller*, 710 F.2d 492 (8th Cir. 1983). On the state level, there are possible sources of protection, such as theft of service statutes. *See, e.g.,* Cal. Penal Code § 593(d); N.Y. Penal Law § 165.15. *See also* § 8.20, *infra*.

[158] H.R. Rep. No. 94–1476, 94th Cong., 2d Sess. 64–65 (1976).

[159] 749 F.2d 154 (3d Cir. 1984).

[160] *Id.* at 158.

to a small group of family or social acquaintances. Because the performance was public under this part of the definition, the court found it unnecessary to examine the second part — the size and composition of the audience.[161] Moreover, the performances were also public under subsection (2) because they were transmitted and it made no difference that the recipients were not located in the same place or at the same time.[162]

Although viewing rooms in videocassette stores are public places, can the same be said for individual rooms in a hotel? If a hotel equips each room with a radio, television or videocassette player, are public performances taking place each time someone plays these machines? This situation is distinguishable from *Redd Horne*, since hotel rooms are living quarters and not rented for the sole purpose of watching movies. They are more akin to renting a movie in the privacy of one's home. The House Report specifically exempts these performances from control by the copyright owner.[163] Thus, so long as the recipients constitute a normal circle of family and social acquaintances, a public performance does not take place. A recent case affirmed the House Report, holding that a hotel is not publicly performing when it merely installed a videodisc player in each private room.[164]

[C]   The Size and Composition of a Public Audience

As indicated in *Redd Horne*, when a performance is not open to the public, the court must analyze the size and composition of the audience to determine whether a performance is public. In the language of the statute, a performance is public

> . . . at any place where a *substantial* number of persons outside of a normal circle of a family and its social acquaintances is gathered.

(Emphasis added.)[165] But how many persons constitute a "substantial" number? The House Report provides little help on this question, except to specify that performances at routine meetings of businesses and governmental personnel do not represent the gathering of a substantial number of persons.[166] On the one hand, a group of 20 persons at a private party or wedding reception would probably not be substantial enough to render a performance public. But what about a gathering of 200 persons? There is no definite point between 20 and 200 at which to draw the

---

[161] As for the size and composition of the audience, the court suggested that it was public in nature, because the showcasing operation was really no different from an exhibition of a film at a conventional theater. *Id.* at 159.

[162] *Id. See also Columbia Pictures Industries, Inc. v. Aveco, Inc.*, 612 F. Supp. 315 (M.D. Pa. 1985), *aff'd*, 800 F.2d 59 (3d Cir. 1986). The Court affirmed the reasoning in *Redd Horne* on similar facts, where customers were given tapes to play for themselves in screening rooms with a twenty-person capacity.

[163] H.R. Rep. No. 94–1476, 94th Cong., 2d Sess. 91–2 (1976).

[164] *See Columbia Pictures Industries, Inc. v. Professional Real Estate Investors, Inc.*, 228 U.S.P.Q. 743 (C.D. Cal. 1986).

[165] 17 U.S.C. § 101.

[166] H.R. Rep. No. 94–1476, 94th Cong., 2d Sess. 64 (1976).

line. In general, the larger and more diverse the gathering, the more likely a performance will be public.[167]

§ 8.17 Non-Profit and Other Exemptions to the Performance Right Under § 110

[A] Generally

Under the 1909 Act, the copyright owner of a musical or non-dramatic literary work could only control public for-profit performances of his work.[168] The rationale for encouraging non-profit performances was to allow easy access to musical and non-dramatic literary works, promoting their performance by non-profit entities such as schools and churches. The 1976 Act rejected the for-profit requirement. The House Report explains that this limitation was dropped because the line between profit and non-profit organizations became too difficult to draw.[169] In addition, many non-profit organizations are financially able to pay copyright royalties. The 1976 Act has not completely abandoned the non-profit exception to the performance right. Rather, it contains a specific set of exceptions to the public performance right. Many of these provisions are based on the non-profit nature of the performance. In short, the 1976 Act accomplishes by specific exemption what the 1909 Act did through its broad non-profit exception.

Section 110 is the vehicle by which certain non-profit performances are exempted. The following sections summarize their key features.

[B] Instructional Exemptions: § 110(1) (Face-to-Face); § 110(2) (By a Transmission)

Section 110(1)[170] exempts performances of copyrighted works given by instructors or pupils in face-to-face, live teaching situations. All varieties of copyrightable subject matter are included under this exemption, unless the person responsible for the performance had reason to know that the copy used was made illegally. The

---

[167] *See* David E. Shipley, *Copyright Law and Your Neighborhood Bar and Grill: Recent Developments in Performances and the Section 110(5) Exemption*, 29 Ariz. L. Rev. 475, 499 (1987).

[168] *See* 17 U.S.C. §§ 1(c) and (e) (1909 Act).

[169] H.R. Rep. No. 94–1476, 94th Cong., 2d Sess. 63 (1976). Under 1909 Act case law, the term "for-profit" was broadly construed. For example, in *Associated Music Publishers, Inc. v. Debs Mem. Radio Fund, Inc.*, 141 F.2d 852 (2d Cir. 1944), a non-profit radio station, because it paid for one-third of its air time by accepting commercial advertising, was held to be performing for-profit, even though it played plaintiff's song on the non-commercial portion of its program.

[170] 17 U.S.C. § 110(1).

educational institution must be non-profit[171] and the performance must occur in a place devoted to teaching.[172]

This exception, for instance, would allow a high school teacher to have the school band play music from Lerner and Loewe's *My Fair Lady* in a classroom before a music appreciation class without obtaining the consent of the copyright owner. This is a typical situation where the exemption applies to an in-class performance in a classroom limited to members of the class. On the other hand, the high school band could not, under this exemption, play the same music in a concert for the entertainment of parents. The latter performance may be exempt under another clause of § 110,[173] but not under § 110(1) which applies to face-to-face teaching situations only.

Section 110(2)[174] also exempts performances during instructional activities. It is both broader and narrower than § 110(1). It is broader because the performance may be transmitted, rather than limited to face-to-face situations as in § 110(1). The section is narrower because the transmitted performance can only be of non-dramatic literary and musical works. Section 110(2) does not apply, for example, to audiovisual works, motion pictures, plays, or show tunes. As in the previous exemption, the performance must be transmitted to classrooms or other places normally devoted to instruction and be directly related to the systematic teaching activities.[175] It cannot be made for entertainment purposes or background music. Both non-profit educational institutions and governmental bodies can use the exemption for transmissions made primarily for the benefit of three groups: students in classrooms, the disabled who are unable to attend class, and governmental workers.[176]

[C] Exemptions for Transmissions to the Blind and Handicapped — §§ 110(8)[177] and 110(9)[178]

Section 110(8) exempts transmissions of performances of a non-dramatic literary work designed for the blind or the handicapped who are unable to read. Performances for the deaf are also included in this provision. The performance must be made without any purpose of direct or indirect commercial advantage, and must be transmitted through a governmental body or noncommercial educational broadcast station, an authorized radio subcarrier or a cable system.

Section 110(9) also applies to transmissions designed for the blind and those unable to read printed material because of their handicaps. As in the preceding

---

[171] This would exclude profit-making institutions such as dance studios and language schools. H.R. Rep. No. 94–1476, 94th Cong., 2d Sess. 82 (1976).

[172] The performance must be confined to an audience made up of members of the class. Excluded from the scope of § 110(1) would be, for example, a play or concert given by students before the entire student body. *Id.*

[173] *See* 17 U.S.C. § 110(4).

[174] 17 U.S.C. § 110(2).

[175] 17 U.S.C. §§ 110(2)(C)(i), (ii).

[176] 17 U.S.C. §§ 110(2)(C)(i)-(iii).

[177] 17 U.S.C. § 110(8).

[178] 17 U.S.C. § 110(9).

exemption, there can be no direct or indirect commercial advantage. The transmission must be made through an authorized radio subcarrier and, unlike § 110(8), can be of a dramatic literary work. The performance, however, may only take place on a single occasion and must be of a work published at least ten years before the date of performance.

[D] Agricultural and Horticultural Fairs — § 110(6);[179] Vending Establishments — § 110(7);[180] and Veterans and Fraternal Organizations — § 110(10)[181]

Performances of non-dramatic musical works by a governmental body or nonprofit agricultural or horticultural organization are exempted by § 110(6). The performance must take place during an agricultural or horticultural fair and must be conducted by the above organizations. This section removes vicarious liability of the organization which sponsored the fair for infringing performances given by concessionaires, businesses, or other persons. These direct infringers, however, remain personally liable.

Section 110(7) provides a limited exemption to vending establishments, allowing performance of non-dramatic musical works for the sole purpose of promoting the retail sale of copies or phonorecords of the work. The performance must take place at the store location or in the immediate vicinity of the sale and may not be transmitted to another location. The performance must occur in a vending establishment open to the public, which charges no direct or indirect admission for entrance.

A 1982 amendment to the Copyright Act added the fraternal organizations exemption under § 110(10).[182] One purpose of this amendment was to allow these organizations an exemption in circumstances which would otherwise violate § 110(4). This section exempts performances of non-dramatic literary and musical works performed during a social function of a veterans or fraternal organization. The event must be one which is not open to the general public, although guests of the organization may be invited. An admission fee may be charged, but whatever proceeds are left after deducting costs must be used for charitable purposes. Social functions of college fraternities and sororities are not included in § 110(10), except for those held solely to raise funds for a specific charitable purpose.

[E] Exemption for Certain Nonprofit Performances: § 110(4)[183]

Section 110(4) contains a general exception to the performance right that covers some of the same provisions as the for-profit limitation of the 1909 Act. This exemption excludes transmissions and is limited to performances given directly by live performers, the playing of phonorecords, or by a receiving apparatus.[184]

---

[179] 17 U.S.C. § 110(6).

[180] 17 U.S.C. § 110(7).

[181] 17 U.S.C. § 110(10).

[182] Although of minor significance from an economic standpoint, § 110(10) is viewed by some as a continuing erosion of the rights of authors by special interest groups. *See* Alvin Deutsch, *Politics and Poker Music Faces the Odds*, 34 J. Copyright L. Soc'y 38 (1986).

[183] 17 U.S.C. § 110(4).

[184] H.R. Rep. No. 94–1476, 94th Cong., 2d Sess. 85 (1976).

The performance must be given without any purpose of direct or indirect commercial advantage. To construe this provision, the House Report indicates that one must look to the case law under the 1909 Act.[185] This case law reveals that a public performance associated with a profit-making activity was a for-profit performance even if no admission was charged. In the leading case of *Herbert v. Shanley Co.*,[186] the Supreme Court held that an orchestra's performance of music for the clientele of a restaurant was a for-profit performance even though the customers were not asked to pay a music charge. The Court's rationale was that the restaurant was profiting from the performance because the music provided an attractive environment for its clientele. They were paying not just for a meal, but for an entire service reflected in the price of the check. By incorporating 1909 Act case law, § 110(4) will not apply to performances which are connected with the profit-making aspect of an enterprise.[187]

In addition to prohibiting direct or indirect commercial advantage, § 110(4) precludes payment of any fee or compensation to performers, promoters, or organizers for the performance in question. The exemption is lost only if the above persons are paid for the performance. It is not affected if the performers receive a salary for duties encompassing the performance.[188] For example, a performance by a school orchestra conducted by a music teacher who is paid an annual salary is exempt, but a performance by that same school orchestra conducted by a band leader hired for the one performance is not.

Even if all of the above conditions are met, the § 110(4) exemption will not apply if there is a direct or indirect admission charge.[189] Admission may be charged, however, if the proceeds, after deducting reasonable production costs, are used exclusively for an educational, religious, or charitable purpose.[190] For performances charging an admission, this section provides the copyright owner with a veto power over the performance if notice is served under the terms of § 110(4)(B).

To illustrate, assume that a high school orchestra plans to hold a concert using tunes by the Beatles and charges a $5.00 admission, and that the proceeds after deducting costs will be used for educational purposes. Section 110(4) gives the copyright owner the right to decide the conditions under which the work is performed, if at all. The copyright owner must serve written notice at least seven days before the date of the performance stating the reasons for objection to the admission charge.[191] According to the House Report, the veto power was given to copyright owners so they would not be compelled to make involuntary donations to fund-raising activities for causes to which they are opposed.[192]

---

[185] *Id.*

[186] 242 U.S. 591 (1917). *See also Associated Music Publishers, Inc. v. Debs Mem. Radio Fund, Inc.*, 141 F.2d 852 (2d Cir. 1944).

[187] *See Quackenbush Music, Ltd. v. Wood*, 381 F. Supp. 904, (M.D. Tenn. 1974), and *MCA, Inc. v. Parks*, 796 F.2d 200, 204 (6th Cir. 1986).

[188] H.R. Rep. No. 94–1476, 94th Cong., 2d Sess. 85 (1976).

[189] 17 U.S.C. § 110(4)(A).

[190] 17 U.S.C. § 110(4)(B).

[191] 17 U.S.C. § 110(4)(B)(ii).

[192] H.R. Rep. No. 94–1976, 94th Cong., 2d Sess. 86 (1976).

This veto power given to the copyright owner raises some perplexing questions.[193] First, the 1976 Act does not explicitly impose an affirmative duty on the user to inform the copyright owner of the forthcoming performance so that he can serve notice within the seven day limit. Should there be a duty to notify? One might argue that the 1976 Act implies that at least a reasonable attempt is required to notify the copyright owner about the performance. This would be consistent with the purpose of the provision, which is to prevent authors from being identified with causes which they do not support. Second, assuming that the copyright owner finds out about the performance and notice of objection is duly filed,[194] the copyright owner must state a reason for objecting to the performance. Would *any* reason suffice? It would appear so. But if any reason may be given, the requirement to provide a reason is rendered meaningless.

§ 8.18   The *Aiken* Exemption — § 110(5) — and the Multiple Performance Doctrine

[A]   The Multiple Performance Doctrine: The 1909 Act Background

Section 110(5), known as the "*Aiken* Exemption," and § 111, the compulsory license for cable television, respond to a long standing controversy about how to treat secondary transmissions (rebroadcasts) of copyrighted works under the 1909 Act. The possibilities of rebroadcasting a copyrighted work can take place in an endless number of settings, ranging from the local barbershop that plays the radio for its clientele, to the cable system that picks up a primary signal and retransmits it to millions of persons. Both are secondary transmitters engaging in a rebroadcast of a primary broadcast. The basic question is whether a rebroadcast of the primary transmission is a public performance. If so, should a copyright owner be entitled to enforce the performance right for every rebroadcast of a work or should the right be limited to the first transmission or in some other way?

Under the 1909 Act, the case law developed incoherently in its approach to secondary transmissions. In *Buck v. Jewell-LaSalle Realty Co.*,[194] the Supreme Court held that a hotel equipped with a master radio was performing when it simultaneously rebroadcast music from a local radio station into private hotel rooms. Plaintiff was the owner of a copyrighted song, broadcast repeatedly by a local radio station without authorization of the copyright owner. Suit was brought against the radio station and the hotel for the rebroadcast. The Court established the multiple performance doctrine, whereby a single rendition of a work can be performed more than once as it is retransmitted from a receiving apparatus.[195]

The issue of secondary transmissions arose again in the 1960s with the development of cable television systems. Despite the *Jewell-LaSalle* multiple performance

---

[193] *See* 2 *Nimmer on Copyright* § 8.15[E](5)(b) (1993).

[194] Notice must comply with formalities set forth in Copyright Office regulations. 17 U.S.C. § 110(4)(B)(iii).

[194] 283 U.S. 191 (1931).

[195] The Court also found a public performance making the analogy to cases where an orchestra plays live music in a restaurant for the entertainment of its clientele. *Id.* at 201.

doctrine, the Supreme Court in two cases refused to hold that cable systems were performing by retransmitting television signals.[196] First came *Fortnightly Corp. v. United Artists Television, Inc.*,[197] in which the Court reasoned that the cable system was not a broadcaster (*i.e.*, performer) but rather like a viewer, because it did no more than enhance the viewer's capacity to receive the original broadcaster's signals. The Court viewed *Jewell-LaSalle* as antiquated authority, and limited it to its specific facts, that is, where the original broadcast was unauthorized by the copyright owner. Several years later, the issue arose again in *Teleprompter Corp. v. Columbia Broadcasting System, Inc.*[198] In this case, the cable system was bringing in distant signals otherwise not available to viewers in the service area. Ignoring *Jewell-LaSalle* completely, the Court again found that cable television served essentially a viewer function, regardless of the distance between the broadcaster and the viewer.[199]

In 1975, one year after *Teleprompter*, the Supreme Court decided *Twentieth Century Music Corp. v. Aiken*,[200] which extended the reasoning of the cable television decisions to a fact situation much like *Jewell-LaSalle*. Defendant owned and operated a small fast food shop (640 square feet) where he installed a radio, and four small ceiling speakers played during business hours to entertain customers and employees. Plaintiff brought suit against Aiken, claiming infringement of the performance right for playing the copyright owner's music without a license. The Supreme Court held that, like the cable television systems, Aiken was not a broadcaster/performer, but fell into the category of viewer/listener. Although *Jewell-LaSalle* was not explicitly overruled, it was limited to its specific facts. The Court maintained that to hold Aiken liable would result in a regime of copyright that would be both unenforceable and inequitable. It would be unenforceable from a practical standpoint because of the infinite number of performances in cafes, bars, beauty shops and like places. It would be inequitable for two reasons: first, Aiken would have no sure way of protecting himself against infringement except by keeping the radio off. Second, it would be inequitable because

> to hold that all in Aiken's position "performed" . . . would be to authorize the sale of an untold number of licenses for what is basically a single public rendition of a copyrighted work. The exaction of such multiple tribute would go far beyond what is required for the economic protection of copyright owners. . . .[201]

---

[196] Cable television systems receive the signals of television broadcasting stations, amplify them, and then transmit these signals by cable or microwave and ultimately send the signals by wire to their paying customers. Once commonly referred to as "CATV" (community antenna television), cable television was originally used to facilitate transmission of television signals to areas such as hilly terrain or cities where normal, direct reception was inadequate. Since these early days, cable systems have greatly expanded their operations and now originate programming as well as retransmit the programs of other creators. *See United States v. Southwestern Cable Co.*, 392 U.S. 157 (1968).

[197] 392 U.S. 390 (1968).

[198] 415 U.S. 394 (1974).

[199] *Id.* at 408.

[200] 422 U.S. 151 (1975).

[201] *Id.* at 162–63.

This dual rationale is the basis behind the *Aiken* exemption in § 110(5) of the 1976 Act.

[B] Secondary Transmissions and the Multiple Performance Under the 1976 Act: The *Aiken* Exemption — § 110(5)

The 1976 Act has completely overturned the Supreme Court's narrow construction of "performance" as found in *Aiken* and the cable television cases. Instead, the Act broadly defines the term "perform," returning to the traditional interpretation of *Jewell-LaSalle*, in which any further transmission of a copyrighted work is considered to be a performance. Thus, under this definition, the playing of a radio or television before a public group is a public performance and an infringing one, if without consent of the copyright owner. The 1976 Act, however, has not turned all bars, beauty parlors, and cafes into infringers of copyright whenever they play a radio or television for their customers. These *de minimis* performances are exempted in § 110(5),[202] known as the "*Aiken* exemption,"[203] which provides:

> communication of a transmission embodying a performance or display of a work by the public reception of the transmission on a single receiving apparatus of a kind commonly used in private homes [is not an infringement of copyright], unless —
>
> (A) a direct charge is made to see or hear the transmission; or
>
> (B) the transmission thus received is further transmitted to the public.

Section 110(5) exempts from copyright liability works performed by the use of standard radio and television sets in small commercial establishments when the works are played for the enjoyment of customers. The rationale behind this exemption is that retransmitted public performances of this type are a *de minimis* invasion of the copyright owner's interest. Accordingly, such establishments should not be forced to obtain a license from the copyright owner. The exemption is a limited one; it applies to transmissions only, excluding performances of recorded music or a videotape in a small commercial establishment. Thus, the local bar that plays a record on the phonograph or a videotape of a movie on the television is not covered by the exemption. Moreover, there can be no admission charge to listen to the performance. Finally, the performance cannot be further transmitted to the public.

The exemption is further limited by the fact situation in the *Aiken* case itself. According to the House Report, the *Aiken* fact situation (standard radio attached to four ceiling speakers) represents the outer limit of the exemption.[204] Liability would be imposed where the proprietor of the establishment has installed a commercial sound system, or has converted a standard receiving apparatus into the equivalent

202 Many, though not all, of the clauses discussed in § 110 are the counterparts of the 1909 Act's for-profit limitation. Section 110(5) is a notable departure from the non-profit origin of this section.

203 Cable television systems are also performing under the Act, but are now subjected to a complicated compulsory licensing provision in § 111. *See* § 8.19, *infra.*

204 H.R. Rep. No. 94–1476, 94th Cong., 2d Sess. 87 (1976).

of a commercial system. The House Report sets forth factors to consider whether the exemption has been exceeded. These would include:

> the size, physical arrangement, and noise level of areas within [the] establishment . . . and the extent to which the receiving apparatus is altered or augmented. . . .[205]

Moreover, as stated in the Conference Report, the exemption does not apply if "the commercial establishment is of sufficient size to justify . . . a subscription to commercial background music service."[206]

From this legislative history, it comes as no surprise that the *Aiken* exemption has created litigation. At what point does a sound system become so sophisticated as to become a commercial sound system? How should one apply the criteria listed in the House Report as to the physical environment justifying the exemption? When is a commercial establishment large enough to justify a subscription to a commercial background music service? The courts have had to grapple with these imponderables.

[C]   The *Aiken* Exemption in the Courts

As a result of a certain vagueness in its terms and a convoluted legislative history, the § 110(5) exemption has generated much more litigation than any other clause in § 110. The case law has generally not exempted commercial establishments which have sophisticated sound systems and are significantly larger than the 640 square foot *Aiken* restaurant. Courts have looked to the legislative history, indicating that the *Aiken* exemption should be limited to smaller commercial establishments which could not justify a subscription to a background commercial music service. Typical is *Sailor Music v. The Gap Stores, Inc.*,[207] where plaintiff sued to enjoin a chain of clothing stores (The Gap) from retransmitting radio broadcasts to their customers in two of their New York City stores. The Second Circuit upheld the injunction and found that the commercial sound systems in the large public areas within the stores greatly exceeded the outer limits of the *Aiken* fact situation. In addition, the Gap Stores were large enough to justify a subscription to a commercial music service. *Sailor* has been reconfirmed in other cases.[208]

Even though the House Report indicates that the *Aiken* fact situation is the outer limit, courts have generally taken a flexible approach, applying the exemption even

205 *Id.*

206 H.R. Conf. Rep. No. 94–1733, 94th Cong., 2d Sess. 75 (1976)

207 516 F. Supp. 923 (S.D.N.Y.), *aff'd*, 668 F.2d 84 (2d Cir. 1981), *cert. denied*, 456 U.S. 945 (1982).

208 *Broadcast Music, Inc. v. United States Shoe Corp.*, 678 F.2d 816 (9th Cir. 1982); *Rodgers v. Eighty-Four Lumber Co.*, 617 F. Supp. 1021 (W.D. Pa. 1985) (public area larger than 10,000 square feet having eight interior and exterior speakers); *Lamminations Music v. P & X Markets, Inc.*, 1985 Copyright L. Dec. ¶ 25 at 19,557 (N.D. Cal. 1985) (supermarkets of 10,000 to 14,500 square feet equipped with sophisticated commercial sound system); *ESPN, Inc. v. Edinburg Community Hotel*, 623 F. Supp. 647 (S.D. Tex. 1985) (satellite dish antennae used to retransmit to individual rooms in a hotel, rather than a "single receiving apparatus of a kind commonly used in private homes").

where some physical aspects of the *Aiken* fact situation are exceeded. Despite the legislative history, some courts have held that the defendant's ability to pay for background music is not relevant in determining whether the § 110 exemption has been exceeded. Moreover, the term "single receiving apparatus" has been construed to mean one apparatus at a particular location even though a chain may have apparatus at each of its several hundred stores. Thus, a chain of stores can avail itself of the exemption so long as each individual store uses homestyle equipment.[209] Nor have the court's been insistent about requiring a maximum square footage to qualify for the *Aiken* exemption. Rather, the focus is on the quality of the sound system used and not on the square footage of the establishment using it.[210] For example, in *Springsteen v. Plaza Roller Dome, Inc.*,[211] a Putt-Putt miniature golf course had a radio receiver and six speakers mounted to light poles over a 7,500 square foot playing area. The Court exempted the performances under § 110(5) and distinguished this fact situation from *Sailor*. As compared with that case, the noise level in an outside Putt-Putt course was much greater and the quality of the sound system was much poorer. In addition, the operation was not of sufficient size to justify, as a practical matter, a subscription to a commercial background music service.

§ 8.19   Secondary Transmissions: § 111

[A]   In General

Section 111 primarily involves the complex compulsory licensing system for retransmission of over-the-air broadcast signals by cable television systems which pick up broadcasts of programs originated by others and retransmit them to paying subscribers. Before the 1976 Act, because of two key Supreme Court decisions, the cable television industry did not have to pay royalties for its retransmission of over-the-air broadcast signals.[212] The cable television conflict became the most hotly debated issue during the revision process, leading to the longest and most complex section in the Copyright Act. The resulting compulsory license represents a delicately woven compromise among industry groups which overturns the earlier Supreme Court decisions. Under § 111, a cable television system is subjected to full copyright liability for its retransmissions unless it complies with the terms of the compulsory license, such as reporting requirements and the payment of royalties. The royalty rate, initially set forth in the 1976 Act, is to be periodically adjusted by copyright arbitration panels[213]

---

[209] *See, e.g., Edison Bros. Stores Inc. v. Broadcast Music, Inc.*, 954 F.2d 1419 (8th Cir. 1992), *cert. denied*, 112 S. Ct. 1995 (1992); *Broadcast Music, Inc. v. Claire's Boutiques, Inc.*, 949 F.2d 1482 (7th Cir. 1991), *cert. denied*, 112 S. Ct. 1942 (1992).

[210] *Edison Bros. Stores Inc. v. Broadcast Music, Inc.*, 954 F.2d 1419, 1424 (8th Cir. 1992), *cert. denied*, 112 S. Ct. 1995 (1992).

[211] 602 F. Supp. 1113 (M.D.N.C. 1985).

[212] *Fortnightly Corp. v. United Artists Television, Inc.*, 392 U.S. 390 (1968), and *Teleprompter Corp. v. CBS, Inc.*, 415 U.S. 394 (1974). For a discussion of these cases, see § 8.18, *supra.*

[213] 17 U.S.C. § 803(b)(1)(A).

[B] Overall Structure of § 111

One can best make sense of this complicated section by keeping in mind its overall structure:

Subsection (a)[214] exempts four kinds of secondary transmissions from infringement of the performance right under § 106(4).

Subsection (b)[215] imposes full liability on secondary transmissions intended for limited audiences such as pay cable and background music services.

Subsection (c)[216] sets up the compulsory license for cable television systems.

Subsection (d)[217] specifies the operation of the compulsory license and defines the responsibility of the Librarian of Congress and Register of Copyrights in the collection and distribution of fees.

Subsection (e)[218] treats certain aspects of off-shore cable systems.

Subsection (f)[219] provides technical definitions of cable matters not found in § 101.

The following discussion primarily concentrates on subsections (a)–(d).

[C] General Exemptions: § 111(a)

[1] Clause (1): Retransmissions to Private Lodgings

Certain secondary transmissions are given a general exemption under clause (1) of § 111(a). The first exemption covers the same situation as *Buck v. Jewell-LaSalle*.[220] It places beyond copyright liability transmissions consisting "entirely of the relaying, by the management of a hotel, apartment house, or similar establishment" of a broadcast to the private lodging of guests or residents who are not charged directly for the secondary transmission.[221] This exemption is limited to a simple relay of the transmission, and the retransmitter cannot adapt or change the signal in any way, such as by cutting out advertisements or running new commercials.[222] Moreover, the term "private lodgings" is limited to private rooms or rooms used for private parties, and does not include dining rooms, meeting halls, or any places that are outside of a normal circle of a family and its social acquaintances.[223] Finally, the House Report specifies that placing an ordinary radio or television set in a private hotel room does not constitute an infringement.

---

[214] 17 U.S.C. § 111(a).
[215] 17 U.S.C. § 111(b).
[216] 17 U.S.C. § 111(c).
[217] 17 U.S.C. § 111(d).
[218] 17 U.S.C. § 111(e).
[219] 17 U.S.C. § 111(f).
[220] 283 U.S. 191 (1931). *See* § 8.18[A], *supra*.
[221] 17 U.S.C. § 111(a)(1).
[222] *See* H.R. Rep. No. 94–1476, 94th Cong., 2d Sess. 91 (1976).
[223] *Id.*

[2]   Clause (2): Instructional Transmissions

Section 111(a)(2) reconfirms that instructional transmissions under § 110(2) are exempt.[224]

[3]   Clause (3): The Passive Carrier Exemption [225]

Section 111(a)(3), known as the "passive carrier exemption," exempts from copyright liability carriers such as AT&T, who merely provide wires and cables for the use of others.[226] The carrier is exempt so long as it neither controls the content nor chooses the recipients of the secondary transmission.[227]

[4]   Clause (4): The Secondary Transmitter Exemption

Section 111(a)(4) exempts secondary transmitters, operating on a nonprofit basis, who provide translators or boosters to improve reception.

Even if the retransmission falls into one of the exempt categories outlined above, under § 111(b) [228] copyright infringement will occur if the primary transmission is intended not for the public at large, but rather for a controlled group. These transmissions include services such as background music services, pay television, or closed circuit broadcasts to theaters. The secondary transmission, even to a controlled group, is not actionable if the primary transmission is made by a broadcast station licensed by the Federal Communications Commission (FCC), the retransmission is required by the FCC, and the transmission is not changed in any manner.

[D]   The Compulsory License for Cable Systems: § 111(c)

Section 111(c) establishes the general contours of the compulsory license, which is conditioned on the reporting requirements and the payment of royalties set forth in § 111(d). The compulsory license applies only to the retransmission of over-the-air broadcast signals and is inapplicable to the secondary transmission of a nonbroadcast primary transmission. This means that a cable system can retransmit only programs originating from a broadcast station licensed by the FCC such as the local CBS affiliate. It cannot, however, retransmit a nonbroadcast program such as one originating with another cable television system.

In retransmitting the broadcast signal, the cable television system cannot willfully change in any way the content of the primary broadcast.[229] For such deletions, full

---

[224] 17 U.S.C. § 110(2).

[225] For an overview, see Stephen R. Barnett, *From New Technology to Moral Rights: Passive Carriers, Teletext, and Deletion as Copyright Infringement — the* WGN *Case*, 31 J. Copyright L. Soc'y 427 (1984).

[226] H.R. Rep. No. 94–1476, 94th Cong., 2d Sess. 92 (1976).

[227] *Compare Eastern Microwave, Inc. v. Doubleday Sports, Inc.*, 691 F.2d 125 (2d Cir. 1982) (exempting microwave and satellite rebroadcasts of Mets baseball games), *with WGN Continental Broadcasting Co. v. United Video, Inc.*, 693 F.2d 622 (7th Cir. 1982) (exemption did not apply to a carrier who deleted material from vertical blanking interval of broadcast signal).

[228] *See* 17 U.S.C. § 111(b); H.R. Rep. No. 94–1476, 94th Cong., 2d Sess. 92 (1976).

[229] One exemption allows changes in commercial advertisements made by those engaged in television commercial advertising market research with the prior consent of the original advertiser. *See* § 111(c)(3).

copyright liability is imposed on the cable television system.[230]

The compulsory licensing system generally does not apply to foreign broadcasts unless carried by a broadcast station licensed by the FCC. Thus, a cable television system would be subjected to full copyright liability if it retransmitted a British television station. An exemption is made for Canadian signals and Mexican signals licensed by a governmental authority.[231] To retransmit a Canadian signal, the cable system must be located within limited geographic zones in the United States.[232] Mexican signals can also be imported pursuant to the compulsory license but the limitation to the qualifying signal is based on technology rather than geography.[233] The above limitations on Canadian and Mexican signals do not apply to a cable system authorized by the FCC before April 15, 1976 to carry these foreign signals. For such cable systems, the compulsory license is available.[234]

[E] Reporting Requirements and Royalty Fees for Cable Systems: § 111(d)

Section 111(d) is a complicated provision setting up the reporting and royalty fee requirements for cable system operators. Failure to comply subjects the cable system to full copyright liability. The cable system must file information in the Copyright Office regarding its subscribers and accounts and must list all signals it regularly carries.[235] The cable system must also file a semiannual statement of account, which includes the royalty fees and various other information concerning the signals carried during that time period. The royalty fees are collected by the Register of Copyright and then deposited with the treasury after deducting reasonable costs incurred by the Copyright Office.[236] Every person claiming to be entitled to royalties must file a claim with the Register of Copyrights during the month of July.[237] The Librarian of Congress on recommendation with the Register of Copyrights is responsible for distributing the royalties and determines whether a controversy exists.[238] If no controversy exists, the funds are distributed to the appropriate copyright owners after deducting reasonable operating expenses.

---

[230] *See WGN Continental Broadcasting Co. v. United Video, Inc.*, 693 F.2d 622, *clarified and rehearing denied*, 217 U.S.P.Q. 151 (1982) (7th Cir. 1982) (§ 111 exemption exceeded by deletion of teletext).

[231] 17 U.S.C. § 111(c)(1).

[232] Applies to areas located within 150 miles from the U.S.-Canadian border, or south from the border to the 42nd parallel of latitude, whichever is greater. *See* 17 U.S.C. § 111(c)(4). Detroit and Pittsburgh could receive the Canadian signals, whereas New York and Chicago, outside the geographic boundaries, could not.

[233] The signal cannot be made

> . . . by means other than direct interception of a free space radio wave emitted by such broadcast television station. . . .

See 17 U.S.C. § 111(c)(4).

[234] 17 U.S.C. § 111(c)(4).

[235] *See* 37 C.F.R. § 201.11.

[236] 17 U.S.C. § 111(d)(2).

[237] 17 U.S.C. § 111(d)(4).

[238] *See* 17 U.S.C. § 111(d)(4).

[F]   The Computation and Distribution of Royalty Fees

The compulsory license entitles the cable system to retransmit all licensed signals, but the royalty fee is based on the retransmission of distant non-network programs. Why are local programming and distant networks excluded from the royalty determination? As for local programming, Congress believed that its retransmission did not harm the copyright owner, who would be compensated for his work within the local markets. As for distant network programming, Congress determined that its retransmission did little harm, because copyright owners were adequately remunerated in their contracts with the networks. On the other hand, Congress found that retransmission of distant non-network programming harmed the copyright owner who would no longer be able to license his work in the community where the work was retransmitted.[239]

The royalty fee to be paid is based on the cable system's use of distant non-network programming and a percentage applied against the cable system's gross receipt base.[240] The computation involves a two-step process. The first step is to determine how many distant non-network programs the cable system has retransmitted. The House Report describes the process as follows:

> First, a value called a "distant signal equivalent" is assigned to all "distant" signals. Distant signals are defined as signals retransmitted by a cable system . . . outside the local service area of the primary transmitter. Different values are assigned to independent, network and educational stations because of the different amounts of viewing of non-network programming carried by such stations. For example, the viewing of non-network programs on network stations is considered to approximate 25 percent. These values are then combined and a scale of percentages is applied to the cumulative total.[241]

Once the total distant signal equivalent (d.s.e.) is determined for the semi-annual accounting period, a schedule of percentages is multiplied against the cable system's gross receipts base [242] for each d.s.e. unit used. Under current rates, the cable system would have to pay 799 one-thousandths of one percent of its gross receipts for the first d.s.e. For the second, third and fourth d.s.e., the percentage falls to 503 one-thousandths of one percent of its gross receipts for each unit used. For the fifth and each additional unit, the percentage falls to 237 one-thousandths of one percent of the gross receipts.[243] For example, suppose the cable system has a gross receipts base of $10 million and has used two d.s.e. units, the computation would look like this:

---

[239] *See* H.R. Rep. No. 94–1476, 94th Cong., 2d Sess. 90 (1976).

[240] 17 U.S.C. § 111(d)(2).

[241] H.R. Rep. No. 94–1476, 94th Cong., 2d Sess. 90 (1976).

[242] Smaller cable systems are required to pay a lesser percentage of their gross receipts base for each d.s.e. used, but are subject to a minimum payment. *See* 17 U.S.C. § 111(d)(2)(C–D); H.R. Rep. No. 94–1476, 94th Cong., 2d Sess. 96 (1976).

[243] For current rates, see 37 C.F.R. § 308.2.

For the 1st d.s.e.: .799 of 1% of $10,000,000 = $79,900
For the 2nd d.s.e.: .503 of 1% of $10,000,000 =   50,300

Total amount owed by the cable system = $130,200

The Register of Copyrights then distributes the royalties to copyright owners whose works were part of non-network distant signal retransmission. The Act does not delineate exactly what process should be used to determine the distribution, leaving it instead to the Register of Copyrights to decide these matters. Copyright owners must file their claims each July,[244] and are granted immunity from the antitrust laws[245] to facilitate agreement among themselves on the division of royalties. By August 1,[246] the Register of Copyrights must determine whether there is a controversy among claimants. If no controversy exists, distribution takes place immediately. However, if a controversy exists, the Register must convene a copyright arbitration royalty panel to determine the distribution of royalties. Before it was abolished in 1993, the collection and distribution functions were carried out by the Copyright Royalty Tribunal. With the numbers of groups involved, and the high stakes,[247] the process generated great controversy, and every Tribunal distribution decision was challenged, leading to endless litigation. The courts, however, in the end have invariably upheld the Tribunal's findings and procedures.[248] It will take some time to find out whether the new regulatory system envisaged by the Copyright Royalty Tribunal Reform Act of 1993, will produce a significantly smoother system.

[G]   Afterthoughts: Is § 111 an Anachronism?

Much has changed since Congress laid down the framework for the cable television compulsory license in 1976. The technological and regulatory environment on which § 111 is premised has largely disappeared. This has led some to question whether § 111 should be repealed or at least seriously modified.

When § 111 was being formulated in the mid-1970s, the Cable industry was strictly regulated by the F.C.C. First, a cable system in one of the top fifty television markets was limited to the number of distant signals it could import. Second, a local station could require a cable system to delete syndicated programming from imported signals if the local station had an exclusive right to the program. These F.C.C. regulations resulted in protecting the dominant position of networks and independent stations from the threat of a fledgling cable industry which was immune

[244] 17 U.S.C. § 111(d)(4)(A).
[245] Id.
[246] 17 U.S.C. § 111(d)(4)(B).
[247] In 1984, more than $86.9 million in cable royalties were received by the Copyright Office. See Ralph Oman, The Compulsory License Redux: Will It Survive in a Changing Marketplace?, 5 Cardozo Arts & Ent. L.J. 37, 44 (1986).
[248] See, e.g., National Ass'n of Broadcasters v. Copyright Royalty Tribunal, 809 F.2d 172 (2d Cir. 1986); National Ass'n of Broadcasters v. Copyright Royalty Tribunal, 675 F.2d 367 (D.C. Cir. 1982); Christian Broadcasting Network, Inc. v. Copyright Royalty Tribunal, 720 F.2d 1295 (D.C. Cir. 1983).

from copyright liability under the *Fortnightly* and *Teleprompter* cases.**249** With this F.C.C. regulatory framework in mind, Congress drafted § 111 establishing liability for cable television in return for the compulsory license. In sum, the new cable provisions were designed to interrelate with F.C.C. regulations, reflecting a delicate and intricate political compromise.

In 1980, the F.C.C. repealed both the distant signal and program exclusivity rules. In just two years after the effective date of the 1976 Act, the regulatory environment on which the mosaic of § 111 was based ceased to exist.

Technological change has also brought into question the basis of § 111. Cable television is hardly the fledgling industry which needs the protective support of the compulsory license. The industry has expanded enormously in the last few years, challenging the once overwhelmingly dominant networks. Developing satellite technology has given cable television an almost unlimited ability to retransmit signals at increasingly lower costs. As a result, the television marketplace is now one of abundance in which cable has to compete with other new technologies such as direct broadcast satellites, low power television, and video disks. Despite these new competing technologies, § 111 favors the cable industry.

These basic changes in the regulatory and technological environment of the cable industry call for a reexamination of § 111 which, short of outright repeal, will probably lead to a more market-oriented system while eliminating the burdensome administrative apparatus used to administer the system.

§ 8.20   The Satellite Retransmission Compulsory License

With the Satellite Home Viewer Act of 1988,**250** Congress again met the challenge of a new technology by establishing a fifth compulsory license. Effective January 1, 1989, the Act established a temporary compulsory license for satellite carrier television transmission to the public for private home viewing. This compulsory license concerns the retransmission of television programming by companies who have rented space on a satellite for this purpose. Satellite carrier companies generally retransmit scrambled signals containing television programming to persons owning backyard satellite dishes. The satellite carrier charges the dish owner a subscription fee which includes a descrambling device. This lucrative business has raised some difficult questions under the 1976 Copyright Act.

Satellite carriers, by retransmitting from satellite to earth, are essentially engaging in secondary transmissions of copyrighted works. As defined by the 1976 Act, the secondary transmission of a copyrighted work constitutes a public performance **251** and is an infringement of copyright without the copyright owner's consent. Although admitting that they are publicly performing works, satellite carriers have argued that they are essentially cable systems, subject to the cable compulsory license, or that they are exempt from liability by falling under the passive carrier exemption.

---

249 For a discussion of these cases, see § 8.18, *supra.*
250 Pub. L. No. 100–667 (1988).
251 *See* 17 U.S.C. § 101 (public performance).

Does this activity fall into the cable compulsory license? The problem is that satellite carriers are not cable systems as defined in the 1976 Act. Under § 111(f) of the 1976 Act, a cable system is defined as "a facility located in any State, Territory, Trust Territory, or possession. . . ."[252] Satellite carriers, however, do not limit their activities to these enumerated locations but carry out their operations on orbiting satellites.

In addition, satellite carriers do not comply with the terms of the passive carrier exemption. Section 111(a)(3)[253] of the 1976 Act exempts liability for secondary transmissions of copyrighted works where the carrier has no direct or indirect control over the content or selection of the primary transmission. Most satellite carriers, however, are hardly passive. They scramble the signals, market descramblers, and package programming. As such, their activities greatly exceed those of passive carriers under the 1976 Act. Thus, secondary transmissions of satellite carriers do not fall within the cable compulsory license and would appear to be an infringement of a copyright owner's public performance right.

The Congressional response to this legal uncertainty was a compulsory license for satellite retransmissions. It was felt that the compulsory license would meet the needs of the industry, compensate copyright owners, and enable continued access to television programming by the growing satellite dish-owning public, particularly those living in rural areas not adequately served by other means.

Under the compulsory license, codified in § 119 of the 1976 Copyright Act, a satellite carrier must pay a statutory royalty per subscriber.[254] The retransmitter can only service customers who live in areas not served by local network affiliates and who have not subscribed to a cable television service for 90 days prior to subscribing to the satellite service. Administration of the compulsory license is similar to others in the 1976 Act, but with some innovations. To facilitate the process, the carrier is required to deposit with the Register of Copyrights a semiannual statement of account to determine royalty fee payments.[255] The royalties are distributed to copyright owners after the Register has deducted administration costs.[256]

The procedures for distributing the royalties are determined by the Register of Copyrights, which also plays an active role in guiding the development of the compulsory license.[257]

---

[252] *See* 17 U.S.C. § 111(f); *Pacific & Southern Co., Inc. v. Satellite Broadcast Networks, Inc.*, 694 F. Supp. 1565 (N.D. Ga. 1988).

[253] *See* 17 U.S.C. § 111(a)(3).

[254] *See* 17 U.S.C. § 119(b)(1)(B).

[255] *See* 17 U.S.C. § 119(a)(1).

[256] *See* 17 U.S.C. § 119(b)(2).

[257] *See* 17 U.S.C. § 119(c)(4).

§ 8.21 The Jukebox License

[A] The Rise and Fall of the Compulsory Jukebox License

Before passage of the 1976 Act, jukebox operators enjoyed a highly controversial[258] blanket exemption from copyright liability. With the 1976 Act, as originally enacted, the jukebox industry lost its total exemption but was able, through political compromise, to carve out for itself a compulsory licensing system with favorable terms. This jukebox compulsory license was deemed to be incompatible with the requirements of the Berne Convention and thus an impediment to U.S. entry into the Convention.[259] Accordingly, the Berne Convention Implementation Act of 1988[260] added a new section 116(A) to the 1976 Copyright Act, modifying the original compulsory license and replacing it with a voluntarily negotiated system.[261]

The original compulsory license was still relevant. It was to be used during an interim period and, more importantly, if copyright owners and jukebox operators were unable to negotiate a license, it was to be readopted. With the Copyright Royalty Tribunal Reform Act of 1993, the compulsory license was repealed, ending an historical peculiarity of American copyright law.

[B] The Jukebox Licensing Procedure: A Voluntary Negotiated License

A newly revised Section 116 creates a voluntary negotiated license covering music played by jukeboxes. Before the 1988 and 1993 amendments to the Copyright Act, a jukebox compulsory license existed whose terms were established entirely by the original provisions of the 1976 Act. With the repeal of the original compulsory licensing system, the current jukebox licensing system is based on voluntary negotiations. Under these provisions, copyright owners of non-dramatic musical works[262] and operators of coin-operated phonorecord players are authorized to negotiate and agree on the terms, rates and distributions of the royalty payments for performances of these works.[263] The purpose of these provisions is to allow negotiations between the performing rights societies (ASCAP, BMI, SESAC)[264] and the Amusement Music Operators of America (AMOA). These negotiations are to be immune from antitrust liability.[265]

---

[258] Under § 1(e) of the 1909 Act, the jukebox industry enjoyed a blanket exemption from copyright liability, which was widely condemned as an anachronistic, historical accident and totally unjustified. *See* H.R. Rep. No. 94–1476, 94th Cong., 2d Sess. 112 (1976).

[259] *See* Berne Convention art. 11(1). For a discussion of the Berne Convention and U.S. entry, see §§ 12.4–12.5, *infra*.

[260] Pub. L. No. 100–568 (1988).

[261] *See* 17 U.S.C. § 116.

[262] For a discussion of what constitutes a non-dramatic musical work, see § 8.22[c], *infra*.

[263] 17 U.S.C. § 116(b)(2).

[264] For a discussion of the role of the performing rights societies, see § 8.22, *infra*.

[265] 17 U.S.C. § 116(b)(2).

§ 8.22   Performing Rights Societies

[A]   Why They Are Needed: Capturing the Valuable But Elusive Performance Right

Every day musical works are publicly performed thousands of times. Each time a musical work is played on the air or before live groups, the event becomes a possible source of revenue for the copyright owner. The performance right is unquestionably the most important of the exclusive rights for composers and publishers of music.[266] The problem is that musical works are performed so extensively, and in such widely diverse settings, that an individual copyright owner is unable to enforce her performance right. Unauthorized performances frequently occur because it is too costly for the copyright owner to police her rights, and too costly for the user to obtain a license.[267]

The performing rights society is the means by which music composers and publishers police, license, and otherwise administer the potentially valuable but elusive performance right.[268] Their membership consists of musical copyright owners who have pooled their copyrights and have authorized the performing rights society to both represent them in licensing these works to users and in policing unauthorized performances. In addition, the performing rights society collects royalties and distributes them to the membership. In short, the performing rights society is a middleman which organizes the market for performance rights, enabling both copyright owners and users to reduce the transaction costs associated with the enforcement and licensing of the performance right. Today, almost every domestic musical composition is in the repertory of ASCAP or BMI, the two largest performing rights societies. The first performing rights society, the American Society of Composers, Authors and Publishers (ASCAP), was founded in 1914. It remains the largest of the performing rights societies,[269] followed in size by Broadcast Music, Inc. (BMI) and several smaller organizations.[270]

---

266 *See* 17 U.S.C. § 106(4).

267 For a recent review of the difficulties music users and copyright owners face regarding licensing, see *Buffalo Broadcasting Co. v. ASCAP,* 546 F. Supp. 274 (S.D.N.Y. 1982), *rev'd,* 744 F.2d 917 (2d Cir. 1984), *cert. denied,* 469 U.S. 1211 (1985).

268 The performing rights societies are recognized in the 1976 Act in § 116(e).

269 ASCAP had approximately 29,400 writer members and 12,007 publisher members as of 1988. *See* Bernard Korman & I. Fred Koenigsberg, *Performing Rights in Music and Performing Rights Societies,* 33 J. Copyright L. Soc'y 332, 352 (1987).

270 The most important of these smaller groups is the privately owned SESAC, originally known as the Society of European Stage, Authors and Composers. See *ACEMLA v. Copyright Royalty Tribunal,* 763 F.2d 101 (2d Cir. 1985), for a discussion of these smaller organizations.

[B] How They Operate: The ASCAP Model[271]

The ASCAP system provides an prime example of how a performing rights society operates. ASCAP membership consists of music writers and publishers who sign an agreement encompassing three major terms. First, the member grants ASCAP the non-exclusive right to license non-dramatic public performance of his works. This provision allows each member to license a work outside the ASCAP system. Second, ASCAP is given the right to bring suit in the name of the member and to police the performance right. Third, the agreement binds the member to ASCAP's method of distributing royalties.

ASCAP simplifies the licensing of its members' performance rights by charging users one fee for the right to use the entire repertory. This agreement is called a "blanket license" under which the user must pay one fee for the three million musical compositions that ASCAP controls. Thus, a television network, radio station, or background music company need not license an individual performance right to play a certain song on a certain date.

Although a single fee is charged, the fee schedule varies greatly between industry groups. Generally, the wealthier are required to pay more.[272] Accordingly, a major television network will be charged more for its blanket license than a small local radio station. License fees generate over $125 million annually.

After deducting operating expenses, ASCAP apportions and distributes the collected royalties to its members. Publishers and writers are paid according to how much and by whom the musical work is performed. ASCAP obtains this information largely by sampling techniques — for example, by taping radio programs on a random basis.[273] These results are subjected to a weighted formula which determines the actual monetary distribution. Thus, a copyright owner of a popular song earns more when it is played on national television than on a local radio station. In short, the copyright owner of a hit song stands to gain handsomely from the performance right royalties.

---

[271] For various discussions of the ASCAP model, see 2 *Nimmer on Copyright* § 8.19 (1993); Sidney Shemel & William M. Krasilovsky, *This Business of Music* Ch. 18 (6th ed. 1990). Other performing rights societies, such as BMI and SESAC, differ in certain significant details.

[272] That the ASCAP fee schedule discriminates in price has been a bone of contention between the Society and industry groups, such as the major television networks, leading to an endless series of antitrust litigation. *See* § 8.22[D], *infra*.

[273] ASCAP also polices live performances as well, developing information by field representatives who locate users, by advertisements in local media, and by copyright owners who alert ASCAP of use of their works. *See* Korman & Koenigsberg, n. 228, at 360.

[C]   Dramatic (Grand Rights) and Non-Dramatic Performing Rights (Small Rights) [274]

Performing rights societies license non-dramatic or *small rights*, whereas dramatic or "grand" rights remain under the control of the copyright owner. Distinguishing between a dramatic as opposed to a non-dramatic performance is not always easy. Generally, a performance is non-dramatic when it is removed from a dramatic context and unrelated to a larger plot structure. Alternatively, a dramatic performance occurs when it is used to develop a story line. The entire drama need not be developed to render a performance dramatic, so long as the performance takes place within a dramatic context and carries forth a plot. The distinctions between dramatic and non-dramatic performances are easy to make at the extremes, but difficult to distinguish at the margins. [275]

Under this definition of "dramatic," a performance need not necessarily depict a plot in which the song originally occurred. [276] Thus, when a night club singer performs the song *I've Grown Accustomed to Her Face* from the musical *My Fair Lady*, unrelated to a larger dramatic context, a non-dramatic performance has taken place. On the other hand, if this same singer performed a significant portion of the musical, singing the songs in sequence or using more songs to carry forth a story line, a dramatic performance has occurred. Because an ASCAP or BMI license does not cover dramatic rights (grand rights), the performer would have to negotiate a license directly from the copyright owner to avoid infringement.

Dramatic performances are treated differently from non-dramatic ones in law and in practice for practical reasons. Non-dramatic performances number in the millions daily and would be impossible to police without a performing rights society. Dramatic performances, by contrast, occur with much less frequency and are more amenable to individually negotiated licenses. They present potentially greater awards to copyright owners since they are performed before paying audiences and present greater problems of artistic control. Because dramatic performances are advertised, they are more easily policed by the copyright owner. [277]

[D]   Antitrust Problems

Almost from the outset, the performing rights societies have been under attack through the antitrust laws by both the Federal Government and various industry groups. Much of the practices engaged in by the performing rights societies came about through consent decrees worked out over a twenty-year period between

---

[274] For a discussion of the difference between dramatic and non-dramatic works, see Korman & Koenigsberg, *Performing Rights in Music and Performing Rights Societies*, 33 J. Copyright L. Soc'y 332 (1987).

[275] *See Robert Stigwood Group, Ltd. v. Sperber*, 457 F.2d 50 (2d Cir. 1972); *Rice v. American Program Bureau*, 446 F.2d 685 (2d Cir. 1971); *Leeds Music Ltd. v. Robin*, 358 F. Supp. 650 (S.D. Ohio 1973).

[276] *See 2 Nimmer on Copyright* § 10.10[3] (1993). Note also that under this definition, any musical work used in a dramatic context is a dramatic performance, even those which were originally composed to be played non-dramatically.

[277] *See* Korman, n. 228, at 335.

ASCAP and the Department of Justice.[278] Some of the more salient provisions are: (1) ASCAP cannot acquire exclusive licenses of its members' performance rights. Individual members can negotiate licenses themselves and receive royalties from them. (2) ASCAP must offer a per program license along with its blanket license on an economically meaningful basis. (3) ASCAP is prohibited from discriminating against similarly situated licensees.[279]

The performing rights societies continue to be challenged on antitrust grounds by national[280] and local broadcasters.[281] The major focus of the attack has been the blanket license, by which a single fee is charged for use of the entire repertory, based on a flat sum or on the users' revenues. The fee is unrelated to the frequency of use of the musical works. Actions under § 1 of the Sherman Act[282] brought by national and local broadcasters alleging price fixing and restraint of trade have largely failed.[283]

---

[278] The first consent decree was entered into in 1941 between the Department of Justice and ASCAP. BMI is covered by its own consent decree. For a discussion of the two consent decrees, see *Broadcast Music, Inc. v. Moor-Law, Inc.*, 484 F. Supp. 357 (D. Del. 1980). The decrees can be found at 1950–51 Trade Cas. ¶ 62,595 (S.D.N.Y. 1950) (ASCAP), and 1966 Trade Cas. ¶ 71,941 (S.D.N.Y. 1966) (BMI). *See also* W. Michael Garner, *United States v. ASCAP: The Licensing Provisions of the Amended Final Judgment of 1950*, 23 Bull. Copyright Soc'y 119 (1976), and Ralph Oman, *Source Licensing: The Latest Skirmish in an Old Battle*, 11 Colum.-VLA J.L. & Arts, 251, 254–56 (1987).

[279] For a discussion of the provisions, see *Broadcast Music, Inc. v. Columbia Broadcasting Sys., Inc.*, 441 U.S. 1 (1979). *See also F.E.L. Publication, Ltd. v. Catholic Bishops of Chicago*, 506 F. Supp. 1127 (N.D. Ill. 1981).

[280] *Columbia Broadcasting System, Inc. v. American Society of Composers, Authors and Publishers*, 620 F.2d 930 (2d Cir. 1980).

[281] *Buffalo Broadcasting Co., Inc. v. American Society of Composers, Authors and Publishers*, 744 F.2d 917 (2d Cir. 1984), *cert. denied*, 469 U.S. 1211 (1985). After losing in the courts, the independent television networks have lobbied for legislation that would prohibit the blanket license. *See, e.g.*, H.R. Rep. No. 3521, 99th Cong., 1st Sess. (1985). These bills, known as source licensing legislation, generally provide that an owner of an audio-visual work may not convey public performance rights in a work to a non-network television station without simultaneously conveying the performance right to the music in the audio-visual work. For an overview of source licensing legislation, see Alvin Deutsch, *The Buffalo Shuffle*, 4 Ent. & Sports Law. 7 (1985), and Ralph Oman, *Source Licensing: The Latest Skirmish in an Old Battle*, 11 Colum.-VLA J.L. & Arts 251 (1987).

[282] 26 Stat. 209 (1980), as amended, 15 U.S.C. §§ 1–7 (1980).

[283] The leading case is *Broadcast Music, Inc. v. Columbia Broadcasting Sys., Inc.*, 441 U.S. 1 (1979), holding that the blanket license does not constitute a *per se* violation of the antitrust laws. *See* Alan J. Hartnick, *The Network Blanket License Triumphant: The Fourth Round of the ASCAP-BMI/CBS Litigation*, 2 Comm. & L. 49 (1980).

§ 8.23 The Compulsory License for Public Broadcasting: § 118[284]

Section 118 sets up a compulsory license for non-commercial broadcasting entities.[285] Under § 118(d), a public broadcasting entity may include in a broadcast the performance and display of *published* non-dramatic musical works and published pictorial, graphic, and sculptural works. The section also allows for the reproduction and distribution of copies of the above programs, and for simultaneous off-the-air videotaping of a transmission by non-profit institutions or governmental bodies for face-to-face teaching purposes. Unlike the three other compulsory licenses, § 118 specifies neither the terms nor the royalties to be assessed for use of the works. Section 118 encourages voluntary agreements between public broadcasters and copyright owners (who are given an exemption from the antitrust laws) to facilitate negotiations between the parties. The agreement must then be filed in the Copyright Office. Absent an agreement, the Librarian of Congress, on recommendation of the Register of Copyrights, shall convene a CARP to determine a schedule of rates for the parties.[286]

§ 8.24 Performance Rights in Sound Recordings (*Droit Voisins*)[287]

Unlike a number of European countries,[288] American copyright law under §§ 106(4) and 114(a) specifically excludes a performance right in sound recordings. As a result, when a radio station plays a popular song, only the copyright owner of the musical work may claim royalties for the performance of the musical composition. Alternatively, the owners of the sound recording, whether they are the record manufacturers or the performers, have no claim. The copyright owner of the song receives all the performance royalties even though the song's success may be due to interpretive musicians or to the artists and technicians who capture the performance in a sound recording. Many have pointed out the illogic of the system, as well as its unfairness.[289] Pursuant to § 114(d), the Register of Copyrights

---

[284] For an overview, see Harriet L. Oler, *Legislating Copyright Protection for Works Used in Public Broadcasting*, 25 Bull. Copyright Soc'y 118 (1977).

[285] 17 U.S.C. § 118(g) defines a public broadcasting entity as a non-commercial, educational, broadcasting station as defined by the FCC. Moreover, any non-profit institution or organization is eligible if it is engaged in the activities described in § 118(d)(2).

[286] 17 U.S.C. § 118(b)(3).

[287] For an exhaustive overview of the subject, see Stewart, *International Copyright and Neighboring Rights* (1983).

[288] *See, e.g.*, France, Law No. 85–660 of July 3, 1985; United Kingdom, Performers Protection Acts 1958/72. Performance rights in sound recording are subject to the *International Convention for the Protection of Performers, Producers of Phonograms and Broadcasting Organizations*. Called the "Rome Convention" and signed at Rome in 1961, some twenty-three countries are members. The convention is based on national treatment setting forth minimum terms of protection for contracting states. For a discussion of the Rome Convention, see § 12.6[A], *infra*.

[289] D'Onofrio, *In Support of Performance Rights in Sound Recordings*, 29 UCLA L. Rev. 168 (1981).

submitted a report recommending an amendment to the section to include a performance right for sound recordings.[290]

Despite a strong sentiment expressed by those favoring performance right bills,[291] it is unlikely that the Copyright Act will be amended to grant a performance right to sound recordings. For one, powerful broadcasting groups vigorously oppose legislation conferring performance rights as a tax every time a record is played on the air, driving marginal stations out of business. Not only would the broadcaster have to buy a license from a performing rights society like ASCAP for the right to perform the musical work, but he or she would also have to negotiate a license to play the sound recording.[292] In addition, drafting an adequate and effective statute taking into account the various interests involved is a difficult task from both a political and practical standpoint. Legislative proposals have provided for a compulsory license, administered by the Copyright Royalty Tribunal (or by the Register of Copyrights and Copyright Arbitration Royalty Panels), to use a sound recording. By this performance right legislation, performers and record companies would equally share the royalties obtained from broadcasters, jukebox box owners and anyone else performing a work.[293]

§ 8.25   The Right of Public Display: § 106(5)

Section 106(5) specifically recognizes the right of public display for the first time in American copyright law. The display right applies to all categories of copyrightable subject matter except for sound recordings and architectural works. Under § 101,

> to display a work means to show a copy of it, either directly or by means of a film, slide, television image, or any other device or process or, in the case of a motion picture or other audiovisual work, to show individual images nonsequentially.[294]

Thus, a series of still photographs of a dancer or a pantomimist would not infringe the performance right, but may infringe the display right in the choreographic work or the pantomime.

---

[290] *Performance Rights in Sound Recordings*, H. Jud. Comm. Print No. 15, 95th Cong., 2d Sess. (1976).

[291] H.R. 1805, Commercial Use of Sound Recordings Amendments, 97th Cong., 2d Sess. (1981).

[292] For a comprehensive critique of performance rights in sound recordings, see Robert L. Bard & Lewis S. Kurlantzick, *A Public Performance Right in Recordings: How to Alter the Copyright System Without Improving It*, 43 Geo. Wash. L. Rev. 152 (1974), who find no convincing argument for such legislation. They argue that performance right legislation will not redress alleged injustices to performers but that the benefits will be divided according to the relative bargaining positions of the parties. As a result, composers, rather than record companies or performers, will be the most likely beneficiaries, contrary to the aims of performance right legislation.

[293] *Id.*

[294] 17 U.S.C. § 101.

Like the performance right, the right of display is limited to *public* displays. The definition of "public" is the same for both performances and displays.[295] Section 101 defines a display as public if it takes place

> at a place open to the public or at any place where a substantial number of persons outside of a normal circle of a family and its social acquaintances is gathered.[296]

Moreover, a display is public, as is a performance, when the display of a copy of the work is transmitted to the public

> whether members of the public . . . receive it in the same place or in separate places and at the same time or at different times.[297]

§ 8.26   Limitations on the Display Right

[A]   Public Display of an Owned Copy: § 109(c)[298]

Under § 109(c), an owner of a lawfully made copy may

> display that copy publicly, either directly or by the projection of no more than one image at a time, to viewers present at the place where the copy is located.[299]

This counterpart of the § 109(a)[300] first sale doctrine applies only if the copy is lawfully owned. Thus, if a museum has bought a work of art from a contemporary artist, it can display the work publicly even though it does not own the copyright on the work. This exemption to the display right applies only if the museum owns the work. The museum could not display or authorize others to display a work on loan from the copyright owner without his permission. Once title to the work passes, the owner of the work not only has the right to display it publicly but may even charge admission for the public to see the work. Absent an agreement to the contrary, § 109(c) gives the copyright owner no right to participate economically in the public display, despite the number of persons who see the work and how much they are charged.[301] Moreover, the owner of a copy of a work can display it directly or

---

[295] For a discussion of what constitutes a public performance or display, see § 8.16, *supra*.

[296] 17 U.S.C. § 101.

[297] *Id. See, e.g., Playboy Enterprises v. Frena*, 839 F. Supp. 1552 (M.D. Fla. 1993) (display right violated where subscribers to a computer bulletin board uploaded photographs from Playboy and defendant bulletin board operator allowed subscribers to download them).

[298] 17 U.S.C. § 109(c).

[299] *Id.*

[300] For a discussion of the first sale doctrine, see § 8.13, *supra*.

[301] For a discussion of the display right as limited by § 109(a), see Thomas A. Goetzl & Stuart A. Sutton, *Copyright and the Visual Artist's Display Right: A New Doctrinal Analysis*, 9 Colum.-VLA J.L. & Arts 15 (1984). The authors argue that the § 109(c) limitation is unfair to artists considering the profits made on these works by museums, galleries, and corporations who display these works publicly before massive paying audiences, sometimes over a million persons, *e.g.*, the Picasso exhibit in 1980. *Id.* at 32. The authors argue for a compulsory licensing system, privately administered to replace the § 109(c) limitation.

indirectly by, for example, an opaque projector, so long as the display occurs at a place where the copy is located. The exemption, however, would not apply if the image of the work were transmitted to members of the public at another location.[302]

Even if the viewing public is located at the same place, § 109(c) will not exempt a display when "more than one image at a time" is projected to viewers. This provision is intended to give copyright owners control over computer uses of their work, because such use may indirectly affect the market for the reproduction and distribution of copies of the work. To illustrate, § 109(c) would not exempt a display in which every person in a lecture hall were provided with a screen at a computer terminal to view the copyrighted work. Here the "one image at a time" limitation would be superseded and permission of the copyright would have to be obtained for the display.[303] Similarly, a transmission of a copyrighted work from one computer terminal to another would violate the display right and fall outside the § 109(c) exemption, whether or not the transmission of the image took place simultaneously or at different times, or whether the computers or terminals are located in the same physical space.

[B] Other Exemptions to the Display Right

Many, but not all of the exemptions for performances outlined in § 110 apply with equal force to displays:

(1) the face-to-face teaching exemption, § 110(1);

(2) the instructional broadcast exemption, § 110(2);

(3) the religious services exemption, § 110(3); and

(4) certain public receptions of transmission (the *Aiken* exemption) § 110(5).[304]

In addition, displays are equally exempt under § 111's provisions concerning secondary transmissions by cable television systems. Finally, § 118 exempts performance displays of copyrighted works made in connection with certain activities of public broadcasting stations.[305]

---

[302] 17 U.S.C. § 109(c).

[303] H.R. Rep. No. 94–1476, 94th Cong., 2d Sess. 80 (1976).

[304] Note that the following § 110 exemptions do not cover the display right, but the performance right only: § 110(4), the not-for-profit performance exemption; § 110(6), the agricultural fair exemption; § 110(7), the record vending establishment exemption; § 110(8), transmissions to the blind and handicapped; § 110(9), transmissions to the blind and handicapped of a dramatic literary work; § 110(10), the fraternal order exemption.

[305] 17 U.S.C. § 118(d); see § 8.23, *supra*, for a discussion of the exemption.

PART V: BEYOND CONVENTIONAL COPYRIGHT PROTECTION: THE MORAL
RIGHT FOR VISUAL ARTISTS AND THE COMPULSORY LICENSE FOR DIGITAL
AUDIO TAPING DEVICES

§ 8.27   The Moral Right [306]

[A]   Generally

The 1976 Act's protection of authors' exclusive rights is based on the economic
principle that the consumer benefits by the incentives given to authors to produce
copyrighted works. By comparison, a number of other countries [307] and signatories
of the Berne Convention [308] recognize the moral right of the author, which treats
the author's work not just as an economic interest, [309] but as an inalienable, natural

---

[306] For an overview of the moral right, see Russel J. DaSilva, Droit Moral *and the Amoral
Copyright: A Comparison of Artists' Rights in France and the United States*, 28 Bull.
Copyright Soc'y 1 (1980); Andre Francon & Jane C. Ginsburg, *Authors' Rights in France:
The Moral Right of the Creator of a Commissioned Work to Compel the Commissioning Party
to Complete the Work*, 9 Law & Arts 381 (1985); Roberta Rosenthal Kwall, *Copyright and
the Moral Right: Is an American Marriage Possible?*, 38 Vand. L. Rev. 1 (1985); John Henry
Merryman, *The Refrigerator of Bernard Buffet*, 27 Hastings L.J. 1023 (1976); 2 *Nimmer on
Copyright* § 8.21 (1993).

[307] The most famous moral rights law is that of France. *See* Law of March 11, 1957 on
Literary and Artistic Property. Although moral rights have found their greatest strength in
Western European Countries, there are some thirty-five countries around the world including
those in Africa, Asia and Latin America that provide for moral rights. *See* Kwall, n. 300,
supra, at 98 (appendix listing countries).

[308] Berne Convention for the Protection of Artistic and Literary Property, July 24, 1971
(Paris) art. 6 *bis*, which reads:

> (1) Independently of the author's economic rights and even after the transfer of the
> said rights, the author shall have the right to claim authorship of the work and to object
> to any distortion, mutilation or other modification of, or other derogatory action in
> relation to, the said work, which would be prejudicial to his honor or reputation.

> (2) The rights granted to the author in accordance with the preceding paragraph
> shall, after his death, be maintained, at least until the expiry of the economic rights,
> and shall be exercisable by the persons or institutions authorized by the legislation
> of the country where protection is claimed. However, those countries whose
> legislation, at the moment of their ratification of or accession to this Act, does not
> provide for the protection after the death of the author of all the rights set out in the
> preceding paragraph may provide that some of these rights may, after his death, cease
> to be maintained.

> (3) The means of redress for safeguarding the rights granted by this Article shall
> be governed by the legislation of the country where protection is claimed.

[309] Two concepts are embodied under French *droit d'auteur*. The first is *droit patrimoniaux*,
analogous to our copyright, which recognizes the author's economic stake in his work, lasts
fifty years after death, and is freely alienable. The second component is *droit moral*, non-
pecuniary in nature, made up of a collection of prerogatives to preserve the integrity of a work
and an artistic personality. *See* Claude Sarraute, *Current Theory on the Moral Right of Authors
and Artists Under French Law*, 16 Am. J. Comp. L. 465 (1968).

right and an extension of the artist's personality.[310] Although the scope of the moral right varies from country to country, it is a composite right consisting generally of three overlapping components:[311]

(1) The right of integrity — the right that the work not be mutilated or distorted;

(2) The right of paternity — the right to be acknowledged as an author of the work; and,

(3) The right of disclosure — the right to decide when and in what form the work will be presented to the public.

Although American copyright law has never adopted an integrated version of the moral right, the concept has made its way incrementally into the law in three ways. First, an author's integrity and attribution rights have been protected piecemeal by various bodies of state and federal law. Second, about a dozen states have passed statutes explicitly recognizing the moral rights of visual artists. Third, in the Visual Artists Rights Act of 1990, federal law has followed the lead of state law by protecting the integrity and attribution rights of visual artists.

[B] Analogues of the Moral Right in State and Federal Law[312]

Although American copyright law has never adopted an integrated version of the moral right, some case law has come very close to achieving the same result in protecting certain aspects of the author's integrity and paternity rights. The leading case is *Gilliam v. American Broadcasting Cos., Inc.*,[313] where plaintiff's right to prevent distortion of his work was protected under both the copyright and unfair competition laws. In *Gilliam*, defendant ABC obtained a license to broadcast several taped shows created by *Monty Python*, the famous British comedy group. The license

---

[310] Colorization of black and white films has generated a debate over recognition of the moral right in the United States. Copyright owners of black and white films have recently begun adapting these films to color by a computer process. Copyright owners colorize films to reach audiences that prefer movies in color. Authors and other persons have vigorously opposed colorization as a mutilation of an artist's work. Copyright owners, however, claim they have a legal right to do what they want with the films to protect their investment. *See* Roger L. Mayer, Rob Word & Buddy Young, *Colorization: The Arguments For*, 17 J. Arts Mgmt. & L. 64 (1987); Woody Allen, Milos Forman, Sidney Pollack, Ginger Rogers & Elliot Silverstein, *Colorization: The Arguments Against*, 17 J. Arts Mgmt. & L. 79 (1987). Unless special legislation is passed, the critics of colorization have lost the battle. The Copyright Office will register colorized films as derivative works. *See* § 2.10, *supra*.

[311] In addition to these three components, some formulations would include: The right of withdrawal — the right to withdraw the work from publication or to make modifications to it, and the right to prevent excessive criticism. *Droit de Suite*, or the resale royalty right, is sometimes considered an aspect of the moral right but is in reality more in the nature of an economic right. For a discussion of the resale royalty right now in existence in California, see § 8.14[E], *infra*.

[312] James M. Treece, *American Law Analogues of the Author's "Moral Right"*, 16 Am. J. Comp. L. 487 (1968).

[313] 538 F.2d 14 (2d Cir. 1976).

provided that shows were to be broadcast in their entirety except for minor editing to adapt the programs for commercials. ABC, however, cut 24 minutes from each 90-minute program. The court held that this truncation violated the terms of the license and constituted an infringement of plaintiff's adaptation right by creating an unauthorized derivative work. In addition, the court found a violation under § 43(a) of the Lanham Act[314] because the abridged version constituted a false designation of origin under the terms of the Act by deforming the work and presenting plaintiff as an author of a work not his own, subjecting him to criticism for a work he did not do. Thus, both copyright and unfair competition laws were invoked to protect the plaintiff's business and personal reputations, providing *de facto* protection of artistic interests akin to the moral rights of integrity and paternity.[315] In addition to copyright and unfair competition laws,[316] American authors have turned to contract,[317] defamation,[318] and privacy[319] laws to protect other aspects of their artistic personality and reputation.

Before Congress passed the Visual Arts Rights Act, several states had adopted their own version of a moral right for visual artists.

[C] State Art Preservation Acts

California, New York, Massachusetts and Louisiana,[320] among others, have passed versions of moral rights statutes, which, except for that of Massachusetts,[321] are limited in their application to works of fine art. The California and New York statutes provide two differing models of moral right protection. The California Art Preservation Act[322] prohibits intentional physical defacement, mutilation, alteration

---

[314] 60 Stat. 427, 15 U.S.C. § 1125(a) (1946).

[315] The court noted that a cause of action to redress a distortion of an artistic work "finds its roots in the continental concept of *droit moral* or moral right." *Id.* at 24.

[316] Section 43(a) of the Lanham Act (false designation of origin) provided the most creative incorporation of moral right principles of paternity and integrity in American law. *See, e.g., Smith v. Montoro*, 648 F.2d 602 (9th Cir. 1981) (upholding plaintiff actor's claim under § 43(a) where defendant film distributor removed plaintiff's name from the credits on the film as well as advertising materials and had substituted the name of another). *See also Geisel v. Poynter Products Inc.*, 283 F. Supp. 261 (S.D.N.Y. 1968), and *Rich v. RCA Corp.*, 390 F. Supp. 530 (S.D.N.Y. 1975).

[317] In addition to *Gilliam, see, e.g., Granz v. Harris*, 198 F.2d 585 (2d Cir. 1952).

[318] *See, e.g., Edison v. Viva Int'l, Ltd.*, 421 N.Y.S.2d 203 (1979) (sustaining action for libel for publication of author's article in substantially different version).

[319] *See, e.g., Zim v. Western Publishing Co.*, 573 F.2d 1318 (5th Cir. 1978) (cause of action under invasion of privacy stated for publication of unauthorized versions of author's work).

[320] La. Rev. Stat. Ann. § 51:2152 (West Supp. 1987).

[321] The Massachusetts law generally follows the California model except that it has broadened the definition of fine art to include

> any original work of visual or graphic art of any media which shall include, but not be limited to, any painting, print drawing, sculpture, craft, object, photograph, audio or video tape, film, hologram, or any combination thereof, of recognized quality.

See Mass. Gen. Laws Ann. Ch. 231 § 85S(b) (West Supp. 1987).

[322] Cal. Civ. Code § 987 (1980).

or destruction of a work of *fine* art.[323] The artist can waive the right, but only in a written instrument. The right passes to his heirs upon his death, and terminates fifty years after the artist's death. The Statute of Limitations for bringing an action is three years.

New York has passed a somewhat different version of a Moral Rights Act. The New York Artists' Authorship Rights Act[324] prevents unauthorized public display, publication, or reproduction of an altered, defaced or mutilated work where such display would reasonably damage the artist's reputation. By precluding mutilation of a work, the California and New York Acts are similar, but their underlying moral right rationale is somewhat different. California emphasizes a broad personal interest in the integrity of the work. The prohibited act is the destruction of a work of fine art in the interest of cultural preservation. By contrast, the New York Act, in prohibiting the *display* of a mutilated work, focuses on the artist's reputational interest. In other words, one violates the California Act by defacing a work of art, whereas one violates the New York Act by displaying the defaced art work.[325] In one way, New York goes a step further into moral rights protection than California: it recognizes not only a right to integrity, but a paternity right as well. The New York Act provides that "the artist shall retain at all times the right to claim authorship."[326] These state moral rights acts present serious questions of federal preemption under § 301 of the Copyright Act and the Visual Artists Rights Act of 1990.[327]

§ 8.28   Copyright Protection of Moral Rights: The Visual Artists Rights Act of 1990 (VARA)

[A]   Generally

The United States became a party to the Berne Convention on March 1, 1989, without passing special legislation designed to comply with Article 6 *bis*[328] of Berne which requires member nations to protect authors' rights of attribution and integrity. Article 6 *bis* provides:

---

[323] Fine art is defined as

an original painting, sculpture, or drawing, or an original work of art in glass of recognized quality, but shall not include work prepared under contract for commercial use by its purchaser.

Cal. Civ. Code § 987.

[324] Effective January 1, 1984. *See* N.Y. Arts & Cultural Affairs Law §§ 14.51–14.59.

[325] *See, e.g., Wojnarowicz v. American Family Association*, 745 F. Supp. 130 (S.D.N.Y. 1990) (unauthorized publication of fourteen photographically reproduced fragments extracted from plaintiff's works constituted actionable mutilation reasonably likely to damage reputation and violate the New York act).

[326] *Id.*

[327] For a discussion of federal preemption of these acts, see § 11.8[D], *infra*.

[328] In the U.C.C. and the Berne Convention, *bis* indicates a statutory article added to the original text and "sandwiched in" so as not to affect the original numbering scheme (much as §§ 106A and 116A were added to the 1976 Copyright Act subsequent to its enactment). The designations *ter* and *quater* indicate the addition of further articles in the same fashion.

Independently of the author's economic rights and even after the transfer of the said rights, the author shall have the right to claim authorship of the work and to object to any distortion, mutilation or other modification of, or other derogatory action in relation to, the said work, which would be prejudicial to his honor or reputation.

Congress justified its decision not to adopt specific moral rights legislation, claiming that the United States already gives *de facto* recognition to moral rights when the entirety of American law is considered. But serious doubts lingered about whether our obligations under Berne had really been met, without specific recognition of moral rights. The proponents of specific legislation quickly prevailed. Congress responded by passing The Visual Artists Rights Act of 1990 (VARA).[329] This legislation adds a new § 106A that confers the rights of attribution and integrity in certain works of visual art.

[B] Summary of the Provisions of VARA

Works protected. The Act does not cover all possible visual art works, but instead is limited (like the state statutes) to works of visual art. Qualifying works include paintings, drawings, prints, sculptures and still photographic images produced for exhibition purposes only, and existing in single copies or in limited editions of 200 or fewer copies, signed by the artist. Works not covered include reproductions of qualifying works, and works destined for commercial purposes, *e.g.*, posters, maps, motion pictures, and works of applied art. Works made for hire are excluded specifically.[330]

Rights of attribution and integrity. The statute creates new rights of attribution and integrity for certain visual artists. The right of attribution includes the artist's rights: (a) to claim authorship of the work; (b) to prevent the use of her name as the author of any work of visual art which she did not create; and (c) to prevent the use of her name as the author of the work in the event of a distortion, mutilation or other modification of the work which would be prejudicial to her honor or reputation. Subject to limitations described in paragraph 5 below, the right of integrity encompasses the rights: (a) to prevent any intentional distortion, mutilation or other modification of the work which would be prejudicial to the artist's honor or reputation; and (b) to prevent any destruction of a work of "recognized stature" (a term which the Act does not define) by an intentional or grossly negligent act.[331]

Scope and exercise of rights. The author of a work of visual art, *i.e.*, has the rights provided in § 106A, whether or not she owns the copyright in the work and whether or not the work qualifies for protection under the national origin provisions of § 104

---

[329] Pub. L. No. 101–650, 104 Stat. 5128 (1990).

[330] 17 U.S.C. § 101 (work of visual art).

[331] 17 U.S.C. § 106A(a). "Recognized stature" has been defined in the case law as describing a work that is meritorious and acknowledged as such by art experts and other members of the artistic community, or by some cross-section of society. *See Carter v. Helmsley-Spear,* 861 F. Supp. 303 (S.D.N.Y. 1994) (removal of a sculptural work incorporated into the lobby of a New York office building would violate VARA).

of the Copyright Act. Persons who jointly create a work of visual art are co-owners of the § 106A rights.[332]

Exceptions. A work is not destroyed, distorted, mutilated or otherwise objectionably modified, for purposes of the integrity right, if the modification is the result of the passage of time or the inherent nature of the materials. Likewise, the integrity right is not violated when a modification is the result of conservation measures or of public presentation, including lighting or placement, unless the modification is caused by gross negligence. Finally, the integrity and attribution rights do not apply to reproductions or other uses of protected works in forms not themselves protected by the Visual Artists Rights Act.[333]

Removal of works from buildings. The Act amends § 113 to establish conditions under which a work of art incorporated as a part of a building may be removed from the building. If the work cannot be removed without being mutilated or destroyed, the owner of the building nonetheless may accomplish such removal if the artist consented to the installation before June 1, 1991, or if thereafter she consented to the eventuality of mutilation or destruction in a signed instrument. If the work can be removed without mutilation or destruction, the work automatically is subject to the artist's attribution and integrity rights unless the owner has tried and failed in a diligent, good faith attempt to notify the artist or her successor-in-interest. If, in such instance, notice succeeds, the artist has 90 days to remove the work or pay for its removal; and that fixation of the work then becomes the artist's property.[334]

Duration of rights. With respect to works of visual art created on or after June 1, 1991, the effective date of the Act, the § 106A rights endure for the life of the artist (for joint works, the life of the last-surviving artist). The artist's § 106 rights (reproduction, adaptation, etc.) are unaffected and endure for the normal life-plus-50 years term.[335]

If the work of visual art was created before June 1, 1991, the Act creates, in certain circumstances, what can only be described as a peculiar situation. Provided that the artist has not parted with title to the copy(ies) of the work, she receives the life-plus-50-years term for both the § 106 rights and the § 106A rights. Whether the artist has parted with title to the work itself is irrelevant. Finally if the work was created before June 1, 1991 and the artist has sold the copy or copies to others, no § 106A rights arise at all.[336]

Transfer and waiver. The artist's attribution and integrity rights cannot be transferred. They can, however, be waived, but only expressly in writing, through an instrument signed by the artist, and only as to works and uses specified in that instrument.[337]

---

[332] 17 U.S.C. § 106A(b).
[333] 17 U.S.C. § 106A(c).
[334] 17 U.S.C. § 113(d).
[335] 17 U.S.C. § 106A(d).
[336] 17 U.S.C. § 106A(d).
[337] 17 U.S.C. § 106A(e).

Infringement. The Act subjects violators of the new attribution and integrity rights in works of visual art to the normal liabilities for infringement, but not to criminal penalties.[338]

Preemption. The statute amends § 301 by preempting any legal or equitable rights at state law that are equivalent to those created by the Act's new provisions. Nothing in the Act, however, annuls or limits any rights or remedies under the common law or statutes of any state with respect to (a) causes of action arising from undertakings commenced before the Act's effective date or (b) activities violating state-created rights that are not equivalent to those created by new § 106A.[339]

[C]   Beyond Moral Rights for Visual Artists?

The VARA is an attempt to accommodate moral rights with federal copyright law. One striking aspect of the Act is its limited scope, protecting only a narrow class of works of art. In addition, the Act protects only works of "recognized stature," a subject matter limitation that, by requiring judges to make aesthetic judgments, would appear to contradict a basic principle of copyright law. Despite these limitations on the scope of moral rights, some consider VARA as only a first step in a more expansive recognition of moral rights, encompassing the full range of literary, musical, and audiovisual works. One should, however, consider the rationale of a minimal ambit for formal recognition of moral rights. One common sense reason for this limitation is that some works are simply not appropriate for moral rights, such as computer programs, and data bases, and other functional works. These kinds of works that have little or no artistic, personality, or cultural heritage are ill suited for moral rights protection.

But even for works with an artistic and cultural dimension, moral rights protection is inappropriate for other reasons. Moral rights protection will inherently clash with the way many works are created in cultural and entertainment industries such as the movies, publishing, and broadcasting. These intensely collaborative endeavors are exploited through subsidiary markets. For example, motion pictures are abridged for television, textbooks are revised and translated, and music is synchronized, adapted, and broadcast in a multiplicity of forms. These lucrative derivative markets, which attract significant investment into the entertainment and cultural industries, are regulated by contractual agreement. But an expansive moral rights concept, presenting a constant threat of legal challenge, brought by any one or more collaborators would tend to undermine the economic expectations and the delicate allocation of rights achieved through private negotiation between authors, users, and labor unions. The result may be less financial support for such collaborate artistic endeavors, ultimately harming the public interest.[340]

---

[338] 17 U.S.C. §§ 501, 506.

[339] 17 U.S.C. § 301(f).

[340] For an elaboration of these criticisms, see Robert A. Gorman, *Federal Moral Rights Legislation: The Need for Caution*, 14 Nova L. Rev. 421 (1990).

§ 8.29   The Audio Home Recording Act of 1992

[A]   The Challenge of New Recording Technology

By the mid-eighties, the recording industry decided to shift its marketing emphasis from analog formats, such as vinyl discs, and magnetic tapes, to a digital format of compact disks. Soon after the public began gravitating to this new format, an even newer technology, originating in Japan, offered a powerful new threat to the industry. This technology, called the digital audio recording technologies (DART), differed from analog recording methods. Unlike analog recording methods, DART would allow the ordinary consumer to make near perfect copies of prerecorded music. The first generation of digital audio tape (DAT) received tepid consumer acceptance, but a new digital recording mini disc format called DCC (3.5 inch), introduced in 1990, has shown great promise to revive a languishing electronics industry. In addition, mini-discs, unlike conventional compact discs, can be used to make copies from all media such as records, tapes, or discs. The record industry feared that these new recording technologies, once readily available, would encourage a new surge of home audio taping and undermine the robust market for CDs. The record industry focused its efforts on ways of legally controlling this new technology.

Whether copyright liability should extend to home audio taping has been a matter of controversy since Congress first recognized protection of sound recordings in 1971.[341] In some ways, audio-taping is a much more serious threat to copyright owners than off-the-air videotaping. Unlike the use of video machines to copy shows off the air, people copy prerecorded sound recordings not just to listen to the music at a more convenient moment, but to avoid buying a record, tape, or disc at full price. For many years, the music industry has maintained that audio recording has greatly decreased sales of prerecorded music.

Industrial relations in the audio field took a more conciliatory path than those involved with videotaping. To clarify the legal status of digital audio recording and avoid wasteful litigation, music and electronics industries entered into negotiations to fashion a compromise that would promote the new technology without harming the record companies. Concluded in 1991, the agreement between these powerful industry groups was transformed into the Audio Home Recording Act of 1992.[342] Breaking new ground in American copyright law, the Act reflects a carefully wrought compromise and an ambitious, if not *sui generis*, legislative undertaking. In addition to erecting a new compulsory license, it creates, for the first time in American copyright law, a new cause of action apart from copyright in infringement.

---

[341] The Supreme Court in the *Betamax* case did not abate the controversy by ruling that private home taping of copyrighted works for time-shifting purposes constituted fair use. It rejected the Court of Appeals' suggestion that a continuing royalty be imposed upon VCR and tape manufacturers based on the sale of VCR's and blank tape. In its narrow ruling, the *Betamax* case left in abeyance the legality of audio copying of prerecorded musical works. For a discussion of *Betamax*, see § 10.11[B].

[342] 102 Pub. L. No. 102–563, 106 Stat. 4237 (1992).

Moreover, for the first time, copyright legislation has placed legal restraints on a technology *per se* rather than on certain uses of that technology.

[B]   Provisions of the Audio Home Recording Act of 1992

The Act, which is now codified as chapter 10 of the Copyright Act, prohibits legal actions for copyright infringement based on the manufacture, importation, or distribution of a digital audio recording device for private non-commercial audio recording.[343] To protect the record industry, the Act requires digital recording machines to be equipped with the Serial Copy Management System that blocks second-generation digital copying — making copies from copies.[344] Original works may be copied without limit. The Act also requires manufacturers and importers of digital hardware and blank digital software to pay compensatory royalties to music creators and copyright owners.[345] In sum, the Act accomplishes two goals: first, it allows manufacturers to sell digital audio recording technology to the consumer, who can use it for home taping within certain limits. Second, it establishes funds to compensate copyright owners likely to be injured by the DART technology.

Subchapter C of the Act[346] establishes procedures to collect and distribute the royalty payments, based on sales of digital audio recording devices, and the audio recording media (the blank tapes or discs). The provisions of the Act are limited to digital audio recording devices such as DCC and DAT as mentioned above. Other audio recording technologies, such as analog audio recording products, diction machines, and personal computers, are excluded.

To compensate copyright owners, the royalty pool is derived from manufacturers and importers who must pay 2% of the transfer price for digital devices and 3% of the transfer price of the tape of disc.[347] Only one payment is due for any digital recording device, blank tape, or disk and only the first person to distribute the item must pay the royalty. The royalty pool is based on prior year sales or air time of their musical works or sound recordings and is preallocated: two thirds of the fund is reserved for the Sound Recordings Fund and the rest earmarked for the Musical Works Fund.[348] The Register of Copyright will administer the royalty system. Royalty-paying parties will file notices, send reports, and make payments to the Register. Interested parties will file claims with the Register of Copyrights. If the Register decides that no controversy exits, it will then distribute the money yearly. If the Register finds the existence of a controversy, the Register must convene a copyright arbitration royalty panel to determine the distribution of royalty fees.[349]

---

[343] 17 U.S.C. § 1008.

[344] 17 U.S.C. § 1002 (a).

[345] *See* Subchapter C, 17 U.S.C. §§ 1003–1007.

[346] 17 U.S.C. §§ 1003–1007.

[347] The royalty rate on recorders is subject to a per unit cap of $8 and a per unit minimum fee of $1. For machines that have two or more digital recorders, the cap is $12. *See* 17 U.S.C. § 1004 (a)(3).

[348] *See* 17 U.S.C. § 1006 (b)(1) and (2).

[349] 17 U.S.C. § 1007(c).

The Act establishes civil remedies for violations of the royalty or SCMS provisions. Any interested party injured by a violation of audio recording provisions can bring an action in federal district court.[350]

The Act authorizes a full battery of remedies, including injunctive relief, damages, costs, and attorney's fees, for failure to observe the serial copying requirements or to pay the required royalties.[351] Penalties are increased for repeat offenders.[352] Liability under the Act is limited to serial copying and royalty requirements. Accordingly, no action can be brought under the Act for copyright infringement for noncommercial home taping by consumers using digital recording equipment and media. In addition, no action for contributory infringement may be based on the manufacture, importation, or distribution of such equipment or media.[353]

Whether the Digital Audio Recording Act will satisfy the expectations of the music and electronics industry will take some time to determine. Ideally, the Act should both protect and compensate copyright owners. It should protect copyright owners against the more harmful forms of unauthorized duplication while compensating them through distributions from the royalty pool. At the same time, the electronics industry reaps benefits as well. Unimpeded by litigation, it can now focus on selling a product that meets consumer demands. We will not soon know whether the Act accomplishes these goals, that is, to see if the royalties are efficiently and properly allocated by the Register of Copyrights, and copying controls adequately protect the copyright owners. But if the Act works as intended, it may well become a model for future compromises between copyright owners and manufacturers of future reprographic technologies.

---

[350] 17 U.S.C. § 1009 (b).

[351] 17 U.S.C. § 1009(d).

[352] 17 U.S.C. § 1009 (d)(2).

[353] 17 U.S.C. § 1008.

CHAPTER 9

INFRINGEMENT AND REMEDIES

§ 9.1 Introduction and Chapter Overview

Copyright infringement occurs when a third party violates one or more of the copyright owner's exclusive rights as enumerated in § 106 of the 1976 Act.[1] Thus, to infringe, the defendant must have reproduced, adapted, distributed, publicly performed, or publicly displayed the copyrighted work in an unprivileged way. Alternatively, if defendant's use of the work does not fall within these enumerated rights, *e.g.*, a private performance, infringement has not occurred. The exclusive rights create the boundaries between an infringement and an allowable use of a copyrighted work.

This chapter is divided into three parts. Part I examines the substantive law of infringement, focusing on the critical issue of substantial similarity. Part II turns to the remedies, legal and equitable, provided in a suit for copyright infringement. Part III examines the suit for copyright infringement in the procedural context, discussing jurisdiction, statute of limitations and the various parties to the suit.

PART I: INFRINGEMENT: SUBSTANTIVE ISSUES

§ 9.2 The Elements: Ownership, Copying, and Improper Appropriation

To sustain an action for infringement, the copyright owner must prove:

(1) ownership of a valid copyright in the work,

(2) copying by the defendant, and

(3) that defendant's copying constitutes an improper appropriation.

To prove ownership, plaintiff must show originality, copyrightable subject matter, compliance with statutory formalities, and the necessary citizenship status. If plaintiff is not the author, he must produce the proper transfer documents or show a relationship which supports the claim for copyright. For most ownership questions, copyright registration constitutes *prima facie* evidence of ownership.[2]

---

[1] 17 U.S.C. § 106.
[2] 17 U.S.C. § 401(c).

In addition to ownership, plaintiff must prove that the defendant *copied* the work. *Copying*[3] is a term of art, an umbrella term embodying two basic issues governing the ultimate determination that plaintiff's exclusive rights have been violated. First, defendant must have taken an improper amount of the plaintiff's work. This is known as the requirement of substantial similarity. Second, even if the works are substantially similar, the requirement of copying has not been met if defendant's work was independently created. In other words, plaintiff must prove that defendant *actually* copied the copyrighted work in creating his own to support a claim of infringement. This concept, fundamental to copyright law, is dictated by the requirement of originality.[4] A work is copyrightable if original and independently created, even though it is identical to another copyrighted work. In marked contrast to patent law, the creator of an original work cannot be an infringer.[5] Independently created, virtually identical works are more than a theoretical possibility and occur with some frequency in fabric designs, popular music, and factual works, where common public domain sources are often used.[6]

§ 9.3 Circumstantial Proof of Copying: Access and Substantial Similarity

Direct evidence of copying is rarely available, for obvious reasons. First, seldom will a defendant admit to copying a work. Second, copying is often carried out secretly or accomplished by non-physical means, *e.g.*, from memory. As a result, few plaintiffs are able to produce a witness who can testify that he saw the defendant physically copying the work. These practical limitations on direct proof of copying do not stop the plaintiff from establishing copying by circumstantial evidence. The circumstantial case is made by proving: (1) access and (2) probative similarity, *i.e.*, similarities between the works probative of copying.[7] In short, if the defendant had access to the plaintiff's work and the defendant's work appears to have made use of the plaintiff's work, there is a high probability that the defendant copied. The

---

[3] The term "copying" is a misnomer. The reproduction, adaptation, and even performance rights involve copying in one way or another. But the term "copying" covers unlawful distribution and display as well, hardly acts of copying as one might use the term in ordinary language.

[4] An original work of authorship for copyright purposes is one that is independently created, *i.e.*, not copied from another source where the author has added more than a *de minimis* amount to the public domain. For a discussion of originality, see § 2.7, *supra*.

[5] Striking similarity between two works can create a presumption against independent creation which forces the defendant to prove independent creation.

[6] *Jewel Music Pub. Co. v. Leo Feist, Inc.*, 62 F. Supp. 596, 599 (S.D.N.Y. 1945); *Arnstein v. Edward B. Marks Music Corp.*, 82 F.2d 275, 277 (2d Cir. 1936).

[7] The term "probative similarity" is taken from Alan Latman, *"Probative Similarity" As Proof of Copying: Toward Dispelling Some Myths in Copyright Infringement*, 90 Colum. L. Rev. 1187 (1990) (Professor Latman's article examines how similarities between the works are used in the litigation process. In this regard, he demonstrates that the term "substantial similarity" is misused by the courts to cover both similarity that is probative of copying and similarity that is necessary to prove improper appropriation).

issue is not whether the defendant copied a sufficient amount to constitute infringement. This aspect of the case concerns another element in infringement litigation, that of improper appropriation. Rather, the issue is whether the defendant copied rather than independently created his work. Thus, to prove the copying element of the infringement action, even proof of copying uncopyrightable features of the protected work may be sufficient for this purpose.

Unfortunately, the courts have used confusing terminology when applying the various issues in infringement litigation.[8]

The issue of indirect copying turns on probabilities: is it more likely than not that defendant copied from plaintiff's work? To prove copying, access and probative similarity are inversely related. Under this notion, the degree of similarity required to establish an inference of access is an inverse ratio to the quantum of direct evidence presented to establish access. Where the case for access is weak, the court will require a correspondingly greater degree of similarity to establish copying. Conversely, where the proof of access is strong, the courts will require a lesser degree of probative similarity. Of course, there are limits. No amount of proof of access will suffice to show copying if there are no similarities.[9]

Although it appears that access and probative similarity are inversely related issues, the courts are often less than explicit in revealing their analytical process on the copying issue. If the similarities between the two works are obvious, many courts do not bother to discuss similarity, focusing entirely on access. Alternatively, if evidence of access is absent, the courts will insist that the similarities be so striking as to preclude the possibility that plaintiff and defendant independently arrived at the same result.[10] Once a sufficient circumstantial case is made, the burden shifts to defendant to disprove copying by showing independent creation[11] or use of common source.[12]

---

[8] *See generally* Howard B. Abrams, *The Law of Copyright*, § 14.01 (1993). Some courts (especially in the Ninth Circuit) use the term "substantial similarity" to refer both to the kind of similarity used to establish indirect proof of copying and the kind required to show improper appropriation. One explanation for this terminological confusion is that in many cases, the same proofs of similarity are used for both purposes. But the type of similarity needed to prove indirect copying is not necessarily the same as that needed to prove improper appropriation. For example, suppose that plaintiff is able to prove certain common errors between his work and the defendant's. These common errors may well be probative for an indirect proof of copying. In themselves, however, these common errors may be inadequate to prove that defendant appropriated enough of plaintiff's work to constitute an improper appropriation. Thus, the term "probative similarity" should be used for similarities referring to indirect copying and the term "substantial similarity" should be employed when improper appropriation is at issue.

[9] *Arnstein v. Porter*, 154 F.2d 464, 468 (2d Cir. 1946).

[10] *Id.*

[11] *Original Appalachian Artworks, Inc. v. Toy Loft, Inc.*, 684 F.2d 821 (11th Cir. 1982).

[12] Defendant can assert other defenses as well, such as plaintiff's authority to use the work. *See Oboler v. Goldin*, 714 F.2d 211, 212 (2d Cir. 1983).

§ 9.4 Access

To prove access, plaintiff must show that defendant had a reasonable opportunity to view or copy the work. Generally, the evidence must be sufficient for the trier of fact to infer a reasonable probability of access. On the other hand, a mere possibility of access, based on conjecture or speculation, is not enough to make the circumstantial case. Accordingly, access has been inferred where the work was in possession of a third party which had done business with both plaintiff and defendant,[13] or where the work was available to employees in defendant corporation's files, one of whom eventually produced a substantially similar work.[14] Alternatively, evidence of access was insufficient to support a claim for infringement where nothing more could be shown other than that the work was available in defendant's city of residence.[15]

Access to a famous, widely-disseminated work may also be inferred where facts suggest that defendant had a reasonable opportunity to view or copy it. In *Bright Tunes Music Corp. v. Harrisongs Music, Ltd.*,[16] plaintiff claimed that George Harrison's *My Sweet Lord* infringed their popular song, *He's So Fine*, which had been played extensively on the radio during a certain time. Harrison denied having copied the song, asserting independent creation. The court found, however, that defendant had access to the copyrighted work because of its popularity as a hit in the United States and abroad. And even though defendant may have unintentionally copied it through subconscious processes, unintentional copying does not constitute a defense against an action for copyright infringement.[17] *Bright Tunes* provides a good example of a situation where defendant's lack of access is simply not plausible.

Another presumption of access, given the facts, arises when the two works are so strikingly similar that independent creation is not a reasonable possibility. To infer access in this situation, plaintiff must show similarities that could only be explained by copying rather than by coincidence, independent creation, or use of a prior common source.[18] The nature of the copyrighted work is the essential factor in making the circumstantial case in this situation. For example, where complex literary works are virtually identical, access may be presumed.[19]

---

[13] *Kamar International, Inc. v. Russ Berrie and Co.*, 657 F.2d 1059 (9th Cir. 1981).

[14] *Meta-Film Associates, Inc. v. MCA, Inc.*, 586 F. Supp. 1346 (C.D. Cal. 1984); *Smith v. Little, Brown & Co.*, 245 F. Supp. 451 (S.D.N.Y. 1965), *aff'd*, 360 F.2d 928 (2d Cir. 1966); *Stanley v. Columbia Broadcasting System, Inc.*, 35 Cal. 2d 653, 221 P.2d 73 (1950). The key aspect of these cases is a close relationship linking the intermediary and the alleged copier, not just a showing that they shared the same employer. *Morrissey v. Proctor & Gamble Co.*, 379 F.2d 675 (1st Cir. 1967).

[15] *Ferguson v. National Broadcasting Co.*, 584 F.2d 111 (5th Cir. 1978).

[16] 420 F. Supp. 177 (S.D.N.Y. 1976).

[17] *Id.* at 181. Although innocent intent is not a defense to copyright infringement, it can affect the extent of damages (particularly statutory damages) plaintiff can recover. *See* § 9.13[B], *infra*.

[18] *Stratchborneo v. Arc Music Corp.*, 357 F. Supp. 1393, 1403 (S.D.N.Y. 1973).

[19] *Association of American Medical Colleges v. Mikaelian*, 571 F. Supp. 144, 150–51 (E.D. Pa. 1983), *aff'd mem.*, 734 F.2d 3 (3d Cir. 1984).

Alternatively, when the works are trite or commonplace and resemble available public sources,[20] the fact that they are similar does not support the inference that the work was copied, and other proof of access showing a reasonable opportunity to view the work will be required.[21] In *Selle v. Gibb*,[22] the question was whether the Bee Gees' international hit song *How Deep Is Your Love* was so strikingly similar to defendant's prior song that proof of access could be inferred. The court held that even striking similarity is not enough to infer access unless there is some evidence making it reasonably possible that plaintiff's work was available to the infringer. Here the reasonable possibility did not exist. The Bee Gees' song was created in France, whereas plaintiff's song was limited to play in the Chicago area. Moreover, the songs did not involve the kind of striking similarity sufficient to overcome the need to show reasonable opportunity to copy. The material here was relatively trite and commonplace, lacking the complexities which would negate an explanation of independent creation.[23]

§ 9.5   Substantial Similarity

[A]   Generally

In an action for copyright infringement, plaintiff must prove that defendant's copying created a substantially similar work.[24] It makes no difference how strong the proof of access is if the works are not substantially similar. Moreover, not every taking or use of another's copyrighted work amounts to substantial similarity. A third party may freely copy the ideas embodied in a work but cannot copy the author's expression beyond what the law allows. And even if some of the expression is copied, there must be a substantial, material taking to constitute infringement. Thus,

---

[20] *Ferguson v. National Broadcasting Co.*, 584 F.2d 111, 113 (5th Cir. 1978) (evidence of striking similarity insufficient for summary judgment).

[21] One such similarity is the presence of similar errors. For example, in *Eckes v. Card Prices Update*, 736 F.2d 859, 863–64 (2d Cir. 1984), there were numerous common errors in defendant's and plaintiff's baseball card price guides, sufficient to support inference of copying. *See also College Entrance Book Co. v. Amsco Book Co.*, 119 F.2d 874 (2d Cir. 1941), and generally 3 *Nimmer on Copyright* § 13.03[C] (1993); Paul Goldstein, *Copyright*, § 7.2.1 (1989).

[22] 741 F.2d 896 (7th Cir. 1984).

[23] On the same issue, *see Scott v. WKJG, Inc.*, 376 F.2d 467 (7th Cir.), *cert. denied*, 389 U.S. 832 (1967). No access was proven where defendant's allegedly infringing play contained no verbatim passages, plaintiff's play was performed a few times, and no copies were distributed to the public.

[24] For an overview of the issue in various contexts, see Gary L. Francione, *Facing the Nation: The Standards for Copyright Infringement and Fair Use of Factual Works*, 134 U. Pa. L. Rev. 519 (1986); Steven B. McKnight, *Substantial Similarity Between Video Games: An Old Copyright Problem in a New Medium*, 36 Vand. L. Rev. 1277 (1983); David May, *So Long as Time Is Music: When Musical Compositions Are Substantially Similar*, 60 S. Cal. L. Rev. 785 (1987); John Pinheiro & Gerard Lacroix, *Protecting the "Look and Feel" of Computer Software*, 1 High Tech L.J. 411 (1986).

to say that the works are substantially similar is to say that the defendant has copied a substantial and material amount of plaintiff's protected expression.

[B] Verbatim Similarity and Pattern Similarity Compared[25]

A defendant can produce a substantially similar work in two ways. One is by verbatim copying; the other by taking the overall pattern and arrangement of the work. These methods are not mutually exclusive. Defendant can produce a work which contains both identical copying and comprehensive pattern copying as well.

[C] Verbatim Similarity

The defendant need not copy the entire work to be guilty of infringement. But if one can infringe by copying less than the entire work, how much of a taking is too much? No arbitrary rule can be formulated, and each case is decided on its own facts using both quantitative and qualitative criteria.[26] Copying a single sentence of a work could theoretically constitute an infringement, depending on the sentence taken.[27] In general, a wider taking is tolerated for copyrighted works, such as compilations of facts and directories, which are made up of essentially public domain materials. For these types of works, near identity will be required to show infringement, because idea and expression are difficult to distinguish. On the other hand, less appropriation would constitute infringement for wholly creative works such as poetry or a novel.[28]

[D] Pattern Similarity

The second way one can create a substantially similar work is by taking the overall pattern of the copyrighted work, even if plaintiff cannot show any instance of verbatim or literal copying. As one court summed it up:

---

[25] The terms "verbatim similarity" and "pattern similarity" are used here as a shorthand to conceptualize broadly the two general types of similarity. Professor Nimmer has adopted a more complicated terminology for these two kinds of similarity: "fragmented literal similarity" and "non-fragmented comprehensive similarity." See 3 *Nimmer on Copyright* § 13.03[A] (1993). Nimmer's terminology is being accepted in the case law. *See, e.g., Walker v. Time-Life Films, Inc.*, 784 F.2d 44 (2d Cir. 1986); and *Smith v. Weinstein*, 578 F. Supp. 1297 (S.D.N.Y. 1984).

[26] The question is how much of plaintiff's work defendant has taken, not how much of defendant's work the taking constitutes.

[27] Infringement can be found even if only a small amount of a copyrighted work is taken, if the part taken is qualitatively significant. *Horgan v. MacMillan, Inc.*, 789 F.2d 157 (2d Cir. 1986). In music infringement cases, copying two bars of plaintiff's work has constituted an infringement. *See Robertson v. Batten, Barton, Durstine & Osborne, Inc.*, 146 F. Supp. 795 (S.D. Cal. 1956). But copying much more than that may not be actionable if qualitatively insignificant. *See Marks v. Leo Feist, Inc.*, 290 F. 959 (2d Cir. 1923).

[28] *Compare Triangle Publications, Inc. v. Sports Eye, Inc.*, 415 F. Supp. 682 (E.D. Pa. 1976) (defendant took nothing more than public domain facts, not their arrangement), *with Schroeder v. William Morrow and Co.*, 566 F.2d 3 (7th Cir. 1977) (defendant infringed plaintiff's gardening directory by taking the selection, ordering, and arrangement of compilation of names and addresses).

[A]n infringement is not confined to literal and exact repetition or reproduction; it includes also the various modes in which the matter of any work may be adopted, imitated, transferred or reproduced, with more or less colorable alterations to disguise the piracy.[29]

What justification is there for the proscription against pattern copying? If infringement were limited to exact copying, a clever plagiarist could avoid a copyright violation by carefully paraphrasing the work. Moreover, absent a concept of infringement by pattern similarity, works could be freely copied in a different medium, such as a novel to film, without copying any specific language or dialogue.[30] In sum, without the proscription against pattern copying, the incentive to create works of authorship would be greatly undermined.

Pattern copying presents greater practical and theoretical problems for a plaintiff trying to prove substantial similarity than does verbatim copying. The difficulty lies in defining the line between use of expression and use of an idea. In attempting to draw that line we are trying to reach an equilibrium between the optimum incentive to create works of authorship and the optimum dissemination of information. It is a difficult line to draw. On the one hand, copyright law should protect against the clever paraphrase to encourage creation; on the other hand, it should not impede the use of ideas and facts revealed in the copyrighted work.[31] Thus, the ultimate issue in determining infringement by pattern copying becomes whether defendant has appropriated the author's copyrightable expression rather than the abstract ideas revealed in the work.

[E]   Determining Pattern Similarity: The Learned Hand Abstractions Test

In *Nichols v. Universal Pictures Corp.*[32] Judge Learned Hand made a famous attempt to draw the line between taking idea and taking expression. In *Nichols*, plaintiff-author of the play *Abie's Irish Rose* sued defendant for its motion picture *The Cohens and the Kelleys*. The issue was whether the play and the movie were substantially similar, given the obvious similarity of the storylines of the two shows. Meticulously comparing the plots, the court concluded that "[T]he only matter common to the two is a quarrel between a Jewish and an Irish father, the marriage of their children, the birth of grandchildren and a reconciliation."[33] To determine how much and what constitutes substantial similarity, Judge Hand formulated what has become well known as his "abstractions" test:

---

[29] *Universal Pictures Co., Inc. v. Harold Lloyd Corp.*, 162 F.2d 354, 360 (9th Cir. 1947).

[30] Copying in a different medium is not a defense to infringement. Substantial similarity can exist across media. *See, e.g., Horgan v. Macmillan, Inc.*, 789 F.2d 157 (2d Cir. 1986) (photographs can infringe choreography); *Filmvideo Releasing Corp. v. Hastings*, 668 F.2d 91 (2d Cir. 1981) (dolls can infringe cartoon characters); *Roy Export Co. Establishment v. Columbia Broadcasting System, Inc.*, 672 F.2d 1095 (2d Cir. 1982) (movies can infringe books).

[31] For a discussion of the idea-expression dichotomy, see § 2.12, *supra*, and 17 U.S.C. § 102(b).

[32] 45 F.2d 119 (2d Cir. 1930).

[33] *Id.* at 122.

Upon any work, and especially upon a play, a great number of patterns of increasing generality will fit equally well, as more and more of the incident is left out. The last may perhaps be no more than the most general statement of what the play is about, and at times might consist only of its title; but there is a point in this series of abstractions where they are no longer protected, since otherwise the playwright could prevent the use of his "ideas," to which, apart from their expression, his property is never extended.[34]

The abstractions test provides insight into how to separate copyrightable expression from non-infringing public domain ideas to determine substantial similarity.[35] The test may be viewed as a continuum with pure idea at one end and pure expression at the other. As the idea travels along the continuum, it gathers concrete detail and becomes more complex. No longer a vague set of generalities, it cannot be summed up in a few words. A taking at this point is a taking of the author's expression.

Although the abstractions test is a useful conceptualization of the problem, it does not clearly indicate where on the continuum an undue amount of plaintiff's expression has been taken. Perhaps all that can be said is that there comes a point where defendant's use of the general theme combines with similarities in details, scenes, sequence of events, characterization, and interplay of characters to constitute infringement.[36]

[F]   Applying the Abstractions Test to Computer Programs: From *Whelan Associates* to *Computer Associates* (*Altai*)

The above approach to substantial similarity works relatively well when dealing with traditional literary works such as plays and novels (*i.e.*, works that tell a story). It has been applied less easily to visual works, music, factual works, and more recently to computer programs. Now that computer programs are copyrightable subject matter and are protected against verbatim copying,[37] the difficult question is to what extent programs are protected against nonliteral copying. The question is whether copyright protection will extend beyond the written code itself to the

---

[34] *Id.* at 121.

[35] Closely related to the abstractions test is the *scenes à faire* doctrine. *Scenes à faire* are incidents, characters or settings which are common to a standard treatment of a topic, such as incidents or sequences of events and stock characters. If *scenes à faire* are the only similarities between two works, a court will not find substantial similarity between the two works. *Scenes à faire* are placed in the realm of unprotectible ideas and are not copyrightable. *See Schwarz v. Universal Pictures Co.*, 85 F. Supp. 270, 275 (S.D. Cal. 1945), where the term *scenes à faire* originated, and *Hoehling v. Universal City Studios, Inc.*, 618 F.2d 972, 979 (2d Cir. 1980) (certain standard devices are used in all historical writing and are not copyrightable). For an excellent overview, see Leslie A. Kurtz, *Copyright: The* Scenes à Faire *Doctrine*, 41 Fla. L. Rev. 79 (1989).

[36] *See Reyher v. Children's Television Workshop*, 533 F.2d 87, 91 (2d Cir.), *cert. denied*, 429 U.S. 980 (1976), and Zechariah Chafee, Jr., *Reflections on the Law of Copyright*, 45 Colum. L. Rev. 503, 513 (1945).

[37] *See* § 3.4, *supra*; *Apple Computer, Inc. v. Franklin Computer Corp.*, 714 F.2d 1240, 1248 (3d Cir. 1983), *cert denied*, 479 U.S. 1033 (1984).

structure of the program and its user interface.[38] The problem of nonliteral copying arises because different lines of computer code can use the same program structure or create similar user interfaces. To determine how far computer programs should be protected against nonliteral copying should ultimately depend on whether the particular approach encourages the optimal production and dissemination of computer programs. Inadequate protection will undermine the incentive to create computer programs, whereas too much protection will unduly impede their dissemination and deprive creators of basic material on which they build their own works.

In these "second generation"[39] computer software copyright cases, the courts have been less than unanimous in developing a conceptual framework to determine the proper scope of protection of computer programs in their nonliteral elements. In *Whelan Associates, Inc. v. Jaslow Dental Laboratory, Inc.*,[40] the Third Circuit became the first Circuit Court of Appeals to confront the issue of nonliteral copying in the computer domain. The heart of inquiry is a definitional one: how does one separate idea from expression in a computer program. In answer to this question, the *Whelan* court defined a program's idea broadly as its purpose or function. The court held that defendant's computer program for managing dental laboratories infringed plaintiff's similarly oriented program. In that regard, copyright protection extended beyond the program's literal codes to its overall structure, sequence, and organization which is not necessitated by the purpose or the functioning of the program.[41] The court reasoned that computer programs are a variety of literary work, a class which includes plays and novels. Like other literary works, such as a play or novel whose overall structure, plots, and themes are protected by the law, so too should a computer program's structure, sequence, and organization receive analogous protection.[42]

The literary analogy should not be pushed too far when computer software is at issue. Unlike books and articles, computer programs are inherently utilitarian, fusing idea, expression, process, and function. Separating idea from expression in such functional works entails a different process than a traditional work of literature. The term "idea" is a loaded term in the copyright lexicon, one which the *Whelan* court took too literally. As Professor Samuelson states: "[T]he term 'idea' in copyright parlance is not confined in its meaning to 'abstract generalized conceptions' such as the general purpose or function of a program; rather, it is a metaphor used in

---

[38] The user interface includes the option menus, labels, key strokes to implement choices or commands, and text describing what the choices accomplish. *See* Raymond T. Nimmer, *The Law of Computer Technology: Rights, Licenses, and Liabilities,* ¶ 1.12, at 1–72 (2d ed. 1992). *See, e.g., Lotus Development Corp. v. Borland Int'l, Inc.*, 831 F. Supp. 616 (1993); *Apple Computer Inc. v. Microsoft Corp.*, 821 F. Supp. 616 (N.D. Cal. 1993); *Lotus Development Corp. v. Paperback Software International*, 740 F. Supp. 37 (D. Mass. 1990).

[39] The term "second generation" was adopted in Peter Menell, *An Analysis of the Scope of Copyright Protection for Application Programs*, 41 Stan. L. Rev. 1045, 1048 (1989) (the first generation cases focused on whether the literal elements could be protected).

[40] 797 F.2d 1222 (3d Cir. 1986), *cert. denied*, 479 U.S. 1031 (1987).

[41] *Id.* at 1234.

[42] The court found that substantial similarity existed between the formats and structures, file structures, screen outputs, and file subroutines. *Id.*

copyright law to describe the unprotectible elements in a copyrighted work."[43] As such, the *Whelan* test has been criticized as taking an overly narrow view of the meaning of "idea" in copyright law. The case suggests that a computer program contains one idea and that everything else in the work is expression unless it is necessary to implement the idea. As a result, *Whelan* ignores § 102(b), which would exclude "processes, procedures, systems, and methods of operation" from copyright protection, even when they are embodied within a copyrighted work. The problem is that the program's structure may be viewed as a process, system, or method of operation, more akin to idea than expression. By taking this bright line approach, *Whelan* appears to reject the traditional abstractions test adopted by Learned Hand in *Nichols*. The abstractions test is a fact-intensive inquiry that tries to determine at each level of abstraction whether there was sufficient expression to confer copyright protection on the work as a whole. The *Whelan* "structure, sequence, organization" test differs considerably from this case-by-case process, resulting in an overinclusive protection of computer programs.

Since *Whelan*, courts have continued to be challenged in determining what degree of non-literal copying constitutes an infringement of a computer program.[44] As a general trend, most courts have either rejected or modified the *Whelan* "structure, sequence, organization" formulation. They have, for the most part, returned to some form of the Hand "abstractions test" in determining how far nonliteral aspects of a program should be protected.[45] The most important of these cases rejecting the *Whelan* approach is *Computer Associates v. Altai, Inc.*[46] In *Altai*, both plaintiff and

[43] Pamela Samuelson, *Computer Program, User Interfaces, and Section 102(b) of the Copyright Act of 1976: A Critique of* Lotus v. Paperback, 55 Law & Contemp. Probs. 311 (1992). *See* Paul Goldstein, *Infringement of Copyright in Computer Programs*, 47 U. Pitt. L. Rev 1119, 1126 (1986) ("Clearly the [*Whelan*] court construed the copyright concept of 'idea' too literally and failed to recognize that, in the copyright lexicon, 'idea' is no more than a metaphor for elements generally belonging in the public domain").

[44] *See Dynamic Solutions, Inc. v. Planning & Control, Inc.*, Copyright L. Dec. (CCH) ¶ 26,062 (S.D.N.Y. 1987) (on hearing for preliminary injunction, operations management programs were substantially similar due to literal and structural similarities which were not functionally mandated).

[45] *See, e.g., Plains Cotton Cooperative Ass'n v. Goodpasture Computer Service, Inc.*, 807 F.2d 1256 (5th Cir. 1987); *Lotus Development Corp. v. Paperback Software Int'l*, 740 F. Supp. 37 (D. Mass. 1990) (in an infringement of Lotus 1-2-3 announcing a three-step test for determining which nonliteral elements merited protection under copyright law: (1) defining the "idea," (2) determining whether idea and expression have merged, and (3) ascertaining whether any remaining protectible expression was a substantial part of the allegedly copyrightable work. Applying this test, Judge Keeton concluded the user interface was protected by copyright); *Lotus Development Corp. v. Borland Int'l, Inc.*, 799 F. Supp. 203 (D. Mass. 1992) (in finding that component parts of Lotus interface program were protected, Judge Keeton modified the three-part test to explicitly include the language of 102(b)); *Brown Bag Software v. Symantec Corp.*, 960 F.2d 1465 (9th Cir.), *cert. denied*, 113 S. Ct. 198 (1992); *Apple Computer, Inc. v. Microsoft Corp.*, 799 F. Supp. 1006 (N.D. Cal. 1992) (in finding that defendant did not infringe the Apple user interface, the court rejected the *Whelan* approach and examined the user interface in light of the doctrines of merger, *scenes à faire*, originality, and § 102(b)).

[46] 982 F.2d 693 (2d Cir. 1992).

defendant marketed a computer program that performed similar functions on IBM mainframe computers. Although the defendant's first version of the program had directly used significant parts of the code structure, the second version contained no program code in common with the plaintiff's software. The defendant conceded liability for copyright infringement for the first version of the program while denying that the second version infringed the plaintiff's copyright. The similarity between the programs, however, raised the question of how far copyright should go to protect the nonliteral elements of a program.

In rejecting the *Whelan* bright line approach, *Altai* adopted a practical inquiry based on the Learned Hand abstractions test. The *Altai* inquiry involves three stages of analysis: abstraction, filtration, comparison. First, one must abstract the program into various layers of generality. Here, in a manner similar to reverse engineering, a court should dissect the copyrighted program's structure and isolate each level of abstraction in it. Second, the merger doctrine can be used to filter out those elements of the program dictated by efficiency or by factors external to the program itself — *e.g.,* mechanical specifications, compatibility requirements — or those taken from the public domain. When abstraction and filtration are accomplished, the third step involves comparing the remaining elements with the corresponding elements of defendant's work. In *Altai*, the court agreed with the district court that the programs were not substantially similar. The court found that defendant's program contained protectible elements similar to plaintiff's program. These similarities, however, were not sufficiently material to the overall program to uphold a finding of infringement.

Although its exact contours are unclear, *Altai* clearly narrows the scope of protection for nonliteral components of computer programs. The tripartite test seems appropriate because it provides a practical framework for distinguishing protectible from unprotectible expression.[47] Its weakness is that it provides little substantive guidance apart from its analytical framework superimposed on a vague and contradictory body of case law. Over time, however, the court's abstraction-filtration-comparison test may provide a useful framework to decide future cases.

§ 9.6 Substantial Similarity in the Litigation Process

[A] Generally

Deciding whether defendant has created a substantially similar work presents special difficulties in the litigation process. The problem is how to present this issue in practical form so that the trier of fact can analyze the question properly. Substantial similarity is a question of fact, but it is a complex question of ultimate fact much like a determination of negligence. For such complex determinations, courts may

---

[47] Not all commentators support *Altai*'s approach; *see* Arthur R. Miller, *Copyright Protection for Computer Programs, Databases, and Computer-Generated Works: Is Anything New Since CONTU?*, 106 Harv. L. Rev. 977, 1001–11 (1993) (arguing that *Altai* merely refines the idea-expression framework begun in *Whelan*, rather than making a complete break with *Whelan*).

present a single question to the trier of fact or break it down into separate issues. Although the proper method of analyzing substantial similarity is still a point of controversy, the courts have generally adopted some form of the ordinary observer or audience test.

[B] The Ordinary Observer or Audience Test

The ordinary observer or audience test is based on the subjective reactions of lay observers. For example, suppose the infringement issue concerns the substantial similarity of two songs. Under the ordinary observer or audience test, the trier of fact would be asked whether defendant took from plaintiff's work so much of what is pleasing to the ears of lay listeners, who comprise the audience for whom such popular music is composed. That is, did defendant wrongfully appropriate something which belonged to the plaintiff.[48] Under the ordinary observer or audience test, neither expert testimony, detailed analysis, nor dissection are a proper basis for determining whether works are substantially similar.[49] Rather, the trier of fact is to fall back on an immediate, visceral reaction to the two works and should consider their total concept and feel. If fabric designs are involved, the ultimate question to be asked is whether the ordinary observer tends to see the works as the same.[50] Similarly, for infringement of a novel by a movie, an ordinary person who has recently read the novel and viewed the movie should detect the piracy without resorting to critical analysis by experts. The reaction of the public to the matter should be both spontaneous and immediate.[51]

Courts have varied in their application of the audience test. Some have used it as the sole measure of infringement, holding that substantial similarity poses just one question: would an average lay observer recognize the alleged copy as having been appropriated from the copyrighted work?[52]

Using the ordinary observer test alone has the advantage of simplicity, but may lead the trier of fact to overlook important issues regarding substantial similarity.[53] Although it may be appropriate for determining whether two fabric designs or popular songs are substantially similar, the ordinary observer test may be less

---

[48] *Arnstein v. Porter*, 154 F.2d 464, 468 (2d Cir. 1946). The term "average lay observer" is not the exclusive term. Other interchangeable terms are the "ordinary reasonable person," and "ordinary lay observer." *See Brubaker v. King*, 505 F.2d 534 (7th Cir. 1974); *International Luggage Registry v. Avery Products Corp.*, 541 F.2d 830, 831 (9th Cir. 1976).

[49] *See Roth Greeting Cards v. United Card Co.*, 429 F.2d 1106, 1110 (9th Cir. 1970); *Bevan v. Columbia Broadcasting System, Inc.*, 329 F. Supp. 601 (S.D.N.Y. 1971).

[50] *See Novelty Textile Mills, Inc. v. Joan Fabrics Corp.*, 558 F.2d 1090 (2d Cir. 1977).

[51] *Harold Lloyd Corp. v. Witwer*, 65 F.2d 1 (9th Cir. 1933).

[52] *See Ideal Toy Corp. v. Fab-Lu Ltd.*, 266 F. Supp. 755, 756 (S.D.N.Y. 1965), *aff'd*, 360 F.2d 1021 (2d Cir. 1966); *Ideal Toy Corp. v. Kenner Prods. Div. of General Mills Fun Group, Inc.*, 443 F. Supp. 291, 303 n. 11. (S.D.N.Y. 1977).

[53] For an excellent discussion of the limitations of the ordinary observer test, see Amy B. Cohen, *Masking Copyright Decisionmaking: The Meaninglessness of Substantial Similarity*, 20 U.C. Davis L. Rev. 719, 733 (1987).

well-suited when more complex works are involved, such as those adapted into different media.[54] For infringement of software programs it is particularly meaningless.[55]

What are the perceived shortcomings of the ordinary observer test? Because it looks at the totality of the works and eschews dissection and use of expert testimony, it is ultimately concerned with surface illusion and the appearance of copying, not its reality. This can lead the trier of fact to find infringement in works independently created, while overlooking situations where a wholesale appropriation has taken place. Professor Nimmer makes the point that an audience's impression of infringement is not the same as actual infringement. He argues that without self-consciously analyzing the similarities and differences between two works, the audience will overlook the similarities between them, particularly for infringement in a different medium. Expression of an author's work in a different medium often hides the resemblances.[56] As a result, by relying solely on the ordinary observer test, the trier of fact may fail to analyze properly whether a work was independently created.

An equally serious criticism is that under an ordinary observer test, the trier of fact may not distinguish between the copying of ideas and the copying of expression. An ordinary observer test alone does not provide the analytical basis necessary to distinguish between similarity derived from copying of expression and similarity due to copying non-copyrightable materials. For these reasons, courts have generally looked to a framework which uses the ordinary observer test, but which also avoids its obvious limitations. The current approach is a two-step process known generally as the "bifurcated test."

[C] Bifurcated Tests: *Arnstein* and *Krofft*

In *Arnstein v. Porter*[57] the court used a bifurcated approach to evaluate whether the works at issue were substantially similar. In this two-step approach, the trier of fact was first to decide whether the defendant copied plaintiff's work. If copying was proved, the trier of fact was then to proceed to the second step: whether the copying amounted to an improper appropriation.

The bifurcated submission of issues first articulated in *Arnstein* avoids certain drawbacks of a simple audience test, allowing the trier of fact to examine the works in different ways for different purposes. On the first issue, the trier of fact examines each work in detail, dissecting them as to their protectible and unprotectible aspects. Most importantly, expert testimony can be used in this "copying" step. If copying has been proved, the second issue, that of unlawful appropriation, is proved by using

---

[54] *See Bevan v. Columbia Broadcasting System, Inc.*, 329 F. Supp. 601, 604 n. 3 (S.D.N.Y. 1971) (finding infringement of novel adapted into film).

[55] *See Whelan Associates, Inc. v. Jaslow Dental Laboratory, Inc.*, 797 F.2d 1222 (3d Cir. 1986), *cert. denied*, 479 U.S. 1031 (1987).

[56] 3 *Nimmer on Copyright* § 13.03[E][2] (1993).

[57] 154 F.2d 464 (2d Cir. 1946).

the ordinary observer or audience test.**58** For this issue, the trier of fact is to rely on the subjective reaction of a lay observer.**59**

In *Sid & Marty Krofft Television Productions, Inc. v. McDonald's Corp.*,**60** the Ninth Circuit modified *Arnstein* and proposed its own two-step test to determine substantial similarity. As set forth in *Krofft*, the first step is an extrinsic test where the trier of fact compares the works for similarity of ideas. This first step is similar to the "copying" stage of *Arnstein*, and the process is one of analytical dissection aided by expert testimony. If substantial similarity of ideas is found, the court proceeds to the second step, called the "intrinsic test." Here, the trier of fact must respond to the works as an ordinary observer, without analytic dissection or use of expert testimony, to determine whether the defendant took enough of what is pleasing to the audience to be held liable.**61**

The *Krofft* test has been criticized as unduly reducing the role of the court when deciding questions of substantial similarity.**62** According to this view, the problem lies in *Krofft*'s *extrinsic* first step, in which plaintiff must prove by any appropriate means that defendant has copied the ideas in the work. Once plaintiff meets this burden, the case proceeds to the jury to determine the copying of expression under an *ordinary observer test*. *Krofft*'s extrinsic test (copying of ideas) improperly frames the inquiry. Similarity in ideas may be probative of copying but does not prove that defendant took plaintiff's protected expression. Thus, if all defendant took were plaintiff's ideas — factual matter, a discovery, method of operation, or a marketing plan — she cannot be liable for copyright infringement. For this reason, decisions since *Krofft* have broadened their inquiry under the extrinsic test, comparing the two works to determine the extent to which defendant's work incorporated the expressive elements contained in plaintiff's.**63** As for the second step in the *Krofft* analysis,

---

58 *Id.* at 473. For example, in *Arnstein*, which involved the alleged infringement of several of Cole Porter's musical compositions, the court articulated the ordinary observer test as:

> whether defendant took from plaintiff's works so much of what is pleasing to the ears of lay listeners, who comprise the audience for whom such popular music is composed, that defendant wrongfully appropriated something which belongs to plaintiff.

59 The terms "ordinary observer test" and "audience test" are used interchangeably. The term "audience" suggests something specific: that substantial similarity should be judged not only by spectator reactions, but by a specific audience composed of people who possess specialized tastes, skills, or knowledge as compared with the average lay observer or the general public. It is not always clear whether courts make the distinction, but some do by assessing the overall effect of the works on the intended audience. *See Clarion Textile Corp. v. Slifka*, 223 F. Supp. 950 (S.D.N.Y. 1961) (dress design); *Arnstein v. Porter*, 154 F.2d 464 (2d Cir. 1946) (musical compositions); *Clarke v. G. A. Kayser and Sons, Inc.*, 472 F. Supp. 481 (W.D. Pa. 1979), *aff'd mem.*, 631 F.2d 725 (3d Cir. 1980) (children's audience for baseball gloves). *See generally* Michael F. Sitzer, *Copyright Infringement Actions: The Proper Role for Audience Reactions in Determining Substantial Similarity*, 54 S. Cal. L. Rev. 385 (1981) (advocating need for clear recognition of the audience test as opposed to a general lay observer test in determining substantial similarity).

60 562 F.2d 1157 (9th Cir. 1977).

61 *Id.* at 1165.

62 *See* 3 *Nimmer on Copyright* § 13.03[E] (1993).

63 *See Shaw v. Lindheim*, 919 F.2d 1353 (9th Cir. 1990).

the intrinsic test, the trend in the Ninth Circuit appears to be to incorporate the more traditional "audience test" in addition to *Krofft*'s "total concept and feel" formulation.[64]

Although it is too early to tell, it would appear that the changes in the *Krofft* test for infringement will render plaintiff's task more difficult in getting a case to the jury in the Ninth Circuit. In general, plaintiffs have had a harder time in overcoming defendant's motion for summary judgment in an *Arnstein* jurisdiction. Under the first step in *Arnstein*, plaintiff has a greater burden in getting the case to the jury because the court may consider both the copying of expression as well as the copying of ideas — that is, a comparison of both protectible and non-protectible material. Thus, the *Arnstein* approach gives the court greater control over the litigation and the ability to dispose of cases before trial as a matter of law than does the *Krofft* approach as originally articulated.

Whatever their merits, the *Krofft* and *Arnstein* bifurcated tests are probably impossible to apply as intended. It is unrealistic to require juries to first dissect a work to determine whether copying has occurred (*Arnstein*) or whether there are similarities in the ideas between the works (*Krofft*). After dissecting the works and listening to expert testimony under the first step of *Arnstein* or *Krofft*, the jury is then asked to forget what they have just heard and apply the second step to determine improper appropriation (*Arnstein*) or copying of expression (*Krofft*). These bifurcated tests require that juries postpone making an immediate overall assessment of the works at issue.[65] The ideal jury in an action for copyright infringement must have a conveniently short, collective memory in order to keep each submission separate and distinct. Such a jury panel probably does not exist.

§ 9.7 Improper Appropriation: Need for a Flexible Approach

It may not be possible to formulate one all-purpose method of administering the substantial similarity issue in the litigation process. The range of copyrighted works and the particular interests involved call for a flexible approach to the issue of substantial similarity and the way it is submitted to the jury. The court should be able to adapt its test of substantial similarity to the medium involved, the variety of copyrightable subject matter, and the fact situation. For example, a single ordinary observer test may be all that is needed in less complicated fabric design or popular music cases. For more complicated literary works, experts may play a useful role in determining whether copying has taken place, and in separating protectible and non-protectible aspects of the work. In either event, the court must exercise control over the litigation process in deciding whether the trier of fact should be allowed to evaluate piracy from an ordinary observer standpoint. In other situations, however, neither the ordinary observer nor the bifurcated test may be appropriate, particularly when complex, difficult media, such as computer programs are involved.

---

[64] *Id.* at 1358.

[65] For a discussion of this point, see Julie J. Bisceglia, *Summary Judgment on Substantial Similarity in Copyright Actions*, 16 Hastings Comm. & Ent. L.J. 51, 82 (1993).

In these instances, the court should adopt a single substantial similarity test admitting both lay and expert testimony, a trend which is developing in the case law.[66]

PART II: REMEDIES

§ 9.8 Preliminary Injunctions

Section 502(a)[67] of the 1976 Act allows a court to grant, at its discretion, both preliminary (temporary) and permanent (final) injunctions. The test for granting injunctions is that

> there must be a showing of possible irreparable injury [to the copyright] owner and either (1) probable success on the merits, or (2) sufficiently serious questions going to the merits to make them a fair ground for litigation and a balance of hardships tipping decidedly toward the party requesting the preliminary relief.[68]

As indicated above, the threshold question in granting a preliminary injunction is the proof of irreparable harm. Accordingly, preliminary injunctions are normally granted where delay would deprive plaintiff of relief and cause him irreparable harm. Typically, these situations occur where plaintiff's work has a short commercial life, for example, fabric designs, and where delay until final relief would effectively deny relief.[69] Alternatively, when damages alone would be adequate, a preliminary injunction will not be issued. Although a showing of irreparable harm is normally required, courts have held that such harm may be presumed when the plaintiff makes out a *prima facie* case of infringement.[70]

Even if plaintiff does not receive a preliminary injunction, a permanent injunction may be issued if there is the probability of continuing infringement. A permanent injunction is not issued as a matter of course, and the plaintiff must show a threat of further infringement to receive this remedy.[71] A copyright owner who has obtained either a preliminary or a permanent injunction can enforce it against a defendant located anywhere in the United States.[72]

---

[66] *See Whelan Associates, Inc. v. Jaslow Dental Laboratory, Inc.*, 797 F.2d 1222 (3d Cir. 1986), *cert. denied*, 479 U.S. 1031 (1987); *E. F. Johnson Co. v. Uniden Corp. of America*, 623 F. Supp. 1485 (D. Minn. 1985).

[67] 17 U.S.C. § 502(a).

[68] *Caulfield v. Board of Education*, 583 F.2d 605, 610 (2d Cir. 1978); *Association of American Medical Colleges v. Carey*, 482 F. Supp. 1358, 1364 (N.D.N.Y. 1980).

[69] *Novelty Textile Mills, Inc. v. Joan Fabrics Corp.*, 558 F.2d 1090 (2d Cir. 1977).

[70] *See Educational Testing Service v. Katzman*, 793 F.2d 533, 543–44 (3d Cir. 1986); *Hasbro Bradley, Inc. v. Sparkle Toys, Inc.*, 780 F.2d 189, 192 (2d Cir. 1985); *Apple Computer, Inc. v. Franklin Computer Corp.*, 714 F.2d 1240, 1254 (3d Cir. 1983), *cert. dismissed*, 464 U.S. 1033 (1984).

[71] *Shapiro, Bernstein & Co. v. 4636 S. Vermont Ave., Inc.*, 367 F.2d 236 (9th Cir. 1966).

[72] 17 U.S.C. § 502(b); H.R. Rep. No. 94–1476, 94th Cong., 2d Sess. 160 (1976).

§ 9.9   Impounding and Destruction of Infringing Articles

Under § 503(a)[73] of the 1976 Act, the court may order the impounding of all copies and phonorecords claimed to have been used to violate the copyright owner's exclusive rights. This remedy extends as well to

. . . all plates, molds, matrices, masters, tapes, film negatives, or other articles by means of which such copies or phonorecords may be reproduced.[74]

It may also be applied against items which, though reproduced and acquired lawfully, have been used for infringing purposes such as rentals, performances and displays.[75] Impounding orders are not issued *ex parte*, and defendant has a right to an adversarial hearing.[76] An *ex parte* impounding order may violate the Fifth Amendment guarantee against the taking of property without due process of law, and may constitute a suppression of speech under the First Amendment.[77]

On final judgment or decree, the court may order destruction or other reasonable disposition of the infringing articles.[78] Although destruction of the article is available as a remedy, it is not the favored solution. More often the court will choose other dispositions, such as ordering the articles sold or delivered to plaintiff, to avoid needless waste while serving the ends of justice.[79]

§ 9.10   Damages and Profits: Generally

According to § 504, a copyright infringer is liable for either:

(1) the copyright owner's actual damages and any additional profits of the infringer, or

(2) statutory damages.[80]

This provision generously allows the plaintiff to recover either actual damages and profits, or statutory damages. Plaintiff may choose the category of recovery at any time before final judgment.[81]

§ 9.11   Actual Damages and Profits: The Prohibition Against Double Counting

Although the 1976 Act allows recovery of both damages and profits, plaintiff can only recover profits which are not taken into account when computing actual

---

[73] 17 U.S.C. § 503(a).

[74] *Id.*

[75] H.R. Rep. No. 94–1476, 94th Cong., 2d Sess. 160 (1976).

[76] *WPOW, Inc. v. MRLJ Enterprises*, 584 F. Supp. 132 (D.D.C. 1984).

[77] *See* 3 *Nimmer on Copyright* § 14.07 (1993)).

[78] 17 U.S.C. § 503(b).

[79] *See* H.R. Rep. No. 94–1476, 94th Cong., 2d Sess. 160 (1976).

[80] 17 U.S.C. § 504(c)(1).

[81] *Id.*

302 □ UNDERSTANDING COPYRIGHT LAW, SECOND EDITION   § 9.12

damages.[82] In other words, double recovery is not allowed. Most often a plaintiff will have to choose between actual damages or profits because they represent the same harm, but the possibility of recovering both damages and profits remains. For example, assume that the plaintiff has created a decorative poster that defendant has infringed. Plaintiff can recover either the lost sales he would have made as actual damages or defendant's profits from the sale of the infringing posters. If defendant's profits were $10,000, plaintiff could recover the entire amount, but could not recover for the diminution of sales in the same market, because this would constitute a double counting, *i.e.*, two recoveries for the same harm. On the other hand, if plaintiff could show that the infringing posters were of inferior quality and damaged plaintiff's future ability to sell his own, or that he lost a major client because of the infringement, not reflected in defendant's sales, the diminution of market value amount could be recovered as damages because it was not reflected in defendant's profits.[83]

Both damages and profits must be proved without employing undue speculation.[84] But some courts have made plaintiff's task easier, holding that once the fact of damage is proved, the extent of the harm does not have to be proved to exact certainty.[85]

§ 9.12   Recovery of Profits

[A]   Advantages to Claiming Lost Profits

Because actual damages are difficult to prove, most plaintiffs concentrate on recovering defendant's profits. Plaintiff is aided by § 504(b) of the 1976 Act, which provides that

> [i]n establishing the infringer's profits, the copyright owner is required to present proof only of infringer's gross revenue. . . .[86]

The defendant then has the burden of proving deductible expenses and elements of profit due to factors other than the infringed work.[87] Which costs can be deducted, how to allocate the costs incurred by the infringing activity, and which profits should be attributable to the infringement have presented difficult problems in infringement litigation.

---

[82] 17 U.S.C. § 504(b); H.R. Rep. No. 94–1476, 94th Cong., 2d Sess. 161 (1976). The 1976 Act departs from the 1909 Act under which a copyright holder could receive a cumulative award of his own damages and the infringer's profits. *See Thomas Wilson & Co. v. Irving J. Dorfman Co.*, 433 F.2d 409, 413 (2d Cir. 1970).

[83] *See Abeshouse v. Ultragraphics, Inc.*, 754 F.2d 467 (2d Cir. 1985) (recognizing the possibility of cumulative damages in addition to profits). In the actual case, plaintiff's proof was not sufficient on this issue to obtain an award.

[84] *See Stevens Linen Associates, Inc. v. Mastercraft Corp.*, 656 F.2d 11, 14 (2d Cir. 1981).

[85] *See Deltak, Inc. v. Advanced Systems, Inc.*, 574 F. Supp. 400, 411 (N.D. Ill. 1983).

[86] 17 U.S.C. § 504(b).

[87] H.R. Rep. No. 94–1476, 94th Cong., 2d Sess. 161 (1976).

[B] Costs Defendant May Deduct

Because the 1976 Act does not specify which expenses defendant can deduct, one has to look to the body of case law for answers. The case law has held that almost all expenses proven with reasonable certainty are deductible if related to producing and selling the infringing work. These expenses normally encompass taxes, royalties to writers, advertising costs, overhead, and material developed to produce the infringing work.[88]

Infringers of a motion picture, popular song, or work of graphic art are often simultaneously engaged in non-infringing activities which share costs with the infringing activity. The general rule is that defendant can deduct only those costs related to the infringing activity. Deciphering which costs are related to the infringement and which are related to the non-infringing aspects of defendant's business poses both practical and theoretical difficulties. For example, one puzzling question of cost allocation is how to treat overhead. In general, overhead can be deducted if defendant proves that it actually contributed to the infringement. Alternatively, defendant cannot deduct overhead if he would have incurred these costs absent the infringement.[89] Mathematical certainty in overhead cost deduction is often impossible and a proportional allocation of overhead expenses to the infringing activity will be accepted if reasonable.[90] Uncertainty about any deduction is resolved in favor of the plaintiff, since defendant has the burden of proof on all cost deduction issues.

[C] Apportionment of Profits to Infringing Activity

Plaintiff can only recover those profits attributable to the infringement.[91] This apportionment issue arises in two situations. One occurs when infringing materials become commingled with non-infringing materials, for example, when one infringing song is placed on an album containing ten songs. Another related pattern occurs when factors other than the use of defendant's work are responsible for some of the profits, for example, if the success of an infringing song is due to the efforts of a famous singer.

Defendant, who has the burden of proof on this issue, can effectively reduce plaintiff's recovery. To illustrate, suppose that plaintiff's novel is made into a motion picture, but has been changed drastically in the process. Suppose also that the movie has become a great success, much more so than the novel, partly because of the changed story line taken from the novel, but also because of famous stars who play the key roles. Proof that defendant's success was attributable to aspects other than the copyrighted work can drastically reduce the percentage of recoverable profits. This example is similar to a leading case on the issue, *Sheldon v. Metro-Goldwyn*

---

[88] *See, e.g., Cream Records, Inc. v. Jos. Schlitz Brewing Co.*, 754 F.2d 826 (9th Cir. 1985) (advertising expenses); *Kamar Int'l, Inc. v. Russ Berrie & Co., Inc.*, 752 F.2d 1327 (9th Cir. 1984) (overhead expenses).

[89] *See Taylor v. Meirick*, 712 F.2d 1112 (7th Cir. 1983).

[90] *Frank Music Corp. v. Metro-Goldwyn-Mayer, Inc.*, 772 F.2d 505, 516 (9th Cir. 1985).

[91] 17 U.S.C. § 504(b).

Pictures Corp.,[92] where the Supreme Court allowed a twenty percent recovery of defendant's profits from the motion picture *Letty Lynton* as attributable to plaintiff's copyrighted play. The motion picture's success was in large part due to aspects unrelated to the copyrighted work, such as the famous movie stars and the MGM screenplay. Despite the virtually impossible task of exact apportionment, *Sheldon* stands for the principle that, when there is a reasonable basis for apportionment, the Court should attempt to apportion, even though error in the process might favor the plaintiff. Of course, mathematical exactness can never be achieved, but to grant plaintiff all the profits would impose an undue penalty on the defendant.[93]

§ 9.13 Statutory Damages

[A] Generally

Damages and profits may not always be a practical remedy for an aggrieved copyright owner. Often, damages to the market for a copyrighted work are difficult to prove. And as for profits, an inefficient infringer may not have made any money from the infringement. Accordingly, the 1976 Act allows a plaintiff in this situation to elect recovery of statutory damages instead of damages and profits. This option to choose statutory damages is open at any time before final judgment.[94] The one major limitation on recovery of statutory damages is that this remedy cannot be sought for infringements commenced before plaintiff has properly registered the copyright, except in the case of published works, which must be registered within three months after publication.[95]

[B] The Method of Computing Statutory Damages

The decision to opt for statutory damages resides with the plaintiff, but the amount of those damages is within the court's discretion.[96] For most infringements, the court may award no less than $500 or more than $20,000.[97] But if the copyright owner can prove willful infringement,[98] the amount can be increased at the court's discretion up to $100,000.[99] If the infringer proves that he or she was unaware of

[92] 309 U.S. 390 (1940).

[93] *See also Abkco Music, Inc. v. Harrisongs Music, Ltd.*, 508 F. Supp. 798 (S.D.N.Y. 1981), *aff'd*, 722 F.2d 988 (2d Cir. 1983) (70% of profits awarded for infringing song reproduced on the flip side of a record), and *MCA Inc. v. Wilson*, 677 F.2d 180 (2d Cir. 1981) (for use of song in musical show, 5% of the profits assessed for infringement).

[94] 17 U.S.C. § 504(c)(1).

[95] 17 U.S.C. § 412. For a discussion of registration formalities, see § 7.5, *supra*.

[96] 17 U.S.C. § 504(c).

[97] 17 U.S.C. § 504(c)(1). For causes of action arising before March 1, 1989, the maximum is $10,000 and the minimum is $250.

[98] "Willfulness" in this context has generally been defined as *knowing* infringement, a more culpable state of mind than a mere intent to infringe. *See* 3 *Nimmer on Copyright* § 14.04[B][3] (1993).

[99] *See* 17 U.S.C. § 504(c)(2). For causes of action arising before March 1, 1989, the maximum amount is $50,000. *See, e.g., Lauratex Textile Corp. v. Allton Knitting Mills*, 517 F. Supp. 900 (S.D.N.Y. 1981).

the infringement, or had no reason to know the acts were infringing, the court has the discretion to reduce recovery to $200.[100] As an exception to the right to recover statutory damages, the 1976 Act specifically disallows them where employees of non-profit educational institutions, libraries, archives, or public broadcasting entities, acting within the scope of their employment, infringe a copyrighted work, having reasonable grounds for believing their acts constituted fair use under § 107.[101] In this situation, statutory damages cannot be recovered.

[C] The Problem of Multiple Infringements

The minimum and maximum amounts recoverable as statutory damages in copyright infringement apply regardless of how many times a defendant has infringed the work or whether the infringing acts were separate, simultaneous, or occurred sequentially.[102] For example, suppose defendant creates an audiovisual work using footage from plaintiff's copyrighted work, and then performs the work hundreds of times in various cities over a two-year period. For these infringing acts, plaintiff can recover only a single award. The extent of the single award, however, will be affected by the number of infringements, as well as by factors including the gravity of the infringement and defendant's fault.

Alternatively, where the suit involves infringement of more than one work, at least minimum statutory damages must be awarded for each work infringed.[103] For example, if defendant's musical review infringes three copyrighted tunes, the copyright owner can recover at least $1500 ($500 x 3) or up to $60,000 ($20,000 x 3) for the infringement.[104]

[D] Multiple Plaintiffs and Defendants

The copyright owner can recover minimum to maximum statutory damages for each copyrighted work infringed, but multiple copyright owners cannot recover statutory damages in separate actions for infringement of their exclusive rights.[105] The one-recovery limitation prevents statutory damages from becoming inordinately extensive where exclusive rights may be divided infinitely under the 1976 Act. For example, suppose defendant has infringed a work of art by reproducing and displaying it. Under the 1976 Act, exclusive rights are infinitely divisible, and each respective owner of the reproduction and display rights has standing to bring suit. Even though A may own the reproduction rights and B may own the display rights, only one recovery of statutory damages will be allowed for the infringing acts.

---

100 17 U.S.C. § 504(c)(2). For causes of action arising after March 1, 1989, a defendant cannot assert a defense of innocent infringement in mitigation of actual or statutory damages when proper notice of copyright appears on published copies or phonorecords of the work to which defendant had access. *See* 17 U.S.C. §§ 401(d) and 402(d). For a discussion of this notice provision, see § 4.10[D] and [E], *supra*.

101 *Id.*

102 H.R. Rep. No. 94–1476, 94th Cong., 2d Sess. 162 (1976).

103 *Id.*

104 The award could be reduced to 3 x $200 for innocent infringement or increased to 3 x $100,000 for willful infringement.

105 H.R. Rep. No. 94–1476, 94th Cong., 2d Sess. 162 (1976).

When multiple defendants are involved, whether plaintiff can recover a full amount from each depends on their status as related defendants. If the defendants are related,[106] for example, two persons who in concert infringe copyright, they are jointly and severally liable and only one recovery can be obtained against any one or all of the defendants. Alternatively, if the defendants are unrelated, as for example, where two record companies independent of each other produce infringing versions of the same copyrighted song, plaintiff may recover two statutory damage awards.[107]

§ 9.14   Costs and Attorney's Fees

Costs and attorney's fees are available in a suit for copyright infringement and are entirely at the court's discretion.[108] The copyright must be registered to recover attorney's fees (not costs), as is required to recover statutory damages.[109]

Reasonable attorney's fees may be given to the "prevailing party." This term of art, undefined in the 1976 Act, merits explanation. The prevailing party can be either plaintiff or defendant, and is the party who was successful at the conclusion of all proceedings, not just trial on the merits. Unlike patent law, which limits attorney's fees to exceptional cases,[110] courts in copyright cases have routinely awarded attorney's fees to prevailing plaintiffs, even though willful infringement has not been proved. In determining the amount of "reasonable" attorney's fees, courts may consider the counsel's skill and reputation, the actual fee charged, the amount of work expended, the monetary recovery allowed, and the result achieved at trial.[111]

When the prevailing party was the defendant, however, courts had tended to allow recovery of attorney's fees only if the plaintiff brought the action frivolously or in bad faith.[112] Defendant did not have to show subjective bad faith on plaintiff's part, although a showing that plaintiff actually knew of the invalidity of the claims would be a strong indication of bad faith.[113]

Why allow recovery of attorney's fees more readily to the prevailing plaintiff than to the prevailing defendant? When the plaintiff prevails, attorney's fees theoretically work as a deterrent against future infringement. But when the defendant is the prevailing party, this policy no longer applies and the courts must look instead to

---

[106] For a discussion of related defendants, see § 9.20, *infra*.

[107] H.R. Rep. No. 94–1476, 94th Cong., 2d Sess. 162 (1976).

[108] 17 U.S.C. § 505.

[109] 17 U.S.C. § 412. *See* § 7.6, *supra*.

[110] 35 U.S.C. § 285.

[111] *Quinto v. Legal Times of Washington, Inc.*, 511 F. Supp. 579 (D.D.C. 1981); *Moorish Vanguard Concert v. Brown*, 498 F. Supp. 830 (E.D. Pa. 1980).

[112] *Jartech, Inc. v. Clancy*, 666 F.2d 403 (9th Cir.), *cert. denied*, 459 U.S. 826 (1982). For an overview of the dual standard in awarding attorney's fees, see Robert S. LaPlante, *Awarding Attorney's Fees in Copyright Infringement Cases: The Sensible Use of a Dual Standard*, 51 Alb. L. Rev. 239 (1987).

[113] *Hughes v. Novi American, Inc.*, 724 F.2d 122 (Fed. Cir. 1984).

the fault, if any, of the plaintiff in bringing the action in bad faith. Thus, stronger policy considerations merit recovery of attorney's fees for prevailing plaintiffs.

In *Fogerty v. Fantasy Inc.*,[114] the United States Supreme Court overruled the case law supporting the favored treatment of plaintiffs on the issue of attorney's fees. The Court held that Congress intended no such disparity between plaintiffs and defendants when, in the 1976 Act, it permitted judges to award a reasonable attorney's fee to the prevailing party. *Fogerty* reverses the accepted rule in the Second, Ninth, Seventh, and District of Columbia Circuits in which attorney's fees were awarded to the prevailing plaintiff as a matter of course. In addition to abrogating the double standard for plaintiffs and defendants, the Court rejected the notion that attorney's fees should be automatic for any prevailing party. According to the Court, if Congress meant reimbursement to be automatic, it would not have used the words "may award" in the 1976 Act. Rather the award of attorney's fees is in the court's discretion.

Writing for the Court, Justice Rehnquist declared that the policies underlying federal copyright law were served not only by vigorous prosecution of copyright claims, but also by vigorous defense against them.[115] Because the boundaries of the copyright monopoly should be demarcated as clearly as possible, the law should encourage defendants to litigate meritorious defenses as vigorously as it should encourage plaintiffs to advance their claims for infringement. Thus, a system that favors plaintiffs in awarding attorney's fees distorts this boundary-making function of copyright litigation and, as such, conflicts with the underlying goals of copyright law.

Although *Fogerty* settled a long-standing conflict in copyright law, it did not specify what standard the courts should use in applying their discretion to award attorney's fees. Probably, the factors supporting an award of attorney's fees will include the frivolousness, motivation, and the objective unreasonableness of the suit.[116] It will probably take some time for the district courts to elaborate on the factors to be considered in exercising their discretion. Whatever elements the courts use, *Fogerty* will probably reduce the incentive to bring suits for infringement. The number of copyright infringement claims might diminish somewhat now that prevailing defendants as well as plaintiffs may recover attorney's fees, but only at the court's discretion, that is non-automatically. The effect of this ruling may well be significant in two important Circuits for copyright matters, the Second and Ninth, that had traditionally awarded attorney's fees automatically to prevailing plaintiffs.

Full costs may also be awarded at the court's discretion[117] against any party except the United States or one of its officers. Full costs are generally not assessed unless some degree of fault or bad faith is shown. Costs recovered have included

---

[114] 114 S. Ct. 1023 (1994).

[115] *Id.* at 1030.

[116] See, *e.g., Lieb v. Topstone Industries Inc.*, 788 F.2d 151, 156 (3d Cir. 1986) for a discussion of the various factors.

[117] 17 U.S.C. § 505. Under the 1909 Act, recovery of full costs was mandatory. 17 U.S.C. § 116 (1909 Act). *See* 3 *Nimmer on Copyright* § 14.09 (1993).

amounts for filing fees, marshal's fees, transcripts, service of process, depositions, photocopying, and postage.[118]

The 1976 Act does not recognize punitive damages.[119] However, the assessment of costs and attorney's fees, as well as statutory damages ($100,000 for willful infringement), can serve much the same deterrent purpose as punitive damages in an infringement action.

§ 9.15   Criminal Penalties

In addition to the remedies available to the copyright owner in a civil action, the government may subject the defendant to criminal penalties.

Under Section 506(a) of the 1976 Act and 18 U.S.C. § 2319,[120] anyone "who infringes a copyright willfully and for purpose of commercial advantage . . . or private financial gain" is subject to felony or misdemeanor punishment. The felony provisions were overhauled in 1992. With the 1992 amendments, the felony copyright statute was for the first time generic in protection of copyrighted works rather than focused on particular categories such as sound recordings, motion pictures, or audiovisual works. Although all copyrighted works are included within the criminal provision, the principal motivation of the amendments was to deter the multibillion dollar business of computer software copyright infringement.[121]

Under this amendment, felony liability will arise where, during any 180-day period, at least 10 copies or phonorecords of one or more copyrighted works having a retail value of more than $2500 are reproduced or distributed without the authorization of the copyright owner. The maximum penalty for such a violation is imprisonment for not more than five years or a fine[122] or both. Second or subsequent offenses will result in a maximum of ten years' imprisonment. Where the requisite number of copies is not made within the specified time periods, or the infringing acts are other than reproduction or distribution, misdemeanor liability will lie. The court may also order forfeiture, destruction, or other disposition of infringing copies and equipment used in their manufacture.

Other provisions of § 506 of the 1976 Act impose criminal sanctions for the fraudulent intent to place copyright notice on any article with knowledge of its falsehood,[123] for removing or altering copyright notice with fraudulent intent,[124] and for knowing, false representation of a material fact in an application for

---

[118] *Quinto v. Legal Times of Washington, Inc.*, 511 F. Supp. 579 (D.D.C. 1981).

[119] The Second Circuit Court of Appeals in *Oboler v. Goldin*, 714 F.2d 211 (2d Cir. 1983), specifically rejected use of punitive damages in statutory copyright infringements.

[120] 17 U.S.C. § 506(a); 18 U.S.C. § 2319.

[121] Act of October 28, 1992 Pub. L. No. 102–561, 106 Stat. 4233. *See* H.R. Rep. No. 102–997, 102d Cong. 2d Sess. (1992).

[122] *See* 18 U.S.C. § 3571(b) (individuals); or 18 U.S.C. § 3571(c) (organizations).

[123] 17 U.S.C. § 506(c).

[124] 17 U.S.C. § 506(d).

copyright registration.[125] These violations carry a maximum penalty of not more than $2,500.

Criminal actions have usually been brought against large-scale, systematic pirates of sound recordings and motion pictures. In general, the government does not have a successful record of curbing criminal infringement actions, largely because of the burden of proof required in a criminal suit. In *U.S. v. Atherton*,[126] involving motion picture tape piracy, the court held that the government was required to prove the following five elements: (1) infringement of copyright (2) of a work that has not been subject to a first sale (3) done willfully (4) with knowledge that the copyrighted work has not been the subject of a first sale and (5) for profit. The difficult element has proved to be whether a criminal defendant knew that the tapes were *not* the subject of a first sale.[127] Unlike the civil preponderance-of-the-evidence standard, the prosecution must prove each element beyond a reasonable doubt. This heavy burden has impeded many criminal prosecutions.

The remedies provided by § 506 of the 1976 Act exhaust criminal relief for copyright violation, and the government has been prevented from using other provisions of federal criminal laws against copyright infringers. For example, in *Dowling v. United States*,[128] criminal suit was brought under the National Stolen Property Act[129] against a bootlegger of Elvis Presley recordings, who had reproduced and distributed copies of Presley's vocals. The Supreme Court limited recovery under the above Act to claims of conversion and fraud involving physical goods, and not conversion of *intangible* property, such as a copyright. After *Dowling*, it appears that federal prosecutors must use the remedies provided under § 506 to bring suit for criminal copyright infringement.

PART III: INFRINGEMENT: PROCEDURAL MATTERS

§ 9.16   Jurisdiction

[A]   "Arising Under" Jurisdiction

28 U.S.C. § 1338(a)[130] gives federal courts exclusive jurisdiction for actions arising under the Copyright Act. When does a case "arise under" the 1976 Copyright Act? According to Judge Friendly's well known synthesis of the issue:

---

[125] 17 U.S.C. § 506(e).

[126] 561 F.2d 747 (9th Cir. 1977).

[127] *See U.S. v. Wise*, 550 F.2d 1180 (9th Cir. 1977). Of course, if the government produces evidence that defendant oversaw reproduction of copies, there is no need to prove lack of first sale. *See United States v. Sachs*, 801 F.2d 839 (6th Cir. 1986). For a discussion of the first sale doctrine, see § 8.13, *supra*.

[128] 473 U.S. 207 (1985).

[129] 18 U.S.C. § 2314.

[130] The section reads:

> The district courts shall have original jurisdiction of any civil action arising under any Act of Congress relating to patents . . . copyrights and trademarks. Such jurisdiction shall be exclusive of the courts of the states in patent . . . and copyright cases.

. . . an action "arises under" the Copyright Act if and only if the complaint is for a remedy expressly granted by the Act, *e.g.*, a suit for infringement or for the statutory royalties for record reproduction . . . or asserts a claim requiring construction of the Act . . . or, at the very least and perhaps more doubtfully, presents a case where a distinctive policy of the Act requires that federal principles control the disposition of the claim. The general interest that copyrights, like all other forms of property, should be enjoyed by their true owner is not enough to meet this last test.[131]

To determine that an action arises under the 1976 Copyright Act requires distinguishing between an action based primarily on a right conferred by the 1976 Copyright Act, and an action incidentally involving issues of copyright law. A suit for statutory copyright infringement is the classic example of an action expressly conferred by copyright, where federal jurisdiction is exclusive.

By comparison, an action brought to enforce an assignment of copyright is essentially an action under contract law.[132] Here, state court jurisdiction would be exclusive, even though the state court may have to interpret aspects of copyright law to determine whether to enforce the assignment. Similarly, an action brought to enforce royalties under a licensing agreement would lie essentially in the domain of state law,[133] as would a will conveying a copyright and an action to foreclose a statutory copyright mortgage.[134]

Even where the action does not involve statutory copyright infringement, exclusive jurisdiction will be conferred if the complaint necessitates construction or application of provisions of the 1976 Copyright Act. Examples are claims as to the extent of royalties under the compulsory licensing provisions,[135] ownership of copyright under the recording priorities, or whether a work constitutes a work made for hire.[136] Actions involving federal preemption of state law also belong on the list.[137] Each of these issues concerns a distinct policy of the 1976 Act, thus requiring that federal principles be controlling.

---

[131] *T. B. Harms Co. v. Eliscu*, 339 F.2d 823, 828 (2d Cir. 1964), *cert. denied*, 381 U.S. 915 (1965); *see Schoenberg v. Shapolsky Publishers, Inc.*, 971 F.2d 926, 932–33 (2d Cir. 1992) (to determine whether a lawsuit arises under the Copyright Act first, the court must determine whether the infringement claim is only "incidental" to the "claim seeking a determination of ownership or contractual rights under the contract." Second, the court must next determine whether the complaint alleges a breach of a condition or of a contract convenant. If breach of a condition is alleged, then the district court has subject matter jurisdiction. If the breach of convenant is so material as to create a right of rescission, then the asserted claim arises under the Copyright Act.

[132] *See* 3 *Nimmer on Copyright* § 12.01[A] (1993).

[133] *Bevan v. Columbia Broadcasting System, Inc.*, 329 F. Supp. 601 (S.D.N.Y. 1971) (failure to pay royalties). *See also Wolfe v. United Artists Corp.*, 583 F. Supp. 52 (E.D. Pa. 1983).

[134] *Republic Pictures Corp. v. Security-First Nat'l Bank of L.A.*, 197 F.2d 767 (9th Cir. 1952).

[135] *T.B. Harms Co. v. Eliscu*, 339 F.2d 823 (2d Cir. 1964), *cert. denied*, 381 U.S. 915 (1965).

[136] *Royalty Control Corp. v. Sanco, Inc.*, 175 U.S.P.Q. (BNA) 641 (N.D. Cal. 1972).

[137] *Morseburg v. Balyon*, 201 U.S.P.Q. (BNA) 518 (C.D. Cal. 1978).

[B] Pendent Jurisdiction

Often a complaint will include both nonfederal as well as federal claims. Under 28 U.S.C. § 1338(a), the federal court must determine whether it has jurisdiction to decide the case under the copyright laws. In addition to copyright claims, the complaint may allege state law claims, such as breach of contract, fraud, and a variety of counts in unfair competition. The question is: once jurisdiction is conferred on the copyright claim, will the district court decide the state law claims as well? At first glance, a policy encouraging the conservation of judicial resources would suggest that all the claims should be handled in one trial. Resolution of all the claims, federal and state, before one tribunal may be desirable, but federal law limits the district courts' power to do so in all situations. Under 28 U.S.C. § 1338(b), a district court has the power to decide the nonfederal claim if three jurisdictional requirements are met: (1) the basis of the nonfederal claim must be "unfair competition," and the federal claim to which it is attached must be both (2) substantial and (3) related.[138]

The first two requirements, that the state claims be "substantial" and constitute "unfair competition" have not presented much controversy. As for the "substantiality" of the federal claim, the courts will deny jurisdiction over the state cause of action if the federal claim is denied on a pretrial motion.[139] As for the requirement that the state claim constitute "unfair competition," the courts have broadly construed that term to include claims of passing off, misappropriation, misrepresentation, conversion, trade secret misappropriation, and breach of contract.[140]

By contrast, the "related" requirement has posed the greatest problems of interpretation. Two views exist on the meaning of "related" for the purpose of pendent jurisdiction. The more restrictive view holds that the two claims are related only if they rest on substantially identical facts.[141] The more liberal view, which appears to be the current trend, holds that the two claims are related if they have the same "factual nucleus," even though they might not derive from identical facts.[142]

---

[138] 28 U.S.C. § 1367(c), amended in 1990, governs the circumstances under which district courts may decline to exercise what is now called "supplemental jurisdiction." The problem is that § 1367 does not expressly state whether it supersedes, or complements, § 1338(b). Although this provision is broad enough to include pendent claims asserted under 28 U.S.C. § 1338(b), as a specific provision relating to pendent jurisdiction in patent and copyright cases, § 1338(b) should govern. But even if § 1367 supersedes § 1338(b), because the intent of § 1367(c) is to codify factors that the Supreme Court has recognized, and those factors apply to § 1338(b), there may be no practical difference.

[139] See, e.g., Scholz Homes, Inc. v. Maddox, 379 F.2d 84, 87 (6th Cir. 1967).

[140] See, e.g., Lone Ranger Television v. Program Radio Corp., 740 F.2d 718, 724 (9th Cir. 1984) (conversion claim lies within ambit of unfair competition).

[141] See Hurn v. Oursler, 289 U.S. 238 (1933).

[142] See, e.g., Friedman, Eisenstein, Raemer & Schwartz v. Afterman, 599 F. Supp. 902 (N.D. Ill. 1984).

§ 9.17   Statute of Limitations

Section 507 of the 1976 Copyright Act provides for a three-year statute of limitations in both civil and criminal actions.[143] The three-year time period is measured from the moment in which the claim accrues,[144] and an action must be brought within the three years or it is irrevocably barred. As in other areas of the law, pinpointing exactly when a cause of action accrues under a statute of limitations can present a thorny problem. One particular conflict in the courts concerns the treatment of a series of infringing acts, where some of the acts occurred more than three years before the action was brought. Some courts would allow recovery for those acts within the statutory period while barring those more than three years old.[145] To these courts, each act of infringement is a distinct harm giving rise to an independent claim for relief. Thus, recovery will be allowed only for those acts occurring within three years of suit, and disallowed for earlier infringing acts.

Other courts have taken the opposite view. In *Taylor v. Meirick*,[146] for example, the Seventh Circuit held that if the infringing acts constituted a continuing wrong, a suit could be brought for all the acts, even those more than three years old.

Plaintiff may also toll the statute of limitations on various equitable grounds recognized by federal law, such as by defendant's fraudulent concealment of the infringement.[147] On the other hand, if defendant can show that plaintiff learned, or by reasonable diligence could have learned, that he had a cause of action, the statute of limitations will not be tolled.[148]

§ 9.18   Parties to Suit: Plaintiff's Standing

Under § 501(b) of the 1976 Act,[149] the legal or beneficial owner of an exclusive right has standing to sue for infringement.[150] The owner of an exclusive right may bring suit on his own behalf without having to join the licensor of the right in the action. By comparison, the non-exclusive licensee has no standing to bring suit. For causes of action brought before March 1, 1989, if suit is brought by anyone other

---

[143] 17 U.S.C. § 507.

[144] Strictly speaking, the language is somewhat different in the statute for civil and criminal actions. Accrual is used for civil actions, whereas the language three years "after the cause of action arose" is used for criminal actions.

[145] *See Rosette v. Rainbo Record Mfg. Corp.*, 354 F. Supp. 1183 (S.D.N.Y. 1973), *aff'd*, 546 F.2d 461 (2d Cir. 1976); *Makedwe Pub. Co. v. Johnson*, 37 F.3d 180 (5th Cir. 1994); *Stone v. Williams*, 970 F.2d 1043 (2d Cir. 1992), *cert. denied*, 113 S. Ct. 2331 (1993); *Robey v. New World Pictures, Ltd.*, 19 F.3d 479 (9th Cir. 1994).

[146] 712 F.2d 1112 (7th Cir. 1983).

[147] *Id.*

[148] *Id.*

[149] 17 U.S.C. § 501(b).

[150] 17 U.S.C. § 205(d). Related to standing is the concept of indispensable parties. Section 501(b) requires that the plaintiff serve written notice on any person whose interest is likely to be affected by a decision in the case. It is unclear under what conditions joinder should be required or permitted. *See* 3 *Nimmer on Copyright* § 12.03 (1993).

than the author, a proper recordation of the instrument of transfer and registration of copyright is a prerequisite for bringing an action for infringement.[151] For causes of action arising on or after March 1, 1989, recordation is no longer required to bring a suit for copyright infringement.[152]

§ 9.19   Standing to Sue Federal and State Governments

[A]   Federal Government

A copyright owner has a statutory right to sue the United States government in the Court of Claims.[153] Also, employees of the United States government are personally liable for their infringing acts, even if carried out in the scope of their employment.[154]

[B]   State Government: The Eleventh Amendment Issue

Whether an action for infringement could be brought against a state government consistent with the Eleventh Amendment's doctrine of sovereign immunity[155] was an ongoing issue of debate until Congress resolved the controversy by legislation in 1990. The Copyright Remedy Clarification Act of 1990 amended the Copyright Act to make states, state instrumentalities, and state officers or employees acting in their official capacity liable for copyright infringement "in the same manner and to the same extent as any non-governmental entity."[156] In addition, the amendments added a new § 511(a) to the Copyright Act, providing that no state entity, or state officer or employee acting in a official capacity, shall be immune "under the Eleventh Amendment of the Constitution of the United States or under any other doctrine of sovereign immunity, from suit in Federal court by any person, including any governmental or non-governmental entity for violation of any of the exclusive rights of copyright.[157] The abrogation of state sovereignty represents the resolution of a continuing clash between two constitutional principles, the Copyright Clause and the Eleventh Amendment to the Constitution, which insulates the states from suit in federal court.[158] Before the 1990 amendments, the trend in the case law

---

[151] 17 U.S.C. § 205(d).

[152] 17 U.S.C. § 205(d), requiring recordation as a prerequisite for bringing a suit for infringement, has been deleted by the Berne Convention Implementation Act of 1988 (Pub. L. No. 100–568 (1988)).

[153] 28 U.S.C. § 1498 (1948). It is now called the "United States Claims Court."

[154] *Towle v. Ross*, 32 F. Supp. 125 (D. Or. 1940).

[155] The Eleventh Amendment of the Constitution states:

> The Judicial power of the United States shall not be construed to extend to any suit in law or equity, commenced or prosecuted against one of the United States by Citizens of another State, or by Citizens or Subjects of any Foreign State.

[156] 17 U.S.C. § 501(a). *See* The Copyright Remedy Clarification Act of 1990, Pub. L. No. 101–553, 104 Stat. 2749 (1990).

[157] Section 511(b) of the Copyright Act, added by the 1990 amendments, makes legal and equitable remedies available against for infringing acts of states and their employees.

[158] 28 U.S.C. § 1338(a) confers exclusive jurisdiction of the federal courts over cases arising under the copyright law.

favored state immunity from suit for damages, allowing the states to freely ignore the rights of copyright owners.[159] As intensive users of copyrighted works, the states represented a real and ever present possibility for systematic abuse. This threat led to the explicit abrogation of sovereign immunity for state governmental entities.[160]

§ 9.20 Related Defendants: Vicarious Liability and Contributory Infringement

[A] Generally

Although not expressly recognized in the 1976 Act, a person can be liable as a related defendant for the infringing activity of another. This general principle is derived from § 106,[161] which grants the copyright owner the exclusive right to authorize others to exploit the exclusive rights of ownership.[162] Through this provision, the principle of related defendants is recognized in the 1976 Copyright Act. As used in following subsections, the term "related defendants" refers to all situations where one can be held liable for the acts of another, including vicarious liability and liability for contributory infringement. It is not coincidental that these terms come from the law of torts, because copyright infringement is a tort. The major focus in the following subsections is on contributory infringement, whereby one can be held liable for actively aiding another to infringe copyright.

Fact situations involving contributory infringement vary widely, but generally have the following attributes: A will be held liable for the infringing acts of B if (1) A supervises or has the power to supervise B's acts of infringement and (2) A benefits or stands to benefit financially from the infringing acts. The easiest cases to find liability for contributory infringement are those where the related defendant has actual knowledge of and comes the closest to directly participating in the infringement.

[B] Actively Inducing Another to Infringe Copyright

Several basic patterns involving related defendants as contributory infringers are apparent from the case law. In one pattern, liability is based on defendant's active

---

[159] See BV Engineering v. University of California, 657 F. Supp. 1246 (C.D. Cal. 1987) (unless Congress has expressly abrogated the immunity or the states have waived it, the states cannot be sued in federal court); Richard Anderson Photography v. Radford University, 633 F. Supp. 1154 (W.D. Va. 1986); Mihalek Corp. v. State of Michigan, 595 F. Supp. 903 (E.D. Mich. 1984); for a leading Supreme Court case, see Atascadero Hospital v. Scanlon, 473 U.S. 234, 239 (1985) (a state may be subjected to damage suits in federal courts only if the state has expressly waived immunity or Congress has expressed its unequivocal intent to abrogate immunity).

[160] For an overview of the issue, see John C. Beiter, Copyright Infringement and the Eleventh Amendment: A Doctrine of Unfair Use, 40 Vand. L. Rev. 225 (1987).

[161] 17 U.S.C. § 106.

[162] H.R. Rep. No. 94–1476, 94th Cong., 2d Sess. 159 (1976).

inducement of and all but direct participation in the infringement. For example, in *Elektra Records Co. v. Gem Electronic Distributors, Inc.*,[163] defendant stores sold blank tapes and, for a fee, loaned shoppers pre-recorded tapes containing the copyrighted musical works. The clientele would then duplicate the tapes on the *Make-A-System* provided for them on the store premises. The court granted a preliminary injunction against the defendants for their all but direct participation in the infringing acts. Although the court's legal basis for granting the relief requested is not altogether clear, the case well illustrates the contributory infringement principle. In effect, defendant controlled the acts of the infringer by supplying all the means necessary to infringe. The only thing defendant did not do was carry out the actual acts of copying. In addition, the defendant had or should have had knowledge of the infringing acts and had a direct financial stake in the infringement.

When the elements of knowledge and control are weaker against the defendant, the case for liability is correspondingly weaker. In *Sony Corp. v. Universal City Studios, Inc.* (the *Betamax* case),[164] the Supreme Court found that the manufacturer of the Betamax machine (VCR) was not liable as a contributory infringer for the off-the-air taping carried out by an individual owner of a Betamax machine.[165] In its decision, the Supreme Court borrowed a principle from patent law [166] that manufacturers of staple articles of commerce, suitable for substantial non-infringing uses, cannot be held as contributory infringers. Otherwise, a finding of contributory infringement would give the plaintiff effective control over the use of the item, placing it within the plaintiff's copyright monopoly. After *Sony*, the seller or manufacturer of copying equipment, such as typewriters, photocopying machines, and VCR's, will not be liable as a contributory infringer even if some buyers will predictably use the machine to infringe copyright.

In addition to the staple article of commerce aspect, the *Betamax* case differs significantly from the mainstream contributory infringement case, such as *Elektra Records*.[167] In the *Betamax* case, Sony had knowledge of possible infringing uses of the machine, but there was much less certainty in that knowledge. In addition, Sony did not control the copying process to the same degree as did the defendant in *Elektra Records*; Sony's participation was less direct, and although it supplied the means to copy, it did not supply the copyrighted work. In this more attenuated case of contributory infringement, it is understandable that the Court did not wish to suppress the development of a worthwhile copying technology. The staple article doctrine, which places limits on liability for contributory infringement, seemed the appropriate analysis for the case.

---

[163] 360 F. Supp. 821 (E.D.N.Y. 1973).

[164] 464 U.S. 417 (1984).

[165] Sony also successfully argued that the taping from the public airwaves for time-shifting purposes in the private home setting constituted a fair use of the copyrighted work. For a discussion of the fair use aspects of the case, see § 10.11, *infra*.

[166] 35 U.S.C. § 271(a).

[167] *Elektra Records Co. v. Gem Electronic Distributors, Inc.*, 360 F. Supp. 821 (E.D.N.Y. 1973).

[C]   Vicarious Liability: The Right to Supervise and a Financial Interest

Another pattern of cases involving related defendants occurs when the defendant has the right or power to supervise the acts of the direct infringer, and has a financial stake in the infringing acts, even though the defendant had no knowledge of, or did not directly participate in, the infringing acts.[168] In *Shapiro, Bernstein & Co. v. H. L. Green Co.*,[169] the defendant retailer was held liable as a related defendant for the infringing acts of its lessee, who had sold pirated records. Liability was found even though the retailer had no knowledge of the infringement because "[w]hen the right and ability to supervise coalesce with an obvious and direct financial interest," liability should be imposed on the financial beneficiary despite lack of knowledge of the infringement.[170] Under the same reasoning, owners of dance halls have been held liable for infringing performances given on their premises by musical groups.[171] In short, although the result may be harsh, particularly where the defendant has no actual knowledge of the infringing activity, it may be justified on basic equitable principles: those who benefit financially from the infringement should compensate the copyright owner.

Liability in the above cases is not based on the doctrine of master-servant (*respondeat superior*) or even the presence of an employment relationship. The rationale is based instead on the right or power to control the infringing acts while financially benefiting from them. Thus, not every landlord whose lessee engages in infringing acts will be liable as a related defendant for contributory infringement. Landlords are not liable due to their status; there must be some proof of control and financial interest.[172] Similarly, a sponsor of radio programs will not be liable vicariously unless one could show the right to supervise or control the infringing performance.[173] On the other hand, lack of knowledge by the related defendant is not a defense to infringement, although it can affect the extent of the remedies provided.[174]

---

[168] *See id. See also Gershwin Publishing Corp. v. Columbia Artists Mgt., Inc.*, 443 F.2d 1159 (2d Cir. 1971) (defendant C.A.M.I. formed and sponsored a community concert association which put on a concert at which there occurred unauthorized performances of copyrighted music; although C.A.M.I. had no formal power to control the local association or the artist for whom it served as agent, the court found C.A.M.I. vicariously liable for being in a position to police the activity, and for deriving substantial financial benefit from the performances; moreover, C.A.M.I. knew that copyrighted music was to be played at the concert and that no one would secure a copyright license).

[169] 316 F.2d 304 (2d Cir. 1963).

[170] *Id.* at 307. *See also Screen Gems-Columbia Music, Inc. v. Mark-Fi Records, Inc.*, 327 F. Supp. 788 (S.D.N.Y. 1971), *rev'd on other grounds*, 453 F.2d 552 (2d Cir. 1972), where an advertising agency defendant was held liable for aiding a client in selling pirated copyrighted music. Liability was based on the ad agency's participation in the commercial exploitation, even though it had not actually engaged in the copying.

[171] *See, e.g., Dreamland Ball Room v. Shapiro, Bernstein & Co.*, 36 F.2d 354 (7th Cir. 1929); *Famous Music Corp. v. Bay State Harness Horse Racing and Breeding Ass'n, Inc.*, 554 F.2d 1213 (1st Cir. 1977).

[172] *See Robert Stigwood Group, Ltd. v. Hurwitz*, 462 F.2d 910 (2d Cir. 1972).

[173] *Bevan v. Columbia Broadcasting System, Inc.*, 329 F. Supp. 601 (S.D.N.Y. 1971).

[174] *Fourth Floor Music, Inc. v. Der Place, Inc.*, 572 F. Supp. 41 (D. Neb. 1983). *See* 17 U.S.C. § 504(c)(2).

CHAPTER **10**

FAIR USE AND OTHER DEFENSES[1] TO COPYRIGHT INFRINGEMENT

§ 10.1 Introduction and Chapter Overview

The doctrine of fair use is a judicially created defense to a suit for copyright infringement which allows a third party to use a copyrighted work in a reasonable manner without consent of the copyright owner. Although codified in the 1976 Act, the doctrine of fair use has retained its nature as an equitable rule of reason to be applied where a finding of infringement would either be unfair or undermine "the progress of science and the useful arts." The current Act sets forth fair use in § 107, which contains a preamble, giving examples of fair use contexts, followed by four broad criteria which must all be applied to determine whether a use is "fair."

---

[1] Fair use is clearly the major defense to an action of copyright infringement, but there are other generally equitable defenses. For example, abandonment of copyright has been successfully asserted where the defendant has shown the necessary intent to abandon by way of an overt act, such as the destruction of the only existing copy of the work. *See Pacific & Southern Co., Inc. v. Duncan*, 572 F. Supp. 1186 (N.D. Ga. 1983), *aff'd*, 744 F.2d 1490 (11th Cir. 1984). Other equitable defenses include estoppel, where plaintiff has induced or aided defendant to infringe, and acquiescence, where the infringing acts are tolerated over a significant period of time. *See 3 Nimmer on Copyright* §§ 13.06–13.07 (1993). Copyright misuse or use of copyright to violate the antitrust laws may impede enforcement of the copyright in an infringement action, although the case law conflicts on this point. *Compare F.E.L. Publications, Ltd. v. Catholic Bishops of Chicago*, 754 F.2d 216 (7th Cir. 1985), and *Blendingwell Music, Inc. v. Moor-Law, Inc.*, 612 F. Supp. 474 (D. Del. 1985) (approving of defense), *with Columbia Pictures Industries v. Redd Horne, Inc.*, 749 F.2d 154 (3d Cir. 1984); *see also Lasercomb America v. Reynolds*, 911 F.2d 970 (4th Cir. 1990) (copyright misuse need not be a violation of the antitrust law); for a criticism of the copyright misuse defense, *see* Marshall A. Leaffer, *Engineering Competitive Policy and Copyright Misuse*, 19 U. Dayton L. Rev. 1087 (1994). The defense of unclean hands has been successfully invoked on occasion in cases of serious plaintiff misconduct, such as falsifying evidence. Other plaintiff misconduct includes fraudulent practices, such as fraud on the Copyright Office, which can result in an invalidation of registration, inability to reregister and enforce the copyright. *See Rohauer v. Killiam Shows, Inc.*, 379 F. Supp. 723 (S.D.N.Y. 1974), *rev'd on other grounds*, 551 F.2d 484 (2d Cir. 1977); *Whimsicality, Inc. v. Rubie's Costumes Co., Inc.*, 891 F.2d 452 (2d Cir. 1989) (purposefully deceiving the Copyright Office invalidates a copyright, rendering it incapable of enforcement. Finally, innocent infringement is not recognized as a defense to an action for copyright infringement, but can affect the remedies provided. *See* 17 U.S.C. § 504(c)(2). *See* §§ 9.12–9.13, *supra*.

This chapter contains three parts. Part I discusses fair use from an historical perspective and then focuses on § 107. Part II is devoted to the four factors and the way in which the Court applies these broad criteria in making a fair use determination. Part III focuses on special situations where particularly difficult use issues have arisen, such as copying with the new technologies and the ever troublesome problem of the use of another's work in a parody. Part III ends with a discussion of how fair use doctrine interrelates with First Amendment rights and values, and concludes with a proposed synthesis of fair use.

PART I: FAIR USE: THE BACKGROUND[2]

§ 10.2   In General

The judicially created doctrine of fair use is by far the most important defense to an action for copyright infringement. It has been defined as a

> privilege in others than the owner of a copyright to use the copyrighted material in a reasonable manner without his consent, notwithstanding the monopoly granted to the owner.[3]

The defense of fair use becomes relevant only after the plaintiff has made out a *prima facie* case for copyright infringement by showing copying and substantial similarity. Once this occurs, the defendant bears the evidentiary burdens of production and persuasion that his otherwise infringing use of the copyrighted work was privileged as a fair use.[4]

Although first articulated in case law in the mid-19th century,[5] fair use was not given its first statutory recognition until the 1976 Act.[6] The 1976 Act, however, does not try to define the doctrine. Instead, in § 107, Congress codified past practice, incorporating an incoherent body of case law into the 1976 Act.[7] As a result, the fair use defense continues to defy precise definition and remains an equitable rule of reason, applied case-by-case, where finding an infringement would undermine the ultimate purpose of copyright law. As one court stated:

---

[2] For an excellent comprehensive overview of the subject, see W. Patry, *The Fair Use Privilege* (1985); *see also* 3 *Nimmer on Copyright* § 13.05 (1993); Howard B. Abrams, *The Law of Copyright*, §§ 15.01–15.06 (1993); Paul Goldstein, *Copyright*, §§ 10.1–10.3 (1989).

[3] *Rosemont Enterprises, Inc. v. Random House, Inc.*, 366 F.2d 303, 306 (2d Cir. 1966), *cert. denied*, 385 U.S. 1009 (1967) (citing H. Ball, *Copyright and Literary Property* 260 (1944)).

[4] Fair use is a mixed question of law and fact. If a reasonable trier of fact could reach only one conclusion, a court may conclude as a matter of law that the challenged use of the copyrighted work qualifies as a fair use. *See Harper & Row, Publishers, Inc. v. Nation Enterprises*, 471 U.S. 539 (1985); *Hustler Magazine, Inc. v. Moral Majority, Inc.*, 796 F.2d 1148, 1150 (9th Cir. 1986).

[5] *Folsom v. Marsh*, 9 F. Cas. 342 (C.C.D. Mass. 1841) (No. 4901).

[6] 17 U.S.C. § 107.

[7] For a discussion of the four criteria to be used in determining fair use, see § 10.6, *infra*.

[t]he doctrine of fair use . . . permits courts to avoid rigid application of the copyright statute when, on occasion, it would stifle the very creativity which that law is designed to foster.[8]

The tradeoff for this flexibility is an elusive legal doctrine, reputed to be the most troublesome in copyright law.[9]

§ 10.3   Historical Origin of the Doctrine of Fair Use: *Folsom v. Marsh*

Although the doctrine of fair use was first articulated in 1841 in *Folsom v. Marsh*,[10] it is surprising how little has changed since that time. In *Folsom*, defendant had taken 353 pages of plaintiff's multi-volume work on George Washington to produce his own biography of the first president. The defendant did not copy the prior work verbatim, but reproduced Washington's letters as they appeared in plaintiff's work, adding only transitional matter. On these facts, Justice Story found infringement, and set forth certain criteria to be evaluated in deciding questions of fair use:

> In short, we must often . . . look to the nature and objects of the selections made, the quantity and value of the materials used, and the degree in which the use may prejudice the sale, or diminish the profits, or supersede the objects, of the original work. . . .[11]

The factors identified by Justice Story in determining fair use are strikingly similar to those incorporated in § 107 of the 1976 Act.[12] Great changes have come about in American society, due in part to the new media and new reproductive technologies, but despite these vast changes, the doctrine of fair use remains rooted in the 19th century, when information was transmitted almost exclusively by the printed word.

§ 10.4   Section 107 of the 1976 Act: Generally

The doctrine of fair use is codified in § 107 of the 1976 Act. The statute, however, does not provide a tight definition of the doctrine. Instead, it sets forth in its preamble the kinds of uses which usually prompt the defense, followed by four criteria which must *all* be applied to determine whether the defense exists. The legislative history of § 107 indicates no intent to freeze the doctrine, but rather to allow its continuing development through the case law and its adaptation to changing times and technology.[13]

---

[8] *Iowa State University Research Foundation, Inc. v. American Broadcasting Companies*, 621 F.2d 57, 60 (2d Cir. 1980).

[9] *Dellar v. Samuel Goldwyn, Inc.*, 104 F.2d 661, 662 (2d Cir. 1939).

[10] 9 F. Cas. 342 (C.C.D. Mass. 1841) (No. 4901).

[11] *Id.* at 348.

[12] In fact, they are virtually the same as those stated in § 107 of the 1976 Act. *See* § 10.6, *infra*.

[13] H.R. Rep. No. 94–1476, 94th Cong., 2d Sess. 66 (1976).

§ 10.5 The Preamble to § 107: Is Fair Use Productive Use?

At the threshold, a party asserting the defense of fair use should show that he is engaged in an activity enumerated in the preamble to § 107.[14] The preamble reads:

> Notwithstanding the provisions of Section 106, the fair use of a copyrighted work, including such use by reproduction in copies or phonorecords or by any other means specified by that section, for purposes such as criticism, comment, news reporting, teaching (including multiple copies for classroom use), scholarship, or research, is not an infringement of copyright.

The examples listed are broad and overlapping. They are meant to be illustrative, not exhaustive, allowing for other contexts in which the fair use defense might arise.[15] For example, parody is not specifically mentioned in the preamble as a sanctioned fair use, but the categories of criticism and comment are broad enough to include parody. Even if parody did not fall into the illustrative categories, one could nevertheless argue that it constitutes a context in which fair use should operate.[16]

Is there a common theme to the diverse uses enumerated in the preamble? One might argue that they are productive uses of a copyrighted work. Productive uses are those that build on the works of others, by adding their own socially valuable creative element.[17] Critics, reporters, and biographers, who use the work of others, copy not for copying's sake, nor for convenience or pleasure, but to produce another separate work of authorship. On the other hand, a non-productive use (*reproductive use*) occurs when a user copies the material to use it for the same intrinsic purpose for which the copyright owner intended it to be used, for example, when A copies B's popular record on his cassette recorder rather than buying it.

Productive use supports the underlying goal of copyright law by increasing our fund of knowledge and information. Accordingly, a productive use should be impeded only when it is so excessive as to undermine unduly the incentive to produce copyrighted works.[18] On the other hand, non-productive (reproductive) use

---

[14] *See Association of American Medical Colleges v. Mikaelian*, 571 F. Supp. 144 (E.D. Pa. 1983), *aff'd*, 734 F.2d 3 (3d Cir. 1984).

[15] *See* 17 U.S.C. § 101. The terms "including" and "such as" are illustrative, not limitative.

[16] *See* § 10.14, *infra*, for a discussion of parody.

[17] *See* Leon E. Seltzer, *Exemptions and Fair Use in Copyright Law* 24 (1978), for the leading statement that a fair use is a productive use. The productive use theory of fair use can plausibly be read into the preamble with the possible exception of the "multiple copies for classroom use." Judge Leval uses the term "transformative" use. The concept is the same. *See* Pierre N. Leval, *Toward a Fair Use Standard*, 103 Harv. L. Rev. 1105, 1111 (1990) (a use is "transformative" if it is productive and employs the quoted matter in a different manner or for a different purpose from the original. It adds value to the original. The quoted matter is raw material that must be "transformed in the creation of new information, new aesthetics, new insights and understandings. . . ."). For an application of Judge Leval's transformative use doctrine, see his opinion in *American Geophysical Union v. Texaco, Inc.*, 802 F. Supp. 1 (S.D.N.Y. 1992) (reproduction of single copies from plaintiff's journals, even for research purposes, is not a transformative use and thus not a fair use).

[18] *See, e.g., Twin Peaks Productions, Inc. v. Publications, Int'l*, 996 F.2d 1366 (2d Cir. 1993) (defendant's detailed report of the plots of a popular television program went far

merely appropriates without creating anything of social value. Because productive uses confer public benefits whereas reproductive uses do not, some would assert that the fair use privilege should be limited to situations where a productive use has been made of a copyrighted work.[19]

The productive use theory is attractive because it is consistent with the underlying goals of copyright law while adding coherence to an amorphous fair use doctrine. It was, however, specifically rejected in *Sony Corp. of America v. Universal City Studios* (the *Betamax* case),[20] where private non-commercial taping of "free" television programming for time-shifting purposes [21] was found to be a fair use. The use made by the defendant did not fall into any of those listed in the preamble to § 107. It was clearly not a productive use, but merely copying for the sake of convenience. Rather than limiting fair use to productive use, the Supreme Court viewed fair use in much broader terms, as an equitable rule of reason to be determined case-by-case. In upholding the fair use defense, the Court focused on the economic impact of the use on the incentives to produce copyrighted work: whether the use was commercial or non-profit. The Court found no harm to the market for the copyrighted work from defendant's private non-commercial use of copyrighted material on "free" television broadcasts. In sum, the *Betamax* case shows that one can successfully assert fair use even if the use does not fall squarely within those listed in the preamble, and even if it is far from being a productive use. Generally, however, the defense of fair use is much easier to prove when defendant has made a productive, rather than an ordinary or reproductive use of the copyright owner's work.[22]

§ 10.6   The Four Criteria

Whether or not the use falls into one of the enumerated categories of the preamble to § 107, one must apply the four factors set forth in the second part of the section to determine whether the use is fair. The four factors which follow the preamble are the heart of the fair use determination. Section 107 states:

> In determining whether the use made of a work in any particular case is a
> fair use the factors to be considered shall include —

---

beyond merely identifying their basic outline for the transformative purposes of comment or criticism).

[19] *Sony Corp. of America v. Universal City Studios, Inc.*, 464 U.S. 417, 475 (1984) (Blackmun, J., dissenting); *Dow Jones & Company, Inc. v. Board of Trade*, 546 F. Supp. 113 (S.D.N.Y 1982).

[20] 464 U.S. 417 (1984). The Supreme Court reversed the Ninth Circuit Court of Appeals which rejected the fair use defense and had based its decision on a productive use theory of fair use. *See Universal City Studios, Inc. v. Sony Corp. of America*, 659 F.2d 963, 970 (9th Cir. 1981).

[21] To "time-shift" means to copy a television program for viewing at a later, more convenient time.

[22] *See Pacific & Southern Co., Inc. v. Duncan*, 744 F.2d 1490 (11th Cir. 1984).

(1) the purpose and character of the use, including whether such use is of a commercial nature or is for nonprofit educational purposes;

(2) the nature of the copyrighted work;

(3) the amount and substantiality of the portion used in relation to the copyrighted work as a whole; and

(4) the effect of the use upon the potential market for or value of the copyrighted work.

According to the legislative history, the four factors represent a codification of fair use.[23] One might ask why Congress would wish to codify the common law of fair use, with all its disarray and its questionable applicability to a world of new technologies and non-print media. The goal was not merely to incorporate the past, but also to allow for a flexible and dynamic future. The House Report states:

> Beyond a very broad statutory explanation of what fair use is and some of the criteria applicable to it, the courts must be free to adapt the doctrine to particular situations on a case-by-case basis. Section 107 is intended to restate the present judicial doctrine of fair use, not to change, narrow, or enlarge it in any way.[24]

Despite Congress's intention to codify fair use, § 107 is, in some important ways, a departure from past practice. First, the major criteria in determining fair use are made explicit for the first time. Second, and more important, is that the court must consider *all* four enumerated factors in determining fair use. The inquiry, however, need not be limited only to those factors. The language "shall include" indicates that the court can, in its discretion, consider other factors as well,[25] such as lack of good faith[26] and industry custom or practice.[27]

Practical application of § 107's four factors has not led to predictable results. In a given case, one may find majority and dissenting opinions disagreeing completely on the application of each factor.[28] This is hardly surprising. The factors are broadly stated, overlapping, and vague, and the legislative history provides little insight as to their meaning, what weight to give them, or how they interrelate. Most *post*–1976 Act cases dealing with fair use examine each factor in sequence, focus on one or more of them — usually the fourth, market effect — and come to a reasoned judgment.[29]

---

[23] H.R. Rep. No. 94–1476, 94th Cong., 2d Sess. 66 (1976); one can trace the four–factor approach back to *Folsom v. Marsh* in 1841, 9 F. Cas. 342 (C.C.D. Mass. 1841) (No. 4901). In fact, the factors in § 107 differ from that early case only by the addition of the second factor, the nature of the copyrighted work.

[24] *Id.*

[25] Section 101 defines "including" and "such as" as illustrative, not limitative.

[26] *Roy Export Co. Establishment v. Columbia Broadcasting System Inc.*, 503 F. Supp. 1137 (S.D.N.Y. 1980), *aff'd*, 672 F.2d 1095 (2d Cir.), *cert. denied*, 459 U.S. 826 (1982).

[27] *Triangle Publications, Inc. v. Knight-Ridder Newspapers, Inc.*, 626 F.2d 1171 (5th Cir. 1980).

[28] *Compare, e.g.,* Justice O'Connor's majority opinion in *Harper & Row, Publishers, Inc. v. Nation Enterprises*, 471 U.S. 539 (1985), *with* Justice Brennan's dissent in that case.

[29] *See, e.g., Association of American Medical Colleges v. Mikaelian*, 571 F. Supp. 144 (E.D. Pa. 1983), *aff'd*, 734 F.2d 3 (3d Cir. 1984).

PART II: THE FOUR FACTORS INDIVIDUALLY EXAMINED

§ 10.7   The Purpose and Character of the Use

As does the preamble, the first factor in § 107 focuses on the nature and purpose of the use. It provides, however, further guidance about the meaning of fair use by emphasizing the distinction between commercial and non-profit educational use. A non-profit educational use is more likely to be a fair use because it is less inclined to harm the market for the copyrighted work than would a commercial use.[30] The focus on the economic impact of the use shows this factor's obvious connection with the fourth factor, the effect of the use on the potential market for the copyrighted work.

A commercial use is one which earns a profit, and as such does not lose its commercial character even though it is ultimately intended for education, news reporting, or any of the other purposes set forth in the preamble to § 107.[31] As one court stated:

> The fair-use doctrine is not a license for corporate theft, empowering a court to ignore a copyright whenever it determines the underlying work contains material of possible public importance.[32]

In short, users should not be able to profit from a copyrighted work without paying the copyright owner.[33]

Generally, if a challenged use of a copyrighted work is for commercial gain, a presumption against fair use arises.[34] A commercial purpose will not conclusively negate a finding of fair use, but "a court should not strain to apply the fair use defense when it is being invoked by a profit-making defendant. . . ."[35] Conversely, a clear non-profit educational use would constitute an important indication of fair use.[36]

---

[30] See Encyclopaedia Britannica Educ. Corp. v. Crooks, 542 F. Supp. 1156 (W.D.N.Y. 1982); Wihtol v. Crow, 309 F.2d 777 (8th Cir. 1962); Sony Corp. of America v. Universal City Studios, Inc., 464 U.S. 417 (1984).

[31] Association of American Medical Colleges v. Mikaelian, 571 F. Supp. 144 (E.D. Pa. 1983), aff'd, 734 F.2d 3 (3d Cir. 1984). In Mikaelian, defendant copied test questions from the Medical College Admissions Test for use in booklets designed for a test preparation course. The court found a commercial rather than a non-profit educational use. "Educational purpose" was defined as the free dissemination of information. Defendant's course cost $485, hardly free, and was profit-making. See also Twin Peaks Prod., Inc. v. Publications, Int'l, Ltd., 996 F.2d 1336 (2d Cir. 1993) (companion book to television show "Twin Peaks" meticulously summarizing plot of the eight shows was commercial use).

[32] Iowa State University Research Foundation, Inc. v. American Broadcasting Companies, Inc., 621 F.2d 57, 61 (2d Cir. 1980).

[33] Harper & Row, Publishers, Inc. v. Nation Enterprises, 471 U.S. 539 (1985).

[34] Sony Corp. of America v. Universal City Studios, Inc., 464 U.S. 417, 451 (1984) ("If the intended use is for commercial gain, that [meaningful] likelihood [of future harm] may be presumed").

[35] Association of American Medical Colleges v. Mikaelian, 571 F. Supp. 144, 153 (E.D. Pa. 1983).

[36] H.R. Rep. No. 94–1476, 94th Cong., 2d Sess. 66–7 (1976).

In considering the first factor, courts have examined purposes other than whether the use is a commercial or non-profit educational use. For example, a use made in bad faith is less likely to be a fair use because fair use presupposes good faith and fair dealing.[37] A use made in bad faith has been found where the defendant has knowingly exploited a stolen manuscript or engaged in verbatim copying without any effort to obtain permission from the copyright owner or to cite the copyright owner as the source of the material.[38]

Alternatively, in *Hustler Magazine, Inc. v. Moral Majority, Inc.*,[39] fair use was sustained for a defendant who had used a copyrighted work to defend himself against personal attack. This situation occurred when *Hustler* magazine published an advertisement which parodied the Reverend Jerry Falwell by portraying his first sexual encounter as an incestuous one with his mother, taking place in an outhouse. Outraged, Falwell reproduced almost a million copies of the advertisement and sent them to his followers for fund-raising purposes. Despite the commercial purpose and the verbatim copying, the court found the purpose of the copying reasonable as comment to rebut the derogatory nature of Hustler's ad.[40] *Hustler* shows that a use can be fair even though it is commercial when other equitable considerations can be shown.

Whether commercial use, non-profit educational use, or use made in good faith, a court must still consider the three remaining factors before coming to its conclusion on the fair use issue.

§ 10.8 Nature of the Copyrighted Work

The basic idea behind this second factor is that to support the public interest there should be greater access to some kinds of works than others. Because the ultimate goal of copyright law is to increase our fund of information, the fair use privilege is more extensive for works of information such as scientific, biographical or historical works than for works of entertainment.[41] Thus, the second factor would allow wider use of a treatise on physics than a video tape of a rock concert. Similarly, if a work is unavailable or out of print, the need for public access and dissemination

---

[37] *Time, Inc. v. Bernard Geis Associates*, 293 F. Supp. 130, 146 (S.D.N.Y. 1968). *See also Harper & Row, Publishers, Inc. v. Nation Enterprises*, 471 U.S. 539 (1985).

[38] *Marcus v. Rowley*, 695 F.2d 1171 (9th Cir. 1983). *See also Harper & Row, Publishers, Inc. v. Nation Enterprises*, 471 U.S. 539 (1985); *Iowa State University Research Foundation, Inc. v. American Broadcasting Companies, Inc.*, 621 F.2d 57 (2d Cir. 1980); *Roy Export Co. Establishment v. Columbia Broadcasting System Inc.*, 503 F. Supp. 1137 (S.D.N.Y. 1980), *aff'd*, 672 F.2d 1095 (2d Cir.), *cert. denied*, 459 U.S. 826 (1982).

[39] 796 F.2d 1148 (9th Cir. 1986).

[40] H.R. Rep. No. 94–1476, 94th Cong., 2d Sess. 73 (1976):

> When a copyrighted work contains unfair, inaccurate, or derogatory information concerning an individual or institution, the individual or institution may copy and reproduce such parts of the work as are necessary to permit understandable comment on the statements made in the work.

[41] *Sony Corp. of America v. Universal City Studios, Inc.*, 464 U.S. 417 (1984).

is greater and, thus, the permissible scope of fair use is broader.[42] On the other hand, the fair use privilege may not be available at all for certain kinds of works particularly susceptible to harm from mass reproduction. For this reason the House Report would preclude all copying for studying or teaching from consumables such as workbooks, exercises, standardized tests, and answer sheets.[43] Any substantial amount of copying of the above materials in teaching situations would destroy the only available market for these works.[44]

Even if a work of information is involved, the fair use privilege narrows for an unpublished work. The author's right to control the publication of the work may outweigh an extensive fair use privilege. This proved to be the critical factor in *Harper & Row, Publishers, Inc. v. Nation Enterprises.*[45] In *Harper & Row*, The Nation magazine obtained, through an undisclosed source, a stolen, as-yet unpublished manuscript of former President Gerald Ford's autobiography, which it hurriedly printed. The article scooped *Time* magazine's planned excerpt from the book, *A Time To Heal*, and *Time* cancelled its contract as a result. The Supreme Court rejected The Nation's fair use defense. Despite the newsworthiness of the subject matter, and The Nation's use of only 300 words verbatim from a 200,000 word manuscript, the Court concluded that

> the unpublished nature of a work is "[a] key, though not necessarily determinative, factor," tending to negate a defense of fair use.[46]

Harper & Row spawned a number of controversial decisions involving fair use of unpublished works, mainly unpublished letters in serious biographies. That an unpublished work is less amenable to fair use was strongly reaffirmed in *Salinger v. Random House, Inc.*,[47] which involved copyrighted letters of the writer J.D. Salinger used by Ian Hamilton in his biography of the writer. The letters, although unpublished, were available to scholars in major libraries and Hamilton incorporated substantial portions of them in his biography. Although publicly accessible, Salinger's letters did not lose their unpublished character because of that fact.[48] Enjoining publication of the biography, the Court emphasized the unpublished nature of the letters as the principal factor in denying the fair use defense. It interpreted *Harper & Row* as holding that unpublished works normally enjoy complete protection against any copying. Thus, a biographer who copies more than minimal amounts of protected unpublished material should be enjoined.[49] A holding contrary

---

[42] S. Rep. No. 94–473, 94th Cong., 1st Sess. 64 (1975); H.R. Rep. No. 94–1476, 94th Cong., 2d Sess. 67 (1976).

[43] H.R. Rep. No. 94–1476, 94th Cong., 2d Sess. 69, 71 (1976). *See Association of American Medical Colleges v. Mikaelian*, 571 F. Supp. 144, 153 (E.D. Pa. 1983).

[44] The same reason is given for a narrow fair use privilege in the case of newsletters as compared with mass circulation periodicals or scientific journals. *See* H.R. Rep. No. 94–1476, 94th Cong., 2d Sess. 74 (1976).

[45] 471 U.S. 539 (1985).

[46] *Id.*, at 554, *citing* S. Rep. No. 94–473, 94th Cong., 1st Sess. 65 (1975).

[47] 650 F. Supp. 413 (S.D.N.Y. 1986), *rev'd*, 811 F.2d 90 (2d Cir. 1987).

[48] See §§ 4.2–4.7, *supra*, for a discussion of publication.

[49] *Salinger* was reconfirmed in dicta in *New Era Publications Int'l v. Henry Holt & Co.*, 873 F.2d 576, *reh'g en banc denied*, 884 F.2d 659 (2d Cir. 1989), *cert. denied*, 493 U.S. 1094 (1990).

to *Salinger* occurred two years later in *Wright v. Warner Books, Inc.*[50] Here, the court affirmed a summary judgment for the author and publisher of a biography of Richard Wright that had quoted and paraphrased a modest amount from his letters and journals. The Court refused to lump all unpublished materials in one category for fair use analysis. In so doing, the Court applied fair use in the traditional way by balancing the competing interests and weighing the enumerated fair use factors set forth in Section 107.

These contradictory decisions left the protection of unpublished works in a confused state, making it a risky proposition for authors and publishers to use unpublished source materials. A remarkable outpouring of interest in the topic provoked much commentary and led to Congressional hearings on proposed amendments to the Copyright Act. This ferment culminated in an amendment to 107 of the Copyright Act[51] adding the following language at the end of that section:

> The fact that a work is unpublished shall not itself bar a finding of fair use if such finding is made upon consideration of all the above factors.[52]

The amendment applies to all unpublished works whether created before or after the date of the enactment. The purpose of this amendment, as indicated in the legislative history, is unambiguous: to ensure that courts do not erect a *per se* rule barring any fair use of unpublished works. In addition, each claim of fair use of an unpublished work should involve a careful consideration of all four statutory factors as well as any other factors the court deems relevant.[53] The House Report also approved of the statement in *Harper & Row* describing the unpublished nature of the work as a "key though not necessarily determinative factor tending to negate the defense of fair use."[54] It remains to be seen how much guidance this language will provide in a given case or to a publisher wishing to use an unpublished letter. The unpublished nature of the work will continue to be an important factor weighing against fair use but will not itself prohibit the use of work.[55]

§ 10.9 The Amount and Substantiality of the Portion Used in Relation to the Copyrighted Work as a Whole

One must distinguish this third factor from the question of substantial similarity,[56] because the fair use defense arises only *after* infringement is proved. This factor properly focuses on whether the defendant has taken more than is necessary to satisfy

---

[50] 953 F.2d 731 (2d Cir. 1991).

[51] 102 Pub. L. No. 492; 106 Stat. 3145 (1992).

[52] 17 U.S.C. § 107.

[53] H.R. Rep. No. 836, 102d Cong., 2d Sess. 9 (1992).

[54] 471 U.S. 539, 554 (1985); H.R. Rep. No. 836, 102d Cong., 2d Sess. 9 (1992).

[55] For an assessment of the amendment, see Lynn I. Miller, *Fair Use, Biographers, and Unpublished Works: Life After H.R. 4412*, 40 J. Copyright Soc'y 349 (1993); and William M. Landes, *Copyright Protection of Letters, Diaries, and Other Unpublished Works: An Economic Approach*, 21 J. Legal Stud. 79 (1992).

[56] For a discussion of substantial similarity in proving copyright infringement, see § 9.5, *supra*.

the specific fair use purpose. Self-defense in tort produces a helpful analogy. In tort law, the scope of the self-defense defense depends on necessity and proportionality: did the defendant need to defend himself and was his reaction commensurate with the threat? Excessive force abrogates the privilege. Similarly, excessive copying not commensurate with the purpose of the use loses the privilege of fair use. This principle is often expressed in parody cases where the issue of fair use invariably focuses on whether the defendant has taken more of the copyright owner's work than is necessary to conjure up the original.[57]

The corollary principle is that verbatim copying invariably exceeds the purpose of the use. For example, a literary critic or biographer may need to quote liberally from plaintiff's work, but may exceed fair use by quoting more than is necessary to make the biographical or critical point.[58] Thus, a literary critic, in evaluating an author's style, would not be allowed to quote two pages of a copyrighted work when two paragraphs would be adequate to support the critic's argument.

Questions of amount and substantiality of the portion used have a qualitative, as well as quantitative, dimension.[59] Even small takings can exceed fair use when the essence of the work is taken. Accordingly, in *Harper & Row,* the verbatim copying of only 300 words out of 200,000 words of plaintiff's book was considered excessive because these words constituted the heart of the work.[60]

The third fair use factor has an obvious connection with the fourth, the harm to the market for the copyrighted work. Fair use is less likely when an entire work is reproduced, because excessive copying may displace the need for the original and destroy its market.[61]

§ 10.10   The Effect of the Use Upon the Potential Market for, or Value of, the Copyrighted Work

The case law frequently states that this factor is the single most important element of fair use. The reason is easy to understand. If the market for the copyright owner's work is harmed, the incentives for creativity that the copyright monopoly is designed to encourage will not work. The fourth factor is related in one way or another to

---

[57] *See* § 10.14, *infra,* for a discussion of parody.

[58] *See Craft v. Kobler,* 667 F. Supp. 120 (S.D.N.Y. 1987), rejecting fair use where the biographer of the musician Igor Stravinsky used excerpts from copyrighted material written by the composer and his assistant, Robert Craft. Even though the takings were a tiny part of the two-million-word Craft-Stravinsky writings, they were, from a qualitative standpoint, considered too numerous to justify defendant's biographical purpose.

[59] *See Meeropol v. Nizer,* 560 F.2d 1061 (2d Cir. 1977), where defendant's popular book on the Rosenberg trial used verbatim portions of 28 copyrighted letters, a total of 1957 words. The court considered this to be substantial despite constituting less than one per cent of defendant's book, particularly since the words were featured prominently in promotional literature advertising the book.

[60] 471 U.S. 539, 569.

[61] *Fisher v. Dees,* 794 F.2d 432, 437 (9th Cir. 1986).

the other three factors, but perhaps most closely to the first factor where presumption of harm arises from commercial use of the copyrighted work.[62]

At one level, the market effect factor is circular in its reasoning. Professor Goldstein has termed this fourth factor hardly more than a theoretical flourish:

> whether a use will affect the potential market for or value of the copyrighted work necessarily turns on whether the use will be proscribed.[63]

Thus, to avoid this circularity, a reviewing court must isolate those uses of a work most directly threatening to the incentives for creativity which copyright tries to protect. These incentives are most threatened when the infringing use tends to diminish the potential sale of the work, or tends to interfere with its marketability, or fulfills the demand for the original.[64]

Potential, not actual harm to the market is the issue.[65] Actual harm need not be shown, although proof of quantifiable harm, such as a lost contract, is the best evidence of harm to the market for the work. But the fact that the copyright owner does not actually market copies of the work does not matter under the potential market language of § 107(4).[66] To prove potential market effect, plaintiff need only show a meaningful likelihood of future harm by a preponderance of the evidence.

PART III: SPECIAL APPLICATIONS OF FAIR USE ANALYSIS: NEW TECHNOLOGIES, PARODY, AND THE FIRST AMENDMENT

§ 10.11 Fair Use and the New Reproductive Technologies: Videotaping and Photocopying

[A] Copyright and the New Reproductive Technologies: Generally

The doctrine of fair use originated in the nineteenth century when printed matter was virtually the only non-oral form in which information was disseminated. At that time, copying was done with pen in hand except for the few who had access to the printing press. With today's new reproductive technologies, anyone can reproduce and transmit a copyrighted work cheaply and inexpensively. The photocopying machine and videocassette recorder come to mind immediately. These devices, however, are only a small part of the radical changes which will take place in the

---

[62] *Sony Corp. of America v. Universal City Studios*, 464 U.S. 417 (1984).

[63] Paul Goldstein, *Copyright, Patent, and Trademark and Related State Doctrines* 780 (2d ed. 1981).

[64] *Hustler Magazine, Inc. v. Moral Majority, Inc.*, 796 F.2d 1148 (9th Cir. 1986).

[65] *See, e.g., Meeropol v. Nizer*, 560 F.2d 1061 (2d Cir. 1977) (the fact that copyrighted letters had been out of print for 20 years did not necessarily mean they had no future market potential which could be injured). *See also Craft v. Kobler*, 667 F. Supp. 120 (S.D.N.Y. 1987), where harm to the potential market was found despite the fact that plaintiff's work was out of print.

[66] *Harper & Row, Publishers, Inc. v. Nation Enterprises*, 471 U.S. 539 (1985). *See Marcus v. Rowley*, 695 F.2d 1171 (9th Cir. 1983), and *Pacific & Southern Co., Inc. v. Duncan*, 744 F.2d 1490 (11th Cir. 1984).

way we receive and transmit information. In the future, the printed word may well become obsolete.[67] Despite these vast technological changes, the doctrine of fair use has changed little from its first judicial recognition in the nineteenth century.

Copying with the new technologies does not comport with the doctrine of fair use as traditionally formulated. For one, the doctrine has normally been invoked in *productive use* contexts where one author builds on the work of another. Second, fair use is normally denied when an entire work has been copied. By comparison, one who photocopies a chapter of a book or videotapes a film off the air is hardly a productive user, but is reproducing an entire work for the same purpose and in the same medium as the original. Nonetheless, as the following sections on videotaping and photocopying will show, courts have rendered decisions which appear to contravene traditional fair use principles. As will be seen, they have employed fair use doctrine where the harm to plaintiff's market appears to be *de minimis* and a finding of infringement would suppress a useful new technology.

[B]   Videotaping: The *Betamax* Case

In the *Betamax* case,[68] plaintiff brought suit against the manufacturer of a video cassette recorder as a contributory infringer for supplying the means to the principal infringer, the home user, to infringe plaintiff's copyrighted works played on the public airwaves. Plaintiff asked for an injunction against Sony as well as profits and damages. In a narrow five-to-four decision, the Supreme Court held that off-the-air taping from the public airwaves for private (time-shifting) purposes constituted a fair use of the copyrighted work. For the majority, Justice Stevens reasoned that for this non-commercial use, harm to the market is not presumed and plaintiffs were not able to prove sufficiently future or potential harm from the time-shifting.[69] In dissent, Justice Blackmun argued that Congress intended to limit fair use to productive use contexts and that extensive reproduction use, as made by the defendants, is an infringement unless specifically exempted.[70]

Off-the-air taping, even for non-commercial, educational purposes, cannot sustain a fair use defense if the economic harm to plaintiff is direct and apparent. Before *Betamax*, the most significant off-the-air taping case was *Encyclopaedia Britannica Educ. Corp. v. Crooks*.[71] In *Crooks*, defendant non-profit corporation had video-taped copyrighted films from television and distributed them to public school districts for educational purposes. The District Court issued a preliminary injunction despite defendant's claim that public education would be disrupted if the practice were enjoined. In refusing the fair use defense, the court emphasized that the substantiality of the copying and the harmful effect on plaintiff's market outweighed the non-commercial educational purpose of the copying.[72]

---

[67] *See* David Ladd, *A Pavan for Print: Accommodating Copyright to the Tele-Technologies*, 29 J. Copyright Soc'y 246 (1982); *see also* I. Pool, *Technologies of Freedom* (1983).

[68] *Sony Corp. of America v. Universal City Studios*, 464 U.S. 417 (1984).

[69] *Id*. at 456.

[70] *Id*. at 480–81.

[71] 542 F. Supp. 1156 (W.D.N.Y. 1982).

[72] *Id*. at 1179.

At first blush, the degree of the harm to plaintiff's market can account for the different results in *Betamax* and *Crooks*. But the cases have other distinguishing features. In *Crooks*, the court pointed out that the defendants could have conveniently entered into a licensing agreement with the plaintiffs.[73] In *Betamax*, however, the copier had no convenient, cost-justified way to negotiate a license.[74] Moreover, in *Betamax*, the plaintiffs sued not only the direct copier, but also Sony, the manufacturer of the VCR, as a contributory infringer. The goal of the plaintiffs was not to resolve a dispute between two parties but rather to impose a court-ordered system of regulation on a new and valuable technology. Although the court based its decision on different grounds, it may have been influenced by the general proposition that the judiciary is better at resolving disputes between parties in a single proceeding than at redistributing wealth, a function best left to the legislature. Many of these same difficult issues can be found in cases dealing with the equally complicated subject of photocopying.

[C] Photocopying: *Williams & Wilkins*

Like the newer VCR technology, the photocopying machine allows access to and dissemination of copyrighted works in ways which were not thought possible until recently. For some years now, they have posed an extreme dilemma for copyright law: how can a court, applying fair use in piecemeal litigation, balance the rights of copyright owners, the public interest in access to information, and the future of a new technology? In *Williams & Wilkins Co. v. United States*,[75] the Court of Claims held that the photocopying of an entire article from a specialized low circulation medical journal constituted fair use. The defendant, through its National Institutes of Health (NIH) and the National Library of Medicine (NLM), photocopied and distributed articles to those requesting them. Generally, the defendant limited requests to no more than one article per journal, no more than fifty pages, and no more than a single copy of an article per request. Plaintiff, a publisher of limited circulation medical and scientific journals, claimed injury because a relatively few lost subscriptions could make the difference between a profit and loss. Even though the NIH had photocopied millions of pages, the court found this activity a fair use because plaintiff failed to prove future harm adequately. The small and speculative future harm to plaintiff was outweighed by the certain harm to medical science if the photocopying were stopped. Thus, the public interest in medical science prevailed over the possible damage to the copyright owner.[76]

[D] The Failure of the Litigation Process

Can the results in *Betamax*, *Williams & Wilkins*, and *Crooks* be reconciled? One general proposition can be derived from these cases: when confronted with disputes

---

[73] *Id.* at 1176.

[74] This idea is discussed in Wendy J. Gordon, *Fair Use as Market Failure: A Structural and Economic Analysis of the* Betamax *Case and its Predecessors*, 82 Colum. L. Rev. 1600 (1982).

[75] 487 F.2d 1345 (1973), *aff'd by an equally divided Court*, 420 U.S. 376 (1975).

[76] For a critique of the Court's reasoning, see David Ladd, *The Harm of the Concept of Harm in Copyright*, 30 J. Copyright Soc'y 421 (1983).

involving the new technologies, courts will use restraint in evoking industry-wide solutions best left to legislatures. One detects a fear, even if not expressed, that a finding of infringement will not merely settle a dispute between the parties but will suppress a new and useful technology. As a result, copyright owners will not fare well when their rights are pitted against a new technological development. In sum, courts are less willing to impose liability when the costs imposed on the public by limiting the use of a copyrighted work are not offset by a correspondingly greater incentive for authors to produce. Accordingly, in *Betamax* and *Williams & Wilkins*, the courts were persuaded that judgment against defendants would deprive the public of videotaping and photocopying without greatly encouraging copyright owners to create more copyrighted works. By comparison, in *Crooks*, the plaintiffs were harmed directly and substantially, and a decision in their favor would not unduly impede access to the distribution of copyrighted works.

Reviewing the several cases involving the new technologies leaves the impression that the litigation process is not capable of solving the issues raised. The reason goes further than the unwieldy and unpredictable doctrine of fair use and is linked to the nature of the litigation process. Court cases are brought to decide grievances between parties at a particular point in time. But in complicated new technology cases the process breaks down. In these cases, a decision can have far reaching ramifications and can result in one court imposing a *de facto* system of regulation on an entire industry. For example, in *Betamax*, the Supreme Court was bound by the record developed at trial in the mid-seventies, but was called upon to reconcile changing technology with the law as it existed at the time of the appeal some ten years later.[77] Other mechanisms, both public and private, seem better able to resolve the challenge of the new reproductive technologies than piecemeal litigation. In short, legislatures, not courts, are much better at finding industry-wide solutions which orchestrate the interests of all concerned rather than just the interest of the parties to a single dispute.

Congress has taken the industry-wide approach to both new and perennial fair use dilemmas in several ways. One method is by an outright exemption of the use from copyright infringement.[78] This approach is evident in the library photocopying provisions of § 108, discussed in subsection § 10.12[A], below. Another method is by the use of voluntary guidelines detailing proper uses of copyrighted works. This approach is discussed in subsection [F], involving classroom photocopying. In addition to legislative efforts, private collecting agencies, such as the Copyright Clearance Center (CCC), may provide an efficient mechanism to enforce the rights of copyright owners.

---

[77] This idea is expressed in Baird, *Changing Technology and Unchanging Doctrine:* Sony Corporation v. Universal Studios, Inc., 1984 Sup. Ct. Rev. 237.

[78] These specific exemptions and limitations are generally found in 17 U.S.C. §§ 108–118. An exemption is sometimes combined with a compulsory license.

§ 10.12   Avoiding Fair Use Determinations: Industry–Wide Resolution of the Photocopying Dilemma

[A]   Library Photocopying Under § 108[79]

To avoid the uncertainties of general fair use doctrine and mindful of the result in *Williams & Wilkins*, Congress has singled out library photocopying for separate treatment under § 108 of the 1976 Act.[80] This provision details the circumstances in which libraries and archives may reproduce and distribute copies of works without infringing copyright. In general, § 108 allows library photocopying for scholarly purposes, unless it is systematic and is a substitute for purchase or subscription. Section 108 sets forth the requirements for exemption but § 107 is still available for those acts exceeding the exemption.[81]

To qualify for the exemption, the library collection must be open to the public or to researchers in a specialized field in addition to researchers affiliated with the library. Two other initial criteria must be met to qualify for the § 108 exception.[82] First, the copy reproduced must be a single copy. Second, it must be made without any purpose of direct or indirect commercial advantage. Before passage of the Berne Convention Implementation Act of 1988, libraries were also required to include a notice of copyright on behalf of the copyright owner. Effective March 1, 1989, it will no longer be an infringement of copyright for a library to distribute a reproduction of a work not containing a notice of copyright.[83]

If the above preconditions are met, the library can make a copy for preservation or security;[84] it may make a copy to replace a damaged, deteriorating, lost or stolen work which cannot be bought at a fair price.[85]

Section 108 takes into account the controversial issue posed by *Williams & Wilkins*,[86] that of reproducing single copies for distribution to users. Under this section, a library can distribute both small amounts of a work and copies of the entire work if certain conditions are met. For small amounts of a work or an article in a periodical issue, the copy can be made in response to user request if the copy becomes the property of the user and the library has no reason to believe that the

---

[79] *See* James M. Treece, *Library Photocopying*, 24 UCLA L. Rev. 1025 (1977), and Young, *Copyright and the New Technologies — The Case of Library Photocopying*, 28 Copyright L. Symp. (ASCAP) 51 (1982).

[80] 17 U.S.C. § 108.

[81] *But see Library Reproduction of Copyrighted Works (17 U.S.C. Section 108): Report of the Register of Copyrights* 93–104 (1983), maintaining that copying beyond the § 108 exemption cannot be defended on general fair use grounds of § 107.

[82] 17 U.S.C. § 108(a).

[83] 17 U.S.C. § 108(a). Repeal of the notice provision does not condone removal or obliteration of notice from a copy of a work before it is reproduced by a library. *See* S. Rep. No. 100–352, 100th Cong., 2d Sess. (1988).

[84] 17 U.S.C. § 108(b).

[85] 17 U.S.C. § 108(c).

[86] *Williams & Wilkins Co. v. United States*, 487 F.2d 1345 (1973), *aff'd by an equally divided Court,* 420 U.S. 376 (1975).

copy will be used for other than private scholarship.[87] In addition, the library must prominently display at its copy order desk and in its order form a warning of copyright.[88] The above provisions apply to user copies of an entire work if the library first determines after reasonable investigation that the work cannot be obtained at a fair price.

Sections 108(g) and (h) impose limitations on copying. Section 108(g) permits the library to distribute isolated, unrelated single copies to users on separate occasions, but prohibits a library from distributing related or concerted reproductions of multiple copies of the same materials. Section 108(g)(2) further prohibits a library from engaging "in the systematic reproduction or distribution of single or multiple copies . . . of" copyrighted works. This subsection allows interlibrary arrangements as well, except when these arrangements involve a distribution "in such aggregate quantities as to substitute for a subscription to or purchase of such work."[89] Finally, § 108(h)[90] limits reproduction and distribution under all of § 108 to books and periodicals, not to musical, pictorial, graphic, or sculptural works, or to motion pictures or other audiovisual works other than those dealing with news.[91]

[B] Multiple Copies for Classroom Use

Classroom teachers have always needed to duplicate materials for their students and most have probably done so without considering copyright law. Congress recognized that need: "multiple copies for classroom use" is listed in the preamble to § 107 and non-profit educational use is explicitly mentioned in the first factor for determining fair use.[92] Although classroom use could be considered a classic fair use context, the case law has been less than accommodating. In *Wihtol v. Crow*,[93] for example, a high school teacher distributed about forty-eight duplicate copies of an arrangement he made of plaintiff's copyrighted song. Despite the non-profit educational use, the teacher's defense of fair use was rejected.[94]

To remedy the uncertainty and vagueness of the law, Congress wished to give special treatment to teachers who make multiple copies of a copyrighted work for classroom use. The help, however, fell short of the blanket exemption the educators lobbied for.[95] Instead, educators, authors and publisher groups produced an

[87] 17 U.S.C. § 108(d).

[88] *Id.*

[89] 17 U.S.C. § 108(g).

[90] 17 U.S.C. § 108(h).

[91] 17 U.S.C. § 108(i) requires the Register of Copyrights to issue a report every five years on library photocopying. The first report was issued in 1983, offering various statutory and non-statutory recommendations. *See Library Reproduction of Copyrighted Works (17 U.S.C. Section 108): Report of the Register of Copyrights* (1983).

[92] 17 U.S.C. § 107.

[93] 309 F.2d 777 (8th Cir. 1962).

[94] *See also MacMillan Co. v. King*, 223 F. 862 (D. Mass. 1914).

[95] H.R. Rep. No. 94–1476, 94th Cong., 2d Sess. at 66–7. *See also* 17 U.S.C. § 504(c)(2), where teachers and other non-profit users of copyrighted materials of innocent infringers cannot be sued for statutory damages.

Agreement on Guidelines for Classroom Copying in Not-For-Profit Educational Institutions,[96] indicating the minimum threshold for fair use. The *Guidelines* are not part of the 1976 Act but are included in the House Report. They are presented as providing a minimum standard for copying, and exceeding them can still be defended as fair use under § 107.[97]

The *Guidelines* apply to not-for-profit educational institutions and are limited to books and periodicals. Part I of the *Guidelines* sets forth what copying a teacher can do for his own scholarly or educational use. Part II deals with the more controversial making of multiple copies for classroom use. Multiple copying for classroom use must meet four basic criteria: (1) brevity, (2) spontaneity, (3) cumulative effect, and (4) each copy must include a notice of copyright. The *Guidelines* further specify in detail the meaning of the above criteria. For example, the *Guidelines* describe "brevity" as

> [e]ither a complete article, story or essay of less than 2,500 words or an excerpt from any prose work of not more than 1,000 words or 10% of the work. . . .[98]

As for spontaneity, the decision to use the work and the moment of its use are to be so close in time that it would be impossible to ask for permission. As for cumulative effect, the copying must be for only one course in the school in which the copies are made. From this brief overview, one might conclude that much classroom copying exceeds fair use. The *Guidelines*, however, provide *minimum* thresholds, and copying exceeding them can be justified under traditional fair use analysis.

The *Guidelines* have become an issue in one litigated case, *Marcus v. Rowley,*[99] which provides an instructive example of how easy it is to violate the *Guidelines* and what is not educational fair use. In *Marcus*, defendant copied eleven of twenty-four pages from plaintiff's cake decorating booklet for use in her food service career classes. Before turning to the *Guidelines*, the court rejected the fair use defense under § 107. The court found that defendant's work was used for the same purpose as plaintiff's, and that defendant showed bad faith in making no attempt to secure permission for the use. In addition, the use made was qualitatively and quantitatively a substantial copy. These aspects dictated against a finding of fair use despite the informational nature of plaintiff's work and lack of specific evidence on the market effect of the use. Moreover, defendant's copying violated all aspects of the *Guidelines*. Copying clearly exceeded the brevity factor. As for spontaneity, defendant had enough time to request permission to use the work. Defendant's use of the work in several classes failed the cumulative effect criterion as well. Finally,

---

[96] H.R. Rep. No. 94–1476, 94th Cong., 2d Sess. 68–70 (1976); *see also Guidelines for Educational Uses of Music, id.* at 70–74, and the 1981 *Guidelines for Off-Air Taping of Copyrighted Works for Educational Use*, H.R. Rep. No. 97–495, 97th Cong., 2d Sess. (1982).

[97] H.R. Rep. No. 94–1476, 94th Cong., 2d Sess. 72 (1976).

[98] *Id.* at 68.

[99] 695 F.2d 1171 (9th Cir. 1983).

the requirement that each copy bear a copyright notice in the owner's name was also violated.[100]

[C] A Private Collecting Agency: The Copyright Clearance Center

An exclusive copyright, whether for reproduction or performance purposes, is only as good as the ability to enforce it. Massive unauthorized reproductions of copyrighted works take place at ever-increasing rates as such locations as corporate and law libraries. In principle, each of these unauthorized reproductions represents a lost royalty. In reality, however, policing the reproduction right, even if possible, would be prohibitively expensive for the copyright owner. The Copyright Clearance Center (CCC), a nonprofit organization, was founded in 1978 to serve as a middleman between publishers and users. It functions as a clearing house that licenses the right to photocopy for a fee, and distributes the collected revenues to copyright owners whose works were copied.

The CCC recovers licensing fees in two distinct ways. The first, the Transactional Reporting System, works on an individualized basis and depends on self-reporting by users. The first page of a covered journal article or other work informs the user of the licensing fee set by the publisher and instructs the user how to forward the fee to the CCC. After deducting for costs, the CCC distributes royalties to the copyright owners. The second collecting method, the Annual Authorization Service (AAS), was designed to reduce the compliance costs associated with the Transactional Reporting System. Under AAS, a representative sample is taken from the users' photocopy machines, from which a statistical model estimates the fees owed. To cut monitoring costs further the CCC has offered to users an alternative statistical method of determining the amount of their copying that avoids individual monitoring of photocopy machines. The CCC has developed statistical models of copying in some 20 industries (*e.g.*, chemical companies). From this statistical model, a user's annual fee is determined based on the amount of copying in a particular industry and the average prices charged by publishers. Users are then free to copy all works registered with the CCC, without limitation on the number of copies made.[101]

In *American Geophysical Union v. Texaco*,[102] the court cited the CCC's existence as a reason why a profit-seeking company's photocopying for research purposes of scientific journal articles is not a fair use. Like many companies, Texaco's corporate library subscribed to a number of scientific and technical journals. Texaco scientists, on learning of a journal article, would have it photocopied and kept for research

---

[100] Another development on the teacher photocopying front occurred when several publishing houses and the Association of American Publishers sued New York University faculty members and an off-campus copying center for infringement due to classroom photocopying practices. *See Addison-Wesley Publishing Co., Inc. v. New York University*, 1983–1984 Copyright L. Dec. (CCH) ¶ 25,544 (S.D.N.Y. 1983). The copying center consented to a stipulated judgment and the university professors agreed to observe the guidelines.

[101] *See generally* Stanley M. Besen & Sheila Nararaj Kirby, *Compensating Creators of Intellectual Property: Collectives That Collect* (1989); Paul Goldstein, *Copyright*, § 5.2.3 (1989).

[102] 37 F.3d 881 (2d Cir. 1994).

purposes. As a defense to a class action brought by journal publishers, Texaco asserted that this practice was a fair use.[103] The court rejected the fair use defense. Even though Texaco was not gaining direct or immediate commercial advantage, its use was for archival purposes, which filled the same need for which additional subscriptions are normally sold, or for which photocopying licenses may be obtained. Texaco's photocopying, despite its research purpose, was not a transformative use. Rather, it was a superseding use because the company's systematic photocopying of articles in their entirety added nothing new or different to the original copyrighted work.

Texaco also argued that scientific research would be impaired without a fair use privilege for its photocopying. A contrary decision would burden the company with oppressive transaction costs every time a scientist wished to copy a journal article. The court was unpersuaded, pointing out that much has changed since *Williams and Wilkins*.[104] Texaco's fears were illusory because the CCC now provides an efficient licensing mechanism that would avoid administrative difficulty, wasteful delay, and inordinate expense in negotiating licenses with individual copyright owners.

§ 10.13   Reverse Engineering of Computer Software: *Sega Enterprises Ltd. v. Accolade, Inc.*

To what extent should software developers be permitted to manipulate their competitors' products to discover the ideas on which those products are based? For example, can a third party reproduce the copyrighted work, not to displace the need for the original, but for the purpose of analyzing the copyrighted work, unearthing its ideas from its expression, so that the third party may create a non-infringing or compatible work? Whether such intermediate copying constitutes a fair use has become a controversial issue in the context of computer software copyright. This need to make intermediate copies for purposes of analysis arises from the inherent nature of computer software.

There are basically three ways in which one can understand a computer program: one can read about the program, read the program itself, or observe the program by running it. Of these methods, reading the program is superior for gaining a complete understanding of it. This can be accomplished, however, only if access to the program is available in a humanly readable form. The problem is that, in most cases, software owners distribute their products only in object code, a form of machine language (a series of 0's and 1's) largely unintelligible to human beings. Thus, to obtain access to the ideas embodied in the program written in object code, a programmer must first translate it into source code, a humanly intelligible language. This entails a process of reverse engineering called "disassembly or

---

[103] Texaco's defense under 17 U.S.C. 108 was rejected. First, § 108 is applicable only if the reproduction is made without commercial purpose. Here, the photocopying was made by a profit-seeking company for profit-motivated research. Second, § 108 permits the marking of "no more than one copy" per customer. Texaco exceeded this limitation.

[104] *See Williams & Wilkins*, 487 F.2d at 1356 (fearing that medicine and medical research would be seriously hurt if NIH and NHL were forbidden from engaging in photocopying).

decompilation"[105] that takes the finished program apart, translates it, and works backward to see how it operates. Once the object code is translated into source code, a skilled programmer can then analyze it to develop noninfringing, compatible or competing software. The problem is that copyright infringement may occur at several stages of the process. Disassembly or decompilation involves reproducing the copyrighted work, presumably an infringement of copyright, even though the ultimate goal of this "intermediate" copying is to produce a noninfringing work.

In *Sega Enterprises, Ltd. v. Accolade, Inc.*,[106] the Ninth Circuit Court of Appeals held that disassembly or decompilation of a computer program to produce a compatible, noninfringing program is a fair use. In this case, the defendant Accolade, an independent developer of video game cartridges, purchased Sega game cartridges, disassembled them, and by reverse engineering techniques, produced a game cartridge that could be played in the Sega game platforms. The court held that Accolade's copying infringed copyright, finding that the plain language of the statute proscribed *intermediate* copying because the Copyright Act does not distinguish between when and for what purpose the defendant has made its unauthorized copies.[107] The court, however, sustained Accolade's intermediate copying for disassembly purposes as a fair use, finding it to be a necessary step in its examination of the unprotected ideas and functional concepts embodied in the code.

In applying the four factors, only the third, the amount and substantiality of the use, weighed in Sega's favor.[108] Both the first factor, the purpose and character of the use, and the closely related fourth factor, market effect, favored the defendant. The court admitted that commercial purpose weighs against fair use, but Accolade's use, though commercial, was intermediate only, and any commercial exploitation resulting from it was indirect. Moreover, Accolade's copying was productive in nature, enabling the copier to produce independently designed works. As for market effect, Accolade's use did not usurp the market for the copyrighted work. Rather, it permitted the company to produce its own works and to compete with works of the same kind. The court added that Sega's attempt to monopolize the market by

---

[105] The distinction is sometimes made between decompilation and disassembly. Decompilation is a procedure by which a high level representation of a program is derived from a machine language program. Disassembly is a procedure for translating the machine language program into an assembly language program. Despite this distinction, the terms are often used interchangeably. Whatever technique is used, the legal issues are identical. *See generally* Office of Technology Assessment, *Finding a Balance: Computer Software, Intellectual Property, and the Challenge of Technological Change* 7 (1992) at pp. 147–150 (discussing the various reverse engineering techniques and providing concrete illustrations of high level language, machine language, and dissembled versions of a program).

[106] 977 F.2d 1510 (9th Cir. 1993); *see also* a case based on a similar fact situation, *Atari Games Corp. v. Nintendo of Am.*, 975 F.2d 832, 842 (Fed. Cir. 1992) (finding that decompilation of a computer program to produce a compatible game cartridge might be fair use but that defendant's program was "substantially similar" to plaintiff's).

[107] *See, e.g., Walker v. University Books*, 602 F.2d 859, 864 (9th Cir. 1979); and *Walt Disney Productions v. Filmation Associates*, 628 F. Supp. 871, 875–76 (C.D. Cal. 1986).

[108] *Sega*, 977 F.2d 1510, 1527 (citing *Sony* for the proposition that even copying the whole work did not preclude a finding of fair use).

making it impossible for others to compete runs counter to the statutory purpose of promoting creative expression.[109]

The court focused on the second factor, the nature of the copyrighted work, recognizing the unique qualities of computer software. Because Sega's video games contained unprotected aspects that could not be examined without copying, the court determined that the games were afforded a lower degree of protection than more traditional literary works. If defendant's reverse engineering through disassembly or decompilation were illegal, the copyright owner world have a *de facto* monopoly over the functional aspects of the work.[110] To be a fair use, however, the disassembly and translation of object code into source code must be the only means of access to the program's unprotected elements. Here, there were no viable alternatives to gaining this access short of disassembly.

As applied in *Sega*, the fair use privilege recognizes the unique attributes of computer software. By restraining the copyright owner from acquiring patent-like protection over the work, the case is consistent with the rationale of § 102(b)[111] that places ideas, processes, and methods of operation in the public domain. Without a fair use privilege for reverse engineering of computer software, the copyright owner could put an idea, process, or method of operation into an unintelligible format and assert copyright infringement against those who try to understand that idea. Thus, *Sega* allows effective access to the ideas underlying the program and prevents software owners from extending their property rights beyond the boundaries provided by copyright law. For these reasons, the court was reluctant to hinder a customary industry practice in a rapidly changing field of technology — particularly a practice that reduces development costs, accelerates innovation, and thereby facilitates competitive entry.[112]

§ 10.14 The Problem of Parody

[A] Generally

A *parody*[113] is an imitation of a serious piece of literature, music, or composition for humorous or satirical effect. A "parodist" is a critic or commentator who exposes the mediocre and pretentious in art and society, forcing us to examine a serious text from a comic standpoint.

Parody, by its very nature, makes use of another's work, sometimes extensively, and because the purpose of this use is satire and ridicule, there is a tension between

---

[109] *Id.* at 1523–24.

[110] *Id.* at 1526.

[111] 17 U.S.C. § 102(b). *See* § 2.12[B][1] *supra*.

[112] For a criticism of *Sega*, see Arthur R. Miller, *Copyright Protection for Computer Programs, Databases, and Computer-Generated Works: Is There Anything New Since CONTU?*, 106 Harv. L. Rev. 977, 1014–34 (1993) (the law imposes no duty on authors to provide access to copyrighted works. Permitting copyright owners to control intermediate copying is desirable because it increases protection against potentially infringing final products.

[113] The term "satire" is often used synonymously with "parody."

the parodist and the copyright owner. As a result, some copyright owners are less than eager to see their work ridiculed and will not license their work for this purpose. Consequently, the parodist must rely on the defense of fair use where substantial use has been made of a copyrighted work and where biting criticism and ridicule may have offended the sensibilities of a copyright owner.

Whether parody, for these reasons, is entitled to a wider fair use privilege than other uses has been the subject of a long, on-going debate.[114] In one sense, a true parody is not just an ordinary taking because it is a productive use, a form of criticism or comment, and as such, a use specifically enumerated in the preamble to § 107. Moreover, the fair use defense is particularly important for the health of this genre because a copyright owner will seldom license a work to be satirized or ridiculed. One could say that the parody defense to copyright infringement exists precisely to make possible a use that generally cannot be bought.[115]

[B] Parody and the Four Factors: *Campbell v. Acuff-Rose*

The four factors listed in § 107 are applied to parody just as to any other fair use issue and follow a consistent pattern. For most parodies, application of the first two factors does not favor a finding of fair use because most parodies are commercial[116] in purpose, and the nature of the copyrighted work they make use of is usually a work of entertainment, not one of information. The close questions usually relate to the third and fourth factors, that of amount and substantiality of the use and the market effect.

In *Campbell v. Acuff-Rose Music, Inc.*[117] the Supreme Court held that a commercial parody may qualify as a fair use. To decide the question of fair use, the court must subject the parody to a an overall balancing process in which the parody's "transformative" character is more important than its commercial purpose. In this case, Acuff-Rose owned the copyright to Roy Orbison's 1964 hit song "Oh, Pretty Woman." The rap group, 2 Live Crew, wrote and recorded a satirical version of the song also called "Pretty Woman" and in 1989 requested a license which Acuff-Rose refused to grant. 2 Live Crew released its satirical version of the Orbison classic anyway. Their version made use of the same drum beat from the original and its distinctive bass line, repeating it eight times throughout the song, while substituting

---

[114] See *Berlin v. E.C. Publications, Inc.*, 329 F.2d 541 (2d Cir.), *cert. denied*, 379 U.S. 822 (1964); *but cf. Walt Disney Prods. v. Air Pirates*, 581 F.2d 751 (9th Cir. 1978), *cert. denied*, 439 U.S. 1132 (1979).

[115] *Maxtone-Graham v. Burtchaell*, 803 F.2d 1253 (2d Cir. 1986); *but see Original Appalachian Artworks, Inc. v. Topps Chewing Gum, Inc.*, 642 F. Supp. 1031 (N.D. Ga. 1986), where bad faith was found on part of defendant who asked for a license to use plaintiff's children's dolls (Cabbage Patch Kids) and was rejected.

[116] The *Sony* presumption of market harm for commercial use should be relaxed for parodies which are invariably commercial. *See* David Goldberg, *Copyright Law*, N.Y.L.J., Nov. 21, 1986; *but see Original Appalachian Artworks, Inc. v. Topps Chewing Gum, Inc.*, 642 F. Supp. 1031 (N.D. Ga. 1986), which applied the *Sony* presumption and rejected the fair use defense primarily for that reason.

[117] 114 S. Ct. 1164 (1994).

its own words such as "big, hairy woman," "bald-headed woman," and "two-timin' woman" in place of Orbison's more genteel lyrics.

The Sixth Circuit had found that 2 Live Crew had infringed Acuff-Rose's "Oh Pretty Woman."[118] Relying on the *Sony* presumption, in which all unauthorized commercial (for profit) uses of copyrighted works are presumptively unfair and have a harmful effect on the market for the work, the court disallowed the fair use defense. The Supreme Court rejected the *Sony* presumption, at least when a parody is at issue, opting for a balancing process that would apply all four fair use factors. As for the first factor, the purpose and character of the use, the court held that the most important inquiry is not whether the use is commercial but whether it is "transforma-tive." The focus should be on whether the work alters the original with "new expression, meaning, and message."[119] The more transformative the new work, the less will be the significance of other factors, like commercialism, that weigh against a finding of fair use. After striking another blow against the *Sony* presumption, the court then turned to an issue that has plagued the courts in determining whether a parody is a fair use: How much can parody take from the original?

[C] How Much Can the Parody Take From the Original?

The third fair use factor, the amount and substantiality of the taking — how much a parody can copy from the original — remains the most controversial issue in determining fair use in the context of parody. The issue arises because the best parodies must take extensively from the original to create the humorous effect. A tension is created with the rights of copyright owners because extensive copying on the part of the parodist may supplant the need for the original. Should there be a wider privilege to take from the original to satisfy the needs of this art form? The issue was not resolved in *Acuff-Rose*. The Court repeated a familiar principle: "the parody must be able to 'conjure up' at least enough of [the] original to make the object of its critical wit recognized."[120] The Court added that the amount necessary to conjure up the original will depend on the persuasiveness of a parodist's justification for the particular copying done and will vary with the purpose and character of the use. Other than articulating these general principles, the court refused to decide whether excessive copying of the music had actually taken place and remanded the case on this issue.[121]

There are some statements in the case law[122] suggesting a wider privilege for parody, but generally courts have not given the parodist *carte blanche* to take indiscriminately from the copyrighted work. In short, the right to make the best parody is balanced against the rights of the copyright owner. The legal standard applied is that the parodist should be allowed to appropriate no greater amount of the original work than is necessary to recall or "conjure up" the object of his satire.[123] As a corollary, near verbatim copying will rarely, if ever, be a fair use.

[118] *Acuff-Rose Music, Inc. v. Campbell*, 972 F.2d 1429 (6th Cir. 1992).
[119] Citing Pierre Leval, *Toward a Fair Use Standard*, 103 Harv. L. Rev. 1105, 1111 (1990).
[120] *Acuff-Rose*, 114 S. Ct. at 1175.
[121] *Id.*
[122] *Berlin v. E.C. Publications, Inc.*, 329 F.2d 541, 545 (2d Cir. 1964).
[123] *Id.*

The "conjure up" test was reaffirmed but applied strictly in *Walt Disney v. Air Pirates*,[124] suggesting that the parodist can take only that which is *minimally* necessary to conjure up the original. In *Air Pirates*, the defendants prepared two magazines of cartoons entitled the *Air Pirates Funnies*, an underground counter-culture comic book which made use of Disney characters placing them in bawdy situations. The court rejected fair use of the Disney characters as the taking exceeded what was necessary to conjure up the original. The court suggested that the conjure up standard will vary from case to case and that a lesser taking was necessary for widely recognizable graphic images of the Disney characters than if the subject of the parody was a less concrete literary work such as a speech.

> By copying the images in their entirety, defendants took more than was necessary to place firmly in the reader's mind the parodied work and those specific attributes that are to be satirized.[125]

Other courts, notably the Second Circuit, apply the conjure up test, allowing a greater taking than that minimally necessary, if the parody builds on the original, contributing something new for humorous effect or commentary.[126]

[D]   Parody and the Fourth Fair Use Factor: Market Effect

The fourth factor, the market effect of the use, will be decided in favor of the parodist absent near verbatim copying.[127] The parody will usually not fulfill the demand for the original and rarely could the plaintiff argue that the market for this type of derivative work has been co-opted by the use.[128]

Thus, no presumption or inference of market harm is applicable unless the parody simply duplicates the original in its entirety for commercial purposes. However, when the second use is transformative, market substitution is less certain and market harm is not so readily inferred.[129] In determining market effect, it is not the impact of the parody as criticism but the economic effect of the use in fulfilling the demand for the original that is the issue.[130] Because of its devastating criticism, an effective

---

[124] *Walt Disney Prods. v. Air Pirates*, 581 F.2d 751 (9th Cir. 1978).

[125] *Id.* at 758.

[126] *Elsmere Music, Inc. v. National Broadcasting Co.*, 623 F.2d 252, 253 n.1 (2d Cir. 1980).

[127] *Benny v. Loew's, Inc.*, 239 F.2d 532 (9th Cir. 1956).

[128] *See Pillsbury Co. v. Milky Way Prods., Inc.*, 215 U.S.P.Q. (BNA) 124 (N.D. Ga. 1981) (fair use and no market harm found for defendant's pornographic depiction in *Screw Magazine* of characters resembling plaintiff's *Poppin* and *Poppin' Fresh* figures).

[129] *Campbell v. Acuff-Rose Music, Inc.*, 114 S. Ct. 1164, 1177 (1994).

[130] *Fisher v. Dees*, 794 F.2d 432 (9th Cir. 1986). The court held that a song parody, *When Sunny Sniffs Glue*, based on the original song, *When Sunny Gets Blue*, was a fair use, primarily because it did not supplant the need for the original. *Cf. Original Appalachian Artworks, Inc. v. Topps Chewing Gum, Inc.*, 642 F. Supp. 1031 (N.D. Ga. 1986) (defendant sold stickers resembling plaintiff's popular children's dolls, Cabbage Patch Kids, but which were much more grotesque in style. The district court rejected the fair use defense because of the commercial nature of defendant's use. The court emphasized the *Sony* presumption of potential market harm, which could also be shown from the fact that the products competed for the same children's market. In addition, the court found defendant's principal purpose was to earn a profit rather than to engage in social commentary).

parody may actually diminish the demand for the original. This is not the kind of market effect which justifies a denial of fair use.[131] The real issue for the fair use determination is whether the parody fulfills the demand for the original, that is, whether consumers are likely to purchase the parody rather than the original because it serves the same purpose as the original.

[E] Does the Parody Have to Satirize the Copyrighted Work?

Whether a parody, to qualify for fair use, has to satirize the copyrighted work itself or whether it may use the copyrighted work for some other humorous purpose has been a point of controversy for some time.[132] The Second Circuit Court of Appeals, which has examined this question in greater depth than any other court, has vacillated on this basic issue but the trend is to require that the parody comment in some way on the original.[133] This view was confirmed by the Supreme Court in *Acuff-Rose*, which sided with the traditional definition of "parody" as a literary or artistic work that imitates the characteristic style of an author or a work for comic effect or ridicule.[134] It rejected the contrary view that would allow use of the original work for humorous effect even though the original was not the object of ridicule or satire.

That a parody need be aimed at least partially at the original is justified by the original purpose of granting to a parody a fair use privilege — to criticize another text through satirical ridicule. When the original is used for general comic purposes or to criticize other targets, the same pressing need to encroach on the original does not exist. In other words, if the copyrighted song is not at least in part an object

---

[131] *Campbell v. Acuff-Rose Music, Inc.*, 114 S. Ct. 1164, 1177 (1994) ("when a lethal parody . . . kills demand for the original, it does not produce a harm cognizable under the Copyright Act").

[132] *Compare Metro-Goldwyn-Mayer, Inc. v. Showcase Atlanta Coop. Prods., Inc.*, 479 F. Supp. 351 (N.D. Ga. 1979) (the musical stage version of *Gone With The Wind*, although comic, did not constitute a parody), *with Fisher v. Dees*, 794 F.2d 432, 436 (9th Cir. 1986).

[133] *See Berlin v. E.C. Publications, Inc*, 329 F.2d 541, 542 (2d Cir.), *cert. denied*, 379 U.S. 822 (1964) (*Mad Magazine*'s lyrics to be sung to the tunes of Irving Berlin and others were ruled a fair use even though the object of the humor was not the songs themselves but the "idiotic world we live in today."); *Elsmere Music, Inc. v. National Broadcasting Co.*, 623 F.2d 252 (2d Cir. 1980) (the primary question is whether the use is a valid satire or parody, not whether it is a parody of the song itself. *But see MCA, Inc. v. Wilson*, 677 F.2d 180 (2d Cir. 1981) (risque version of the Andrews Sisters' classic, "The Boogie Woogie Bugle Boy of Company B," entitled "Cunnilingus Champion of Company C," not a fair use). Generally, pornographic parodies do not receive a fair use privilege. *See, e.g., Dallas Cowboys Cheerleaders v. Scoreboard Posters, Inc.*, 600 F.2d 1184 (5th Cir. 1979); *Pillsbury Co. v. Milky Way Prods., Inc.*, 215 U.S.P.Q. (BNA) 124 (N.D. Ga. 1981); *Walt Disney Prods. v. Mature Pictures Corp.*, 389 F. Supp. 1397 (S.D.N.Y. 1975); *Walt Disney Prods. v. Air Pirates*, 581 F.2d 751 (9th Cir. 1978).

[134] *Campbell v. Acuff-Rose Music, Inc.*, 114 S. Ct. 1164, 1171 (1994); *see also Rogers v. Koons*, 960 F.2d 301 (2d Cir. 1992) (Three dimensional wood sculpture in unnatural color scheme based on black and white photographs of a photograph of puppies, was not a fair use. Although it may be a satirical critique of the "materialist" society in which we live, there was no parody of the photograph itself).

of the parody, there is no need to conjure it up. Thus, parody must do more than merely achieve comic effect but must make some critical comment or statement about the original work. Otherwise, the parodist should be required to obtain permission from the copyright owner to use the work.[135]

§ 10.15   Fair Use and the First Amendment

[A]   Generally: No Irreconcilable Tension

A few courts,[136] and more commentators [137] have referred to a tension between copyright and the First Amendment to the Constitution that "Congress shall make no law . . . abridging the freedom of speech. . . ."[138] Copyright appears to encroach on the freedom of speech and First Amendment values because it prohibits the right to reproduce the expression of others. But does this produce an irreconcilable tension between the two constitutional provisions: the Patent and Copyright Clause and the First Amendment?

Despite the amount of space devoted to this subject in law reviews, only one court has ever held that the First Amendment prevents the enforcement of copyright.[139] It has now been universally accepted that copyright's idea-expression dichotomy supplies the necessary definitional balance allowing access to and dissemination of ideas and facts while protecting the author's expression.[140] Moreover, the defense of fair use can be invoked where rigid application of the Copyright Act would unreasonably prevent the dissemination of information.[141] Viewed in this way, copyright law optimizes First Amendment values by encouraging production of works of authorship without prohibiting the free communication of facts and ideas embodied in these works. Copyright law does not impede the flow of information

---

[135] *See* Julie Bisceglia, *Parody & Copyright Protection: Turning the Balancing Act into a Juggling Act*, 34 Copyright L. Symp. (ASCAP) 1, 26 (1987). *See also* Richard A. Posner, *When Is Parody Fair Use?*, 21 J. Legal Stud. 67 (1992) (parody is fair use when used to target the original, not when it is used a weapon for humorous effect or to ridicule society at large).

[136] *Triangle Publications, Inc. v. Knight-Ridder Newspapers, Inc.*, 626 F.2d 1171 (5th Cir. 1980); *Schnapper v. Foley*, 471 F. Supp. 426 (D.D.C. 1979); *Maxtone-Graham v. Burtchaell*, 631 F. Supp. 1432 (S.D.N.Y. 1986).

[137] To mention a few: Robert C. Denicola, *Copyright and Free Speech: Constitutional Limitations on the Protection of Expression*, 67 Calif. L. Rev. 283 (1979); Paul Goldstein, *Copyright and the First Amendment*, 70 Colum. L. Rev. 983 (1970); Nimmer, *Does Copyright Abridge the First Amendment Guarantees of Free Speech and Press?*, 17 UCLA L. Rev. 1180 (1970); Lyman Ray Patterson, *Private Copyright and Public Communication: Free Speech Endangered*, 28 Vand. L. Rev. 1161 (1975).

[138] U.S. Const. amend. I.

[139] *Triangle Publications, Inc. v. Knight-Ridder Newspapers, Inc.*, 626 F.2d 1171 (5th Cir. 1980). *See also Schnapper v. Foley*, 471 F. Supp. 426 (D.D.C. 1979).

[140] *See Sid & Marty Krofft Television Prods., Inc. v. McDonald's Corp.*, 562 F.2d 1157 (9th Cir. 1977).

[141] *Consumers Union of United States, Inc. v. General Signal Corp.*, 724 F.2d 1044, 1046 (2d Cir. 1983).

per se, and is not an obstacle to the free flow of ideas, but provides positive incentives to encourage the flow.[142] As one court phrased it,

> The judgment of the Constitution is that free expression is enriched by protecting the creations of authors from exploitation by others. . . . The First Amendment is not a license to trammel on legally recognized rights of intellectual property.[143]

Accordingly, if plaintiff can demonstrate a substantial likelihood of copyright infringement, a court in its discretion can grant a preliminary injunction barring publication of the infringing work despite the First Amendment preclusion of prior restraints on speech.[144]

[B] The Merger of Idea and Expression

One may agree that no inherent irreconcilable conflict exists between copyright law and the First Amendment. But could there be certain situations in which the First Amendment would mandate copying beyond the furthest reaches of fair use? In *Triangle Publications, Inc. v. Knight-Ridder Newspapers, Inc.*,[145] the defendant publisher of the *Miami Herald* used the cover of *T.V. Guide* in its comparative advertisement campaign to promote its own television supplement. The District Court held that the defendant's use of the *T.V. Guide* cover was not a fair use but found it privileged under the commercial speech branch of the First Amendment.[146] The Court of Appeals affirmed the result but not the lower court's First Amendment rationale. It held that defendant's use of the cover was a fair use, primarily because it did not affect the market for the work.[147]

A concurring opinion in *Knight-Ridder* suggested that there might be situations in which the First Amendment would have a role to play but not in the current case. Professor Nimmer, who has written extensively on the subject, would agree, but only where idea and expression are so inextricably wedded that one could not use the idea in the copyright without using its expression.[148] To Nimmer, it is difficult to come up with appropriate examples where the merger of idea and expression occur, necessitating use of a copyrighted work beyond the fair use privilege. He does, however, cite the example of a newsphoto which would have to be reproduced and displayed in its entirety to express the idea embodied in it.[149] His rationale: how

---

[142] *See, e.g., Pacific and Southern Co., Inc. v. Duncan*, 744 F.2d 1490 (11th Cir. 1984).

[143] *Dallas Cowboys Cheerleaders, Inc. v. Scoreboard Posters, Inc.*, 600 F.2d 1184, 1187–88 (5th Cir. 1979).

[144] *Id.* at 1188; *Salinger v. Random House, Inc.*, 811 F.2d 90 (2d Cir. 1987) (enjoining publication of a biography of the writer J.D. Salinger); *see also Craft v. Kobler*, 667 F. Supp. 120 (S.D.N.Y. 1987), where a forthcoming biography of Igor Stravinsky, the composer, was enjoined because the appropriations of copyrighted material were too extensive and important and their justification too slight to support an overall claim of fair use.

[145] 626 F.2d 1171 (5th Cir. 1980).

[146] *Triangle Publications v. Knight-Ridder Newspapers, Inc.*, 445 F. Supp. 875 (S.D. Fla. 1978).

[147] 626 F.2d 1171, 1178 (5th Cir. 1980).

[148] 1 *Nimmer on Copyright* § 110[e] (1993).

[149] This situation approximates *Time, Inc. v. Bernard Geis Associates*, 293 F. Supp. 130 (S.D.N.Y. 1968), in which the court allowed extensive verbatim copying for commercial

else could the idea of horror or revulsion in a picture of a rioting crowd, an assassinated political leader, or a natural disaster be conveyed? According to Nimmer, other than in this narrow newsphoto exception, there are few, if any, instances where First Amendment values would conflict with copyright.

The merger of idea and expression as a First Amendment defense was asserted by the defendant in the *Nation* case, but was ultimately rejected by the Supreme Court.[150] According to *The Nation* magazine, not only the facts contained in the Ford memoirs but the precise manner in which he expressed them were as newsworthy as what he said. The Supreme Court disagreed, finding that in *The Nation*'s case, quoted portions of the unpublished manuscript were excessive and were not protected under fair use. As for the First Amendment, the Court reasoned that copyright's idea-expression dichotomy provided the proper definitional balance between copyright and the First Amendment, and even public figures who write newsworthy memoirs should be able to enjoy the market for their original expression. The Court stated

> [i]n our haste to disseminate news, it should not be forgotten that the Framers intended copyright itself to be the engine of free expression. By establishing a marketable right to the use of one's expression, copyright supplies the economic incentive to create and disseminate ideas.[151]

As the Supreme Court noted, there should be no public figure exception to copyright protection,[152] otherwise public figures would have less incentive to record their impressions. In short, the Copyright Act and the First Amendment are mutually supportive.

---

purposes of the Zapruder film taken of the Kennedy assassination. Frames of the film were closely rendered in drawings for a *Life* magazine article on the assassination. The court justified the taking on fair use grounds stating that

> the public interest in having the fullest information available on the murder of President Kennedy outweighed the copyright owner's interest in the work.

See also Rosemont Enterprises, Inc. v. Random House, Inc., 366 F.2d 303 (2d Cir. 1966), *cert. denied*, 385 U.S. 1009 (1967), where the court sustained a fair use defense on public interest grounds despite defendant's substantial use of copyrighted magazine articles. It is not clear in either *Rosemont* or *Time* whether the court has adopted the public interest as a separate fair use factor. Instead, reference to the public interest appears to incorporate First Amendment values into the fair use determination.

[150] *See Harper & Row, Publishers, Inc. v. Nation Enterprises*, 471 U.S. 539 (1985).
[151] *Harper & Row, Publishers, Inc. v. Nation Enterprises*, 471 U.S. 539, 558 (1985).
[152] *Id.* at 559.

§ 10.16   Fair Use: A Synthesis[153]

After almost one hundred fifty years, the doctrine of fair use remains as elusive as ever. But despite its amorphous codification in § 107, and a conflicting body of case law, certain general principles do surface. The fair use determination supports the underlying goals of copyright law: to create conditions for the optimum amount of production and dissemination of works of authorship. In applying fair use, a court ultimately must decide whether the interest in dissemination outweighs possible harm to the economic incentives to produce copyrighted works. Courts, in determining fair use issues, if not always explicitly, appear to concentrate on two dimensions[154] more than others: (1) the public benefit of the defendant's use, whether the use is productive or reproductive; and (2) the harm to the market for the copyrighted work, whether the use is commercial or non-commercial. The analysis is illustrated by the following chart:

---

[153] For other attempts to synthesize the doctrine, see Stephen Freid, *Fair Use and the New Act*, 22 N.Y.L.S. L. Rev. 497 (1977); Wendy J. Gordon, *Fair Use as Market Failure: A Structural and Economic Analysis of the* Betamax *Case and its Predecessors*, 82 Colum. L. Rev. 1600 (1982); Note, *Toward A Unified Theory of Copyright Infringement for an Advanced Technological Era*, 96 Harv. L. Rev. 450 (1982); Leo J. Raskind, *A Functional Interpretation of Fair Use*, 31 J. Copyright Soc'y 601 (1984).

[154] The term "dimensions" is used here rather than "factors" although the dimensions loosely relate to factors one and four of § 107 respectively.

Extent of Commercial Exploitation

		Non-commercial	Commercial
	Productive	Strongest case for Fair Use	Hard cases, *e.g.*, Parody
Public Benefit of the Use	Reproductive	Hard cases, *e.g.*, *Betamax* case	Weakest case for Fair Use

The easiest cases to justify on fair use grounds are those where defendant has made a productive, non-commercial use[155] of plaintiff's work, as for example, where a scholar writing an article for a learned journal quotes from plaintiff's copyrighted work. Here defendant's use is consistent with the ultimate public interest goal of copyright law, which is to encourage the optimal amount of production and dissemination of works of authorship. Access is given to plaintiff's work to enable another to build on it and to produce another work of authorship. The public is benefited, and because the market for the work is not harmed, the incentives to produce works of authorship are not suppressed. Alternatively, the easiest case against fair use occurs when a non-productive (reproductive) commercial use is made of a work. Here, ordinary infringement has occurred and fair use cannot be justified.

The more difficult fair use issues arise when defendant has made a reproductive but non-commercial use of plaintiff's work. The interplay of fair use and the new technologies often involves this issue, as for example, in the *Betamax*[156] case. In these situations, other factors must be considered. Fair use will often be found in the interest of dissemination of the copyrighted work, particularly when the copyright owner would gain little from prohibiting access to his work and it would be impractical for the defendants to negotiate for the use of a copyrighted work.[157]

---

[155] *See* § 10.5, *supra*.

[156] *Sony Corp. of America v. Universal City Studios*, 464 U.S. 417 (1984).

[157] *See* Wendy J. Gordon, *Fair Use as Market Failure: A Structural and Economic Analysis of the* Betamax *Case and its Predecessors*, 82 Colum. L. Rev. 1600 (1982), justifying

Moreover, implicit in these cases is an awareness of effects of the ruling on a new technology.

When defendant's use is productive but commercial, another difficult issue in fair use analysis is presented. Here the courts will look to the nature of the copyrighted work and the amount and substantiality of the use, as was done in the *Nation*[158] case. Parody often presents this mix of productive and commercial use, and the critical issue is how much of plaintiff's work is needed to be used to conjure up the original for the purposes of parody. Thus, if a parody builds on but does not supplant the original through excessive use, the public is benefited. It has received a net increase in information available, a new work of authorship, and possible harm to the economic incentives for future creation is not sufficient to offset the use.[159]

---

application of fair use doctrine in situations where the copier would be unable to reach an agreement with the copyright owner and no corresponding reward to the copyright owner would offset disallowing access to the work. *See also* Douglas G. Baird, *Changing Technology and Unchanging Doctrine*: Sony Corporation v. Universal Studios, Inc., 1984 Sup. Ct. Rev. 237.

[158] *Harper & Row, Publishers, Inc. v. Nation Enterprises*, 471 U.S. 539, 558 (1985).

[159] *See* § 10.14, *supra*.

CHAPTER **11**

COPYRIGHT LAW IN A FEDERAL SYSTEM: PREEMPTION OF STATE LAW

§ 11.1   Introduction and Chapter Overview

An extensive system of state law protection of intangibles has always coexisted with federal intellectual property law. State trade secret, common law copyright, and unfair competition laws overlap federal patent, trademark, and copyright laws both in the subject matter involved and in the rights protected. The coexistence, however, has not always been harmonious, and the overlapping forms of intellectual property protection have created tensions within the federal system. The vehicle for regulating these tensions is the Supremacy Clause of the Constitution[1] which dictates that a federal statute preempts, *i.e.*, displaces, state law, when the state law, "stands as an obstacle to the accomplishment and execution of the full purposes and objectives of Congress."[2] As applied to forms of intellectual property protection, the issue under the Supremacy Clause is not whether states have the power to protect intellectual property but rather, under what circumstances does state protection unduly interfere with the objectives and policies of federal protection? Deciding this difficult question has often led to irreconcilable results and conflicting doctrine as, for example, in copyright law, where the preemption doctrine was in disarray under the 1909 Act. One objective of Congress in promulgating the new Copyright Act in 1976 was to clarify preemption doctrine. Unfortunately, the 1976 Act has done little, if anything, to solve the problem.

---

[1] U.S. Const., art. VI, cl. 2 reads:

> This Constitution, and the Laws of the United States . . . shall be the supreme Law of the Land; and the Judges in every State shall be bound thereby, any Thing in the Constitution or Laws of any State to the Contrary notwithstanding.

[2] *Hines v. Davidowitz*, 312 U.S. 52, 67 (1941). *See also Synercom Technology, Inc. v. University Computing Co.*, 474 F. Supp. 37, 42 (N.D. Tex. 1979). Traditionally, courts have found that a state law is preempted in two situations. First, when Congress has so occupied the field in question that state legislation is foreclosed. Courts have found federal occupation in the express terms of the federal legislation or by implication. *See, e.g., Roy v. Atlantic Richfield Co.* 435 U.S. 151 (1978) (clear Congressional decision for national uniformity of standards). Second, state law will be preempted when it conflicts with the basic objectives of a federal statute. *See, e.g., Pacific Gas & Electric Co. v. State Energy Resources Conservation Comm'n*, 461 U.S. 190, 203–04 (1983). Generally, courts have been reluctant to preempt state law unless there is an express Congressional intent to do so, or in instances where there is a high degree of federal-state conflict. *See, e.g., Maryland v. Louisiana*, 451 U.S. 725, 746 (1981).

Some of the confusion under the 1909 Act[3] was caused by the bifurcated nature of copyright law, where the dividing line between state and federal copyright protection was publication.[4] State common law copyright protected unpublished works and federal copyright began when a work was published. But even after a work was published, it was never quite clear how far the states could go to protect writings of authors.[5]

Effective January 1, 1978, the Copyright Act of 1976 eliminated the dual system, replacing it with a single national system whereby virtually all works of authorship, whether published or unpublished, were made exclusively the subject of federal law. Partly in anticipation of conflicts between federal and state law, and partly to avoid the uncertainties of the pre-1976 preemption doctrine, § 301 of the 1976 Act sets forth specific criteria for preemption. Under the 1976 Act, state law is specifically preempted under § 301[6] when two conditions are met: first, the state law must protect the same rights conferred in § 106,[7] and second, the state law must protect the same subject matter enumerated in §§ 102 and 103.[8] Although § 301 was intended to clarify the preemption doctrine as it applied to copyright law, it has instead superimposed another set of problems on this already complicated and confusing subject.

To understand § 301, it is important to consider preemption doctrine as it developed before the 1976 Act. Part I of this chapter provides the *pre*-1976 background to the preemption issue. Its three sections trace the development of state copyright protection and the way in which the Supreme Court used preemption doctrine in trying to harmonize state law not just with federal copyright law, but also with federal law in related areas of intellectual property, particularly federal patent law. Much of the controversy has concerned the misappropriation doctrine, a broad and amorphous, basically equitable concept, used by courts to protect intangible property which failed to meet federal intellectual property standards. Part II examines preemption under § 301 of the 1976 Copyright Act. Most of the discussion is devoted to the meaning of rights equivalent, one of the two elements that must be found for preemption to take place. The conclusion reached is that Congress largely failed to provide a bright line guide to preemption and, as a consequence, one must look to traditional preemption doctrine much as it was before the 1976 Act.

---

[3] Ch. 320, 35 Stat. 1075, revised by 17 U.S.C. §§ 101–914 (1982 and Supp. III 1985).

[4] For a discussion of publication doctrine, see § 4.2, *supra*.

[5] U.S. Const., art. I, § 8, cl. 8.

[6] 17 U.S.C. § 301.

[7] 17 U.S.C. § 106.

[8] 17 U.S.C. §§ 102, 103.

PART I: Preemption Before the 1976 Act

§ 11.2   The Misappropriation Doctrine and Other State Attempts to Protect Intellectual Property: The 1909 Act Background[9]

[A]   Two Divergent Tendencies

Federal intellectual property protection constitutes a relatively well-defined body of law, despite the intangible nature of its subject matter. In general, federal law, as exemplified by the copyright and patent statutes, attempts to balance the property rights of creators against the public's right of access to the intangible creation. Copyright law strikes this balance by protecting only certain categories of works. It also imposes limits on that protection, such as the fair use doctrine, the idea-expression dichotomy, and the limited duration of a copyright. Patent law[10] also balances access with incentive to create, but in a significantly different way from copyright law. In return for disclosure of the invention, the patentee is given a highly exclusive monopoly right. That right, much more limited in duration than a copyright, lasts no more than seventeen years. Further, it is much more difficult to acquire than copyright because of the rigorous standards of patentability.

Through the years, two general attitudes have been expressed about how expansive state law should be in protecting valuable intangibles we call intellectual property. The expansive view would permit an active role for state law in filling gaps in protection left by federal law. This view would allow the state to actively regulate intellectual property, except in clear instances of conflict with federal law. The opposing minimal view would treat common law protection for intellectual property with much suspicion because of its tendency to take information out of the public domain. This view favors federal intellectual property law and the public domain over an active regime of state regulation of intellectual property.[11]

[B]   The Classic Statement: The *INS* Case

Courts have wavered between these two divergent views, which found their classic statement in *International News Service v. Associated Press*.[12] In this *pre-Erie* case,[13] a majority of the Supreme Court recognized broad common law[14]

---

[9] For an excellent overview, see Howard B. Abrams, *Copyright, Misappropriation and Preemption: Constitutional and Statutory Limits of State Law Protection*, 1983 Sup. Ct. Rev. 509; 1 *Nimmer on Copyright* § 1.01 (1993); Paul Goldstein, *Copyright* §§ 15–15.34 (1989).

[10] For a general discussion of patent law, see § 1.11, *supra*.

[11] The power of the states to regulate matters of copyright dates back to the first copyright case in the Supreme Court, *Wheaton v. Peters*, 33 U.S. (8 Pet.) 591 (1834), where the Court acknowledged state protection of published works. This dichotomous system of copyright protection lasted until the 1976 Act unified copyright law under a single federal system.

[12] 248 U.S. 215 (1918).

[13] In *Erie R.R. v. Tompkins*, 304 U.S. 64 (1938), the Supreme Court held that the federal courts must apply state substantive law on non-federal questions.

[14] *INS* was a diversity case which based its decision on federal common law. A major issue in the case was whether the misappropriation doctrine under federal common law impinged

power to regulate intangible interests by upholding the misappropriation doctrine as a vehicle for protecting intellectual property. The Court forbade the International News Service (INS), a rival news organization, from copying the Associated Press's (AP) hot news stories and publishing them on the West coast before AP was able to do so. "Passing off" — unfair competition in the traditional sense of the term — was not involved; the I.N.S. was not trying to deceive consumers about the origin of these stories. They simply took valuable information without permission or payment. The news stories themselves may not have qualified for copyright protection, having been published without notice, or perhaps not demonstrating sufficient originality. Nonetheless, the Supreme Court held that INS's acts constituted a "misappropriation" because "he who has fairly paid the price should have the beneficial use of the property."[15] The misappropriation doctrine is based on a natural rights theory which recognizes the right of an individual to the fruits of his labor.

Justice Brandeis, in dissent, eloquently stated the case for a narrower field of protection:

> . . . [T]he fact that a product of the mind has cost its producer money and labor, and has a value for which others are willing to pay, is not sufficient to ensure to it this legal attribute of property. The general rule of law is, that the noblest of human productions — knowledge, truths ascertained, conceptions, and ideas — become, after voluntary communication to others, free as the air to common use. Upon these incorporeal productions the attribute of property is continued after such communication only in certain classes of cases where public policy has seemed to demand it.[16]

The sentiment expressed by Brandeis reflects a hostile attitude toward expansive state protection of intangibles. To Brandeis, any protection conferred on intellectual property should be limited and, except in narrow circumstances, should be a matter of federal statutory law.

The far-reaching equitable doctrine recognized in the *INS* case, known as the "misappropriation doctrine," provided broad, though vaguely defined, protection against the taking of intangible values.[17] Because state misappropriation laws

---

on federal statutory protection of intellectual property law. The *INS* case has also been read to permit state law to operate in the intellectual property field despite federal statutory patent and copyright law. If it were not read in this way, it would only be an historical curiosity because a general federal common law no longer exists after *Erie*.

Indeed, the argument has been made that the *INS* case is no longer authoritative because it was decided before *Erie* had abolished federal common law. *See, e.g., DeCosta v. Columbia Broadcasting Sys., Inc.*, 520 F.2d 499 (1st Cir. 1975), *cert. denied*, 433 U.S. 1073 (1976). Other courts have based their decisions on the *INS* case despite its pre-*Erie* status. *See Board of Trade v. Dow Jones & Co., Inc.*, 108 Ill. App. 3d 681, 439 N.E.2d 526 (1982).

[15] 248 U.S. 215, 240 (1918).

[16] *Id.* at 250.

[17] The elusive doctrine has been defined as follows:

> 1. Plaintiff has created an intangible product through extensive time, labor, skill and money. 2. The free riding defendant, a competitor, makes use of that product and

overlapped federal patent and copyright law, it was inevitable that the preemption issue would rise again.

Beginning in the 1930's, the pendulum began to swing against permitting broad state protection of intangibles,[18] but the culmination of this anti-state sentiment occurred in 1964 when the Supreme Court confronted the preemption issue in the *Sears* and *Compco* cases. These two Supreme Court cases, decided the same day, appeared to narrow drastically the scope of state law in protecting intellectual property.

§ 11.3   Preemption Reborn: *Sears* and *Compco*[19]

In *Sears, Roebuck & Co. v. Stiffel Co.*[20] and *Compco Corp. v. Day-Brite Lighting, Inc.*,[21] the Supreme Court reasserted preemption under the Supremacy Clause, invalidating state law protection of intangible property rights. With these two cases, the Court seemed to declare the end of the misappropriation doctrine, and other state law causes of action protecting intellectual property. In sum, the pendulum appeared to have swung in the direction of the Brandeis dissent in *INS*.

In *Sears* and *Compco*, plaintiffs brought actions under the Illinois unfair competition law for copying product shapes, pole lamps in *Sears* and fluorescent lighting fixtures in *Compco*. Neither product shape qualified for either mechanical or design patent protection, and neither manufacturer had sought copyright protection. The Supreme Court invalidated Illinois's unfair competition law, finding that the state law was preempted because it conflicted with federal copyright and patent law. The Court appeared to reject the misappropriation doctrine and any similar state regulation, providing intellectual property rights beyond those granted by federal law. The key language in *Compco* is:

---

gains a special advantage because the defendant is not burdened with the same costs of production. 3. Plaintiff suffers commercial damage.

Synercom Technology, Inc. v. University Computing Co., 474 F. Supp. 37, 39 (N.D. Tex. 1979). Some courts do not require a competitive relationship but have rather focused on the unjust enrichment aspect of defendant's actions. *See, e.g., Metropolitan Opera Ass'n v. Wagner-Nichols Recorder Corp.*, 101 N.Y.S.2d 483, 492 (Sup. Ct. 1950), *aff'd*, 279 A.D. 632, 107 N.Y.S.2d 795 (1951) (misappropriation claim upheld where defendant transcribed radio broadcasts of plaintiff's operatic performances and sold them to the retail market). *See also Standard & Poor's Corp. v. Commodity Exch., Inc.*, 683 F.2d 704 (2d Cir. 1982) (upholding injunction preventing the Commodity Exchange from creating a market for futures contracts based on Standard & Poor's 500 Index (S&P 500)).

[18] *See, e.g., Cheney Bros. v. Doris Silk Corp.*, 35 F.2d 279 (2d Cir. 1929), where Learned Hand refused to extend the *INS* rationale to protect dress designers. *See also R.C.A. Mfg. Co. v. Whiteman*, 114 F.2d 86 (2d Cir.), *cert. denied*, 311 U.S. 712 (1940) (restrictive legend on a phonograph record cannot prevent subsequent broadcast of the record).

[19] For an overview, see J. Thomas McCarthy, *Trademarks and Unfair Competition* §§ 10.23–10.34 (2d ed. 1984).

[20] 376 U.S. 225 (1964).

[21] 376 U.S. 234 (1964).

. . . [W]hen an article is unprotected by a patent or a copyright, state law may not forbid others to copy that article.[22]

Similar to the Brandeis dissent in the *INS* case, these decisions reflect a strong policy favoring competitive copying unencumbered by state law, unless the subject matter was protected by federal intellectual property law.

§ 11.4   The Aftermath of *Sears* and *Compco* [23]

Lower courts applied *Sears* and *Compco* inconsistently. Some adopted the broadest preemptive reading of these cases.[24] Other courts, however, struggled to reconcile *Sears* and *Compco* with the seeming inequity of allowing imitators to take a free ride on another's intellectual creation, simply because the creation was not protected by copyright or other federal intellectual property law. These courts often relied on trivial differences to distinguish *Sears* and *Compco* from the case at bar.[25] Given the uncertainty of state law protection following *Sears* and *Compco*, plaintiffs looked elsewhere to protect intangible values from imitation. One result was a heightened interest in § 43(a) [26] of the Lanham Act, a federal unfair competition law, which circumvented the preemption problem because it was federal law.[27]

In *Goldstein v. California*,[28] the broad preemptive thrust of *Sears* and *Compco* was substantially narrowed when the Supreme Court held that states have concurrent power with the federal government to protect works of authorship. *Goldstein* involved a criminal statute prohibiting the copying of musical recordings without permission. At the time the cause of action arose, sound recordings were not protected under federal copyright law and record piracy was rife. The criminal statute in *Goldstein* attempted to protect an important state industry threatened by

---

[22] *Id.* at 237.

[23] For an overview, see Ralph S. Brown, Jr., *Publication and Preemption in Copyright Law: Elegiac Reflections on* Goldstein v. California, 22 UCLA L. Rev. 1022 (1975).

[24] *Columbia Broadcasting Sys., Inc. v. DeCosta*, 377 F.2d 315 (1st Cir. 1967).

[25] During this time, there were several state efforts to protect record producers against the unauthorized duplication of tape and records. Until the Sound Recording Act of 1971, the copyright law (1909 Act) did not recognize sound recordings as copyrightable subject matter. Record producers looked to state remedies, *see, e.g., Tape Industries Ass'n of America v. Younger*, 316 F. Supp. 340 (C.D. Cal. 1970), and *Capitol Records, Inc. v. Erickson*, 2 Cal. App. 3d 526, 82 Cal. Rptr. 798 (1969), *cert. denied*, 398 U.S. 960 (1970), reasoning that tape duplication is not "copying" within the meaning of *Sears-Compco*, but rather misappropriation of the owner's labors. The distinction between copying and misappropriation is clearly a fiction. When one misappropriates, one is merely reproducing another's work. *See also Pottstown Daily News Publishing Co. v. Pottstown Broadcasting Co.*, 247 F. Supp. 578 (E.D. Pa. 1965); and *Capitol Records, Inc. v. Greatest Records, Inc.*, 43 Misc. 2d 878, 252 N.Y.S.2d 553 (Sup. Ct. 1964) (upholding State's power to protect sound recordings as unpublished works).

[26] 15 U.S.C. § 1025(a).

[27] *See, e.g., Truck Equipment Service Co. v. Freuhauf Corp.*, 536 F.2d 1210 (8th Cir.), *cert. denied*, 429 U.S. 861 (1976).

[28] 412 U.S. 546 (1973).

this widespread piracy. The issue in *Goldstein* was whether the California anti-piracy statute was preempted by federal law.

The Court analyzed the preemption issue on two different levels. The first level involved whether the Copyright Clause of the Constitution totally precluded the states from legislating in that area. The second level concerned whether the California tape piracy statute was implicitly preempted by federal copyright law.

The Court found no broad-based preemption under the Copyright Clause of the Constitution. First, nothing in the Constitution explicitly indicated that Congress had been granted exclusive power to protect writings of authors.[29] Second, the power given to Congress to protect writings of authors was not a matter of such national interest that state legislation in the field would inevitably lead to conflicts with federal law.[30]

The Court also held that the California statute was not preempted under the Supremacy Clause; it found no conflict between federal copyright policy and California's protection of sound recordings.[31] The opinion distinguished *Sears* and *Compco* as cases involving patent policy where the requirement for uniform national protection of limited duration is greater than in copyright.[32] As for any conflict with copyright policy, the Court stated:

> No comparable conflict between state law and federal law arises in the case of recordings of musical performances. In regard to this category of "Writings", Congress has drawn no balance; rather, it has left the area unattended, and no reason exists why the State should not be free to act.[33]

One year later, the Supreme Court, in *Kewanee Oil Co. v. Bicron Corp.*,[34] took a similar position on the power of the states to protect trade secrets, further narrowing the preemption doctrine as articulated in *Sears* and *Compco*. In *Kewanee*, plaintiff had developed a process for a new synthetic crystal for use in detecting ionizing radiation. The process was potentially patentable, but the plaintiff decided not to seek patent protection; instead, it tried to enforce its rights to the process under Ohio's trade secret law. The Court found that state trade secret law was not preempted by federal patent law because the state law neither clashed with the objectives of federal patent law nor obstructed congressional purposes.[35] Thus *Goldstein* and *Kewanee* erased the bright line presumption favoring preemption as set forth in *Sears* and *Compco*. The new approach focused on whether state and federal law could exist harmoniously in the same field, and whether Congress had a clearly stated policy in favor of preemption. In short, by 1974, the pendulum had now swung toward the expansionist view, giving the states a wide ambit in which to regulate matters of intellectual property, at least in those areas not directly occupied by federal law or those which clearly stand as an obstacle to federal

[29] *Id.* at 557.
[30] *Id.* at 559.
[31] *Id.* at 561.
[32] *Id.* at 567.
[33] *Id.* at 570.
[34] 416 U.S. 470 (1974).
[35] *Id.* at 491.

policy.[36] This principle was reconfirmed by the Supreme Court in its 1989 *Bonito Boats* opinion.[37] Here the Court applied the policy of the *Sears-Compco* decisions in determining the preemptive scope of federal patent law. The Court held that, under the Supremacy Clause, the Patent Act preempted a Florida "plug molding statute," which prevented the duplication of industrial product designs by a direct molding process. In a unanimous decision, the Court held that the statute, in effect, created a state mini-patent law. As a result, the "plug molding" statute improperly restricted competition in prohibiting the free imitation of designs in general circulation, unprotected by federal patent law. The Supreme Court's decision in *Bonito Boats* shows that the preemptive thrust of *Sears-Compco* is still alive, and will be used to preclude state law protection for the designs of useful articles. In sum, although its contours are not entirely clear, *Bonito Boats* appears to be limited to state law that provides patent-like protection to design and utilitarian aspects of products rather than applying to the full range of state intellectual property law.[38]

PART II: PREEMPTION UNDER § 301 OF THE 1976 ACT[39]

§ 11.5 Section 301: Generally

The uncertainty left by inconsistent lines of cases led Congress to attempt to clarify the preemption doctrine in the 1976 Copyright Act. Section 301 abolishes common law copyright and sets forth explicit criteria to resolve preemption issues. Section 301[40] reads:

> (a) On and after January 1, 1978, all legal or equitable rights that are equivalent to any of the exclusive rights within the general scope of copyright as specified by section 106 in works of authorship that are fixed in a tangible medium of expression and come within the subject matter of copyright as specified by sections 102 and 103, whether created before or after that date and whether published or unpublished, are governed exclusively by this title. Thereafter, no person is entitled to any such right or equivalent right in any such work under the common law or statutes of any State.

---

[36] *See also Zacchini v. Scripps-Howard Broadcasting Co.*, 433 U.S. 562 (1977).

[37] 489 U.S. 141 (1989).

[38] For a penetrating analysis of *Bonito Boats*, see John Shepard Wiley Jr., Bonito Boats: *Uninformed but Mandatory Innovation Policy*, 1989 Sup. Ct. Rev. 283 (1990) (criticizing the opinion's vague scope and lack of credible justification); David E. Shipley, *Refusing to Rock the Boat: The* Sears/Compco *Preemption Doctrine Applied to* Bonito Boats v. Thunder Craft, 25 Wake Forest L. Rev. 385 (1990) (approving of the opinion because it more precisely defines the sweep of preemption analysis than *Goldstein* and *Kewanee*).

[39] For an overview of the subject, see Ralph S. Brown, Jr. *Unification: A Cheerful Requiem for Common Law Copyright*, 24 UCLA L. Rev. 1070 (1977); Henry David Fetter, *Copyright Revision and the Preemption of State "Misappropriation" Law: A Study in Judicial and Congressional Interaction*, 27 Copyright L. Symp. (ASCAP) 1 (1982); Paul Goldstein, *Preempted State Doctrines, Involuntary Transfers and Compulsory Licenses: Testing the Limits of Copyright*, 24 UCLA L. Rev. 1107 (1977).

[40] 17 U.S.C. § 301.

(b) Nothing in this title annuls or limits any rights or remedies under the common law or statutes of any State with respect to —

(1) subject matter that does not come within the subject matter of copyright as specified by sections 102 and 103, including works of authorship not fixed in any tangible medium of expression; or

(2) any cause of action arising from undertakings commenced before January 1, 1978; or

(3) activities violating legal or equitable rights that are not equivalent to any of the exclusive rights within the general scope of copyright as specified by section 106.

This section effectively abolishes the 1909 Act's dual system of federal and state copyright protection whose dividing line was publication. In place of the bifurcated system, § 301 creates a single system of federal protection for all published and unpublished works of authorship fixed in a tangible medium of expression. Under § 301, once a work of authorship is fixed in a tangible medium of expression, it is governed by federal copyright law. By doing away with the 1909 Act's dual system, Congress attempted to create a more unified, simplified, and effective copyright law to protect the writings of authors.

In addition to abolishing common law copyright, § 301(a) establishes specific criteria for preemption to prevent state law from unduly intruding into the field of copyright law. It sets forth three conditions, all of which must be met for state law to be preempted: (1) the right protected by state law must be equivalent to any of the exclusive rights within the general scope of copyright as specified by § 106; (2) the right must be in a work of authorship fixed in a tangible medium of expression; and (3) the work of authorship must come within the subject matter of copyright specified in §§ 102 and 103.

Both conditions must be met for preemption to occur. For example, assume that a state passed a law prohibiting the unauthorized copying of computer software. To decide whether the state law will be preempted, under the first prong one must determine whether the law provides a right equivalent to copyright. Here the right granted by unauthorized copying is equivalent to the reproduction right of § 106(1). The first prong being met, one must also meet the second requirement for preemption to take place: does the state law cover the same subject matter as that covered by federal copyright? The state law clearly covers the subject matter under § 102(1) because computer software is a literary work. Thus, the state law is preempted, having met the dual requirements — rights equivalent and subject matter — of § 301.

The above hypothetical provides a straightforward example of how the preemption provision should work. As stated in the House Report, the purpose of § 301 is to avoid ambiguity and uncertainty in a murky area of the law. The preemption principles set forth in § 301 are

. . . intended to be stated in the clearest and most unequivocal language possible, so as to foreclose any conceivable misinterpretation of its unqualified intention that Congress shall act preemptively, and to avoid the development of any vague borderline areas between State and Federal protection.[41]

Despite the intended goal, § 301 has fallen far short of creating bright line criteria for matters of preemption. The problem is that neither the statute nor the legislative history answer some puzzling questions about the meaning of rights equivalent and when such rights come within the subject matter of copyright. Because of the ambiguities left by § 301, in difficult cases one must return, ironically enough, to traditional preemption doctrine expressed in the Supreme Court's inconsistent interpretations of the Supremacy Clause.[42] As always, the ultimate determination is whether the state law improperly interferes with the policies of federal copyright law.

§ 11.6 Rights Equivalent: The Language of the Statute and the Legislative History

[A] Rights Equivalent: The Peculiar Structure of § 301

The major difficulty in construing § 301 has proven to be the first prong of the preemption test. There are several basic reasons for this difficulty. First, and most important, the Act does not define "equivalency," a meaningless term which lends itself to varied interpretations. Second, the legislative history concerning § 301, rather than clarifying Congressional intent, actually obfuscates the issue of what constitutes a right equivalent. In addition to those basic deficiencies, § 301 is peculiarly drafted. The problem lies in § 301(b)(3),[43] which sets forth generally what is *not* preempted. This section preserves for state control activities relating to violations of "legal or equitable rights that are not equivalent to any of the exclusive rights within the general scope of copyright as specified by section 106."[44] The language of this section is almost, but not quite, the mirror image of § 301(a). What is the purpose of this apparently redundant provision, and what does it add in defining the scope of rights equivalent? To understand the puzzling redundancy, it is helpful to consider the legislative history of § 301.

[B] The Legislative Odyssey of § 301

As originally drafted, § 301(b)(3) listed examples of claims involving non-equivalent rights not preempted by the Copyright Act. By 1975, the section, as drafted and amended, read as follows:

> (b) Nothing in this title annuls or limits any rights or remedies under the common law or statutes of any State with respect to:

. . . .

---

[41] H.R. Rep. No. 94–1476, 94th Cong., 2d Sess. 130 (1976).
[42] *E.g., Goldstein v. California*, 412 U.S. 546 (1973).
[43] 17 U.S.C. § 301(b)(3).
[44] *Id.*

(3) activities violating legal or equitable rights that are not equivalent to any of the exclusive rights within the general scope of copyright as specified by section 106, *including rights against misappropriation not equivalent to any of such exclusive rights, breaches of contract, breaches of trust, trespass, conversion, invasion of privacy, defamation, and deceptive trade practices such as passing off and false representation.*[45]

(Emphasis added.)

On the eve of passage, the examples listed in clause (3) were deleted from § 301(b)(3), leaving the section as it now reads. The italicized language was deleted because the Justice Department objected to the inclusion of misappropriation, fearing that states' misappropriation laws would be construed so broadly as to render the preemption section meaningless. The following dialogue ensued between Congressman Seiberling, who offered the amendment deleting the examples, and Congressman Railsback, the ranking Republican on the House Subcommittee reporting out the bill:

> MR. RAILSBACK: Mr. Chairman, may I ask the gentleman from Ohio, for the purpose of clarifying the amendment that by striking the word misappropriation, the gentleman in no way is attempting to change the existing state of the law, that is as it may exist in certain States that have recognized the right of recovery relating to misappropriation; is that correct?

> MR. SEIBERLING: That is correct. All I am trying to do is prevent the citing of them as examples in a statute. We are, in effect, adopting a rather amorphous body of State law and codifying it, in effect. Rather I am trying to have this bill leave the State law alone and make it clear we are merely dealing with copyright laws, laws applicable to copyrights.

> MR. RAILSBACK: Mr. Chairman, I personally have no objection to the gentleman's amendment in view of that clarification and I know of no objections from this side.

> . . . .

> MR. KASTENMEIER: Mr. Chairman, I too have examined the gentleman's amendment and was familiar with the position of the Department of Justice. Unfortunately, the Justice Department did not make its position known to the committee until the last day of markup.

> MR. SEIBERLING: I understand.

> MR. KASTENMEIER: However, Mr. Chairman, I think that the amendment the gentleman is offering is consistent with the position of the Justice Department and accept it on this side as well.[46]

This amendment was accepted just before passage of the bill, giving little time to consider its effect. Considering the 21 years of meticulous revision process, it is unfortunate that such an important amendment was added to the 1976 Act in this

---

[45] S. Rep. No. 94–22, 94th Cong., 2d Sess. (1976); H.R. Rep. No. 94–1476, 94th Cong., 2d Sess. 276 (1976).

[46] 122 Cong. Rec. H32015 (Sept. 22, 1976).

haphazard way. But how should this curious legislative history be treated? More specifically, how should a court take into account the deleted examples and the above exchange concerning them?

§ 11.7 Rights Equivalent: The Case Law Applying § 301

[A] The Extra Elements Approach

To interpret a legislative provision, courts normally turn to the legislative history and the various drafts of the statute, but that process will not work here. The legislative history as reflected in the above exchange is simply too ambiguous to be helpful in determining whether a right equivalent has been provided by state law. The exchange on the House floor does not explain why all the examples were deleted, nor does it shed much light on the continuing scope of the misappropriation doctrine. As a result, most courts have ignored the legislative history and instead focused on what the state law cause of action does, whether labelled misappropriation, *quantum meruit*, or conversion.[47]

Overall, a right granted by state law is regarded as equivalent and preempted when the state law provides an infringement action for the acts of reproduction, adaptation, performance, and display, as set forth in § 106. Alternatively, a state cause of action is not preempted when it differs in nature from the rights and remedies conferred by copyright law, and when it requires elements other than those set forth in § 106. As one court phrased it, the question is whether the state protected rights "are *qualitatively* different from the rights of reproduction, performance, distribution or display."[48] Thus, if the rights and remedies provided by state law are qualitatively different from those enumerated in § 106, preemption will not take place.[49] For example, if A violates a relationship of trust and appropriates B's trade secret, A has committed an act of reproduction under § 106. However, preemption will not occur because the crux of the cause of action involves the breach of trust, quite unlike anything covered in § 106 of the Copyright Act.

The courts have generally used this mode of analysis, and for the most part have decided against preemption when the state law confers an important element in addition to the exclusive rights of § 106.[50] On the whole, the legitimate claims brought under the various causes of action deleted from § 301(b)(3)[51] pass muster

---

[47] *See Peckarsky v. American Broadcasting Co., Inc.*, 603 F. Supp. 688 (D.D.C. 1984); *see also Mitchell v. Penton Indus. Pub. Co., Inc.*, 486 F. Supp. 22 (N.D. Ohio 1979) (plaintiff's broad misappropriation claim preempted).

[48] *Schuchart & Associates v. Solo Serve Corp.*, 540 F. Supp. 928, 943 (W.D. Tex. 1982), *citing Harper & Row, Publishers, Inc. v. Nation Enterprises*, 501 F. Supp. 848, 852 (S.D.N.Y. 1980) (emphasis supplied).

[49] *See* 1 *Nimmer on Copyright* § 1.01 (1988).

[50] *See* Robert A. Gorman, *Fact or Fancy? The Implications for Copyright*, 29 J. Copyright Soc'y 560, 608 (1982).

[51] *See* § 11.6[B], *supra.*

when they truly constitute breaches of trust[52] or contract,[53] conversion,[54] passing-off[55] or defamation,[56] or infringe privacy[57] or publicity rights.[58]

Contract law provides a good example of a state law that should not be susceptible to preemption under the extra elements test. The terms of a contract may prohibit, or regulate, in some way, the acts of reproduction, adaptation, distribution, performance or display of a work. However, contract law, in addition to these acts, requires proof of a bargained-for exchange, an element not required in an action for copyright infringement. The preemption of state contract law arose in *National Car Rental Systems, Inc. v. Computer Associates International, Inc.*[59] In this case, National had entered into a contract with Computer Associates, which was to create programs to analyze National's data. The contract stipulated that National would use the program only to process its own data but not data of third parties. Computer Associates asserted that National had breached the license agreement by allowing third parties to use the programs. In response, National claimed that the limitation on the uses to which a licensee may put a licensed work are preempted by federal copyright law. The Court rejected the preemption argument because the contractual restriction on use of the programs constituted an extra element that made the cause of action qualitatively different from one for copyright.

In deciding whether a cause of action is preempted, a court must look beyond the label to determine whether, in fact, a right conferred by state law qualitatively differs from the exclusive rights of § 106 of the 1976 Copyright Act.[60] For example, a defamation action involves a claim vindicating one's relationship with society, a passing off action involves a deception about the origin of goods or services, and a privacy action involves the right to be let alone. Each of these actions include elements substantially different from copyright and unlike anything covered under the five exclusive rights enumerated in § 106. On the other hand, an action for *quantum meruit* or commercial immorality does not essentially involve anything different from the rights granted under federal copyright law, and thus should be preempted under § 301.

---

[52] *See Warrington Associates, Inc. v. Real-Time Engineering Systems, Inc.*, 522 F. Supp. 367 (N.D. Ill. 1981) (trade secret claim not preempted).

[53] *Smith v. Weinstein*, 578 F. Supp. 1297, 1307 (S.D.N.Y. 1984); *see also Werlin v. Reader's Digest Ass'n, Inc.*, 528 F. Supp. 451 (S.D.N.Y. 1981).

[54] *See, e.g., Oddo v. Ries*, 743 F.2d 630, 636 (9th Cir. 1984) (conversion and breach of fiduciary duty).

[55] *See Warner Bros., Inc. v. American Broadcasting Co.*, 720 F.2d 231 (2d Cir. 1983); *see also* H.R. Rep. No. 94–1476, 94th Cong., 2d Sess. 132 (1976).

[56] *See Allied Artists Pictures Corp. v. Rhodes*, 496 F. Supp. 408 (S.D. Ohio 1980), *aff'd*, 679 F.2d 656 (6th Cir. 1982).

[57] H.R. Rep. No. 94–1476, 94th Cong., 2d Sess. 132 (1976).

[58] *See, e.g., Factors, Inc. v. ProArts, Inc.*, 496 F. Supp. 1090 (S.D.N.Y. 1980) (right to publicity not preempted).

[59] 991 F.2d 426 (8th Cir. 1993).

[60] *See generally* 1 *Nimmer on Copyright* § 1.01[B] (1988). As one Court phrased it,

> Plaintiff cannot merely rephrase the same claim citing contract law and thereby obtain relief equivalent to that which he has failed to obtain under copyright law.

Smith v. Weinstein, 578 F. Supp. 1297, 1307 (S.D.N.Y. 1984).

Mayer v. Josiah Wedgwood & Sons, Ltd.,[61] provides an example of how a court looked beyond the language of the pleading to determine whether the state law cause of action was equivalent to or qualitatively different from those provided under § 106. In *Mayer*, plaintiff designed and published, but did not copyright, a snowflake design. Her complaint alleged that the Wedgwood Company misappropriated the design for use on a Christmas tree ornament. In 1979, Mayer had contacted Wedgwood about using the design on Christmas plates, but her proposal was rejected. Years later the design suddenly appeared on Wedgwood's Christmas ornaments. Plaintiff demanded remuneration and brought an action under state law for conversion and unfair competition. The design itself was apparently in the public domain and not copyrightable under federal law, so plaintiff had to seek redress under state law.

Was the cause of action preempted by § 301? The court found equivalent subject matter under §§ 102 and 103 and considered the second prong of the preemption test — whether the rights asserted were the same as those protected by § 106. Using this analysis, the court in *Mayer* found no extra element which would qualitatively distinguish plaintiff's conversion and misappropriation claims from the rights specifically addressed by federal copyright law.[62] Because the conversion claim was a functional equivalent of the reproduction and distribution rights outlined in § 106, it did not state the extra element needed to avoid preemption. Similarly, plaintiff's misappropriation claim, based on commercial immorality, added no extra qualitative element.[63] In effect, plaintiff was merely alleging that defendant had acted intentionally and improperly. According to the Court, such an allegation, if proved, might alter the scope of action but not its nature.[64] In sum, the nature of plaintiff's conversion and misappropriation claims were both the same once the court looked behind the language used: they were simply claims of copyright infringement asserted under state law and as such, were preempted by § 301.[65]

Other courts have not adopted the *Mayer* approach; instead, they appear to accept almost any colorable additional element claimed which would save the plaintiff's state claim from preemption. For example, in *Schuchart & Associates v. Solo Serve Corp.*,[66] plaintiff alleged that its architectural drawings were used without permission by defendants in a construction project. One of the claims[67] in the complaint was for unjust enrichment — *quantum meruit*. The court found the cause of action in *quantum meruit* fundamentally different from a copyright claim, because plaintiffs did not seek damages analogous to actual damages in a copyright action under

---

[61] 601 F. Supp. 1523 (S.D.N.Y. 1985).

[62] *Id.* at 1535.

[63] *Id.* at 1536.

[64] *Id.* at 1534.

[65] Plaintiff also asserted both breach of confidentiality and unjust enrichment, which could possibly not be equivalent to a copyright claim. Because the design was in the public domain, plaintiff had lost her property interest in it. Accordingly, defendant was not unjustly enriched. The breach of confidentiality claim failed as well. The publication of the design removed the secrecy that a breach of confidentiality requires. *Id.* at 1536.

[66] 540 F. Supp. 928 (W.D. Tex. 1982).

[67] Plaintiff's misappropriation claim, however, was preempted.

§ 504(b) of the 1976 Act, but asked instead for the value of services rendered to defendants.[68]

This approach, as exemplified by the holding in *Schuchart*, seems to be too permissive because almost any state law claim can be worded so that it differs from a copyright claim. The question should be whether the extra element changes the nature of the cause of action under state law and makes it into something qualitatively different from a copyright claim.

[B]   The Failure of the Extra Elements Approach

As explained above, courts generally apply the extra elements approach when deciding whether the state cause of action is qualitatively different from copyright and, thus, not preempted by federal copyright law. This approach simply states a conclusion. When is a right provided by state law qualitatively different, and how different in nature must it be to escape preemption? In all but the simplest cases, the extra elements test cannot be applied with any certainty.

When a court concludes that a state cause of action contains extra elements and qualitative differences, it is expressing an overall judgment that the purpose and effect of the state legislation or case law does not unduly interfere with federal copyright law. Both the purpose and effect of the state statute must be scrutinized to determine whether the state cause of action is equivalent to the federal. The reason that both purpose and effect must be considered is to avoid a preemptive effect either too broad or too narrow. If a court were to look just at the stated purpose of the state law, many state laws, covering essentially the same ground as federal copyright law, would escape preemption because a state legislature can always indicate a noncopyright purpose for its legislation. On the other hand, if a court were to consider only the effect of the state law, preemption would cut too wide a path. State trade secret, defamation, publicity, and contract law all provide similar relief to copyright law, but it was not Congress' intention that these state causes of action be displaced. A court must strike a balance between these two extremes and, in difficult cases, this determination takes reasoned judgment.[69]

Thus, the basic question of preemption cannot be avoided: does the state cause of action interfere with the objectives and policies of federal copyright law? This, of course, is a traditional restatement of the preemption doctrine under the Supremacy Clause of the Constitution. Although § 301 of the 1976 Act was drafted in part to simplify preemption analysis, this result did not occur, and the courts are forced to base their analysis on basic constitutional doctrine with little additional guidance from Congress.

---

[68] *Id.* at 945; *see* 17 U.S.C. § 504(b).

[69] Professor Gorman has proposed that the economic purpose of the state law should determine what constitutes a right equivalent. He would find preemption of a state cause of action which provides relief for the same economic harm as does copyright law, *i.e.*, harm from copying in its various forms. On the other hand, state causes of action such as those for privacy and defamation which provide recovery against personal harm and reputation are different in economic focus than copyright and should survive preemption. *See* Robert A. Gorman, *Fact or Fancy? The Implications for Copyright*, 29 J. Copyright Soc'y 560, 608–10 (1982).

§ 11.8 The Necessary Return to Traditional Preemption Analysis: Four Examples

[A] State Anti-Blind-Bidding Statutes

State anti-blind-bidding statutes provide an excellent example of the futility of a mechanical application of § 301. These statutes exist in eighteen states and typically require suppliers of motion pictures to screen their films in the state before any negotiations can be completed or bids taken. In effect, they prohibit the practice of blind bidding, whereby a motion picture producer (the copyright owner) requires theater operators to bid on a picture without a prior trade screening within the state. Motion picture producers have argued that these statutes are preempted by the 1976 Copyright Act because they interfere with distribution and performance rights and generally impede the objectives and policies of the 1976 Copyright Act. The Circuit courts have disagreed on the preemption question, but have analyzed it both under § 301 and under general Supremacy Clause principles.[70]

The following sections discuss other situations where the preemption issue cannot be determined by a mechanical application of § 301 nor by a single-minded search for extra elements and qualitative differences.

[B] State Law Conferring Broader or Narrower Rights

Is a state law preempted if it creates a right either broader or narrower than the exclusive rights enumerated in § 106? The basic problem in addressing this question is that neither the statute nor the legislative history define "equivalency," a term hopelessly ambiguous absent some indication of which features must be similar and which can diverge.[71] As a result, one must ultimately retreat to the basic policy which motivated the equivalency test and reexamine the essential question: whether the state law improperly interferes with the goals and policies of the 1976 Copyright Act. For example, § 106(4), the performance right, covers public performances only; a private performance is not an infringing act.[72] If a state were to pass a law providing a private performance right for musical works, a right broader than

---

[70] *See Associated Film Distribution Corp. v. Thornburgh*, 520 F. Supp. 971 (E.D. Pa. 1981), *rev'd and rem'd*, 683 F.2d 808 (3d Cir. 1982), *on remand*, 614 F. Supp. 1100 (E.D. Pa. 1985). The court initially found the state statute preempted as impeding the basic objectives of the Copyright Act. Summary judgment on the issue of preemption was overturned on appeal and the case was remanded to determine at trial whether in fact the statute interfered with federal law. After a trial on the merits the court decided against preemption. *See also Allied Artists Pictures Corp. v. Rhodes*, 496 F. Supp. 408 (S.D. Ohio 1980), *aff'd in part and rem'd in part*, 679 F.2d 656 (6th Cir. 1982) (state anti-blind-bidding statute did not frustrate the basic objectives of the Copyright Act).

[71] To take a crude example, suggested by Professor William Richman, consider the comparison of these three items: a black dog, a yellow dog and a black cat. If the relevant feature is color, items one and three are equivalent and item two is not. On the other hand, if the relevant feature is species, items one and two are equivalent and item three is not.

[72] 17 U.S.C. § 106(4). For a discussion of the performance right as it applies to private performances, see § 8.16, *supra*.

§ 106(4), would the state law be preempted as "equivalent to any of the exclusive rights within the general scope of copyright as specified by Section 106?"[73] One could argue that the state law should be preempted because a private performance right falls within the general scope of § 106(4), the right to perform the work publicly. But this argument simply states a conclusion; it provides no principled reason why a state law extending protection to private performances should be preempted or not.

A better method is to interpret equivalency according to the basic goal Congress intended to accomplish by § 301. According to this analytical method, it would seem that the broader private performance right conferred by the hypothetical state law would interfere with the basic goals of copyright law and would therefore be preempted. Otherwise, the states could greatly enlarge the range of copyright law by conferring a private performance right despite Congress' intention to limit copyright owners' control to public performances only.

[C] Are Rights Equivalent Those Provided Under §§ 107–120?

A related question involving the meaning of rights equivalent is whether this term applies to §§ 107–120, as well as to § 106. The problem is that § 301 limits its application of rights equivalent to those provided in § 106, referring to no other sections of the 1976 Act. Once again, neither the statute nor the legislative history provide any help in deciding this question. Because preemption analysis should concern the ultimate question of whether state law unduly interferes with the objectives of copyright law, the entire range of limitations on exclusive rights outlined in §§ 107–120 should be considered in determining whether the state law confers rights equivalent.

For example, would a state law be preempted if it gave motion picture copyright owners the right to prohibit the rental of their movies by video stores that legally obtained copies of the films? This state law would conflict with § 109(a) of the 1976 Act, known as the "first sale doctrine," which gives the owner of a copy or phonorecord the right to sell, rent, or otherwise dispose of the possession of that copy.[74] Here a strong argument could be made for preemption because the state law would effectively annul the first sale doctrine of § 109 whose basic policy, the free alienability of goods, would be effectively undermined by the state law. Similarly, a state law which would change the terms of the various compulsory licenses[75] would be preempted under the same reasoning, as would a state attempt

---

[73] 17 U.S.C. § 301(a).

[74] 17 U.S.C. § 109(a) reads as follows:

> Notwithstanding the provisions of section 106(3), the owner of a particular copy or phonorecord lawfully made under this title, or any person authorized by such owner, is entitled, without the authority of the copyright owner, to sell or otherwise dispose of the possession of that copy or phonorecord.

[75] For example, a state would be preempted from raising the royalty to be paid for the mechanical license. See 17 U.S.C. § 115. For a discussion of the mechanical license, see § 8.7, *supra*.

to place a fee on the right of broadcasters to make ephemeral recordings under § 112.[76]

[D] The California Resale Royalty Act

California's Resale Royalty Act,[77] which allows artists a percentage of the resale price of their works, poses many of the same preemption questions as moral rights legislation. The preemption issue has already been litigated in a 1909 Act case, *Morseburg v. Baylon*,[78] where the court applied traditional preemption analysis to find that the Resale Royalty Act was not preempted by the 1909 Copyright Act. The court found the restrictions the Resale Royalty Act placed upon the first sale doctrine and the distribution right were not serious enough interferences with the purposes and objectives of federal copyright to warrant preemption.

Morseburg, however, did not definitively settle the preemption issue because the case was decided under the 1909 Act. Whether the California Resale Royalty Act will fare as well, if the preemption issue is litigated again under the 1976 Act, is an open question. Here the problem is that the right granted by state law is similar to, though narrower than, the distribution right under § 106(3). In addition, California law also modifies the effect of the first sale doctrine in § 109(a) of the 1976 Act. One could plausibly argue that the Resale Royalty Act does nothing more than restrict the first sale doctrine of § 109(a) and modify the distribution right of § 106(3).[79] But even if this is so, the Resale Royalty Act unduly interferes with basic copyright policy under §§ 109(a) and 106(3), whose purpose is to promote the free alienability of material objects embodying the copyrighted work. Moreover, the interference would become even greater if other states passed resale royalty acts whereby more than one resale royalty would be imposed on the same sale. This possibility for conflict among state laws which may impede the distribution of copyrighted works indicates a basic conflict with federal copyright principles.

§ 11.9 Subject Matter: The Second Requirement for Preemption of State Law

The second prong of the preemption test requires that the subject matter covered by the state law come within the subject matter of copyright, as specified in §§ 102 and 103. This test involves two special problems of interpretation. First, can a work be protected under state law, but for some reason be uncopyrightable? Examples would include a work which fails to meet the standard of originality, or has fallen into the public domain, or constitutes uncopyrightable subject matter (idea, fact, process) under § 102(b). Second, can state law protect subject matter which Congress has considered, but decided not to protect, such as typeface design, literary characters, or industrial design?

---

[76] 17 U.S.C. § 112. For a discussion of ephemeral recordings, see § 8.8, *supra*.

[77] Cal. Civ. Code § 986 (1983). For a discussion of the California Resale Royalty Act, see § 8.14[E], *supra*.

[78] 621 F.2d 972 (9th Cir.), *cert. denied*, 449 U.S. 983 (1980).

[79] For a discussion of the first sale doctrine and the distribution right, see § 8.13, *supra*.

[A] Non-Original Works, and Works in the Public Domain or Excluded by § 102(b)

According to the House Report,[80] states cannot protect a work within §§ 102 or 103 that fails to achieve copyright protection because it is minimal or lacking in originality, or because it has fallen into the public domain. Otherwise, the states could confer unlimited protection on that which was unfit for even limited protection under federal law. Thus, a state law which protects a work of art that fails to meet the federal standard of originality, or is injected into the public domain for failure to meet notice formalities, would be preempted by § 301 or by general principles of the Supremacy Clause of the Constitution.

A similar question is whether state law can protect facts, ideas, systems or processes because these are excluded from copyrightable subject matter under § 102(b). For example, suppose a state misappropriation law protects the taking of facts and ideas presented in an autobiography of a president. One might argue that the subject matter test is not met because copyright protects the arrangements of facts, not the facts themselves. As for ideas, copyright protects the expression of an idea, not the idea itself. Despite these arguments, preemption is appropriate because the entire work in question falls within the general category of copyrightable subject matter — it is a copyrightable literary work, even though it contains uncopyrightable portions which are the object of the state law protection. Preemption is proper; otherwise, state law protection would create "vague borderline areas between State and Federal protection" and circumvent one of the central purposes of the 1976 Act, the establishment of comprehensive federal standards.[81] In addition to these arguments favoring federal preemption of state protection of facts, such protection may also be suspect under the First Amendment.[82]

[B] Subject Matter Which Congress Could Have, But Did Not Include

Congress chose not to include certain categories of subject matter in §§ 102 and 103 of the 1976 Act. Examples include typeface designs, literary characters and industrial design. If a state were to pass a law protecting typeface design, or one protecting the design of useful articles, would such a law be preempted by federal copyright law as constituting works of authorship coming within §§ 102 or 103? To answer this question, one must first determine whether typeface or industrial design fall within the general categories of copyrightable subject matter. The initial

---

[80] H.R. Rep. No. 94–1476, 94th Cong., 2d Sess. 131 (1976).

[81] *Harper & Row, Publishers, Inc. v. Nation Enterprises*, 723 F.2d 195, 200 (2d Cir. 1983), *rev'd on other grounds*, 471 U.S. 539 (1985).

[82] Courts and commentators do not always adhere to the above analysis. *See, e.g.*, Paul Goldstein, *Preempted State Doctrines, Involuntary Transfers and Compulsory Licenses: Testing the Limits of Copyright*, 24 UCLA L. Rev. 1107, 1119 (1977). In *Bromhall v. Rorvik*, 478 F. Supp. 361 (E.D. Pa. 1979), the court upheld claims for the misappropriation of plaintiff's ideas regarding the cloning of rabbits which were expressed in plaintiff's thesis and later used in defendant's work on human cloning. The state law claims were not preempted because copyright protection under § 102(b) extends only to the expression of an idea, not the idea itself.

response is that they fall generally within pictorial, graphic, and sculptural works as such terms are used in § 102.[83] But does Congress's specific exclusion of these items indicate that the states are free to occupy the field? This is another area where Courts must turn again to general preemption analysis based on the Supremacy Clause, that is, they must decide whether the state law conflicts with basic copyright policy. In the examples cited above, a strong argument could be made that a state law conferring protection would improperly interfere with the objectives of federal copyright law. Congress has apparently decided as a matter of policy that these forms of writings should not be given monopoly protection and should be in the public domain instead.[84] One cannot argue, as in *Goldstein v. California*,[85] that Congress left these forms of subject matter unattended so that state law could fill the void. Each was specifically considered by Congress, which decided that characters, typeface, and industrial design should not receive protection and should rest in the public domain.[86]

§ 11.10   Non-Preempted Works

Section 301 leaves certain works outside its preemptive effect. First, this section, consistent with the Constitution, applies only to works fixed in a tangible medium of expression.[87] Unfixed works, such as purely oral works, improvised music, spontaneous speeches, and other unfixed performances, are not covered, and state law governing such works would not be preempted. Second, § 301 does not apply to any cause of action arising before January 1, 1978.[88] Third, for sound recordings fixed before February 15, 1972, rights and remedies under the common law are not affected until February 15, 2047.[89] Fourth, nothing in § 301 affects rights and remedies under any other federal statute.[90] From a practical standpoint, this last aspect is the most significant. Examples of federal statutes covering the same terrain as copyright and exempted from preemption provisions are the Federal Communications Act,[91] the Patent Act,[92] and, most particularly, the Lanham Act.[93] This latter federal statute involves federal trademark protection and provides for the registration of words, names, symbols and devices.

---

[83] *See* H.R. Rep. No. 94–1476, 94th Cong., 2d Sess. 55 (1976).

[84] *See Second Supplementary Report of the Register of Copyright on the General Revision of the U.S. Copyright Law: 1975 Revision Bill* Ch. 1 (draft ed. 1975).

[85] 412 U.S. 546 (1973).

[86] For two cases refusing to register typeface designs, see *Eltra Corp. v. Ringer*, 579 F.2d 294 (4th Cir. 1978) (upholding Register's refusal to register typefaces as works of art); and *Leonard Storch Enterprises, Inc. v. Mergenthaler Linotype Co.*, 208 U.S.P.Q. (BNA) 58 (E.D.N.Y. 1980) (denying protection of typeface under state unfair competition law but holding that typeface was not preempted because typeface designs are uncopyrightable).

[87] 17 U.S.C. § 301(b)(1).

[88] 17 U.S.C. § 301(b)(2).

[89] 17 U.S.C. § 301(c).

[90] 17 U.S.C. § 301(d).

[91] 47 U.S.C. §§ 151–611.

[92] 35 U.S.C. §§ 1–140 (1952).

[93] 15 U.S.C. §§ 1051–1127.

§ 11.11   Other Preemption Provisions of the Copyright Act

[A]   The Visual Artists Rights Act of 1990: § 301(f)

Section 301(f)[94] preempts state laws that give rights equivalent to § 106A's rights of attribution and integrity falling within the subject matter covered by that section's protection of works of visual art. The same two conditions, as are found in § 301(a), must be met for preemption of state law. First, the subject matter of state law must be a work of visual art as defined in § 101, which is limited to painting, graphic arts, and sculpture. According to the legislative history, Congress did not intend to preempt state art preservation acts that confer protection on such subject matter as audiovisual works, or photographs that are not included in § 101's definition of a "work of visual art."[95] For example, the Massachusetts statute[96] includes movies, and television productions and to that extent would not be preempted by § 301(f). Second, § 301(f)(2) will preempt state law only if it is equivalent to § 106A's rights of attribution or integrity. Thus, a state law that includes some extra element not included in § 106A, such as an affirmative obligation to attribute authorship of a work of visual art, will not be preempted.[97] Similarly, § 301(f)(2)(C) will not preempt a state statute that extends protection beyond the life of the author. Unlike the rights conferred under § 106, which last the life of the author plus fifty years, the rights under the Visual Artists Rights Act expire on the death of the author. Thus, the state provision conferring a *post mortem* right will become operative when federal protection under § 106A ends, *i.e.*, when the author dies.

[B]   The Architectural Works Protection Act of 1990: § 301(b)(4)

The Architectural Works Copyright Protection Act enacted on the same date as the Visual Artists Rights Act of 1990, also takes preemption into account to avoid any preemptive effect the law may have on state law concerning landmarks, historic preservation, zoning, or building codes. Section 301(b)(4)[98] provides:

> (b) Nothing in this title annuls or limits any rights or remedies under the common law or statutes of any State with respect to:
>
> . . . .
>
> (4) state and local landmarks, historic preservation, zoning, or building codes relating to architectural works protected under section 102(a)(8).

---

[94] 17 U.S.C. § 301(f).

[95] *See* H.R. Rep. No. 101–514, 101st Cong. 2d Sess. 21 (1990).

[96] *See* Mass. Gen. Laws Ann. ch. 231 § 855 (West Supp. 1986).

[97] Section 106A grants the author the right to claim authorship of the work and prevent the use of his or her name as the author of the work of visual art in the event of a mutilation or other modification of the work which would be prejudicial to his or her honor or reputation. *See* 17 U.S.C. § 106A(a).

[98] 17 U.S.C. § 301(b)(4).

AN OVERVIEW OF INTERNATIONAL COPYRIGHT

§ 12.1 Introduction and Chapter Overview

In our information age, the international dimension of copyright law grows in importance with each day. Satellite communications as well as other developing technologies permit access to copyrighted works worldwide as never before. Copyrighted works can be copied cheaply and disseminated quickly, unimpeded by time, space, or national boundaries. The result of these developments, particularly when coupled with systematic piracy in certain foreign countries, is that copyright owners have less and less control over their creations. As the world's largest user and producer of copyrighted works, the United States has a special interest in an orderly and responsive international regime of copyright protection. This recognition is reflected in the United States' adherence (effective March 1, 1989) to the Berne Convention, the oldest and preeminent multinational copyright treaty.

This chapter, which is divided into four parts, provides a brief overview of international copyright matters. Part I examines the international copyright conventions. The major focus is on the provisions of the Berne Convention, and the changes in American law that permitted the United States to adhere to this important international arrangement.

Part II treats the broad-based protection of foreign authors conferred by § 104 of the 1976 Copyright Act. It also discusses issues involving the conflicts of laws in international copyright.

Part III provides an outline of various trade regulation laws affecting copyright. The first topic in Part III concerns the regulation of importation under §§ 602 and 603 of the 1976 Copyright Act, which designates the Customs Service as the agency to police importation of infringing articles. The second topic concerns § 337 of the Tariff Act, administered by the International Trade Commission, which prohibits unfair methods of competition in the importation of goods into the United States. The third topic in Part III reviews forms of international trade regulation, Generalized System of Preferences and the Caribbean Basin Recovery Act, designed to encourage countries to provide adequate protection of U.S. intellectual property interests. Part IV focuses on international and regional trade agreements as they concern copyright law. It treats the recently concluded Trade Related Aspects of Intellectual Property (TRIPS) agreement arising out of the Uruguay Round of the General Agreement on Tariffs and Trade (GATT). This Part also discusses regional trade agreements, namely the European Union and the recently completed North

American Free Trade Agreement (NAFTA). Multilateral and regional trade agreements are the newest development in international copyright relations and may prove to be a powerful force for change on the international stage.

PART I: THE MAJOR INTERNATIONAL TREATIES INVOLVING COPYRIGHT

§ 12.2   Generally

Worldwide copyright does not exist. The principal treaties, the Berne Union[1] and the Universal Copyright Convention (U.C.C.), do not automatically protect an author's works throughout the world under a supranational copyright law. No matter what the international agreement, protection against infringement in any given country depends on the national laws of that country. Thus, an author who wishes to protect his work abroad must comply with the pertinent national laws.

Falling short of establishing an international copyright, the U.C.C., and particularly the Berne Union, have simplified the requirements for obtaining foreign copyright protection. This has been accomplished by establishing convention *minima*, that is, minimum rights which may be claimed in all member countries, regardless of any other national legislation. The difference between the two major international conventions is the substantiality of the conventions' *minima*.[2]

From 1891 until its entry into the U.C.C. in 1955, the United States relied on a series of bilateral agreements[3] to protect its copyright interests internationally. These piecemeal arrangements became increasingly less adequate in an ever shrinking world of new communication technologies which recognize no national boundaries. By the 1950's, when the United States emerged as the major exporter of copyrighted works, the need for American participation in a truly integrated system of international copyright became readily apparent. The gap was filled by the United States' entry into the Universal Copyright Convention.

---

[1] Convention concerning the creation of an International Union for the Protection of Literary and Artistic Works (Sept. 9, 1886, revised in 1908, 1928, 1948, 1967, 1971), hereinafter cited as the "Berne Convention."

[2] For an excellent comparison of the characteristics of the Berne Convention and the U.C.C., see the text of a speech made by Lewis Flacks, Policy Planning Adviser for the U.S. Register of Copyrights, contained in *Out of UNESCO and Into Berne: Has the United States Participation in the Berne Convention for International Copyright Protection Become Essential?*, 4 Cardozo Arts & Ent. L.J. 216–26 (1985).

[3] *See* 1 *Nimmer on Copyright* § 5.05[B][2][c] (1988). For a list of the bilateral agreements in force, see *Copyright Office Circular* 38(a).

§ 12.3　The Universal Copyright Convention (U.C.C.)

[A]　Generally

The United States was the motivating force behind the formation of the U.C.C. At that time, the Copyright Act of 1909 was in force and its features[4] precluded United States entry into the Berne Convention, the major international copyright convention. The U.C.C. was negotiated as a stop-gap measure to protect U.S. copyright interests temporarily, and as a bridge to eventual U.S. entry into Berne.[5] The U.C.C. turned out to be more than a temporary measure. It took more than 30 years and major revisions of American copyright law before the United States was able to adhere to the Berne Convention. Although the U.C.C. has now been supplanted by the United States' adherence to the Berne Convention, it is still important for American copyright interests because a number of countries are members of the U.C.C. but are not members of Berne.[6]

The Universal Copyright Convention took effect in the United States on September 16, 1955. A revision of the Convention occurred at Paris in 1971, and became effective in 1974. The U.C.C. is administered by UNESCO and because the United States has withdrawn from this United Nations agency,[7] some have questioned our continued reliance on this Convention to provide effective protection for U.S. copyright interests.[8]

[B]　Basic Provisions of the U.C.C.

The basis of the U.C.C. is "national treatment,"[9] which requires all member countries to accord to foreign works eligible under the U.C.C. the same protection granted its own nationals. Additionally, the Convention specifies certain minimum legal obligations for each contracting state. Its more important elements can be summarized as follows:

---

[4] Most important of the features impeding entry into Berne was duration of copyright and required compliance with formalities imposed by American copyright law. For a discussion of Berne and its convention *minima*, see § 12.4, *infra*.

[5] Evidence of U.S. intent to enter the Berne Union eventually can be found in the House Report on the 1976 Act. *See* H.R. Rep. No. 94–1476, 94th Cong., 2d Sess. 135 (1976). *See* Barbara A. Ringer, "The Universal Copyright Convention and its Future," *reprinted in The Copyright Act of 1976: Dealing With the New Realities* 339 (1977).

[6] As of January 1, 1989, some 26 countries are members of the U.C.C. but are not Berne adherents. These include certain developing countries in Africa and several Latin American countries.

[7] The U.S. gave the requisite one-year notice of intent to withdraw from the United Nations Educational, Scientific, and Cultural Organization (UNESCO), which administers the U.C.C., on December 29, 1983. *See U.S. Notifies UNESCO of Intent to Withdraw*, 84 U.S. Dept. of State Bull. No. 2083, 41 (1984).

[8] A country does not have to be a member of UNESCO to participate in the U.C.C., but without membership, the United States would not be able to influence the future direction and policy on international copyright matters within the organization that administers the U.C.C. *See* S. Rep. No. 100–352, 100th Cong., 2d Sess. 4 (1988).

[9] *See* 3 *Nimmer on Copyright* § 17.04[B] n. 6 (1988).

[1] General Obligations

The contracting states must provide for adequate and effective protection of the rights of authors and other copyright proprietors.[10]

[2] Basis of Protection

The published works of nationals of a contracting state must receive the same protection as the contracting state accords to works of its nationals first published in its own territory. The same applies for unpublished works.[11] The convention is not retroactive and those works in the public domain of a contracting state remain there.

[3] Formalities

Formalities such as notice, registration and manufacture which may be part of a contracting state's copyright law, are satisfied for a foreign U.C.C. work

> if from the time of first publication all the copies of the work . . . bear the symbol © accompanied by the name of the copyright proprietor and the year of first publication placed in such manner and location as to give reasonable notice of claim of copyright.[12]

A member state may, however, require additional formalities, such as deposit, registration, and manufacturing requirements, for works first published within its territory by foreign nationals or by its own nationals, wherever they may be published. Thus, pursuant to this provision, formalities are not excused for works first published in the U.S. by either a U.S. citizen or a foreign national. In addition, a work first published abroad by a U.S. citizen was always subject to formalities under U.S. law.

[4] Minimum Term of Protection

Member states must grant a minimum copyright term of 25 years from publication, or life of the author plus 25 years.[13]

[5] Exclusive Rights

Contracting states must grant exclusive translation rights to foreign authors of other member states for at least seven years. After this term expires, a compulsory licensing arrangement can be instituted.[14]

[6] Berne Safeguard Clause

The U.C.C. contains a Berne Safeguard Clause, which prohibits a Berne Convention country from denouncing Berne and relying on the U.C.C. in its copyright relations with members of the Berne Convention.[15] This provision came about through the efforts of Berne Union members who feared the U.C.C. was a step backwards, and wanted to prevent Berne principles from being undermined by the U.C.C. adherence of its members. Thus, the United States, now a member of Berne,

---

[10] *U.C.C.* art. 1 (Paris Act).
[11] *U.C.C.* art. 2 (Paris Act).
[12] *U.C.C.* art. 3 (Paris Act).
[13] *U.C.C.* art. 4 (Paris Act).
[14] U.C.C. art. 5 (Paris Act).
[15] *U.C.C.* art. 15 and Appendix Declaration (Paris Act).

cannot look to the U.C.C. for protection of any work originating from a Berne country, even though that country may also adhere to the U.C.C.

[C]   The Paris Revision of the U.C.C.

The U.C.C. was revised in Paris in 1971 in response to demands made by developing countries.[16] The revision, effective in 1974, allows developing countries to obtain compulsory licenses under certain conditions to translate copyrighted works for teaching, scholarship, and research purposes. It also allows reproduction of copyrighted works for use in systematic instructional activities.

The Paris revision strengthened Convention *minima* for adequate and effective protection by adding basic rights which ensure an author's economic interest. These included the rights of reproduction, public performance and broadcasting, three rights which are to be interpreted broadly. However, protection of the author's moral rights[17] was specifically excluded. In addition, the Berne Safeguard Clause was suspended, permitting developing countries to withdraw from Berne and adhere to the U.C.C.[18]

§ 12.4   The Berne Convention

[A]   Generally

Until its adherence on March 1, 1989, the United States was the only major western country[19] not a member of the International Union for the Protection of Literary and Artistic Works (known as the Berne Union or Berne Convention), the oldest multilateral copyright convention. The Berne Union was first established in 1886 in Berne, Switzerland, and has been revised six times. The current text, the

---

[16] The United Nations General Assembly designates "developing countries" by a nation's cultural, social, and economic development; for example, Algeria, Barbados, Cambodia, Dahomey, and Ecuador are considered "developing countries." *See* Heinz Dawid, *Basic Principles of International Copyright*, 21 Bull. Copyright Soc'y 1 (1973). *See also* U.C.C. art. 5 *bis* (Paris Act) *reprinted in* 4 *Nimmer on Copyright* Appendix 25 (1988).

[17] Many countries recognize an artist's moral or personal right in his work to prevent mutilation, alteration and false suggestion even after the work is legally transferred. In contrast, American copyright law is rooted in economic rights and once copyright of the work is transferred, the author can no longer control use of his work. For a discussion of moral rights and their lack of express recognition under American law, see § 8.27, *supra*.

[18] The Berne Safeguard Clause prohibits a Berne Convention country from denouncing Berne and relying on the U.C.C. in its copyright relations with members of the Berne Convention. The Paris revisions reflected the desire of developing nations to reduce their treaty obligations, granting wider translation and instructional privileges in the U.C.C., plus more latitude in withdrawing from Berne without abandoning protections previously accorded their authors. *See also* "Appendix Declaration Relating to Article XVII" of the U.C.C. as revised at Paris, July 10, 1974, *reprinted in* 4 *Nimmer on Copyright* Appendix 25 (1988).

[19] As of January 1, 1989, the other notable non-adherents to Berne were the Soviet Union and China. Since that time, China has joined the Union and Russia appears be on the verge of doing so.

one to which the United States and most other countries have adhered, is that of Paris, 1971.[20] The Berne Convention is administered by the World Intellectual Property Organization (WIPO), an intergovernmental organization with headquarters in Geneva, Switzerland.[21]

[B] Berne Convention: Summary of its Basic Provisions

The substantive provisions of Berne are found in the first twenty Articles, followed by administrative provisions and an Appendix incorporating special provisions for developing countries. These substantive provisions include both specific and general obligations imposed on its membership. Other rules are optional with the member country. Similar to the U.C.C., the Berne Union is based on national treatment and compliance with Convention *minima*. However, as the following summary will reveal, the Berne Union has established Convention *minima* more substantial than those found in the U.C.C.

[1] Subject Matter

Under Article 2(1) the scope of subject matter is broad, encompassing

> literary and artistic works [which] shall include every production in the literary and artistic domain whatever may be the mode or form of its expression.[22]

This article provides an illustrative list of such works as choreography, painting, and architecture. Compilations and derivative works are to be given protection as well.[23] The *Convention* expressly excludes from obligatory protection "news of the day or . . . miscellaneous facts having the character of mere items of press information."[24] Protection of industrial design is optional and is left to national law.[25]

[2] Basis of Protection

The Berne Convention requires that protection be given to published or unpublished works of an author who is a national of a member state. Berne protection is also required for a work of a non-national of a member state if the work is first published in a member state or simultaneously published in a non-member and member state. Under the Paris and Brussels texts of Berne, a work is published simultaneously if it is published in a member country within 30 days of its first publication in a non-member country.[26]

---

[20] The Berne Convention, signed Sept. 9, 1886, was supplemented by the Additional Act and Declaration signed at Paris, May 4, 1896. The Convention was revised at Berlin, Nov. 13, 1908; Rome, June 2, 1928; Brussels, June 26, 1948; Stockholm, July 14, 1967, (but not ratified); Paris, July 24, 1971.

[21] WIPO is a specialized agency with the United Nations system. Its central role is to conduct studies and provide services designed to facilitate protection of intellectual property. Its Director General is chief of the Berne Union.

[22] Protection of unfixed works is left to the discretion of each member state. Berne Convention art. 2(2) (Paris text).

[23] Berne Convention arts. 2(3) and (5) (Paris text).

[24] Berne Convention art. 2(8) (Paris text).

[25] Berne Convention art. 2(7) (Paris text).

[26] Berne Convention art. 3(2) (Paris text).

Even before the United States' entry into Berne, American authors were able to enjoy Berne privileges by simultaneously publishing their works in a Berne country. For example, American authors had often published their works in Canada within 30 days of publication in the United States. Because Canada adhered to the Paris text of Berne, American authors benefited from Berne despite the United States' non-adherence. This technique of obtaining the benefits of Berne has become known as the "back door to Berne."

Simultaneous publication did not prove to be the panacea it may have appeared on first glance.[27] First, it could be costly, rendering the less wealthy author unable to avail himself of the privilege. Second, seeking protection under the simultaneous publication privilege was not altogether certain in conferring the benefits of Berne. This uncertainty lies in the meaning of "publication" under the Berne Convention. One view is that the term "publication" in the Berne context means that the author must supply enough copies to satisfy the public's need for the work. Under this definition of publication, an American author would have to do much more than send a couple of copies of a book to a Canadian distributor to meet Berne publication requirements, even though this act would constitute publication under U.S. law.[28] Apart from these difficulties, an author taking the "back door" route had to verify that the country chosen adhered to a text of Berne that allowed the 30-day publication privilege. For those countries adhering to the Rome text only, simultaneous publication means that publication must take place on the same day in the two countries, a task impossible to fulfill for many authors.[29]

[3] Preclusion of Formalities

Berne requires that the work be protected without formalities outside the country of origin. Thus, if a work originates from a member country, it must be protected in all Berne countries without being subjected to any formalities as prerequisite to copyright protection.[30] The Berne Convention does not govern protection of works in their countries of origin. This means that formalities can be imposed on a work in its country of origin.

[4] Minimum Term of Protection

The Berne Convention has established a minimum term of protection of life-plus-50-years or an alternative of 50 years from publication for anonymous or pseudonymous works.[31] As is generally the case for all Berne provisions, the member country can grant a term of protection in excess of the minimum term.[32]

[5] Exclusive Rights

The Berne Convention requires that certain exclusive rights be protected under national law. These rights are on the whole are quite similar to the array of economic

---

[27] For a detailed overview, see 3 *Nimmer on Copyright* § 17.04[D] (1988).

[28] *See* 17 U.S.C. § 101 (publication) for a discussion of publication.

[29] Berne Convention art. 4(3) (Rome text).

[30] Berne Convention art. 5(2) (Paris text).

[31] Berne Convention arts. 7(1) and (3) (Paris text).

[32] Berne Convention art. 7(6) (Paris text).

rights found in § 106 of the 1976 Copyright Act.[33] Berne, in some ways, is not as comprehensive as American law. For example, Berne is silent on distribution and display rights, both of which are specifically provided for under American law. Berne also recognizes certain limitations on the exclusive rights, such as a fair use[34] privilege, and a possible limitation of the right of recording of musical works, such as found in § 115 of the 1976 Act. In addition to these exclusive economic rights, Berne also requires that the author's moral right be recognized and endure beyond the life of the author.[35] This concept is alien to United States copyright law, but may have received *de facto* recognition when considered in the entire context of American unfair competition and defamation law.[36] Finally, in 1990, with the Visual Artists Rights Act, the U.S. for the first time gave explicit, but hardly complete, recognition to a moral right.[37]

§ 12.5 U.S. Entry Into Berne

[A] Generally

Before its entry into Berne on March 1, 1989, the United States was the only major western country which was not a party to the Convention.[38] Because the United States has been for some time the world's largest exporter of copyrighted works,[39] it had a strong interest in joining the world's largest, preeminent copyright convention, particularly because Berne, by then, encompassed 85 nations including America's major trading partners. By the late 80's, the impetus for joining Berne was greater than ever, because the United States had withdrawn from UNESCO, the United Nations organization which administers the U.C.C. As a result, it was felt that the United States could no longer influence the policy within UNESCO even though its withdrawal does not preclude its membership in the U.C.C. With the increase of organized international piracy of copyrighted works of American

---

[33] *See* Berne Convention arts. 8(1) (translation right); 9(1) (reproduction); 11(1) (public performance); 12 (adaptation) (Paris text).

[34] Berne Convention arts. 9(2), 10, and 10 *bis* (Paris text).

[35] *See* Berne Convention art. 6 *bis* which provides in part:

(1) Independently of an author's economic rights and even after the transfer of said rights, the author shall have the right to claim authorship of the work and to object to any distortion, mutilation or other modification of, or other derogatory action in relation to, the said work, which would be prejudicial to his honor or reputation.

(2) The rights granted to the author in accordance with the preceding paragraph shall, after his death, be maintained, at least until the expiry of the economic rights. . . .

[36] For a discussion of the moral right and its American analogs, see § 8.26, *supra*.

[37] The Act confers a right of integrity and paternity on certain works in the visual arts. *See* § 8.28, *supra*.

[38] *See* S. Rep. No. 100–352, 100th Cong., 2d Sess. 2 (1988).

[39] Export value of American motion pictures now exceeds the value of our steel imports. *U.S. Adherence to the Berne Convention Hearings Before the Subcomm. on Patents, Copyrights and Trademarks of the Senate Comm. on the Judiciary*, 99th Cong., 1st and 2d Sess. 5 (1987).

authors, it had often been pointed out how critically important it was for the United States to have a major role in influencing the direction of international copyright matters.[40] The entry of the United States into Berne appeared to be the logical solution to its current isolation in the world copyright system.

Major changes have taken place in American copyright law and attitudes since the initial refusal of the United States to enter into Berne at the outset in 1886.[41] The United States had taken a more international orientation in joining the U.C.C. and thereby recognizing the principle of national treatment.[42] More importantly, the provisions of the 1976 Act eliminated many of the impediments to Berne adherence. The 1976 Act, however, still fell far short of compliance with certain substantial and explicit Convention *minima* required for Berne membership, and major amendments to the 1976 Act were needed to make membership possible.[43]

[B]   The Berne Convention Implementation Act of 1988

On March 1, 1989, with the passage of the Berne Convention Implementation Act of 1988,[44] the United States officially entered the Berne Convention. Section 2(1) of the Implementation Act declares that the Berne Convention is not self-executing under U.S. law.[45] This means that rights and responsibilities dealing with copyright matters will be resolved under the domestic law, state and federal, of the United States. Thus, because the Berne Convention is not self-executing, special implementing legislation was needed, modifying the current Copyright Act to comply with the general and specific obligations of Berne adherence.

In drafting the implementing legislation, Congress took what has been termed as a minimalist approach. As used here, the term "minimalist" means that only the essential changes necessary to comply with Convention obligations would be made to American law.[46] An example of this minimalist approach can be found in the treatment of moral rights, which are specifically recognized in Article 6 *bis* of the Berne Convention. Congress believed that the protection afforded by the entirety of American copyright, unfair competition, defamation, privacy and contract law served to prevent improper alterations of an author's work, and were thus sufficient

---

[40] S. Rep. No. 100–352, 100th Cong., 2d Sess. 4 (1988).

[41] United States refusal to enter Berne in 1886 was the result of rivalries between American and British publishing houses over the national treatment doctrine and the extension of protection to non-resident foreigners.

[42] The national treatment principle requires that persons entitled to Convention benefits enjoy in each member nation the advantages accorded to nationals of the forum country.

[43] At the request of the U.S. State Department, individuals with significant experience in copyright formed an Ad Hoc Working Group on U.S. Adherence to the Berne Convention to consider possible U.S. adherence to Berne. The final report addresses items of conflict, including notice and registration. For the complete, detailed text, see Final Report of the Ad Hoc Working Group on U.S. Adherence to the Berne Convention, *reprinted in* 10 Colum.–VLA J.L. & Arts 513 (1986) [hereinafter referred to as the "Ad Hoc Working Group"].

[44] Pub. L. No. 100–568 (1988).

[45] *Id.* at § 2(1).

[46] 134 Cong. Rec. S14552 (daily ed. Oct. 5, 1988) (statement of Sen. Patrick J. Leahy).

to meet the needs of Berne adherence.[47] The major aspects of the implementing legislation and amendments to the 1976 Act are summarized as follows:

[1] Formalities

Article 5(2) of the Berne Convention provides that the enjoyment and exercise of an author's rights shall not be subject to any formality. Thus, to enter Berne, the United States had to eliminate certain formalities, such as notice and registration requirements, contained in the 1976 Act. Under American law, omission of notice[48] could lead to forfeiture of copyright and registration,[49] a prerequisite for bringing suit for infringement and obtaining certain remedies. These requirements were contrary to Berne because they affect the "enjoyment and exercise of rights under copyright."[50]

The most significant change to American copyright law brought about by the Berne Convention Implementation Act of 1988 Amendments is the abrogation of required notice for publicly distributed works on or after March 1, 1989. For these publicly distributed works, notice of copyright is permissive and omission of notice can no longer forfeit copyright.[51] Although notice is no longer required for publicly distributed works, it is still highly recommended. In fact, the Berne amendments encourage the affixation of proper notice. For causes of action arising on or after March 1, 1989, proper notice on a work will preclude a defendant from asserting a defense of innocent infringement in mitigation of actual or statutory damages.[52] The new permissive notice provisions are not retroactive and a work publicly distributed before the effective date of the BCIA will be governed by the prior provisions and is still subject to possible forfeiture.[53]

Before the Berne amendments, recordation of an interest in a copyright was a condition prerequisite to bringing a suit for copyright infringement. Now, for causes of action arising on or after March 1, 1989, recordation is no longer a prerequisite.[54] However, recordation remains, even on or after March 1, 1989, a highly recommended procedure for the owner of an interest in a copyright. One reason is that recordation is still important in determining the priority between conflicting transfers.

Opinions differed whether registration as a prerequisite for bringing an infringement suit was a formality incompatible with Berne. The Berne amendments took a compromise approach to this issue. Instead of flatly repealing § 411, the legislation adopted a two-tier approach to registration. For works originating from a Berne country, the Berne amendments have abrogated the registration requirement as a

[47] For a discussion of moral rights, see § 8.27, *supra*; see also 2 *Nimmer on Copyright* § 8.21 (1988), for a discussion of the moral right as recognized in Article 6 *bis* of the *Berne Convention*.
[48] *See* 17 U.S.C. § 405. For a discussion of notice, see §§ 4.8–4.14, *supra*.
[49] *See* 17 U.S.C. §§ 401, 411. For a discussion of registration, see §§ 7.2–7.8, *supra*.
[50] Berne Convention art. 5(2) (Paris text).
[51] *See* 17 U.S.C. § 401(a).
[52] *See* 17 U.S.C. §§ 401(d), 402(d).
[53] *See* 17 U.S.C. §§ 405(a), (b), (f).
[54] *See* 17 U.S.C. § 205. For a discussion of recordation, see § 5.12, *supra*.

precondition to bringing suit. Alternatively, registration will still be required to bring suit when a work is first published (or simultaneously published) in the United States or for an unpublished work when all the authors are nationals, domiciliaries, or permanent residents of the United States.[55]

Although registration is no longer required for Berne works, the incentives to register continue, unaffected by the Berne amendments. First, the *prima facie* evidentiary value of the certificate of registration, which shifts the burden of proof to the benefit of the copyright owner in an infringement suit, is unchanged. Second, registration remains a prerequisite for obtaining statutory damages and attorney's fees. Moreover, statutory damages for infringement of copyrighted works have been doubled, thereby further encouraging registration of copyright.

In sum, as to formalities, the Berne amendments (with the exception of permissive notice) have done little to weaken the necessity of complying with formalities, and in some cases, have increased the rewards of such compliance. Although the Berne amendments have modified the formalities of notice, recordation and registration, a copyright owner in order to effectively protect and enforce his rights is greatly encouraged to place proper notice on his work, register it, and record his ownership interest in the Copyright Office.

[2] Architectural Works

The Berne Convention includes architectural works and works of applied art as part of minimum subject matter protection.[56]

Traditionally, the "useful articles" doctrine of American copyright law has restricted the protection of architectural designs. Even so, consistent with the "minimalist" approach, which characterized United States adherence to the Berne Convention in 1988, no changes were then made in the domestic law relating to architectural works. As was the case for moral rights, however, Berne adherence has had a delayed effect on U.S. copyright law. After a 1989 Copyright Office study recommended change, Congress passed legislation establishing protection of architectural works.[57]

[3] Jukebox Compulsory License [58]

This compulsory license, contained in § 116 of the 1976 as originally enacted, clearly contravened the requirements of the Berne Convention. The relevant Berne provision, Article 11, prescribes an exclusive right to authorize the public performance of a musical work.[59] The jukebox license under the original § 116 was a

---

[55] *See* 17 U.S.C. § 411. *See also* 17 U.S.C. § 101 (defining country of origin of a Berne Convention work). In addition, registration will be required to bring an infringement suit when a work is published in a foreign nation that does not adhere to the Berne Convention and all the authors are nationals, domiciliaries, or permanent residents of, or in the case of an audiovisual work, legal entities with headquarters in, the United States. *Id.* For a discussion of copyright registration, see § 7.6, *supra.*

[56] Berne Convention art. 2(1) (Paris text).

[57] *See* Pub. L. No. 101–650 (Title VII), 104 Stat. 5089 (1990): H.R. Rep. No. 101–735, 101st Cong., 2d Sess. (1990). For a discussion of copyright in architectural works, see § 3.15, *supra.*

[58] For a discussion of the jukebox license, see § 8.21, *supra.*

[59] 17 U.S.C. § 116.

limitation on the copyright owner's performance right in a nondramatic musical work because it allowed the public performance of such works without the copyright owner's consent and for a non-negotiated compensation. To harmonize the jukebox license with Berne requirements, the BCIA enacted a new § 116A to replace the compulsory license with a voluntarily negotiated one, but if the parties were not able to formulate a negotiated license, then the previous compulsory licensing system was to be reinstituted. All vestiges of the compulsory license were repealed by legislation in 1993. Section 116 as originally enacted is now replaced by a renumbered § 116A.[60]

[4] Works in the Public Domain: Retroactivity

Retroactivity of protection was one of the most controversial issues raised in the discussions leading to Berne adherence. Article 18 of Berne provides that "(t)his Convention shall apply to all works which, at the moment of its coming into force, have not yet fallen into the public domain in the country of origin through the expiry of protection." This would appear to mean that, under the treaty, the only reason a country may use for not protecting a member country's work is the expiration of its copyright in either the country of origin or the forum country. But article 18 also provides that "the respective countries of the Union shall determine, each insofar as it is concerned, the conditions of application of this principle."[61] Whatever may be the proper interpretation of Art. 18, Congress did nothing to protect works in the public domain as of March 1, 1989. Section 12 of the BCIA provides that no retroactive protection is provided for any work that is in the public domain in the United States.[62] Thus, the obligations of the United States under the Berne Convention will apply to works that are protected in the United States on the effective date of the BCIA. In addition, § 13(b) provides that the Berne Convention Implementation Act does not apply to causes of action arising before its effective date.[63] Although steadfast against retroactivity for Berne adherence, the United States in 1993 allowed for retroactivity pursuant to negotiations leading to the completion of NAFTA. To implement its obligations under NAFTA, the United States agreed to retroactive protection for Mexican and Canadian motion pictures that had fallen into the public domain for failure to comply with the notice provisions of the 1976 Act.[64]

In more dramatic fashion, the Uruguay Round Agreements Act passed at the end of 1994 greatly expanded the relatively modest NAFTA restoration provisions. This legislation, whose purpose is to implement United States obligations under the new World Trade Organization, restored copyright in certain foreign works that had fallen into the public domain for failure to comply with U.S. copyright formalities.[65]

---

[60] 17 U.S.C. § 116A.

[61] Berne Convention art. 18(3) (Paris text).

[62] Berne Convention Implementation Act of 1988 § 12, Pub. L. No. 100–568 (1988).

[63] Berne Convention Implementation Act of 1988 § 13(b), Pub. L. No. 100–568 (1988).

[64] *See* 17 U.S.C. § 104A.

[65] 17 U.S.C. § 104A. Section 104A restores copyright in works of foreign origin — *i.e.,* works from Berne or WTO countries — but leaves works of U.S. origin in the public domain. Copyright restoration is discussed in §§ 4.18-4.19 *supra.*

Thus, after many years of resistance, the concept of "retroactivity" has become firmly entrenched in U.S. law. This change in fundamental attitude shows once again the increasing influence of international norms on U.S. copyright law, the globalization of markets for copyrighted works, and the need to ensure full and reciprocal treatment of U.S. works in foreign countries.

[5]　Copyright Infringement Remedies

Unrelated to Berne compatibility, the Berne amendments doubled the amount of statutory damages that can be recovered in lieu of actual damages and profits in copyright infringement actions.[66] Doubling the statutory damages enhances the incentives to register a work because statutory damages cannot be sought without a registration, even for works whose origin is a Berne country.

[C]　Benefits to American Authors and Copyright Owners from Berne Membership

One immediate benefit of entry into Berne is that American authors and copyright owners no longer have to rely on the costly and risky use of the back-door Berne procedure to protect their works in some 24 Berne countries with which the United States has had no other copyright relations. For the most part, however, the tangible benefits that Berne membership will bring to American copyright owners may not be felt immediately. They will manifest themselves over the long term due to the United States' more effective influence over the direction of international copyright policy.[67]

§ 12.6　Other Copyright-Related Conventions

[A]　Convention for the Protection of Producers of Phonograms Against Unauthorized Duplication of Their Phonograms

Signed in Geneva in 1971 and effective in 1974 in the United States, this Convention was created to provide international protection for sound recordings. Each member nation agrees to protect nationals of other member nations against the unauthorized manufacture, importation, and distribution of copies of sound recordings. The Convention is based on national protection and has minimum requirements for participation, such as a 25-year minimum term as measured from fixation (*i.e.*, embodied in tangible form in a phonorecord, cassette, disc, etc.) or first publication, and a notice requirement, identical to U.S. law,[68] which is deemed to satisfy all other formalities. Compulsory licenses are limited, and are allowed only for teaching or scientific research.

The 1971 Geneva Convention should be distinguished from the Rome Convention of 1961, entitled the International Convention for the Protection of Performers,

---

[66] *See* 17 U.S.C. § 504(c) (as amended by the BCIA). For a discussion of statutory damages, see § 9.13, *supra.*

[67] Entry enabled the United States to have copyright relations with some 24 new countries. *See* S. Rep. No. 100–352, 100th Cong., 2d Sess. 3 (1988).

[68] *See* 17 U.S.C. § 402.

Producers of Phonograms and Broadcasting Organizations.[69] The Rome Convention, unlike later phonogram conventions, protects performances embodied in sound recordings. The United States, which does not protect performance rights in sound recordings, has not ratified the Rome Convention.[70]

[B] Brussels Satellite Convention

In 1984 the United States ratified the Convention relating to the Distribution of Programme-Carrying Signals Transmitted by Satellite, known as the "Brussels Satellite Convention."[71] Established in 1974, its purpose is to combat the misappropriation of satellite signals on an international level. The need for a special international agreement covering satellite transmission was apparent from its inadequate treatment in the major international copyright conventions. Although the U.C.C. (art. IV *bis*) and the Berne Convention (art. 11 *bis*) provide for the exclusive right to broadcast, it is unclear whether "broadcasting" in these conventions covers satellite transmissions. To fill this void, the Brussels Satellite Convention was conceived.

The Convention creates no new rights for programs transmitted by satellite. Implementation of the treaty is left to the contracting states, who agree to provide adequate protection against satellite signal piracy.[72] The United States viewed its copyright and communication laws as adequate in this regard; thus, unlike adherence to the Berne Convention, there was no perceived need for specific implementing legislation to join the Brussels Convention.

The Convention focuses on the unauthorized distribution of signals, not their unauthorized reception. Thus, the private reception of signals for private use does not violate the Brussels Convention. Moreover, the signal is the object of protection, not the content of the material sent by the signal. Accordingly, the Convention is designed to protect the emitter or carrier, not the copyright owner of the program material.

[C] Copyright in the Americas: Buenos Aires Convention

The United States and 17 Latin American nations adhere to the Buenos Aires Convention, which took effect in 1911.[73] Article 3, the basic provision of the

---

[69] For an overview, see Robert Dittrich, *The Practical Application of the Rome Convention*, 26 Bull. Copyright Soc'y 287 (1979).

[70] For a discussion of performance rights in sound recordings, see § 8.24, *supra*.

[71] The United States signed the treaty in 1974 but did not ratify it until 1984.

[72] Satellite signal piracy is also referred to as "signal poaching" or the unauthorized use of program-carrying satellite signals. *See generally* Heather Dembert, *Securing Authors' Rights in Satellite Transmissions: U.S. Efforts to Extend Copyright Protection Abroad*, 24 Colum. J. Transnat'l L. 73, n. 2 (1985).

[73] The Buenos Aires Convention was not the first inter-American treaty governing copyright in which the United States participated. The first was the Mexico City Treaty of 1902 which governed copyright relations between the U.S. and El Salvador, until that country's adherence to the U.C.C. in 1979. For an overview, see Alfred L. Rinaldo, Jr. *The Scope of Copyright Protection in the United States Under Existing Inter-American Relations: Abrogation of the Need for U.S. Protection Under the Buenos Aires Convention by Reliance Upon the U.C.C.*, 22 Bull. Copyright Soc'y 417 (1975).

Convention, requires that once copyright is obtained for a work in one member country, protection is given by all member countries without further formalities, provided that there appears in the work a statement that property rights are reserved. Usually this statement appears as *All Rights Reserved* or similar language. The U.S. Copyright Office, however, takes the position that Buenos Aires works have no special status under American law, that works must satisfy all formalities imposed on national authors, and that use of the words "all rights reserved" is insufficient notice of copyright.[74] Today, virtually all of the countries of the Americas are members of Berne or the U.C.C. or both — each of which is more effective than the Buenos Aires Convention. Nonetheless, publishers, by force of habit, continue to affix on the title page of a work the Buenos Aires notice "All Rights Reserved" which, if nothing more, has a nice ring to it. One might question whether the Buenos Aires Convention serves any practical purpose because virtually all the countries in the Americas are members of the U.C.C. The U.C.C. provides much the same protection as does the Buenos Aires Convention; its terms are clearer and the number of adherents is much greater than under the Buenos Aires Convention.

PART II: FOREIGN AUTHORS AND CONFLICTS OF LAW IN INTERNATIONAL COPYRIGHT

§ 12.7   Foreign Authors

[A]   Unpublished Works

Nationals and domiciliaries of foreign nations may protect their works in the United States as an American citizen can, if the foreign author meets the conditions set forth in § 104 of the 1976 Act.[75] These conditions vary depending on whether the work is published or unpublished. The rule for unpublished works of foreign authors is simple and all inclusive: all works qualifying for statutory copyright are protected from the moment of creation, no matter what the nationality or domicile of the author. So long as the work has not gone into the public domain, an unpublished work of a foreign author is protected in the United States no differently than that of an American author.[76]

[B]   Published Works: The Five Bases for Protection in § 104(b)[77]

Section 104(b) of the 1976 Copyright Act sets forth five broad, overlapping categories for published works, any of which the foreign author must fall within to be eligible for protection in the United States like any other citizen.

---

[74] *See Compendium of Copyright Office Practices II* §§ 1005.01(b) and 1104.02.

[75] 17 U.S.C. § 104.

[76] *See* 17 U.S.C. § 104(a). *See also* 1 *Nimmer on Copyright* § 5.05 (1988).

[77] 17 U.S.C. § 104(b) (as amended by the BCIA).

First, one or more of the authors must be a national or domiciliary of the United States or a country with which the United States has copyright relations under a treaty, or the author may be a stateless person.[78]

The term "domicile," as used in § 104, consists of two elements: (1) residence in the United States, and (2) an intent to remain in the United States. Mere residency without the requisite intent is insufficient for status as a domiciliary in the United States. The resident must manifest the requisite intent by establishing ties such as declarations, marriage, payment of taxes, voting, or establishing a home.

Even foreign authors not domiciled in the United States may claim copyright under United States law if on the date of publication, the author is a domiciliary or national of a treaty nation. Treaty nations are those adhering to the Berne Union, the Universal Copyright Convention (U.C.C.),[79] the Buenos Aires Convention,[80] or countries with which the United States has bilateral arrangements, such as China, Romania, Thailand, and the Philippines.[81]

Second, if the work is first published in the United States or in a country that is a party to the U.C.C., it will receive non-discriminatory protection under U.S. law.[82]

When a work is first published in a U.C.C. country, the publication must have occurred no earlier than September 15, 1955, the date on which the United States became a member of the U.C.C.. If the work was published before that date, it is irrevocably in the public domain unless it can be protected on some other basis.

Third, a published work of a foreign author receives protection if it was published by the United Nations or by any of its specialized agencies, or by the Organization of American States.[83]

Fourth, the work is a Berne Convention work.[84] A work is a Berne Convention work if it is unpublished, and one or more of the authors is a national of a nation

---

[78] 17 U.S.C. § 104(b)(1).

[79] Universal Copyright Convention, Sept. 6, 1952, 6 U.S.T. 2732, T.I.A.S. No. 3324, 753 U.N.T.S. 368, *amended by* Universal Copyright Convention, July 24, 1971, 25 U.S.T. 1341, T.I.A.S. No. 7868.

[80] Pan American Copyright Convention (Buenos Aires), Aug. 11, 1910, 38 Stat. 1785, T.S. No. 593, 155 I.N.T.S. 1979.

[81] The texts of these agreements are reprinted in the appendices in 4 *Nimmer on Copyright* (1988). *See also International Copyright Relations of the United States*, Circular R38(a), U.S. Copyright Office. What constitutes a valid bilateral arrangement is not free from doubt. For example, in 1946, the United States signed a Friendship, Commerce and Navigation Treaty ("FCN") with the Republic of China committing both countries to honor each other's copyrights. In 1948, with the Chinese Revolution, the Nationalist government was overthrown and established itself in Taiwan. In 1978, the President signed a memorandum recognizing the People's Republic of China and terminating diplomatic relations with Taiwan. *New York Chinese TV Programs, Inc. v. U.E., Inc.*, 944 F.2d 847 (1992), raised the question whether Taiwanese works still enjoy protection in this country under the 1946 Treaty. The Court held that the Treaty should be recognized because of the deference we owe to the political branches of the government in treaty matters. Although the U.S. may not have diplomatic relations with a country, it does honor its treaty obligations.

[82] 17 U.S.C. § 104(b)(2).

[83] 17 U.S.C. § 104(b)(3).

[84] *See* 17 U.S.C. § 104(b)(4) (as amended by the BCIA).

adhering to the Berne Convention.[85] For published works, a work is a Berne work if first published in a Berne country.[86] Because the United States has adhered to the Paris text of the Berne Convention, a work that is first published simultaneously in a nation adhering to Berne and one not adhering to Berne will be protected under U.S. law. Under the Paris revision of Berne, a work is considered to have been simultaneously published in two or more nations if the dates of publication are within 30 days of one another.[87] If the basis of protection is publication in a Berne member country, the publication must have taken place after the United States' effective entry into the Convention, on March 1, 1989.

Fifth, the work is protected if covered by a Presidential proclamation extending protection to works originating in a specific country which extends protection to U.S. works on substantially the same basis given to its own works.[88]

§ 12.8   International Copyright and Conflicts of Law

[A]   The Application of Foreign Copyright Law by U.S. Courts

As a general principle, copyright law is territorial in nature and, as such, is considered effective only within the borders of an individual country. But when an act of infringement occurs in a foreign country, a U.S. court may, nevertheless, have jurisdiction to hear the case. To understand why, one must make a distinction between jurisdiction to adjudicate and the choice of law to be applied. The Federal courts may have jurisdiction if the claim of copyright infringement is considered a transitory cause of action, even if the cause of action arose in the foreign jurisdiction. 28 U.S.C. § 1332(a)(2) confers jurisdiction in a federal court if the requirements of diversity of citizenship (citizens of a State and citizens or subjects of a foreign state) and jurisdictional amount ($50,000) are met. Even though U.S. law may not apply, a U.S. court might retain jurisdiction over an action for copyright infringement, and in so doing, apply the copyright law of the foreign jurisdiction. For example, in *London Film Productions Ltd. v. Intercontinental Communications, Inc.*[89] a British plaintiff sued a New York corporation for alleged acts of infringement occurring in Chile and other Latin American countries. The Court declared that it was competent to pass on the issues of the case and apply foreign law. Moreover, no principles of comity, such as the need to pass on the validity of acts of foreign officials, made it inappropriate for the U.S. court to adjudicate the controversy.

---

[85] *See* 17 U.S.C. § 101 (as amended by the BCIA).

[86] *Id.*

[87] 17 U.S.C. § 101 (defining a Berne Convention work).

[88] 17 U.S.C. § 104(b)(5). Presidential proclamations issued under the 1909 Act remain in force today. *See* 17 U.S.C. Trans. & Supp. Prov. § 104.

[89] 580 F. Supp. 47 (S.D.N.Y. 1984).

[B] The Application of U.S. Law to Foreign Infringing Acts

As already stated, when acts of infringement occur abroad, the copyright laws of the United States do not apply. The courts, however, will relax this principle when the infringing acts committed abroad result in infringement taking place in the United States. Thus, U.S. Copyright law was applied to defendant's sales in Germany to a German exporter of bottled water bearing allegedly infringing labels that were destined for U.S. distribution.[90] But what about the other side of the coin? Will U.S. copyright law be applied to infringing acts begun in the U.S. whose purpose is to infringe copyright in a foreign country? Here, the courts will apply U.S. copyright law so long as some of the infringing *acts* occurred in the United States. On the other hand, United States copyright law will not reach acts of infringement that take place entirely abroad, even though these acts were authorized in the United States.[91]

[C] Choice of Law Rules in International Copyright Conflicts

The rights conferred by international conventions are territorially limited whereby national law decides both substance and procedure. Thus, an American author who wishes to enforce her copyrighted work in France will be subject to French law. Because the U.S. and France are members of the major international conventions (*i.e.*, Berne, U.C.C.), the American author must be afforded national treatment. What this means in practical terms is that a work originating in the United States is entitled to protection in France to the same degree as if it had been created by a French citizen.[92]

From the above principles, the law that a court will apply is that of the county in which the rights are claimed. Difficult conflicts of law issues, however, may arise when a work of foreign origin is exploited in the forum country pursuant to a contract executed in the country of origin. Sometimes the parties in their contract will chose the pertinent law (choice of law clause) to be applied. Normally, the law chosen by the parties is the applicable law unless the law so chosen offends the public policy of the forum state. If the parties have not stipulated their choice of law, the court must make this decision. In this situation, it would apply the traditional choice of law rule, that is, the law where the contract was executed. But again, a strong public policy may override this traditional rule.

---

[90] *See, e.g., G.B. Marketing U.S.A. Inc. v. Gerolsteiner Brunnen GmbH & Co.*, 782 F. Supp. 763 (W.D.N.Y. 1991); *see also Update Art, Inc. v. Modiin Publishing, Ltd.*, 843 F.2d 67 (2d Cir. 1988) (award of damages from Israeli newspaper's unauthorized publication of a photograph of U.S. citizen's "Ronbo" poster later reproduced in the U.S.).

[91] *Subafilms, Ltd. v. MGM-PATHE Communications Co.*, 24 F.3d 1088 (9th Cir. 1994).

[92] One exception to the principle of national treatment is the doctrine of the shorter term, (Article 7(8) Berne Convention). This doctrine provides that a Berne Union country can grant works, originating in other Union states, a shorter term of protection than the country provides for equivalent domestic works. But it may do so only if the term of protection of the work's country of origin is less than that provided in the county where protection is claimed. *See* § 6.4, *supra*, for a discussion of the doctrine.

Moral rights laws provide a good a example of the tension between choice of law rules and the overriding public policy of the forum country. In contrast to the U.S., moral rights in France are both inalienable and perpetual. Thus, a film director who has transferred all economic interest in a work still preserves the right to oppose violations of the work's integrity and paternity. This discrepancy between U.S. and French law arose in the choice of law context where the heirs of the American director, John Huston, sought to prevent the broadcast on French television of a colorized version of his film, *The Asphalt Jungle*. The heirs brought suit in France and asked the French court to apply the French moral rights law to prohibit this distortion of the work. In *Huston v. la Cinq*[93] the intermediate court applied American law and determined that the heirs had no standing to bring the action under their moral rights theory. In choosing American law, the court applied the prevailing choice of law rule that recognizes the rules of the country of origin on authorship status and copyright ownership. The French Supreme court reversed, applying French law that would allow heirs of an author to defend the work's right of integrity. The Court abandoned the traditional choice of laws analysis because of the imperative nature of moral rights protection.

The *Huston* case highlights the need to develop a uniform set of principles governing the conflicts of laws arising from the ever-growing international exploitation of copyrighted works. Moral rights law is not the only area in which a court may consider overturning a traditional choice of law rule for public policy reasons. Many countries are much more paternalistic in their view of contracts concerning the use and ownership of copyright. For example, some countries specify in their copyright laws the number of years in which a grant may be given, the percentage of profits that an author must receive, and other such protective provisions. Suppose a U.S. work is exploited in a country that explicitly stipulates certain contractual provisions that are more favorable to the copyright owner than those of contract. In this situation, should the public policy of the forum override the traditional choice of law rule and entitle the U.S. author to the benefits of local law? Unfortunately, there are no convenient answers to these issues. Ultimately, a new international agreement may be required to harmonize the law concerning copyright, contracts, and the conflicts of law.[94]

---

[93] *Huston v. la Cinq*, Judgment of May 28, 1991; for an excellent analysis of the case, see Jane C. Ginsburg and Pierre Sirinelli, *Authors and Exploitations in International Private Law: The French Supreme Court and the Huston Film Colorization Controversy*, 15 Colum.-VLA J.L. & Arts 135 (1991).

[94] *See* Paul Edward Geller, *Harmonizing Copyright-Contract Conflicts Analysis*, 25 Copyright 49 (1989).

PART III: TRADE REGULATION AFFECTING INTERNATIONAL COPYRIGHT MATTERS

§ 12.9 Infringing Importation of Copies or Phonorecords

[A] Sections 602 and 603 of the 1976 Copyright Act

International commercial counterfeiting is a big business and an ever-expanding one. As a result, §§ 602 and 603[95] of the 1976 Copyright Act, which prohibit the importation of infringing copies or phonorecords acquired abroad, have become more important than ever to U.S. copyright owners. The United States Customs Service, an arm of the Department of the Treasury, may seize and "forfeit" the imported infringing articles.[96] Regulations implementing the provisions of § 602 have been issued by the Customs Service.

Unlawful importation of copyrighted works can be attacked both by private actions as well as by Customs Office enforcement. Although private enforcement is available, Customs enforcement is clearly the more effective remedy against the importation of unlawful goods. In general, customs enforcement is less expensive and time-consuming. By preventing the goods from entering into the stream of commerce, Customs enforcement provides a global, one-stop remedy against unlawful importation. By comparison, a private action works in a less effective, piecemeal fashion. Private injunctive remedies prevent the sale of the goods, not their original importation. In a private action, an injunction applies only to the individual distributors but not to others who were not parties to the suit. As a result, some unlawful goods are more likely to elude interdiction and will continue to be sold to the public.

To benefit from § 602 and its regulations, the copyright owner must record his registered copyright with the U.S. Customs Service. Each application must be accompanied by a registration certificate issued by the U.S. Copyright Office, five copies of any copyrighted work, and the required filing fee. Once the copyright is recorded, Customs Service officers are issued a copyright notice accompanied by identifying documents and information about suspected infringing copies or phonorecords.[97]

The Customs Office may hold articles suspected of being "pirated" (i.e., infringing) copies of copyrighted works, and officials will notify the importer, who is given 30 days to file a denial that the articles are piratical.[98] If the importer does not file the denial within 30 days, the articles are deemed piratical and are subject to seizure and forfeiture.[99]

Customs service regulations set forth a procedure used to substantiate the claims of the parties.[100] The copyright owner must file a bond to compensate the importer

---

[95] 17 U.S.C. §§ 602, 603.

[96] 17 U.S.C. § 603(c).

[97] 19 C.F.R. § 133.33.

[98] 19 C.F.R. § 133.43(a). For a definition of "pirated goods," see 19 C.F.R. § 133.42.

[99] Id.

[100] 19 C.F.R. § 133.43(b)(2).

for any loss he may wrongly suffer,[101] and has the burden of proving that the articles are piratical.[102] The ultimate decision is made by the Commissioner of Customs and is based on evidence submitted by the parties. If the copyright owner wins, the articles are forfeited (*i.e.*, destroyed or sent back to the country of origin); if the importer's position is upheld, the bond is forfeited to him.

Although Customs can be effective in excluding infringing goods at the border, it is not above reproach. Customs has been criticized for its confidentiality restrictions that prevent the service from giving intellectual property owners sufficient information to facilitate judicial action against manufacturers, importers, and distributors. Newly proposed regulations would endow the agency with authority to expedite the release of such data.[103]

[B] Section 337 of the Tariff Act of 1930: The U.S. International Trade Commission[104]

Section 337 of the Tariff Act of 1930[105] provides for relief against unfair methods of competition and unfair acts in the importation of articles into, or their sale thereafter in, the United States. The acts protected against include any patent, trademark, copyright, and mask work infringement that occurs in connection with the importation of goods into the United States. The burden varies, depending on whether the copyright or mask work is registered or unregistered. For registered copyright and mask works, a complainant must show that an industry in the United States relating to the articles protected by the copyright or mask work exists or is in the process of being established. Under the statute, an industry exists, for the articles at issue, if there is in the United States: "(A) significant investment in plant and equipment; (B) significant employment of labor or capital; or (C) substantial investment in its exploitation, including engineering, research and development, or licensing."[106] For unregistered copyright or mask works, a complainant has an extra burden in having to prove injury to a U.S. industry.[107] The U.S. International Trade Commission (USITC) administers the statute and is required to make its determination based on an administrative hearing similar to federal court litigation. Under the Commission's rules, the complaint must contain a detailed statement of facts that

---

[101] *Id.*

[102] 19 C.F.R. § 133.43(c)(1).

[103] 19 C.F.R. § 133.43(b)(2).

[104] For an overview, see R. V. Lupo, *International Trade Commission Section 337 Proceedings and Their Applicability to Copyright Ownership*, 32 J. Copyright Soc'y 193 (1985).

[105] 19 U.S.C. § 1337.

[106] 19 U.S.C. § 1337(a)(3).

[107] The Omnibus Trade and Competitiveness Act of 1988 has amended § 337 of the Tariff Act, which had required that the plaintiff prove that imports would destroy or injure a U.S. industry, an industry that was efficient and economically operated. *See* Trade and Competitiveness Act, Pub. L. No. 100–418, § 1342, 102 Stat. 1107, 1212–16 (1988) (codified as 19 U.S.C. § 1337(a) (1988)). The Omnibus Act also made a number of procedural improvements to § 337 practice as well as changes relating to preliminary relief, cease and desist orders, fines, and default judgments. *See* H.R. Conf. Rep. No. 100–576, 100th Cong., 2d Sess. 632–39, *reprinted in* 1988 U.S. Code, Cong. & Admin. News 1665–72.

consists of more than mere allegations.[108] Within 30 days after receipt of a complaint, the Commission must decide whether to go forward with an investigation.[109] If there is a positive decision by the USITC, the matter is assigned to an administrative law judge (ALJ), who is in charge of the investigation.[110] The Commission is empowered to issue temporary exclusion orders prohibiting the entry of merchandise during the pendency of an investigation.

Section 337 cases are litigated before an ALJ who conducts the litigation similar to a federal court judge. If the ALJ finds a violation, and no appeal is made to the USITC, an *in rem* order excluding the infringing articles from the United States may be issued. This is known as an exclusion order, and is often a more effective remedy than an injunction, which would require personal jurisdiction over foreign manufacturers or exporters. In addition, articles subject to an exclusion order can be seized and forfeited in certain clear instances of bad faith shown by the owner or importer of the articles.[111]

The exclusion order does not take effect immediately. The President has 60 days to review it for possible veto. At the end of 60 days, the order becomes effective, although review of the Commission's determination is available by the Court of Appeals for the Federal Circuit. Unlike private litigation, the plaintiff does not have to bear the cost of service and enforcement.

The 1988 Omnibus Act's revision of § 337 has triggered a European Community complaint under the General Agreement on Tariffs and Trade, and a GATT panel subsequently found § 337 to violate GATT standards.[112] From a GATT perspective, § 337 was discriminatorily applied and thus constituted a barrier to free trade.[113] Congress finally addressed these concerns in the Uruguay Round Agreements Act, passed in 1994 to implement the new World Trade Organization agreement (GATT).[114]

---

[108] 19 C.F.R. § 210.20.

[109] *Id.* at § 210.12.

[110] *Id.* at § 210.24.

[111] Those instances are when " . . . the owner, importer or consignee previously attempted to import the article into the United States" or the article was previously denied entry into the United States by a previous exclusion order. 19 U.S.C. § 1337(i) (1988).

[112] See United States — Section 337 of the Tariff Act of 1930, Report by the Panel Adopted on 7 November 1989 (L/6439), General Agreement on Tariffs and Trade: Basic Instruments and Selected Documents 345, 396 (36th Supp. 1990).

[113] For background, see "ABA Delegates Adopt Resolution Supporting Amendment of Section 377," BNA Int'l Trade Reporter, Aug. 13, 1993.

[114] Congress took a minimalist approach in changing § 337. 19 U.S.C. § 1337 now requires that the ITC make its determinations at the earliest practicable times. Counterclaims by respondents are also allowed as well as termination or arbitration by mutual agreement of the parties. 19 U.S.C. § 1337(c). Bonding procedures under § 337(e), (f), and (g) are amended to make them more analogous to District Court procedures. Finally, District Courts handling actions involving parties who are also parties to an ITC proceeding must grant a motion to stay the District Court proceeding until the ITC determinations become final. *See* 28 U.S.C. § 1659.

[C] Broad Based Trade Legislation

A major U.S. export, and a bright spot in an otherwise dismal balance of trade, intellectual property rights have become a major focus in U.S. trade negotiations.[115] Unfortunately, organized and systematic piracy of U.S. intellectual property has become a major industry in some countries. Alarm over this ever-increasing piracy and concern about the balance of trade has led to the passage of new and amended federal legislation. The major thrust of this legislation is to use economic reward and punishment to encourage other countries to provide adequate protection to American intellectual property owners.

The Generalized System of Preferences (GSP), enacted in 1974 and revised with amendments as part of the International Trade and Investment Act of 1984,[116] is one such legislative attempt to encourage proper protection of American interests. To reward protection within the foreign country, the GSP confers duty-free treatment on specific categories of goods exported to the United States by certain developing countries. To punish improper treatment of American intellectual property rights, the GSP contains both discretionary and mandatory sanctions. The most harsh mandatory provision of the GSP dictates that countries shall automatically lose their duty-free benefits for acts of nationalization and seizure of U.S. patents, trademarks and copyrights. The President may allow certain countries benefits if they provide "adequate and effective protection"[117] for U.S. intellectual property. Information on trade losses is provided by the U.S. Trade Representative in an annual report.

Instituted in 1983, the Caribbean Basin Economic Recovery Act is similar to the GSP, and[118] it confers duty-free status on certain products exported by Caribbean countries. To obtain this favored status, a country must accord adequate protection of U.S. intellectual property. The legislation includes both mandatory and discretionary criteria for inclusion in the program.

The 1988 amendments to the Trade Act of 1974 have continued the trend toward increased sanctions against foreign countries which deny adequate and effective protection to intellectual property. The United States Trade Representative (USTR) is required to identify "priority" nations that deny this protection. These "priority" countries would then become the target of unfair trade investigation. If the foreign country's acts are found to deny adequate protection, the USTR must recommend trade sanctions to the President, who is required to meet certain deadlines in taking the necessary action. These sanctions can include cessation of trade concessions, the imposition of duties, and withdrawal of designation under the Generalized System of Preferences.[119]

The 1988 amendments have created a new "Super 301" and special 301 procedures. Super 301 proceedings are initiated by the USTR against countries deemed

---

[115] S. Rep. No. 100–352, 100th Cong., 2d Sess. 2 (1988).

[116] Pub. L. No. 98–573, 98 Stat. 3000 (1984).

[117] *See* 19 U.S.C. § 2462(c)(5).

[118] Pub. L. No. 98–67, 97 Stat. 384 (1983).

[119] 19 U.S.C. §§ 2411–2416 (as amended by the Omnibus Trade and Competitiveness Act of 1988).

to be particularly serious offenders of established norms.[120] One device that the USTR has used to exercise leverage over countries providing inadequate intellectual property protection is to place the country on a "watch list," and a country so designed will be considered a candidate for serious scrutiny. The watch list procedure has enjoyed some success. For example, Taiwan, after being placed on the "watch list," enacted a new cable TV law and entered into a bilateral copyright agreement with the U.S.[121] Some countries, such as Brazil and Thailand, have proved to be less responsive to the carrot-and-stick approach of Super 301. Both were designated as priority countries in May, 1993. Since that time, Thailand has undertaken strong anti-piracy measures and has drafted a new copyright law. On the other hand, Brazil has proven to be less cooperative, particularly in protecting U.S. computer software.[122] Other countries under review have included Poland, Pakistan, Korea, and Cyprus.

PART IV: MULTILATERAL AND REGIONAL APPROACHES TO INTERNATIONAL COPYRIGHT PROTECTION

§ 12.10 Beyond the International Treaties: A GATT Solution

[A] The Shortcomings of the International Treaties

The 1988 amendments to the Trade Act have provided U.S. negotiators with a strong bargaining chip in bilateral dealings with developing countries. These efforts, however, have their inherent limitations: the problem of organized piracy is simply too large, and too diverse, for one country, even one as powerful as the U.S., to solve the problem acting alone. The reluctance of developing countries to enforce copyright adequately is related to economic realities in the third world. For developing countries, there is little to gain from costly efforts to enforce copyright. After all, third world countries are consumers of these new technologies and need access to them for economic progress. Thus, developing countries have little incentive to pass substantive laws in the areas of software or mask works. Clearly, a more comprehensive multilateral approach was needed to combat organized piracy in developing countries. For this purpose, industry groups and governmental agencies turned to the General Agreement on Tariffs and Trade as the mechanism to resolve this worldwide problem.[123]

---

[120] The Uruguay Round Agreements Act, passed at the end of 1994, further strengthened the USTR's ability to identify offending countries. *See* 19 U.S.C. § 2242(d), amended to provide that a country may be identified for "special 301" treatment if it denies market access to products protected by intellectual property law, notwithstanding its compliance with the GATT, TRIPS agreement.

[121] Office of the USTR Notice, 58 Fed. Reg. 31788, June 4, 1993.

[122] Office of the USTR Notice, 58 Reg. 31788, June 4, 1993.

[123] For a background on the international protection of intellectual property leading to a GATT solution, see Marshall A. Leaffer, *Protecting United States Intellectual Property Abroad: Toward a New Multilateralism*, 76 Iowa L. Rev. 273 (1991).

The search for a new multilateral mechanism was brought about by the shortcomings of the traditional international conventions.[124] Although the international conventions have served an important function, they have failed, from a U.S. perspective, in certain significant ways. For one, they have lagged in providing adequate substantive coverage of new technological developments. But even more important, they contain no flexible dispute resolution mechanisms when member states neglect to meet their treaty obligations. By the early 1980's, the United States and other western countries began to look for an innovative solution to the piracy dilemma and the shortcomings of the conventions. In this context, the General Agreement on Tariffs and Trade (GATT) offered itself as the international institution best equipped to provide the needed remedy.

[B]   From the GATT to the World Trade Organization

The GATT, renamed and reformulated as of January 1, 1995 the World Trade Organization (or WTO), is the most important international agreement regulating trade among nations. It was formed after the Second World War through negotiations between the United States and the United Kingdom, and came into effect on January 1, 1948. At the outset, the GATT was conceived as an ancillary tariff agreement to work within a broadly designed institution to be called the International Trade Organization. Its goal was to engage its member countries in multilateral trade negotiations for the encouragement of free trade. Intended to be no more than interim measures, the GATT provisions were to be incorporated into the larger organization. The International Trade Commission never materialized, but the GATT has remained in place since the late 1940's. Despite its ambiguous origins and incoherent organizational structure, the GATT has been surprisingly successful.[125] Through the years, GATT has undergone periodic multilateral negotiations called "Rounds." The latest and most ambitious of these rounds, the Uruguay Round, placed intellectual property prominently on its agenda.

One might ask how the protection of intellectual property relates to the concept of free trade. The answer is that inadequate protection of intellectual property undermines the goal of free trade because it leads to trade distortions. Absent sufficient protection, creators can no longer recover the cost of their investment in research and development, resulting in lower production, fewer trading opportunities, and higher costs to the consumer. Despite the obvious need for its successful completion, it appeared until the last minute that the negotiations might fail. But on December 15, 1993, the Uruguay Round was successfully concluded, incorporating within its framework the standards set forth in TRIPS.

The culmination of the Uruguay Round negotiations, taking eight years to finish, was a sweeping world trade agreement. In addition to the intellectual property provisions, the trade pact slashes tariffs globally by roughly 40% and tightens rules on investment and trade in services. As of January 1, 1995, the 47-year old GATT

---

[124] For a compendium of intellectual property treaties, see Marshall A. Leaffer, *International Treaties on Intellectual Property* (1990).

[125] *See generally* Robert Hudec, *The GATT Legal System and World Trade Diplomacy* 9–10, 45–46 (1975).

no longer exists. In its place, the new World Trade Organization (WTO) will oversee the trade agreement.[126]

[C] Intellectual Property Under the WTO: The TRIPS Agreement

In its substantive features, the TRIPS agreement covers all phases of intellectual property. TRIPS provides both national treatment and very detailed rules for minimum standards of protection for intellectual property rights. TRIPS also provides for Most Favored Nation (MFN) treatment with limited exceptions. MFN requires that any advantage, favor, privilege or immunity granted by a party to the nationals of any other country shall be accorded immediately and unconditionally to the nationals of all other World Trade Organization (WTO) members. In addition, TRIPS provides for transitional implementation: one year for developed countries, up to five years for developing countries, and extendable ten-year periods for the least developed countries.[127]

As for its substantive aspects concerning copyright law, TRIPS has taken a "Berne plus" approach to protection. The agreement incorporates by reference essentially the minimum standard contained in Articles 1–21 of the 1971 Berne Convention. At the insistence of the United States, the one exclusion is Article 6 *bis* of Berne conferring moral rights. In certain other of its provisions, TRIPS goes further than Berne by explicitly requiring protection for computer programs and other compilations of data.[128] Even more than its substantive aspects, TRIPS enforcement provisions are perhaps its principal innovative feature. They require contracting parties to provide civil and administrative procedures and remedies for the enforcement of intellectual property rights. These enforcement provisions include preliminary measures for prohibiting the importation of infringing goods as well as criminal penalties for willful infringement.

But what happens if a member does not comply with the substantive or enforcement provisions? Here is where the WTO dispute settlement procedures are triggered. The WTO provides for consultations between the parties to resolve the dispute. If the consultations fail, a disputant may refer the matter to the Contracting Parties, who, through a panel, make recommendations to the disputants. If these settlement procedures fail, the Contracting Parties may suspend the application of concessions or other obligations to the offending party required under the WTO. These dispute settlement features of the WTO distinguish it from the supposedly "toothless" quality of the international conventions.

---

[126] The provisions of the Uruguay Round were named "The Dunkel Draft" after Arthur Dunkel, the ex-director of GATT. *See* "The Dunkel Draft" from the GATT Secretariat, collected and edited by the Institute for International Legal Information, (W.S. Hein 1992). On December 8, 1994, President Clinton signed the Uruguay Round Agreements Act, whose provisions implement the standards set forth in TRIPS. In addition to patent and trademark provisions, the Act dictates important changes in United States copyright law. See §§ 4.18–4.19 *supra* for a discussion of restoration of public domain copyrights, and § 2.3[B] *supra* for a discussion of the anti-bootleg provisions.

[127] TRIPS, Articles 65, and 66.

[128] TRIPS Agreement, Article 10.

[D]   WIPO Responds to GATT: The Berne Protocol

The GATT initiative has not received universal approbation. Prominent among GATT critics was the World Intellectual Property Organization (WIPO) that saw TRIPS as a threat to the stability of the international copyright system. Partly in response to the GATT negotiations, WIPO, in 1989, announced proposals to develop a "Protocol" — a side agreement — to the Berne Convention. The Protocol was designed to resolve the problems that the new technologies, such as computer programs and databases, posed for copyright. Why was the protocol procedure chosen instead of a full revision of the Berne Convention? The reason was one of convenience: a full revision of Berne would require the unanimous consent of all the member states, which would take a long time to obtain. By comparison, the Protocol would require less than unanimity, and an agreement of this kind could be achieved within a reasonable time.

Since WIPO began deliberating on the Protocol, its focus has changed. Computer software is now apparently off the agenda. In addition, the sound recording protection is now part of an effort to develop into a new instrument that may eventually take the place of the Rome and Geneva Conventions. Deliberations on the Protocol have been redirected to two topics of current interest: distribution rights and national treatment. As for distribution rights, the issue is to clarify minimum standards for the protection of rental rights on works ranging from movies to computer software and rights of unauthorized importation.[129] The other issue of the moment and certainly more controversial, concerns the principle of "national treatment."[130] Recently, the U.S. has become alarmed at the increasing trend toward reciprocity among European countries. For example, when France developed a mechanism to collect and distribute royalties to compensate copyright owners for home audio and video recording, it specified that foreign copyright owners could not share in the returns unless their national laws accorded equivalent rights to French copyright owners. In addition, the European Union has proposed a directive to protect databases under which the EU states would provide a right of remuneration to foreign database proprietors on a reciprocal basis. The question of "national treatment" remains one of the thorniest issues in the domain of international copyright.

§ 12.11   Regional Integration and Copyright Law: The European Union and NAFTA

[A]   The European Union (EU)

The original treaties of the European Union did not specifically address intellectual property within the member states. What regulation there was of intellectual property arose under the general provisions of the Treaty of Rome, such as those covering the free movement of goods (article 30), services (article 59), and the rules

---

[129] 46 BNA PTCJ 6 (May 6, 1993).
[130] 46 BNA PTCJ 116 (June 3, 1993).

preventing the distortion of competition (articles 85 and 86). But differences in intellectual property among the member states distort trade by raising transactions costs, contrary to the community policy of economic integration. Thus, even though the Community was not ready for uniform intellectual property laws, it began a serious effort for its harmonization.[131] In 1988, the Commission issued a Green Paper on Copyright in which it began its efforts to harmonize the Community's copyright laws.[132] Five specific copyright issues were covered: piracy, audio visual home copying, distribution and rental rights, computer programs, and databases. Several of these issues are the subject of EU directives, to which the member states are obligated to conform their laws.

The first of these issues to receive final action was rights in computer software, with a Council directive requiring EU countries to extend specific statutory copyright protection to software.[133] The directive establishes the scope of protection for computer software, and allows a limited reverse engineering right (decompilation for purposes of interoperability).[134] In 1992, the EU completed its second copyright directive covering rental rights.[135] This directive requires each member state to enact legislation protecting the rental right for works protected under copyright and neighboring rights regimes. It also allows states to adopt schemes of compulsory licensing or collective administration whereby owners of rental rights would receive "equitable remuneration." The United States does not recognize a rental right for audiovisual works or sound recordings and the directive is silent on whether the EU countries must extend "national treatment" to works of U.S. origin. As indicated above, this very question has been vigorously debated in discussions relating to the Berne Protocol.[136]

Other efforts at harmonization would require members states to extend the copyright term to seventy years as opposed to life plus fifty years. Another proposed directive is the controversial "database directive" that would establish a two-tier system of protection for databases. Under the directive, those databases manifesting intellectual creation would receive full copyright protection whereas others that represent capital investment without true authorship (like the white pages in *Feist*), would receive a ten-year period of protection against unfair extraction.

---

[131] Beryl R. Jones, *An Introduction to the European Economic Community and Intellectual Properties*, 23 Brooklyn J. Int'l L. 665 (1992).

[132] Green Paper on Copyright and the Challenge of Technology — Copyright Issues Requiring Immediate Action, COM(88)172 final.

[133] Directive 91/250 on the legal protection of computer programs, O.J. Eur. Comm. No. L122/42 (May 14, 1991).

[134] One should compare the European resolution of the reverse engineering dilemma with that of the position taken in *Sega Enterprises, Ltd. v. Accolade, Inc.*, 977 F.2d 1510 (9th Cir. 1993), which found that disassembly and decompilation of a computer program necessary to create a compatible or non-infringing program was a fair use. The European directive, by contrast, provides a narrower privilege. It would allow such reverse engineering only to create an interoperable (compatible) program.

[135] Directive 92/100 on rental right, lending right, and on certain rights related to copyright, O.J. Eur. Comm. No. L346 (November 11, 1992).

[136] *See* § 12.10 (D), *supra*.

[B]   The North American Free Trade Agreement (NAFTA)

NAFTA is an agreement creating a free trade area for the North American market. Based partially on the United States' current free trade agreement with Canada, NAFTA was entered into on December 17, 1993, and took effect on January 1, 1994. Similar to all free trade agreements, NAFTA's goal is to assure relatively free access to the markets of the member states by eliminating tariff and non-tariff barriers that impede trade between its members. Because inadequate protection of intellectual property can constitute a trade barrier, NAFTA has included provisions to harmonize Canadian, Mexican and U.S. standards covering the entire range of intellectual property.[137]

The intellectual property provisions of the treaty are based on national treatment. Under this principle, each party to the treaty must accord to nationals of another party treatment no less favorable than it accords to its own nationals. As for copyright, the treaty requires the protection of computer programs as literary works, the protection of databases as compilations, and rental rights for sound recordings and software. It also places limits on compulsory licensing, and requires recognition of rights against unauthorized importation of copies of protected works. Perhaps the most significant aspect of NAFTA is its emphasis on effective enforcement of intellectual property rights. In that regard, it requires signatories to make pretrial injunctive relief available in intellectual property cases. This requirement is designed to overturn the reluctance of Mexican courts to confer such preliminary relief. To comply with NAFTA's requirements, both Canada and Mexico had to make major amendments to their intellectual property laws.[138] As for the United States, NAFTA implementation requires less significant legislative change, except that the U.S. had to restore certain Mexican and Canadian motion pictures previously in the public domain.[139]

What role do these regional agreements play in the multilateral system of trade in intellectual property? One might argue that regionalism, which these agreements represent, threatens to fragment and undermine the multilateral trading system. The threat is real as, for example, the conflict between the U.S. and European Union over national treatment and reciprocity has shown. On the other hand, true multilateral agreements are difficult to negotiate and take years to complete. Once achieved, they become snapshots in time and may already be obsolete in some ways — another example of how legal change adapts slowly to technological change.

This gap, however, is particularly dramatic when a world body confronts a technologically driven body of law such as copyright or some other aspect of intellectual property law. By comparison, regional agreements can be concluded more quickly and produce more dramatic legal change. NAFTA, for example, goes further

---

[137] The intellectual property provisions are included in Chapter 17 of the Treaty. For a draft of the treaty, see North American Free Trade Agreement, reprinted in *North American Free Trade Agreements*, Dobbs Ferry: Oceana (1993).

[138] *See* Cristina Del Valle, 4 No. 11 J. Proprietary Rts. 8 (1992).

[139] 17 U.S.C. § 104A. The Uruguay Round Agreements Act passed at the end of 1994 amended § 104A to include much more substantial coverage of the restoration of public domain copyrights of foreign origin.

than TRIPS in many of its provisions. This is hardly surprising. An agreement among three countries (NAFTA) as opposed to more than a hundred (TRIPS) involves less intricate political compromise. Once concluded, regional agreements may actually enhance the multilateral system. Ideally, a NAFTA can operate as a beacon for change to spur the multilateral system toward quicker action and perhaps encourage the completion of side agreements within the multinational framework. Of course, it will take some time to evaluate what effect, salutary or otherwise, these regional agreements will have on the larger system. But they are clearly here to stay and we can probably expect to find a larger role for them as time passes.

TABLE OF CASES

[References are to sections.]

A

Abeshouse v. Ultragraphics, Inc. 9.11

Abkco Music, Inc. v. Harrisongs Music, Ltd.
. . . . 9.12[C]

Abli, Inc. v. Standard Brands Paint Co. . . . .
4.14[D]

Academy of Motion Pictures Arts and Sciences v.
Creative House Promotions, Inc. . . 4.5[C]

ACEMLA v. Copyright Royalty Tribunal . . .
8.22[A]

Acuff-Rose Music, Inc. v. Campbell . . . . . .
Preface; 10.14[B]–[E]

Addison-Wesley Publishing Co. v. Brown . . .
8.5; 10.12[B]

Advertisers Exch., Inc. v. Anderson . . 4.14[D]

Aitken, Hazen, Hoffman, Miller P.C. v. Empire
Constr. Co. . . . . 3.15[B][2]

Alberto-Culver Co. v. Andrea Dumon, Inc. . .
2.7[C]

Aldon Accessories, Ltd. v. Spiegel, Inc. . . . .
5.2[C], [D]

Aldrich v. Remington Rand, Inc. . . 2.12[B][2]

Alfred Bell & Co. v. Catalda Fine Arts, Inc. . .
2.7[B]; 2.9[D]

Allied Artists Pictures Corp. v. Rhodes . . . .
11.7[A]; 11.8[A]

Alva Studios, Inc. v. Winninger . . . . 2.9[D]

American Code Co. v. Bensinger . . . 4.14[B]

American Geophysical Union v. Texaco, Inc.
. . . . 10.5; 10.12[C]

American Greetings Corp. v. Kleinfarb Corp.
. . . . 4.14[E]

American Tobacco Co. v. Werckmeister . . . .
4.7[B]

American Visuals Corp. v. Holland . . 4.5[B]

American Vitagraph, Inc. v. Levy . . . 4.5[B]

Amsterdam v. Triangle Publications, Inc. . . .
3.17

Amusement & Music Operators Ass'n v. Copyright Royalty Tribunal . . . . 8.3[B]

Anderson v. Stallone . . . . 2.12[C]

Ansehl v. Puritan Pharmaceutical Co. . . . . .
2.7[C]

Apple Computer, Inc. v. Formula Int'l, Inc. . .
3.6[D]; 8.6

Apple Computer, Inc. v. Franklin Computer Corp.
. . . . 3.3; 3.6[A]; 9.5[F]; 9.8

Apple Computer, Inc. v. Microsoft Corp. . . .
2.12[B][2]; 9.5[F]

Application of (see name of applicant)

Arnstein v. Edward B. Marks Music Corp. . . .
9.2

Arnstein v. Porter . . . . 9.3; 9.6[B], [C]

Arrhythmia Research Technology, Inc. v. Corazonix Corp. . . . . 3.8[B]

Arthur Retlaw & Assocs., Inc. v. Travenol Laboratories, Inc. . . . . 3.2[B]

Associated Film Distribution Corp. v. Thornburgh
. . . . 11.8[A]

Associated Music Publishers, Inc. v. Debs Mem.
Radio Fund, Inc. . . . . 8.17[A], [E]

Association of American Medical Colleges v.
Carey 9.8

Association of American Medical Colleges v.
Mikaelian 9.4; 10.5; 10.6; 10.7; 10.8

Atari Games Corp. v. Nintendo of Am. . . . .
10.13

Atari Games Corp. v. Oman 3.22

Atari, Inc. v. Amusement World, Inc. . . . 2.5

Atari, Inc. v. JS & A Group, Inc. 8.6

Atari, Inc. v. North Am. Philips Consumer Electronics Corp. 2.5

Atascadero Hospital v. Scanlon . . . . 9.19[B]

Atherton; United States v. . . . . 8.13[A]; 9.15

Aymes v. Bonelli . . . . 5.2[D]

B

Bailie v. Fisher . . . . 2.7[C]

Baker v. Selden . . . . 2.12[A], [B]; 3.6[D];
3.15[B][2]

Bartok v. Boosey & Hawkes, Inc. . . . 6.6[B]

Bartsch v. Metro-Goldwyn-Mayer, Inc. . . 5.10

Basevi v. Edward O'Toole Co. . . . . 4.14[E]

Beacon Looms, Inc. v. S. Lichtenberg & Co., Inc.
. . . . 4.11[B][2], [C]

Belcher v. Tarbox . . . . 2.13[A]

Bellsouth Advtg. & Pub. Corp. v. Donnelley
Information Pub., Inc. . . . . 2.11[C]

Benny v. Loew's, Inc. . . . . 10.14[D]

Bentley v. Tibbals . . . . 4.17[B]

Berlin v. E.C. Publications, Inc. . . . 10.14[A],
[C], [E]

Bessett v. Germain . . . . 4.14[A]

Bevan v. Columbia Broadcasting System, Inc.
. . . . . . 9.6[B]; 9.16[A]; 9.20[C]

[References are to sections.]

Bleistein v. Donaldson Lithographing Co. . . . 2.1; 2.2; 2.7[C]; 3.11

Blendingwell Music, Inc. v. Moor-Law, Inc. . . 10.01

Blisscraft of Hollywood v. United Plastics Co. . . . . 3.16[A]

BMG Music v. Perez . . . . 8.14[C]

Board of Trade v. Dow Jones & Co. . . . . . . 1.14[E]; 11.2[B]

Bonito Boats v. Thunder Craft 11.4

Brandir Int'l, Inc. v. Cascade Pacific Lumber Co. 3.14

Brattleboro Publishing Co v. Winmill Publishing Corp. 5.3

Brenner v. Mason (1966) . . . . 1.11[D]

Bright Tunes Music Corp. v. Harrisongs Music, Ltd. 9.4

Broadcast Music, Inc. v. Claire's Boutiques, Inc. . . . . 8.18[C]

Broadcast Music, Inc. v. Columbia Broadcasting Sys., Inc. . . . . 8.22[D]

Broadcast Music, Inc. v. Moor-Law, Inc. . . . . 8.22[D]

Broadcast Music, Inc. v. United States Shoe Corp. . . . . 8.18[C]

Bromhall v. Rorvik . . . . 11.9[A]

Brown Bag Software v. Symantec Corp. . . . . 9.5[F]

Brubaker v. King . . . . 9.6[B]

Buck v. Jewell-LaSalle Realty Co. . . 8.18[A], [B]; 8.19[C][1]

Buffalo Broadcasting Co. v. ASCAP . . . . . . 8.22[A], [D]

Building Officials & Code Admin. v. Code Technology, Inc. . . . . 2.13[B]

Burke v. National Broadcasting Co., Inc. . . . . 4.3; 4.5[C]

Burns v. Rockwood Dist. Co. . . . . . 5.12[A]

Burroughs v. Metro-Goldwyn-Mayer, Inc. . . . 6.13

Burrow-Giles Lithographic Co. v. Sarony . . . 2.2

BV Engineering v. University of California . . 9.19[B]

C

C. M. Paula Co. v. Logan . . . . 8.5; 8.13[A]

Campbell v. Acuff-Rose Music, Inc. . . . . . . 10.14[B]–[E]

Capitol Records, Inc. v. Erickson 11.4

Capitol Records, Inc. v. Greatest Records, Inc. 11.4

Capitol Records, Inc. v. Mercury Records Corp. 2.2[A], [C]

Carol Barnhart Inc. v. Economy Cover Corp. 3.14

Carson v. Here's Johnny Portable Toilets, Inc. . . . . 1.14[D]

Carter v. Hawaii Transportation Co. 2.8; 3.17

Carter v. Helmsley-Spear . . . . 8.28[B]

Caulfield v. Board of Education 9.8

Cheney Bros. v. Doris Silk Corp. . . . 1.14[E]; 11.2[B]

Childress v. Taylor . . . . 5.4[A], [B]

Christian Broadcasting Network, Inc. v. Copyright Royalty Tribunal . . . . . . 8.3[B]; 8.19[F]

Clarion Textile Corp. v. Slifka . . . . . 9.6[C]

Clarke v. G. A. Kayser and Sons, Inc. . . . . . 9.6[C]

Cohen v. Paramount Pictures Corp. 5.10

College Entrance Book Co. v. Amsco Book Co. 9.4

Columbia Broadcasting Sys., Inc. v. DeCosta . . . . 11.2[B]; 11.44

Columbia Broadcasting System v. Scorpio Music Distributors, Inc. . . . . 8.14[C]

Columbia Broadcasting System, Inc. v. American Society of Composers, Authors and Publishers . . . . 8.22[D]

Columbia Pictures Industries, Inc. v. Aveco, Inc. . . . . 8.16[B]

Columbia Pictures Industries, Inc. v. Professional Real Estate Investors, Inc. . . . . 8.16[B]

Columbia Pictures Industries, Inc. v. Redd Horne, Inc. . . . . 8.16[B], [C]; 10.1

Community for Creative Non-violence v. Reid . . . . . Preface; 5.2[C]–[E]; 5.4[C]

Compco Corp. v. Day-Brite Lighting, Inc. . . . 1.14[E]; 11.2[B]; 11.3; 11.4

Computer Associates v. Altai, Inc. . . Preface; 2.12[B][2]; 3.6[D]; 9.5[F]

Conner v. Mark I, Inc. . . . . 4.14[F]

Consumers Union of United States, Inc. v. General Signal Corp. . . . . 10.15[A]

Continental Casualty Co. v. Beardsley . . . . . 2.12[B][2]

Cosmair, Inc. v. Dynamite Enterprises, Inc. . . 8.14[C]

Costello Publications Co. v. Rotelle . . . 8.12

Coventry Ware, Inc. v. Reliance Picture Frame Co. . . . . 4.14[C]

Craft v. Kobler . . . . . 10.9; 10.10; 10.15[A]

Cream Records, Inc. v. Jos. Schlitz Brewing Co. . . . . 9.12[B]

Crume v. Pacific Mutual Life Ins. Co. . . . . . 2.12[B][2]

[References are to sections.]

D

Dallas Cowboys Cheerleaders v. Scoreboard Posters, Inc. . . . . 10.14[E]; 10.15[A]
Dan Kasoff, Inc. v. Palmer Jewelry Mfg. Co. . . . . 4.14[B]
Davies v. Krasna . . . . 2.12[A]
Davis v. United Artists, Inc. . . . . . . 3.2[B]
DC Comics, Inc. v. Filmation Assocs. . . . . . 2.12[C]
DeCosta v. Columbia Broadcasting Sys., Inc. . . . . 11.2[B]; 11.4
DeJonge & Co. v. Breaker de Kassler Co. . . . 4.14[C]
Dellar v. Samuel Goldwyn, Inc. 10.2
Deltak, Inc. v. Advanced Systems, Inc. . . 9.11
Demetriades v. Kaufmann . . . . . 3.15[B][2]
Desny v. Wilder . . . . 2.12[A]
DeSylva v. Ballentine . . . . 6.6[B]; 6.8
Diamond v. Chakrabarty . . . . 1.11[D]
Diamond v. Diehr . . . . . . 1.11[D]; 3.8[B]
Digital Communications Associates, Inc. v. Softklone Distributing Corp. 7.5
Donahue v. Ziv Television Programs, Inc. . . . 2.12[A]
Donaldson v. Beckett . . . . . 1.2; 1.3; 4.2[B]
Donna v. Dodd, Mead & Co., Inc. . . . 5.4[A], [C]
Dow Jones & Company, Inc. v. Board of Trade 10.5
Dowling v. United States 9.15
Dreamland Ball Room v. Shapiro, Bernstein & Co. . . . . 9.20[C]
Duchess Music Corp. v. Stern . . . . . 8.7[C]
Dumas v. Gommerman . . . . 5.2[D]
Durham Industries v. Tomy Corp. . . . 2.9[D]
Dynamic Solutions, Inc. v. Planning & Control, Inc. . . . . 9.5[F]

E

E. F. Johnson Co. v. Uniden Corp. of America 9.7
Easter Seal Society for Crippled Children and Adults of Louisiana, Inc. v. Playboy Enterprises . . . . 5.2[C], [D]
Eastern Microwave, Inc. v. Doubleday Sports, Inc. . . . . 8.19[C][3]
Eckes v. Card Prices Update . . . 2.11[C]; 9.4
Eden Toys v. Florelee Undergarment Co. . . . 2.9[D]; 5.11[A]
Edison v. Viva Int'l, Ltd. . . . . . . 8.27[B]
Edison Bros. Stores Inc. v. Broadcast Music, Inc. . . . . 8.18[C]
Educational Testing Service v. Katzman . 9.8

Edward B. Marks Music Corp. v. Foullon . . . 8.7[C]
Effects Assocs. Inc. v. Cohen . . . . . 5.11[A]
Eggers v. Sun Sales Corp. 2.8
E.I. du Pont de Nemours & Co. v. Christopher . . . . 1.14[A]
Elektra Records Co. v. Gem Electronic Distributors, Inc. . . . . 9.20[B]
Elsmere Music, Inc. v. National Broadcasting Co. . . . . 10.14[C][E]
Eltra v. Ringer . . . . 3.2[B]; 11.9[B]
Encyclopaedia Britannica Educ. Corp. v. Crooks . . . . 10.7; 10.11[B], [D]
Epoch Producing Corp. v. Killiam Shows, Inc. . . . . 6.7[D]; 6.8
Erickson v. Trinity Theatre . . . . 5.4[A]
Erie R.R. v. Tompkins . . . . 11.2[B]
ESPN, Inc. v. Edinburg Community Hotel . . . 8.18[C]
Esquire, Inc. v. Ringer . . . . . . 3.2[D]; 3.13; 3.15[B][1]
Estate of (see name of party)
Evans Newton, Inc. v. Chicago Systems Software . . . . 5.2[C]
Ewer v. Coxe 4.9
Excel Promotions Corp. v. Babylon Beacon, Inc. . . . . 4.14[F]

F

Factors, Inc. v. ProArts, Inc. . . . . . 11.7[A]
Falwell v. Penthouse International, Ltd. . . 2.6
Famous Music Corp. v. Bay State Harness Horse Racing and Breeding Ass'n, Inc. . . 9.20[C]
Fantastic Fakes, Inc. v. Pickwick Int'l, Inc. . . 4.9; 4.12[B]; 5.9
Fawcett Publications, Inc. v. Eliot Pub. Co. . . 8.13[A]
Feist Publications, Inc. v. Rural Telephone . . . Preface; 2.7[A]; 2.11[A]–[D]; 2.12[D]; 3.17
F.E.L. Publication, Ltd. v. Catholic Bishops of Chicago . . . . 8.22[D]; 10.1
Ferguson v. National Broadcasting Co. . . 9.4
Ferris v. Frohman . . . . 4.7[A]
Filmvideo Releasing Corp. v. Hastings . . . . 6.10[A]; 9.5[D]
Financial Information v. Moody's Investors Service . . . . 2.11[C], [D]
First Am. Artificial Flowers, Inc. v. Joseph Markovits, Inc. . . . . 4.7[D]
Fisher v. Dees . . . . . . 10.9; 10.14[D], [E]
Fitch v. Shubert . . . . 6.10[A]
Fleischer Studios, Inc. v. Ralph A. Freundlich, Inc. . . . . 4.14[B]

[References are to sections.]

Flora Kung, Inc. v. Items of Cal., Inc. . . . . . 4.11[B]

Florence Art Co. v. Quartite Creative Corp. . . 4.14[D], [E]

Fogerty v. Fantasy . . . . Preface; 9.14

Folsom v. Marsh 10.2; 10.3; 10.6

Ford Motor Co. v. Summit Motor Prods., Inc. . . . . 4.11[B]

Fortnightly Corp. v. United Artists Television, Inc. . . . . 8.18[A]; 8.19[A], [G]

Fourth Floor Music, Inc. v. Der Place, Inc. . . 9.20[C]

Frank Music Corp. v. Metro-Goldwyn-Mayer, Inc. . . . . 9.12[B]

Fred Fisher Music Co. v. M. Witmark & Sons 6.8; 6.11

Fredrick Music Co. v. Sickler . . . 6.8; 6.9[A]

Friedman, Eisenstein, Raemer & Schwartz v. Afterman . . . . 9.16[B]

G

G. & C. Merriam Co. v. United Dictionary Co. . . . . 4.14[F]

Gardenia Flowers, Inc. v. Joseph Markovits, Inc. . . . . 2.7[C]; 4.14[E]

Gay Toys, Inc. v. Buddy L. Corp. 3.13

G.B. Marketing U.S.A. Inc. v. Gerolsteiner Brunnen GmbH & Co. . . . . 12.8[B]

Geisel v. Poynter Products Inc. . . . . 8.27[B]

Georgia v. The Harrison Company . . 2.13[B]

Gershwin Publishing Corp. v. Columbia Artists Mgt., Inc. . . . . 9.20[C]

Gilliam v. American Broadcasting Co., Inc. . . 8.5; 8.27[B]

Goldsmith v. Max . . . . 4.10[A]

Goldstein v. California . . . 1.14[C], [E]; 2.2; 2.3[A]; 3.2[A][8]; 11.4; 11.5; 11.9[B]

Goodis v. United Artists Television, Inc. 5.9; 5.10

Gracen v. Bradford Exchange . . . . . . 2.9[D]

Graham v. John Deere Co. . . . . 1.11[D]; 2.1

Grand Upright Music, Ltd. v. Warner Bros. Records 1.9

Granz v. Harris . . . . 8.27[B]

Grove Press, Inc. v. Greenleaf Publishing Co. . . . . 2.9[B]; 6.10[A]; 8.5

H

H. M. Kolbe Co., Inc. v. Armgus Textile Co. . . . . 4.14[C]

Hadden, In re . . . . 3.16[A]

Haelan Laboratories, Inc. v. Topps Chewing Gum, Inc. . . . . 1.14[D]

Hagendorf v. Brown . . . . 4.11[C][2]

Hamilton; United States v. 3.17

Harcourt, Brace & World, Inc. v. Graphic Controls Corp. . . . . 2.12[B][2]

Harold Lloyd Corp. v. Witwer . . . . . 9.6[B]

Harper & Row, Publishers, Inc. v. Nation Enterprises . . . . 10.2; 10.6; 10.7; 10.8; 10.9; 10.10; 10.15[B]; 10.16; 11.7[A]; 11.19[A]

Hasbro Bradley, Inc. v. Sparkle Toys, Inc. . . . 4.11[C][2]; 4.14[F]; 9.8

Hearst Corp. v. Stark . . . . 8.14[C]

Heim v. Universal Pictures Co. . . . . 4.14[F]

Hemingway, Estate of v. Random House, Inc. . . . . 2.6; 4.5[C]

Herbert v. Shanley Co. . . . . 8.17[E]

Herbert Rosenthal Jewelry Corp. v. Kalpakian . . . . 2.12[B][2]

Hesse v. Brunner 2.8

Hill & Range Songs, Inc. v. London Records, Inc. . . . . 4.14[F]

Hines v. Davidowitz 11.1

Hirsch v. S.C. Johnson & Son, Inc. . . 1.14[D]

Hirshon v. United Artists Corp. . . . . . 4.5[B]

Hoehling v. Universal City Studios, Inc. . . . . 2.12[D]; 9.5[E]

Hoffenberg v. Kaminstein . . . . 4.17[B], [C]

Hollywood Jewelry Mfg. Co. v. Dushkin . . . 4.14[B]

Horgan v. MacMillan, Inc. . . . . 3.21; 9.5[C], [D]

Hruby, In re (1967) . . . . 3.16[A]

Hubbard Broadcasting, Inc. v. Southern Satellite Systems, Inc. . . . . 5.8[A]

Hughes v. Novi American, Inc. 9.14

Hurn v. Oursler . . . . 9.16[B]

Hustler Magazine, Inc. v. Moral Majority, Inc. 10.2; 10.7; 10.10

Huston v. La Cinq . . . . 12.8[C]

I

Ideal Toy Corp. v. Fab-Lu Ltd. . . . . . 9.6[B]

Ideal Toy Corp. v. Kenner Products Div. of General Mills Fun Group, Inc. . . . 3.15[B][2]; 9.6[B]

Ilyin v. Avon Publications, Inc. . . . . . 5.8[B]

Imperial Homes Corp. v. Lamont . . . . 3.15[B][2]

In re (see name of party)

International Luggage Registry v. Avery Products Corp. . . . . 9.6[B]

International News Service v. Associated Press . . . . . 1.6; 1.14[E]; 11.2[B]; 11.3

International Trade Management, Inc. v. United States . . . . 7.5[A]

[References are to sections.]

Iowa State University Research Foundation, Inc. v. American Broadcasting Companies 10.2; 10.7

J

J. A. Richards, Inc. v. New York Post, Inc. . . 4.14[E]
Jartech Inc. v. Clancy . . . . . . 2.13[A]; 9.14
Jewel Music Pub. Co. v. Leo Feist, Inc. . . 9.2

K

K Mart Corp. v. Cartier, Inc. . . . . . 8.14[C]
Kamar International, Inc. v. Russ Berrie and Co. . . . . 9.4; 9.12[B]
Kern River Gas Transmission Co. v. Coastal Corp. . . . . 2.12[B][2]; 3.17
Kewanee Oil Co. v. Bicron Corp. 11.4
Key Publications, Inc. v. Chinatown Today Publishing Enterprises, Inc. . . . . 2.11[C]
Key West Hand Print Fabrics, Inc. v. Serbin, Inc. . . . . 4.7[D]
Kieselstein-Cord v. Accessories By Pearl, Inc. 3.14
King v. Burnett . . . . 4.11[B]
King v. Mister Maestro, Inc. . . 4.5[C]; 4.7[A]
Kitchens of Sara Lee, Inc. v. Nifty Foods Corp. . . . . 2.7[C]
Klein v. Beach 5.10
Kongsberg Int'l, Inc. v. Rice . . . . . 5.11[A]
Korzybski v. Underwood & Underwood, Inc. . . . . 3.16[A]
Krafft v. Cohen . . . . 4.14[E]
Kregos v. Associated Press . . . . . . 2.11[C]

L

L. Batlin & Son, Inc. v. Snyder . . . . 2.9[D]
Ladd v. Law and Technology Press . . . 7.10
Lamminations Music v. P & X Markets, Inc. . . . . 8.18[C]
Lasercomb America v. Reynolds 10.01
Lauratex Textile Corp. v. Allton Knitting Mills . . . . 9.13[B]
L.C. Page & Co. v. Fox Film Corp. . . . 5.10
Leeds Music Ltd. v. Robin . . . . . . 8.22[C]
Leigh v. Gerber . . . . 4.14[D]
Leon v. Pacific Telephone & Telegraph Co. . . 2.11[B]
Leon B. Rosenblatt Textiles, Ltd. v. M. Lowenstein & Sons, Inc. . . . . 4.14[E]
Leonard Storch Enterprises, Inc. v. Mergenthaler Linotype Co. . . . . 11.9[B]
Letter Edged in Black Press, Inc. v. Public Bldg. Comm . . . . 4.3; 4.7[B]; 5.9

Lewis Galoob Toys, Inc. v. Nintendo of Am. Inc. 8.5
Library Publications, Inc. v. Medical Economics Co. . . . . 5.8[A]
Lieb v. Topstone Industries Inc. 9.14
London Film Productions Ltd. v. Intercontinental Communications, Inc. . . . . 12.8[A]
Lone Ranger Television v. Program Radio Corp. . . . . 9.16[B]
Lotus Dev. v. Paperback Software Int'l . . . . 2.12[B][2]; 9.5[F]
Lotus Development Corp. v. Borland Int'l, Inc. . . . . 9.5[F]

M

MacMillan Co. v. King . . . . 10.12[B]
Madsen, In re . . . . 2.13[A]
MAI Systems Corp. v. Peak Computer Inc. . . 2.3[A]
Makedwe Pub. Co. v. Johnson 9.17
Manners v. Morosco 5.10
Manufacturers Technologies, Inc. v. Cams, Inc. . . . . 2.12[B][2]
Marco v. Accent Publishing Co. . . . . 5.2[D]
Marcus v. Rowley . . . 10.7; 10.10; 10.12[B]
Marks v. Leo Feist, Inc. . . . . 9.5[C]
Martin Luther King, Jr. Center for Social Change, Inc. v. American Heritage Products, Inc. . . 1.14[D]
Maryland v. Louisiana 11.1
Masascalco v. Fantasy, Inc. . . . 6.8; 6.9[A]
Mason v. Montgomery Data, Inc. . . . . 2.12[B][2]; 3.17
Matter of (see name of party)
Maxtone-Graham v. Burtchaell . . . 10.14[A]; 10.15[A]
May v. Morganelli-Heumann & Assoc. . . 5.3
Mayer v. Josiah Wedgwood & Sons, Ltd. . . . 11.7[A]
Mazer v. Stein . . . . 1.8[A]; 2.12[B][2]; 3.11; 3.13; 8.10
MCA, Inc. v. Parks . . . . 8.17[E]
MCA Inc. v. Wilson . . . . 9.12[C]
McIntyre v. Double-A Music Corp. 2.10
McKay v. Barbour . . . . 4.14[F]
Meccano, Ltd. v. Wagner . . . . 4.17[C]
Meeropol v. Nizer 10.9; 10.10
Meltzer v. Zoller . . . . 5.3; 5.4[C]
Memphis Development Found. v. Factors, Etc. . . . . 1.14[D]
Meta-Film Associates, Inc. v. MCA, Inc. 9.4
Metro-Goldwyn-Mayer, Inc. v. Showcase Atlanta Cooperative Productions, Inc. . . . . . 8.5; 10.14[F]

[References are to sections.]

Metropolitan Opera Association v. Wagner-Nichols Recorder Corp. . . . 1.14[E]; 11.2[B]

Micro-Sparc Inc. v. Amtype Corp. 8.6

Midler v. Ford Motor Co. . . . . 1.14[D]

Midway Mfg. Co. v. Artic Int'l, Inc. . . . 2.5; 4.11[C][2]; 8.6

Mihalek Corp. v. State of Michigan . . 9.19[B]

Millar v. Taylor . . . . 1.2; 4.2[B]

Miller v. Universal City Studios, Inc. . . . . . 2.12[D]

Miller Music Corp. v. Charles N. Daniels, Inc. 6.8

Mills Music, Inc. v. Snyder 6.14; 6.15

Minniear v. Tors . . . . 2.12[A]

Mirage Editions, Inc. v. Albuquerque A.R.T. Co. . . . . 8.5; 8.13[A]

Mitchell v. Penton Indus. Pub. Co., Inc. . . . . 11.7[A]

Mitchell Brothers Film Group v. Cinema Adult Theater . . . . 2.13[A]

Moore; United States v. . . . . 8.13[A]

Moorish Vanguard Concert v. Brown . . . 9.14

Morrissey v. Procter & Gamble Co. . . . . . 2.12[B][2]; 3.6[D]; 9.4

Morseburg v. Balyon . . . . 8.14[D]; 9.16[A]; 11.8[D]

Movie Systems, Inc. v. Heller . . . 8.16[A][2]

Murray v. Gelderman 5.3

N

Nalbandian, In re . . . . 3.16[A]

Nash v. CBS . . . . 2.12[D]

National Association of Broadcasters v. Copyright Royalty Tribunal . . . . 8.3[B]

National Business Lists, Inc. v. Dun & Bradstreet, Inc. . . . . 2.11[B]

National Car Rental Systems, Inc. v. Computer Associates International, Inc. . . . . 11.7[A]

National Geographic Soc'y v. Classified Geographic . . . . 8.13[A]

NEC Corp. v. Intel Corp. . . . . 3.6[D]

New Era Publications Int'l v. Henry Holt & Co. 10.8

New York Chinese TV Programs, Inc. v. U.E., Inc. . . . . 12.7[B]

Nichols v. Universal Pictures Corp. . . . . 2.12[A], [C]; 9.5[E]

Nintendo of America, Inc. v. Elcon Industries, Inc. . . . . 8.14[C]

Norris Indus., Inc. v. International Tel. & Tel. Corp. 3.13; 7.5

Northern Music Corp. v. King Record Distributing Co. 3.18

Novelty Textile Mills, Inc. v. Joan Fabrics Corp. . . . . 2.6[B]; 9.8

Nucor Corp. v. Tennessee Forging Steel Serv., Inc. . . . . 4.5[C]

O

Oboler v. Goldin 9.3; 9.14

Oddo v. Ries . . . . . 5.4[C]; 5.11[A], 11.7[A]

O'Neill v. General Film Co. . . . . 4.7[D]

Original Appalachian Artworks, Inc. v. Topps Chewing Gum, Inc. . . . . . . 10.14[A][D]

Original Appalachian Artworks, Inc. v. Toy Loft, Inc. . . . . 4.11[A]; 4.14[A]; 9.3

P

Pacific & Southern Co., Inc. v. Duncan . . . . 10.1; 10.5; 10.10; 10.15[A]

Pacific Gas & Electric Co. v. State Energy Resources Conservation Comm'n 11.1

Pantone, Inc. v. A. I. Friedman, Inc. . . . 2.10

Pardo, In re . . . . 3.8[B]

Parfums Givenchy, Inc. v. Drug Emporium, Inc. . . . . 8.14[C]

Pavesich v. New England Life Ins. Co. . . . . 1.14[D]

Peckarsky v. American Broadcasting Co., Inc. . . . . 11.7[A]

Peregrine v. Lauren Corp. . . . . . 5.2[C], [D]

Peter Pan Fabrics, Inc. v. Martin Weiner Corp. . . . . 3.11; 4.11[B]; 4.14[C]

Picture Music, Inc. v. Bourne, Inc. . . . 5.4[C]

Pillsbury Co. v. Milky Way Prods., Inc. . . . . 10.14[D], [E]

Plains Cotton Cooperative Ass'n v. Goodpasture Computer Service, Inc. . . . . 9.5[F]

Platinum Record Co., Inc. v. Lucasfilm, Ltd. 5.10

Platt & Munk Co. v. Republic Graphics, Inc. . . . . 8.13[B]

Playboy Enterprises v. Frena 8.25

Plymouth Music Co. v. Magnus Organ Corp. 3.18

Poe v. Missing Persons 3.14

Pottstown Daily News Publishing Co. v. Pottstown Broadcasting Co. 11.4

Prestige Floral S.A. v. California Artificial Flower Co. . . . . 2.7[C]

Proulx v. Hennepin Technical Centers . . . . . 7.6[A]; 7.7

Public Affairs Associates, Inc. v. Rickover . . . 4.5[C]

Puddu v. Buonamici Statuary, Inc. . . 4.14[B], [E]

Pushman v. New York Graphic Society, Inc. 5.7

[References are to sections.]

Q

Quackenbush Music, Ltd. v. Wood . . 8.17[E]
Quinto v. Legal Times of Washington, Inc. . . .
4.10[A]; 4.11[D]; 4.12[B]; 4.13[B];
5.6; 9.14

R

Rand McNally & Co. v. Fleet Management Sys.,
Inc. . . . . 2.11[B]
R.C.A. Mfg. Co. v. Whiteman . . . . . 11.2[B]
Recording Industry Association of America v.
Copyright Royalty Tribunal . . . . . 8.3[B];
8.7[B]
Red Baron-Franklin Park, Inc. v. Taito Corp.
. . . . 8.14[B]
Republic Pictures Corp. v. Security-First Nat'l
Bank of L.A. . . . . 9.16[A]
Rexnord, Inc. v. Modern Handling Sys., Inc.
. . . . 4.14[E]
Reyher v. Children's Television Workshop . .
2.8; 3.6[D]; 9.5[E]
Rice v. American Program Bureau . . 8.22[C]
Rich v. RCA Corp. . . . . 8.27[B]
Richard Anderson Photography v. Radford Uni-
versity . . . . 9.19[B]
Ricordi & Co. v. Paramount Pictures, Inc. . . .
6.10[A]
Robert Stigwood Group, Ltd. v. Hurwitz . . . .
9.20[C]
Robert Stigwood Group, Ltd. v. Sperber . . . .
8.22[C]
Robertson v. Batten, Barton, Durstine & Osborne,
Inc. . . . . 9.5[C]
Robey v. New World Pictures, Ltd. . . . 9.17
Rodgers v. Eighty-Four Lumber Co. . . . . . .
8.18[C]
Rogers v. Koons . . . . 10.14[E]
Rohauer v. Killiam Shows . . . 6.10[A]; 9.20;
10.01
Rosemont Enterprises, Inc. v. Random House, Inc.
. . . . 2.12[D]; 10.2; 10.15[B]
Rosette v. Rainbo Record Mfg. Corp. . . . . .
4.7[C]; 9.17
Roth v. Pritikin . . . . 5.3; 5.5; 6.6[A]; 6.7[D]
Roth Greeting Cards v. United Card Co. . . . .
2.8; 9.6[B]
Roy v. Atlantic Richfield Co. 11.1
Roy Export Co. Establishment v. Columbia Broad-
casting System, Inc. . . . 9.5[D]; 10.6; 10.7
Royalty Control Corp. v. Sanco, Inc. . . . . . .
9.16[A]
Royalty Designs, Inc. v. Thrifticheck Serv. Corp.
. . . . 3.11
Rubin v. Boston Magazine Co. . . . 2.12[D]

Runsdorf, In re . . . . 2.13[A]
Russell v. Price . . . . 2.9[B]; 6.10[A]

S

Sachs; United States v. 9.15
Sailor Music v. The Gap Stores, Inc. . . . . . .
8.18[C]
Salinger v. Random House, Inc. 10.8;
10.15[A]
Sargent v. American Greetings Corp. . . . 2.10
Scarves by Vera, Inc. v. United Merchants &
Mfrs., Inc. . . . . 4.14[C]
Scherr v. Universal Match Co. . . . . 2.13[A]
Schiller & Schmidt, Inc. v. Nordisco Corp. . .
5.2[B][E]
Schmid Bros., Inc. v. W. Goebel Porzellanfabrik,
K.G. . . . . 6.7[C]
Schnapper v. Foley . . . . . 2.13[B]; 10.15[A]
Schoenberg v. Shapolsky Publishers, Inc. . . .
9.16[A]
Scholz Homes, Inc. v. Maddox . . . . 9.16[B]
Schroeder v. William Morrow and Co. . . . . .
2.11[B]; 9.5[C]
Schuchart & Associates v. Solo Serve Corp. . .
11.7[A]
Schwarz v. Universal Pictures Co. . . . 9.5[E]
Scott v. WKJG, Inc. 9.4
Screen Gems-Columbia Music, Inc. v. Mark-Fi
Records, Inc. . . . . 9.20[C]
Sears, Roebuck & Co. v. Stiffel Co. . . . . . .
1.14[E]; 3.16[A]; 11.2[B]; 11.3;
11.4
Sebastian Int'l, Inc. v. Consumer Contacts Ltd.
. . . . 8.14[C]
Sega Enterprises, Ltd. v. Accolade, Inc. . . . .
Preface; 3.6[D]; 8.6; 10.13;
12.11[A]
Seiff v. Continental Auto Supply, Inc. . . . . .
4.14[E]
Selle v. Gibb 9.4
Shapiro & Son Bedspread Corp. v. Royal Mills
Associates . . . . 4.11[C], [D]
Shapiro, Bernstein & Co. v. 4636 S. Vermont
Ave., Inc. 9.8
Shapiro, Bernstein & Co. v. H. L. Green Co.
. . . . 9.20[C]
Shapiro, Bernstein & Co. v. Jerry Vogel Music Co.
. . . . 2.8; 5.5; 7.8
Shapiro, Bernstein & Co. v. Miracle Record Co.,
Inc. . . . . 2.7[C]
Shaw v. Lindheim . . . . 9.6[C]
Sheldon v. Metro-Goldwyn Pictures Corp. . . .
2.7[B]; 9.12[C]
Sid & Marty Krofft Television Productions,
Inc. v. McDonald's Corp. . . . . . 9.6[C];
10.15[A]

[References are to sections.]

Smith v. Little, Brown & Co. 9.4
Smith v. Montoro . . . . 8.27[B]
Smith v. Weinstein . . . . . 9.5[B]; 11.7[A]
Sony Corp. v. Universal City Studios, Inc. . . .
  8.29[A]; 9.20[B]; 10.5; 10.7; 10.8;
  10.10; 10.11[B], [D]; 10.14[D];
  10.16
S.O.S., Inc. v. Payday, Inc. . . . . 5.4[A]
Southern Bell Tel. & Tel. Co. v. Associated Tel.
  Directory Publishers . . . . 2.11[B]
Southwestern Cable Co.; United States v. . . .
  8.18[A]
Springsteen v. Plaza Roller Dome, Inc. . . . . .
  8.18[C]
Standard & Poor's Corp. v. Commodities Ex-
  change, Inc. . . . . 1.14[E]; 11.2[B]
Stanley v. Columbia Broadcasting System, Inc.
  . . . . 9.4
State of (see name of state)
Stern v. Remick & Co. 4.3
Stern Electronics, Inc. v. Kaufman 2.5;
  3.6[A]; 3.22
Stevens Linen Associates, Inc. v. Mastercraft
  Corp. 9.11
Stewart v. Abend . . . Preface; 2.9[B]; 6.9[C];
  6.10[A]–[C]
Stone v. Williams . . . . 6.6[B]; 9.17
Stonehill Communications, Inc. v. Martuge . .
  4.16[B]
Stratchborneo v. Arc Music Corp. 8.5;
  8.7[C]; 9.4
Strauss v. Penn Printing & Publishing Co. . . .
  4.14[E]
Subafilms, Ltd. v. MGM-PATHE Communica-
  tions Co. . . . . 12.8[B]
Swarovski, Ltd. v. Silver Deer Ltd. . . 5.12[A]
Sweet Music, Inc. v. Melrose Music Corp. . . . .
  5.4[C]
Sygma Photo News, Inc. v. Globe International,
  Inc. . . . . 5.2[C]
Synercom Technology, Inc. v. University Comput-
  ing Co. . . . . 11.1; 11.2[B]

T

T. B. Harms Co. v. Eliscu . . . . . . 9.16[A]
Tandy Corp. v. Personal Micro Computers, Inc.
  . . . . 2.5; 3.6[B]
Tape Industries Ass'n of America v. Younger
  . . . . 11.4
Taylor v. Meirick . . . . 9.12[B]; 9.17
Taylor Instrument Co. v. Fawley-Brost Co. . . .
  2.12[B][2]
Ted Arnold Ltd. v. Silvercraft Co. 3.11
Teleprompter Corp. v. Columbia Broadcasting
  System, Inc. . . . . 8.18[A], [C]

Telex Corp. v. I.B.M. Corp. . . . . . . 3.8[A]
Thomas Wilson & Co. v. Irving J. Dorfman Co.
  . . . . 9.11
Time, Inc. v. Bernard Geis Associates . . 10.7;
  10.15[B]
Toksvig v. Bruce Publishing Co. . . . 2.12[D]
Towle v. Ross . . . . 9.19[A]
Trademark Cases . . . . 1.12[A]
Triangle Publications, Inc. v. Knight-Ridder
  Newspapers, Inc. . . . . 10.6; 10.15[A], [B]
Triangle Publications, Inc. v. Sports Eye, Inc.
  . . . . 9.5[C]
Trifari, Krussman & Fishel, Inc. v. Charel Co., Inc.
  . . . . 4.14[C]
Truck Equipment Service Co. v. Freuhauf Corp.
  . . . . 11.4
Twentieth Century Music Corporation v. Aiken
  . . . . 1.8[B]; 8.18[A]
Twin Peaks Productions, Inc. v. Publications, Int'l
  . . . . 10.5; 10.7

U

United Christian Scientists v. Christian Science
  Bd. . . . . 6.5[C]
United States v. (see name of defendant)
United Thrift Plan, Inc. v. National Thrift Plan,
  Inc. . . . . 4.14[A], [C]
Universal City Studios, Inc. v. Sony Corp. of
  America 10.5
Universal Pictures Co., Inc. v. Harold Lloyd Corp.
  . . . . 9.5[D]
Update Art, Inc. v. Modiin Publishing, Ltd. . . .
  12.8[B]

V

Vanna White v. Samsung Electronics America,
  Inc. . . . . 1.14[D]
Vault Corp. v. Quaid Software Ltd. 8.6
Videotronics, Inc. v. Bend Elec. . . . 4.10[A];
  4.11[C][2]

W

W. T. Rogers Co., Inc. v. Keene 3.16
Walker v. Time Life Films, Inc. . . . . 9.5[B]
Walker v. University Books 10.13
Walt Disney Prod. v. Air Pirates . . . 2.12[C];
  10.14[A], [C], [E]
Walt Disney Prods. v. Mature Pictures Corp.
  . . . . 10.14[E]
Walt Disney Productions v. Basmajian . . . . .
  8.13[A]
Walt Disney Productions v. Filmation Associates
  10.13

[References are to sections.]

Walter, In re . . . . 3.8[B]

Warner Bros, Inc. v. American Broadcasting Co.,
Inc. . . . . 2.12[C]; 11.7[A]

Warner Bros. Pictures, Inc. v. Columbia Broadcasting System . . . . 2.12[C]

Warrington Associates, Inc. v. Real-Time Engineering Systems, Inc. . . . . 11.7[A]

Washingtonian Publishing Co. v. Pearson . . .
7.8

Weinstein v. University of Illinois . . 5.2[B][1]

Weissman v. Freeman . . . . 5.4[B]

Werlin v. Reader's Digest Ass'n, Inc. . . . . .
11.7[A]

West Publishing Co. v. Mead Data Central Inc.
. . . . 2.11[D]

WGN Continental Broadcasting Co. v. United
Video, Inc. . . . . . . 3.22; 8.19[C][3], [D]

Wheaton v. Peters . . . 1.3; 4.2[B]; 4.9; 11.2A

Whelan Assoc., Inc. v. Jaslow Dental Laboratory,
Inc. . . . . . 3.6[D]; 7.5; 9.5[F]; 9.6[B]; 9.7

Whimsicality, Inc. v. Rubie's Costume Co., Inc.
. . . . 10.01

White v. Kimmell . . . . 4.5[C]

White-Smith Music Publishing Co. v. Apollo Co.
. . . . 2.4; 3.6[B]; 4.7[C]

Wihtol v. Crow . . . . 10.7; 10.12[B]

Wildman v. New York Times Co. . . . 4.14[D],
[E]

Williams and Wilkins Co. v. United States . .
8.3[C]; 10.11[C], [D]; 10.12[A], [C]

Williams Electronics, Inc. v. Artic Int'l, Inc. . .
2.5; 3.6[A], [C]

Wise; United States v. . . . . 8.13[A]

Wise; U.S. v. 9.15

Wojnarowicz v. American Family Association
. . . . 8.27[C]

Wolfe v. United Artists Corp. . . . . . 9.16[A]

WPOW, Inc. v. MRLJ Enterprises 9.9

Wright v. Warner Books, Inc. 10.8

Y

Yardley, In re . . . . 3.16[A]

Z

Zacchini v. Scripps-Howard Broadcasting Co.
. . . . 11.4

Zachary v. Western Publishing Co. . . 3.16[A]

Zahn, In re . . . . 3.16[A]

Zim v. Western Publishing Co. . . . . 8.27[B]

TABLE OF STATUTES, REGULATIONS, AND TREATIES

[References are to sections.]

ACT OF MAY 31, 1790
Generally 1.3

26 STAT. 1106 (1891)
Generally 4.15

ACT OF DEC. 12, 1980
Sec. 10(b) . . . . 3.4[A]

ACT OF OCT. 15, 1971
Generally . . . . 6.3[E]

ACT OF OCT. 28, 1992
Also see 18 USC § 2319(b)
Generally 9.15

ARCHITECTURAL WORKS PROTECTION ACT OF 1990
Generally . . 3.15[A],[C]; 11.11[B]; 12.5[B][2]

AUDIO HOME RECORDING ACT OF 1992
Generally . . . . . 8.1; 8.3[A],[C]; 8.29[A],[B]

AUTOMATIC RENEWAL AMENDMENT
Generally . . . . 6.5[B]

BERNE CONVENTION or BERNE UNION
Generally . . . 1.4[B]; 1.5[C],[D]; 1.5[D], 1.7;
2.6, 4.4; 4.6[C]; 4.8[A]; 4.11[A];
4.15; 4.18; 5.12[A]; 6.2; 6.4; 7.6[A];
8.28[A]; 12.1; 12.2;
12.3[A],[B][6],[C]; 12.4[A],[B];
12.5[A],[B],[C]; 12.6[B],[C];
12.7[B]; 12.8[C]; 12.10[C],[D]
Arts. 1–21 . . . . 4.19[B]; 12.10[C]
Art. 2(1) . . . . 12.4[B][1]; 12.5[B][2]
Art. 2(2) . . . . 12.4[B][1]
Art. 2(3) . . . . 12.4[B][1]
Art. 2(5) . . . . 12.4[B][1]
Art. 2(7) . . . . 12.4[B][1]
Art. 2(8) . . . . 12.4[B][1]

Art. 3(2) . . . . 12.4[B][2]
Art. 4(3) . . . . 12.4[B][2]
Art. 5(2) . . . . . 1.5[B]; 4.1; 4.8[A]; 6.9[A];
12.4[B][3]; 12.5[B][1]
Art. 6 bis . . . . 8.28[A]; 12.4[B][5]; 12.5[B];
12.10[C]
Art. 7 . . . . 1.4[B]
Art. 7(1) . . . . 6.2; 12.4[B][4]
Art. 7(3) . . . . 12.4[B][4]
Art. 7(6) . . . . 12.4[B][4]
Art. 7(8) . . . . 6.4; 12.8[C]
Art. 8(1) . . . . 12.4[B][5]
Art. 9(1) . . . . 12.4[B][5]
Art. 9(2) . . . . 12.4[B][5]
Art. 10 . . . . 12.4[B][5]
Art. 10 bis . . . . 12.4[B][5]
Art. 11 . . . . 12.5[B][3]; 12.6[B]
Art. 11(1) . . . . 8.21[A]; 12.4[B][5]
Art. 12 . . . . 12.4[B][5]
Art. 18 . . . . 4.18; 12.5[B][4]
Art. 18(3) . . . . 12.5[B][4]
Appendix . . . . 4.19[B]
Protocol . . . . 12.10[D]; 12.11[A]

BERNE CONVENTION IMPLEMENTATION ACT OF 1988
Also see 17 USC
Generally . . . . . 1.5[B],[D]; 4.1; 4.4; 4.6[B];
4.8[A],[B]; 4.9; 4.11[A]; 4.12[A];
4.13[A]; 4.14[A]; 4.17[C]; 5.12[A];
8.3[B]; 8.21[A]; 9.18; 10.12[A];
12.5[B]; 12.7[B]
Sec. 2(1) . . . . 12.5[B]
Sec. 12 . . . . 12.5[B][4]
Sec. 13(b) . . . . 12.5[B][4]

BUENOS AIRES CONVENTION
Generally . . . . 12.6[C]; 12.7[B]

CALIFORNIA ART PRESERVATION ACT
Sec. 987 . . . . 8.27[C]

[References are to sections.]

CALIFORNIA CIVIL CODE

Sec. 980(a) 2.6
Sec. 982(c) 5.7
Sec. 986 . . . . 8.14[E]; 11.8[D]
Sec. 987 . . . . 8.27[C]
Sec. 990 . . . . 1.14[D]
Sec. 3344 . . . . 1.14[D]

CALIFORNIA PENAL CODE

Sec. 593(d) . . . . 8.16[A]

CARIBBEAN BASIN ECONOMIC RECOVERY ACT

Generally . . . . 12.1; 12.9[C]

CODE OF FEDERAL REGULATIONS
Title 19

Sec. 133.33 . . . . 12.9[A]
Sec. 133.43(a) . . . . 12.9[A]
Sec. 133.43(b)(2) . . . . 12.9[A]
Sec. 133.43(c)(1) . . . . 12.9[A]
Sec. 210.12 . . . . 12.9[B]
Sec. 210.20 . . . . 12.9[B]
Sec. 210.24 . . . . 12.9[B]

Title 37

Secs. 201.1–201.2 . . . . 7.2
Sec. 201.2(d) 7.2
Sec. 201.5 . . . . 7.3
Sec. 201.10 . . . . 6.13
Sec. 201.10(b)(ii) 6.13
Sec. 201.20 . . . . 4.10[E]
Sec. 202 . . . . 2.10; 4.11[A]
Sec. 202.1 . . . . 2.7[C]
Sec. 202.1(a) . . . . 2.7[C]
Sec. 202.1(b) . . . . 2.12[B][2]
Sec. 202.2 . . . . 4.12[A]
Sec. 202.3(b)(2)(3) 7.5
Sec. 202.8(a) 3.11
Sec. 202.10(c) 3.11
Secs. 202.19–.21 . . . . 7.10
Sec. 202.19 . . . . 7.13
Sec. 202.19(b)(iii) 7.12
Sec. 202.19(f) 7.13
Secs. 202.20–.21 . . . . 7.12
Sec. 202.20 . . . . 3.18; 7.5; 7.12
Sec. 202.20(c)(2)(vii)(C) 7.5
Sec. 202.21 . . . . 7.5
Sec. 307 . . . . 8.7[B]
Sec. 307.3 . . . . 8.7[B]

CONVENTION FOR THE PROTECTION OF PRODUCERS OF PHONOGRAMS AGAINST UNAUTHORIZED DUPLICATION OF THEIR PHONOGRAMS (GENEVA CONVENTION)

Generally . . . . 12.6[A]; 12.10[D]

CONVENTION RELATING TO THE DISTRIBUTION OF PROGRAMME-CARRYING SIGNALS TRANSMITTED BY SATELLITE (BRUSSELS SATELLITE CONVENTION)

Generally . . . . 12.6[B]

COPYRIGHT ACT OF 1909

Also see 17 USC
Generally . . . . 1.3; 1.4[A],[B],[C];
1.5[A],[B],[D]; 1.14[C]; 2.7[A],[C];
2.12[A]; 3.2[A],[C]; 3.13; 3.17;
3.21; 4.1; 4.3; 4.5[A],[C]; 4.7[B];
4.8[B]; 4.9; 4.13[B];
4.14[A],[B],[C],[D],[E],[F]; 4.15;
5.1; 5.2[B]; 5.5; 5.6; 5.7; 5.8[B];
5.9; 5.11[B]; 6.3[A]; 6.5[A]; 6.7[D];
6.8; 6.11; 7.8; 7.11; 8.17[A];
8.18[A],[B]; 9.11; 9.14; 11.1; 11.2;
11.4; 11.5; 11.8[C]; 12.3[A]
Sec. 1(c) . . . . 8.17[A]
Sec. 1(e) . . . . 8.17[A]; 8.21[A]
Sec. 4 . . . . 1.4[A]; 3.2[A]
Sec. 5 . . . . 3.2[C]
Sec. 9 . . . . 4.14[F]
Sec. 10 . . . 1.4[A],[B]; 4.4; 4.11[A]; 4.12[A];
4.14[A],[F]; 5.9; 6.2
Sec. 12 . . . . 6.2
Sec. 13 . . . . 7.8; 7.11
Sec. 14 . . . . 7.8
Sec. 16 . . . . 4.15; 4.17[A]
Sec. 17 . . . . 4.17[A]
Sec. 18 . . . . 4.17[A]
Secs. 19–21 . . . . 4.14[B]
Sec. 19 . . . . 4.14[C],[D],[F]; 5.9
Sec. 20 . . . . 4.14[C],[F]
Sec. 21 . . . . 4.11[B]; 4.14[D],[E]
Sec. 24 . . . 1.4[A]; 4.2[A]; 5.5; 6.2; 6.5[A];
6.6[A],[B]; 6.7[A]; 6.8
Sec. 26 . . . . 5.3
Sec. 28 . . . . 5.11[B]

[References are to sections.]

COPYRIGHT ACT OF 1976

Also see 17 USC

Generally . . . . . 1.4[A]; 1.5[A],[B],[C],[D];
1.14[C]; 2.6; 3.3; 4.7[B]; 4.11[B];
4.14[F]; 4.15; 5.11[A],[B]; 5.3;
6.3[G]; 6.5[A]; 6.9[A]; 6.13; 6.14;
8.17[A]; 8.19[A]; 8.20; 8.21[A],[B];
8.24; 8.27[A]; 9.11; 9.12[B];
9.13[D]; 9.14; 9.16[A]; 9.20[A];
10.2; 10.12[B]; 10.15[A],[B]; 11.1;
11.2[A]; 11.5; 11.6[B];
11.8[A],[B],[C],[D]; 11.9[A];
12.5[A],[B][1],[3]

Sec. 101 . . . . 3.4[A]
Sec. 102(a) . . . . 2.1; 2.8; 3.2[A],[C]
Sec. 102(b) . . . . 2.11[A]
Sec. 103(a) . . . . 2.9[C]
Sec. 104 . . . . 12.1
Sec. 104A . . . . 1.5[C]; 4.11[A]
Sec. 105 . . . . 2.12[B]
Sec. 106A . . . . 8.28[A],[B]
Secs. 107–120 . . . . 8.1
Sec. 116A . . . . 8.28[A]
Sec. 117 . . . . 3.4[A]
Sec. 119 . . . . 8.20
Sec. 202 . . . . 5.7
Sec. 203 . . . . 6.1
Sec. 204(a) . . . . 5.11[A]
Sec. 301 . . . . 1.5[A]; 1.14[E]; 4.2[A]
Sec. 301(a) . . . . 1.14[C]; 4.14[B]
Sec. 301(c) . . . . 3.19[C]; 6.3[E]
Sec. 302 . . . . 6.3[F]
Sec. 302(a) . . 1.5[A]; 4.2[A]; 4.5[B]; 4.6[D];
6.3[B]
Sec. 302(b) . . . . 5.5; 6.3[D]
Sec. 302(c) . . . . . . 1.5[A]; 4.6[D]; 5.2[A];
6.3[C],[E]
Sec. 302(d) . . . . 4.6[D]; 6.3[F]
Sec. 302(e) . . . . 4.6[D]; 6.3[F]
Sec. 303 . . . . 6.3[G]
Sec. 304(a) . . . . 6.7[A],[B]
Sec. 304(a)(2)(A)(1) 6.8
Sec. 304(a)(2)(B)(1) 6.8
Sec. 304(c) . . . . . . 6.1; 6.10[A]; 6.11; 6.12
Sec. 304(c)(1) 6.12
Sec. 304(c)(2) 6.12
Sec. 304(c)(3) 6.12
Sec. 304(c)(4) 6.12
Sec. 304(c)(5) 6.11
Sec. 304(c)(6)(F) 6.11; 6.12
Sec. 305 . . . . 6.3[A]
Secs. 401–412 . . . . 7.1
Sec. 401 . . . . 4.10[B]
Sec. 401(a) . . . . 1.5[A]; 4.6[B]; 4.8[A]; 4.9;

Sec. 401(b)(1) . . . . 4.10[A],[B]
Sec. 401(b)(2) . . . . 4.7[D]; 4.10[C]
Sec. 401(c) . . . . 4.10[A]
Sec. 401(d) . . . . . 4.8[B]; 4.9; 4.12[A],[C];
4.13[A],[B]
Sec. 402 . . . . 4.10[B]
Sec. 402(a) . . . . 4.6[B]
Sec. 402(d) . . . . . 4.9; 4.12[A],[C]; 4.13
Sec. 403 . . . . 4.13[A]
Sec. 404 . . . . 4.3; 5.9; 4.13[B]
Sec. 404(a) 5.9
Sec. 405 . . . . . 1.5[A],[B]; 4.6[B]; 4.11[A];
4.12[D]; 4.13[A]; 7.4
Sec. 405(a) . . . . . 4.1; 4.8[B]; 4.11[A],[B];
4.14[A]
Sec. 405(a)(1) . . . . . 4.11[B]; 4.14[A],[E]
Sec. 405(a)(2) . . . . 4.11[A],[C]
Sec. 405(a)(3) . . . . 4.11[B],[C]
Sec. 405(b) . . . . 4.11[B]; 4.12[A]
Sec. 405(c) . . . . 4.9; 4.11[B]
Sec. 406 . . . . 4.12[B]; 7.4
Sec. 406(a) . . . . 4.12[B]; 4.13[B]
Sec. 406(a)(1),(2) . . . . 4.12[C]
Sec. 406(b) . . . . 4.12[C]
Sec. 406(c) . . . . 4.12[D]
Sec. 407(a) . . . . 4.6[B]
Sec. 407(d) . . . . 4.6[B]
Sec. 408 . . . . 2.2
Sec. 412 . . . . 7.6[A]
Sec. 602 . . . . 12.1
Sec. 603 . . . . 12.1

COPYRIGHT REFORM BILL OF 1993

Generally . . . . 7.6[C]

COPYRIGHT REMEDY CLARIFICATION ACT OF 1990

Generally . . . . 9.19[B]

COPYRIGHT RENEWAL ACT OF 1992

Generally . . . . 6.8; 6.9[A],[B],[C]

COPYRIGHT ROYALTY TRIBUNAL REFORM ACT OF 1993

Generally . . 1.5[A]; 8.3[B]; 8.19[F]; 8.21[A]

EUROPEAN UNION

Dir. 91/250 . . . . 12.11[A]
Dir. 92/100 . . . . 12.11[A]

FEDERAL BANKRUPTCY ACT

[References are to sections.]

FEDERAL COMMUNICATIONS ACT
Title 47
Generally 11.10
Sec. 705(a) . . . . 8.16[A]

GENERAL AGREEMENT ON TARIFFS AND TRADE (GATT) (also World Trade Organization or WTO)
Also see Trade Related Aspects of Intellectual Property (TRIPS) Agreement
Generally . . Preface; 1.5[D]; 2.3[B]; 4.11[A]; 4.15; 4.19[B]; 12.9[B]; 12.10[A],[B],[C]
Art. XXIII . . . . 12.10[C]

GENERALIZED SYSTEM OF PREFERENCES (GSP)
Also see International Trade and Investment Act of 1984
Generally . . . . 12.9[C]

INTERNATIONAL CONVENTION FOR THE PROTECTION OF PERFORMERS, PRODUCERS OF PHONOGRAMS, AND BROADCASTING ORGANIZATIONS (ROME CONVENTION)
Generally . . . . 12.6[A]; 12.10[D]

INTERNATIONAL TRADE AND INVESTMENT ACT OF 1984
Generally . . . . 12.9[C]

LANHAM ACT
Also see 15 USC
Generally . . 1.12[B]; 2.13[B]; 8.14[C]; 11.10
Sec. 43(a) 11.4

MASSACHUSETTS GENERAL LAWS ANNOTATED
Chapter 231
Sec. 855 . . . . 11.11[A]
Sec. 855(b) . . . . 8.27[C]

MEXICO CITY TREATY OF 1902
Generally

NEW YORK ARTISTS' AUTHORSHIP RIGHTS ACT, N.Y. Arts & Cultural Affairs Law
Secs. 14.51–14.59 . . . . 8.27[C]

NEW YORK GENERAL BUSINESS LAW
Secs. 223–24 . . . . 5.7

NEW YORK PENAL CODE
Sec. 165.15 . . . . 8.16[A]

NORTH AMERICAN FREE TRADE AGREEMENT (NAFTA)
Generally . . Preface; 1.5[C]; 4.8[B]; 4.11[A]; 12.1; 12.5[B][4]; 12.11[B]

OMNIBUS TRADE AND COMPETITIVENESS ACT OF 1988
Sec. 1342 . . . . 12.9[B]

PAN AMERICAN COPYRIGHT CONVENTION (BUENOS AIRES CONVENTION)
Generally . . . . 12.6[C]; 12.7[B]
Art. 3 . . . . 12.6[C]

PATENT ACT
Also see 35 USC
Generally 11.4; 11.10

PRIV. L. NO. 92–60, 85 STAT. 857 (1971)
(protecting works of Mary Baker Eddy)
Generally . . . . 6.5[C]

RECORD RENTAL AMENDMENT OF 1984
Generally . . . . 1.5[B]; 8.14[A]

RESALE ROYALTY ACT
Generally . . . . 8.14[E], 11.8[D]

RESTATEMENT (SECOND) OF AGENCY
Sec. 220 (1958) . . . . 5.2[C]

RESTATEMENT (FIRST) OF TORTS

[References are to sections.]

RESTATEMENT (THIRD) OF UNFAIR COMPETITION

Secs. 2–6 . . . . 1.14[B]

ROME CONVENTION
(See International Convention for the Protection of Performers, Producers of Phonograms and Broadcasting Organizations)

SATELLITE HOME VIEWER ACT OF 1988

Also see 17 USC
Generally . . . . 1.5[B]; 8.20

SEMICONDUCTOR CHIP PROTECTION ACT OF 1984

Also see 17 USC §§ 900 et seq.
Generally . . . . 1.5[A]; 3.9[B]
Sec. 902(b)(1),(2) . . . . 3.9[B]
Sec. 904 . . . . 3.9[B]
Sec. 905 . . . . 3.9[B]
Sec. 908(a) . . . . 3.9[B]
Sec. 908(e) . . . . 3.9[B]
Sec. 909(a) . . . . 3.9[B]
Sec. 909(b) . . . . 3.9[B]
Sec. 910(a) . . . . 3.9[B]
Sec. 910(b) . . . . 3.9[B]
Sec. 911 . . . . 3.9[B]
Sec. 911(d) . . . . 3.9[B]

SHERMAN ACT

Sec. 1 . . . . 8.22[D]

SOFTWARE RENTAL AMENDMENTS ACT OF 1990

Also see 17 USC § 109(b)
Generally . . . . 8.14[B]

SOUND RECORDING ACT OF 1971

Generally . . . . 3.19[C]; 4.7[C]; 11.4

STATUTE OF ANNE (1710)

Generally 1.2; 1.3
8 Anne; Ch. 19 . . . . 4.2[B]

TARIFF ACT OF 1930

Sec. 337 . . . . 12.1; 12.9[B]
Sec. 337(e),(f),(g) . . . . 12.9[B]

TRADE ACT OF 1974

12.9[C]

TRADE RELATED ASPECTS OF INTELLECTUAL PROPERTY AGREEMENT (TRIPS)

Also see General Agreement on Tarffs and Trade (GATT)
Generally . . . . 4.19[B]; 12.1; 12.10[A],[B],[C],[D]; 12.11[B]
Art. 9 . . . . 4.19[B]
Art. 10 . . . . 12.10[C]
Art. 65 . . . . 4.19[B]; 12.10[C]
Art. 66 . . . . 12.10[C]

TREATY OF ROME

Generally . . . . 12.11[A]
Art. 30 . . . . 12.11[A]
Art. 59 . . . . 12.11[A]
Art. 85 . . . . 12.11[A]
Art. 86 . . . . 12.11[A]

UNIFORM COMMERCIAL CODE

Sec. 2–703 . . . . 8.13[B]
Sec. 2–706 . . . . 8.13[B]

UNIFORM SALES ACT

Sec. 60 . . . . 8.13[B]

UNITED KINGDOM'S PUBLIC LENDING RIGHT ACT OF 1979

Generally . . . . 8.14[D]

UNITED STATES CODE

Title 15

Sec. 1025(a) 11.4
Sec. 1051(b)(1)(A) . . . . 1.12[A]
Secs. 1051–1127 . . . . . . §§ 1.12[B]; 11.10
Sec. 1052(a) . . . . 1.12[B]; 2.13[A]
Sec. 1052(d) . . . . 1.12[B],[C]
Sec. 1052(e) . . . . 1.12[B]
Sec. 1057(b) . . . . 1.12[B]
Sec. 1065 . . . . 1.12[B]
Sec. 1072 . . . . 1.12[B]
Sec. 1111 . . . . 1.12[B]
Secs. 1116–1120 . . . . 1.12[B]
Sec. 1124 . . . . 1.12[B]
Sec. 1125(a) . . . . 8.27[B]
Sec. 1127 . . . . 1.12[A]

Title 17

Sec. 1(e) . . . . 8.7[A]
Sec. 4 . . . . 1.4[A]; 3.2[A]
Sec. 5 . . . . 3.2[C]
Sec. 9 . . . . 4.14[F]
Sec. 10 . . . 1.4[A],[B]; 4.4; 4.11[A]; 4.12[A]; 4.14[F]; 5.9; 6.2

[References are to sections.]

Sec. 12 . . . . 6.2
Sec. 16 . . . . 4.15; 4.17[A]
Sec. 17 . . . . 4.17[C]
Sec. 18 . . . . 4.17[C]
Sec. 19 . . . . 4.14[B],[D],[F]; 5.19
Secs. 19–21 . . . . 4.14[B]
Sec. 20 . . . . 4.14[C],[F]
Sec. 21 . . . . 4.14[E]
Sec. 24 . . . . 1.4[A]; 4.2[A]; 5.5; 6.2; 6.5[A];
        6.6[A],[B]; 6.7[A],[B]; 6.8
Sec. 26 . . . . 5.3
Sec. 28 . . . . 5.11[B]
Sec. 101 . . . . 1.5[C]; 2.2; 2.3[A]; 2.7[B]; 2.8;
        2.9[D]; 2.11[D]; 3.3; 3.4[A]; 3.6[B];
        3.10; 3.12; 3.13; 3.15[B],[C];
        3.19[A]; 3.22; 4.3; 4.7[A],[D]; 4.9;
        5.2[B]; 5.4[A]; 5.6; 5.8[A]; 5.11[A];
        6.6[B]; 6.7[C]; 7.4; 7.6[A]; 7.12;
        8.4; 8.8; 8.15; 8.16[A],[C]; 8.17[E];
        8.19[B]; 8.20; 8.25; 8.28[B]; 10.5;
        10.6; 11.11[A]; 12.4[B][2];
        12.5[B][1]; 12.7[B]
Secs. 101–914 . . . . 11.1
Sec. 102 . . . . . 2.2; 2.8; 11.1; 11.5; 11.7[A];
        11.9[A],[B]
Sec. 102(a) . . . 1.5[A]; 1.14[C]; 2.1; 2.2; 2.4;
        2.6; 3.2[A],[B],[C]; 3.6[B]; 4.2[A];
        4.11[D]; 7.4; 11.5
Sec. 102(a)(2) 3.18
Sec. 102(a)(5) 3.10
Sec. 102(a)(8) . . . . . . 1.5[A],[C]; 3.15[C]
Sec. 102(b) . . 2.1; 2.10; 2.11[A]; 2.12[A],[B];
        3.6[D]; 3.15[C]; 9.5[D]; 10.13;
        11.9[A]
Sec. 103 . . 1.5[D]; 2.2; 2.8; 4.4; 11.1; ; 11.5;
        11.7[A]; 11.9[B]
Sec. 103(a) . . . . 2.9[C]
Sec. 104 . . . 4.6[D]; 5.2[A]; 8.28[B]; 12.7[A]
Sec. 104(a) . . . . 12.7[A]
Sec. 104(b) . . . . 7.4; 12.7[B]
Sec. 104(b)(1) . . . . 12.7[B]
Sec. 104(b)(2) . . . . 12.7[B]
Sec. 104(b)(3) . . . . 12.7[B]
Sec. 104(b)(4) . . . . 12.7[B]
Sec. 104(b)(5) . . . . 12.7[B]
Sec. 104A . . 1.5[C],[D]; 4.4; 4.8[B]; 4.11[A];
        4.14[A]; 4.19[B]; 12.5[B][4];
        12.5[B][4]; 12.11[B]
Sec. 104A(a)(1)(B) . . . . 4.19[B]
Sec. 104A(b) . . . . 4.19[A]
Sec. 104A(c) . . . . 4.19[A]
Sec. 104A(d) . . . . 4.19[A]
Sec. 104A(d)(2)(A) . . . . 8.14[D]
Sec. 104A(d)(2)(B) . . . . 8.14[D]
Sec. 104A(d)(3)(B) . . . . 4.19[B]

Sec. 104A(e)(1) . . . . 4.19[B]
Sec. 104A(h) . . . . 4.19[A]
Sec. 104A(h)(3) . . . . 4.19[B]
Sec. 104A(h)(4) . . . . 4.19[B]
Sec. 104A(h)(6)(B) . . . . 4.19[B]
Sec. 104A(h)(6)(C) . . . . 4.19[B]
Sec. 104A(h)(6)(D) . . . . 4.19[B]; 6.5[B]
Sec. 104A(h)(8) . . . . 4.19[B]
Sec. 105 . . . . . . 2.13[B]; 4.13[A]; 5.2[A]
Sec. 106 . . . 1.5[A]; 3.21; 5.8; 8.12; 8.28[B];
        9.1; 9.20[A]; 11.1; 11.6[A]; 11.7[A];
        11.8[B]; 11.11[A]; 12.4[B][5]
Sec. 106(1) 8.4; 11.5
Sec. 106(2) . . . . 3.15[C]; 8.5
Sec. 106(3) . . . . 8.12; 11.8[D]
Sec. 106(4) . . . 8.9; 8.15; 8.19[B]; 8.22[A];
        8.24; 11.8[B]
Sec. 106(5) 8.25
Sec. 106A . . . . . 1.5[A],[C]; 7.6[A]; 8.28;
        11.11[A]
Sec. 106A(a) . . . . 8.28[B]; 11.11[A]
Sec. 106A(b) . . . . 8.28[B]
Sec. 106A(c) . . . . 8.28[B]
Sec. 106A(d) . . . . 8.28[B]
Sec. 106A(e) . . . . 8.28[B]
Sec. 107 . . 1.5[A]; 4.13[B]; 10.1; 10.2; 10.3;
        10.4; 10.5; 10.6; 10.7; 10.8;
        10.12[A],[B]; 10.14[B]; 10.16
Sec. 107(4) 10.10
Secs. 107–120 . . . . . 1.5[A]; 8.15; 11.8[C]
Sec. 108 . . . . 4.6[D]; 10.12[A]
Secs. 108–118 . . . . 10.11[D]
Sec. 108(a) . . . . 10.12[A]
Sec. 108(b) . . . . 10.12[A]
Sec. 108(c) . . . . 10.12[A]
Sec. 108(d) . . . . 10.12[A]
Sec. 108(g) . . . . 10.12[A]
Sec. 108(g)(2) . . . . 10.12[A]
Sec. 108(h) . . . . 3.2[D]; 10.12[A]
Sec. 108(i) . . . . 10.12[A]
Sec. 109 . . . . 11.8[C]
Sec. 109(a) . . . . . . 4.19[B]; 8.13[A],[B];
        8.14[B],[D],[F]; 8.26[A];
        11.8[B],[C],[D]
Sec. 109(b) . . . 1.5[C]; 8.7[B]; 8.14[A],[B]
Sec. 109(b)(1)(A) . . . . 8.14[B]
Sec. 109(b)(1)(3)(ii) . . . . 8.14[B]
Sec. 109(b)(2)(A) . . . . 8.14[B]
Sec. 109(c) . . . . 8.26[A]
Sec. 109(e) . . . . 8.14[B]
Sec. 110 . . 8.17[A],[B]; 8.18[B],[C]; 8.26[B]
Sec. 110(1) . . . . 8.17[B]; 8.26[B]
Sec. 110(2) . . . . 3.20; 8.8; 8.17[B]; 8.19[C];
        8.26[B]
Sec. 110(3) . . . .

[References are to sections.]

Sec. 110(3) . . . . 8.26[B]
Sec. 110(4) . . . . . 8.17[B],[D],[E]; 8.26[B]
Sec. 110(4)(A) . . . . 8.17[D]
Sec. 110(4)(B) . . . . 8.17[E]
Sec. 110(4)(B)(ii) . . . . 8.17[E]
Sec. 110(4)(B)(iii) . . . . 8.17[E]
Sec. 110(5) . . . . 8.18[B],[C]; 8.26[B]
Sec. 110(6) . . . . 8.17[D]; 8.26[B]
Sec. 110(7) . . . . 8.17[D]; 8.26[B]
Sec. 110(8) . . . . . . 8.8; 8.17[C]; 8.26[B]
Sec. 110(9) . . . . 8.17[C]; 8.26[B]
Sec. 110(10) . . . . 8.17[D]; 8.26[B]
Sec. 111 . . 1.5[A]; 8.3[A],[C]; 8.18[A]; 8.19;
8.26[B]
Sec. 111(a) . . . . 8.19[C]
Sec. 111(a)(1) . . . . 8.19[C]
Sec. 111(a)(2) . . . . 8.19[C]
Sec. 111(a)(3) . . . . 8.19[C]; 8.20
Sec. 111(a)(4) . . . . 8.19[C]
Sec. 111(b) . . . . 8.19[B],[C]
Sec. 111(c) . . . . 8.19[B],[D]
Sec. 111(c)(1) . . . . 8.19[D]
Sec. 111(c)(3) . . . . 8.19[D]
Sec. 111(c)(4) . . . . 8.19[D]
Sec. 111(d) . . . . 8.19[B],[E]
Sec. 111(d)(2) . . . . 8.19[E],[F]
Sec. 111(d)(2)(C-D) . . . . 8.19[F]
Sec. 111(d)(4) . . . . 8.19[E]
Sec. 111(d)(4)(A) . . . . 8.19[F]
Sec. 111(e) . . . . 8.19[B]
Sec. 111(f) . . . . 8.19[B]; 8.20
Sec. 112 . . . . 8.8; 11.8[C]
Sec. 112(a) 8.8
Sec. 112(b) 8.8
Sec. 112(c) 8.8
Sec. 112(d) 8.8
Sec. 112(e) 8.8
Sec. 113 . . . . 8.10; 8.28[B]
Sec. 113(a) 8.10
Sec. 113(b) . . . . . 3.9[A]; 3.15[B][2]; 8.10
Sec. 113(c) 8.10
Sec. 113(d) . . . . 8.28[B]
Sec. 113(d)(2) 8.11
Sec. 114 . . . . 3.2; 3.19[A]
Sec. 114(a) 8.8; 8.9; 8.24
Sec. 114(b) 8.9
Sec. 114(c) 8.9
Sec. 114(d) 8.24
Sec. 115 . . . . 1.5[A]; 3.2[D]; 3.20; 8.3[A];
8.7[A]; 11.8[C]; 12.4[B][5]
Sec. 115(a)(1) . . . . 8.7[C]
Sec. 115(a)(2) . . . . 8.7[C]
Sec. 115(b)(1) . . . . 8.7[B],[D]
Sec. 115(b)(2) . . . . 8.7[D]

Sec. 116 . . . . . 1.5[A],[C]; 8.21[A]; 9.14;
12.5[B][3]
Sec. 116(b)(2) . . . . 8.21[B]
Sec. 116(e) . . . . 8.22[A]
Sec. 116A . . . . 1.5[C]; 8.21[A]; 12.5[B][3]
Sec. 117 . . . . 1.5[A]; 3.4[A]; 8.6
Sec. 117(1) 8.6
Sec. 117(2) 8.6
Sec. 118 . . . . 1.5[A]; 4.6[D]; 8.3[A]; 8.23
Sec. 118(b) . . . . 4.6[A]
Sec. 118(b)(3) 8.23
Sec. 118(d) . . . . 4.6[A]; 8.26[B]
Sec. 118(d)(2) 8.23
Sec. 118(g) 8.23
Sec. 119 . . . . 1.5[A]; 8.3[A]
Sec. 119(a)(1) 8.20
Sec. 119(b)(1)(B) 8.20
Sec. 119(b)(2) 8.20
Sec. 119(c)(4) 8.20
Sec. 120(a) . . . . 3.15[C]; 8.11
Sec. 120(b) . . . . 3.15[C]; 8.11
Sec. 201(a) 5.1
Sec. 201(b) . . . . 5.2[A],[B]
Sec. 201(c) 5.6
Sec. 201(d) . . . . 1.5[A]; 5.8[A]
Sec. 201(d)(2) . . . . 5.8[A]
Sec. 201(e) 5.13
Sec. 202 . . . . 1.5[A]; 2.2; 5.7
Sec. 203 . . 5.2; 6.1; 6.10[A]; 6.11; 6.15; 6.16;
6.17[A],[B]
Sec. 203(a) . . . . 5.2[E]; 6.15
Sec. 203(a)(1) 6.15
Sec. 203(a)(2) 6.15
Sec. 203(a)(3) . . . . 4.6[A]; 6.15
Sec. 203(a)(4) 6.13; 6.15
Sec. 203(a)(5) 6.11
Sec. 203(b) 6.15; 6.16
Sec. 203(b)(1) 6.15
Sec. 203(b)(3) 6.15
Sec. 203(b)(6) 6.11
Sec. 204 . . . . 5.8[A]
Sec. 204(a) . . . . 5.4[C]; 5.11[A]
Sec. 204(b) . . . . 5.11[A]
Sec. 205 . . . . . 1.5[A]; 5.12[A]; 12.5[B][1]
Sec. 205(c) . . . . . 5.12[A],[B]; 7.5; 7.6[A],[D]
Sec. 205(c)(2) . . . . 5.12[A]
Sec. 205(d) . . . . 1.5[C]; 5.12[A],[B]; 7.6[D];
9.18
Sec. 205(e) . . . . 5.12[A],[C]
Sec. 301 . . . 1.5[A]; 1.14[E]; 4.2[A]; 8.27[C];
8.28[B]; 11.1; 11.5; 11.6[A],[B];
11.7[A],[B]; 11.8[A],[B],; 11.9[A];
11.10
Sec. 301(a) . . . . . . 1.14[C]; 4.14[A]; 11.5;
11.6[A]; 11.8[B]; 11.11[A]

[References are to sections.]

Sec. 301(b)(1) 11.10
Sec. 301(b)(2) 11.10
Sec. 301(b)(3) . . . . . 11.6[A],[B]; 11.7[A]
Sec. 301(b)(4) . . . . 11.11[B]
Sec. 301(c) . . . . . . 3.19[C]; 6.3[E]; 11.10
Sec. 301(d) 11.10
Sec. 301(f) . . . . 8.28[C]; 11.11[A]
Sec. 301(f)(2) . . . . 11.11[A]
Sec. 301(f)(2)(C) . . . . 11.11[A]
Sec. 302 . . . . 6.3; 6.36
Sec. 302(a) . . 1.5[A]; 4.2[A]; 4.5[B],[D]; 4.6;
6.3[B]
Sec. 302(b) . . . . 5.5; 6.3[D]
Sec. 302(c) . . . . . . 1.5[A]; 4.6[D]; 5.2[A];
6.3[C],[E]
Sec. 302(d) . . . . 4.6[D]; 6.3[F]
Sec. 302(e) . . . . 4.6[D]; 6.3[F]
Sec. 303 . . . . 3.15[C]; 4.6[D]; 6.3[G]
Sec. 304 . . . . 4.5[B]; 5.2[A]
Sec. 304(a) . . 6.5[B]; 6.6[A],[B]; 6.7[A],[B];
6.17[B]; 7.3; 7.4
Sec. 304(a)(2)(A)(i) 6.8
Sec. 304(a)(2)(B) . . . . 6.8; 6.9[B]
Sec. 304(c) . . . 6.1; 6.10[A]; 6.11; 6.12; 6.13;
6.14; 6.15; 6.16; 6.17[A]
Sec. 304(c)(1) 6.12
Sec. 304(c)(2) 6.12
Sec. 304(c)(3) 6.12
Sec. 304(c)(4) 6.12; 6.13
Sec. 304(c)(5) 6.11
Sec. 304(c)(6)(A) 6.14
Sec. 304(c)(6)(C) 6.12
Sec. 304(c)(6)(D) 6.12
Sec. 304(c)(6)(F) 6.11; 6.12
Sec. 305 . . . . 6.3[A]
Sec. 401 . . . . . 1.5[B]; 4.10[B]; 12.5[B][1]
Sec. 401(a) . . . . 1.5[A]; 4.6[B]; 4.8[A]; 4.9;
4.14[F]; ; 7.1; 7.4; 12.5[B][1]
Sec. 401(b) . . . . 4.10[A]
Sec. 401(b)(1) . . . . 4.10[B]
Sec. 401(b)(2) . . . . . . 4.7[D]; 4.10[A],[C]
Sec. 401(b)(3) . . . . 4.10[D]
Sec. 401(c) . . . . 4.10[A]; 9.2
Sec. 401(d) . . . . . 4.8[D]; 4.9; 4.12[A],[C];
4.13[B]; 9.13[B]; 12.5[B][1]
Sec. 402 . . . . 4.10[B]; 12.6[A]
Sec. 402(a) . . . . 4.6[B]
Sec. 402(b) . . . . 4.10[B]
Sec. 402(b)(1) . . . . 4.10[B]
Sec. 402(b)(2) . . . . 4.10[C]
Sec. 402(b)(3) . . . . 4.10[B],[D]
Sec. 402(c) . . . . 4.10[A],[B]
Sec. 402(d) . . . 4.9; 4.12[A],[C]; 4.13[A],[B];
9.13[B]; 12.5[B][1]
Sec. 402

Sec. 404 . . . . 4.13[B]; 5.9
Sec. 404(a) . . . . 4.13[B]; 5.9
Sec. 405 . . . . 1.5[A],[B]; 4.6[B]; 4.12[C];
4.13[A]; 7.4; 12.5[B][1]
Sec. 405(a) . . . . . 4.1; 4.8[B]; 4.11[A],[B];
4.14[A]; 7.4; 12.5[B][1]
Sec. 405(a)(1) . . . . 4.11[B]; 4.14[E]
Sec. 405(a)(2) . . . . 4.11[A],[C]; 7.1
Sec. 405(a)(3) . . . . 4.11[B],[C]
Sec. 405(b) . . . . . . 4.11[B],[D]; 4.12[A];
12.5[B][1]
Sec. 405(c) . . . . 4.9; 4.11[B]
Sec. 405(f) . . . . 12.5[B][1]
Sec. 406 . . . . 4.12[A]; 7.4
Sec. 406(a) . . . . 4.12[A]; 4.13[B]
Sec. 406(a)(1),(2) . . . . 4.12[C]
Sec. 406(b) . . . . 4.12[C]
Sec. 406(c) . . . . 4.12[D]
Sec. 407 . . . . 7.10; 7.13
Sec. 407(a) . . . . 4.6[B]
Sec. 407(a)(1) 7.10; 7.12
Sec. 407(a)(2) 7.10; 7.12
Sec. 407(c) 7.10; 7.12
Sec. 407(d) . . . . 4.6[B]
Sec. 407(d)(3) 7.11
Sec. 408 . . . . 2.2; 7.5; 7.10; 7.13
Secs. 408–412 . . . . 4.6[B]
Sec. 408(a) 7.4
Sec. 408(b)(1) 7.13
Sec. 408(b)(3) 7.13
Sec. 408(c)(1) . . . . 3.2[D]
Sec. 408(d) 7.3
Sec. 409 . . . . 7.5
Sec. 410(a) 7.5
Sec. 410(c) . . . . . 4.6[B]; 7.3; 7.4; 7.6[B]
Sec. 410(d) . . . . 4.11[C]; 7.5
Sec. 411 . . 1.5[A],[C]; 7.4; 7.6[A]; 12.5[B][1]
Sec. 411(a) . . . . 7.6[A],[C]; 7.7
Sec. 411(b) . . . . 7.6[C]
Sec. 412 . . . 4.6[B]; 7.4; 7.6[A],[C]; 9.13[A];
9.14
Sec. 412(1) . . . . 7.6[C]
Sec. 412(2) . . . . 7.6[C]
Sec. 501 . . . . 8.28[B]
Sec. 501(a) . . . . 9.19[B]
Sec. 501(b) 9.8; 9.18
Secs. 502–505 . . . . 2.3[B]
Sec. 502(a) 9.8
Sec. 503(a) 9.9
Sec. 503(b) 9.9
Sec. 504 . . . . 6.9[C]
Sec. 504(b) . . . . . 9.11; 9.12[A],[C]; 11.7[A]
Sec. 504(c) . . . . 1.5[C]; 7.6[C]; 9.13[B];
12.5[B][5]

[References are to sections.]

Sec. 504(c)(2) . . . . . 9.13[B]; 10.1; 10.12[B]
Sec. 504(c)(2)(ii) . . . . 4.6[D]
Sec. 505 . . . . 6.9[C]; 9.14
Sec. 505(a) 9.15
Sec. 505(a) 9.15
Sec. 506(c) 9.15
Sec. 506(d) 9.15
Sec. 506(e) 9.15
Sec. 507 . . . . 9.17
Sec. 601 . . . . 3.20; 4.15
Sec. 601(a) . . . . 4.15; 4.16[A]
Sec. 601(b) . . . . 4.16[C]
Sec. 601(c) . . . . 4.16[A]
Sec. 601(d) . . . . 4.16[D]
Sec. 601(d)(3) . . . . 4.16[D]
Sec. 602 . . . . 4.15; 8.13[4]; 12.9[A]
Sec. 602(a) . . . . 8.14[C]
Sec. 602(b) . . . . 8.14[C]
Sec. 603 . . . . 12.9[A]
Sec. 603(a) . . . . 4.16[D]
Sec. 603(c) . . . . 12.9[A]
Sec. 701(a) 7.2
Sec. 705 . . . . 7.2
Sec. 706 . . . . 7.2
Secs. 801–803 . . . . 1.5[C]
Secs. 801–810 . . . . 1.5; 8.3[B]
Sec. 803(a) . . . . 8.3[B]
Sec. 803(b)(1)(A) . . . . 8.19[A]
Sec. 810 . . . . 8.3[B]
Sec. 902(b) . . . . 3.9[B]
Sec. 904 . . . . 3.9[B]
Sec. 905 . . . . 3.9[B]
Sec. 908(a) . . . . 3.9[B]
Sec. 908(e) . . . . 3.9[B]
Sec. 909(a) . . . . 3.9[B]
Sec. 909(b) . . . . 3.9[B]
Sec. 910(a) . . . . 3.9[B]
Sec. 910(b) . . . . 3.9[B]
Sec. 911 . . . . 3.9[B]
Sec. 911(d) . . . . 3.9[B]
Secs. 1001–1010 . . . . 8.3[A]
Sec. 1002(a) . . . . 8.29[B]
Secs. 1003–1007 . . . . 8.29[B]
Sec. 1004(a)(3) . . . . 8.29[B]
Sec. 1006(b)(1),(2) . . . . 8.29[B]
Sec. 1007(c) . . . . 8.29[B]
Sec. 1008 . . . . 8.29[B]
Sec. 1009(b) . . . . 8.29[B]
Sec. 1009(d) . . . . 8.29[B]
Sec. 1009(d)(2) . . . . 8.29[B]
Sec. 1101 . . . . 1.5[C]
Sec. 1101(a)(1) . . . . 2.3[B]

Title 18

Sec. 2319 . . . . 9.15
Sec. 2319A . . . . 1.15[C]; 2.3[B]
Sec. 3571(b),(c) 9.15

Title 19

Sec. 1337 . . . . 12.9[B]
Sec. 1337(a) . . . . 12.9[B]
Sec. 1337(a)(3) . . . . 12.9[B]
Sec. 1337(i) . . . . 12.9[B]
Secs. 2411–2416 . . . . 12.9[C]
Sec. 2462(c)(5) . . . . 12.9[C]

Title 28

Sec. 1332(a)(2) . . . . 12.8[A]
Sec. 1338(a) . . . . . 9.16[A],[B]; 9.19[B]
Sec. 1338(b) . . . . 9.16[B]
Sec. 1367(c) . . . . 9.16[B]
Sec. 1498 . . . . 9.19[A]
Sec. 1659 . . . . 12.9[B]

Title 35

Secs. 1–140 . . . . 11.10
Sec. 101 . . . . . 1.11[C],[D]; 2.7[B]; 3.8[B]
Sec. 102 . . . . 2.7; 2.12; 3.8[B]
Sec. 102(a) . . . . 1.11[D]
Sec. 102(b) . . . . 1.11[D]
Sec. 103 . . . . 1.11[B],[D]; 2.12; 3.8[B]
Secs. 111–115 . . . . 1.11[B]
Sec. 154 . . . . 1.11; 2.12
Sec. 154(c)(1) . . . . 1.11[B]
Sec. 161 . . . . 1.11[C]
Sec. 171 . . . . 1.11[C]; 3.16[A]
Sec. 271 . . . . . 1.11[D],[E]; 2.7[B]; 3.8[B]
Sec. 271(a) . . . . 1.11[D]; 3.8; 9.20[B]
Secs. 281–294 . . . . 1.11[E]
Sec. 285 . . . . 9.14

Title 47

Secs. 151–611 . . . . 11.10

UNITED STATES CONSTITUTION

Copyright Clause (Art. 1, § 8, cl. 8) . . . 1.3;
1.8[A]; 1.14[C]; 2.2; 2.3[A];
2.12[A]; 2.13[A]; 3.4[B]; 3.7;
4.2[C]; 4.18; 6.1; 9.19[B]; 10.15[A];
11.1; 11.4
Due Process Clause 4.18; 5.3
Eleventh Amendment . . . . 9.19[B]
First Amendment . . . . 2.12[A]; 10.15[A],[B]
Fourteenth Amendment 5.3
Supremacy Clause . . . . . 1.14[E]; 11.1; 11.3;
11.5; 11.8[A]; 11.9[A],[B]
Takings Clause (Fifth Amendment) . . . . . .
4.11[A]; 4.19[B]

[References are to sections.]

UNIVERSAL COPYRIGHT CONVENTION

Generally . . . . 1.4[C]; 1.5[B]; 8.28[A]; 12.2;
12.3; 12.5[A]; 12.6; 12.7[B];
12.8[C]
Art. 1 (Paris Act) . . . . 12.3[B][1]
Art. 2 (Paris Act) . . . . 12.3[B][2]
Art. 3 (Paris Act) . . . . 12.3[B][3]
Art. 4 (Paris Act) . . . . . 12.1[B][4]; 12.6[B]
Art. 5 (Paris Act) . . . . 12.3[B][5]
Art. 15 (Paris Act) . . . . 12.3[B][6]
Appendix Declaration (Paris Act) . . . .
12.3[B][6]

UNIVERSAL DECLARATION OF HUMAN RIGHTS

Art. 27(2) 1.7

URUGUAY ROUND AGREEMENTS ACT

Also see Generalized Agreement on Tariffs and
Trade, 17 USC § 104A
Generally . . . . 1.11[B]; 2.3[B]; 4.4; 4.11[A];
4.14[A]; 4.19[B]; 6.5[B]; 6.6[A];
8.14[D]; 12.5[B][4]; 12.10[B],
12.11[B]
Sec. 514(h)(2)(A) . . . . 4.19[B]

VISUAL ARTISTS RIGHTS ACT OF 1990 (VARA)

Generally . . . . 8.27; 8.28; 11.11; 12.4[B][5]

INDEX

[References are to sections.]

A

ADAPTATION RIGHTS
Generally 8.5
Limitations on
    Architectural works 8.11
    Computer software; CONTU 8.6
    Ephemeral recordings 8.8
    Mechanical licenses (See MECHANICAL LICENSES)
    Sound recordings 8.9
    Useful articles, rights for pictorial, graphic, and sculptural works embodied in . . . .
    8.10

**AMERICAN SOCIETY OF COMPOSERS, AUTHORS AND PUBLISHERS
(ASCAP)** (See PERFORMING RIGHTS SOCIETIES)

AMUSEMENT MUSIC OPERATORS OF AMERICA (AMOA)
Performing rights societies and, jukebox license negotiations between . . . . . 8.21[B]

ANONYMOUS WORKS
Term of copyright for . . . . . 6.3[C]

ANTITRUST ISSUES
Performing rights societies, arising from . . . . . 8.22[D]
Public broadcasting arrangements, exemption for copyright owners entering into . . 8.23

ARCHITECTURAL WORKS
Generally . . . . . 3.15[A]
Adaptation and reproduction rights, limitations on 8.11
Architectural Works Protection Act of 1990
    Generally . . . . . 1.5[C]; 3.15[C]
    Preemption of state law protection by . . . . . 11.11[B]
Berne Convention Implementation Act of 1988, protection under . . . . . 12.5[B][2]
Plans, models and drawings . . . . . 3.15[B][2]
Preemption of state law protection for . . . . . 11.11[B]
Separability test applicable to . . . . . 3.15[B][1]
Structures . . . . . 3.15[B][1]

ARCHITECTURAL WORKS PROTECTION ACT OF 1990
Generally . . . . . 1.5[C]; 3.15[C]
Preemption of state law protection by . . . . . 11.11[B]

ARRANGEMENT OF DATA (See COMPILATIONS)

ATTORNEY'S FEES
Generally 9.14
Registration as prerequisite to . . . . . 7.6[A], [C]

[References are to sections.]

AUDIO HOME RECORDING ACT OF 1992
Generally . . . . . 8.29[A], [B]

AUDIOVISUAL WORKS
Generally 3.22
Colorization 2.10
Commissioned works . . . . . 5.2[B]
Fixation requirement 2.5
Motion pictures 3.22
Works made for hire . . . . . 5.2[B]

AUTHORS AND AUTHORSHIP
Anonymous works, term of copyright for . . . . . 6.3[C]
Child of author defined . . . . . 6.6[B]
Collective works (See COLLECTIVE WORKS)
Corporations . . . . . 6.7[C]
Death of author . . . . . 6.3[F]
Derivative works (See DERIVATIVE WORKS)
Foreign authors
    Eligibility for protection . . . . . 12.7[B]
    Restoration of copyright for work of (See RESTORATION OF COPYRIGHT)
    Unpublished works of, protection of . . . . . 12.7[A]
Government works (See GOVERNMENT WORKS)
Joint works (See JOINT WORKS)
Posthumous works
    Generally . . . . . 6.3[C]
    Renewal rights for, vesting of . . . . . 6.7[B]
Renewal rights vesting in (See RENEWAL OF COPYRIGHT REGISTRATION)
Survivors of authors, vesting of renewal rights in . . . . . 6.6[B]
Widow of author defined . . . . . 6.6[B]
Works made for hire (See WORKS MADE FOR HIRE)
Works of authorship (See WORKS OF AUTHORSHIP)

B

BANKRUPTCY
Involuntary transfer due to 5.13

BERNE CONVENTION
Generally . . . . . 12.4[A], [B]
Basis of protection under . . . . . 12.4[B][2]
Benefits of . . . . . 12.5[C]
Berne Convention Implementation Act of 1988 (See BERNE CONVENTION
   IMPLEMENTATION ACT OF 1988)
Exclusive rights . . . . . 12.4[B][5]
Formalities, preclusion of . . . . . 12.4[B][3]
Infringement suits under, registration not required for . . . . . 7.6[A]
Minimum term of protection . . . . . 12.4[B][4]
New technologies protocol . . . . . 12.10[D]
Publication and . . . . . 4.6[C]
Registration as bar to U.S. entry into . . . . . 6.9[A]

[References are to sections.]

BERNE CONVENTION—Cont.
Restoration of copyright for U.S. public domain works 4.18
Subject matter . . . . . 12.4[B][1]
U.S. entry into . . . . . 1.4[B]; 6.9[A]; 12.5[A]; 12.5[C]

BERNE CONVENTION IMPLEMENTATION ACT OF 1988
Generally . . . . . 12.5[B]
Architectural works . . . . . 12.5[B][2]
Formalities, removal of . . . . . 1.5[B]; 12.5[B][1]
Infringement remedies . . . . . 12.5[B][5]
Jukebox license . . . . . 12.5[B][3]
1976 Act, amending . . . . . 1.5[B]
Notice requirement and . . . . . 4.8[B]
Public domain, retroactive protection of works in . . . . . 12.5[B][4]

BOOKS
(See also specific subject headings)
Manufacturing clause test . . . . . 4.16[B]
Public lending right . . . . . 8.14[F]

BOOTLEGGING
Generally . . . . . 2.3[A], [B]
Convention for the Protection of Producers of Phonograms Against Unauthorized
    Duplications of their Phonograms . . . . . 12.6[A]
Uruguay Round Agreements Act . . . . . 2.3[B]

BROADCAST MUSIC, INC. (BMI) (See PERFORMING RIGHTS SOCIETIES)

BROADCASTS
Ephemeral recordings of 8.8

BRUSSELS SATELLITE CONVENTION
Generally . . . . . 12.6[B]

BUENOS AIRES CONVENTION
Generally . . . . . 12.6[C]

C

CABLE TELEVISION LICENSES
Generally . . . . . 8.3[A]
Applicability of . . . . . 8.19[D]
Compulsory license . . . . . 8.19[D]
Instructional purposes exemption . . . . . 8.19[C][2]
International broadcasts . . . . . 8.19[D]
Liability . . . . . 8.19[A]–[G]
Modification of . . . . . 8.19[G]
Non-profit secondary transmitters . . . . . 8.19[C][4]
Passive carrier exemption . . . . . 8.19[C][3]
Private lodgings exemption . . . . . 8.19[C][1]
Reporting requirements . . . . . 8.19[E]
Royalty fees . . . . . 8.19[E], [F]

[References are to sections.]

CALIFORNIA RESALE ROYALTY ACT
Generally . . . . . 8.14[E]
Preemption of . . . . . 11.8[D]

CHOREOGRAPHIC WORKS
Generally 3.21

COLLECTIVE WORKS
(See also COMPILATIONS; JOINT WORKS)
Composite works compared to . . . . . 6.7[C]
Deposit requirements, individual contributions exempt from 7.12
Notice requirements for contributions to . . . . . 4.13[B]
Ownership of copyright in 5.6

COMMERCIAL USE
Fair use doctrine applied to 10.16
Infringement defense 10.7
Non-profit use distinguished from 10.7
Parody . . . . . 10.14[B]; 10.16

COMMISSIONED WORKS (See WORKS MADE FOR HIRE)

COMMON LAW COPYRIGHT
Generally . . . . . 1.14[C]; 2.6
Abolition of 11.5
Civil law approach distinguished from 1.1
Oral works 2.6; 11.10
Preemption . . . . . 1.5[A]
Trade secrets . . . . . 1.14[C]
Unpublished works . . . . . 1.4[A]

COMPILATIONS
Generally 2.8
Originality in . . . . . 2.11[A]
"Yellow pages" cases . . . . . 2.11[C]

COMPOSITE WORKS
Renewal rights for . . . . . 6.7[C]

COMPULSORY LICENSES
Generally . . . . . 8.3[A]
Cable television (See CABLE TELEVISION LICENSES)
Copyright Arbitration Royalty Panels (CARPs), administration by 8.2
Copyright Royalty Tribunal (CRT), administration by . . . . . 8.2; 8.3[B]
Digital audio tape devices . . . . . 8.3[A]
Jukebox license (See JUKEBOX LICENSES)
Justifications for . . . . . 8.3[C]
Mechanical licenses (See MECHANICAL LICENSES)
1976 Act . . . . . 1.5[A]
Public broadcasting license 8.23
Satellite retransmission license 8.20

COMPUTERS
Computer-generated works 3.7

[References are to sections.]

COMPUTERS—Cont.
Graphical user interface (GUI), merger doctrine applicable to . . . . . 2.12[B][2]
Hardware . . . . . 3.5[A]
Mask works
    Generally . . . . . 3.9[A]
    Notice . . . . . 3.9[B]
Semiconductor chips (See SEMICONDUCTOR CHIPS)
Software (See COMPUTER SOFTWARE)

COMPUTER SOFTWARE
Generally . . . . . 3.4[A]
Adaptation and reproduction rights 8.6
Apple Computers, Inc. v. Franklin Computer Corp. . . . . . . 3.6[A]–[D]
Applications software . . . . . 3.5[C]
Commission of New Technology Uses of Copyrighted Works (CONTU) . . . 3.4[A]; 8.6
Copyrightability . . . . . 3.4[B]
Developmental stages . . . . . 3.5[B]
Distribution rights for . . . . . 8.14[B]
Object code . . . . . 3.6[B]
Operating systems . . . . . 3.6[C], [D]
Reverse engineering 10.13
ROM, programs embodied in . . . . . 3.6[C]

CONSTITUTIONAL CONSIDERATIONS
Copyright Clause 1.3
Due Process Clause 4.18
First Amendment issues
    Generally . . . . . 10.15[A]
    Idea/expression dichotomy . . . . . 10.15[B]
Restoration of copyright for U.S. public domain works 4.18
Standing . . . . . 9.19[B]
Takings Clause 4.18

CONTU (See NATIONAL COMMISSION ON NEW TECHNOLOGICAL USES OF COPYRIGHTED WORKS (CONTU))

COPIES
Defined 2.2
Deposit of (See DEPOSIT REQUIREMENT)
Display right limitations on owners of lawfully made . . . . . 8.26[A]
Manufacturing clause exception . . . . . 4.16[C]
Notice on . . . . . 4.10[A]
Photocopies, fair use doctrine applied to (See FAIR USE DOCTRINE, subhead: Photocopies)

COPYING
Access to original 9.4
Circumstantial proof of 9.3
Defined 9.2
Idea/expression dichotomy . . . . . 2.12[B][1]
Proof of
    Generally 9.2

[References are to sections.]

COPYING—Cont.
Proof of—Cont.
    Access to work, proof of 9.3; 9.4
    Substantial similarity (See SUBSTANTIAL SIMILARITY)

COPYRIGHT ACT OF 1790
Generally 1.3

COPYRIGHT ACT OF 1909
Generally . . . . . 1.4[A]
Notice (See NOTICE)
Publication 4.4
Public domain, applicability to works in . . . . . 1.5[D]
Registration under 7.8
Term of copyright under . . . . . 1.4[A], [B]; 6.2
Transfer of copyright, writing required for . . . . . 5.11[B]
Works of authorship, comparison to 1976 Act regarding . . . . . 3.2[C]

COPYRIGHT ACT OF 1976
Compulsory licenses available under . . . . . 1.5[A]
Copyright Royalty Tribunal (CRT) . . . . . 1.5[A]
Durational system of . . . . . 1.5[A]
Exclusive rights . . . . . 1.5[A]
Fair use doctrine
    Generally 10.4
    Productive uses 10.5
Formalities under . . . . . 1.5[A]
Industrial design 3.12
Manufacturing clause under . . . . . 4.16[A]–[C]
Notice . . . . . 4.9; 4.10[A]–[E]
Ownership under . . . . . 1.5[A]
Publication . . . . . 4.6[A]
Public domain, applicability to works in . . . . . 1.5[D]
Renewal of registration . . . . . 6.5[B]–[D]
State common law copyright preempted by . . . . . 1.5[A]
Subject matter . . . . . 1.5[A]
Term of copyright . . . . . 1.5[A]; 6.2
Trade regulation . . . . . 12.9[A]
Transfer of copyright . . . . . 5.11[A]
Works of authorship, comparison to 1909 Act regarding . . . . . 3.2[C]

COPYRIGHT ARBITRATION ROYALTY PANELS (CARPS)
Generally . . . . . 8.2; 8.3[B]; 8.23

COPYRIGHT CLEARANCE CENTER (CCC)
Generally . . . . . 10.12[C]

COPYRIGHT LAW
Common law (See COMMON LAW COPYRIGHT)
Constitutional basis 1.3
Economic law theory . . . . . 1.8[A], [B]
Historical background 1.2; 1.3

[References are to sections.]

COPYRIGHT LAW—Cont.
Natural law theory 1.7
State law (See STATE REGULATION)
Statute of Anne 1.2
Technological impacts on future 1.9

COPYRIGHT OFFICE
Generally 7.2
Registration 7.5

COPYRIGHT RENEWAL ACT OF 1992
Generally . . . . . 6.9[A]

COPYRIGHT ROYALTY TRIBUNAL (CRT)
Compulsory licenses . . . . . 8.2; 8.3[B]
Establishment of . . . . . 1.5[A]
Secondary transmissions . . . . . 8.19[F]

COUNTERFEITING
1976 Act, customs office enforcement under . . . . . 12.9[A]
U.S. International Trade Commission . . . . . 12.9[B]

CREATIVITY (See ORIGINALITY)

CRIMINAL INFRINGEMENT
Generally 9.15

CUSTOMS OFFICE, U.S.
Enforcement authority of . . . . . 12.9[A]

D

DAMAGES
Generally . . . . . 9.13[A]
Computation . . . . . 9.13[B]
Costs 9.14
Multiple infringement cases . . . . . 9.13[C], [D]
Registration prerequisite . . . . . 9.13[C], [D]
Statutory damages . . . . . 7.6[A], [C]; 9.13[A]

DEFENSES
Commercial use 10.7
Criminal infringement 9.15
Fair use doctrine (See FAIR USE DOCTRINE)
Parody (See PARODY)

DEPOSIT REQUIREMENT
Generally 7.1; 7.9
Exemption from requirement 7.12
Failure to comply 7.11
Form . . . . . App. to ch. 7
Library of Congress deposit compared to deposit for registration 7.13
Mandatory nature of 7.10

[References are to sections.]

DEPOSIT REQUIREMENT—Cont.
Reproduction of deposit copies 7.2

DEPOSIT REQUIREMENTS
Advertising exemption 7.12

DERIVATIVE WORKS
Generally 2.8
Adaptation right 8.5
Art reproductions . . . . . 2.9[D]
Colorization as 2.10
Joint works compared to . . . . . 5.4[C]
Lawful use requirement . . . . . 2.9[C]
Musical arrangements 3.18
Originality in . . . . . 2.9[A], [D]
Ownership of copyright . . . . . 5.4[B]
Publication of . . . . . 4.7[D]
Public domain, use of derivative work in . . . . . 2.9[B]
Renewal . . . . . 6.9[C]
Renewal of . . . . . 6.10[B], [C]
Sound recordings 8.9
Termination of transfer 6.14

DESIGN PROTECTION
Graphic design 3.11
Industrial design (See INDUSTRIAL DESIGN)
Patent law . . . . . 1.11[C]; 3.16[A]

DISPLAY RIGHTS
Generally 8.25
Exemptions
    Aiken exemption . . . . . 8.26[B]
    Instructional broadcast exemption . . . . . 8.26[B]
    Lawfully made copies, exemption for owners of . . . . . 8.26[A]
    Public broadcast exemption . . . . . 8.26[B]
    Religious services exemption . . . . . 8.26[B]
    Secondary transmission exemption . . . . . 8.26[B]
    Teaching exemption . . . . . 8.26[B]

DISTRIBUTION
Exclusive right . . . . . 8.12; 8.13[A], [B]
First sale doctrine (See FIRST SALE DOCTRINE)
Non-consensual transfers . . . . . 8.13[B]
Oral dissemination . . . . . 4.7[A]
Preemption of state law . . . . . 11.8[D]
Publication, by . . . . . 4.3; 4.7[C]

DIVISIBILITY OF COPYRIGHT
Generally . . . . . 5.8[A]
1909 Act, under 5.9
1976 Act, under . . . . . 1.5[A]
Standing to sue and . . . . . 5.8[B]

[References are to sections.]

DRAMATIC WORKS
Generally 3.20

DURATION OF COPYRIGHT (See TERM OF COPYRIGHT)

E

EDUCATIONAL USES
Display right limitation for . . . . . 8.26[B]
Fair use doctrine applicable to photocopying for
    Guidelines . . . . . 10.12[B]
    Productive use 10.5
Manufacturing clause exception . . . . . 4.16[C]
Performance right exemption . . . . . 8.17[B]

EPHEMERAL RECORDINGS
Generally 8.8

EUROPEAN UNION (EU)
Generally . . . . . 12.11[A]

EXCLUSIVE RIGHTS
Generally 8.1; 8.2
Adaptation rights (See ADAPTATION RIGHTS)
Berne Convention, under . . . . . 12.4[B][5]
Categorization affecting . . . . . 3.2[D]
Display rights (See DISPLAY RIGHTS)
Distribution rights (See DISTRIBUTION RIGHTS)
Divisibility of 8.2
Fair use doctrine as limitation on 8.2
Limitations on
    Generally 8.2
    Compulsory licenses (See COMPULSORY LICENSES)
    Fair Use doctrine (See FAIR USE DOCTRINE)
    Mechanical license (See MECHANICAL LICENSES)
Performance rights (See PERFORMANCE RIGHTS)
Reproduction rights (See REPRODUCTION RIGHT)
Violation of (See INFRINGEMENT)

F

FAIR USE DOCTRINE
Generally 10.2
Amount and substantiality of portion of work used, applicability determined by . . 10.6; 10.9
Applicability 10.6; 10.7
Commentary 10.5
Computer software 10.13
Copyright Clearance Center (CCC) . . . . . 10.12[C]
Criticism 10.5
Defined 10.2
Educational uses 10.5

[References are to sections.]

FAIR USE DOCTRINE—Cont.
Exclusive rights limited by 8.2
First amendment issues
    Generally . . . . . 10.15[A]
    Idea/expression dichotomy . . . . . 10.15[B]
General principles of, synthesis of 10.16
History 10.3
Market impact 10.6; 10.10
Nature of copyrighted work 10.6; 10.8
News reporting 10.5
1976 Act
    Generally 10.4
    Productive uses 10.5
Parody (See PARODY)
Photocopies
    Generally . . . . . 10.11[C]
    Classroom use, guidelines for . . . . . 10.12[B]
    Copyright Clearance Center (CCC), licensing by . . . . . 10.12[C]
    Library photocopying, exemption for . . . . . 10.12[A]
Productive uses 10.5
Reproductive technology . . . . . 10.11[A]; 10.11[D]
Research 10.5
Reverse engineering of computer software 10.13
Scholarship 10.5
Unpublished works 10.8
Use, purpose and character of 10.6
Videotaping . . . . . 10.11[A], [B]

FICTIONAL CHARACTERS
Exclusion from copyright protection . . . . . 3.2[B]
Idea/expression dichotomy, applicability of . . . . . 2.12[C]

FINE ARTS
Moral right protection . . . . . 8.27[C]
Preemption of state law . . . . . 11.11[A]
Reproductions . . . . . 2.9[D]
Visual Artists Rights Act (VARA) (See VISUAL ARTISTS RIGHTS ACT (VARA))

FIRST AMENDMENT
Generally . . . . . 10.15[A]
Idea/expression dichotomy . . . . . 10.15[B]

FIRST SALE DOCTRINE
Generally . . . . . 8.13[A]
Exceptions to
    Computer software rental . . . . . 8.14[B]
    Phonorecord rental . . . . . 8.14[A]
    Public lending rights . . . . . 8.14[F]
    Resale royalty right (*droit de suite*) . . . . . 8.14[E]
Gray market goods . . . . . 8.14[C]
Non-consensual transfers . . . . . 8.13[B]

[References are to sections.]

FIXATION REQUIREMENT
Generally 2.2
Audiovisual images 2.5
Choreographic works 3.21
Live broadcasts . . . . . 2.3[A]
Machine or device, perception by 2.4
Tangible medium of expression . . . . . 2.3[A]; 3.21
Video games 2.5

FOREIGN AUTHORS
Eligibility for protection, categories of . . . . . 12.7[B]
Restoration of copyright for work of (See RESTORATION OF COPYRIGHT)
Unpublished works, protection of . . . . . 12.7[A]

FORFEITURE OF COPYRIGHT (See PUBLIC DOMAIN)

FORMALITIES
Generally 4.1
Berne Convention Implementation Act of 1988 (BCIA), modification by . . . . . 1.4[B];
    12.5[B][1]
Buenos Aires Convention . . . . . 12.6[C]
Fixation (See FIXATION REQUIREMENT)
Manufacturing clause (See MANUFACTURING CLAUSE)
1976 Act . . . . . 1.5[A]
Notice (See NOTICE)
Publication (See PUBLICATION REQUIREMENT)

G

GATT (GENERALIZED AGREEMENT ON TARIFFS AND TRADE) (See WORLD
    TRADE ORGANIZATION (WTO))

GOVERNMENT WORKS
Exclusion from copyright protection . . . . . 2.12[A]
Notice requirements . . . . . 4.13[A]

GRAPHIC WORKS
Generally 3.10; 3.11
Applied art, works of 3.11
Architectural works (See ARCHITECTURAL WORKS)
Industrial design (See INDUSTRIAL DESIGNS)
Maps 3.17
Useful objects 3.11

GRAY MARKET GOODS
Generally . . . . . 8.14[C]

I

IDEA/EXPRESSION DICHOTOMY
Generally . . . . . 2.12[A]
Fictional characters, applicability to . . . . . 2.12[C]

[References are to sections.]

IDEA/EXPRESSION DICHOTOMY—Cont.
Functional works, applicability to . . . . . 2.12[B][1], [2]

INDUSTRIAL DESIGN
Exclusion from copyright . . . . . 3.2[B]
Legislation, proposed . . . . . 3.16[B]
1976 Act 3.12
Pictorial works distinguished from . . '. . . . 3.12
Separability
    Conceptual separability 3.14
    Physical separability 3.13

INFRINGEMENT
Generally 9.1
Attorney's fees 9.14
Berne Convention Implementation Act (BCIA), remedies available under . . . 12.5[B][5]
Berne Convention, registration not required for suits under 7.6
Computer programs . . . . . 9.5[F]
Contributory infringement . . . . . 9.20[A], [B]
Copying, proving (See COPIES AND COPYING)
Costs, recovery of 9.14
Criminal penalties for 9.15
Damages (See DAMAGES)
Defenses (See DEFENSES)
Fair use defense (See FAIR USE DOCTRINE)
Inducement to infringe . . . . . 9.20[B]
Jurisdiction (See JURISDICTION)
Multiple infringements . . . . . 9.13[C]
Multiple parties . . . . . 9.13[D]
Ownership, proving 9.2
Parties to 9.18
Proving improper appropriation 9.2; 9.3; 9.7
Registration as prerequisite . . . . . 7.6[A]; 7.7
Remedies
    Berne Convention Implementation Act (BCIA) . . . . . 12.5[B][5]
    Damages (See DAMAGES)
    Destruction of infringing items 9.9
    Impounding of infringing items 9.9
    Preliminary injunctions 9.8
    Profits, recovery of
        Advantages to . . . . . 9.12[A]
        Apportionment of profits for . . . . . 9.12[C]
        Costs of defendant deductible from . . . . . 9.12[B]
        Double counting of damages and 9.11
Similarity (See SUBSTANTIAL SIMILARITY)
Standing
    Generally 9.18
    Federal government, against . . . . . 9.19[A]
    State governments, against . . . . . 9.19[B]
Statute of limitations 9.17
Substantial similarity (See SUBSTANTIAL SIMILARITY)

[References are to sections.]

INFRINGEMENT—Cont.
Vicarious liability . . . . . 9.20[A], [C]

INJUNCTIONS
Generally 9.8

INTERNATIONAL COPYRIGHT
Generally 12.2
Berne Convention (See BERNE CONVENTION)
Brussels Satellite Convention . . . . . 12.6[B]
Buenos Aires Convention . . . . . 12.6[C]
Conflict of law . . . . . 12.8[A]–[C]
Convention for the Protection of Producers of Phonograms Against Unauthorized
   Duplications of their Phonograms . . . . . 12.6[A]
European Union (EU) . . . . . 12.11[A]
NAFTA (North American Free Trade Agreement) . . . . . 4.11[A]; 12.11[B]
Universal Copyright Convention (UCC) (See UNIVERSAL COPYRIGHT
   CONVENTION (UCC))
Uruguay Round Agreements Act (See URUGUAY ROUND AGREEMENTS ACT)
World Intellectual Property Organization (WIPO) . . . . . 12.10[D]
World Trade Organization (WTO) (See WORLD TRADE ORGANIZATION (WTO))

**INTERNATIONAL UNION FOR THE PROTECTION OF LITERARY AND
   ARTISTIC WORKS** (See BERNE CONVENTION)

J

JOINT WORKS
Generally . . . . . 5.4[C]
Derivative works compared to . . . . . 5.4[C]
Intent to create . . . . . 5.4[A], [B]
Ownership . . . . . 5.4[A], [B]
Renewal of copyright . . . . . 6.6[B]
Term of copyright . . . . . 6.3[D]

JUKEBOX LICENSES
Generally . . . . . 8.21[A]
Berne Convention Implementation Act of 1988 . . . . . 12.5[B][3]
Procedure for obtaining . . . . . 8.21[B]

JURISDICTION
"Arising under" jurisdiction . . . . . 9.16[A]
Mask works, infringement of . . . . . 3.9[B]
Pendent jurisdiction . . . . . 9.16[B]
Preemption (See PREEMPTION)

L

LIBRARIES
Photocopying exemption . . . . . 10.12[A]
Public lending right . . . . . 8.14[F]

[References are to sections.]

LIBRARY OF CONGRESS
Generally 7.2
Deposit
    Generally 7.9
    "Best edition," of 7.12
    Failure to deposit 7.11
    Mandatory deposits 7.10
    Registration deposits compared to 7.13
    Unsuitable works for deposit 7.12

LICENSES
ASCAP . . . . . 8.22[B]
Broadcast Music, Inc. (BMI) . . . . . 8.22[B]
Cable television license (See CABLE TELEVISION LICENSE)
Compulsory licenses (See COMPULSORY LICENSES)
Exclusive license 7.5
Mechanical license (See MECHANICAL LICENSES)
Nonexclusive license 6.13
Performing rights societies . . . . . 8.22[B]

LITERARY WORKS
Generally 3.3
Computer software (See COMPUTER SOFTWARE)
Preemption of state law . . . . . 11.9[B]

LIVE BROADCASTS
Generally . . . . . 2.3[A]

M

MANUFACTURING CLAUSE
Generally 4.15
Braille works exception . . . . . 4.16[C]
1909 Act . . . . . 4.17[A]–[C]
1976 Act . . . . . 4.16[A]–[C]
Scholarly materials exception . . . . . 4.16[C]

MAPS
Generally 3.17

MECHANICAL LICENSES
Generally . . . . . 8.3[A]; 8.7[A], [B]
Non-dramatic musical works . . . . . 8.7[C]
Notice of intention to obtain . . . . . 8.7[D]
Procedures for obtaining . . . . . 8.7[D]
Royalties . . . . . 8.7[D]

MORAL RIGHTS PROTECTION
Generally . . . . . 8.27[A]
Art Preservation Acts . . . . . 8.27[C]
Colorization controversy . . . . . 8.27[A]
Conflict of laws . . . . . 12.8[C]

[References are to sections.]

MORAL RIGHTS PROTECTION—Cont.
Federal law . . . . . 8.27[B]
Lanham Act . . . . . 8.27[A]
State law
   Generally . . . . . 8.27[B]
   Art Preservation Acts . . . . . 8.27[C]
Visual Artists Rights Act (VARA) (See VISUAL ARTISTS RIGHTS ACT OF 1990 (VARA))

MOTION PICTURES
(See also AUDIOVISUAL WORKS)
Generally 3.22

MUSICAL WORKS
Generally 3.18
Compulsory license . . . . . 8.7[C]
Originality standard applicable to 3.18

N

NAFTA (NORTH AMERICAN FREE TRADE AGREEMENT)
Generally . . . . . 4.11[A]; 12.11[B]
Restoration of copyright for foreign works under . . . . . 4.19[A]

NATIONAL COMMISSION ON NEW TECHNOLOGICAL USES OF COPYRIGHTED WORKS (CONTU)
Generally 8.6
Computer software . . . . . 3.4[a]

NON-PROFIT USES
Cable television license for . . . . . 8.19[C][4]
Commercial use distinguished from 10.7
Performance rights exemption . . . . . 8.17[E]

NOTICE
Generally . . . . . 4.8[A]
Berne Convention Implementation Act (BCIA) . . . . . 4.8[B]
Collective works, contributions to . . . . . 4.13[B]
Date . . . . . 4.10[C]; 4.12[A], [C], [D]; 4.14[D]
Error in . . . . . 4.12[A], [C]
Foreign publication of U.S. works . . . . . 4.14[F]
Government works, publication containing . . . . . 4.13[A]
Innocent infringement . . . . . 4.11[D]; 4.12[A]
Name . . . . . 4.10[D]; 4.12[A], [B], [D]; 4.12[D]
1909 Act . . . . . 4.14[A]–[D]
1976 Act, under . . . . . 4.9; 4.10[A]–[E]
Omission of
   Generally . . . . . 4.11[A]
   Forfeiture of copyright . . . . . 4.11[B]
   Innocent infringement due to, remedies for . . . . . 4.11[D]
   1909 Act, under . . . . . 4.14[E]
   Savings provision and . . . . . 4.11[C]

[References are to sections.]

O

ORAL WORKS
Common law copyright protection 2.6
Preemption by federal law of state protection 11.10

ORIGINALITY
Generally . . . . . 2.7[A]
Artistic merit . . . . . 2.7[C]
Choreographic works 3.21
Compilations (See COMPILATIONS)
Computer databases . . . . . 2.11[D]
Derivative works (See DERIVATIVE WORKS)
Feist standard . . . . . 2.11[B]
Independent creation . . . . . 2.7[B]
Industrious effort . . . . . 2.11[B]
Quantum of originality in creative authorship . . . . . 2.7[C]
Registration as prima facie evidence of . . . . . 7.6[B]
Selection and arrangement of information . . . . . 2.11[C]
Substantial similarity (See SUBSTANTIAL SIMILARITY)
"Sweat of the brow" doctrine . . . . . 2.12[D]

OWNERSHIP OF COPYRIGHT
Academic writings . . . . . 5.2[B]
Collective works 5.6
Derivative works . . . . . 5.4[B]
Employees, works made by (See WORKS MADE FOR HIRE)
Infringement actions 9.2
Joint ownership 5.5
Joint works . . . . . 5.4[A], [B]
Material object ownership distinguished 5.7
1909 Act, under 5.3
Registration (See REGISTRATION)
Works made for hire (See WORKS MADE FOR HIRE)

P

PANTOMIME
Generally 3.21

PARODY
Generally . . . . . 10.5; 10.14[A]
Four-factor test
Generally . . . . . 10.14[B]
Amount and substantiability of use . . . . . 10.14[C]
Market impact on used work . . . . . 10.14[D]
Satire as element of . . . . . 10.14[E]

PATENT LAW
Generally . . . . . 1.10; 1.11[A]; 2.12[B][1]
Computer programs protected under . . . . . 3.8[B]

[References are to sections.]

PATENT LAW—Cont.
Copyright law compared
    Generally 1.10
    Chart 1.13
Design patents . . . . . 1.11[C]; 3.16[A]
Infringement . . . . . 1.11[E]
Plant patents . . . . . 1.11[C]
Procedural aspects . . . . . 1.11[B]
Trademark law compared
    Generally 1.10
    Chart 1.13
Utility patents
    Generally . . . . . 1.11[C]
    Novelty requirement . . . . . 1.11[D]

PERFORMANCE RIGHTS
Generally . . . . . 8.15; 8.16[A]–[C]
Exemptions
    Generally . . . . . 8.17[A]
    Agricultural and horticultural fairs . . . . . 8.17[D]
    Aiken exemption . . . . . 8.18[A]–[C]
    Blind persons . . . . . 8.17[C]
    Charitable functions . . . . . 8.17[D]
    Disabled persons . . . . . 8.17[C]
    Fraternal organization functions . . . . . 8.17[D]
    Instructional purposes . . . . . 8.17[B]
    Non-profit performances . . . . . 8.17[E]
    Public broadcasting exemption 8.23
    Retail establishment promotions . . . . . 8.17[D]
    Veterans organization functions . . . . . 8.17[D]
Public performance . . . . . 8.16[A]–[C]
Secondary transmissions . . . . . 8.18[A]–[C]
Societies protecting (See PERFORMING RIGHTS SOCIETIES)
Sound recordings . . . . . 3.19[A]; 8.24

PERFORMING RIGHTS SOCIETIES
Generally . . . . . 8.22[A], [B]
American Society of Composers, Authors and Publishers (ASCAP) . . . . . 8.22[B]
Amusement Music Operators of America (AMOA) and, license negotiations between . . 8.21[B]
Antitrust issues arising from . . . . . 8.22[D]
Broadcast Music, Inc. (BMI) . . . . . 8.22[A]
Dramatic (grand) rights . . . . . 8.22[C]
Licensing by . . . . . 8.22[B]
Non-dramatic (small) rights . . . . . 8.22[C]
Non-dramatic works 3.20

PHONOGRAMS (See SOUND RECORDINGS)

PHONORECORDS
Generally 2.2

[References are to sections.]

PHONORECORDS—Cont.
Bootlegging, protection against (See BOOTLEGGING)
Distribution . . . . . 4.7[C]
Ephemeral recordings 8.8
First sale doctrine . . . . . 8.14[A]
Manufacture and distribution of, license for (See MECHANICAL LICENSES)
Notice . . . . . 4.10[B]
Sound recordings distinguished . . . . . 3.19[A]

PHOTOCOPYING
Generally . . . . . 10.11[C]
Fair use doctrine applicable to (See FAIR USE DOCTRINE)

PICTORIAL WORKS
Generally 3.10
Applied art 3.11
Architectural works (See ARCHITECTURAL WORKS)
Graphic design 3.11
Industrial design (See INDUSTRIAL DESIGNS)
Industrial designs distinguished from 3.12
Maps 3.17
Useful objects 3.11; 8.10

POSTHUMOUS WORKS
Generally . . . . . 6.3[C]
Renewal rights for . . . . . 6.7[B]

PREEMPTION
Generally . . . . . 11.1[A]; 11.5; 11.9
Application of, inconsistency in 11.4
Architectural works . . . . . 11.11[B]
Architectural Works Protection Act of 1990 . . . . . 11.11[A]
California Resale Royalty Act . . . . . 11.8[D]
Common law copyright . . . . . 1.5[A]
Facts, systems, ideas and processes . . . . . 11.9[A]
History . . . . . 11.2[A]–[B]
Industrial design . . . . . 11.9[B]
Literary characters . . . . . 11.9[B]
Misappropriation doctrine 11.2
Non-original works . . . . . 11.9[A]
Non-preempted works 11.10
Public domain works . . . . . 11.9[A]
"Rights equivalent" doctrine . . . . . 11.6[A], [B]
State law . . . . . 11.2[B]; 11.8[A]–[D]
Typefaces . . . . . 11.9[B]
Visual art works . . . . . 11.11[A]

PRODUCTIVE USES
Generally 10.5

PSEUDONYMOUS WORKS
Term of copyright for . . . . . 6.3[C]

[References are to sections.]

PUBLICATION REQUIREMENT
Generally . . . . . 4.2[A]
Berne Convention, under . . . . . 4.6[C]
Definition of 4.3
Derivative works . . . . . 4.7[D]
Display, publication by . . . . . 4.7[B]
Divestive publication . . . . . 4.5[B]
Formalities . . . . . 4.6[B]
General publication . . . . . 4.5[C]
Historical development of doctrine . . . . . 4.2[B]
International copyright and . . . . . 4.6[C]
Investive publication . . . . . 4.5[B]
Justification for . . . . . 4.2[C]
Limited publication . . . . . 4.5[C]
1909 Act 4.4
1976 Act . . . . . 4.6[A]
Performance, publication by . . . . . 4.7[A]
Phonorecord distribution, publication by . . . . . 4.7[C]
Sound recordings . . . . . 4.7[C]
Term of copyright affected by . . . . . 4.6[D]

PUBLIC BROADCASTING
Generally 8.23

PUBLIC DOMAIN
Berne Convention Implementation Act (BCIA) . . . . . 12.5[B][4]
Derivative works in, use of . . . . . 2.9[B]
1909 Act . . . . . 1.5[D]
1976 Act . . . . . 1.5[D]
Restoration of copyright in works fallen into (See RESTORATION OF COPYRIGHT)

R

RECORDATION
Generally . . . . . 5.12[A]
Priority in . . . . . 5.12[B], [C]

RECORD RENTAL AMENDMENT
Generally . . . . . 8.14[A]

REGISTER OF COPYRIGHTS
Generally 7.2; 7.5

REGISTRATION OF COPYRIGHT
Generally 7.1; 7.4
Advantages of 7.4
Attorney's fees, as prerequisite to statutory . . . . . 7.6[A], [C]
Berne Convention . . . . . 6.9[A]
Condition of copyright, as 7.4
Copyright Office, administration by 7.2
Damages, as prerequisite to statutory . . . . . 7.6[A], [C]
Death records of authors, maintenance of . . . . . 6.3[F]

[References are to sections.]

REGISTRATION OF COPYRIGHT—Cont.
Effect of 7.4
Evidentiary weight of . . . . . 6.9[C]
Form TX . . . . . App to ch. 7
Infringement suits . . . . . 7.6[A]; 7.7
Invalid claim, refusal of 7.5
Justifications for 7.3
1909 Act 7.8
Originality, as prima facie evidence of . . . . . 7.6[B]
Procedures 7.5
Recordation of transfer of copyright . . . . . 7.6[D]
Refusal of invalid claims 7.7
Remedies for infringement broadened by . . . . . 6.9[C]
Renewal (See RENEWAL OF COPYRIGHT REGISTRATION)
Timing of 7.4
Validity, as prima facie evidence of . . . . . 7.6[B]

RELIGIOUS PURPOSES
Display right exemption for . . . . . 8.26[B]
Manufacturing clause exception for copies made for . . . . . 4.16[C]

REMEDIES (See INFRINGEMENT, subheads: Damages; Injunctions)

RENEWAL OF COPYRIGHT REGISTRATION
Generally . . . . . 6.5[A]; 6.6[A]; 6.9[A]
Automatic renewal . . . . . 6.9[A]–[C]
Berne Convention . . . . . 6.9[A]
Claimants . . . . . 6.6[B]
Compilations . . . . . 6.7[C]
Composite works . . . . . 6.7[C]
Copyright Renewal Act of 1992 . . . . . 6.9[A]
Corporations, rights of . . . . . 6.7[C]
Derivative works . . . . . 6.9[C]; 6.10[B], [C]
Duration of . . . . . 6.5[D]
Joint works . . . . . 6.6[B]
1976 Act . . . . . 6.5[B]–[D]
Posthumous works . . . . . 6.7[B]
Registration requirement . . . . . 6.5[B]
Term 6.4
Transfer of term 6.8
Works made for hire . . . . . 6.7[D]

REPRODUCTION RIGHT
Generally 8.4
Architectural works 8.11
Computer software 8.6
Ephemeral recordings 8.8
Mechanical license (See MECHANICAL LICENSES)
Pictorial, graphic, and sculptural works embodied in useful articles 8.10
Sound recordings 8.9
Useful articles, rights for pictorial, graphic, and sculptural works embodied in . . . 8.10

[References are to sections.]

RESALE ROYALTY RIGHT (*DROIT DE SUITE*)
Generally . . . . . 8.14[E]

RESEARCH ACTIVITIES
Exclusion from copyright protection . . . . . 2.12[D]
Photocopying exemption for library uses . . . . . 10.12[A]
Productive use 10.5

RESTORATION OF COPYRIGHT
Generally 4.18; 4.19
Constitutional implications 4.18
Foreign works
    Berne Convention, under 4.18
    NAFTA . . . . . 4.19[A]
    Uruguay Round Agreements Act . . . . . 4.19[B]; 8.14[D]; 12.5[B][4]
    World Trade Organization (WTO) 4.18; 4.19

ROYALTIES
Cable television license . . . . . 8.19[E], [F]
California Resale Royalty Act . . . . . 8.14[E]; 11.8[D]
Copyright Royalty Arbitration Panels (CARPs) . . . . . 8.2; 8.3[B]; 8.23
Copyright Royalty Tribunal (CRT) . . . . . 8.2; 8.3[B]; 8.19[F]
Mechanical license . . . . . 8.7[D]
Resale royalty right (*droit de suite*) . . . . . 8.14[E]

S

SATELLITE TRANSMISSIONS
Brussels Satellite Convention . . . . . 12.6[B]
Compulsory licenses 8.20

SATIRE (See PARODY)

SCULPTURAL WORKS
Generally 3.10
Architectural works (See ARCHITECTURAL WORKS)
Deposit requirements 7.12
Industrial design (See INDUSTRIAL DESIGNS)
Useful objects 3.11; 8.10

SECONDARY TRANSMISSIONS
Cable television license . . . . . 8.19[C][4]
Display rights exemption . . . . . 8.26[B]
Non-profit secondary transmitters . . . . . 8.19[C][4]
Performance rights . . . . . 8.18[A]–[C]

SEMICONDUCTOR CHIP PROTECTION ACT
Generally . . . . . 3.9[B]

SEMICONDUCTOR CHIPS
Generally . . . . . 3.9[A]
Mask works . . . . . 3.9[A], [B]
Semiconductor Chip Protection Act . . . . . 3.9[B]

[References are to sections.]

SOUND RECORDING ACT OF 1971
Generally . . . . . 3.19[C]
Publication under . . . . . 4.7[C]

SOUND RECORDINGS
Generally . . . . . 3.19[A]
Adaptation rights for, limitations on 8.9
Bootlegging (See BOOTLEGGING)
Convention for the Protection of Producers of Phonograms Against Unauthorized
    Duplications of their Phonograms . . . . . 12.6[A]
Derivative works, as . . . . . 3.19[B]
Exclusion of pre-1972 recordings . . . . . 3.19[C]
Motion picture soundtracks . . . . . 3.22[C]
Notice . . . . . 4.10[B]
Originality in . . . . . 3.19[B]
Performance rights . . . . . 3.19[A]; 8.24
Phonorecord, distinguished from . . . . . 3.19[A]
Phonorecords (See PHONORECORDS)
Preemption of state protection 11.10
Publication . . . . . 4.7[C]
Registration 7.5
Reproduction and adaptation rights 8.9
Sound Recording Act of 1971
    Generally . . . . . 3.19[C]
    Publication under . . . . . 4.7[C]
State law protection . . . . . 3.19[C]

STATE REGULATION
Common law copyright (See COMMON LAW COPYRIGHT)
Expansive view . . . . . 11.2[A], [B]
Minimal view . . . . . 11.2[A], [B]
Misappropriation doctrine . . . . . 1.14[E]; 11.2[B]
Moral rights protection . . . . . 8.27[B], [C]
Preemption by federal law (See PREEMPTION)
Publicity rights . . . . . 1.14[D]
"Rights equivalent" clause . . . . . 11.6[A], [B]; 11.7[A], [B]
Sound recordings before 1972, protection for . . . . . 3.19[C]
Trademarks . . . . . 1.12[A]
Trade secrets . . . . . 1.14[A]
Unfair competition . . . . . 1.14[B]

STATUTE OF LIMITATIONS
Generally 9.17
Mask works . . . . . 3.9[B]

SUBJECT MATTER
Audiovisual works (See AUDIOVISUAL WORKS)
Berne Convention . . . . . 12.4[B][1]
Categories . . . . . 1.5[A]; 3.2[A]–[D]
Choreographic works 3.21
Dramatic works 3.20

[References are to sections.]

SUBJECT MATTER—Cont.
Excluded subject matter
    Facts . . . . . 2.12[D]
    Fictional characters . . . . . 3.2[B]
    Functional works . . . . . 2.12[A]
    Government works . . . . . 2.12[B]
    Historical research . . . . . 2.12[D]
    Idea/expression dichotomy (See IDEA/EXPRESSION DICHOTOMY)
    Illegal works . . . . . 2.13[A]
    Immoral works . . . . . 2.13[A]
    Industrial design . . . . . 3.2[B]
    Obscene works . . . . . 2.13[A]
    Originality requirement (See ORIGINALITY)
    Titles . . . . . 3.2[B]
    Typefaces . . . . . 3.2[B]
    Useful objects . . . . . 2.12[A]
Graphic works (See GRAPHIC WORKS)
Literary works (See LITERARY WORKS)
Motion pictures 3.22
1976 Act . . . . . 1.5[A]
Pantomimes 3.21
Pictorial works (See PICTORIAL WORKS)
Preemption (See PREEMPTION)
Sculptural works (See SCULPTURAL WORKS)
Sound recordings (See SOUND RECORDINGS)
Works of authorship (See WORKS OF AUTHORSHIP)

SUBSTANTIAL SIMILARITY
Generally . . . . . 9.5; 9.6[A]
Arnstein test . . . . . 9.6[C]
Audience test . . . . . 9.6[B]
Bifurcated test . . . . . 9.6[C]
Krofft test . . . . . 9.6[C]
Ordinary observer test . . . . . 9.6[B]
Pattern similarity
    Generally . . . . . 9.5[B], [D]
    Learned Hand abstractions test
        Generally . . . . . 9.5[E]
        Computer programs, applicability to . . . . . 9.5[F]
Verbatim similarity . . . . . 9.5[B], [C]

SYMBOL (See NOTICE)

T

TERM OF COPYRIGHT
Generally 6.1
Anonymous works . . . . . 6.3[C]
Basic term 1.3; 6.1; 6.4
Berne Convention . . . . . 12.4[B][4]
Death of author . . . . . 6.3[F]

[References are to sections.]

TERM OF COPYRIGHT—Cont.
Duration . . . . . 6.2; 6.3[A], [B]
Extension of basic term 6.4
GATT, effect of . . . . . 4.19[A]
Joint works . . . . . 6.3[D]
NAFTA . . . . . 4.19[A]
1909 Act . . . . . 1.4[A], [B]; 6.2
1976 Act . . . . . 1.5[A]; 6.2
Pseudonymous works . . . . . 6.3[C]
Renewal (See RENEWAL OF COPYRIGHT REGISTRATION)
Sound recordings . . . . . 6.3[E]
Uruguay Round Agreements Act . . . . . 4.19[B]
Works made for hire . . . . . 6.3[C]
World Trade Organization (WTO) . . . . . 4.19[B]

TRADEMARK LAW
Generally . . . . . 1.12[A]
Copyright law compared
    Generally 1.10
    Chart 1.13
Infringement . . . . . 1.12[C]
Patent law compared
    Generally 1.10
    Chart 1.13
Registration requirements, federal . . . . . 1.12[B]

TRADE REGULATION
Caribbean Basin Economic Recovery Act . . . . . 12.9[C]
European Union . . . . . 12.11[A]
Generalized System of Preferences (GSP) . . . . . 12.9[C]
Limitations on . . . . . 12.10[A]
NAFTA . . . . . 1.14[A]
1976 Act . . . . . 12.9[A]
U.S. International Trade Commission . . . . . 12.9[B]
World Trade Organization (WTO) (See WORLD TRADE ORGANIZATION (WTO))

TRADE SECRETS
Generally . . . . . 1.14[A]
Computer programs protected as . . . . . 3.8[A]

TRANSFER OF COPYRIGHT
Involuntary transfer 5.13
License (See LICENSES)
1909 Act . . . . . 5.11[B]
1976 Act . . . . . 5.11[A]
Recordation of . . . . . 7.6[D]
Termination of
    Generally . . . . . 6.11; 6.15; 6.16; 6.17[A], [B]
    Derivative works 6.14
    Formalities 6.13
    Notice of 6.13

[References are to sections.]

TRANSFER OF COPYRIGHT—Cont.
Termination of—Cont.
    Renewal term 6.12
Writing requirement . . . . . 5.11[A], [B]

U

UNFAIR COMPETITION
Generally . . . . . 1.14[B]
Antitrust (See ANTITRUST)

UNIVERSAL COPYRIGHT CONVENTION (UCC)
Generally . . . . . 12.2; 12.3[A], [B]
Basis of protection . . . . . 12.3[B][2]
Berne Safeguard Clause . . . . . 12.3[B][6]
Exclusive rights . . . . . 12.3[B][5]
Formalities . . . . . 12.3[B][3]
Minimum term of protection . . . . . 12.3[B][4]
Obligations . . . . . 12.3[B][1]
Paris revision . . . . . 12.3[C]
Publication and . . . . . 4.6[C]
Ratification by U.S. . . . . . 1.4[C]

UNPUBLISHED WORKS
Common law protection for . . . . . 1.4[A]
Fair use 10.8
Foreign authors . . . . . 12.7[A]
Infringement of . . . . . 7.6[C]

URUGUAY ROUND AGREEMENTS ACT
Bootlegging prohibited . . . . . 2.3[B]
Formalities . . . . . 4.11[A]
Restoration of copyright . . . . . 4.19[B]; 8.14[D]

USEFUL OBJECTS
Generally 3.11
Adaptation rights for works embodied in, limitations on 8.10
Industrial design (See INDUSTRIAL DESIGN)

V

VIDEOTAPING
Fair use doctrine . . . . . 10.11[A], [B]

VISUAL ARTISTS RIGHTS ACT OF 1990 (VARA)
Moral rights protected under . . . . . 8.28[A]–[C]
1976 Act . . . . . 1.5[C]
Preemption . . . . . 11.11[A]

W

WORKS MADE FOR HIRE
Academic writings . . . . . 5.2[B]

[References are to sections.]

WORKS MADE FOR HIRE—Cont.
Definition of . . . . . 5.2[B]
Independent contractors and . . . . . 5.2[C], [D]
Ownership of copyright in . . . . . 5.2[A], [C]
Renewal rights . . . . . 6.7[D]
Term of copyright . . . . . 6.3[C]

WORKS OF AUTHORSHIP
Audiovisual works 3.22
Categorization . . . . . 3.2[C], [D]
Choreographic works 3.21
Computer software (See COMPUTER SOFTWARE)
Copyright subsisting in 2.2
Dramatic works 3.20
Excluded works (See EXCLUSION FROM COPYRIGHT PROTECTION)
Graphic works (See GRAPHIC WORKS)
Industrial designs . . . . . 3.2[B]
Literary works 3.3
Motion pictures 3.22
Musical works (See MUSICAL WORKS)
Pantomimes 3.21
Pictorial works (See PICTORIAL WORKS)
Property rights in . . . . . 1.8[B]
Sculptural works (See SCULPTURAL WORKS)
Sound recordings (See SOUND RECORDINGS)
Titles, exclusion of . . . . . 3.2[B]
Typefaces, exclusion of . . . . . 3.2[B]

WORLD INTELLECTUAL PROPERTY ORGANIZATION (WIPO)
GATT, reaction to . . . . . 12.10[D]

WORLD TRADE ORGANIZATION (WTO)
Generally . . . . . 12.10[B]
Most Favored Nation (MFN) . . . . . 12.10[C]
Restoration of copyright (See RESTORATION OF COPYRIGHT)
Trade-Related Aspects of Intellectual Property (TRIPS) . . . . . 12.10[B], [C]
Uruguay Round Agreements Act (See URUGUAY ROUND AGREEMENTS ACT)
World Intellectual Property Organization (WIPO) reaction to . . . . . 12.10[D]